The Practical Skeptic
Readings in Sociology

Third Edition

Lisa J. McIntyre
Washington State University

Higher Education

Boston   Burr Ridge, IL   Dubuque, IA   Madison, WI   New York   San Francisco   St. Louis
Bangkok   Bogotá   Caracas   Kuala Lumpur   Lisbon   London   Madrid   Mexico City
Milan   Montreal   New Delhi   Santiago   Seoul   Singapore   Sydney   Taipei   Toronto

 **Higher Education**

PRACTICAL SKEPTIC: READINGS IN SOCIOLOGY

Published by McGraw-Hill, a business unit of The McGraw-Hill Companies, Inc., 1221
Avenue of the Americas, New York, NY, 10020. Copyright © 2006, 2002, 1999 by The McGraw-
Hill Companies, Inc. All rights reserved. No part of this publication may be reproduced or
distributed in any form or by any means, or stored in a database or retrieval system, without
the prior written consent of The McGraw-Hill Companies, Inc., including, but not limited to,
in any network or other electronic storage or transmission, or broadcast for distance learning.

Some ancillaries, including electronic and print components, may not be available to
customers outside the United States.

This book is printed on acid-free paper.

1 2 3 4 5 6 7 8 9 0 DOC/DOC 0 9 8 7 6 5

ISBN 0-07-288530-0

Editor in Chief: *Emily Barrosse*
Publisher: *Phillip A. Butcher*
Sponsoring Editor: *Sherith H. Pankratz*
Developmental Editor: *Kate Scheinman*
Senior Marketing Manager: *Daniel M. Loch*
Managing Editor: *Jean Dal Porto*
Project Manager: *Catherine R. Iammartino*
Manuscript Editor: *Barbara Hacha*
Art Director: *Jeanne Schreiber*
Design Manager: *Laurie J. Entringer*
Cover Designer: *Kiera Pohl*
Art Manager: *Robin Mouat*
Photo Research Manager: *Brian Pecko*
Cover Credit: © *Digital Vision*
Senior Print Supplements Producer: *Louis Swaim*
Senior Media Project Manager: *Nancy Garcia*
Production Supervisor: *Janean A. Utley*
Composition: *10/12 Book Antiqua by International Typesetting and Composition*
Printing: *45 # New Era Matte, R.R. Donnelley and Sons, Inc./Crawfordsville, IN*

Library of Congress Cataloging-in-Publication Data

The practical skeptic : readings in sociology / [edited by] Lisa J. McIntyre. — 3rd ed.
    p. cm.
    Includes bibliographical references.
    ISBN 0-07-288530-0 (alk paper)
    1. Sociology. 2. Social problems. 3. United States — Social conditions. I. McIntyre, Lisa J.
HM585 .P73 2006
301 — dc22   2005047999

The Internet addresses listed in the text were accurate at the time of publication. The inclusion
of a website does not indicate an endorsement by the authors of McGraw-Hill, and McGraw-
Hill does not guarantee the accuracy of the information presented at these sites.

www.mhhe.com

Preface

There are dozens of anthologies available for introductory-level sociology classes, but I think that this one is different. It's different because as I compiled and edited these articles, I kept the needs of introductory students in mind. That's important. When sociologists write for their professional colleagues, they take for granted (as they should) that their readers are equipped with a great deal of knowledge. Student readers, by contrast, generally lack this sort of preparation; consequently, many students find that reading the works of sociologists is not so much a challenge as an onerous chore. I suspect that beginning students assigned to read sociology feel much like the theatergoer who stumbles into a foreign film that lacks subtitles. No matter how dramatic or comedic the action, unless one can follow the dialogue, the movie is boring.

In this volume, I have tried to bridge the gap between the sociologists who wrote these articles and the students who will read them. Each article begins with a brief introduction to help orient students to the author's aims and point of view, includes footnotes containing explanations of concepts that are likely to be unfamiliar to novice sociologists, and concludes with some questions that will help students sort through and make sense of what they have read. My goal is to replace boredom with intellectual challenge, to make sociology not "easy," but accessible.

Both classic and contemporary articles were selected because they help to illustrate the importance of understanding the social contexts through which people move and to highlight some of the core concepts that sociologists and other social observers use to make sense of the social world. The classic articles especially were selected to illustrate the foundational concepts that most contemporary writers take for granted. But while these fundamentals might seem old hat to professional sociologists, they still contain important revelations for beginners.

New to This Edition

This third edition of the reader continues to emphasize articles that provide students the opportunity to explore the work of sociologists and to challenge the lay understanding of the social world. For the most part, the new additions to the reader are intended to challenge students to reevaluate familiar social arenas: the college classroom, televised sports shows, restaurants, doctors' offices, and even public restrooms. As always, the essential lesson is this: There is much that goes on in the social world that escapes the sociologically untrained eye.

ACCOMPANYING TEST BANK

For the benefit of instructors, I have written a test bank to accompany the reader. The test bank includes multiple-choice, true-false, and short answer/ essay questions as well as suggested short paper assignments.

The Practical Skeptic: Core Concepts in Sociology

Created to serve as a companion to the reader, *The Practical Skeptic: Readings in Sociology,* this text focuses on core concepts as the central building blocks for understanding sociology. Written in a lively, conversational style, this text includes numerous pedagogical features to help students grasp key sociological concepts.

ACKNOWLEDGMENTS

The following colleagues reviewed the manuscript and choice of articles for the first edition and made many helpful suggestions: Sheila Cordray, Oregon State University; Rebecca Erickson, University of Akron; Allen Scarboro, Augusta State University; and Martha L. Shockey, St. Ambrose University.

For the second edition, the following individuals provided thoughtful reviews and recommendations: Deborah J. Baiano Berman, Framingham State College; Jerry Barrish, Bellevue Community College; Valerie S. Brown, Cuyahoga Community College; Margo Rita Capparelli, Framingham State College; Debra Cornelius, Shippensburg University; Jamie Dangler, SUNY Cortland; Laurel R. Davis, Springfield College; Gloria Y. Gadsden, Fairleigh Dickinson University; Alan G. Hill, Delta College; Susan E. Humphers-Ginther, Moorhead State University; Katherine Johnson, Niagara County Community College; Barbara Karcher, Kennesaw State University; Debra C. Lemke, Western Maryland College; Patricia A. Masters, George Mason University; Susan McWilliams, University of Southern Maine; Kristy McNamara, Furman University; Dan Pence, Southern Utah University; Marcella Thompson, University of Arkansas; and Brenda S. Zicha, Charles Stewart Mott Community College.

I would like to thank the reviewers of the third edition for their insightful feedback: Deborah A. Abowitz, Bucknell University; Jarl Ahlkvist, University of Colorado-Colorado Springs; Cheryl Albers, Buffalo State College; Sue Cox, Bellevue Community College; Derek Greenfield, Highline Community College; Tiffany Hayes, Green River Community College; Louise Hull, Green River Community College;Barbara Karcher, Kennesaw State University; John Poindexter; West Shore Community College; Susan Ross, Lycoming College; Ericka Stange, Central Washington University; Ann S. Stein, College of Charleston; Deborah Thorne, Ohio University; and Jamee K. Wolfe, Roanoke College.

Contents

Part Two   *THE RESEARCH CRAFT*

Part Three   *CULTURE*

In most schools, girls and boys sit in the same classrooms, read the same books, and listen to the same teachers. That means they learn the same lessons, right? Wrong.

reasons that college students give for cheating. How persuasive do you find their explanations?

"My speedometer cable is broken and I had no idea I was driving so fast!" "My alarm didn't go off this morning—that's why I missed the final exam." "My printer stopped working so I can't turn in the paper on time." It's routine to offer explanations or "accounts" to excuse or justify our misdeeds so that people won't condemn our behavior. But what happens if we get caught doing something really wrong? In this article, you will read the accounts offered by men convicted of white-collar crimes.

Sociologists' obsession with inequality surprises many laypeople (and most students). Why is that? Historian Loewen claims it's because most students leave high school as "terrible sociologists."

In this classic discussion of stratification, Tumin shows the illogic of traditional theories of social inequality in society.

Ehrenreich has written a lot of books and articles, but in 1998 she left home to try to discover how people survive working minimum wage jobs. She wasn't a great success in this part of the real world.

In their account of the problems faced by workers in the inner cities, Newman and Lennon provide an important warning for anyone who thinks that there are easy answers to unemployment.

·1·

The Promise

C. Wright Mills

"The Promise," published in 1959 by C. Wright Mills, is probably the most famous essay ever written by a modern sociologist. In this article, Mills captures the essential lesson of sociology: To truly understand people's behavior, we must look beyond those individuals to the larger social contexts in which they live. Individuals make choices, to be sure, but their choices are constrained by social, historical, cultural, political, and economic factors. Most important, people frequently do not even realize the extent to which their lives are affected by things that are external to them and outside of their control. Mills's point is that if we are to understand people's behavior, we must take into account these nonindividual factors. (This is not an especially easy article to read, but it is fundamental. You might find it helpful to read the section on Mills in *The Practical Skeptic: Core Concepts in Sociology,* chapter 2, before you tackle this reading.)

Nowadays men often feel that their private lives are a series of traps. They sense that within their everyday worlds, they cannot overcome their troubles, and in this feeling, they are often quite correct: What ordinary men are directly aware of and what they try to do are bounded by the private orbits in which they live; their visions and their powers are limited to the close-up scenes of job, family, neighborhood; in other milieux[1] they move vicariously and remain spectators. And the more aware they become, however vaguely, of ambitions and of threats which transcend their immediate locales, the more trapped they seem to feel.

Underlying this sense of being trapped are seemingly impersonal changes in the very structure of continent-wide societies. The facts of contemporary history are also facts about the success and the failure of individual men and women. When a society is industrialized, a peasant becomes a worker; a feudal lord is liquidated or becomes a businessman. When classes rise or fall, a man is employed or unemployed; when the rate of investment goes up or down, a man takes new heart or goes broke. When wars happen, an insurance salesman becomes a rocket launcher; a store clerk, a radar man; a wife lives alone; a child grows up without a father. Neither the life of an individual nor the history of a society can be understood without understanding both.

Yet men do not usually define the troubles they endure in terms of historical change and

---

[1]*Milieux* is French; it means "social environments." (*Milieux* is plural; *milieu* is singular.) — Ed.

institutional contradiction.[2] The well-being they enjoy, they do not usually impute to the big ups and downs of the societies in which they live. Seldom aware of the intricate connection between the patterns of their own lives and the course of world history, ordinary men do not usually know what this connection means for the kinds of men they are becoming and for the kinds of history-making in which they might take part. They do not possess the quality of mind essential to grasp the interplay of man and society, of biography and history, of self and world. They cannot cope with their personal troubles in such ways as to control the structural transformations that usually lie behind them.

Surely it is no wonder. In what period have so many men been so totally exposed at so fast a pace to such earthquakes of change? That Americans have not known such catastrophic changes as have the men and women of other societies is due to historical facts that are now quickly becoming "merely history." The history that now affects every man is world history. Within this scene and this period, in the course of a single generation, one sixth of mankind is transformed from all that is feudal and backward into all that is modern, advanced, and fearful. Political colonies are freed; new and less visible forms of imperialism installed. Revolutions occur; men feel the intimate grip of new kinds of authority. Totalitarian societies rise, and are smashed to bits—or succeed fabulously. After two centuries of ascendancy, capitalism is shown up as only one way to make society into an industrial apparatus. After two centuries of hope, even formal democracy is restricted to a quite small portion of mankind. Everywhere in the underdeveloped world, ancient ways of life are broken up and vague expectations become urgent demands. Everywhere in the overdeveloped world, the means of authority and of violence become total in scope and bureaucratic in form. Humanity itself now lies before us, the super-nation at either pole concentrating its most coordinated and massive efforts upon the preparation of World War Three.

The very shaping of history now outpaces the ability of men to orient themselves in accordance with cherished values. And which values? Even when they do not panic, men often sense that older ways of feeling and thinking have collapsed and that newer beginnings are ambiguous to the point of moral stasis. Is it any wonder that ordinary men feel they cannot cope with the larger worlds with which they are so suddenly confronted? That they cannot understand the meaning of their epoch for their own lives? That—in defense of selfhood—they become morally insensible, trying to remain altogether private men? Is it any wonder that they come to be possessed by a sense of the trap?

It is not only information that they need—in this Age of Fact, information often dominates their attention and overwhelms their capacities to assimilate it. It is not only the skills of reason that they need—although their struggles to acquire these often exhaust their limited moral energy.

---

[2]Mills is using the term *institution* in its sociological sense—which is a bit different from the way this term is used in everyday or conventional speech. To the sociologist, institution refers to *a set of social arrangements, an accepted way of resolving important social problems.* Thus, the institution of the family is our society's way of resolving the important social problem of raising children. The institution of the economy is how we resolve the problem of distributing goods and services (for example, in the case of the United States, capitalism). The concept of institutional contradiction refers to situations in which the demands of one institution are not compatible with the demands of another institution. For example, there is institutional contradiction when the institution of the family is based on the norm that dad goes to work and mom stays home with the kids but the institution of the economy is such that it takes two employed adults to support a family. You will find more examples of institutional contradictions in reading 2 by Stephanie Coontz. You can read more about the nature of institutions in *The Practical Skeptic: Core Concepts in Sociology,* chapter 9, "Society and Social Institutions." —Ed.

What they need, and what they feel they need, is a quality of mind that will help them to use information and to develop reason in order to achieve lucid summations of what is going on in the world and of what may be happening within themselves. It is this quality, I am going to contend, that journalists and scholars, artists and publics, scientists and editors are coming to expect of what may be called the sociological imagination.

1

The sociological imagination enables its possessor to understand the larger historical scene in terms of its meaning for the inner life and the external career of a variety of individuals. It enables him to take into account how individuals, in the welter of their daily experience, often become falsely conscious of their social positions. Within that welter, the framework of modern society is sought, and within that framework the psychologies of a variety of men and women are formulated. By such means the personal uneasiness of individuals is focused upon explicit troubles and the indifference of publics is transformed into involvement with public issues.

The first fruit of this imagination—and the first lesson of the social science that embodies it—is the idea that the individual can understand his own experience and gauge his own fate only by locating himself within his period, that he can know his own chances in life only by becoming aware of those of all individuals in his circumstances. In many ways it is a terrible lesson; in many ways a magnificent one. We do not know the limits of man's capacities for supreme effort or willing degradation, for agony or glee, for pleasurable brutality or the sweetness of reason. But in our time we have come to know that the limits of "human nature" are frighteningly broad. We have come to know that every individual lives, from one generation to the next, in some society; that he lives out a biography, and that he lives it out within some historical sequence. By the fact of his living he contributes, however minutely, to the shaping of this society and to the course of its history, even as he is made by society and by its historical push and shove.

The sociological imagination enables us to grasp history and biography and the relations between the two within society. That is its task and its promise. . . . And it is the signal of what is best in contemporary studies of man and society.

No social study that does not come back to the problems of biography, of history and of their intersections within a society has completed its intellectual journey. Whatever the specific problems of the classic social analysts, however limited or however broad the features of social reality they have examined, those who have been imaginatively aware of the promise of their work have consistently asked three sorts of questions:

1. What is the structure of this particular society as a whole? What are its essential components, and how are they related to one another? How does it differ from other varieties of social order? Within it, what is the meaning of any particular feature for its continuance and for its change?

2. Where does this society stand in human history? What are the mechanics by which it is changing? What is its place within and its meaning for the development of humanity as a whole? How does any particular feature we are examining affect, and how is it affected by, the historical period in which it moves? And this period—what are its essential features? How does it differ from other periods? What are its characteristic ways of history-making?

3. What varieties of men and women now prevail in this society and in this period? And what varieties are coming to prevail? In what ways are they selected and formed, liberated and repressed, made sensitive and blunted? What kinds of "human nature" are revealed in the conduct and character we observe in this society in this period? And what is the meaning for "human nature" of each and every feature of the society we are examining?

Whether the point of interest is a great power state or a minor literary mood, a family, a prison, a creed — these are the kinds of questions the best social analysts have asked. They are the intellectual pivots of classic studies of man in society — and they are the questions inevitably raised by any mind possessing the sociological imagination. For that imagination is the capacity to shift from one perspective to another — from the political to the psychological; from examination of a single family to comparative assessment of the national budgets of the world; from the theological school to the military establishment; from considerations of an oil industry to studies of contemporary poetry. It is the capacity to range from the most impersonal and remote transformations to the most intimate features of the human self — and to see the relations between the two. Back of its use there is always the urge to know the social and historical meaning of the individual in the society and in the period in which he has his quality and his being.

That, in brief, is why it is by means of the sociological imagination that men now hope to grasp what is going on in the world, and to understand what is happening in themselves as minute points of the intersections of biography and history within society. In large part, contemporary man's self-conscious view of himself as at least an outsider, if not a permanent stranger, rests upon an absorbed realization of social relativity and of the transformative power of history. The sociological imagination is the most fruitful form of this self-consciousness. By its use men whose mentalities have swept only a series of limited orbits often come to feel as if suddenly awakened in a house with which they had only supposed themselves to be familiar. Correctly, or incorrectly, they often come to feel that they can now provide themselves with adequate summations, cohesive assessments, comprehensive orientations. Older decisions that once appeared sound now seem to them products of a mind unaccountably dense. Their capacity for astonishment is made lively again. They acquire a new way of thinking, they experience a transvaluation of values; in a word, by their reflection and by their sensibility, they realize the cultural meaning of the social sciences.

2

Perhaps the most fruitful distinction with which the sociological imagination works is between "the personal troubles of milieu" and "the public issues of social structure." This distinction is an essential tool of the sociological imagination and a feature of all classic work in social science.

Troubles occur within the character of the individual and within the range of his immediate relations with others; they have to do with his self and with those limited areas of social life of which he is directly and personally aware. Accordingly, the statement and the resolution of troubles properly lie within the individual as a biological entity and within the scope of his immediate milieu — the social setting that is directly open to his personal experience and to some extent his willful activity. A trouble is a private matter: values cherished by an individual are felt by him to be threatened.

Issues have to do with matters that transcend these local environments of the individual and the range of his inner life. They have to do with the organization of many such milieux into the institutions of an historical society as a whole, with the ways in which various milieux overlap and interpenetrate to form the larger structure of social and historical life. An issue is a public matter: some value cherished by publics is felt to be threatened. Often there is a debate about what that value really is and about what it is that really threatens it. This debate is often without focus if only because it is the very nature of an issue, unlike even widespread trouble, that it cannot very well be defined in terms of the immediate and everyday environments of ordinary men. An issue, in fact, often involves a crisis in institutional arrangements, and often too it involves what Marxists call "contradictions" or "antagonisms."

In these terms, consider unemployment. When, in a city of 100,000, only one man is unemployed, that is his personal trouble, and for its relief we properly look to the character of the man, his skills, and his immediate opportunities. But when in a nation of 50 million employees, 15 million men are unemployed, that is an issue, and we may not hope to find its solution within the range of opportunities open to any one individual. The very structure of opportunities has collapsed. Both the correct statement of the problem and the range of possible solutions require us to consider the economic and political institutions of the society, and not merely the personal situation and character of a scatter of individuals.

Consider war. The personal problem of war, when it occurs, may be how to survive it or how to die in it with honor; how to make money out of it; how to climb into the higher safety of the military apparatus; or how to contribute to the war's termination. In short, according to one's values, to find a set of milieux and within it to survive the war or make one's death in it meaningful. But the structural issues of war have to do with its causes; with what types of men it throws up into command; with its effects upon economic and political, family and religious institutions, with the unorganized irresponsibility of a world of nation-states.

Consider marriage. Inside a marriage a man and a woman may experience personal troubles, but when the divorce rate during the first four years of marriage is 250 out of every 1,000 attempts, this is an indication of a structural issue having to do with the institutions of marriage and the family and other institutions that bear upon them.

Or consider the metropolis—the horrible, beautiful, ugly, magnificent sprawl of the great city. For many upper-class people, the personal solution to "the problem of the city" is to have an apartment with private garage under it in the heart of the city, and forty miles out, a house by Henry Hill, garden by Garrett Eckbo, on a hundred acres of private land. In these two controlled environments—with a small staff at each end and a private helicopter connection—most people could solve many of the problems of personal milieux caused by the facts of the city. But all this, however splendid, does not solve the public issues that the structural fact of the city poses. What should be done with this wonderful monstrosity? Break it all up into scattered units, combining residence and work? Refurbish it as it stands? Or, after evacuation, dynamite it and build new cities according to new plans in new places? What should those plans be? And who is to decide and to accomplish whatever choice is made? These are structural issues; to confront them and to solve them requires us to consider political and economic issues that affect innumerable milieux.

In so far as an economy is so arranged that slumps occur, the problem of unemployment becomes incapable of personal solution. In so far as war is inherent in the nation-state system and in the uneven industrialization of the world, the ordinary individual in his restricted milieu will be powerless—with or without psychiatric aid—to solve the troubles this system or lack of system imposes upon him. In so far as the family as an institution turns women into darling little slaves and men into their chief providers and unweaned dependents, the problem of a satisfactory marriage remains incapable of purely private solution. In so far as the overdeveloped megalopolis and the overdeveloped automobile are built-in features of the overdeveloped society, the issues of urban living will not be solved by personal ingenuity and private wealth.

What we experience in various and specific milieux, I have noted, is often caused by structural changes. Accordingly, to understand the changes of many personal milieux we are required to look beyond them. And the number and variety of such structural changes increase as the institutions within which we live become more embracing and more intricately connected with one another. To be aware of the idea of social structure and to use it with sensibility is to be capable of tracing such linkages among a great variety of milieux. To be able to do that is to possess the sociological imagination. . . .

Questions

1. What is the sociological imagination? (You might begin with quoting Mills's definition, but try to describe this phenomenon in your own words as well.)

2. In brief, what kinds of questions are asked by those who possess a sociological imagination?

3. What are "personal troubles of milieu"? What are "public issues of social structure"? Why does Mills say that the distinction between troubles and issues is "an essential tool of the sociological imagination"?

·2·

How History and Sociology Can Help Today's Families

Stephanie Coontz

In this 1997 article (the introductory chapter to her book *The Way We Really Are*), Stephanie Coontz demonstrates the sociological imagination as she discusses the nature of relations between men and women and between parents and kids. Again, these issues *seem* personal; but Coontz demonstrates how taking the larger—sociological and historical—view is very important if we want to find practical answers to such crucial questions as "What's wrong with male–female relationships in modern society?" and "What's happening to today's youth?"

When lecture audiences first urged me to talk about how family history and sociology were relevant to contemporary life, I wasn't sure I wanted to abandon the safety of my historical observation post. But my experiences in recent years have convinced me that people are eager to learn whether historians and social scientists can help them improve their grasp of family issues. And I've come to believe that it's our responsibility to try.

I don't want to make false promises about what history and sociology offer. I can't give you five tips to make your relationship last. I don't have a list of ten things you can say to get your kids to do what *you* want and make them think it's what *they* want. Nor can I give kids many useful pointers on how to raise their parents.

But a historical perspective can help us place our personal relationships into a larger social context, so we can distinguish individual idiosyncrasies or problems from broader dilemmas posed by the times in which we live. Understanding the historical background and the current socioeconomic setting of family changes helps turn down the heat on discussion of many family issues. It can alleviate some of the anxieties of modern parents and temper the recriminations that go back and forth between men and women. Seeing the larger picture won't make family dilemmas go away, but it can reduce the insecurity, personal bitterness, or sense of betrayal that all of us, at one time or another, bring to these issues. Sometimes it helps to know that the tension originates in the situation, not the psyche.

Putting Teen–Parent Conflicts in Perspective

Consider the question of what's happening to American youth. It's extremely difficult for parents today to look at a specific problem they may have with their teenager, whether that is sneaking out at night or experimenting with alcohol and drugs, without seeing it as a sign of the crisis we are told grips modern youth. Parents tell me they are terrified by headlines about the "epidemic" of teen suicide and by chilling television stories about kids too young to drive a car but old enough to carry an AK-47.

Concerns over adolescent behavior are not entirely new. "Let's Face It," a *Newsweek* cover story of September 6, 1954, declared: "Our Teenagers Are Out of Control." The 1955 film, *Blackboard Jungle,* claimed that teens were "savage" animals because "gang leaders have taken the place of parents." Still, there *are* new structural and historical changes in American life that have recently complicated the transition from early adolescence to young adulthood, making youth–adult relations seem more adversarial.

It doesn't help us understand these changes, however, when people exaggerate the problems of today's teens or turn their normal ups and downs into pathologies. Most teens do not get involved in violence, either as criminals or victims. While teen suicide rates have indeed been increasing, any growth from a low starting point can sound dramatic if presented as a percentage. For example, a 1995 report from the Centers for Disease Control stated that suicides among 10- to 14-year-old youths had "soared" between 1980 and 1992. What this meant in real figures, points out researcher Mike Males, was that 1 in 60,000 youths in this age group killed themselves in 1992, compared to 1 in 125,000 in 1980. The actual death rate among teens from firearms and poisoning has scarcely changed since the 1950s, but the proportion attributed to suicide has risen dramatically, while the proportion attributed to accident has declined (Holinger 1994; Males 1996).

Furthermore, many "teen" suicide figures are overstated because they come from a database that includes people aged 15 to 24. Suicide rates for actual teenagers, aged 13 to 19, are among the lowest of any age group. In fact, notes Kirk Astroth, "teens as a whole are *less likely* to commit suicide than any other age group *except* preteens. . . . Occupational surveys consistently show that parents and teachers are *twice* as likely, counselors and psychologists are *four* times as likely, and school administrators are *six* times as likely to commit suicide as are high school students" (Astroth, 1993, 413). (When I read this statistic to a teenage acquaintance of mine, he told me dourly, "Yeah, but they'll just say we drove them to it.")

It's not that we have more bad parents or more bad kids today than we used to. It's not that families have lost interest in their kids. And there is no evidence that the majority of today's teenagers are more destructive or irresponsible than in the past. However, relations between adults and teens are especially strained today, not because youths have lost their childhood, as is usually suggested, but because they are not being adequately prepared for the new requirements of adulthood. In some ways, childhood has actually been prolonged, if it is measured by dependence on parents and segregation from adult activities. What many young people have lost are clear paths for gaining experience doing responsible, socially necessary work, either in or out of the home, and for moving away from parental supervision without losing contact with adults.

The most common dilemma facing adolescents, and the one that probably causes the most conflicts with adults, is their "rolelessness" in modern society. A rare piece of hard data in all the speculation about what makes adolescents tick is that young people do better on almost every level when they have meaningful involvement in useful and necessary tasks. This effect exists independently of their relationships with parents and friends. Teens also benefit from taking responsibility for younger or less-fortunate children. As one author observes, teens "need some experience of being older, bigger, stronger, or wiser" (Hamburg 1992, 201; Maton 1990, 297).

But today's adolescents have very few opportunities to do socially necessary work. The issue of rolelessness has been building for eighty years, ever since the abolition of child labor, the extension of schooling, and the decline in farm work that used to occupy many youths in the summer. The problem has accelerated recently, as many of the paths that once led teenagers toward mastery of productive and social roles have turned into dead ends. Instead of having a variety of routes to adulthood, as was true for most of American history, most youngsters are now expected to stay in high school until age 17 or 18.

High schools were originally designed for the most privileged sector of the population. Even now they tend to serve well only that half of the high school population that goes on to college. Non-college-bound students often tell me they feel like second-class citizens, not really of interest to the school. And in recent decades a high school degree has lost considerable value as a ticket to a stable job. Even partial college work confers fewer advantages than in the past. Because of these and other trends, researcher Laurence Steinberg claims, adolescence "has become a social and economic holding period" (1992, 30).

Parents are expected to do the holding. In 1968, two researchers commented that most teen–parent conflicts stemmed from the fact that "readiness for adulthood comes about two years *later* than the adolescent claims and about two years *before* the parent will admit" (Stone and Church 1968, 447; emphasis added). There is some evidence that the level of miscalculation has widened for *both* parents and kids.

From the point of view of parents, it is more necessary than ever for kids to stay in school rather than seek full-time work, and to delay marriage or pregnancy. After all, the age at which youths can support themselves, let alone a *family*, has reached a new high in the past two decades. From the kids' point of view, though, this waiting period seems almost unbearable. They not only know a lot more than their folks about modern technology but they feel that they also know more about the facts of life than yesterday's teens. Understandably, they strain at the leash.

The strain is accentuated by the fact that while the age of economic maturation has been rising, the age of physical maturation has been falling. The average age of puberty for girls, for instance, was 16 in 1820, 14 in 1900, and 13 in 1940. Today it is 12, and may still be dropping. For boys, the pace and timing of pubertal development is the most important factor in determining the age at which they first have sex; the influence of parents, friends, income, and race is secondary. Although parents and friends continue to exert considerable influence on the age at which girls begin to have sex, there are obvious limits to how long parents can hold their teenagers back (Nightingale and Wolverton 1988, 1994).

And even as the job market offers fewer and fewer ways for teens to assert their independence and show that they are more grown up than younger kids, consumer markets and the media offer more and more. Steinberg points out that while teens "have less autonomy to pursue societally-valued *adult* activities" than in the past, they "have more autonomy than did their counterparts previously in matters of leisure, discretionary consumption, and grooming." As a result, adolescents "find it easier to purchase illicit drugs than to obtain legitimate employment" (Steinberg 1992, 30).

Another problem for parent–child relations is society's expectation that teens abide by rules and habits that grown-ups have abandoned, and that parents ought to be able to *make* them do so. In preindustrial societies most kids were integrated into almost all adult activities, and right up until the twentieth century there were few separate standards or different laws for teens and adults. For centuries, youth and adults played the same games by the same rules, both literally and figuratively. From "blind man's bluff" to "follow the leader," games we now leave to children were once played by adults as well. There were few special rules or restrictions that applied solely to teens. *All* premarital sex was supposedly out of line in the nineteenth century; teen sex was not singled out as a special problem. In fact, as late as 1886, the "age of consent" for girls was only 10 in more than half the states in the union (Luker 1996). However, girls or women who *did* consent to premarital sex were ostracized, regardless of their age.

Today's adults have moved on to new amusements and freedoms, but we want teens to play the old games by the old rules. There may be some good reasons for this, but any segregated group soon develops its own institutions, rules, and value systems, and young people are no exception.

Sports is virtually the only adult-approved and peer-admired realm where teens can demonstrate successive gains in competency, test their limits, and show themselves bigger, stronger, and better than younger children. But for teens who aren't good at sports, or those who reject it as busywork designed to keep them out of trouble, what's left? Music, clothes, drugs, alcohol—the choices differ. Many kids experiment and move on. Others get caught in the quagmire of seeking their identity through consumption. What we often call the youth culture is actually adult marketers seeking to commercially exploit youthful energy and rebellion. But sometimes consumerism seems the only way teens can show that they are growing up and experimenting with new social identities while adults try to keep them suspended in the children's world of school or summer camp.

Of course, many teens get a lot out of school and summer camp. But the dilemmas of rolelessness often put adolescents and their parents on a collision course. Young people feel that adults are plying them with make-work or asking them to put their lives on hold as they mature. They're pretty sure we didn't put *our* lives on hold at comparable levels of maturity, so they suspect us of hypocrisy. Often, they have a point.

On the other hand, while many parents recognize that risk taking among teenagers hasn't changed much since their own youth, they feel that there are more serious consequences for those behaviors than there used to be, given the presence of AIDS (acquired immune deficiency syndrome), high-tech weapons, and new potent drugs. So adults are not necessarily being hypocritical when they hold kids to higher standards than they met themselves. Many of us fear that the second chances and lucky breaks we got may not be available to the next generation.

Balancing the legitimate fears of adults against the legitimate aspirations of teens is not easy. But it helps for both teens and adults to realize that many of their conflicts are triggered by changes in social and economic arrangements, not just family ones. The best way I've found to personally confirm the sociological studies of rolelessness is to ask older men to talk about their life histories. Some of the most interesting discussions I've had over the past few years have been with men over age 60, whose memories extend beyond the transitional period of the 1960s and 1970s to what teen life was like in the 1930s, 1940s, or early 1950s.

The conversations usually start with comments on irresponsible behavior by today's teenage males. "I'd have had my hide tanned if I'd been caught doing that," someone always says, which generally leads to examples of how they got "whomped" or "taught a lesson." Soon, though, the subject switches to the things these upstanding men *didn't* get caught doing in their youth. And most of the time, it turns out the first lesson they learned by getting whomped was how not to get caught.

When they talk about what *really* set them on the right path, almost every older man I've talked with recalls his first job. "I was supporting myself when I was 17" (16, 18, 19, even 15), or "I was in the army with a job to do," the stories go: "What's the matter with today's kids?" And soon they provide their own answers. The typical job a teenager can get today provides neither the self-pride of economic independence nor the socializing benefits of working alongside adult mentors. Teens work in segregated jobs where the only adult who ever comes around is the boss, almost always in an adversarial role. Few jobs for youth allow them to start at the bottom and move up; the middle rungs of the job ladder have been sawed off. Marking time in dead-end jobs that teach no useful skills for the future, teens remain dependent on their parents for the basic necessities of life, simultaneously resenting that dependence and trying to manipulate it.

The stories older men tell about their first jobs are quite different from those told by today's teens. Even men who later became businessmen or highly educated professionals say that their first jobs were in construction, factory work, or some menial setting where they worked beside older men who were more skilled or highly paid. The senior men teased the youngsters, sending them out for a left-handed hammer or making them the butt of sometimes painful practical jokes, but they also showed kids the ropes and helped protect them from the foreman or boss. And they explained why "putting up with the crap" was worth it. After older men talk for a while about what these work experiences meant to them, they are almost always surprised to find themselves agreeing that the loss of nonparental male mentoring may be a bigger problem for boys today than the rise of single-mother homes.

Even allowing for nostalgia, such work relations seem to have been critical experiences for the socialization of many young men in the past. Such jobs integrated youths into adult society, teaching skills they would continue to use as they aged, instead of segregating them in a separate peer culture. As late as 1940, about 60 percent of employed adolescents aged 16–17 worked in traditional workplaces, such as farms, factories, or construction sites. The jobs they did there, or at least the skills they used, might last well into their adult lives. By 1980, only 14 percent worked in such settings (Greenberger and Steinberg 1986).

Girls, who were excluded from many such jobs, have lost less in this arena of life. Up through the 1960s an adolescent girl typically had more responsibilities at home, from washing dishes to taking care of siblings, than she does today. While such tasks may have prepared girls for adult roles as wives and mothers, they also held girls back from further education or preparation for future work outside the home. The change in work patterns for girls has thus made it *easier* for them to see that they have paths toward adult independence. On the other hand, it raises a different set of tensions between girls and their parents. The decline of the sexual double standard, without an equal decline in economic and social discrimination against women, leads parents to worry that their daughters may have too much opportunity, too early, to engage in sexual risk taking for which girls still pay a far higher price than boys.

Another issue facing teens of both sexes is their increasing exclusion from public space. People talk about how kids today are unsupervised, and they often are; but in one sense teens are under *more* surveillance than in the past. Almost anyone about the age of 40 can remember places where young people could establish real physical, as opposed to psychic, distance from adults. In the suburbs it was undeveloped or abandoned lots and overgrown woods, hidden from adult view, often with old buildings that you could deface without anyone caring. In the cities it was downtown areas where kids could hang out. Many of these places are now gone, and only some kids feel comfortable in the malls that have replaced them.

Much has been written about the gentrification of public space in America, the displacement of the poor or socially marginal from their older niches, followed by fear and indignation from respectable people suddenly forced to actually see the homeless doing what they always used to do. Over the years we have also seen what I think of as an "adultification" of public space. Kids are usually allowed there, as long as they're young enough to be in their parents' charge. But where in your town are teenagers welcome on their own?

Teens today have fewer opportunities than in the past for gradual initiation into productive activities, both at home and in public, and fewer places to demonstrate their autonomy in socially approved ways. At the same time, though, they have more access to certain so-called adult forms of consumption than ever before. This makes it hard for adults to avoid the extremes of overly controlling, lock-'em-up positions on the one hand and frequent breakdowns of supervision on the other. Some parents clearly underprotect their kids. We've all seen parents who are too stressed to monitor their kids effectively or who have had their limits overrun so many times that they have given up. Other parents, however, overprotect their kids, trying to personally compensate for the loss of wider adult contacts and of safe retreats. Both extremes drive kids away. But, in most cases, both are reactions to structural dilemmas facing parents and teens rather than abdications of parental responsibility.

What Social Science Tells Us About Male—Female Conflicts

The same kind of perspective can be useful in sorting through conflicts between modern couples. I vividly remember the first people who forced me to bring my historical and social analysis down to individual cases. Following one of my talks, a couple stood up and described a conflict they were having in their marriage. She complained about how unappreciative he was of the effort she took in making gourmet dinners and keeping the house clean. He said: "Hang on a minute. I never asked her to do any of those things. I can't help it if she has higher standards than I do. I don't *care* what we have for dinner. I don't *care* if the floor gets mopped twice a week." They wanted me to comment on their situation.

This is not fair, I thought, as I tried to wriggle out of doing so. I've just summed up the history of family diversity and changing gender roles since colonial times and they want me to settle a marital argument—over housework, of all things? I'm not a counselor; I don't know anything about mediating these issues. I tried to change the subject, but they wouldn't let up, and the audience was clearly on their side. You think family history is relevant, they seemed to be saying. Prove it.

Trapped, but unwilling to pretend I had therapeutic expertise, I cast about for something in my own research or training that might by any stretch of the imagination be helpful. The only thing that came to mind was a concept I had read about in an academic journal. "So," I said, feeling a bit silly, "perhaps the problem we have here lies in what social scientists would call your 'situated social power'" (Wartenberg 1988).

It sounded very academic, even downright pompous, but the more we talked about it, the more I realized this *was* a useful concept for them. In plain English it means that various groups in society have unequal access to economic resources, political power, and social status, and these social differences limit how fair or equal a personal relationship between two individuals from different groups can really be. Such social imbalances affect personal behavior regardless of sincere intentions of both parties to "not let it make a difference."

Teachers, for example, have social power over students. I tell my students that I want them to speak their minds and express their disagreements with me. And I mean it. But often I don't even notice that they continue to defer until someone finally gets angry at me for "dominating the discussion." Even after all these years, my initial reaction is usually indignation. "I told you to speak up," I want to say; "it's not my fault if you hold back." Then I remind myself that in any situation of unequal power, it's the party with the most power who always assumes that other people can act totally free of outside constraints.

When a person with power pretends not to have it, people with less power feel doubly vulnerable. Although they continue to be unequal, they are now asked to put aside the psychological defenses they have constructed against that inequality, including a certain amount of self-protective guardedness. So they clam up or get sore, which leaves the more powerful person feeling that his or her big-hearted gestures are being rebuffed. This tension arises between people of different races and classes, between employees and supervisors, and between men and women, as well as between my students and me.

With this awareness, I try to remember that my students are never going to feel as free criticizing my work as I'm going to feel criticizing theirs. I have to adjust the structure of my class to facilitate discussion. I need to institute protected spaces for criticism, such as providing anonymous evaluation forms for assessing my performance. But I also have to recognize that our power imbalance will always create tensions between us. I should neither blame my students for that nor feel that I've failed to communicate my "authentic self" to them. None of us exists independently of the social relations in which we operate.

Remembering how helpful this concept is to me in depersonalizing conflicts with students, I reminded the couple that men and women have different options in our society, outside and independent of their personal relationships. Research shows that men are happiest in a relationship when they don't have to do much housework and yet meals get made, clothes get ironed, and the house looks good. This doesn't mean they are chauvinist pigs. Who *wouldn't* be happier under those conditions?

But the wives of such men tend to be depressed. A wife may feel, especially if she jeopardized her earning power by taking time off to raise children, that she can't give up the domestic services she performs, because if her husband *does* get dissatisfied, she has fewer options than he does in the work world, and will be far worse off after a divorce.

Consciously or not, the wife in this particular marriage seemed to be assessing the risk of not keeping a nice house or putting delicious meals on the table, and finding it too high to just relax and let the housework go. But she was also resenting her husband's unwillingness to help out. This very common pattern of seemingly voluntary sacrifice by the woman, followed by resentment for the man's failure to reciprocate, originates outside the individual relationship. The man was probably completely sincere about not caring if the work got done, but he was missing the point. His wife had looked around, seen what happened to wives who failed to please their husbands, and tried extra hard to make her husband happy. He could not understand her compulsion, and resented being asked to participate in what he saw as unnecessary work. Counseling and better communication might help, but would probably not totally remove the little kernel of fear in the wife's heart that stems from her perfectly reasonable assessment of the unequal social and economic options for men and women.

Similarly, two people trying to raise a child while they both work full-time are going to get stressed or angry. Part of the problem may be that the man isn't doing enough at home (on average, research shows, having a man in the house *adds* hours to a woman's workday) (Brace, Lloyd, and Leonard 1995; Hartmann 1981). Part of the problem may be that the woman is sabotaging her own stated desire to have the man do more—treating him as an unskilled assistant, refusing to relinquish her control over child-raising decisions, and keeping her domestic standards too high for him to meet. But another part of the problem will remain even if they are the most enlightened individuals in the world.

There's no nonstressful way to divide three full-time jobs between two individuals. Better communication can make the sacrifices more fair, or help clear away the side issues that get entangled with the stress, but the strains are a social problem existing outside the relationship. The solution does not lie in Martians learning to talk Venusian or Venusians being tolerant of the cultural oddities of Martians, as one pop psychologist describes the differences between men and women, but in changing the job structures and social support networks for family life. Until businesses and schools adjust their hours and policies to the realities of two-earner families, even the best-intentioned couples are going to have difficult times.

Improving communication or using the shortcuts offered by self-help books can alleviate some of the conflicts between men and women in this period of rapidly changing roles and expectations. But addressing communication problems alone ignores the differing social options and the patterned experiences of inequality that continually *re-create* such problems between men and women. So people move from one self-help book to another; they try out new encounter groups and memorize new techniques; they slip back and must start all over again. They are medicating the symptoms without solving the problem.

For example, the Venusian–Martian reference comes from best-selling author John Gray, who has found a strikingly effective analogy for getting men and women to realize that they bring different assumptions and experiences to relationships: Men and women, he says, come from different planets. They need to learn each other's culture and language. Gray tells women why men's periodic withdrawals from communication do not mean lack of interest in a relationship. Martians, he says, like to retreat to caves in times of stress, while Venusians tend to crowd around, offering each other support and empathy. He explains to men that women are often just asking for reassurance, not trying to control men's lives, when they pursue subjects past the male comfort zone (Gray 1992).

But Gray doesn't urge either sex to make any big changes, merely to take "tiny steps toward understanding the other." He offers women hints on how to ask their partners for help without antagonizing them or making them feel manipulated, but he doesn't demand that men share housework or that women accept the responsibilities that go with egalitarian relationships. For Gray, a healthy relationship exists "when both partners have permission to ask for what they want and need, and they both have permission to say no if they choose." This is certainly better than no one feeling free to ask, but it leaves a rather large set of issues unresolved (Gray 1992, 265; Peterson 1994).

The problem is that many advice books refuse to ask hard questions about the division of household work and decision-making power. In a section called "scoring points with the opposite sex," for example, Gray's advice to women revolves around issues such as not criticizing men for their driving or choice of restaurants. Men, by contrast, are advised: "offer to make dinner," "occasionally offer to wash the dishes," "compliment her on how she looks," "give her four hugs a day," and "don't flick the remote control to different channels when she is watching TV with you" (Gray 1992; Sen 1983).

Now, most women will say that the book would be worth its weight in gold if their husbands would just follow that last tip, but the fact remains that the unequal bargaining power and social support systems for men and women are not addressed, *or even acknowledged,* in this kind of advice. In the long run, failure to address the roots of gender differences perpetuates the problem of communication, or merely replaces one set of misunderstandings with another. As therapist Betty Carter writes, communicating about feelings rather than addressing issues of power and daily behavior can lead to manipulation that eventually degenerates into mutual blame and psychological name-calling (Carter 1996).[1] If we're going to think of men and women as being from different planets, they need more than guidebooks and language translations; we must make sure that the social, economic, and political treaties they operate under are fair to both parties.

It's not only women's dissatisfactions that are addressed by a historical and sociological perspective. Men often complain that feminists ignore male insecurities and burdens, and they have a point. Men *do* feel injured and alienated, despite their economic and political advantages over women of the same social group. But history and sociology can identify the sources of men's pain a lot more accurately than myths about the loss of some heroic age of male bonding when Australian aborigines, Chinese sun kings, and Greek warriors marched to their own drumbeat. Going "back to the woods" makes a nice weekend retreat,

but it doesn't help men restructure their long-term relationships or identify the social, economic, and political changes they need to improve their family lives (Bly 1990).[2]

Male pain is the other side of male power. Not all men, contrary to the rhetoric of masculinity, can be at the top of the pyramid. The contrast between rhetoric and reality is very painful for men whose race, class, health, or even height does not allow them to wield power, exercise authority, or just cut a figure imposing enough to qualify as a "real man." Even successful men pay a high price for their control and authority. The competitive, hierarchical environments men are encouraged to operate in cut them off from intimacy and penalize them for letting down their guard. The myth that male power is all individually achieved, not socially structured, means masculinity can be lost if it is not constantly proven in daily behavior (Brines 1994; Lehne 1989).

Structural analysis helps us get beyond the question of "who hurts more" to explore the different rewards and penalties that traditional gender roles impose on today's men and women. For girls, societal pressures descend heavily at about age 11 or 12, penalizing them for excelling and creating a sharp drop in their self-esteem. There is overwhelming evidence, for example, that girls are treated in ways that hinder their academic and intellectual development. But sometimes this discrimination takes the form of too easy praise and too little pressure to complete a task, leading boys to feel that "girls get off easy." And almost any parent can testify that boys are subject to a much earlier, more abrupt campaign to extinguish the compassion, empathy, and expression of feelings that young boys initially display as openly as girls. The list of derogatory words for boys who don't act masculine is

---

[1] As Andrew Greeley points out (1989), women's morale has declined far more significantly than men's. Unless their frustrations with the marriage bargain are addressed more directly, not just placated, men and women *could* end up on different planets.

[2] For a critique of Bly's point of view, see Connell 1992.

miles longer than the list of disparaging words for girls who don't act feminine. Boys who don't get the message quickly enough are treated brutally. Those who do get the message find that the very success of their effort to "be a man" earns mistrust and fear as well as admiration. In an article that my male students invariably love, Eugene August points out that people always talk about "innocent women and children" in describing victims of war or terrorism. Is there no such thing as an innocent man? (August 1992; Gilligan and Brown 1992; Gilligan, Lyons, and Hammer 1990; Kann 1986; Ornstein 1994; Sadker and Sadker 1994).

It's good to get past caricatures of female victims and male villains, but it is too simplistic to say that we just have to accept our differences. A man's fear of failure and discomfort with intimacy, for example, come from his socially structured need to constantly have others affirm his competence, self-reliance, or superiority. This is the downside of what he must do to exercise power and privilege. For women, lack of power often leads to fear of *success*. The downside of women's comfort with intimacy is discomfort with asserting authority.

As three researchers in the psychology of gender summarize the tradeoffs, boys "get encouraged to be independent and powerful, possibly at the cost of distancing themselves from intimacy." The result is that boys "tend to be overrepresented in the psychopathologies involving aggression." Girls, by contrast, "get rewarded for being compliant and for establishing intimate relations, possibly at the cost of achieving autonomy and control over their choices." This may be why girls are "overrepresented in the psychopathologies involving depression" (Cowan, Cowan, and Kerig 1993, 190).

The solution suggested by historical and social analysis is not for men and women to feel each other's pain but to equalize their power and access to resources. That is the only way they can relate with fairness and integrity, so that unequal and therefore inherently dishonest relations do not deform their identities. Men must be willing to give up their advantages over women if they hope to build healthy relationships with either sex. Women must be willing to accept tough criticism and give up superficial "privileges" such as being able to cry their way out of a speeding ticket if they hope to develop the inner resources to be high achievers. . . .

References

Astroth, Kirk. 1993. "Beyond Ephebiphobia: Problem Adults or Problem Youths?" *Phi Delta Kappan,* January.

August, Eugene. 1992. "Real Men Don't: Anti-Male Bias in English." Pp. 131–141 in Melita Schaum and Connie Flanagan (eds.), *Gender Images: Reading for Composition.* Boston: Houghton Mifflin.

Bly, Robert. 1990. *Iron John: A Book About Men.* Reading, MA: Addison-Wesley.

Brace, Judith, Cynthia Lloyd, and Ann Leonard, with Patrice Engle and Niev Duffy. 1995. *Families in Focus: New Perspectives on Mothers, Fathers, and Children.* New York: The Population Council.

Brines, Julie. 1994. "Economic Dependency, Gender, and the Division of Labor at Home." *American Journal of Sociology* 100.

Carter, Betty. 1996. *Love, Honor, and Negotiate: Making Your Marriage Work.* New York: Pocket Books.

Connell, R. W. 1992. "Drumming Up the Wrong Tree." *Tikkun* 7.

Cowan, Philip A., Carolyn Pape Cowan, and Patricia K. Kerig. 1993. "Mothers, Fathers, Sons and Daughters: Gender Differences in Family Formation and Parenting Styles" in Philip Cowan et al., (eds.), *Family, Self, and Society: Toward a New Agenda for Family Research.* Hillsdale, NJ: Erlbaum.

Gilligan, Carol, and Lynn Mickel Brown. 1992. *Meeting at the Crossroads: Women's Psychology and Girls' Development.* Cambridge, MA: Harvard University Press.

Gilligan, Carol, Nona Lyons, and Trudy Hammer. 1990. *Making Connections: The Relational World of Adolescent Girls at Emma Willard School.* Cambridge, MA: Harvard University Press.

Gray, John. 1992. *Men Are from Mars, Women Are from Venus.* New York: HarperCollins.

Greeley, Andrew. 1989. "The Declining Morale of Women." *Sociology and Social Research* 73.

Greenberger, Ellen, and Laurence Steinberg. 1986. *When Teenagers Work: The Psychological and Social Costs of Adolescent Employment.* New York: Basic Books.

Hamburg, David. 1992. *Today's Children: Creating a Future for a Generation in Crisis.* New York: Times Books.

Hartmann, Heidi. 1981. "The Family as the Locus of Gender, Class and Political Struggle: The Example of Housework." *Signs* 6.

Holinger, Paul. 1994. *Suicide and Homicide Among Adolescents.* New York: Guilford.

Kann, Mark. 1986. "The Costs of Being on Top." *Journal of the National Association for Women Deans* 49.

Lehne, Gregory. 1989. "Homophobia Among Men: Supporting and Defining the Male Role." Pp. 416–429 in Michael Kimmel and Michael Messner (eds.), *Men's Lives.* New York: Macmillan.

Luker, Kristin. 1996. *Dubious Conceptions: The Politics of Teenage Pregnancy.* Cambridge, MA: Harvard University Press.

Maddrick, Jeffrey. 1995. *The End of Affluence: The Causes and Consequences of America's Economic Dilemma.* New York: Random House.

Males, Mike. 1996. *The Scapegoat Generation: America's War on Adolescents.* Monroe, ME: Common Courage Press.

Maton, Kenneth. 1990. "Meaningful Involvement in Instrumental Activity and Well-Being: Studies of Older Adolescents and At Risk Urban Teen-Agers." *American Journal of Community Psychology* 18.

Nightingale, Elena, and Lisa Wolverton. 1988. "Adolescent Rolelessness in Modern Society." Working paper, Carnegie Council on Adolescent Development, September.

_____. 1994. "Sex and America's Teenagers." New York: Alan Guttmacher Institute.

Orenstein, Peggy. 1994. *School Girls: Young Women, Self-Esteem, and the Confidence Gap.* New York: Doubleday.

Peterson, Karen. 1994. "A Global Ambassador Between the Sexes." *USA Today,* March 28.

Sadker, Myra, and David Sadker. 1994. *Failing at Fairness: How American Schools Cheat Girls.* New York: Scribner.

_____. 1992. *How Schools Shortchange Girls: The AAUW Report: A Study of Major Findings on Girls and Education.* Washington, DC: AAUW Educational Foundation.

Sen, Amartya. 1983. "Economics and the Family." *Asian Development Review* 1.

Steinberg, Laurence. 1992. "The Logic of Adolescence." In Peter Edelman and Joyce Ladner (eds.), *Adolescence and Poverty: Challenge for the 1990s.* Washington, DC: Center for National Policy Press.

Stone, L. J., and J. Church. 1968. *Childhood and Adolescence: A Psychology of the Growing Person.* New York: Random House.

Wartenberg, Thomas. 1988. "The Situated Concept of Social Power." *Social Theory and Practice* 14.

Questions

1. Would Mills conclude that Coontz has a sociological imagination? Why or why not?

2. What is "rolelessness"? As a teenager, did you experience (or are you now experiencing) this phenomenon? Explain.

3. What is "situated social power"? Describe an example of situated social power that you have experienced or witnessed personally.

4. Consider the concept of "adultification." To what extent did it exist in the place(s) where you grew up? Explain. How might this problem be resolved?

·3·

Hernando Washington

Lisa J. McIntyre

One of the things that sets sociologists apart from ordinary people is their concern for the social. In their professional lives, sociologists tend to ignore individual cases and focus on aggregates or groups. For example, Émile Durkheim studied suicide in order to discover what factors contributed to fluctuations in the overall rates of suicide; he had no interest in what might lead particular individuals to take their lives.

Professional sociologists study *social* facts simply because these are interesting (at least to us). But to the layperson trying to live life in society, social facts may seem irrelevant. Why a society's crime rate goes up and down seems much less intriguing than why *my* house was robbed, or why *I* was mugged on the street. Likewise, the social forces that propel the unemployment rate are not nearly as interesting as the matter of why I am having a difficult time finding a job.

As C. Wright Mills pointed out, however, having a sociological imagination allows us to make connections between individuals and the societies in which they live. And, for the student of sociology, the acquisition of this imagination brings with it an enhanced ability to make sense of the behavior of individuals. Recall what Mills stressed as the "first fruit" of the sociological imagination: "the idea that the individual can understand his own experience and gauge his own fate only by locating himself within his period." It was in this sense that Stephanie Coontz (in the previous reading) brought to bear the sociological concept of "situated social power" to help her understand her own relationships with her teaching assistants, as well as the personal troubles of the woman whose husband did not appreciate her heroic housework.

From the viewpoint of the professional sociologist, the following reading may seem out of place in a sociology reader, because its focus is on an individual and how he responded to his immediate social milieu. But I have included it for the benefit of nonsociologists; written in 1999, it provides an example of how having an understanding of the impact of the social milieu can help us to understand the all-too-frequently unintelligible behaviors of individuals in our environment.

To get a Ph.D., one has to write something called a dissertation. It's essentially a research paper, and sometimes a very long research paper. Mine, for example, ended up being two hundred plus pages. I wrote my dissertation on public defenders—those attorneys who are paid by the state to defend people who are accused of crimes but can't afford to hire their own lawyer. The basic question was this: How can these attorneys defend individuals they know are guilty of crimes, especially if they are terrible crimes? Ultimately, I arrived at my answer by looking not just at the private consciences of the public defenders but also at what Mills would have called their social milieux or surroundings.

I met a number of murderers in the course of my research, but Hernando was my first one; and in part because he was my first, he left a large impression on me. But this crime also made a big impression on me because it seemed so bizarre. It never should have happened the way it did. But you can judge for yourself. I will tell you the story as I learned it.

Warning: The first time I heard this story, I remember being shocked. I remember, in fact, feeling nauseous. It's not because anyone showed me terrible pictures of the crime scene; it's just because the whole thing seemed so awful. And it *seemed* so awful because it *was* awful. That led me to wonder, Should I share this story with college students? Possibly, no one is (or should be) worldly enough to hear about this sort of thing.

The Case

This story takes place in Chicago. The major player in the story is a man named Hernando Washington. At various times, his nicknames included the Reverend and the Deacon, because he was president of the youth choir. His other nickname was Prince, because he was so charming and good-looking.

Before I get to the story, let me tell you a bit about the neighborhood in which Hernando lived, or as Mills would put it, his *social milieu*. It was on the South Side of Chicago. In a song from the 1970s, Jim Croce called the South Side of Chicago "the baddest part of town." That was an astute observation. It is

the baddest part of town; chances are, if you lived on the South Side, you'd never be able to get a cab driver to take you home at night; some cabs won't even venture there in the daytime.

The police refer to a murder that involves a man and woman on the South Side as a "South Side divorce." A great deal of its reputation involves the fact that the South Side of Chicago is heavily populated by people who are poor — mostly African Americans. Perhaps that's why the police tend to disrespect the people who live there. The police often call murders that involve African American killers and victims as "63rd Street misdemeanors." Police also take much longer to respond to calls on the South Side. The clear message to the people who live there is that they really aren't a part of the community that the Chicago police are pledged to "serve and to protect." This, I think, is an important fact.

On April 1, 1978, Hernando "Prince" Washington was arrested and charged with robbery, aggravated kidnapping, rape, and murder. His victim, 29-year-old Sarah Gould, was the wife of a physician and the mother of a small child. Sarah Gould had the great misfortune to be one of the 787 people in Chicago and one of the 20,432 people in the United States who were murdered that year.

When I say that Sarah had the "great misfortune" to be murdered, I mean that. Statistically, she should not have been a murder victim. Nationally, the murder rate for white women in 1978 was 2.8 per 100,000 population. For white men, it was 9.0; for black women, 12.8; and for black men, 58.1. Not only was Sarah white, but she was killed by a stranger. And in 1978, most murder victims were killed by people they knew — friends, lovers, family members, acquaintances, or neighbors. Of all the recorded acts of criminal violence — batteries, assaults, murders — in 1978, less than a third were committed by strangers. This was especially true for women: When the violent act was committed by a stranger, the victim was typically male.

Finally, Sarah Gould was white while Hernando was black. This was one of the more unusual aspects of the case. Most violence, and certainly most murders, involve persons of the same race.

So, the odds were really against Sarah Gould being murdered — however you want to look at it.

That year, April 1, April Fool's Day, fell on a Saturday. The story actually begins two days earlier. That Thursday afternoon, Hernando went out to do his sister Leah a favor. She had just bought a car, a used two-year-old Oldsmobile Cutlass, and the dealer had called the day before to tell her it was ready to be picked up. Hernando offered to do this for her, partly because he wanted to drive the car. His sister, who is ten years older than Hernando, said that would be fine as long as Hernando came to pick her up when she was done with work. Leah worked at the post office and got off work ten minutes before midnight.

Hernando picked up the car, but of course he didn't drive it straight home. Instead, he cruised around his South Side neighborhood for a while. However, he didn't see any of his friends, so he decided to cruise up to the north part of the city.

For Sarah Gould, that was a fatal decision.

Hernando later said he didn't have any particular plan, but eventually he admitted that just maybe, in the back of his mind, he thought he might rob someone. But it was nothing definite. He would simply drive around and see what happened.

Once up north, he drove to Northwestern University's hospital parking lot. He got out of his car and sat on the steps of a nearby building.

ROBBERY AND ABDUCTION

Around 7:30 P.M., Hernando saw a woman getting out of a reddish-orange VW Rabbit.

He approached her, gun in hand, and demanded her money. Sarah gave him $25, explaining that it was all the money she had, but he grabbed her by the arm, dragged her back to his car, and shoved her inside.

Later, when asked why he did that, he told his lawyers that he'd noticed a bunch of people walking toward them and he didn't want them to know that he had just robbed this woman. He said he was afraid that she'd scream or run or something.

Once Hernando got Sarah into the car, he was still afraid that she'd somehow make trouble, so he ordered her to take off her slacks and underpants. He threw her clothing underneath her car and then drove off.

In his confession to the police, Hernando had this to say:

> She was real excited, you know, asking me not to hurt her and I was constantly telling her I wouldn't hurt her, that all I want is money. She was sitting in the front seat alongside of me. We drove off, and she asked me, "What are you going to do to me?" and I told her that I would take her away from the area, so I would have a chance, you know, to get away without being caught.

He kept assuring her that he would not hurt her.

THE PHONE CALL

After Hernando drove around for several hours, Sarah said that he should let her go because her husband and son would be getting worried about her. He considered this for a while and then asked her if she'd like to call home. He stopped at a gas station that was closed for the evening but it had a phone booth.

Sarah's husband, who was indeed worried about her, later told police that she had said something to the effect that she was okay. He asked her, "When are you coming home?" There was a pause, and then he could hear

Sarah asking someone when she'd be home. In the background, he heard a male voice saying "an hour." He then asked, "Where are you?" She asked, "Where are we?" Her husband heard the answer: "You'll be home in an hour, bitch, come on."

After the phone call, Hernando told police,

I turned from the phone, going around the car and at this time, when I, you know, walked around to my car, she broke and ran. I was running after her. I asked her, I said, "Why are you acting like that? I have not hurt you, I told you I will let you go, I just want to make it as safe for me as you want it safe for yourself."

Then, as it was approaching midnight, Hernando pulled the car into a dark alley. He explained to Sarah that he had to go pick someone up and that she couldn't stay in the front seat of the car while he did this. Perhaps for a moment Sarah thought he was going to let her go, but instead, he forced her into the trunk telling her that if she was quiet, everything would be okay.

At exactly 11:50 P.M., Hernando was where he was supposed to be—in the car in front of the main post office. His sister Leah came out and got into the front seat with him. As he drove her home, they talked about the sorts of things that you would expect a brother and sister to talk about—mostly about the new car.

When they got home, Hernando waited in the car until Leah was inside the house. He had always been very concerned about her safety.

A few years earlier, Leah had been raped on her way home from work. Two men grabbed her, dragged her into an alley, stripped off her clothes, and raped her repeatedly. Afterwards, she crawled out of the alley and was relieved to see a police car there. The two officers looked at her, a black woman with her face bleeding and her clothes torn up, and said "Get home by yourself, bitch." Maybe they didn't want her to mess up the back of their patrol car.

Usually, Hernando met his sister after work—but that night he'd had a bike accident and was running late.

Indeed, Hernando's family had not had a great deal of luck when it came to dealing with the police. A few years earlier, Hernando's brother James had been at a party when he was shot by one of the neighborhood guys. Some of James's friends took him to the emergency room, but they were afraid to stay with him because gunshot wounds tend to attract attention. They left him in the emergency room, where he bled to death before the medical staff got to him. "Everyone knew" who had shot Hernando's brother, but for some reason the police didn't take him into custody. It was at that point that Hernando bought his first gun.

Then Hernando drove a few blocks away, stopped, and let Sarah out of the trunk. She reminded him of his promise to let her go, but he said they'd have to go back and get her clothes, because he didn't want to let her go until she was fully dressed again. He drove back to the hospital parking lot, but her clothes were gone; by now, the police had them.

When Sarah had driven into that parking lot earlier in the evening, she was on her way to a Lamaze class she was supposed to teach that night. Eventually, her students became worried about her, called her husband, and found out that she wasn't home. And, of course, he thought she was in class. Next, the class notified hospital security, which investigated and found Sarah's car in the parking lot. When they saw her keys in the ignition and her pants and underpants under the car, the security officers were naturally concerned. They called her husband, who immediately called the police to file a missing person's report.

Finding the clothes missing from under the car scared Hernando. Sarah told him that it didn't matter, that she could go home without them—she was covered enough, she said, by her long raincoat. But he was adamant that he wasn't going to let her go until he'd found her something to wear or, as he put it, until she was "decent" again. He said, "I've got to think of somewhere to get you some clothes."

THE RAPE

By now, it was well past midnight. Hernando thought it was much too late to go to a friend's house and borrow some clothes, so instead, he drove them back down to the South Side. On the way, he stopped and bought a pint of rum, leaving Sarah alone in the car for a moment. Then, he drove to a motel, got out of the car (again leaving Sarah in the front seat alone), registered for a room—in his name. He later told police, "I let her wash up. First she was kind of skeptical. I guess she was frightened. I kept reassuring her that I would not do anything to her. After a while, she went into the bathroom and washed up." Then, he told police, they both went to sleep.

But that was a lie. What really happened next, as Hernando admitted to his attorneys, was that he raped Sarah.

The next morning, Hernando left Sarah alone in the room while he checked out. After they left the motel, he stopped the car and put her back into the trunk. Then he drove to his parents' house to get a change of clothing for himself.

A few blocks later, Hernando let Sarah out of the trunk. Then he drove to a northwestern suburb where he had an appointment. On the way, he again stopped in an alley and forced her into the trunk while he "took care of some business."

What was this urgent appointment? Hernando's "appointment" was in one of the felony trial courtrooms in Cook County, Illinois. At the time all this was going on, Hernando was out on bail. A year earlier, Hernando had been arrested on charges of rape and aggravated kidnapping. His parents had taken out a loan, paid his bail, and hired him a private lawyer, who told Hernando that he would probably beat the rap and not to worry.

In any case, that Friday, March 31, was the scheduled trial date for the year-old rape case. When the case was called, however, the prosecutor requested a continuance, which the judge granted. Feeling good, Hernando walked out of the courtroom a relatively free man; he even offered his lawyer's assistant a ride back downtown.

When Hernando got back to his car, he saw a couple of people standing near it, seemingly talking to his trunk. Hernando told them to get lost and sped away. But one of the people got Hernando's license plate number and called it in to the police. The dispatcher who took the call about a "woman in the trunk" relayed the message to the detective division; someone placed it on a detective's desk.

Unfortunately, that particular detective had taken off—unannounced—for the weekend, and so no one found the message until the next morning. By then, it was too late. Sarah was dead.

Hernando let Sarah out of the trunk and told her he was disappointed that she'd tried to get help. After all, hadn't he told her that he wasn't going to hurt her and that he would let her go as soon as she got some clothes?

Hernando drove around for a while, and then, as he later told his lawyers, he noticed how dirty her raincoat was. Once again, he told Sarah that he just had to find some decent clothes for her. And once again, she protested that it really wasn't necessary, that she could get home without being fully dressed. Instead, Hernando went to the home of an old girl-friend to borrow some clothes. But he ended up not getting any clothes, claiming that he just didn't quite know how to ask and that her boyfriend was home and he didn't want the boyfriend to hear.

So he released Sarah from the trunk and drove around some more.

As evening approached, Hernando put Sarah back into the trunk of the car and went to meet some friends at a bar. Actually, they ended up going to several bars. He was, he said, getting pretty tired, but he liked being with his friends. And he was "reluctant" to go back to his car because he knew he'd have to deal with this problem. Finally, well after midnight, he returned to the car.

At this point, as they were listening to Hernando tell his story, one of his attorneys asked him, "If you were beginning to be uncomfortable about your situation, why didn't you just let her go, then and there?" Hernando said, "Because the neighborhood I was in wasn't a safe neighborhood for a white woman to be alone in."

Instead of letting her go, he took Sarah to another motel and again raped her. Details about the rape are sketchy because Hernando was a "little shy," as he put it, when it came to talking about "sex." And that's how he referred to the rapes — as sex.

THE MURDER

Early the next morning, Hernando checked out of the motel, drove around for about an hour, and then came to a decision: Clothing or no clothing, it was time to let Sarah go. He parked the car on a residential street, gave her some change, and told her to get on the bus. He said he told her, "All you got to do is walk straight down the street there and get on the bus. Go straight home."

And Sarah, as Hernando always emphasized when he got to this part of the story, Sarah Gould *promised* him that she would get on the bus and go straight home. And, of course, she *promised* not to tell the police.

Hernando let Sarah out of the car, and as he drove away, she was walking toward the bus stop. But, as soon as he was out of sight, she changed her course, walked up to a house, and rang the doorbell.

The house belonged to a Chicago firefighter, who was getting ready for work. He opened the door and saw Sarah — messy, dirty, bruised, and distraught. She told him that she needed help; he told her that he would call the police and that she should stay right there on the porch. Then he closed the door and went to phone the police.

Meanwhile, Hernando had begun to wonder whether Sarah had kept her promise and gotten on the bus. So he doubled back to where he had left her. He saw Sarah standing on the porch of that house; he saw the firefighter talking to her; he saw the firefighter close the door.

As Hernando recounted it, he felt betrayed — she had broken her promise to him. He parked and got out of the car. He said that he called out to her. In Hernando's words, here's what happened next:

I called to her and she came down. I took her by the arm and around the corner to the alley.

I said, "What are you doing? All you had to do was get on the bus. You promised that you would get on the bus."

She protested that I was hurting her, that I was going to kill her.

I said, "No. All you had to do was get on the bus!"

She screamed, "You are going to kill me!"

I said, "No, you said you was going to get on the bus. All you had to do was to get on the bus. Stop screaming. I'm not going to hurt you."

She said, "You are going to kill me."

I said, "I am not going to kill you, shut up, stop screaming."

She said, "You are going to kill me. You are going to kill me."

I said, "I am not going to kill you."

She said, "You are going to kill me. I know you are going to kill me."

So I shot her. Then I shot her again. She fell. I looked at her, then I broke and ran to my car.

The Chicago firefighter kept his promise and called the police, but they were too late to save Sarah. Around one of her wrists was a cloth stamped with Hernando's father's name. When the police asked the firefighter why he didn't let Sarah into his home, he said that when he saw how beat up she was and saw a black man out on the street calling to her, he assumed it was a domestic dispute and didn't want to get in the middle of it.

Shortly thereafter, the police found Hernando at his parents' home, washing the trunk of his car. At first, he denied everything. Then, when police confronted him with the fact that witnesses had said he had a woman in the trunk of his car, he said it was a prostitute. He varied his story every time the police introduced more information. The police were gentle with him; they read him his Miranda rights, they offered him food and drink. But they confused him with their questions, and it didn't take too long for Hernando to confess to having robbed, kidnapped, and murdered Sarah.

But when police asked Hernando to sign the confession, he refused, saying that it might make his attorney mad. It didn't matter. That attorney didn't really want to have anything to do with Hernando the murderer, and besides, his parents had no money left to pay him.

Before his trial, his new attorneys—public defenders—persuaded him that his only chance to beat the death penalty was to plead guilty. This was one of those cases that defense attorneys in Chicago, not without a certain amount of irony, call a "dead bang loser case"—one in which "the state has everything but a videotape of the crime." At first, Hernando didn't want to plead guilty; he didn't want his parents to know that he was guilty. But ultimately, in hopes of saving his own life, he did plead guilty.

It didn't work. In January 1980, Hernando was sentenced to death. Finally, on March 25, 1995, after his appeals were exhausted, Hernando was executed by lethal injection.

Hernando's lawyers spend a lot of time trying to find some explanation for what happened. Maybe if they could understand what had been going on in his mind, it would help to save his life. But Hernando couldn't really

say. What he kept saying, in essence, was, "What is the big deal? Why is everyone so upset with me?" It was not that, in his mind, Hernando did not understand that robbery, kidnapping, rape, and murder are against the law. The fact that he at first denied doing them helped to prove that. So, Hernando was not legally insane—in the sense that he didn't know right from wrong. It was simply that he could not understand why everyone was so worked up about what he had done.

This is difficult for most of us to understand. Why would someone be surprised at getting into really serious trouble for robbing, kidnapping, raping, and murdering another human being? At first, I could not make any sense of Hernando's confusion on this point. But eventually, as my horror receded, I was able to bring a more sociological perspective to bear on the whole subject. In other words, I had to call upon my sociological imagination—I had to look for the general in the particular.

Let me begin my explanation with an analogy. Last semester, in my introductory class, two students decided to turn in the same paper. They weren't in the same section, so I guess they thought they could get away with it. Unfortunately for them, in my department the professors discuss the papers because we want to be sure that we are all grading consistently. We noticed that the two students had submitted the same paper, so we called them in and said, "Hey, you cheated. And, as it says in the syllabus, if you cheat, you flunk."

At first, in each case, the students denied the accusation. However, when confronted with positive proof (copies of the papers with their names on them), they admitted what they had done. But, they said, our reaction was way out of line. Yes, they had read in the syllabus that getting caught cheating meant flunking the course. But flunking was simply *too much* punishment. In one case, flunking meant more than getting an F; it meant losing scholarship and loan money.

Hernando's reaction was much the same: "Okay, I did this, but you shouldn't punish me; certainly you shouldn't punish me this much."

You may be thinking that my analogy isn't really appropriate, that there is no way to compare students who cheat with people who murder. And, of course, I would not compare the behaviors. What I am comparing is how the individuals thought about their acts, and especially their reactions to the punishment.

Both the murder and the cheating were done in hopes of not getting caught; and in neither case did the perpetrators plan on getting caught. Furthermore, when they were caught, each thought the punishment was way out of proportion to the crime. In the case of the students, they argued that the consequences were much too severe, that cheating on a paper wasn't that bad and that losing a scholarship is unfair. In part, too, I think the students were shocked to find that we actually were going to flunk them. I suspect that to the degree they thought about it in advance, they expected to be given another chance, or to receive some lesser punishment. It's possible that they knew of other students who had been caught but not punished for cheating. In any case, their view was that punishment was unfair.

Hernando's reaction was much the same. He acted as if he thought that people were simply too worked up over his deeds. Being sentenced to death was just not acceptable to him. Like our students, he showed no real remorse for what he had done. He was only sorry that he had been caught and had to deal with the consequences.

Again, I suspect that some of you won't like my analogy. Perhaps you can understand why the students might feel that the punishment for cheating was too harsh. But you might wonder how Hernando could think that he should not be given the more serious punishment for what he'd done wrong.

This is where having a sociological imagination becomes helpful. The students felt abused because they did not see cheating as such a horrendous crime. After all, cheating happened all the time, and in any case, it was only a class paper.

The same kind of logic can be used to explain Hernando's reaction. Recall that Hernando had grown up on Chicago's South Side, where, when a husband killed his wife, it was jokingly referred to by police as a "South Side divorce." That sort of attitude from officials teaches people that life is not very valuable. And, as I mentioned previously, Hernando had learned some more personal, and painful, lessons about the low value placed on life. When his sister was raped, the police would not help her; they would not even give her a ride home. Also, when his brother was murdered, no one moved to identify the killer, much less to arrest him.

What I did not stress was the degree to which Hernando himself had committed violent acts against others. I did mention that he was out on bail on a rape and kidnapping charge, but in addition to that, he had raped at least three other women. No charges were brought in any of those cases—perhaps because they were not reported, for his victims knew there would be little point. *Those* victims also lived on the South Side.

What about the one charge he did have against him? Hernando's parents had mortgaged their home to get him a private lawyer, who told him he would beat the rape charge. Again, Hernando got the same message: His acts had no consequences. As a result of his life experiences, Hernando had learned that human life doesn't count for too much and that it's okay to take what you want. That's why he was so surprised that he was in so much trouble.

Let's look at what two psychiatrists had to say about Hernando.

> He appeared to mask any signs of strong emotions and states that "this is typical for me." He gave an example of—if he were upset about something and it pertained mostly to himself, he wouldn't reveal it to anyone. He would give the

impression that he didn't have any feelings, and that he does not reveal his real emotions. . . . He shows a recall of dates and times not in synchrony with reality—this, together with his difficulty with complex problem solving and concept formation—shows impairment, possibly indicative of minimal brain dysfunction. . . .

The evaluation of this man indicates that he is suffering from a borderline personality disorder with episodic deterioration in reality testing and thought processes with episodic psychotic thinking. There is the impression of someone who may be seen as withdrawn or aloof, with a superficial intellectual achievement in the use of language which masks a lowered intellectual achievement. There is also the indication of a minimal brain damage, which combined with his psychological profile, would indicate that at times of stress (as existed prior to the commission of the alleged offense) he lacks the ability to plan and to comprehend to the consequences of action.

He has at best a fragile purchase on reality. He feels overwhelmed by external stimulation and must constantly narrow his perceptual field in order to manage it. These overwhelmed feelings include those of inferiority and paranoia. While he generally stays close to the normal bounds of reality, he does occasionally lapse into abnormal perception and thinking. His capacity to recover from such lapses is the major reason for forgoing a diagnosis of schizophrenia. In general, his thinking and perception are idiosyncratic. He often does not see what others see. The mode of this distortion is to experience and understand the world in ways that are egocentric and sociopathic. . . . [The results of projective tests] present a picture of a highly impoverished internal world where fantasy and imagination are often enacted according to the most basic laws of "kill or be killed," or "eat or be eaten."

Note that this second psychiatrist stressed his expert opinion that *Hernando did not have much of a grasp of reality.* The psychiatrist made that judgment because Hernando persisted in seeing the world as a jungle in which the rule is to kill or be killed.

If this psychiatrist had possessed a sociological imagination, he might have realized that Hernando actually had an uncannily accurate grasp of reality. The understanding of his world as one in which the most basic law was kill or be killed was no delusion or misunderstanding; that was the way things worked on the South Side of Chicago. The very structure of social life in that part of the city meant that people were vulnerable—without help from the police, they had only themselves to fall back on.

But Hernando, too, lacked a sociological imagination—the ability to see beyond his own immediate social milieu, to understand that there are different rules for different people in places like Chicago. On the South Side, where the population is mostly poor and mostly African American, people don't have much power to call on "the establishment" to help them, so life is like a jungle. But on the North Side, things are different. When Hernando drove his sister's car to the North Side of Chicago, he made a fatal error because he drove into a part of the world where life does have value.

On the face of it, we seemingly can never understand what Hernando did. However, it is easier to understand if we use our sociological imagination (as Mills told us to do) and look past Hernando to his social milieu or environment. Then, things begin to make sense.

Don't get me wrong! I'm not saying that we should excuse Hernando for what he did because of the harsh environment in which he grew up. That's not the point. And certainly, that's not the *sociological* point. The goal of sociology is to understand and make predictable people's behavior, to explain what can lead people to act as they do.

What's the benefit of this sort of sociological thinking? What if it were your job to help prevent such crimes? Wouldn't you want to understand how the social environment affects people so that you could, if possible, make changes in that environment? Wouldn't you want to have a sociological imagination?

Mini-Glossary

borderline personality disorder   a personality disorder characterized by a long-standing pattern of instability in mood, interpersonal relationships, and self-image. Frequently severe enough to cause extreme distress or interfere with social and occupational functioning.

egocentric   centered around and focused on the self.

idiosyncratic   a personal reaction (not shared by other people).

minimal brain dysfunction   a relatively mild impairment of brain function which has subtle effects on perception, behavior, and academic ability.

psychotic   a form of thinking in which the individual has inaccurate perceptions. Specific symptoms of psychosis include delusions, hallucinations, markedly incoherent speech, disorientation, and confusion. Psychotic individuals generally do not know that they are confusing reality and fantasy.

sociopathic   like "psychopathic," a term for what is now usually called "antisocial personality disorder." This disorder is characterized by chronic and continuous antisocial behavior (and is not due to severe mental retardation, schizophrenia, or manic episodes). This behavior pattern, which is more common in males than in females, generally begins before the age of 15 with such infractions as lying, stealing, fighting, truancy, vandalism, theft, drunkenness, and substance abuse. It then continues after age 18 with at least four of the following manifestations: inability to work consistently, inability to function as a responsible parent, repeated violations of the law, inability to maintain an enduring sexual relationship, frequent fights and beatings inside and outside the home, failure to repay debts and provide child support, travel from place to place without planning, repeated lying and conning, and extreme recklessness in driving and other activities.

Questions

1. After I tell them about Hernando, students frequently ask me: "Why didn't Sarah Gould escape? She seemed to have so many chances, why didn't she take advantage of them?" Because I never had an opportunity to speak with Sarah, I will never know the answers for sure, but like my students, I can't help but wonder about it.

   The sociologist Max Weber introduced sociologists to the concept of *verstehen* — that's a German term meaning "empathic understanding." According to Weber, one way to better our understanding of people's behavior is to use empathy to put ourselves in their places to determine what they were thinking and feeling about their situations. With this concept in mind, why do you think Sarah didn't try to escape from Hernando?

2. Assume that you are a sociologist who is presented with the opportunity to act as an investigator for Hernando's defense team. In that role, you have the opportunity to ask questions of everyone involved in the case — Hernando himself; his attorneys, family, friends, and psychiatrists; and Sarah Gould's family and friends. Who would you want to interview? What questions would you ask?

3. Suppose you are the mayor of Chicago and you've just read all the facts of Hernando's murder of Sarah Gould. In a memo to your chief of police, what suggestions might you make to improve the structure of the city's law enforcement to help prevent this sort of crime happening again?

·4·

Men as Success Objects and Women as Sex Objects
A Study of Personal Advertisements

Simon Davis

As the following 1990 article recounts, Simon Davis used what social scientists refer to as an "unobtrusive method" to conduct his research. Unlike obtrusive methods—surveys, experiments, participant observation—in which the researcher's presence may have an effect on the people being studied, unobtrusive measures do not. Specifically Davis studied the personal ads that people place in newspapers. The research is unobtrusive because it is done after the fact, and none of the people being studied is aware of what's going on.

To give himself (and the readers) confidence in his findings, Davis used a basic statistical test known as "chi-square" (χ^2). This test enables the researcher to determine whether it's valid to say that a relationship exists between the variables being studied. How does that work?

Suppose you are gambling with a coin. We would expect, simply by chance, that the coin would come up heads about 50 percent of the time. But what if you got heads two times in a row? Would you conclude that something was fishy? No, two heads in a row is not that different from what you would expect from chance. But what if you got heads fifty times in a row? In this case, you would rightly be suspicious that something was wrong with the coin, that something other than random chance was operating.

If two heads are okay but fifty heads make you suspicious, what about three heads? Four heads? Ten heads? At what point do you begin to suspect that the outcome is not owing to random chance? To determine where to draw the line, we would use something like a chi-square test. Doing a chi-square test allows us to determine if what we actually get is significantly different statistically from what we would expect to get by chance.

The bottom line is this: When researchers report that their findings are "significant" or "statistically significant," they are saying that there is most likely a real relationship between the variables, that their findings are not owing merely to random chance.

Previous research has indicated that, to a large extent, selection of opposite-sex partners is dictated by traditional sex stereotypes (Urberg 1979). More specifically, it has been found that men tend to emphasize sexuality and physical attractiveness in a mate to a greater extent than women (e.g., Deaux and Hanna 1984; Harrison and Saeed 1977; Nevid 1984); this distinction has been found across cultures, as in the study by Stiles and colleagues (1987) of American and Icelandic adolescents.

The relatively greater preoccupation with casual sexual encounters demonstrated by men (Hite 1987, 184) may be accounted for by the greater emotional investment that women place in sex; Basow (1986, 80) suggests that the "gender differences in this area (different meaning attached to sex) may turn out to be the strongest of all gender differences."

Women, conversely, may tend to emphasize psychological and personality characteristics (Curry and Hock 1981; Deaux and Hanna 1984), and to seek longevity and commitment in a relationship to a greater extent (Basow 1986, 213).

Women may also seek financial security more so than men (Harrison and Saeed 1977). Regarding this last point, Farrell (1986, 25) suggests that the tendency to treat men as success objects is reflected in the media, particularly in advertisements in women's magazines. On the other hand, men themselves may reinforce this stereotype in that a number of men still apparently prefer the traditional marriage with working husband and unemployed wife (Basow 1986, 210).

Men have traditionally been more dominant in intellectual matters, and this may be reinforced in the courting process: Braito (1981) found in his study that female coeds feigned intellectual inferiority with their dates on a number of occasions. In the same vein, Hite, in her 1981 survey, found that men were less likely to seek intellectual prowess in their mate (108).

The mate selection process has been characterized in at least two ways. Harrison and Saeed (1977) found evidence for a matching process, where individuals seeking particular characteristics in a partner were more likely to offer those characteristics in themselves. This is consistent with the observation that "like attracts like" and that husbands and wives tend to resemble one another in various ways (Thiessen and Gregg 1980). Additionally, an exchange process may be in operation, wherein a trade-off is made with women offering "domestic work and sex for financial support" (Basow 1986, 213).

With respect to sex stereotypes and mate selection, the trend has been for "both sexes to believe that the other sex expects them to live up to the gender stereotype" (Basow 1986, 209).

Theoretical explanations of sex stereotypes in mate selection range from the sociobiological (Symons 1987) to radical political views (Smith, 1973). Of interest in recent years has been demographic influences, that is, the lesser availability of men because of population shifts and marital patterns (Shaevitz 1987, 40). Age may differentially affect women, particularly when children are desired; this, combined with women's generally lower economic status [particularly when unmarried (Halas 1981, 124)], may mean that the need to "settle down" into a secure, committed relationship becomes relatively more crucial for women.

The present study looks at differential mate selection by men and women as reflected in newspaper companion ads. Using such a forum for the exploration of sex stereotypes is not new; for instance, in the study by Harrison and Saeed (1977) cited earlier, the authors found that in such ads women were more likely to seek financial security and men to seek attractiveness; a later study by Deaux and Hanna (1984) had similar results, along with the finding that women were more likely to seek psychological characteristics, specific personality traits, and to emphasize the quality and longevity of the relationship. The present study may be seen as a follow-up of this earlier research, although on this occasion using a Canadian setting. Of particular interest was the following: Were traditional stereotypes still in operation, that is, women being viewed as sex objects and men as success objects (the latter defined as financial and intellectual accomplishments)?

Method

Personal advertisements were taken from the *Vancouver Sun,* which is the major daily newspaper serving Vancouver, British Columbia. The *Sun* is generally perceived as a conservative, respectable journal—hence it was assumed that people advertising in it represented the "mainstream." It should be noted that people placing the ads must do so in person. For the sake of this study, gay ads were not included. A typical ad would run about 50 words, and included a brief description of the person placing it and a list of the attributes desired by the other party. Only the parts pertaining to the attributes desired in the partner were included for analysis. Attributes that pertained to hobbies or recreations were not included for the purpose of this study.

The ads were sampled as follows: Only Saturday ads were used, since in the *Sun* the convention was for Saturday to be the main day for personal ads, with 40 to 60 ads per edition—compared to only 2 to 4 ads per edition on weekdays. Within any one edition *all* the ads were included for analysis. Six editions were randomly sampled, covering the period of September 30, 1988, to September 30, 1989. The attempt to sample through the calendar year was made in an effort to avoid an unspecified seasonal effect. The size of the sample (six editions) was large enough to meet goodness-of-fit requirements for statistical tests.

The attributes listed in the ads were coded as follows:

1. *Attractive:* specified that a partner should be, for example, "pretty" or "handsome."

2. *Physique:* similar to 1; however, this focused not on the face but rather on whether the partner was "fit and trim," "muscular," or had "a good figure." If it was not clear if body or face was being emphasized, this fell into variable (1) by default.

3. *Sex:* specified that the partner should have, for instance, "high sex drive," or should be "sensuous" or "erotic," or if there was a clear message that this was an arrangement for sexual purposes ("lunch-time liaisons—discretion required").

4. *Picture:* specified that the partner should include a photo in his/her reply.

5. *Profession:* specified that the partner should be a professional.

6. *Employed:* specified that the partner should be employed, e.g., "must hold steady job" or "must have steady income."

7. *Financial:* specified that the partner should be, for instance, "financially secure" or "financially independent."

8. *Education:* specified that the partner should be, for instance, "well educated" or "well read," or should be a "college grad."

9. *Intelligence:* specified that the partner should be "intelligent," "intellectual," or "bright."

10. *Honest:* specified, for instance, that the partner should be "honest" or have "integrity."

11. *Humor:* specified "sense of humor" or "cheerfulness."

12. *Commitment:* specified that the relationship was to be "long term" or "lead to marriage," or some other indication of stability and longevity.

13. *Emotion:* specified that the partner should be "warm," "romantic," "emotionally supportive," "emotionally expressive," "sensitive," "loving," "responsive," or similar terms indicating an opposition to being cold and aloof.

In addition to the 13 attribute variables, two other pieces of information were collected: The length of the ad (in lines) and the age of the person placing the ad. Only if age was exactly specified was it included; if age was vague (e.g., "late 40s") this was not counted.

Variables were measured in the following way: Any ad requesting one of the 13 attributes was scored once for that attribute. If not explicitly mentioned, it was not scored. The scoring was thus "all or nothing," e.g., no matter how many times a person in a particular ad stressed that looks were important it was only counted as a single score in the "attractive" column; thus, each single score represented one person. Conceivably, an individual ad could mention all, some, or none of the variables. Comparisons were then made between the sexes on the basis of the variables, using percentages and chi-squares. Chi-square values were derived by cross-tabulating gender (male/female) with attribute (asked for/not asked for). Degrees of freedom in all cases equaled one. Finally, several of the individual variables were collapsed to get an overall sense of the relative importance of (a) physical factors, (b) employment factors, and (c) intellectual factors.

Results

A total of 329 personal ads were contained in the six newspaper editions studied. One ad was discarded in that it specified a gay relationship, leaving a total sample of 328. Of this number, 215 of the ads were placed by men (65.5%) and 113 by women (34.5%).

The mean age of people placing ads was 40.4. One hundred and twenty-seven cases (38.7%) counted as missing data in that the age was not specified or was vague. The mean age for the two sexes was similar: 39.4 for women (with 50.4% of cases missing) and 40.7 for men (with 32.6% of cases missing).

Sex differences in desired companion attributes are summarized in Table 1. It will be seen that for 10 of the 13 variables a statistically significant difference was detected. The three largest differences were found for attractiveness, professional and financial status. To summarize the table: in the case of attractiveness, physique, sex, and picture (physical attributes) the men were more likely than the women to seek these. In the case of professional status, employment status, financial status, intelligence, commitment, and emotion (nonphysical attributes) the women were more likely to seek these. The women were also more likely to specify education, honesty and humor, however not at a statistically significant level.

The data were explored further by collapsing several of the categories: the first 4 variables were collapsed into a "physical" category, variables 5–7 were collapsed into an "employment" category, and variables 8 and 9 were collapsed into an "intellectual" category. The assumption was that the collapsed categories were sufficiently similar (within the three new categories) to make the new larger categories conceptually meaningful; conversely, it was felt the remaining variables (10–13) could not be meaningfully collapsed any further.

Sex differences for the three collapsed categories are summarized in Table 2. Note that the Table 2 figures were not derived simply by adding the numbers in the Table 1

Table 1 Gender Comparison for Attributes Desired in Partner

| | Gender | | |
Variable	Desired by Men (*n* = 215)	Desired by Women (*n* = 113)	Chi-square
1. Attractive	76 (35.3%)	20 (17.7%)	11.13[a]
2. Physique	81 (37.7%)	27 (23.9%)	6.37[a]
3. Sex	25 (11.6%)	4 (3.5%)	6.03[a]
4. Picture	74 (34.4%)	24 (21.2%)	6.18[a]
5. Profession	6 (2.8%)	19 (16.8%)	20.74[a]
6. Employed	8 (3.7%)	12 (10.6%)	6.12[a]
7. Financial	7 (3.2%)	22 (19.5%)	24.26[a]
8. Education	8 (3.7%)	8 (7.1%)	1.79 (ns)
9. Intelligence	22 (10.2%)	24 (21.2%)	7.46[a]
10. Honest	20 (9.3%)	17 (15.0%)	2.44 (ns)
11. Humor	36 (16.7%)	26 (23.0%)	1.89 (ns)
12. Commitment	38 (17.6%)	31 (27.4%)	4.25[a]
13. Emotion	44 (20.5%)	35 (31.0%)	4.36[a]

[a]Significant at the .05 level.

Table 2 Gender Comparison for Physical, Employment, and Intellectual Attributes Desired in Partner

| | Gender | | |
Variable	Desired by Men (*n* = 215)	Desired by Women (*n* = 113)	Chi-square
Physical	143	50	15.13[a]
(collapsing variables 1–4)	(66.5%)	(44.2%)	
Employment	17	47	51.36[a]
(collapsing variables 5–7)	(7.9%)	(41.6%)	
Intellectual	29	31	9.65[a]
(collapsing 8 and 9)	(13.5%)	(27.4%)	

[a]Significant at the .05 level.

categories: recall that for variables 1–4 a subject could specify all, one, or none; hence simply adding the Table 1 figures would be biased by those individuals who were more effusive in specifying various physical traits. Instead, the Table 2 categories are (like Table 1) all or nothing: whether a subject specified one or all four of the physical attributes it would only count once. Thus, each score represented one person.

In brief, Table 2 gives similar, although more exaggerated, results to Table 1. (The exaggeration is the result of only one item of several being needed to score within a collapsed category.) The men were more likely than the women to specify some physical attribute. The women were considerably more likely to specify that the companion be employed, or have a profession, or be in good financial shape. And the women were more likely to emphasize the intellectual abilities of their mate. . . .

Discussion

SEX DIFFERENCES

This study found that the attitudes of the subjects, in terms of desired companion attributes, were consistent with traditional sex role stereotypes. The men were more likely to emphasize stereotypically desirable feminine traits (appearance) and deemphasize the non-feminine traits (financial, employment, and intellectual status). One inconsistency was that emotional expressiveness is a feminine trait but was emphasized relatively less by the men. Women, on the other hand, were more likely to emphasize masculine traits such as financial, employment, and intellectual status, and valued commitment in a relationship more highly. One inconsistency detected for the women concerned the fact that although emotional expressiveness is not a masculine trait, the women in this sample asked for it, relatively more than the men, anyway. Regarding this last point, it may be relevant to refer to Basow's (1986, 210) conclusion that "women prefer relatively androgynous men, but men, especially traditional ones, prefer relatively sex-typed women."

These findings are similar to results from earlier studies, e.g., Deaux and Hanna (1984), and indicate that at this point in time and in this setting sex role stereotyping is still in operation. . . .

METHODOLOGICAL ISSUES

Content analysis of newspaper ads has its strengths and weaknesses. By virtue of being an unobtrusive study of variables with face validity, it was felt some reliable measure of gender-related attitudes was being achieved. That the mean age of the men and women placing the ads was similar was taken as support for the assumption that the two sexes in this sample were demographically similar. Further, sex differences in desired companion attributes could not be attributed to differential verbal ability in that it was found that length of ad was similar for both sexes.

On the other hand, there were some limitations. It could be argued that people placing personal ads are not representative of the public in general. For instance, with respect to this study, it was found that the subjects were a somewhat older group—mean age of 40—than might be found in other courting situations. This raises the possibility of age being a confounding variable. Older singles may emphasize certain aspects of a relationship, regardless of sex. On the other hand, there is the possibility that age differentially affects women in the mate selection process, particularly when children are desired. The strategy of controlling for age in the analysis was felt problematic in that the numbers for analysis were fairly small, especially given the missing data, and further, that one cannot assume the missing cases were not systematically different (i.e., older) from those present.

References

Basow, S. 1986. *Gender Stereotypes: Traditions and Alternatives*. Pacific Grove, CA: Brooks/Cole.

Curry, T., and R. Hock. 1981. "Sex Differences in Sex Role Ideals in Early Adolescence." *Adolescence* 16: 779–789.

Deaux, K., and R. Hanna. 1984. "Courtship in the Personals Column: The Influence of Gender and Sexual Orientation." *Sex Roles* 11: 363–375.

Farrell, W. 1986. *Why Men Are the Way They Are.* New York: Berkeley Books.

Halas, C. 1981. *Why Can't a Woman Be More Like a Man?* New York: Macmillan.

Harrison, A., and L. Saeed. 1977. "Let's Make a Deal: An Analysis of Revelations and Stipulations in Lonely Hearts Advertisements." *Journal of Personality and Social Psychology* 35: 257–264.

Hite, S. 1981. *The Hite Report on Male Sexuality.* New York: Knopf.

___. 1987. *Women and Love: A Cultural Revolution in Progress.* New York: Knopf.

Nevid, J. 1984. "Sex Differences in Factors of Romantic Attraction." *Sex Roles* 11: 401–411.

Shaevitz, M. 1987. *Sexual Static.* Boston: Little, Brown.

Stiles, D., J. Gibbon, S. Hardardottir, and J. Schnellmann. 1987. "The Ideal Man or Woman as Described by Young Adolescents in Iceland and the United States." *Sex Roles* 17: 313–320.

Symons, D. 1987. "An Evolutionary Approach." In J. Geer and W. O'Donohue (eds.), *Theories of Human Sexuality.* New York: Plenum Press.

Thiessen, D., and B. Gregg. 1980. "Human Assortive Mating and Genetic Equilibrium: An Evolutionary Perspective." *Ethology and Sociobiology* 1: 111–140.

Urberg, K. 1979. "Sex Role Conceptualization in Adolescents and Adults." *Developmental Psychology* 15: 90–92.

Questions

1. What does Davis mean by "sex objects" and "success objects"?

2. According to Davis's findings, what are the major differences between the personal ads placed by men and those placed by women?

3. In the research reported here, Davis wants to investigate whether mate selection continues to be influenced by traditional sex stereotypes. Sociologists are always concerned about whether their results can be used to make generalizations about the larger population. This works only to the degree that there are no important differences between the general population and those who place ads. Think about it—why might we hesitate before saying that the findings from this study of personal ads can inform us about the influence of sex-role stereotypes in mate selection more generally?

4. Since Davis conducted his research, have gender relations changed much? If you replicated this study today, do you think your results would be similar or different? Why?

·5·

Student Participation in the College Classroom

David A. Karp
William C. Yoels

The reluctance of many students to participate in class is the bane of many college professors' existence: "It's like pulling teeth to get students to talk!" Notwithstanding their expertise in things social, many sociology professors are baffled by the silence. This research by David Karp and William Yoels, however, suggests that the failure of students to participate (or the professor's inability to provoke lively discussions) isn't a "personal trouble." As you read this article, look for evidence that the level of student participation depends on the nature of the "milieu" of the college classroom.

A recent report on the employment of sociologists and anthropologists indicated that 97 percent of the sociologists in the United States were teaching either full-time or part-time in an institution of higher education. While sociologists earn their "daily bread" by teaching, they earn their scholarly reputations by engaging in research studies of almost every conceivable kind of social setting except, it seems, that of the college classroom. The failure to explore the "routine grounds" of our everyday lives as teachers is testimony to the existence of the college classroom as part of what Alfred Schutz (1962) referred to as "the world as taken-for-granted."

There has been considerable research on the classroom, but typically investigators have centered their inquiries on primary and secondary school settings. Several works have portrayed the social structure and operation of the classroom as it is influenced by broader institutional arrangements. Other investigators have concerned themselves with more specific features of the primary and secondary school classrooms. Among other issues, researchers have been concerned with teacher effectiveness, leadership style, teacher expectation effects, the nature of classroom interaction, communication structures in the classroom, and the like.

While there has been, alternatively, a good deal written about higher education in general, there has been comparatively little research specifically on the *college classroom*. That which has been done reflects largely the work of educational psychologists and focuses on student/teacher personality characteristics as they relate to various aspects of classroom interaction. With the exception of Robert Sommer's (1967, 1969) work on "classroom ecology," which employed observational techniques, the research on college classrooms relies heavily on

David A. Karp and William C. Yoels, "The College Classroom: Some Observations on the Meaning of Student Participation," from *Sociology and Social Research*, Vol. 60, No. 4.

"Student Participation in the College Classroom" by David A. Karp and William C. Yoels from *Sociology & Social Research*, Vol. 60, No. 4, 1976. Reprinted by permission of the authors.

questionnaires administered to students and teachers. The intent of these questionnaires has been to measure various personality dimensions of students and teachers and to relate these to a number of classroom behaviors. The present study is based on the premise that the types of studies briefly characterized above do not uncover certain salient elements of the college classroom as a special social context.

Rarely have researchers attempted to consider the processes through which students and teachers formulate definitions of the classroom as a social setting. The problem of how students and teachers assign "meaning" to the classroom situation has been largely neglected in the various studies mentioned.

The present study focuses on the meanings of student participation in the college classroom. Our examination of this problem will center on the way in which definitions of classrooms held by students and teachers relate to their actual behavior in the classroom.

Methods of Study

In an attempt to investigate the issues mentioned above we initiated an exploratory study of classroom behavior in several classes of a private university located in a large city in the northeastern United States. Our familiarity with the literature on the "words-deeds" problem (Deutscher, 1973; Phillips, 1971) led us to employ a two-fold process of data collection — namely, systematic observation of classroom behavior in selected classes, accompanied by questionnaires administered at the end of the semester in the classes under observation.[1]

None of the previously reviewed studies employed this type of research strategy, and it was hoped that such an approach would yield insights not attainable from reliance on a single data gathering procedure. In addition to the foregoing procedures we also drew upon our numerous years of experience as both students and teachers in college classrooms.

Ten classes were selected for observation. The observers were undergraduate and graduate sociology students who were doing the research as part of a Readings and Research arrangement. The classes were not randomly selected but were chosen in terms of the observers' time schedules and the possibility of their observing behavior in the classrooms on a regular basis throughout the semester. The observed classes were located in the following departments: sociology, philosophy, English, psychology, economics, theology. While the classes are certainly not a representative sample of all classes taught in this university, questionnaire responses from an additional sample of students in classes selected at random at the end of the semester indicate a remarkable similarity to the questionnaire responses of the students in the ten classes under observation.

At the end of the semester a questionnaire was distributed in class to the students in the ten classes which had been under prior observation. A shortened version of this questionnaire was also given to the teachers of these classes. Questionnaire items centered on factors deemed important in influencing students' decisions on whether to talk or not in class.

Findings

Table 1 presents a summary of selected observational items by class size. Classes with fewer than 40 students have a higher average number of interactions per session than those with more than 40 students. More important, however, is the fact that in both categories of class size the

---

[1]The "words-deeds" problem acknowledges the fact that there is frequently a disjunction between what people say and what people do. The discrepancy between words and deeds is not necessarily a product of intentional dishonesty — frequently, people misreport their behavior simply because they cannot provide an accurate account it. In this case, Karp and Yoels "triangulated" their research by using two different research strategies: they asked people about their behavior and they actually observed the behavior — Ed.

Table 1 Student Interactions (Questions, Answers, Comments, etc.) by Class Size

Class Size	Average Number of Interactions per Class	Average Number of Students Participating	Average Percent of Students Present Participating	Average Number of Students Making Two or More Comments	Percent of Those Present Making Two or More Comments	Percent of Total Interactions Accounted for by Those Making Two or More Comments
Fewer than 40 students*	25.96	9.83	47.84	4.64	25.06	75.61
More than 40 students	19.40	9.88	23.98	2.70	5.74	51.00

*The smallest class had 12 students; the largest class had 65 students.

average number of students participating is almost identical. Moreover, a handful of students account for more than 50 percent of the total interactions in both under 40 and over 40 classes. In classes with fewer than 40 students, between 4 and 5 students account for 75 percent of the total interactions per session; in classes of more than 40 students between 2 and 3 students account for 51 percent of the total interactions per session. From the limited data presented here it would appear that class size has relatively little effect on the average number of students participating in class. Such a finding is particularly interesting in view of the fact, as indicated in Table 5, that more than 65 percent of both male and female students indicated that the large size of the class was an important factor in why students would choose not to talk in class.

Data also indicate that students have a conception of classroom participation as being concentrated in the hands of a few students. Ninety-three percent of the males and 94 per cent of the females strongly agreed or agreed with the item "In most of my classes there are a small number of students who do most of the talking." Such a conception is in congruence with the observations of actual classroom behavior noted in Table 1.

The students' conception that a handful of students do most of the talking is also coupled with annoyance on the part of many students at those who "talk too much." Responses to a questionnaire item indicated that 62 percent of the males and 61 percent of the females strongly agreed or agreed with the item "I sometimes find myself getting annoyed with students who talk too much in class."

Students also believe it possible to make a decision very early in the semester as to whether professors really want class discussion. Ninety-four percent of the males and 96 percent of the females strongly agreed or agreed with the item "students can tell pretty quickly whether a professor really wants discussion in his/her class."

Students were also asked whether the teacher's sex is likely to influence their participation in class. The overwhelming response of both male and female students to this question is that the professor's sex makes *no difference* in their likelihood of participating in class. Over 93 percent of the males and 91 percent of the female students answered "No Difference" to this question. In effect, then, both male and female students tend to define the classroom as a situation in which the sexual component of the professor's identity is completely irrelevant.

The contrast between what students say about the previous item and what they actually do in classroom is highlighted in Table 2. The data indicate a very clearcut relationship between the sex of the teacher and the likelihood of male or female participation in class. In male taught classes men account for 75.4 percent of the interactions, three times the percentage for women—24.6 percent. In female taught classes, men still account for more of the interactions than women—57.8 percent to 42.2 percent—but the percentage of female participation increases almost 75 percent from 24.7 percent in male taught classes to 42.2 percent in female taught classes. Female student participation is maximized under the influence of female professors.

The participation of men and women may be a function of their proportion in class, [but] in both male and female taught classes the percentage of male and female students is almost equal, therefore eliminating the possibility that the rate of male-female participation is a function of male student over-representation in these classes. (See Table 2.)

Table 3 presents observational data regarding what the students were responding to when they participated in classroom interactions. There was very little student-to-student interaction occurring in the ten classes under observation. Ten percent of the total number of classroom interactions involved cases in which students responded to the questions or comments of other students. Table 3 indicates quite dramatically that the actions of the teacher are indeed most crucial in promoting classroom interaction. Questions posed by the teacher and teacher comments accounted for 88 percent of the classroom interactions. Especially significant is the fact

Table 2 Interactions (Questions, Answers, Comments, etc.) by Sex of Student and Sex of Teacher

	Male Student	Female Student	Total Interactions	(n)*
Male Teacher	75.4%	24.6%	100%	(565)
Female Teacher	57.8%	42.2%	100%	(774)

*On average, classes were 52% male and 42% female.

Table 3 Source of Interaction by Sex of Student

	Source (Initiator) of Interaction							
Sex of Student	Teacher Question[a] Direct	Indirect	Teacher Comment	Student Question	Student Comment	Source Not Specified	Total	(n)*
Male	10.0%	46.5%	31.9%	3.6%	6.3%	1.5%	99.8%	(840)
Female	9.8%	45.9%	31.3%	1.6%	8.9%	2.2%	99.7%	(437)
							Total	(1277)

*62 cases were excluded because of insufficient information.

[a]Questions from the teacher may be "direct" (as when the teacher asks a particular student a question) or "indirect" (as when the teacher addresses a question to the class as a whole).

that very few cases occur in which the teacher directly calls on a particular student to answer a question. The percentage for the Direct Question category is 9.9 percent, compared to 46.3 percent for the Indirect Question in which the teacher poses a question to the class in general. Indeed, it might be argued that the current norm in college classrooms is for both students and teachers to avoid any type of direct *personal confrontation* with one another.

Table 4 indicates that in male taught classes male students are more likely than female students to be directly questioned by the instructor (7.1 percent to 3.1 percent). In addition, men are twice as likely as female students (30.3 percent to 15.0 percent) to respond to a comment made by a male teacher. In female taught classes the percentage of male and female responses are almost identical in each category under observation. Of interest here is the fact that female teachers are equally likely to directly question male and female students (12.8 percent versus 12.5 percent).

Table 5 presents the student responses to a series of items concerning why students would choose not to talk in class. The items are ranked in terms of the percentage of students who indicated that the particular item was important in keeping them from talking. As the rankings indicate, male and female students are virtually identical in their conceptions of what factors inhibit or promote their classroom participation. The items accorded the most importance—not doing the assigned reading, ignorance of the subject matter, etc.—are in the highest ranks. The lowest ranking items are those dealing with students and teachers not respecting the student's point of view, the grade being negatively affected by classroom participation, etc.

In comparing the teachers' rankings of these same items with that of the students, it appears that, with one important exception, the rankings are very similar. About 42 percent of both male and female students ranked as important the item concerning the possibility that other

Table 4 Source of Interaction by Sex of Student and Sex of Teacher

| Sex of Student | Teacher Question[a] | | Teacher Comment | Student Question | Student Comment | Source Not Specified | Total | (n) |
	Direct	Indirect						
				Male Teacher				
Male	7.1%	55.3	30.1%	1.9%	2.6%	2.6%	99.8%	(419)
Female	3.1%	67.4%	15.0%	3.9%	3.9%	6.3%	99.6%	(126)
							Total	(545)
				Female Teacher				
Male	12.8%	37.7%	33.4%	5.4%	9.9%	.4%	99.6%	(421)
Female	12.5%	37.2%	37.9%	.6%	10.9%	.6%	99.7%	(311)
							Total	(732)

[a]Questions from the teacher may be "direct" (as when the teacher asks a particular student a question) or "indirect" (as when the teacher addresses a question to the class as a whole).

Table 5 Percentage of Students Who Indicated That an Item Was an Important Factor in Why Students Would Choose Not to Talk in Class, by Sex of Student

	Males			Females	
Rank	Item	%	Rank	Item	%
1.	I had not done the assigned readings.	80.9	1.	The feeling that I don't know enough about the subject matter.	84.8
2.	The feeling that I don't know enough about the subject matter.	79.6	2.	I had not done the assigned readings.	76.3
3.	The large size of the class.	70.4	3.	The feeling that my ideas are not well enough formulated.	71.1
4.	The feeling that my ideas are not well enough formulated.	69.8	4.	The large size of the class.	68.9
5.	The course simply isn't meaningful to me.	67.3	5.	The course simply isn't meaningful to me.	65.1
6.	The chance that I would appear unintelligent in the eyes of the teacher.	43.2	6.	The chance that I would appear unintelligent in the eyes of other students.	45.4
7.	The chance that I would appear unintelligent in the eyes of other students.	42.9	7.	The chance that I would appear unintelligent in the eyes of the teacher.	41.4
8.	The small size of the class.	31.0	8.	The small size of the class.	33.6
9.	The possibility that my comments might negatively affect my grade.	29.6	9.	The possibility that my comments might negatively affect my grade.	24.3
10.	The possibility that other students in the class would not respect my point of view.	16.7	10.	The possibility that the teacher would not respect my point of view.	21.1
11.	The possibility that the teacher would not respect my point of view.	12.3	11.	The possibility that other students in the class would not respect my point of view.	12.5

students would find them unintelligent. Eighty percent of the teachers, on the other hand, indicated that this was likely an important factor in keeping students from talking.

Discussion

Although we did not begin this study with any explicit hypotheses to be tested, we did begin with some general guiding questions. Most comprehensive among these, and of necessary importance from a symbolic interactionist perspective, was the question, "What is a college classroom?" We wanted to know how both students and teachers were defining the social setting, and how these definitions manifested themselves in the activity that goes on in the college classrooms. More specifically, we wanted to understand what it was about the definition of the situation held by students and teachers that led to, in most instances, rather little classroom interaction.

What knowledge, we might now ask, do students have of college classrooms that makes the decision not to talk a "realistic" decision? There would seem to be two factors of considerable importance as indicated by our data.

First, students believe that they can tell very early in the semester whether or not a professor really wants class discussion. Students are also well aware that there exists in college classrooms a rather distinctive "consolidation of responsibility." In any classroom there seems almost inevitably to be a small group of students who can be counted on to respond to questions asked by the professor or to generally have comments on virtually any issue raised in class. Our observational data (Table 1) indicated that on the average a very small number of students are responsible for the majority of all talk that occurs in class on any given day. The fact that this "consolidation of responsibility" looms large in students' consciousness is indicated by the fact, reported earlier, that more than 90 percent of the students strongly agreed or agreed with the statement "In most of my classes there are a small number of students who do most of the talking."

Once the group of "talkers" gets established and identified in a college classroom the remaining students develop a strong expectation that these "talkers" can be relied upon to answer questions and make comments. In fact, we have often noticed in our own classes that when a question is asked or an issue raised the "silent" students will even begin to orient their bodies toward and look at this coterie of talkers with the expectation, presumably, that they will shortly be speaking.

Our concept of the "consolidation of responsibility" is a modification of the ideas put forth by Latane and Darley (1970) in *The Unresponsive Bystander*. In this volume Latane and Darley developed the concept of "the diffusion of responsibility" to explain why strangers are often reluctant to "get involved" in activities where they assist other strangers who may need help.[2] They argue that the delegation of responsibility in such situations is quite unclear and, as a result, responsibility tends to get assigned to no one in particular—the end result being that no assistance at all is forthcoming. In the case of the classroom interaction, however, we are dealing with a situation in which the responsibility for talking gets assigned to a few who can be relied upon to carry the "verbal load"—thus the *consolidation of responsibility*. As a result, the majority of students play a relatively passive role in the classroom and see themselves as recorders of the teacher's information. This expectation is mutually supported by the professor's reluctance to directly call on *specific* students, as indicated in Table 3.

---

[2]Latane and Darley coauthored a whole series of research articles on what came to be known as the "bystander intervention" problem. The problem came to public attention in 1964: On March 13, in Queens (Kew Gardens), New York City, a man named Winston Mosley killed Katherine ("Kitty") Genovese. The murder was brutal: He stabbed her, and she got away; he caught her and stabbed her some more. All of this was done in full view of Kitty's neighbors. It was as if Mosley knew that Kitty's screams would go unheard and that no one would call the police. Kitty's screams did not go unheard: twenty-eight neighbors heard Kitty's cries for help. Some even opened their doors to look outside to see what was going on; some pulled chairs up to their windows to watch the event; a few called other neighbors to ask what to do. No one called the police: "I didn't want to get involved"; "It looked like a lovers' quarrel."

People were outraged! How could such a vicious murder take place in full view of dozens of people? Why didn't anyone call for help?

Latane and Darley (and others) conducted several research projects to understand what had happened. Most of the research involved staging situations in which a person needed help—under what conditions would a bystander respond? Ultimately, Latane and Darley discovered that the greater the number of witnesses there were, the less likely it was that anyone would help. This led to the notion of "diffusion of responsibility": If bystanders know that there are others around who could do something, then it is unlikely that they themselves will take action. On the other hand, if there is only one bystander in a position to help, he or she is likely to come to the victim's assistance. (William Mosley was eventually caught, tried, and sentenced to death. His sentence was overturned on appeal and he received life in prison. While serving his sentence, he earned a BA in sociology.)—Ed.

While students expect that only a few students will do most of the talking, and while these talkers are relied upon to respond in class, the situation is a bit more complicated than we have indicated to this point. It would appear that while these talkers are "doing their job" by carrying the discussion for the class as a whole, there is still a strong feeling on the part of many students that they ought not to talk *too much*. As noted earlier, more than 60 percent of the students responding to our questionnaire expressed annoyance with students who "talk too much in class." This is interesting to the extent that even those who talk very regularly in class still account for a very small percentage of total class time. While we have no systematic data on time spent talking in class, the comments of the observers indicate that generally a total of less than five minutes of class time (in a fifty-minute period) is accounted for by student talk in class.

A fine balance must be maintained in college classes. Some students are expected to do most of the talking, thus relieving the remainder of the students from the burdens of having to talk in class. At the same time, these talkers must not be "rate-busters.[3] We are suggesting here that students see "intellectual work" in much the same way that factory workers define "piece-work." Talking too much in class, or what might be called "linguistic rate-busting," upsets the normative arrangement of the classroom and, in the students' eyes, increases the probability of raising the professor's expectations vis-a-vis the participation of other students. It may be said, then, that a type of "restriction of verbal output" norm operates in college classrooms, in which those who engage in linguistic rate-busting or exhibit "over-involvement" in the classroom get defined by other students as "brown-noses" and "apostates" from the student "team." Other students often indicate their annoyance with these "rate-busters" by smiling wryly at their efforts, audibly sighing, rattling their notebooks and, on occasion, openly snickering.

A second factor that ensures in students' minds that it will be safe to refrain from talking is their knowledge that only in rare instances will they be directly called upon by teachers in a college classroom. Our data (Table 3) indicate that of all the interaction occurring in the classes under observation only about 10 percent were due to teachers calling directly upon a specific student. The unwillingness of teachers to call upon students would seem to stem from teachers' beliefs that the classroom situation is fraught with anxiety for students. It is important to note that teachers, unlike students themselves, viewed the possibility that "students might appear unintelligent in the eyes of other students" as a very important factor in keeping students from talking (Table 6). Unwilling to exacerbate the sense of risk which teachers believe is a part of student consciousness, they refrain from directly calling upon specific students.

The direct result of these two factors is that students feel no obligation or particular necessity for keeping up with reading assignments so as to be able to participate in class. Such a choice is made easier still by the fact that college students are generally tested infrequently. Unlike high school, where homework is the

---

[3] A "rate-buster" is anyone who is overly enthusiastic about completing his or her assigned tasks and who, in consequence, makes others look bad. Suppose a group of factory workers earn $20 an hour to assemble widgets. Suppose further that the typical worker manages to assemble 8 widgets an hour (for a total of 64 widgets a day). A new worker joins the group: she manages to assemble 12 widgets an hour (for a total of 96 widgets a day). When management discovers that this new worker is much more productive than the others (who are earning the same amount of money), they will be inclined to pressure the entire group of workers to be more productive. That new worker is a "rate-buster."

Alternatively, suppose your sociology instructor gave a really hard test and the average student scored a 54 percent. Naturally, many students will complain that the test was too hard. But if one student managed to earn 99 percent on the test, the professor will judge that the difficulty of the exam was appropriate—that lone A student is a "rate-buster."—Ed.

Table 6 Percentage of Teachers Who Indicated That an Item Was an Important Factor in Why Students Would Choose Not to Talk in Class

Rank	Item	%
1.5	The large size of the class.	80
1.5	The chance that I would appear unintelligent in the eyes of other students.	80
4	The feeling that I don't know enough about the subject matter.	70
4	The feeling that my ideas are not well-enough formulated.	70
4	The possibility that my comments might negatively affect my grade.	70
6	The course simply isn't meaningful to me.	50
7.5	I had not done the assigned reading.	40
7.5	The chance that I would appear unintelligent in the eyes of the teacher.	40
9.5	The possibility that the teacher would not respect my point of view.	30
9.5	The possibility that other students in the class would not respect my point of view.	30
11	The small size of the class.	10

teacher's "daily insurance" that students are prepared for classroom participation, college is a situation in which the student feels quite safe in coming to class without having done the assigned reading and, not having done it, safe in the secure knowledge that one won't be called upon. It is understandable, then, why such items as "not having done the assigned reading" and "the feeling that one does not know enough about the subject matter" would rank so high (Table 5) in students' minds as factors keeping them from talking in class.

In sum, we have isolated two factors relative to the way that classrooms actually operate that make it "practically" possible for students not to talk in class. These factors make it possible for the student to pragmatically abide by an early decision to be silent in class. We must now broach the somewhat more complicated question: what are the elements of students' definitions of the college classroom situation that prompt them to be silent in class? To answer this question we must examine how students perceive the teacher as well as their conceptions of what constitutes "intellectual work."

By the time that students have finished high school they have been imbued with the enormously strong belief that teachers are "experts" who possess the "truth." They have adopted, as Freire (1970) has noted, a "banking" model of education. The teacher represents the bank, the huge "fund" of "true" "knowledge. As a student it is one's job to make weekly "withdrawals" from the fund, never any "deposits." His teachers, one is led to believe, and often led to believe it by the teachers themselves, are possessors of the truth. Teachers are in the classroom to *teach*, not to *learn*.

If the above contains anything like a reasonable description of the way that students are socialized in secondary school, we should not find it strange or shocking that our students find our requests for criticism of ideas a bit alien. College students still cling to the idea that they are knowledge seekers and that faculty members are knowledge dispensers. Their view of intellectual work leaves little room for the notion that ideas themselves are open to negotiation. It is simply not part of their view of the classroom that ideas are generated out of dialogue, out of persons questioning and taking issue with one another, out of persons being *critical* of each other.

It comes as something of a shock to many of our students when we are willing to give them, at best, a "B" on a paper or exam that is "technically" proficient. When they inquire about their grade, they want to know what they did "wrong." Intellectual work is for them dichotomous. It is either good or bad, correct or incorrect. They are genuinely surprised when we tell them that nothing is wrong, that they simply have not been critical enough and have not shown enough reflection on the ideas. Some even see such an evaluation as unfair. They claim a kind of incompetence at criticism. They often claim that it would be illegitimate for them to disagree with an author.

Students in class respond as uncritically to the thoughts of their professors as they do to the thoughts of those whom they read. Given this general attitude toward intellectual work, based in large part on students' socialization, and hence their definition of what should go on in classrooms, the notion of using the classroom as a place for generating ideas is a foreign one.

Part of students' conceptions of what they can and ought to do in classrooms is, then, a function of their understanding of how ideas are to be communicated. Students have expressed the idea that if they are to speak in class they ought to be able to articulate their point logically, systematically, and above all completely. The importance of this factor in keeping students from talking is borne out by the very high ranking given to the item (Table 5) "the feeling that my ideas are not well enough formulated."

In their view, if their ideas have not been fully formulated in advance, then the idea is not worth relating. They are simply unwilling to talk "off the top of their heads." They feel, particularly in an academic setting such as the college classroom, that there is a high premium placed on being articulate. This feeling is to a large degree prompted by the relative articulateness of the teacher. Students do not, it seems, take into account the fact that the teacher's coherent presentation is typically a function of the time spent preparing his/her ideas. The relative preparedness of the teacher leads to something of a paradox vis-a-vis classroom discussion.

We have had students tell us that one of the reasons they find it difficult to respond in class involves the professor's preparedness; that is, students have told us that because the professor's ideas as presented in lectures are (in their view) so well formulated they could not add anything to those ideas. Herein lies something of a paradox. One might suggest that, to some degree at least, the better prepared a professor is for his/her class, the less likely are students to respond to the elements of his lecture.

We have both found that some of our liveliest classes have centered around those occasions when we have talked about research presently in progress. When it is clear to the student that we are ourselves struggling with a particular problem, that we cannot fully make sense of a phenomenon, the greater is the class participation. In most classroom instances, students read the teacher as the "expert," and once having cast the professor into that role it becomes extremely difficult for students to take issue with or amend his/her ideas.

It must also be noted that students' perceptions about their incapacity to be critical of their own and others' ideas leads to an important source of misunderstanding between college students and their teachers. In an open-ended question we asked students what characteristics they thought made for an "ideal" teacher. An impressionistic reading of these responses indicated that students were overwhelmingly uniform in their answers. They consensually found it important that a teacher "not put them down" and that a teacher "not flaunt his/her superior knowledge." In this regard the college classroom is a setting pregnant with possibilities for mutual misunderstanding. Teachers are working under one set of assumptions about "intellectual work" while students proceed under another. Our experiences as college teachers lead us to believe that teachers tend to value *critical* responses by students and tend to respond critically themselves to the comments and questions of college students. Students tend to perceive these critical comments as in some way an assault on their "selves" and find it difficult to separate a critique of their thoughts from a critique of themselves. Teachers are for the most part unaware of the way in which students interpret their comments.

The result is that when college teachers begin to critically question a student's statement, trying to get the student to be more critical and analytical about his/her assertions, this gets interpreted by students as a "putdown." The overall result is the beginning of a "vicious circle" of sorts. The more that teachers try to instill in students a critical attitude toward one's own ideas, the more students come to see faculty members as condescending, and the greater still becomes their reluctance to make known their "ill formulated" ideas in class. Like any other social situation where persons are defining the situation differently, there is bound to develop a host of interactional misunderstandings.

Before concluding this section, let us turn to a discussion of the differences in classroom participation rates of male versus female students. Given the fact that men and women students responded quite similarly to the questionnaire items reported here, much of our previous discussion holds for both male and female students. There are some important differences, however, in their *actual behavior* in the college classroom (as revealed by our observational data) that ought to be considered. Foremost among these differences is the fact that the sex of the teacher affects the likelihood of whether male or female students will participate in class (Table 2). Clearly, male and female

teachers in these classes are "giving off expressions" that are being interpreted very differently by male and female students. Male students play a more active role in all observed classes regardless of the teacher's sex, but with female instructors the percentage of female participation sharply increases. Also of interest, as indicated in Table 4, is the fact that the male instructors are more likely to directly call on male students than on female students (7.1 percent to 3.1 percent), whereas female instructors are just as likely to call on female students as on male students (12.5 percent to 12.8 percent). Possibly female students in female taught classes interpret the instructor's responses as being more egalitarian than those of male professors and thus more sympathetic to the views of female students. With the growing involvement of women faculty and students in feminist "consciousness" groups it may not be unreasonable to assume that female instructors are more sensitive to the problem of female students both inside and outside the college classroom.

Implications

For the reasons suggested in the last few pages, it may be argued that most students opt for non-involvement in their college classroom. This being the case, and because organizational features of the college classroom allow for non-involvement (the consolidation of responsibility, the unwillingness of professors to directly call on specific students, the infrequency of testing), the situation allows for a low commitment on the part of students. The college classroom, then, rather than being a situation where persons must be deeply involved, more closely approximates a situation of "anonymity" where persons' obligations are few.

We can now perceive more clearly the source of the dilemma for college instructors who wish to have extensive classroom dialogues with students. To use the terminology generated by

Goffman (1963) in *Behavior In Public Places*, we can suggest that instructors are treating the classroom as an instance of "focused" interaction while students define the classroom more as an "unfocused" gathering. Focused gatherings are those where persons come into one another's audial and visual presence and see it as their obligation to interact. These are to be distinguished from unfocused gatherings where persons are also in a face-to-face situation but either feel that they are not privileged to interact or have no obligation to do so.

It may very well be that students more correctly "read" how professors interpret the situation than vice versa. Knowing that the teacher expects involvement, and having made the decision not to be deeply involved, students reach a compromise. Aware that it would be an impropriety to be on a total "away" from the social situation, students engage in what might be called "civil *attention.*" They must *appear* committed enough to not alienate the teacher without at the same time showing so much involvement that the situation becomes risky for them. Students must carefully create a show of interest while maintaining non-involvement. A show of too great interest might find them more deeply committed to the encounter than they wish to be.

So, students are willing to attend class regularly and they do not hold private conversations while the teacher is talking; they nod their heads intermittently, and maintain enough attention to laugh at the appropriate junctures during a lecture, and so on. Students have become very adept at maintaining the social situation without becoming too involved in it. Teachers interpret these "shows" of attention as indicative of a real involvement (the students' performances have proved highly successful) and are, therefore, at a loss to explain why their involvement is not even greater—why they don't talk very much in class.

References

Adams, R.S. 1969. "Location as a Feature of Instructional Interaction," *Merrill-Palmer Quarterly of Behavior and Development* 15: 309–321.

Bales, R.F. 1952. "Some Uniformities of Behavior in Small Social Systems," in G.E. Swanson *et al.*, (eds.), *Readings in Social Psychology*, revised edition. New York: Holt, pp. 146–159.

Bavelas, A. 1962. "Communication Patterns in Task-Oriented Groups," in D. Cartwright and A. Zander (eds.), *Group Dynamics*, Evanston, Ill.: Row, Peterson and Company, pp. 669–682.

Blumer, H. 1956. "Sociological Analysis and the Variable." *American Sociological Review* 21: 683–690.

_____. 1969. Symbolic Interactionism. Englewood Cliffs, N.J.: Prentice-Hall.

Boocock, S. 1972. *An Introduction to the Sociology of Learning*. Boston: Houghton Mifflin.

Bowers, N.D. and R.S. Soar 1962. "The Influence of Teaching Personality on Classroom Interaction," *Journal of Experimental Education* 30: 309–311.

Brophy, J. and T. Good 1974. *Teacher-Student Relationships: Causes and Consequences*. New York: Holt, Rinehart and Winston.

Cogan, M.L. 1958. "The Behavior of Teachers and the Productive Behavior of Their Pupils," *Journal of Experimental Education* 27: 89–124.

Deutscher, I. 1973. What We Say/What We Do. Glenview, Ill.: Scott, Foresman and Company.

Feenberg, L. 1972. "Faculty-Student Interaction: How Students Differ." *Journal of College Student Personnel* 13:24–27.

Flanders, N. 1960. Teacher Influence, Pupil Attitudes and Achievements. U.S. Department of Health, Education and Welfare, Office of Education, Cooperative Research Monograph No. 12.

Freire, P. 1970. *Pedagogy of the Oppressed*. New York: Seabury Press. Glaser, B. and A.L. Strauss.

Goffman, E. 1963. *Behavior in Public Places*. New York: Free Press.

Hollingshead, A.B. 1949. *Elmtown's Youth*. New York: Wiley.

Holt, J. 1964. *How Children Fail*. New York: Delta.

_____. 1967. *How Children Learn*. New York: Pitman.

Latane, B. and J. Darley 1970. *The Unresponsive Bystander: Why Doesn't He Help?* New York: Appleton-Century-Crofts.

Phillips, D. 1971. *Knowledge From What?* Chicago: Rand McNally and Co.

Schutz, A. 1962. *Collected Papers: I. The Problem of Social Reality*. Edited by Maurice Natanson, The Hague: Martinus Nijhoff.

Sommer, R. 1967. "Classroom Ecology." *Journal of Applied Behavior Science* 3: 489–503.

_____. 1969. *Personal Space*. Englewood Cliffs, N.J.: Prentice-Hall.

Questions

1. Karp and Yoels suggest that students "believe it possible to make a decision very early in the semester as to whether professors really want class discussion." In your personal experience, is this true? What clues do professors give or give off to encourage or discourage discussion?

2. Compare the data shown in Table 5 with those shown in Table 6. What are the important differences between students' and teachers' points of view on why students do or do not participate? Why might students and teachers see things differently?

3. The authors of this article suggest that students view "intellectual work" as "dichotomous." What do they mean by this? Do you agree or disagree with their assessment?

4. Karp and Yoels suggest that students tend to view the classroom as an "unfocused gathering." What do they mean by this? Do you tend to agree or disagree with their assessment? How might instructors make classrooms more focused?

·6·
Doing the Right Thing
Ethics in Research

Lisa J. McIntyre

There is more to doing sociological research than choosing variables, picking respondents, gathering data, and doing an analysis. More than ever before, every choice the social researcher makes must be informed by considerations of ethics. At base, doing the right thing means not subjecting the people we study and (those around them) to unnecessary risk of harm. What's behind the increasing stress on ethics in research? What are the responsibilities of the ethical researcher? Above all, what is "harm"? This 1999 paper explores these questions.

Ethical guides are not simply prohibitions; they also support our positive responsibilities. For example, scientists have an obligation to advance knowledge through research. They also have a responsibility to conduct research as competently as they can and to communicate their findings accurately to other scientists.

— Diener and Crandall 1978

To begin, it is important to note that the term *ethics* has both a conventional (or everyday) meaning and a technical meaning. The fact that there are two ways to use this term causes a great deal of confusion. In the conventional or everyday sense, ethics is synonymous with morality, and doing the ethical thing simply means doing the moral thing. Conversely, unethical behavior is immoral behavior.

Ethics: Technical Meaning and Origins

In the technical sense, ethics and morals are different. Although in many cases there may

be an overlap between ethical and moral behavior, there are no guarantees that this will occur. The following two scenarios give examples of how morals and ethics may diverge.

Scenario 1

Chris confesses to a friend to having killed someone and hidden the body under a pile of garbage near an old shack at the lake. The police can't find the missing victim, nor do they know that Chris is the killer. The friend calls the police and tells them where to find Chris and the victim's body.

Has the friend done something moral or immoral? In spite of the fact that there is a widely accepted rule in society against snitching on one's friends, most people probably would say that the friend did the moral thing. It is not right to allow murderers to go free, and the victim certainly has a right to a proper burial.

Scenario 2

Chris hires an attorney and then confesses the murder and burial to that attorney. The police can't find the missing victim, nor do they know that Chris is the killer. The lawyer isn't all that sure about Chris's story and drives up to the lake to check it out. A search through the garbage reveals the body. After taking a Polaroid of the body, the lawyer reburies it in the garbage. Returning to town, the lawyer urges Chris to go to the police but does not call the police.[1]

Because the lawyer does not turn in the murderer, he or she does not seem to be acting morally. But there is an important consideration: Whereas in scenario 1 the friend may have a moral obligation to turn Chris in to the police, the lawyer has an ethical obligation to keep the client's confidence—even when the client is a murderer! This is not a gray area, either; this ethical requirement is spelled out clearly in the legal profession's *Code of Professional Responsibility:* "The lawyer must hold in strictest confidence the disclosures made by the client in the professional relationship. The first duty of an ethical attorney is 'to keep the secrets of his clients'" (Ethical Consideration 4-1). Preserving a client's secrets is such an important ethical obligation that had the lawyer turned Chris in, that attorney could have been disbarred and never again allowed to practice law.

In the technical sense, *behavior is ethical insofar as it follows the rules that have been specifically oriented to the welfare of the larger society and not to the self-interests of the professional.* So, ethics are designed to promote the welfare of others. You might be wondering how this lawyer could be promoting the welfare of others. The short answer is this: The legal profession is committed to the idea that people are innocent until proved guilty, that everyone accused of a crime has a right to the best defense, and that this is possible only if those accused of crimes can trust their attorneys. No client would trust an attorney who did not keep his or her secrets.

To be ethical, professionals have the burden of having to do things that others might consider to be immoral. For lawyers, in addition to keeping possibly nasty secrets, being ethical involves the duty to defend what may be unpopular cases and vicious criminals.

To become a professional, one must promise to abide by the relevant professional ethical codes. This is not a matter of personal choice—if you want to be a physician, you must follow the medical rules of ethics. To act unethically is to act unprofessionally.

It is important to be precise here: What do I mean by "professional"? In conventional language, we use the term at least three different ways. Sometimes, we apply the word to a job that is well done: "You did a very professional job of building that doghouse." Other times, we label someone a professional because he or she is paid to do something, regardless of the quality of the outcome: "John was a professional baseball player—but he never could hit a curve ball."

When sociologists use the term *professional,* however, they generally mean something else. Sociologically speaking, a professional is a member of a special kind of occupational group. Originally, only three occupational groups qualified as professions: lawyers, physicians, and clergy. These three groups have several things in common that set them apart from other occupations:

1. Their practitioners study for years to acquire technical knowledge and skills.

2. The knowledge they possess involves traditions and secrets that are not shared by outsiders.

3. Their knowledge is useful to outsiders and frequently means the difference between life and death.

---

[1]A very similar case happened several years ago in Lake Pleasant, New York.

From the first three characteristics of the professional derives a fourth—and this is really what sets the professional apart from other workers:

4. The work of a professional cannot be judged or supervised by anyone who is not a member of the same profession.

As sociologists see it, these qualities are characteristics of doctors, lawyers, and clergy, but not of plumbers or hairstylists. Although people in any occupational group may refer to themselves as professionals ("I am a professional hairstylist" or "I am a professional plumber"), relatively few occupations really are professions.[2]

The nature of the professional's job is such that *how* it is done is as important as (if not more important than) what the outcome is. The problem is that as laypeople, we cannot judge how well the job was done. For example, if patient Q's family suspects that the surgeon wasn't competent and that this incompetence led to Q's death, they might want to sue the surgeon for malpractice. Q's family might feel righteous in claiming that if the surgeon had done the job right, Q would still be alive. But that is not necessarily true (recall the old saying, "The operation was a success, but the patient died"). The views of Q's family are legally irrelevant and will hold no water in court. According to the law, only another physician can judge whether the surgeon was truly negligent. So, Q's family will have to find another surgeon who is willing to testify that it was the poor quality of the surgeon's work that led to the patient's death.[3]

Even though they could not tell if their doctor, lawyer, priest, or rabbi was doing all that ought to be done, for a long time people trusted these professionals to do the right thing. But by the mid-nineteenth century, many people were growing increasingly suspicious of professionals and were beginning to suggest that perhaps professionals ought not to be given so much freedom and autonomy.

Professionals responded by emphasizing the fact that their actions were prompted not by self-interest, but by their concern for their clients, patients, or parishioners. According to members of the medical profession, then, doctors do not perform surgery simply to make money, but to relieve people's suffering. And according to members of the legal profession, then, lawyers do not represent clients simply for the money, but because everyone has a right to representation.

One of the ways that professionals emphasized their commitment to the public welfare over self-interest was to promulgate or announce codes of ethics. They promised that they would follow these codes of ethics and punish any member of their profession who failed to do so. As we moved into the twentieth century, however, it became increasingly clear that at least one aspect of professional work was not being regulated properly by the professionals themselves: research.

Research Atrocities

Gross abuses of professional power in research became public knowledge after World War II. When Nazi physicians were brought to trial at Nuremberg in the late 1940s, the tales of their "research" horrified the world:

> Physicians forced people [in concentration camps] to drink seawater to find out how long a man might survive without fresh water. At Dachau, Russian prisoners of war were immersed in icy waters to see how long a pilot might survive when shot down over the

---

[2] I do not mean to disrespect members of any occupational group by claiming that they are not professionals. I simply mean to illustrate how sociologists use the term *professional* to highlight the qualities of certain occupational groups.

[3] There are exceptions. Some errors are so obvious that the law does not require an expert witness to testify—as when a surgeon cuts off the wrong leg or sews a surgical instrument into the wound. (The legal phrase for such exceptions is *res ipsa loquitur*, a Latin term meaning "the thing speaks for itself.")

English Channel and to find out what kinds of protective gear or rewarming techniques were most effective. Prisoners were placed in vacuum chambers to find out how the human body responds when pilots are forced to bail out at high altitudes. . . . At Auschwitz, physicians experimented with new ways to sterilize or castrate people as part of the plan to repopulate Eastern Europe with Germans. Physicians performed limb and bone transplants (on persons with no medical need) and, in at least one instance, injected prisoners' eyes with dyes to see if eye color could be permanently changed. At Buchenwald, Gerhard Rose infected prisoners with spotted fever to test experimental vaccines against the disease; at Dachau, Ernst Grawitz infected prisoners with a broad range of pathogens to test [different cures]. . . . Hundreds of people died in these experiments; many of those who survived were forced to live with painful physical or psychological scars. (Annas and Grodin 1992, 26)

At their trials, many Nazi physicians protested that they "had only been following orders." But much evidence suggested otherwise: "Contrary to postwar apologies, doctors were never forced to perform such experiments. Physicians volunteered — and in several cases, *Nazi officials actually had to restrain overzealous physicians from pursuing even more ambitious experiments*" (Annas and Grodin 1992, 26; emphasis added).

What could have motivated these physicians, these professional healers, to misapply their professional skills so horribly? At the time, many Americans believed that there was something fundamentally wrong with the German "personality type." For one thing (or so it was thought), Germans were all too quick to follow orders without exercising independent judgment. Certainly, such things could never happen in the United States!

What many people did not know or appreciate was the long tradition among U.S. physicians of conducting questionable research. For example, in the nineteenth century, orphans, the "feeble-minded," and hospital patients frequently were made the unwilling victims of medical experiments.

> In his autobiography, physician J. Marion Sims described how, between 1845 and 1849, he kept several black female slaves at his hospital to test his discovery of a repair for vesicovaginal fistula. The fistulas, allowing urine or feces to leak through the vaginal opening, caused great discomfort and distress. . . . Sims performed dozens of operations on the women — this in the days before anesthetics — and praised their "heroism and bravery." (Lederer 1995, 115–116)

There have even been cases in which U.S. military personnel were required to participate in surgical experiments — under threat of court-martial!

In any case, outraged at the evidence they heard, the judges at Nuremberg promulgated the Nuremberg Code. The ten principles of the code were written to protect the rights of research subjects. Never again, the judges said, would humans be placed at risk of serious harm by being used as unwilling guinea pigs. But less than 30 years later, there was another research scandal. This time, the physicians were not only Americans but were employed by the United States Public Health Service! This study, known as the Tuskegee Syphilis Experiment, began in 1932 when public health workers came to Macon County, Georgia, in search of African American men who suffered from syphilis. The physicians preyed on the poverty of the men and recruited research subjects by offering to "pay" for their participation — free medical exams, transportation to and from the medical facilities where the exams would be held, and free meals on examination days. The biggest incentive was that the families of each subject would be paid $50 to help with burial expenses.

Not one of the subjects was told that he had syphilis — though each was told that he had "bad blood." And, although a cure for syphilis was widely available throughout most of the

The nuremberg code

1. The voluntary consent of the human subject is absolutely essential. . . .

2. The research should be such as to yield fruitful results for the good of society, unprocurable by other methods or means. . . .

3. The research should be so designed . . . so that the anticipated results will justify the performance of the experiment.

4. The research should be so conducted as to avoid all unnecessary physical and mental suffering and injury.

5. No research should be conducted where there is . . . reason to believe that death or disabling injury will occur.

6. The degree of risk to be taken should never exceed that determined by the humanitarian importance of the problem to be solved by the research.

7. Proper preparations should be made . . . to protect the research subject against even remote possibilities of injury, disability, or death.

8. The research should be conducted only by scientifically qualified persons. . . .

9. During the course of the research the human subject should be at liberty to bring the research to an end if he has reached the physical or mental state where continuation of the research seems to him to be impossible.

10. During the course of the research the scientist in charge must be prepared to terminate the research at any stage, if he has probable cause to believe . . . the continuation of the research is likely to result in injury, disability, or death to the research subject.

Note: The writers of the original code emphasized the need to protect subjects in experimental research. Because social scientists use a variety of techniques, I have substituted the word "research" for "experiment."

30-year period during which the study was conducted, not one of the men was given this medication despite the fact that it would have saved his life.[4] You see, the researchers were intent on studying the effects of *untreated* syphilis. The study continued until 1972 when its existence became public. At that point, the research was terminated because of public outrage (Jones 1981).

The Case for Sociological Research

You might well think that members of the general public have little to fear from sociologists. After all, what harm can a bunch of geeks with clipboards do by asking questions?

There is potential for harm in any sort of research that involves human subjects. The potential harm in sociological research frequently

[4]Alexander Fleming discovered the cure (penicillin) in 1928, but it would be another decade before the drug was used by medical practitioners. In the late 1930s, just in time for World War II, two British researchers, Ernst Chain and Howard Florey, discovered a process that purified penicillin and made it safe. The drug was widely used by the military in the war and in the civilian sector after the war.

involves not what we do or do not do to our research subjects, but what we find out about them. Sociologists and other social scientists find out information that people often would prefer to keep private.

One of the most famous examples of social science research that many believed crossed the ethical lines was Laud Humphreys' study, which he titled *Tearoom Trade* (1970).

Technically speaking, *Tearoom Trade* was a study of impersonal sexual activity between male homosexuals. Less technically speaking, Humphreys began his research (or so he later said) by trying to find an answer to a question posed by his graduate advisor: "Where does the average guy go just to get a blow job?"

As Humphreys discovered, the answer to that particular question was "a tearoom" (that is, a restroom in a public park). In these tearooms, Humphreys did observational research. More specifically, to hide the fact that he was a researcher, he took on the role of "watch queen" (a third man who serves as a lookout for those engaged in homosexual acts and obtains voyeuristic pleasure from his observations).

From his observations, Humphreys obtained a great deal of information about how men approach each other and negotiate sex. But, given the circumstances, he could not very well find out much else. Humphreys wanted to know, Who are these men? How do they spend the rest of their time?

So, in addition to making his secret observations, Humphreys recorded each participant's license plate number. He then took this list of numbers to the police, told them he was doing "market research," and obtained the names and addresses of each man.

But, then what? He could hardly show up at the men's doorsteps and announce, "Hi, I saw you engaging in homosexual sex in the park last month, and now I would like to ask you a few questions about the rest of your life." (Sometimes, the most straightforward approach simply does not work.)

Around that time, another researcher at the same university was conducting a study on issues related to health care. Humphreys persuaded this researcher to include the names of his tearoom players on the list of subjects for the health study and schedule them for interviews. Humphreys himself would interview these men. To reduce the chances that the men would recognize him, Humphreys waited a year and changed his hairstyle. Then, no doubt armed with that ubiquitous clipboard, Humphreys visited and interviewed each of the men. This way, posing as a health-care researcher, he was able to find out all about the men's socioeconomic status (mostly middle class), their educational level (pretty high), and their family life (mostly married with children). Humphreys discovered that the only nonconventional thing about these men was that they visited tearooms for anonymous sex.

What might be ethically questionable about Humphreys' research? Although some might object that the very topic of Humphreys' research was immoral, the nature of the topic is not an *ethical* concern. What is of concern ethically is the fact that Humphreys deceived his subjects—they never knew that they were participating in research, and they didn't have the opportunity to choose to participate. Moreover, Humphreys conducted his research during a time when homosexual behavior was illegal where the research was conducted. By recording their names and addresses, Humphreys was placing his research subjects in great jeopardy. After his book was published, what if the police had demanded that Humphreys turn over his list of subjects' names and addresses? There was a great risk not only of legal prosecution but of psychological and social harm as well. And, had their names been discovered, some of the men might even have been subjected to extortion.

Humphreys defended his research by pointing out that it is important for sociologists to know about such men and their activities in order to understand them. In point of fact, Humphreys' research did contradict many social myths about men who have sex in public bathrooms. Most were established members of the community with wives and children, and in practicing consensual sex, they were not hurting anyone and certainly not bothering children. Humphreys' research was published and widely cited and may well have played a role in decriminalizing some sexual acts between consenting adults.

Humphreys' research was perhaps extreme in this respect, but it is not unusual for sociologists to uncover embarrassing details. Sometimes, what we learn not only is embarrassing but may place the research subject in legal jeopardy. In such cases, we have to figure out what our duty is—do we keep the secrets only of those whom we respect as "good people"? The problem may be compounded by the fact that the people we study are often those who have little power in society: it almost seems as if sociologists are obsessed with marginalized people (the poor, the homeless, street criminals, and so on).[5]

There are few hard-and-fast rules about what is and is not ethical behavior in sociological research. As far as I am concerned, the only thing that is consistently unethical is to not think through the possible consequences of our research.

As we think through the possible consequences of our research, we need to remember that we have an obligation not only to our research subjects but to other sociologists, to the university, and to members of the community at large. Making ethical decisions involves weighing the costs and benefits of the research to all of these groups.

This takes a great deal of thought; frequently, our research may have consequences that extend beyond the obvious. For example, in the early 1960s, a woman named Kitty Genovese was raped and murdered in New York City. What set the Genovese murder apart from the many other murders that happened that year was the fact that a number of people had heard her screams for help, which lasted for many minutes, but not a single one called the police.

The Genovese murder caught the imagination of social researchers in a big way. Under what conditions would people help strangers in trouble? What followed was a multitude of so-called bystander intervention studies. Some of these were pretty benign, such as a boy on crutches dropping all of his school books to see whether anyone would stop to help. Other versions included scenes of staged violence, such as a woman yelling from the bushes, "Help, rape." Soon, people grew leery and distrustful as they walked around college campuses and nearby neighborhoods—there were so many researchers out and about that one never knew when one might become an involuntary research subject.

Then, the inevitable but still unthinkable happened:

> At the University of Washington in Seattle in 1973, a male student accosted another student on campus and shot him. Students on their way to class did not stop to aid the victim, nor did anyone follow the assailant (who was caught anyway). When the campus reporters asked some students about their lack of concern over the murder, they said they thought it was just a psychology experiment. (Diener and Crandall 1978, 87)

In this case, the harm caused by the overdoing of bystander and other sorts of research in the field did not affect only the research subjects. It contaminated the researcher's world by making people distrust researchers. And, far worse, it may have contributed to the death of a college student.

---

[5]Part of the reason for this apparent obsession is that it is much easier to gain access to people with little power. It's easier to get permission to examine, say, prison inmates than executives of Ford Motor Company.

> ### The nature of informed consent
>
> "Informed consent is the procedure in which individuals choose whether to participate in an investigation after being informed of facts that would be likely to influence their decision. Informed consent includes several key elements: (a) subjects learn that the research is voluntary; (b) they are informed about aspects of the research that might influence their decision to participate; and (c) they exercise a continuous free choice to participate that lasts throughout the study. The greater the possibility of danger in the study and the greater the potential harm involved, or the greater the rights relinquished, the more thorough must be the procedure of obtaining informed consent" (Diener and Crandall 1978).

Institutional Review Boards: The Dawn of a New Era

These days, before any member of the university community (student, faculty, or staff) can conduct research that involves humans, they must submit a research proposal to a university officer or committee charged with ensuring that research is done ethically. If there is any question of risk to the human subjects, a committee consisting of both faculty (from a variety of disciplines) and community members will scrutinize the proposal. These committees are commonly called Institutional Review Boards (IRBs). If the members of the IRB judge that the researcher has not created sufficient safeguards to protect the rights of the research subjects and the general public, and even the researcher him- or herself, the researcher is prohibited from going on.

Like the Nuremberg Code, contemporary ethical guidelines place a great deal of emphasis on treating research subjects with respect. In many cases, researchers must obtain not merely *consent* from potential subjects but *informed consent*. As a general rule, deception must be kept to the absolute minimum. Members of IRBs are particularly skeptical of any research that places research subjects at risk of injury (physical, psychological, emotional, or

legal) greater than the risk that surrounds the routine activities of everyday life.

How Heroic Must an Ethical Researcher Be?

To what extremes must the sociological researcher go to fulfill his or her ethical duty? As I noted previously, one of the reasons Laud Humphreys was criticized when he published *Tearoom Trade* was that homosexual acts were prohibited by law where he did his research. In theory, the district attorney could have subpoenaed the list of names and addresses of Humphreys' subjects and prosecuted these men.[6] Would being ethical have required Humphreys to choose jail over releasing his information? In fact, this course of action apparently was contemplated, though it never materialized.

A little over a decade later, another sociologist came even closer to being forced to decide between breaching confidentiality and

---

[6] A subpoena (sa-PEE-na) is nothing to fool around with. It is a command from a legal authority to appear and give testimony. If you refuse to comply with a subpoena, you can be charged with contempt of court and sent to jail until you change your mind (or until the judge accepts the fact that nothing is going to change your mind).

going to jail. Mario Brajuhas, a graduate student at the State University of New York at Stony Brook, was doing participant observation research as a waiter in a restaurant. When the restaurant burned down, the police suspected arson. Investigators knew of Brajuhas's research and of the fact that he had taken copious field notes; they suspected that those field notes might help identify the arsonist. The local prosecutor subpoenaed the notes, but Brajuhas refused to hand them over, even when threatened with jail. Finally (after 2 years), the major suspects in the fire died, and the prosecutor dropped the case.

In the early 1990s, Rik Scarce, a graduate student at Washington State University, took a vacation. He left an acquaintance of his, Rodney Coronado, behind as a housesitter. Scarce and Coronado had become acquainted when Scarce, prior to going to graduate school, had been researching a book on radical environmentalists entitled *Eco-Warriors: Understanding the Radical Environmental Movement* (1990). Coronado was involved with the Animal Liberation Front (ALF), which was adamantly opposed to the use of animals for research.

While Scarce was on vacation, the ALF raided a research laboratory at Washington State University. Several animals were set free, and the researchers' computers were destroyed. The university estimated the damage at about $100,000. Several months later, Scarce was subpoenaed and commanded to appear before a grand jury that had been convened to investigate the crime. Scarce did appear and answer several questions, but he declined to answer questions that, he said, required him to breach the confidentiality of his research subjects. Scarce quoted from the American Sociological Association's Code of Ethics, which states that "confidential information provided by research participants must be treated as such, even when this information enjoys no legal protection or privilege and legal force is applied." As Scarce later explained, "I told the judge that I feared for my ability to earn a living as a sociologist if I were compelled to testify. Research subjects might not be willing to speak with me, and institutions might not be willing to hire an unethical researcher" (Scarce 1994).

The judge was not moved by Scarce's explanation. Ultimately, after he continued to refuse to testify, Scarce was sent to jail as a "recalcitrant [unwilling] witness." He spent more than 5 months in jail before the judge, finally convinced that Scarce could not be compelled to testify, freed him.

The Scarce case sounded a warning bell to sociologists everywhere. According to their ethical code, they have an obligation to keep confidential information to themselves even when they have no legal right to do so. This puts sociologists in a different position than lawyers and doctors. Communication between lawyers and clients and between doctors and patients is *legally privileged*. Lawyers and physicians have not only an *ethical duty* to keep information confidential but the *legal right* to do so. Sociologists, on the other hand, have no such clear legal right, although they do have an ethical duty.

References

Annas, George J., and Michael A. Grodin. 1992. *The Nazi Doctors and the Nuremberg Code.* New York: Oxford University Press.

Diener, Edward, and Rick Crandall. 1978. *Ethics in Social and Behavioral Research.* Chicago: University of Chicago Press.

Humphreys, Laud. 1970. *Tearoom Trade: Impersonal Sex in Public Places.* Chicago: Aldine.

Jones, James H. 1981. *Bad Blood: The Tuskegee Syphilis Experiment.* New York: Free Press.

Lederer, Susan E. 1995. *Subjected to Science: Human Experimentation in America Before the Second World War.* Baltimore: Johns Hopkins University.

Scarce, Rik. 1994. "(No) Trial (But) Tribulations: When Courts and Ethnography Conflict." *Journal of Contemporary Ethnography* 23: 123–149.

Scarce, Rik, 1990. *Eco-Warriors: Understanding the Radical Environmental Movement.* Chicago: Noble Press.

Questions

1. One problem that often crops up in survey research is that many people do not fill out and return questionnaires. Researchers have learned that it helps increase the "response rate" if survey respondents are sent a reminder a week or so after they are sent the questionnaire. This doesn't sound controversial, does it? Well, consider the following situation:

   > For her senior research project, Mary is doing an anonymous survey. In other words, she has stated on the cover of each questionnaire that responses will be totally anonymous—no names will be asked for or in any way recorded.
   >
   > From reading the literature on response rates, Mary expects that only about a third of those to whom she mails the questionnaire will send it back. She knows that she can perhaps double her response rate if she sends everyone a reminder. However, she barely had enough money to send out the questionnaire in the first place, and she can't afford to send a postcard reminder to everyone. She comes up with what she thinks is a great plan. She will embed a secret symbol somewhere in each questionnaire—a different symbol for each respondent. As each survey is returned, she will locate the symbol, consult the master list, and determine the name of each respondent.
   >
   > That way, she will be able to check off the name of each respondent who has returned his or her questionnaire. After a week or so, Mary will send reminder cards to respondents who have not yet returned their questionnaires.

   You are Mary's thesis advisor. What ethical issues would you raise with her?

2. A sociology professor offers her students extra credit for participating in an experiment. As far as the students are concerned, the down side is the fact that participating in this particular experiment will expose them to embarrassing situations; the up side is that obtaining the extra credit will have a big impact on their grades.

   Is a student's participation really voluntary when to not participate means he or she will miss out on some valuable rewards and possibly fail the class? What might this professor do to make her plan more ethical?

3. Bob is writing his senior thesis on "The Functions of Symbols in the Secret Rituals of College Fraternities." He plans to ask his fraternity brothers to give him their views on the ceremonies of their fraternity. In addition, he plans to secretly record an upcoming fraternity initiation ritual.

   As his thesis advisor, what ethical issues would you feel compelled to raise with Bob about his research?

·7·

If Hitler Asked You to Electrocute a Stranger, Would You? Probably

Philip Meyer

When he reflected back on the tales of Nazi horror that surfaced after World War II, Stanley Milgram wanted to know how ordinary people could be led to participate in such brutality. Like many others, Milgram had persuaded himself that it was something about the German character or culture that allowed the Holocaust to happen; such a horrible thing could never take place, for example, in the United States. Milgram's original plan was to go to Germany to test his hypothesis. Before he could do that, however, he needed a point of comparison. So, he tried out his experiment in New Haven and Bridgeport, Connecticut. As Philip Meyer explains in this 1970 article, Milgram never got to Germany.

In the beginning, Stanley Milgram was worried about the Nazi problem. He doesn't worry much about the Nazis anymore. He worries about you and me, and perhaps, himself a little bit too.

Stanley Milgram is a social psychologist, and when he began his career at Yale University in 1960 he had a plan to prove, scientifically, that Germans are different. The Germans-are-different hypothesis has been used by historians, such as William L. Shirer,[1]

[1]William Lawrence Shirer began his career as a journalist. Shirer went to work for CBS in 1937, broadcasting the events of the war from both Europe and the United States. In 1940, Shirer took a job with the New York *Herald Tribune,* for which he wrote a column for a couple of years. In 1960, his book *The Rise and Fall of the Third Reich* won the National Book Award.—Ed.

to explain the systematic destruction of the Jews by the Third Reich. One madman could decide to destroy the Jews and even create a master plan for getting it done. But to implement it on the scale that Hitler did meant that thousands of other people had to go along with the scheme and help to do the work. The Shirer thesis, which Milgram set out to test, is that Germans have a basic character flaw which explains the whole thing, and this flaw is a readiness to obey authority without question, no matter what outrageous acts the authority commands.

The appealing thing about this theory is that it makes those of us who are not Germans feel better about the whole business. Obviously, you and I are not Hitler, and it seems equally obvious that we would never do Hitler's dirty work for him. But now, because of Stanley Milgram, we are compelled to wonder. Milgram developed a laboratory experiment which provided a systematic way to measure obedience. His plan was to try it out in New Haven on Americans and then go to Germany and try it out on Germans. He was strongly motivated by scientific curiosity, but there was also some moral content in his decision to pursue this line of research, which was, in turn, colored by his own Jewish background. If he could show that Germans are more obedient than Americans, he could then vary the conditions of the experiment and try to find out just what it is that makes some people more obedient than others. With this understanding, the world might, conceivably, be just a little bit better.

But he never took his experiment to Germany. He never took it any farther than Bridgeport. The first finding, also the most unexpected and disturbing finding, was that we Americans are an obedient people: not blindly obedient, and not blissfully obedient, just obedient. "I found so much obedience," says Milgram softly, a little sadly, "I hardly saw the need for taking the experiment to Germany."

There is something of the theatre director in Milgram, and his technique, which he learned from one of the old masters in experimental psychology, Solomon Asch, is to stage a play with every line rehearsed, every prop carefully selected, and everybody an actor except one person. That one person is the subject of the experiment. The subject, of course, does not know he is in a play. He thinks he is in real life. The value of this technique is that the experimenter, as though he were God, can change a prop here, vary a line there, and see how the subject responds. Milgram eventually had to change a lot of the script just to get people to stop obeying. They were obeying so much, the experiment wasn't working—it was like trying to measure oven temperature with a freezer thermometer.

The experiment worked like this: If you were an innocent subject in Milgram's melodrama, you read an ad in the newspaper or received one in the mail asking for volunteers for an educational experiment. The job would take about an hour and pay $4.50. So you make an appointment and go to an old Romanesque stone structure on High Street with the imposing name of The Yale Interaction Laboratory. It looks something like a broadcasting studio. Inside, you meet a young, crew cut man in a laboratory coat, who says he is Jack Williams, the experimenter. There is another citizen, fiftyish, Irish face, an accountant, a little overweight, and very mild and harmless-looking. This other citizen seems nervous and plays with his hat while the two of you sit in chairs side by side and are told that the $4.50 checks are yours no matter what happens. Then you listen to Jack Williams explain the experiment.

It is about learning, says Jack Williams in a quiet, knowledgeable way. Science does not know much about the conditions under which people learn and this experiment is to find out about negative reinforcement. Negative reinforcement is getting punished when you do something wrong, as opposed to positive reinforcement which is getting rewarded when you do something right. The negative reinforcement in this case is electric shock. You notice a book on the table, titled *The Teaching-Learning Process*, and you assume that this has something to do with the experiment.

Then Jack Williams takes two pieces of paper, puts them in a hat, and shakes them up. One piece of paper is supposed to say, "Teacher" and the other, "Learner." Draw one and you will see which you will be. The mild-looking accountant draws one, holds it close to his vest like a poker player, looks at it, and says, "Learner." You look at yours. It says, "Teacher." You do not know that the drawing is rigged, and both slips say "Teacher." The experimenter beckons to the mild-mannered "learner."

"Want to step right in here and have a seat, please?" he says. "You can leave your coat on the back of that chair . . . roll up your right sleeve, please. Now what I want to do is strap down your arms to avoid excessive movement on your part during the experiment. This electrode is connected to the shock generator in the next room.

"And this electrode paste," he says, squeezing some stuff out of a plastic bottle and putting it on the man's arm, "is to provide a good contact and to avoid a blister or burn. Are there any questions now before we go into the next room?"

You don't have any, but the strapped-in "learner" does.

"I do think I should say this," says the learner. "About two years ago I was at the veterans' hospital . . . they detected a heart condition. Nothing serious, but as long as I'm having these shocks, how strong are they — how dangerous are they?"

Williams, the experimenter, shakes his head casually. "Oh, no," he says. "Although they may be painful, they're not dangerous. Anything else?"

Nothing else. And so you play the game. The game is for you to read a series of word pairs: for example, blue-girl, nice-day, fat-neck. When you finish the list, you read just the first word in each pair and then a multiple-choice list of four other words, including the second word of the pair. The learner, from his remote, strapped-in position, pushes one of four switches to indicate which of the four answers he thinks is the right one. If he gets it right, nothing happens and you go on to the next one. If he gets it wrong, you push a switch that buzzes and gives him an electric shock. And then you go to the next word. You start with 15 volts and increase the number of volts by 15 for each wrong answer. The control board goes from 15 volts on one end to 450 volts on the other. So that you know what you are doing, you get a test shock yourself, at 45 volts. It hurts. To further keep you aware of what you are doing to that man in there, the board has verbal descriptions of the shock levels, ranging from "Slight Shock" at the left-hand side,

through "Intense Shock" in the middle, to "Danger: Severe Shock" toward the far right. Finally, at the very end, under 435- and 450-volt switches, there are three ambiguous X's. If, at any point, you hesitate, Mr. Williams calmly tells you to go on. If you still hesitate, he tells you again.

Except for some terrifying details, which will be explained in a moment, this is the experiment. The object is to find the shock level at which you disobey the experimenter and refuse to pull the switch.

When Stanley Milgram first wrote this script, he took it to fourteen Yale psychology majors and asked them what they thought would happen. He put it this way: Out of one hundred persons in the teacher's predicament, how would their break-off points be distributed along the 15-to-450-volt scale? They thought a few would break off very early, most would quit someplace in the middle and a few would go all the way to the end. The highest estimate of the number out of one hundred who would go all the way to the end was three. Milgram then informally polled some of his fellow scholars in the psychology department. They agreed that very few would go to the end. Milgram thought so too.

"I'll tell you quite frankly," he says, "before I began this experiment, before any shock generator was built, I thought that most people would break off at 'Strong Shock' or 'Very Strong Shock.' You would get only a very, very small proportion of people getting out to the end of the shock generator, and they would constitute a pathological fringe."

In his pilot experiments, Milgram used Yale students as subjects. Each of them pushed the shock switches, one by one, all the way to the end of the board.

So he rewrote the script to include some protests from the learner. At first, they were mild, gentlemanly, Yalie protests, but, "it didn't seem to have as much effect as I thought it would or should," Milgram recalls. "So we had more violent protestation on the part of the person getting the shock. All of the time, of course, what we were trying to do was not to create a macabre situation, but simply to generate disobedience. And that was one of the first findings. This was not only a technical deficiency of the experiment, that we didn't get disobedience. It really was the first finding: that obedience would be much greater than we had assumed it would be and disobedience would be much more difficult than we had assumed."

As it turned out, the situation did become rather macabre. The only meaningful way to generate disobedience was to have the victim protest with great anguish, noise, and vehemence. The protests were tape-recorded so that all the teachers ordinarily would hear the same sounds and nuances, and they started with a grunt at 75 volts, proceeded through a "Hey, that really hurts," at 125 volts, got desperate with, "I can't stand the pain, don't do that," at 180 volts, reached complaints of heart trouble at 195, an agonized scream at 285, a refusal to answer at 315, and only heart-rending, ominous silence after that.

Still, sixty-five percent of the subjects, twenty- to fifty-year-old American males, everyday, ordinary people like you and me, obediently kept pushing those levers in the belief that they were shocking the mild-mannered learner, whose name was Mr. Wallace, and who was chosen for the role because of his innocent appearance, all the way up to 450 volts.

Milgram was now getting enough disobedience so that he had something he could measure. The next step was to vary the circumstances to see what would encourage or discourage obedience. There seemed very little left in the way of discouragement. The victim was already screaming at the top of his lungs and feigning a heart attack. So whatever new impediment to obedience reached the brain of the subject had to travel by some route other than the ear. Milgram thought of one.

He put the learner in the same room with the teacher. He stopped strapping the learner's hand down. He rewrote the script so that at 150 volts the learner took his hand off the shock plate and declared that he wanted out of the experiment. He rewrote the script some more so that the experimenter then told the teacher to grasp the learner's hand and physically force it down on the plate to give Mr. Wallace his unwanted electric shock.

"I had the feeling that very few people would go on at that point, if any," Milgram says. "I thought that would be the limit of obedience that you would find in the laboratory."

It wasn't.

Although seven years have now gone by, Milgram still remembers the first person to walk into the laboratory in the newly rewritten script. He was a construction worker, a very short man. "He was so small," says Milgram, "that when he sat on the chair in front of the shock generator, his feet didn't reach the floor. When the experimenter told him to push the victim's hand down and give the shock, he turned to the experimenter, and he turned to the victim, his elbow went up, he fell down on the hand of the victim, his feet kind of tugged to one side, and he said, 'Like this, boss?' ZZUMPH!"

The experiment was played out to its bitter end. Milgram tried it with forty different subjects. And thirty percent of them obeyed the experimenter and kept on obeying.

"The protests of the victim were strong and vehement, he was screaming his guts out, he refused to participate, and you had to physically struggle with him in order to get his hand down on the shock generator," Milgram remembers. But twelve out of forty did it.

Milgram took his experiment out of New Haven. Not to Germany, just twenty miles down the road to Bridgeport. Maybe, he reasoned, the people obeyed because of the prestigious setting of Yale University. If they couldn't trust a center of learning that had been there for two centuries, whom could they trust? So he moved the experiment to an untrustworthy setting.

The new setting was a suite of three rooms in a run-down office building in Bridgeport. The only identification was a sign with a fictitious name: "Research Associates of Bridgeport." Questions about professional connections got only vague answers about "research for industry."

Obedience was less in Bridgeport. Forty-eight percent of the subjects stayed for the maximum shock, compared to sixty-five percent at Yale. But this was enough to prove that far more than Yale's prestige was behind the obedient behavior.

For more than seven years now, Stanley Milgram has been trying to figure out what makes ordinary American citizens so obedient. The most obvious answer—that people are mean, nasty, brutish and sadistic—won't do. The subjects who gave the shocks to Mr. Wallace to the end of the board did not enjoy it. They groaned, protested, fidgeted, argued, and in some cases, were seized by fits of nervous, agitated giggling.

"They even try to get out of it," says Milgram, "but they are somehow engaged in something from which they cannot liberate themselves. They are locked into a structure, and they do not have the skills or inner resources to disengage themselves."

Milgram, because he mistakenly had assumed that he would have trouble getting people to obey the orders to shock Mr. Wallace, went to a lot of trouble to create a realistic situation.

There was crew cut Jack Williams and his grey laboratory coat. Not white, which might denote a medical technician, but ambiguously authoritative grey. Then there was the book on the table, and the other appurtenances of the laboratory which emitted the silent message that things were being performed here in the name of science, and were therefore great and good.

But the nicest touch of all was the shock generator. When Milgram started out, he had only a $300 grant from the Higgins Fund of Yale University. Later he got more ample support from the National Science Foundation, but in the beginning he had to create this authentic-looking machine with very scarce resources except for his own imagination. So he went to New York and roamed around the electronic shops until he found some little black switches at Lafayette Radio for a dollar apiece. He bought thirty of them. The generator was a metal box, about the size of a small footlocker, and he drilled the thirty holes for the thirty switches himself in a Yale machine shop. But the fine detail was left to professional industrial engravers. So he ended up with a splendid-looking control panel dominated by the row of switches, each labeled with its voltage, and each having its own red light that flashed on when the switch was pulled. Other things happened when a switch was pushed. Besides the ZZUMPHing noise, a blue light labeled "voltage energizer" went on, and a needle on a dial labeled "voltage" flicked from left to right. Relays inside the box clicked. Finally, in the upper left-hand corner of the control panel was this inscription, engraved in precise block letters:

SHOCK GENERATOR TYPE ZLB
DYSON INSTRUMENT COMPANY
WALTHAM, MASS.
OUTPUT: 15 VOLTS–450 VOLTS

One day a man from the Lehigh Valley Electronics Company of Pennsylvania was passing through the laboratory, and he stopped to admire the shock generator.

"This is a very fine shock generator," he said. "But who is this Dyson Instrument Company?" Milgram felt proud at that, since Dyson Instrument Company existed only in the recesses of his imagination.

When you consider the seeming authenticity of the situation, you can appreciate the agony some of the subjects went through. It was pure conflict. As Milgram explains to his students, "When a parent says, 'Don't strike old ladies,' you are learning two things: the content and, also, to obey authority. This experiment creates conflicts between the two elements."

Here is a partial transcription from one of the experiments. The naïve "teacher" is a heavyset, worried-looking man with prematurely grey hair. He is wearing a polo shirt. He is very polite. He has just pushed the 180-volt lever. A hidden camera is recording the performance.

LEARNER (*who, from the teacher's point of view is heard but not seen, an offstage voice*): Ow, I can't stand the pain. Don't do that. . . .

TEACHER (*pivoting around in his chair and shaking his head*): I can't stand it. I'm not going to kill that man in there. You hear him hollering?

EXPERIMENTER: As I told you before, the shocks may be painful, but—

TEACHER: But he's hollering. He can't stand it. What's going to happen to him?

EXPERIMENTER (*His voice is patient, matter-of-fact.*): The experiment requires that you continue, Teacher.

TEACHER: Aaah, but, unh, I'm not going to get that man sick in there . . . know what I mean?

EXPERIMENTER: Whether the learner likes it or not, we must go on, through all the word pairs.

TEACHER: I refuse to take the responsibility. He's in there hollering!

EXPERIMENTER: It's absolutely essential that you continue, Teacher.

TEACHER (*indicating the unused questions*): There's too many left here, I mean, Geez, if he gets them wrong, there's too many of them left. I mean who's going to take the responsibility if anything happens to that gentleman?

EXPERIMENTER: I'm responsible for anything that happens to him. Continue please.

TEACHER: All right. (*Consults list of words.*) The next one's "Slow—walk, truck, dance, music." Answer, please. (*A buzzing sound indicates the learner has signaled his answer.*) Wrong.

A hundred and ninety-five volts. "Dance." (*Zzumph!*)

LEARNER: Let me out of here. My heart's bothering me! (*Teacher looks at experimenter.*)

EXPERIMENTER: Continue, please.

LEARNER (*screaming*): Let me out of here, you have no right to keep me here. Let me out of here, let me out, my heart's bothering me, let me out! (*Teacher shakes head, pats the table nervously.*)

TEACHER: You see, he's hollering. Hear that? Gee, I don't know.

EXPERIMENTER: The experiment requires. . . .

TEACHER (*interrupting*): I know it does, sir, but I mean—hunh! He don't know what he's getting in for. He's up to 195 volts! (*Experiment continues, through 210 volts, 225 volts, 240 volts, 255 volts, 270 volts, delivered to the man in the electric chair, at which point the teacher, with evident relief, runs out of word-pair questions.*)

EXPERIMENTER: You'll have to go back to the beginning of that page and go through them again until he's learned them all correctly.

TEACHER: Aw, no. I'm not going to kill that man. You mean I've got to keep going up with the scale. No sir. He's hollering in there. I'm not going to give him 450 volts.

EXPERIMENTER: The experiment requires that you go on.

TEACHER: I know it does, but that man is hollering in there, sir.

EXPERIMENTER (*same matter-of-fact tone*): As I said before, although the shocks may be painful . . .

TEACHER (*interrupting*): Awwww. He—he—he's yelling in there.

EXPERIMENTER: Start with "Blue," please, at the top of the page. Continue, please, Teacher. Just go ahead.

TEACHER (*concentrating intently on list of words in front of him, as if to shut everything else out*): "Blue—boy, girl, grass, hat." (*Buzz indicates answer.*) Correct. "Night—day, sky, job, chair." (*Buzz*) Wrong. The answer is "day." Two hundred and eighty-five volts. (*Zzumph!*)

LEARNER: *Ohhhuhhuuhhh!*

EXPERIMENTER: Continue, please.

TEACHER: "Fat—man, lady, tub, neck." Answer, please. (*Buzz*) Wrong. The answer is "neck." Three hundred volts. (*Zzumph!*)

LEARNER: Ohhh. I absolutely refuse to answer any more. (*Shouting urgently, now*) Let me out of here. You can't hold me here. Get me out. Get—me—out—of—here.

EXPERIMENTER: Continue. The next word is "Green," please.

TEACHER: "Green—grass, hat, ink, apple." (*Nothing happens. No answering buzz. Just gloomy silence.*)

TEACHER: I don't think he is going to answer.

EXPERIMENTER: If the learner doesn't answer in a reasonable time, about four or five seconds, consider the answer wrong. And follow the same procedures you have been doing for wrong answers. Say "Wrong," tell him the number of volts, give him the punishment, read him the correct answer. Continue, please.

TEACHER: "Green—grass, hat, ink, apple." Answer, please. (*More silence. Teacher just sits there.*)

EXPERIMENTER: Go on with the procedure, please, Teacher.

TEACHER: Three hundred and fifteen volts. The answer is "ink." (*Zzumph!*)

LEARNER: Ohh, Ooohh.

TEACHER (*relieved to hear response*): Next one . . .

LEARNER: I absolutely refuse to answer.

TEACHER: You got to. You get a shock if you don't answer. (*Experiment continues with learner refusing to answer, and finally failing even to grunt or groan. At 375 volts, the teacher stands up. Has he had enough? Will he break off the experiment? Will he disobey?*)

TEACHER: I think something's happened to that fellow in there. I don't get no answer. He was hollering at less voltage. Can't you check in and see if he's all right, please?

EXPERIMENTER (*same detached calm*): Not once we've started. Please continue, Teacher.

TEACHER (*sits down, sighs deeply*): "Cool—day, shade, water, paint." Answer, please. Are you all right in there? Are you all right?

EXPERIMENTER: Please continue, Teacher. Continue, please. (*Teacher pushes lever. Zzumph!*)

TEACHER (*swiveling around in his chair*): Something's happened to that man in there. (*Swiveling back*) Next one. "Low—dollar, necklace, moon, paint." (*Turning around again*) Something's happened to that man in there. You better check in on him, sir. He won't answer or nothing.

EXPERIMENTER: Continue. Go on, please.

TEACHER: You accept all responsibility.

EXPERIMENTER: The responsibility is mine. Correct. Please go on. (*Teacher returns to his list, starts running through words as rapidly as he can read them, works through to 450 volts.*)

TEACHER: That's that.

EXPERIMENTER: Continue using the last switch on the board, please. The four-fifty switch for each wrong answer. Continue, please.

TEACHER: But I don't get no anything!

EXPERIMENTER: Please continue. The next word is "White."

TEACHER: Don't you think you should look in on him, please.

EXPERIMENTER: Not once we've started the experiment.

TEACHER: But what if something has happened to the man?

EXPERIMENTER: The experiment requires that you continue. Go on, please.

TEACHER: Don't the man's health mean anything?

EXPERIMENTER: Whether the learner likes it or not . . .

TEACHER: What if he's dead in there? (*Gestures toward the room with the electric chair*) I mean, he told me he can't stand the shock, sir. I don't mean to be rude, but I think you should look in on him. All you have to do is look in the door. I don't get no answer, no noise. Something might have happened to the gentleman in there, sir.

EXPERIMENTER: We must continue. Go on, please.

TEACHER: You mean keep giving him what? Four hundred fifty volts, what he's got now?

EXPERIMENTER: That's correct. Continue. The next word is "White."

TEACHER (*now at a furious pace*): "White—cloud, horse, rock, house." Answer, please. The answer is "horse." Four hundred and fifty volts. (*Zzumph!*) Next word. "Bag—paint, music, clown, girl." The answer is "paint." Four hundred and fifty volts. (*Zzumph!*) Next word is "Short—sentence, movie . . ."

EXPERIMENTER: Excuse me, Teacher. We'll have to discontinue the experiment.

(*Enter Milgram from camera's left. He has been watching from behind one-way glass.*)

MILGRAM: I'd like to ask you a few questions. (*Slowly, patiently, he dehoaxes the teacher, telling him that the shocks and screams were not real.*)

TEACHER: You mean he wasn't getting nothing? Well, I'm glad to hear that. I was getting upset there. I was getting ready to walk out. (*Finally, to make sure there are no hard feelings, friendly, harmless Mr. Wallace comes out in coat and tie. Gives jovial greeting. Friendly reconciliation takes place. Experiment ends.*)

Subjects in the experiment were not asked to give the 450-volt shock more than three times. By that time, it seemed evident that they would go on indefinitely. "No one," says Milgram, "who got within five shocks of the end ever broke off. By that point, he had resolved the conflict."

Why do so many people resolve the conflict in favor of obedience?

Milgram's theory assumes that people behave in two different operating modes as different as ice and water. He does not rely on Freud or sex or toilet-training hang-ups for this theory. All he says is that ordinarily we operate in a state of autonomy, which means we pretty much have and assert control over what we do. But in certain circumstances, we operate under what Milgram calls a state of agency (after agent, n . . . one who acts for or in the place of another by authority from him; a substitute; a deputy. —*Webster's Collegiate Dictionary*). A state of agency, to Milgram, is nothing more than a frame of mind.

"There's nothing bad about it, there's nothing good about it," he says. "It's a natural circumstance of living with other people. . . . I think of a state of agency as a real transformation of a person: if a person has different properties when he's in that state, just as water can turn to ice under certain conditions of temperature, a person can move to the state of mind that I call agency . . . the critical thing is that you see yourself as the instrument of the execution of another person's wishes. You do not see yourself as acting on your own. And there's a real transformation, a real change of properties of the person."

To achieve this change, you have to be in a situation where there seems to be a ruling authority whose commands are relevant to some legitimate purpose; the authority's power is not unlimited.

But situations can be and have been structured to make people do unusual things, and not just in Milgram's laboratory. The reason, says Milgram, is that no action, in and of itself, contains meaning.

"The meaning always depends on your definition of the situation. Take an action like killing another person. It sounds bad.

"But then we say the other person was about to destroy a hundred children, and the only way to stop him was to kill him. Well, that sounds good.

"Or, you take destroying your own life. It sounds very bad. Yet, in the Second World War, thousands of persons thought it was a good thing to destroy your own life. It was set in the proper context. You sipped some saki from a whistling cup, recited a few haiku. You said 'May my death be as clean and as quick as the shattering of crystal.' And it almost seemed like a good, noble thing to do, to crash your kamikaze plane into an aircraft carrier. But the main thing was, the definition of what a kamikaze pilot was doing had been determined by the relevant authority. Now, once you are in a state of agency, you allow the authority to determine, to define what the situation is. The meaning of your action is altered."

So, for most subjects in Milgram's laboratory experiments, the act of giving Mr. Wallace his painful shock was necessary, even though unpleasant, and besides they were doing it on behalf of somebody else and it was for science. There was still strain and conflict, of course. Most people resolved it by grimly sticking to their task and obeying. But some broke out. Milgram tried varying the conditions of the experiment to see what would help break people out of their state of agency.

"The results, as seen and felt in the laboratory," he has written, "are disturbing. They raise the possibility that human nature, or more specifically the kind of character produced in American democratic society, cannot be counted on to insulate its citizens from brutality and inhumane treatment at the direction of malevolent authority. A substantial proportion of people do what they are told to do, irrespective of the content of the act and without limitations of conscience, so long as they perceive that the command comes from a legitimate authority. If, in this study, an anonymous experimenter can successfully command adults to subdue a fifty-year-old man and force on him painful electric shocks against his protest, one can only wonder what government, with its vastly greater authority and prestige, can command of its subjects."

This is a nice statement, but it falls short of summing up the full meaning of Milgram's work. It leaves some questions still unanswered.

The first question is this: Should we really be surprised and alarmed that people obey? Wouldn't it be even more alarming if they all refused to obey? Without obedience to a relevant ruling authority there could not be a civil society. And without a civil society, as Thomas Hobbes pointed out in the seventeenth century, we would live in a condition of war, "of every man against every other man," and life would be "solitary, poor, nasty, brutish and short."

In the middle of one of Stanley Milgram's lectures at C.U.N.Y. recently, some mini-skirted undergraduates started whispering and giggling in the back of the room. He told them to cut it out. Since he was the relevant authority in that time and that place, they obeyed, and most people in the room were glad that they obeyed.

This was not, of course, a conflict situation. Nothing in the coeds' social upbringing made it a matter of conscience for them to whisper and giggle. But a case can be made that in a conflict situation it is all the more important to obey. Take the case of war, for example. Would we really want a situation in which every participant in a war, direct or indirect—from front-line soldiers to the people who sell coffee and cigarettes to employees at the Concertina barbed-wire factory in Kansas—stops and consults his conscience before each action? It is asking for an awful lot of mental strain and anguish from an awful lot of people. The value of having civil order is that one can do his duty, or whatever interests him, or whatever seems to benefit him at the moment, and leave the agonizing to others. When Francis Gary Powers was being tried by a Soviet military tribunal after his U-2 spy plane was shot down, the presiding judge asked if he had thought about the possibility that his flight might have provoked a war. Powers replied with Hobbesian clarity: "The people who sent me should think of these things. My job was to carry out orders. I do not think it was my responsibility to make such decisions."

It was not his responsibility. And it is quite possible that if everyone felt responsible for each of the ultimate consequences of his own tiny contributions to complex chains of events, then society simply would not work. Milgram, fully conscious of the moral and social implications of his research, believes that people should feel responsible for their actions. If someone else had invented the experiment, and if he had been the naïve subject, he feels certain that he would have been among the disobedient minority.

"There is no very good solution to this," he admits, thoughtfully. "To simply and categorically say that you won't obey authority may resolve your personal conflict, but it creates more problems for society which may be more serious in the long run. But I have no doubt that to disobey is the proper thing to do in this [the laboratory] situation. It is the only reasonable value judgment to make."

The conflict between the need to obey the relevant ruling authority and the need to follow your conscience becomes sharpest if you insist on living by an ethical system based on a rigid code—a code that seeks to answer all questions in advance of their being raised. Code ethics cannot solve the obedience problem. Stanley Milgram seems to be a situation ethicist, and situation ethics does offer a way out: When you feel conflict, you examine the situation and then make a choice among the competing evils. You may act with a presumption in favor of obedience, but reserve the possibility that you will disobey whenever obedience demands a flagrant and outrageous affront to conscience. This, by the way, is the philosophical position of many who resist the draft. In World War II, they would have fought. Vietnam is a different, an outrageously different, situation.

Life can be difficult for the situation ethicist, because he does not see the world in straight lines, while the social system too often assumes such a God-given, squared-off structure. If your moral code includes an injunction against all war, you may be deferred as a conscientious objector. If you merely oppose this particular war, you may not be deferred.

Stanley Milgram has his problems, too. He believes that in the laboratory situation, he would not have shocked Mr. Wallace. His professional critics reply that in his real-life situation he has done the equivalent. He has placed innocent and naïve subjects under great emotional strain and pressure in selfish obedience to his quest for knowledge. When you raise this issue with Milgram, he has an answer ready. There is, he explains patiently, a critical difference between his naïve subjects and the man in the electric chair. The man in the electric chair (in the mind of the naïve subject) is helpless, strapped in. But the naïve subject is free to go at any time.

Immediately after he offers this distinction, Milgram anticipates the objection.

"It's quite true," he says, "that this is almost a philosophic position, because we have learned that some people are psychologically incapable of disengaging themselves. But that doesn't relieve them of the moral responsibility."

The parallel is exquisite. "The tension problem was unexpected," says Milgram in his defense. But he went on anyway. The naïve subjects didn't expect the screaming protests from the strapped-in learner. But they went on.

"I had to make a judgment," says Milgram. "I had to ask myself, was this harming the person or not? My judgment is that it was not. Even in the extreme cases, I wouldn't say that permanent damage results."

Sound familiar? "The shocks may be painful," the experimenter kept saying, "but they're not dangerous."

After the series of experiments was completed, Milgram sent a report of the results to his subjects and a questionnaire, asking whether they were glad or sorry to have been in the experiment. Eighty-three and seven-tenths percent said they were glad and only 1.3 percent were sorry; 15 percent were neither sorry nor glad. However, Milgram could not be sure at the time of the experiment that only 1.3 percent would be sorry.

Kurt Vonnegut Jr. put one paragraph in the preface to *Mother Night*, in 1966, which pretty much says it for the people with their fingers on the shock-generator switches, for you and me, and maybe even for Milgram. "If I'd been born in Germany," Vonnegut said, "I suppose I would have *been* a Nazi, bopping Jews and gypsies and Poles around, leaving boots sticking out of snowbanks, warming myself with my sweetly virtuous insides. So it goes."

Just so. One thing that happened to Milgram back in New Haven during the days of the experiment was that he kept running into people he'd watched from behind the one-way glass. It gave him a funny feeling, seeing those people going about their everyday business in New Haven and knowing what they would do to Mr. Wallace if ordered to. Now that his research results are in and you've thought about it, you can get this funny feeling too. You don't need one-way glass. A glance in your own mirror may serve just as well.

Questions

1. Ultimately, Milgram conducted this experiment with thousands of individuals from all walks of life. One series of experiments involved the use of women in the teacher role. Milgram notes that their performance was "virtually identical to the performance of men," although women experienced a higher level of conflict than men did. One variation that Milgram did not attempt was using women as "learners." What effect might this have had on, say, male teachers' performance?

2. In your judgment, if the technician ("Jack Williams") had been female, would this have changed the outcome of the experiment? Why or why not?

3. Milgram has been criticized for being unethical in conducting this research. Why? How did he respond to these criticisms? Are you more persuaded by Milgram or by his critics? Why?

4. Meyer implies that Milgram's motives were something other than purely scientific—that his decision was in part a "moral one," "colored by his own Jewish background." Did Milgram's moral convictions lead him to invalid findings? Why or why not?

5. Elsewhere, Milgram wrote this:

   The problem of obedience, therefore, is not wholly psychological. The form and shape of society and the way it is developed have much to do with it. There was a time, perhaps, when men were able to give a fully human response to any situation because they were fully absorbed in it as human beings. But as soon as there was a division of labor among men, things changed. Beyond a certain point, the breaking up of society into people carrying out narrow and very special jobs takes away from the human quality of work and life. A person does not get to see the whole situation but only a small part of it, and is thus unable to act without some kind of over-all direction. He yields to authority but in so doing is alienated [separated] from his own actions. (Milgram, *Obedience to Authority* [New York: Harper & Row, 1975], p. 11)

   Do you agree or disagree with Milgram? Why?

·8·

Queer Customs

Clyde Kluckhohn

Clyde K. M. Kluckhohn (1905–1960) was born in Iowa and studied anthropology at Princeton, Wisconsin, Vienna, and Oxford universities. In 1935, Kluckhohn accepted a position at Harvard University, where he stayed for the remainder of his career. Kluckhohn's particular area of expertise was the Navajo. The following essay is excerpted from his 1949 book *Mirror for Man,* which Kluckhohn wrote in order to explain cultural theory to the lay public.

Why do the Chinese dislike milk and milk products? Why would the Japanese die willingly in a Banzai[1] charge that seemed senseless to Americans? Why do some nations trace descent through the father, others through the mother, still others through both parents? Not because different peoples have different instincts, not because they were destined by God or Fate to different habits, not because the weather is different in China and Japan and the United States. Sometimes shrewd common sense has an answer that is close to that of the anthropologist: "because they were brought up that way." By "culture" anthropology means the total life way of a people, the social legacy the individual acquires from his group. Or culture can be regarded as that part of the environment that is the creation of man.

This technical term has a wider meaning than the "culture" of history and literature. A humble cooking pot is as much a cultural product as is a Beethoven sonata. In ordinary speech a man of culture is a man who can speak languages other than his own, who is familiar with history, literature, philosophy, or the fine arts. In some cliques that definition is still narrower. The cultured person is one who can talk about James Joyce, Scarlatti, and Picasso.[2] To the anthropologist, however, to be human is to be cultured. There is culture in general, and then there are the specific cultures such as Russian, American, British, Hottentot,[3] Inca. The general abstract notion serves to remind us that we cannot explain acts solely in terms of the biological properties of the people concerned, their individual past experience, and the immediate situation. The past experience of other men in the form of culture enters into almost every event. Each specific culture constitutes a kind of blueprint for all of life's activities.

---

[1] Banzai is a Japanese war cry. — Ed.

"Queer Customs" from *Mirror for Man* by Clyde Kluckhohn, pp. 17–20, 24–27, 30–33. Copyright © 1949 George E. Taylor. Reprinted by permission of George E. Taylor.

[2] So, are you a cultured person by this definition? James Joyce (1882–1941) was an Irish author. His best-known book, *Ulysses,* was a novel about a day in Dublin (June 4, 1904). It was published in Paris in 1922 but was banned in the United States until 1937. Alessandro Scarlatti (1660–1725) was a Sicilian composer noted mostly for his operas. Pablo Picasso (1881–1973) was a prolific artist. Born in Spain (in Málaga), he spent much of his life in France. During his lifetime, he created more than 50,000 works—drawings, paintings, sculptures, and even ceramics and lithographs. — Ed.

[3] More properly called the *Khoikhoi*—a people mostly of Namibia, Africa. Nomadic and pastoral, their numbers were decimated by Dutch colonists in the seventeenth and eighteenth centuries—Ed.

One of the interesting things about human beings is that they try to understand themselves and their own behavior. While this has been particularly true of Europeans in recent times, there is no group which has not developed a scheme or schemes to explain man's actions. To the insistent human query "why?" the most exciting illumination anthropology has to offer is that of the concept of culture. Its explanatory importance is comparable to categories such as evolution in biology, gravity in physics, disease in medicine. A good deal of human behavior can be understood, and indeed predicted, if we know a people's design for living. Many acts are neither accidental nor due to personal peculiarities nor caused by supernatural forces nor simply mysterious. Even those of us who pride ourselves on our individualism follow most of the time a pattern not of our own making. We brush our teeth on arising. We put on pants—not a loincloth or a grass skirt. We eat three meals a day—not four or five or two. We sleep in a bed—not in a hammock or on a sheep pelt. I do not have to know the individual and his life history to be able to predict these and countless other regularities, including many in the thinking process, of all Americans who are not incarcerated in jails or hospitals for the insane.

To the American woman a system of plural wives seems "instinctively" abhorrent. She cannot understand how any woman can fail to be jealous and uncomfortable if she must share her husband with other women. She feels it "unnatural" to accept such a situation. On the other hand, a Koryak woman of Siberia, for example, would find it hard to understand how a woman could be so selfish and so undesirous of feminine companionship in the home as to wish to restrict her husband to one mate.

Some years ago I met in New York City a young man who did not speak a word of English and was obviously bewildered by American ways. By "blood" he was as American as you or I, for his parents had gone from Indiana to China as missionaries. Orphaned in infancy, he was reared by a Chinese family in a remote village. All who met him found him more Chinese than American. The facts of his blue eyes and light hair were less impressive than a Chinese style of gait, Chinese arm and hand movements, Chinese facial expression, and Chinese modes of thought. The biological heritage was American, but the cultural training had been Chinese. He returned to China.

Another example of another kind: I once knew a trader's wife in Arizona who took a somewhat devilish interest in producing a cultural reaction. Guests who came her way were often served delicious sandwiches filled with a meat that seemed to be neither chicken nor tuna fish yet was reminiscent of both. To queries she gave no reply until each had eaten his fill. She then explained that what they had eaten was not chicken, not tuna fish, but the rich, white flesh of freshly killed rattlesnakes. The response was instantaneous—vomiting, often violent vomiting. A biological process is caught in a cultural web.

A highly intelligent teacher with long and successful experience in the public schools of Chicago was finishing her first year in an Indian school. When asked how her Navaho pupils compared in intelligence with Chicago youngsters, she replied, "Well, I just don't know. Sometimes the Indians seem just as bright. At other times they just act like dumb animals. The other night we had a dance in the high school. I saw a boy who is one of the best students in my English class standing off by himself. So I took him over to a pretty girl and told them to dance. But they just stood there with their heads down. They wouldn't even say anything." I inquired if she knew whether or not they were members of the same clan. "What difference would that make?"

"How would you feel about getting into bed with your brother?" The teacher walked off in a huff, but, actually, the two cases were quite comparable in principle. To the Indian the type of bodily contact involved in our social dancing has a directly sexual connotation. The incest taboos between members of the same clan are as severe as between true brothers and sisters. The shame of the Indians at the suggestion that a clan brother and sister should dance and the indignation of the white teacher at the idea that she should share a bed with an adult brother represent equally nonrational responses, culturally standardized unreason. . . .

Culture and Society

Since culture is an abstraction, it is important not to confuse culture with society. A "society" refers to a group of people who interact more with each other than they do with other individuals—who cooperate with each other for the attainment of certain ends. You can see and indeed count the individuals who make up a society. A "culture" refers to the distinctive ways of life of such a group of people. Not all social events are culturally patterned. New types of circumstances arise for which no cultural solutions have as yet been devised.

A culture constitutes a storehouse of the pooled learning of the group. A rabbit starts life with some innate responses. He can learn from his own experience and perhaps from observing other rabbits. A human infant is born with fewer instincts and greater plasticity. His main task is to learn the answers that persons he will never see, persons long dead, have worked out. Once he has learned the formulas supplied by the culture of his group, most of his behavior becomes almost as automatic and unthinking as if it were instinctive. There is a tremendous amount of intelligence behind the making of a radio, but not much is required to learn to turn it on.

The members of all human societies face some of the same unavoidable dilemmas, posed by biology and other facts of the human situation. This is why the basic categories of all cultures are so similar. Human culture without language is unthinkable. No culture fails to provide for aesthetic expression and aesthetic delight. Every culture supplies standardized orientations toward the deeper problems, such as death. Every culture is designed to perpetuate the group and its solidarity, to meet the demands of individuals for an orderly way of life and for satisfaction of biological needs.

However, the variations on these basic themes are numberless. Some languages are built up out of twenty basic sounds, others out of forty. Nose plugs were considered beautiful by the predynastic Egyptians but are not by the modern French. Puberty is a biological fact. But one culture ignores it, another prescribes informal instructions about sex but no ceremony, a third has impressive rites for girls only, a fourth for boys and girls. In this culture, the first menstruation is welcomed as a happy, natural event; in that culture the atmosphere is full of dread and supernatural threat. Each culture dissects nature according to its own system of categories. The Navaho Indians apply the same word to the color of a robin's egg and to that of grass. A psychologist once assumed that this meant a difference in the sense organs, that Navahos didn't have the physiological equipment to distinguish "green" from "blue." However, when he showed them objects of the two colors and asked them if they were exactly the same colors, they looked at him with astonishment. His dream of discovering a new type of color blindness was shattered.

Every culture must deal with the sexual instinct. Some, however, seek to deny all sexual expression before marriage, whereas a Polynesian adolescent who was not promiscuous would be distinctly abnormal. Some cultures enforce lifelong monogamy; others, like our own, tolerate serial monogamy; in still other cultures, two or more women may be joined to one man or several men to a single woman. Homosexuality has been a permitted pattern in the Greco-Roman world, in parts of Islam, and in various primitive tribes. Large portions of the population of Tibet, and of Christendom at some places and periods, have practiced complete celibacy. To us marriage is first and foremost an arrangement between two individuals. In many more societies marriage is merely one facet of a complicated set of reciprocities, economic and otherwise, between two families or two clans.

The essence of the cultural process is selectivity. The selection is only exceptionally conscious and rational. Cultures are like Topsy. They just grew.[4] Once, however, a way of handling a situation becomes institutionalized, there is ordinarily great resistance to change or deviation. When we speak of "our sacred beliefs," we mean of course that they are beyond criticism and that the person who suggests modification or abandonment must be punished. No person is emotionally indifferent to his culture. Certain cultural premises may become totally out of accord with a new factual situation. Leaders may recognize this and reject the old ways in theory. Yet their emotional loyalty continues in the face of reason because of the intimate conditionings of early childhood.

A culture is learned by individuals as the result of belonging to some particular group, and it constitutes that part of learned behavior which is shared with others. It is our social legacy, as contrasted with our organic heredity. It is one of the important factors which permits us to live together in an organized society, giving us ready-made solutions to our problems, helping us to predict the behavior of others, and permitting others to know what to expect of us.

Culture regulates our lives at every turn. From the moment we are born until we die there is, whether we are conscious of it or not, constant pressure upon us to follow certain types of behavior that other men have created for us. Some paths we follow willingly, others we follow because we know no other way, still others we deviate from or go back to most unwillingly. Mothers of small children know how unnaturally most of this comes to us—how little regard we have, until we are "culturalized," for the "proper" place, time, and manner for certain acts such as eating, excreting, sleeping, getting dirty, and making loud noises. But by more or less adhering to a system of related designs for carrying out all the acts of living, a group of men and women feel themselves linked together by a powerful chain of sentiments. Ruth Benedict gave an almost complete definition of the concept when she said, "Culture is that which binds men together." . . .

No participant in any culture knows all the details of the cultural map. The statement frequently heard that St. Thomas Aquinas was the last man to master all the knowledge of his society is intrinsically absurd. St. Thomas would have been hard put to make a pane of cathedral glass or to act as a midwife. In every culture there are what Ralph Linton has called "universals, alternatives, and specialties." Every Christian in the thirteenth century knew that it was necessary to attend mass, to go to confession, to ask the Mother of God to intercede with her Son. There were many other universals in the Christian culture of Western Europe. However, there were also alternative cultural patterns even in the realm of religion. Each individual had his own patron saint, and

---

[4]To grow like Topsy means to flourish without being purposefully tended. The roots of this odd-sounding expression are to be found in *Uncle Tom's Cabin,* by Harriet Beecher Stowe. In 1850, the Congress enacted a Fugitive Slave Act which required the return of runaway slaves who fled to states where slavery had been abolished. Beecher Stowe's novel was written in a protest against this law and slavery in general. The character Topsy was a young slave girl of about eight or nine years old. Purchased from an abusive family, Topsy is brought to New England to be raised by the pious Ophelia St. Clare. Asked by Miss Ophelia how old she is, Topsy says she has no idea: Another slave explains to Miss Ophelia that it is common practice in the South for speculators to purchase black infants and raise them for the slave market. When queried about her parents, Topsy says, "I spect I growed. Don't think nobody never made me." —Ed.

different towns developed the cults of different saints. The thirteenth-century anthropologist could have discovered the rudiments of Christian practice by questioning and observing whomever he happened to meet in Germany, France, Italy, or England. But to find out the details of the ceremonials honoring St. Hubert or St. Bridget he would have had to seek out certain individuals or special localities where these alternative patterns were practiced. Similarly, he could not learn about weaving from a professional soldier or about canon law from a farmer. Such cultural knowledge belongs in the realm of the specialties, voluntarily chosen by the individual or ascribed to him by birth. Thus, part of a culture must be learned by everyone, part may be selected from alternative patterns, part applies only to those who perform the roles in the society for which these patterns are designed.

Many aspects of a culture are explicit. The explicit culture consists in those regularities in word and deed that may be generalized straight from the evidence of the ear and the eye. The recognition of these is like the recognition of style in the art of a particular place and epoch. If we have examined twenty specimens of the wooden saints' images made in the Taos valley of New Mexico in the late eighteenth century, we can predict that any new images from the same locality and period will in most respects exhibit the same techniques of carving, about the same use of colors and choice of woods, a similar quality of artistic conception. Similarly, if, in a society of 2,000 members, we record 100 marriages at random and find that in 30 cases a man has married the sister of his brother's wife, we can anticipate that an additional sample of 100 marriages will show roughly the same number of cases of this pattern.

The above is an instance of what anthropologists call a behavioral pattern, the practices as opposed to the rules of the culture. There are also, however, regularities in what people say they do or should do. They do tend in fact to prefer to marry into a family already connected with their own by marriage, but this is not necessarily part of the official code of conduct. No disapproval whatsoever is attached to those who make another sort of marriage. On the other hand, it is explicitly forbidden to marry a member of one's own clan even though no biological relationship is traceable. This is a regulatory pattern—a Thou Shalt or a Thou Shalt Not. Such patterns may be violated often, but their existence is nevertheless important. A people's standards for conduct and belief define the socially approved aims and the acceptable means of attaining them. When the discrepancy between the theory and the practice of a culture is exceptionally great, this indicates that the culture is undergoing rapid change. It does not prove that ideals are unimportant, for ideals are but one of a number of factors determining action.

Cultures do not manifest themselves solely in observable customs and artifacts. No amount of questioning of any save the most articulate in the most self-conscious cultures will bring out some of the basic attitudes common to the members of the group. This is because these basic assumptions are taken so for granted that they normally do not enter into consciousness. This part of the cultural map must be inferred by the observer on the basis of consistencies in thought and action. Missionaries in various societies are often disturbed or puzzled because the natives do not regard "morals" and "sex code" as almost synonymous. The natives seem to feel that morals are concerned with sex just about as much as with eating—no less and no more. No society fails to have some restrictions on sexual behavior, but sex activity outside of marriage need not necessarily be furtive or attended with guilt. The Christian tradition has tended to assume that sex is inherently nasty as well as dangerous. Other cultures assume that sex in itself is not only natural but one of the good things of life, even though sex acts with certain persons under certain circumstances are forbidden. This is implicit culture, for the natives do not announce their premises. The missionaries would get further if they said, in effect, "Look, our morality starts from different assumptions. Let's talk about those assumptions," rather than ranting about "immorality." . . .

In our highly self-conscious Western civilization that has recently made a business of studying itself, the number of assumptions that are literally implicit, in the sense of never having been stated or discussed by anyone, may be negligible. Yet only a trifling number of Americans could state even those implicit premises of our culture that have been brought to light by anthropologists. If one could bring to the American scene a Bushman who had been socialized in his own culture and then trained in anthropology, he would perceive all sorts of patterned regularities of which our anthropologists are completely unaware. In the case of the less sophisticated and less self-conscious societies, the unconscious assumptions characteristically made by individuals brought up under approximately the same social controls bulk even larger. But in any society, as Edward Sapir said, "Forms and significances which seem obvious to an outsider will be denied outright by those who carry out the patterns; outlines and implications that are perfectly clear to these may be absent to the eye of the onlooker." . . .

Questions

1. According to Kluckhohn, what is the difference between culture and society? (Many people improperly use these terms interchangeably, but now that you know the difference you can avoid that error.)

2. What does Kluckhohn mean by the phrase "culturally standardized unreason"? Can you think of any examples of this sort of unreason from your own culture?

3. What does Kluckhohn mean by the concept of "behavioral pattern"? What is a "regulatory pattern"? Give a couple of examples from your own culture of instances in which behavioral and regulatory patterns are consistent. Then, give examples from your own culture in which behavioral and regulatory patterns are inconsistent. (Which was harder to do — to find examples of consistency or of inconsistency between behavioral patterns and regulatory patterns? Why do you think this is?)

·9·

Body Ritual Among the Nacirema

Horace Miner

The American anthropologist Horace Miner was one of the first to make public the results of anthropological research on the Nacirema. Although in the decades that followed the 1956 publication of Miner's work many more studies have been published, none more dramatically reveals the role of myth, magic, and ritual in the lives of this rather exotic group of people.

The anthropologist has become so familiar with the diversity of ways in which different peoples behave in similar situations that he is not apt to be surprised by even the most exotic customs. In fact, if all of the logically possible combinations of behavior have not been found somewhere in the world, he is apt to suspect that they must be present in some as yet undescribed tribe. This point has, in fact, been expressed with respect to clan organization by Murdock (1949, 71). In this light, the magical beliefs and practices of the Nacirema present such unusual aspects that it seems desirable to describe them as an example of the extremes to which human behavior can go.

Professor Linton first brought the ritual of the Nacirema to the attention of anthropologists [over sixty] years ago (1936, 326), but the culture of this people is still very poorly understood. They are a North American group living in the territory between the Canadian Cree, the Yaqui and Tarahumare of Mexico, and the Carib and Arawak of the Antilles. Little is known of their origin, although tradition states that they came from the east. According to Nacirema mythology, their nation was originated by a culture hero, Notgnihsaw, who is otherwise known for two great feats of strength—the throwing of a piece of wampum across the river Po-To-Mac and the chopping down of a cherry tree in which the Spirit of Truth resided.

Nacirema culture is characterized by a highly developed market economy which has evolved in a rich natural habitat. While much of the people's time is devoted to economic pursuits, a large part of the fruits of these labors and a considerable portion of the day are spent in ritual activity. The focus of this activity is the human body, the appearance and health of which loom as a dominant concern in the ethos of the people. While such a concern is certainly not unusual, its ceremonial aspects and associated philosophy are unique.

The fundamental belief underlying the whole system appears to be that the human body is ugly and that its natural tendency is to debility and disease. Incarcerated in such a body, man's only hope is to avert these characteristics through the use of the powerful influences of ritual and ceremony. Every household has one or more shrines devoted to this purpose. The more powerful individuals in the society have several shrines in their houses and, in fact, the opulence of a house is often referred to in terms of the number of such ritual centers it possesses. Most houses are of wattle and daub construction, but the

"Body Ritual Among the Nacirema" by Horace Miner is reproduced by permission of the American Anthropological Association and the Estate of Horace Miner from *American Anthropologist* 58:3, June 1956. Not for further reproduction.

shrine rooms of the more wealthy are walled with stone. Poorer families imitate the rich by applying pottery plaques to their shrine walls.

While each family has at least one such shrine, the rituals associated with it are not family ceremonies but are private and secret. The rites are normally only discussed with children, and then only during the period when they are being initiated into these mysteries. I was able, however, to establish sufficient rapport with the natives to examine these shrines and to have the rituals described to me.

The focal point of the shrine is a box or chest which is built into the wall. In this chest are kept the many charms and magical potions without which no native believes he could live. These preparations are secured from a variety of specialized practitioners. The most powerful of these are the medicine men, whose assistance must be rewarded with substantial gifts. However, the medicine men do not provide the curative potions for their clients, but decide what the ingredients should be and they write them down in an ancient and secret language. This writing is understood only by the medicine men and by the herbalists who, for another gift, provide the required charm.

The charm is not disposed of after it has served its purpose, but is placed in the charmbox of the household shrine. As these magical materials are specific for certain ills, and the real or imagined maladies of the people are many, the charm-box is usually full to overflowing. The magical packets are so numerous that people forget what their purposes were and fear to use them again. While the natives are very vague on this point, we can only assume that the idea in retaining all the old magical materials is that their presence in the charm-box, before which the body rituals are conducted, will in some way protect the worshipper.

Beneath the charm-box is a small font. Each day every member of the family, in succession, enters the shrine room, bows his head before the charm-box, mingles different sorts of holy water in the font, and proceeds with a brief rite of ablution. The holy waters are secured from the Water Temple of the community, where the priests conduct elaborate ceremonies to make the liquid ritually pure.

In the hierarchy of magical practitioners, and below the medicine men in prestige, are specialists whose designation is best translated "holy-mouth-men." The Nacirema have an almost pathological horror of and fascination with the mouth, the condition of which is believed to have a supernatural influence on all social relationships. Were it not for the rituals of the mouth, they believe that their teeth would fall out, their gums bleed, their jaws shrink, their friends desert them, and their lovers reject them. They also believe that a strong relationship exists between oral and moral characteristics. For example, there is a ritual ablution of the mouth for children which is supposed to improve their moral fiber.

The daily body ritual performed by everyone includes a mouth-rite. Despite the fact that these people are so punctilious about care of the mouth, this rite involves a practice which strikes the uninitiated stranger as revolting. It was reported to me that the ritual consists of inserting a small bundle of hog hairs into the mouth, along with certain magical powders, and then moving the bundle in a highly formalized series of gestures.

In addition to the private mouth-rite, the people seek out a holy-mouth-man once or twice a year. These practitioners have an impressive set of paraphernalia, consisting of a variety of augers, awls, probes, and prods. The use of these objects in the exorcism of the evils of the mouth involves almost unbelievable ritual torture of the client. The holy-mouth-man opens the client's mouth and, using the above mentioned tools, enlarges any holes which decay may have created in the teeth. Magical materials are put into these holes. If there are no naturally occurring holes in the teeth, large sections of one or more teeth are gouged out so that the supernatural substance can be applied. In the client's view, the purpose of these ministrations is to arrest decay and to draw friends. The extremely sacred and traditional character of the rite is evident in the fact that the natives return to the holy-mouth-men year after year, despite the fact that their teeth continue to decay.

It is to be hoped that, when a thorough study of the Nacirema is made, there will be careful inquiry into the personality structure of these people. One has but to watch the gleam in the eye of a holy-mouth-man, as he jabs an awl into an exposed nerve, to suspect that a certain amount of sadism is involved. If this can be established, a very interesting pattern emerges, for most of the population shows definite masochistic tendencies. It was to these that Professor Linton referred in discussing a distinctive part of the daily body ritual which is performed only by men. This part of the rite involves scraping and lacerating the surface of the face with a sharp instrument. Special women's rites are performed only four times during each lunar month, but what they lack in frequency is made up in barbarity. As part of this ceremony, women bake their heads in small ovens for about an hour. The theoretically interesting point is that what seems to be a preponderantly masochistic people have developed sadistic specialists.

The medicine men have an imposing temple, or *latipso,* in every community of any size. The more elaborate ceremonies required to treat very sick patients can only be performed at this temple. These ceremonies involve not only the thaumaturge but a permanent group of vestal maidens who move sedately about the temple chambers in distinctive costume and headdress.

The *latipso* ceremonies are so harsh that it is phenomenal that a fair proportion of the really sick natives who enter the temple ever recover. Small children whose indoctrination is still incomplete have been known to resist attempts to take them to the temple because "that is where you go to die." Despite this fact, sick adults are not only willing but eager to undergo the protracted ritual purification, if they can afford to

do so. No matter how ill the supplicant or how grave the emergency, the guardians of many temples will not admit a client if he cannot give a rich gift to the custodian. Even after one has gained admission and survived the ceremonies, the guardians will not permit the neophyte to leave until he makes still another gift.

The supplicant entering the temple is first stripped of all his or her clothes. In every-day life the Nacirema avoids exposure of his body and its natural functions. Bathing and excretory acts are performed only in the secrecy of the household shrine, where they are ritualized as part of the body-rites. Psychological shock results from the fact that body secrecy is suddenly lost upon entry into the *latipso.* A man, whose own wife has never seen him in an excretory act, suddenly finds himself naked and assisted by a vestal maiden while he performs his natural functions into a sacred vessel. This sort of ceremonial treatment is necessitated by the fact that the excreta are used by a diviner to ascertain the course and nature of the client's sickness. Female clients, on the other hand, find their naked bodies are subjected to the scrutiny, manipulation and prodding of the medicine men.

Few supplicants in the temple are well enough to do anything but lie on their hard beds. The daily ceremonies, like the rites of the holy-mouth-men, involve discomfort and torture. With ritual precision, the vestals awaken their miserable charges each dawn and roll them about on their beds of pain while performing ablutions, in the formal movements of which the maidens are highly trained. At other times they insert magic wands in the supplicant's mouth or force him to eat substances which are supposed to be healing. From time to time the medicine men come to their clients and jab magically treated needles into their flesh. The fact that these temple ceremonies may not cure, and may even kill the neophyte, in no way decreases the people's faith in the medicine men.

There remains one other kind of practitioner, known as a "listener." This witch-doctor has the power to exorcise the devils that lodge in the heads of people who have been bewitched. The Nacirema believe that parents bewitch their own children. Mothers are particularly suspected of putting a curse on children while teaching them the secret body rituals. The counter-magic of the witch-doctor is unusual in its lack of ritual. The patient simply tells the "listener" all his troubles and fears, beginning with the earliest difficulties he can remember. The memory displayed by the Nacirema in these exorcism sessions is truly remarkable. It is not uncommon for the patient to bemoan the rejection he felt upon being weaned as a baby, and a few individuals even see their troubles going back to the traumatic effects of their own birth.

In conclusion, mention must be made of certain practices which have their base in native esthetics but which depend upon the pervasive aversion to the natural body and its functions. There are ritual fasts to make fat people thin and ceremonial feasts to make thin people fat. Still other rites are used to make women's breasts larger if they are small, and smaller if they are large. General dissatisfaction with breast shape is symbolized in the fact that the ideal form is virtually outside the range of human variation. A few women afflicted with almost inhuman hypermammary development are so idolized that they make a handsome living by simply going from village to village and permitting the natives to stare at them for a fee.

Reference has already been made to the fact that excretory functions are ritualized, routinized, and relegated to secrecy. Natural reproductive functions are similarly distorted. Intercourse is taboo as a topic and scheduled as an act. Efforts are made to avoid pregnancy by the use of magical materials or by limiting intercourse to certain phases of the moon. Conception is actually very infrequent. When pregnant, women dress so as to hide their condition. Parturition takes place in secret, without friends or relatives to assist, and the majority of women do not nurse their infants.

Our review of the ritual life of the Nacirema has certainly shown them to be a magic-ridden people. It is hard to understand how they have managed to exist so long under the burdens which they have imposed upon themselves. But even such exotic customs as these take on real meaning when they are viewed with the insight provided by Malinowski when he wrote (1948, 70):

> Looking from far and above, from our high places of safety in the developed civilization, it is easy to see all the crudity and irrelevance of magic. But without its power and guidance early man could not have mastered his practical difficulties as he has done, nor could man have advanced to the higher stages of civilization.

References

Linton, Ralph. 1936. *The Study of Man.* New York: Appleton-Century.

Malinowski, Bronislaw. 1948. *Magic, Science, and Religion.* Glencoe, IL: Free Press.

Murdock, George P. 1949. *Social Structure.* New York: Macmillan.

Questions

1. What is a thaumaturge?

2. Why would it be ethnocentric to think of the Nacirema as weird—or even silly—for their beliefs?

3. Can you see any signs that Miner experienced "culture shock" as he investigated the Nacirema? Explain.

4. Do you think you would enjoy taking a vacation in the land of the Nacirema? Why or why not?

·10·

The Young, the Rich, and the Famous
Individualism as an American Cultural Value

Poranee Natadecha-Sponsel

At first, many visitors to the United States are struck by how warm and open Americans seem to be. But it doesn't take a visitor long to discover that what seems like friendliness is really something else. Professor Natadecha-Sponsel, who was born and raised in Thailand, now teaches at the University of Hawaii at Manoa. In this 1998 article she describes some of the truths of American culture that go unnoticed by Americans themselves.

"Hi, how are you?" "Fine, thank you, and you?" These are greetings that everybody in America hears and says every day—salutations that come ready-made and packaged just like a hamburger and fries. There is no real expectation for any special information in response to these greetings. Do not, under any circumstances, take up anyone's time by responding in depth to the programmed query. What or how you may feel at the moment is of little, if any, importance. Thai people would immediately perceive that our concerned American friends are truly interested in our welfare, and this concern would require polite reciprocation by spelling out the details of our current condition. We become very disappointed when we have had enough experience in the United States to learn that we have bored, amused,

or even frightened many of our American acquaintances by taking the greeting "How are you?" so literally. We were reacting like Thais, but in the American context where salutations have a different meaning, our detailed reactions were inappropriate. In Thai society, a greeting among acquaintances usually requests specific information about the other person's condition, such as "Where are you going?" or "Have you eaten?"

One of the American contexts in which this greeting is most confusing and ambiguous is at the hospital or clinic. In these sterile and ritualistic settings, I have always been uncertain exactly how to answer when the doctor or nurse asks "How are you?" If I deliver a packaged answer of "Fine," I wonder if I am telling a lie. After all, I am there in the first place precisely because I am not so fine. Finally, after debating for some time, I asked one nurse how she expected a patient to answer the query "How are you?" But after asking this question, I then wondered if it was rude to do so. However, she looked relieved after I explained to her that people from different cultures have different ways to greet other people and that for me to be asked how I am in the hospital results in awkwardness. Do I simply answer, "Fine, thank you," or do I reveal in accurate detail how I really feel at the moment? My suspicion was verified when the nurse declared that "How are you?" was really no more than a polite greeting and that she didn't expect any answer more elaborate than simply "Fine." However, she told me that some patients do answer her by describing every last ache and pain from which they are suffering.

A significant question that comes to mind is whether the verbal pattern of greetings reflects any social relationship in American culture. The apparently warm and sincere greeting may initially suggest interest in the person, yet the intention and expectations are, to me, quite superficial. For example, most often the person greets you quickly and then walks by to attend to other business without even waiting for your response! This type of greeting is just like a package of American fast food! The person eats the food quickly without enjoying the taste. The convenience is like many other American accoutrements of living such as cars, household appliances, efficient telephones, or simple, systematic, and predictable arrangements of groceries in the supermarket. However, usually when this greeting is delivered, it seems to lack a personal touch and genuine feeling. It is little more than ritualized behavior.

I have noticed that most Americans keep to themselves even at social gatherings. Conversation may revolve around many topics, but little, if anything, is revealed about oneself. Without talking much about oneself and not knowing much about others, social relations seem to remain at an abbreviated superficial level. How could one know a person without knowing something about him or her? How much does one need to know about a person to really know that person?

After living in this culture for more than a decade, I have learned that there are many topics that should not be mentioned in conversations with American acquaintances or even close friends. One's personal life and one's income are considered to be very private and even taboo topics. Unlike my Thai culture, Americans do not show interest or curiosity by asking such personal questions, especially when one just meets the individual for the first time. Many times I have been embarrassed by my Thai acquaintances who recently arrived at the University of Hawaii and the East–West Center. For instance, one day I was walking on campus with an American friend when we met another Thai woman to whom I had been introduced a few days earlier. The Thai woman came to write her doctoral dissertation at the East–West Center where the American woman worked, so I introduced them to each other. The American woman greeted my Thai companion in Thai language, which so impressed her that she felt immediately at ease. At once, she asked the American woman numerous personal questions such as, How long did you live in Thailand? Why were you there? How long were you married to the Thai man? Why did you divorce him? How long have you been divorced? Are you going to marry a Thai again or an American? How long have you been working here? How much do you earn? The American was stunned. However, she was very patient and more or less answered all those questions as succinctly as she could. I was so uncomfortable that I had to interrupt whenever I could to get her out of the awkward situation in which she had been forced into talking about things she considered personal. For people in Thai society, such questions would be appropriate and not considered too personal, let alone taboo.

The way Americans value their individual privacy continues to impress me. Americans seem to be open and yet there is a contradiction because they are also aloof and secretive. This is reflected in many of their behavior patterns.

By Thai standards, the relationship between friends in American society seems to be somewhat superficial. Many Thai students, as well as other Asians, have felt that they could not find genuine friendship with Americans. For example, I met many American classmates who were very helpful and friendly while we were in the same class. We went out, exchanged phone calls, and did the same things as would good friends in Thailand. But those activities stopped suddenly when the semester ended.

Privacy as a component of the American cultural value of individualism is nurtured in the home as children grow up. From birth they are given their own individual, private space, a bedroom separate from that of their parents. American children are taught to become progressively independent, both emotionally and economically, from their family. They learn to help themselves at an early age. In comparison, in Thailand, when parents bring a new baby home from the hospital, it shares the parents' bedroom for two to three years and then shares another bedroom with older siblings of the same sex. Most Thai children do not have their own private room until they finish high school, and some do not have their own room until another sibling moves out, usually when the sibling gets married. In Thailand, there are strong bonds within the extended family. Older siblings regularly help their parents to care for younger ones. In this and other ways, the Thai family emphasizes the interdependence of its members.

I was accustomed to helping Thai babies who fell down to stand up again. Thus, in America when I saw babies fall, it was natural for me to try to help them back on their feet. Once at a summer camp for East–West Center participants, one of the supervisors brought his wife and their ten-month-old son with him. The baby was so cute that many students were playing with him. At one point he was trying to walk and fell, so all the Asian students, males and females, rushed to help him up. Although the father and mother were nearby, they paid no attention to their fallen and crying baby. However, as the students were trying to help and comfort him, the parents told them to leave him alone; he would be all right on his own. The baby did get up and stopped crying without any assistance. Independence is yet another component of the American value of individualism.

Individualism is even reflected in the way Americans prepare, serve, and consume food. In a typical American meal, each person has a separate plate and is not supposed to share or taste food from other people's plates. My Thai friends and I are used to eating Thai style, in which you share food from a big serving dish in the middle of the table. Each person dishes a small amount from the serving dish onto his or her plate and finishes this portion before going on with the next portion of the same or a different serving dish. With the Thai pattern of eating, you regularly reach out to the serving dishes throughout the meal. But this way of eating is not considered appropriate in comparison to the common American practice where each person eats separately from his or her individual plate.

One time my American host, a divorcée who lived alone, invited a Thai girlfriend and myself to an American dinner at her home. When we were reaching out and eating a small portion of one thing at a time in Thai style, we were told to dish everything we wanted onto our plates at one time and that it was not considered polite to reach across the table. The proper American way was to have each kind of food piled up on your plate at once. If we were to eat in the same manner in Thailand, eyebrows would have been raised at the way we piled up food on our plates, and we would have been considered to be eating like pigs, greedy and inconsiderate of others who shared the meal at the table.

Individualism as a pivotal value in American culture is reflected in many other ways. Material wealth is not only a prime status marker in

American society but also a guarantee and celebration of individualism—wealth allows the freedom to do almost anything, although usually within the limits of law. The pursuit of material wealth through individual achievement is instilled in Americans from the youngest age. For example, I was surprised to see an affluent American couple, who own a large ranch house and two BMW cars, send their nine-year-old son to deliver newspapers. He has to get up very early each morning to deliver the papers, even on Sunday! During summer vacation, the boy earns additional money by helping in his parents' gift shop from 10 A.M. to 5 P.M. His thirteen-year-old sister often earns money by babysitting, even at night.

In Thailand, only children from poorer families work to earn money to help the household. Middle- and high-income parents do not encourage their children to work until after they have finished their education. They provide economic support in order to free their children to concentrate on and excel in their studies. Beyond the regular schooling, families who can afford it pay for special tutoring as well as training in music, dance, or sports. However, children in low- and middle-income families help their parents with household chores and the care of younger children.

Many American children have been encouraged to get paid for their help around the house. They rarely get any gifts free of obligations. They even have to be good to get Santa's gift at Christmas! As they grow up, they are conditioned to earn things they want; they learn that "there is no such thing as a free lunch." From an early age, children are taught to become progressively independent economically from their parents. Also, most young people are encouraged to leave home at college age to be on their own. From my viewpoint as a Thai, it seems that American family ties and closeness are not as strong as in Asian families whose children depend on family financial support until joining the workforce after college age. Thereafter, it is the children's turn to help support their parents financially.

Modern American society and economy emphasize individualism in other ways. The nuclear family is more common than the extended family, and newlyweds usually establish their own independent household rather than initially living with either the husband's or the wife's parents. Parents and children appear to be close only when the children are very young. Most American parents seem to "lose" their children by the teenage years. They don't seem to belong to each other as closely as do Thai families. Even though I have seen more explicit affectionate expression among American family members than among Asian ones, the close interpersonal spirit seems to be lacking. Grandparents have relatively little to do with the grandchildren on any regular basis, in contrast to the extended family, which is more common in Thailand. The family and society seem to be graded by age to the point that grandparents, parents, and children are separated by generational subcultures that are evidently alienated from one another. Each group "does its own thing." Help and support are usually limited to whatever does not interfere with one's own life. In America, the locus of responsibility is more on the individual than on the family.

In one case I know of, a financially affluent grandmother with Alzheimer's disease is taken care of twenty-four hours a day by hired help in her own home. Her daughter visits and relieves the helper occasionally. The mature granddaughter, who has her own family, rarely visits. Yet they all live in the same neighborhood. However, each lives in a different house, and each is very independent. Although the mother worries about the grandmother, she cannot do much. Her husband also needs her, and she divides her time between him, her daughters and their children, and the grandmother. When the mother needs to go on a trip with her husband, a second hired attendant is required to care for the grandmother temporarily. When I asked why the granddaughter doesn't temporarily care for the grandmother, the reply was that she has her own life, and it would not be fair for the granddaughter to take care of the grandmother, even for a short period of time. Yet I wonder if it is fair for the grandmother to be left out. It seems to me that the value of individualism and its associated independence account for these apparent gaps in family ties and support.

In contrast to American society, in Thailand older parents with a long-term illness are asked to move in with their children and grandchildren if they are not already living with them. The children and grandchildren take turns attending to the grandparent, sometimes with help from live-in maids. Living together in the same house reinforces moral support among the generations within the extended family. The older generation is respected because of the previous economic, social, and moral support for their children and grandchildren. Family relations provide one of the most important contexts for being a "morally good person," which is traditionally the principal concern in the Buddhist society of Thailand.

In America, being young, rich, and/or famous allows one greater freedom and independence and thus promotes the American value of individualism. This is reflected in the mass appeal of major annual television events like the Super Bowl and the Academy Awards. The goal of superachievement is also seen in more mundane ways. For example, many parents encourage their children to take special courses and to work hard to excel in sports as a shortcut to becoming rich and famous. I know one mother who has taken her two sons to tennis classes and tournaments since the boys were six years old, hoping that at least one of them will be a future tennis star like Ivan Lendl. Other parents focus their children on acting, dancing, or musical talent. The children have to devote much time and hard work as well as sacrifice the ordinary activities of youth in order to develop and perform their natural talents and skills in prestigious programs. But those who excel in the sports and entertainment industries can become rich and famous, even at an early age, as for example Madonna, Tom Cruise, and Michael Jackson. Television and other media publicize these celebrities and thereby reinforce the American value of individualism, including personal achievement and financial success.

Although the American cultural values of individualism and the aspiration to become rich and famous have had some influence in Thailand, there is also cultural and religious resistance to these values. Strong social bonds, particularly within the extended family, and the hierarchical structure of the kingdom run counter to individualism. Also, youth gain social recognition through their academic achievement. From the perspective of Theravada Buddhism, which strongly influences Thai culture, aspiring to be rich and famous would be an illustration of greed, and those who have achieved wealth and fame do not celebrate it publicly as much as in American society. Being a good, moral person is paramount, and ideally Buddhists emphasize restraint and moderation.

Beyond talent and skill in the sports and entertainment industries, there are many other ways that young Americans can pursue wealth. Investment is one route. One American friend who is only a sophomore in college has already invested heavily in the stock market to start accumulating wealth. She is just one example of the 1980s trend for youth to be more concerned with their individual finances than with social, political, and environmental issues. With less attention paid to public issues, the expression of individualism seems to be magnified through emphasis on lucrative careers, financial investment, and material consumption—the "Yuppie" phenomenon. This includes new trends in dress, eating, housing (condominiums), and cars (expensive European imports). Likewise, there appears to be less of a long-term commitment to marriage. More young couples are living together without either marriage or plans for future marriage. When such couples decide to get married, prenuptial agreements are made to protect their assets. Traditional values of marriage, family, and sharing appear to be on the decline.

Individualism as one of the dominant values in American culture is expressed in many ways. This value probably stems from the history of the society as a frontier colony of immigrants in search of a better life with independence, freedom, and the opportunity for advancement through personal achievement. However, in the beliefs and customs of any culture there are some disadvantages as well as advantages. Although Thais may admire the achievements and material wealth of American society, there are costs, especially in the value of individualism and associated social phenomena.

Questions

1. Recently, while browsing in a bookstore in London, I came across a paperback book titled *Xenophobe's Guide to the Americans*. The authors' goal was to explain various aspects of American culture that really puzzle visitors from other countries. As I read it through, it seemed to me that book was chock full of wonderfully accurate insights. For example, here's part of their description of the American Thanksgiving celebration:

   > Thanksgiving, the third Thursday in November, is time for far-flung families to join around a common table. Grown children brave the busiest travel season of the year to return to their ancestral nest, where they eat too much, drink too much, and pick up year-old arguments as though they'd never left home. . . .
   >
   > The goal is to eat so much that nobody can move, and then watch football on television. On this day it is traditional to bow one's head and give thanks for life's many blessings. However, most celebrants are actually silently giving thanks that they only see their families once a year.

   Suppose that you are asked to contribute a brief section to the next edition of the *Xenophobe's Guide to the Americans* titled "Americans and Privacy." What would you write? (Your contribution should be no longer than 250 words.)

2. Read back through the part of the article that describes how parents in the United States encourage and even train their children to be independent. Then, think back to your own childhood. What sorts of things contributed to your growing up to be independent? What sorts of things did your parents do to teach you to value your privacy?

3. Professor Natadecha-Sponsel observes that, in the United States, it is considered ill-mannered to "regularly reach out to the serving dishes" throughout a meal. So, when Americans dine in a restaurant, each person usually orders his or her own dinner. But there are exceptions, aren't there? How do people (even Americans) order and eat their meals in Chinese or Thai restaurants? Why do you think we do this?

·11·

Rule Enforcement Without Visible Means
Christmas Gift Giving in Middletown

Theodore Caplow

A closer look at everyday and routine events can be revealing. In this 1984 article, Theodore Caplow analyzes the "rules" that underlie gift giving in Christian homes during Christmas in "Middletown." As Caplow makes clear, although these rules are not anywhere published, most people seem to know to follow them scrupulously.

The Middletown III study is a systematic replication of the well-known study of a midwestern industrial city conducted by Robert and Helen Lynd in the 1920s (Lynd and Lynd 1929/1959) and partially replicated by them in the 1930s (Lynd and Lynd 1937/1963). The fieldwork for Middletown III was conducted in 1976–79; its results have been reported in *Middletown Families* (Caplow et al. 1982) and in 38 published papers by various authors; additional volumes and papers are in preparation. Nearly all this material is an assessment of the social changes that occurred between the 1920s and the 1970s in this one community, which is, so far, the only place in the United States that provides such long-term comprehensive sociological data. The Middletown III research focused on those aspects of social structure described by the Lynds in order to utilize the opportunities for longitudinal comparison their data afforded, but there was one important exception. The Lynds had given little attention to the annual cycle of religious-civic family festivals (there were only two inconsequential references to Christmas in *Middletown* and none at all to Thanksgiving or Easter), but we found this cycle too important to ignore. The celebration of Christmas, the high point of the cycle, mobilizes almost the entire population for several weeks, accounts for about 4% of its total annual expenditures, and takes precedence over ordinary forms of work and leisure. In order to include this large phenomenon, we interviewed a random sample of 110 Middletown adults early in 1979 to discover how they and their families had celebrated Christmas in 1978. The survey included an inventory of all Christmas gifts given and received by these respondents. Although the sample included a few very isolated individuals, all of these had participated in Christmas giving in the previous year. The total number of gifts inventoried was 4,347, a mean of 39.5 per respondent. The distribution of this sample

"Rule Enforcement Without Visible Means: Christmas Gift Giving in Middletown" by Theodore Caplow from *American Journal of Sociology*, 89: 6 (1984): pp. 1306–1323. Reprinted by permission of The University of Chicago Press.

of gifts by type and value, by the age and sex of givers and receivers, and by gift-giving configurations has been reported elsewhere (Caplow 1982). . . .

In this paper, I discuss a quite different problem: How are the rules that appear to govern Christmas gift giving in Middletown communicated and enforced? There are no enforcement agents and little indignation against violators. Nevertheless, the level of participation is very high.

Here are some typical gift-giving rules that are enforced effectively in Middletown without visible means of enforcement and indeed without any widespread awareness of their existence:

The Tree Rule

> Married couples with children of any age should put up Christmas trees in their homes. Unmarried persons with no living children should not put up Christmas trees. Unmarried parents (widowed, divorced, or adoptive) may put up trees but are not required to do so.

Conformity with the Tree Rule in our survey sample may be fairly described as spectacular. . . .

Nobody in Middletown seems to be consciously aware of the norm that requires married couples with children of any age to put up a Christmas tree, yet the obligation is so compelling that, of the 77 respondents in this category who were at home for Christmas 1978, only one—the Venezuelan woman—failed to do so. Few of the written laws that agents of the state attempt to enforce with endless paperwork and threats of violence are so well obeyed as this unwritten rule that is promulgated by no identifiable authority and backed by no evident threat. Indeed, the existence of the rule goes unnoticed. People in Middletown think that putting up a Christmas tree is an entirely voluntary act. They know that it has some connection with children, but they

do not understand that married couples with children of any age are effectively required to have trees and that childless unmarried people are somehow prevented from having them. Middletown people do not consciously perceive the Christmas tree as a symbol of the complete nuclear family (father, mother, and one or more children). Those to whom we suggested that possibility seemed to resent it. . . .

The Wrapping Rule

> Christmas gifts must be wrapped before they are presented.

A subsidiary rule requires that the wrapping be appropriate, that is, emblematic, and another subsidiary rule says that wrapped gifts are appropriately displayed as a set but that unwrapped gifts should not be so displayed. Conformity with these rules is exceedingly high.

An unwrapped object is so clearly excluded as a Christmas gift that Middletown people who wish to give something at that season without defining it as a Christmas gift have only to leave the object unwrapped. Difficult-to-wrap Christmas gifts, like a pony or a piano, are wrapped symbolically by adding a ribbon or bow or card and are hidden until presentation. . . .

In nearly every Middletown household, the wrapped presents are displayed under or around the Christmas tree as a glittering monument to the family's affluence and mutual affection. Picture taking at Christmas gatherings is clearly a part of the ritual; photographs were taken at 65% of the recorded gatherings. In nearly all instances, the pile of wrapped gifts was photographed; and individual participants were photographed opening a gift, ideally at the moment of "surprise." Although the pile of wrapped gifts is almost invariably photographed, a heap of unwrapped gifts is not a suitable subject for the Christmas photographer. Among the 366 gatherings we recorded, there was a single instance in which a participant, a small boy, was photographed with all his unwrapped gifts. To display unwrapped gifts as a set seems to invite the invidious comparison of gifts—and of the relationships they represent.

The Decoration Rule

> Any room where Christmas gifts are distributed should be decorated by affixing Christmas emblems to the walls, the ceiling, or the furniture.

This is done even in nondomestic places, like offices or restaurant dining rooms, if gifts are to be distributed there. Conformity to this rule was perfect in our sample of 366 gatherings at which gifts were distributed, although, once again, the existence of the rule was not recognized by the people who obeyed it.

The same lack of recognition applies to the interesting subsidiary rule that a Christmas tree should not be put up in an undecorated place, although a decorated place need not have a tree. Unmarried, childless persons normally decorate their homes, although they have no trees, and decorations without a tree are common in public places, but a Christmas tree in an undecorated room would be unseemly. . . .

It goes without saying that Christmas decorations must be temporary, installed for the season and removed afterward (with the partial exception of outdoor wreaths, which are sometimes left to wither on the door). A room painted in red and green, or with a frieze of plaster wreaths, would not be decorated within the meaning of the rule.

The Gathering Rule

> Christmas gifts should be distributed at gatherings where every person gives and receives gifts.

Compliance with this rule is very high. More than nine-tenths of the 1,378 gifts our respondents received, and of the 2,969 they gave, were distributed in gatherings, more than three-quarters of which were family gatherings. Most gifts mailed or shipped by friends and relatives living at a distance were double wrapped, so that the outer unceremonious wrappings could be removed and the inner packages could be placed with other gifts to be opened at a gathering. In the typical family gathering, a number of related persons assemble by prearrangement at the home of one of them where a feast is served; the adults engage in conversation; the children play; someone takes photographs; gifts are distributed, opened, and admired; and the company then disperses. The average Middletown adult fits more than three of these occasions into a 24-hour period beginning at Christmas Eve, often driving long distances and eating several large dinners during that time.

The Dinner Rule

> Family gatherings at which gifts are distributed include a "traditional Christmas dinner."

This is a rule that participants in Middletown's Christmas ritual may disregard if they wish, but it is no less interesting because compliance is only partial. Presumably, this rule acquired its elective character because the pattern of multiple gatherings described above requires many gatherings to be scheduled at odd hours when dinner either would be inappropriate or, if the dinner rule were inflexible, would require participants to overeat beyond the normal expectations of the season. However, 65% of the survey respondents had eaten at least one traditional Christmas dinner the previous year.

There appears to be a subsidiary rule that traditional Christmas dinners served in homes should be prepared exclusively by women. There was not a single reported instance in this survey of a traditional Christmas dinner prepared by a man.

The Gift Selection Rules

A Christmas gift should (*a*) demonstrate the giver's familiarity with the receiver's preferences; (*b*) surprise the receiver, either by expressing more affection—measured by the aesthetic or practical value of the gift—than the receiver might reasonably anticipate or more knowledge than the giver might reasonably be expected to have; (*c*) be scaled in economic value to the emotional value of the relationship.

The economic values of any giver's gifts are supposed to be sufficiently scaled to the emotional values of relationships that, when they are opened in the bright glare of the family circle, the donor will not appear to have disregarded either the legitimate inequality of some relationships by, for example, giving a more valuable gift to a nephew than to a son, or the legitimate equality of other relationships by, for example, giving conspicuously unequal gifts to two sons.

Individuals participating in these rituals are not free to improvise their own scales of emotional value for relationships. The scale they are supposed to use, together with its permissible variations, is not written down anywhere but is thoroughly familiar to participants. From analysis of the gifts given and received by our survey respondents, we infer the following rules for scaling the emotional value of relationships.

The Scaling Rules

(*a*) A spousal relationship should be more valuable than any other for both husband and wife, but the husband may set a higher value on it than the wife. (*b*) A parent–child relationship should be less valuable than a spousal relationship but more valuable than any other relationship. The parent may set a higher value on it than the child does. (*c*) The spouse of a married close relative should be valued as much as the linking relative. (*d*) Parents with several children should value them equally throughout their lives. (*e*) Children with both parents still living, and still married to each other, may value them equally or may value their mothers somewhat more than their fathers. A married couple with two pairs of living, still-married parents should value each pair equally. Children of any age with divorced, separated, or remarried parents may value them unequally. (*f*) Siblings should be valued equally in childhood but not later. Adult siblings who live close by and are part of one's active network should be equally valued, along with their respective spouses, but siblings who live farther away may be valued unequally. (*g*) Friends of either sex, aside from sexual partners treated as quasi-spouses, may be valued as much as siblings but should not be valued as much as spouses, parents, or children. (*h*) More distant relatives—like aunts or cousins—may be valued as much as siblings but should not be valued as much as spouses, parents, or children.

It is a formidable task to balance these ratios every year and to come up with a set of Christmas gifts that satisfies them. Small wonder that Middletown people complain that Christmas shopping is difficult and fatiguing. But although they complain, they persist in it year after year without interruption. People who are away from home for Christmas arrange in advance to have their gifts distributed to the usual receivers and to open their own gifts ceremoniously. People confined by severe illness delegate others to do shopping and wrapping. Although our random sample of Middletown adults included several socially isolated persons, even the single most isolated respondent happened to have an old friend with whom he exchanged expensive gifts.

Given the complexity of the rules, errors and failures in gift selection can be expected to occur, and they frequently do. Indeed, the four or five shopping days immediately after Christmas are set aside in Middletown stores for return or exchange of badly selected gifts.

A number of respondents described relatives who make a point of being impossible to please, like the grandfather in Renata Adler's story:

> The grandfather, who pretended not to care about the holiday, every year, until the precise moment when the door to the study, where the piano stood, was opened and the presents were revealed, became every year, at that moment, hopeful, eager, even zealous and then dejected utterly. No one had ever found a present that actually pleased him. "Very nice," he would say, in a tight voice, as he unwrapped one thing after another. "Very nice. Now I'll just put that away." The year his sons gave him an electric razor, he said, "Very nice. Of course I'll never use it. I'm too old to change the way I shave." When they asked him at least to try it, he said "No, I'm sorry. It's very nice. No I'll just put that away." (Adler 1978, 136–37)

The standard disappointing gift is an article of clothing in the wrong size. Women are particularly resentful of oversized items that seem to say the giver perceives them as "fat." Children are often insulted by inattentive relatives who give them toys that are too "young." The spouse's or lover's gift that is disliked by the receiver is a sign of alienation. Two of the five couples in our sample for whom such gifts were reported at Christmas 1978 had separated by the time of the interview several weeks later.

The rigor of the Selection Rules is softened by several devices—joint gifts from and to married couples, from children to parents, and from two or three siblings to another are common. Such arrangements make it difficult to determine whether the comparative value of relationships has been correctly translated into gifts, and that is the more or less conscious intention. Two families in our sample drew lots for their gifts. That practice is nearly standard at nonfamilial Christmas gatherings, like ward parties for hospitalized children, where presents are distributed without any attempt to particularize relationships.

Fitness Rules

Rules about the fitness of gifts (e.g., women should not give cut flowers to men) are too numerous to specify, but one deserves passing attention. Money is an appropriate gift from senior to junior kin, but an inappropriate gift from junior to senior kin, regardless of the relative affluence of the parties. This is another rule which appears to be unknown to the people who obey it. Of 144 gifts of money given by persons in our sample to those in other generations, 94% went to junior kin, and of the 73 money gifts respondents received from persons in other generations, 93% were from senior kin. A gift certificate may be given to a parent or grandparent to whom an outright gift of money would be improper, but we did not record a single instance of a gift certificate having been given to a child or a grandchild, no substitution being called for.

The Reciprocity Rule

> Participants in this gift system should give (individually or jointly) at least one Christmas gift every year to their mothers, fathers, sons, daughters; to the current spouses of these persons; and to their own spouses.

By the operation of this rule, participants expect to receive at least one gift in return from each of these persons excepting infants. Conformity runs about 90% for each relationship separately and for the aggregate of all such relationships. Gifts to grandparents and grandchildren seem to be equally obligatory if these live in the same community or nearby, but not at greater distances (see Caplow 1982, table 6). Christmas gifts to siblings are not required. Only about one-third of the 274 sibling relationships reported by the sample were marked by Christmas gifts. The proportion was no higher for siblings living close than for those farther away. However, gifts to siblings do call for a return gift; this obligation is seldom scanted.

Gift giving to siblings' children, and parents' siblings and their respective spouses, appears to be entirely elective; fewer than half of these are reciprocated. We have no way of knowing whether such gifts may be reciprocated at another Christmas, but there were no references to deferred reciprocation in the interviews.

The Reciprocity Rule does not require reciprocated gifts to be of equal value. Parents expect to give more valuable and more numerous gifts to their minor children and to their adult children living at home than they receive in return. This imbalance is central to the entire ritual. The iconography of Middletown's secular Christmas emphasizes unreciprocated giving to children by the emblematic figure of Santa Claus, and the theme of unreciprocated giving provides one of the few connections between the secular and religious iconography of the festival — the Three Wise Men coming from a distant land to bring unreciprocated gifts to a child.

Equivalence of value tends to be disregarded in gift giving between husbands and wives and between parents and their adult children. Husbands often give more valuable gifts to wives than they receive from them. The gifts of parents to adult children are approximately balanced in the aggregate — about the same number of substantial gifts are given in each direction — but there is no insistence on equivalence in particular cases, and when we examine such relationships one by one, we discover many unbalanced exchanges, which seem to be taken for granted.

Only in the relationship between siblings and sibling couples do we find any active concern that the gifts exchanged be of approximately equal value, and even there it is more important to give gifts of approximately equal value to several siblings than to exchange gifts of equal value with each of them.

Empirically, the gift giving between adults and children in our sample was highly unbalanced, in both quantity and value. Respondents

gave 946 gifts to persons under 18 and received 145 in return; 89 of these were of substantial value and six of the return gifts were. In about one-third of these relationships, no gift was returned to the adult either by the child or in the child's name. In most of the remaining relationships, the child returned a single gift of token or modest value.

There is little reciprocity in the gift giving between non-kin. A large number of the gifts in this category are addressed to persons who provide minor services; reciprocation in those cases would be bizarre. Gifts from employers to employees, from grateful patients to physicians, and from pupils to teachers do not call for reciprocation. The Christmas gifts exchanged en masse at club meetings and office parties are reciprocal to the extent that each participant gives and receives some small gift, but there is no direct exchange between giver and receiver.

Discussion

Since the problem is to account for the uniformities of gift-giving behavior revealed by the data, speaking of rules begs the question to some extent. Although we infer from the uniformities observed in Middletown's Christmas gift giving that, somewhere in the culture, there must be statements to which the observed behavior is a response, the crucial point is that we cannot find those statements in any explicit form. Indeed, they are not recognized by participants in the system. In effect, the rules of the game are unfamiliar to the players, even though they can be observed to play meticulously by the rules. Instructions for Christmas gift giving are not found in administrative regulations or popular maxims or books of etiquette; they are not *promulgated*. Neither do they seem to be enforced by what Durkheim called "the public conscience" (Durkheim 1895/1964, 2–3). People who scanted their Christmas obligations would not be disapproved of by the public conscience in Middletown because Christmas gift giving is visualized there as both a private and a voluntary activity. We never heard anyone make an even indirect reference to community opinion in connection with Christmas gift giving. As far as we can tell, there are no customary forms of moral disapproval reserved for persons who neglect their Christmas duties (which are not, of course, considered to be duties). The moral drift goes the other way. Among Middletown's Protestant fundamentalists there are still vestiges of the violent Puritan objection to the celebration of Christmas as a "wanton Bacchanalian feast" (Barnett 1954, 1–23), which is commonly expressed in sermons about the "degradation" and "commercialization" of the festival. . . .

Gift exchange, in effect, is a language that employs objects instead of words as its lexical elements. In this perspective, every culture (there may be exotic exceptions, but I am unaware of them) has a language of presentation to express important interpersonal relationships on special occasions, just as it has a verbal language to create and manage meaning for other purposes. The language of prestation, like the verbal language, begins to be learned in early childhood and is used with increasing assurance as the individual matures and acquires social understanding. These "natal" languages are seldom completely forgotten, although new languages may be learned by translation and practice. The problem of accounting for the enforcement of gift-giving rules without visible means is simplified if we take them to be linguistic rules, or at least as similar to them, because linguistic rules, for the most part, are enforced among native speakers of a language without visible means and without being recognized explicitly. It may be objected that school teachers do make linguistic rules explicit and then enforce them by reward and punishment, but that is a rather special case of learning a new language or relearning a natal language in more elegant form. The acquisition of language does not depend on schooling, and the gram-

matical rules that are made explicit in school are only a small fraction of the rules that native speakers obey without being aware of their existence. The process whereby grammatical rules acquire consensual support is partly instinctual, partly cultural, and partly social. The tendency to follow linguistic rules without explicit awareness appears to be innate in the construction of new verbal combinations: young children acquire the language of the people who raise them along with other elements of the ambient culture; and linguistic rules are self-enforcing insofar as the effective transmission of messages rewards both senders and receivers.

Visualizing Christmas gift giving as a language—or, more precisely, as a dialect or code (Douglas 1972, 1979)—helps to explain, among other matters, the insistence on wrapping and other signs to identify the objects designated for lexical use and the preference for the simultaneous exchange of gifts at family gatherings rather than in private.

In most cases such a gathering is composed of a parent–child unit containing one or two parents and one or more children together with other persons who are tied to that unit by shared membership in another parent–child unit, such as children's children, children's spouses, parents' siblings, or parents' parents. Although there is room at a family gathering for a friend or distant relative who otherwise might be solitary at Christmas, there is no convenient way of including any large number of persons to whom no gift messages are owed.

Under the Scaling Rules, gift messages are due from every person in a parent–child relationship to every other. The individual message says "I value you according to the degree of our relationship" and anticipates the response "I value you in the same way." But the compound message that emerges from the unwrapping of gifts in the presence of the whole gathering allows more subtle meanings to be conveyed. It permits the husband to say to the wife "I value you more than my parents" or the mother to say to the daughter-in-law "I value you as much as my son so long as you are married to him" or the brother to say to the brother "I value you more than our absent brothers, but less than our parents and much less than my children." These statements, taken together, would define and sustain a social structure, if only because, by their gift messages, both parties to each dyadic relationship confirm that they have the same understanding of the relationship and the bystanders, who are interested parties, endorse that understanding by tacit approval. The compound messages would have a powerful influence even if they were idiosyncratic and each parent–child unit had its own method of scaling relationships. In fact, there are some observable differences in scaling from one Middletown family to another and from one subcultural group to another, but the similarities are much more striking than the differences. We attribute this commonality to the shared dialect of Christmas gift giving, hyperdeveloped in Middletown and elsewhere in the United States in response to commercial promotion, stresses in the family institution, and constant reiteration by the mass media. Once the dialect is reasonably well known, these factors continue to enlarge its vocabulary and its domain.

Another circumstance facilitating the standardization of the dialect is that nearly every individual in this population belongs to more than one parent–child unit for Christmas gift-giving purposes. Because these units are linked and cross-linked to other units in a network that ultimately includes the larger part of the community, they would probably tend to develop a common set of understandings about appropriate kinship behavior, even without the reinforcement provided by domestic rituals.

The most powerful reinforcement remains to be mentioned. In the dialect of Christmas gift giving, the absence of a gift is also a lexical sign, signifying either the absence of a close relation, as in the Christmas contact of cousins, or the desire to terminate a close relationship, as when a husband gives no gift to his wife. People who have once learned the dialect cannot choose to forget it, nor can they pretend to ignore messages they understand. Thus, without any complicated normative machinery, Middletown people find themselves compelled to give Christmas gifts to their close relatives, lest they inadvertently send them messages of hostility. In this community, where most people depend on their relatives for emotional and social support, the consequences of accidentally sending them a hostile message are too serious to contemplate, and few are willing to run the risk.

In sum, we discover that the participants in this gift-giving system are themselves the agents who enforce its complex rules, although they do so unknowingly and without conscious reference to a system. The dialect, once learned, imposes itself by linguistic necessity, and the enforcement of its rules is the more effective for being unplanned.

References

Adler, Renata. 1978. *Speedboat.* New York: Popular Library.

Barnett, James H. 1954. *The American Christmas: A Study of National Culture.* New York: Macmillan.

Caplow, Theodore. 1982. "Christmas Gifts and Kin Networks." *American Sociological Review* 47: 383–392.

Caplow, Theodore, Howard H. Bahr, Bruce A. Chadwick, Reuben Hill, and Margaret Holmes Williamson. 1982. *Middletown Families: Fifty Years of Change and Continuity.* Minneapolis: University of Minnesota Press.

Douglas, Mary. 1972. "Deciphering a Meal." *Daedalus* 101: 31–81.

———. 1979. *The World of Goods.* New York: Basic Books.

Durkheim, Émile. 1895/1964. *Rules of Sociological Method.* New York: Free Press.

Lynd, Robert, and Helen Merell Lynd. 1929/1959. *Middletown: A Study in American Culture.* New York: Harcourt Brace.

———. 1937/1963. *Middletown in Transition: A Study in Cultural Conflicts.* New York: Harcourt Brace.

Questions

1. In your judgment, why is it deemed inappropriate by Middletown families to display or photograph *unwrapped* gifts?

2. Which of the rules mentioned by Caplow are followed by you and your family or (if you don't celebrate the holiday) by others known to you? Which aren't followed?

3. Caplow suggests that people who break the rules regarding gift giving run no risk of sanction. Do you agree? Let us say, for example, that you found shopping to be more trouble than it's worth and decided to give your parents or your partner/spouse gift certificates for generous amounts. Would you be sanctioned in any way? How so? Likewise, suppose you violated the "scaling rule" by giving every person in your family the exact same thing. What would be their response?

4. Consider other special times when gift giving is deemed appropriate—Chanukah or birthdays, for example. What rules govern those sorts of interaction?

·12·

The Code of the Streets

Elijah Anderson

Except in the most general sense, it is wrong to speak of "American" culture as if it were a single entity. American society is not homogeneous, nor is its culture. In this 1994 article, Elijah Anderson focuses on a particular *subculture* that exists within the larger culture. In this subculture, the ubiquitous human search for respect creates what has been called a "perverse etiquette of violence," one from which it may well be impossible to escape.

Of all the problems besetting the poor inner-city black community, none is more pressing than that of interpersonal violence and aggression. It wreaks havoc daily in the lives of community residents and increasingly spills over into downtown and residential middle-class areas. Muggings, burglaries, carjackings, and drug-related shootings, all of which may leave their victims or innocent bystanders dead, are now common enough to concern all urban and many suburban residents. The inclination to violence springs from the circumstances of life among the ghetto poor—the lack of jobs that pay a living wage, the stigma of race, the fallout from rampant drug use and drug trafficking, and the resulting alienation and lack of hope for the future.

Simply living in such an environment places young people at special risk of falling victim to aggressive behavior. Although there are often forces in the community which can counteract the negative influences, by far the most powerful being a strong, loving, "decent" (as inner-city residents put it) family committed to middle-class values, the despair is pervasive enough to have spawned an oppositional culture, that of "the streets," whose norms are often consciously opposed to those of mainstream society. These two orientations—decent and street—socially organize the community, and their coexistence has important consequences for residents, particularly children growing up in the inner city. Above all, this environment means that even youngsters whose home lives reflect mainstream values—and the majority of homes in the community do—must be able to handle themselves in a street-oriented environment.

This is because the street culture has evolved what may be called a code of the streets, which amounts to a set of informal rules governing interpersonal public behavior, including violence. The rules prescribe both a proper comportment and a proper way to respond if challenged. They regulate the use of violence and so allow those who are inclined to aggression to precipitate violent encounters in an approved way. The rules have been established and are enforced mainly by the street-oriented, but on the streets the distinction between street and decent is often irrelevant; everybody knows that if the rules are violated, there are penalties. Knowledge of the code is thus largely defensive; it is literally necessary for operating in public. Therefore, even though

"The Code of the Streets" by Elijah Anderson from *The Atlantic Monthly,* May 1994. Reprinted by permission of the author.

families with a decency orientation are usually opposed to the values of the code, they often reluctantly encourage their children's familiarity with it to enable them to negotiate the inner-city environment.

At the heart of the code is the issue of respect—loosely defined as being treated "right," or granted the deference one deserves. However, in the troublesome public environment of the inner city, as people increasingly feel buffeted by forces beyond their control, what one deserves in the way of respect becomes more and more problematic and uncertain. This in turn further opens the issue of respect to sometimes intense interpersonal negotiation. In the street culture, especially among young people, respect is viewed as almost an external entity that is hard-won but easily lost, and so must constantly be guarded. The rules of the code in fact provide a framework for negotiating respect. The person whose very appearance—including his clothing, demeanor, and way of moving—deters transgressions feels that he possesses, and may be considered by others to possess, a measure of respect. With the right amount of respect, for instance, he can avoid "being bothered" in public. If he is bothered, not only may he be in physical danger but he has been disgraced or "dissed" (disrespected). Many of the forms that dissing can take might seem petty to middle-class people (maintaining eye contact for too long, for example), but to those invested in the street code, these actions become serious indications of the other person's intentions. Consequently, such people become very sensitive to advances and slights, which could well serve as warnings of imminent physical confrontation.

This hard reality can be traced to the profound sense of alienation from mainstream society and its institutions felt by many poor inner-city black people, particularly the young. The code of the streets is actually a cultural adaptation to a profound lack of faith in the police and the judicial system. The police are most often seen as representing the dominant white society and not caring to protect inner-city residents. When called, they may not respond, which is one reason many residents feel they must be prepared to take extraordinary measures to defend themselves and their loved ones against those who are inclined to aggression. Lack of police accountability has in fact been incorporated into the status system: the person who is believed capable of "taking care of himself" is accorded a certain deference, which translates into a sense of physical and psychological control. Thus the street code emerges where the influence of the police ends and personal responsibility for one's safety is felt to begin. Exacerbated by the proliferation of drugs and easy access to guns, this volatile situation results in the ability of the street-oriented minority (or those who effectively "go for bad") to dominate the public spaces.

Decent and Street Families

Although almost everyone in poor inner-city neighborhoods is struggling financially and therefore feels a certain distance from the rest of America, the decent and the street family in a real sense represent two poles of value orientation, two contrasting conceptual categories. The labels "decent" and "street," which the residents themselves use, amount to evaluative judgments that confer status on local residents. The labeling is often the result of a social contest among individuals and families of the neighborhood. Individuals of the two orientations often coexist in the same extended family. Decent residents judge themselves to be so while judging others to be of the street, and street individuals often present themselves as decent, drawing distinctions between themselves and other people. In addition, there is quite a bit of circumstantial behavior—that is, one person may at different times exhibit both decent and street orientations, depending on the circumstances. Although these designations result from so much social jockeying, there do exist concrete features that define each conceptual category.

Generally, so-called decent families tend to accept mainstream values more fully and attempt to instill them in their children. Whether married couples with children or single-parent (usually female) households, they are generally "working poor" and so tend to be better off financially than their street-oriented neighbors. They value hard work and self-reliance and are willing to sacrifice for their children. Because they have a certain amount of faith in mainstream society, they harbor hopes for a better future for their children, if not for themselves. Many of them go to church and take a strong interest in their children's schooling. Rather than dwelling on the real hardships and inequities facing them, many such decent people, particularly the increasing number of grandmothers raising grandchildren, see their difficult situation as a test from God and derive great support from their faith and from the church community.

Extremely aware of the problematic and often dangerous environment in which they reside, decent parents tend to be strict in their child-rearing practices, encouraging children to respect authority and walk a straight moral line. They have an almost obsessive concern about trouble of any kind and remind their children to be on the lookout for people and situations that might lead to it. At the same time, they are themselves polite and considerate of others, and teach their children to be the same way. At home, at work, and in church, they strive hard to maintain a positive mental attitude and a spirit of cooperation.

So-called street parents, in contrast, often show a lack of consideration for other people and have a rather superficial sense of family and community. Though they may love their children, many of them are unable to cope with the physical and emotional demands of parenthood, and find it difficult to reconcile their needs with those of their children. These families, who are more fully invested in the code of the streets than the decent people are, may aggressively socialize their children into it in a normative way. They believe in the code and judge themselves and others according to its values.

In fact the overwhelming majority of families in the inner-city community try to approximate the decent-family model, but there are many others who clearly represent the worst fears of the decent family. Not only are their financial resources extremely limited, but what little they have may easily be misused. The lives of the street-oriented are often marked by disorganization. In the most desperate circumstances people frequently have a limited understanding of priorities and consequences, and so frustrations mount over bills, food, and, at times, drink, cigarettes, and drugs. Some tend toward self-destructive behavior; many street-oriented women are crack-addicted ("on the pipe"), alcoholic, or involved in complicated relationships with men who abuse them. In addition, the seeming intractability of their situation, caused in large part by the lack of well-paying jobs and the persistence of racial discrimination, has engendered deep-seated bitterness and anger in many of the most desperate and poorest blacks, especially young people. The need both to exercise a measure of control and to lash out at somebody is often reflected in the adults' relations with their children. At the least, the frustrations of persistent poverty shorten the fuse in such people—contributing to a lack of patience with anyone, child or adult, who irritates them.

In these circumstances a woman—or a man, although men are less consistently present in children's lives—can be quite aggressive with children, yelling at and striking them for the least little infraction of the rules she has set down. Often little if any serious explanation follows the verbal and physical punishment. This response teaches children a particular lesson. They learn that to solve any kind of interpersonal problem one must quickly resort to hitting or other violent behavior. Actual peace and quiet, and also the appearance of calm, respectful children conveyed to her neighbors and friends, are often what the young mother most desires, but at times she will be very aggressive in trying to get them. Thus she may be quick to beat her children, especially if they defy her law, not because she hates them but because this is the way she knows to control them. In fact, many street-oriented women love their children dearly. Many mothers in the community subscribe to the notion that there is a "devil in the boy" that must be beaten out of him or that socially "fast girls need to be whupped." Thus much of what borders on child abuse in the view of social authorities is acceptable parental punishment in the view of these mothers.

Many street-oriented women are sporadic mothers whose children learn to fend for themselves when necessary, foraging for food and money any way they can get it. The children are sometimes employed by drug dealers or become addicted themselves. These children of the street, growing up with little supervision, are said to "come up hard." They often learn to fight at an early age, sometimes using short-tempered adults around them as role models. The street-oriented home may be fraught with anger, verbal disputes, physical aggression, and even mayhem. The children observe these goings-on, learning the lesson that might makes right. They quickly learn to hit those who cross them, and the dog-eat-dog mentality prevails. In order to survive, to protect oneself, it is necessary to marshal inner resources and be ready to deal with adversity in

a hands-on way. In these circumstances physical prowess takes on great significance.

In some of the most desperate cases, a street-oriented mother may simply leave her young children alone and unattended while she goes out. The most irresponsible women can be found at local bars and crack houses, getting high and socializing with other adults. Sometimes a troubled woman will leave very young children alone for days at a time. Reports of crack addicts abandoning their children have become common in drug-infested inner-city communities. Neighbors or relatives discover the abandoned children, often hungry and distraught over the absence of their mother. After repeated absences, a friend or relative, particularly a grandmother, will often step in to care for the young children, sometimes petitioning the authorities to send her, as guardian of the children, the mother's welfare check, if the mother gets one. By this time, however, the children may well have learned the first lesson of the streets: survival itself, let alone respect, cannot be taken for granted; you have to fight for your place in the world.

Campaigning for Respect

These realities of inner-city life are largely absorbed on the streets. At an early age, often even before they start school, children from street-oriented homes gravitate to the streets, where they "hang" — socialize with their peers. Children from these generally permissive homes have a great deal of latitude and are allowed to "rip and run" up and down the street. They often come home from school, put their books down, and go right back out the door. On school nights eight- and nine-year-olds remain out until nine or ten o'clock (and teenagers typically come in whenever they want to). On the streets they play in groups that often become the source of their primary social bonds. Children from decent homes tend to be more carefully supervised and are thus likely to have curfews and to be taught how to stay out of trouble.

When decent and street kids come together, a kind of social shuffle occurs in which children have a chance to go either way. Tension builds as a child comes to realize that he must choose an orientation. The kind of home he comes from influences but does not determine the way he will ultimately turn out—although it is unlikely that a child from a thoroughly street-oriented family will easily absorb decent values on the streets. Youths who emerge from street-oriented families but develop a decency orientation almost always learn those values in another setting—in school, in a youth group, in church. Often it is the result of their involvement with a caring "old head" (adult role model).

In the street, through their play, children pour their individual life experiences into a common knowledge pool, affirming, confirming, and elaborating on what they have observed in the home and matching their skills against those of others. And they learn to fight. Even small children test one another, pushing and shoving, and are ready to hit other children over circumstances not to their liking. In turn, they are readily hit by other children, and the child who is toughest prevails. Thus the violent resolution of disputes, the hitting and cursing, gains social reinforcement. The child in effect is initiated into a system that is really a way of campaigning for respect.

In addition, younger children witness the disputes of older children, which are often resolved through cursing and abusive talk, if not aggression or outright violence. They see that one child succumbs to the greater physical and mental abilities of the other. They are also alert and attentive witnesses to the verbal and physical fights of adults, after which they compare notes and share their interpretations of the event. In almost every case the victor is the person who physically won the altercation,

and this person often enjoys the esteem and respect of onlookers. These experiences reinforce the lessons the children have learned at home: might makes right, and toughness is a virtue, while humility is not. In effect they learn the social meaning of fighting. When it is left virtually unchallenged, this understanding becomes an ever more important part of the child's working conception of the world. Over time the code of the streets becomes refined.

Those street-oriented adults with whom children come in contact—including mothers, fathers, brothers, sisters, boyfriends, cousins, neighbors, and friends—help them along in forming this understanding by verbalizing the messages they are getting through experience: "Watch your back." "Protect yourself." "Don't punk out." "If somebody messes with you, you got to pay them back." "If someone disses you, you got to straighten them out." Many parents actually impose sanctions if a child is not sufficiently aggressive. For example, if a child loses a fight and comes home upset, the parent might respond, "Don't you come in here crying that somebody beat you up; you better get back out there and whup his ass. I didn't raise no punks! Get back out there and whup his ass. If you don't whup his ass, I'll whup your ass when you come home." Thus the child obtains reinforcement for being tough and showing nerve.

While fighting, some children cry as though they are doing something they are ambivalent about. The fight may be against their wishes, yet they may feel constrained to fight or face the consequences—not just from peers but also from caretakers or parents, who may administer another beating if they back down. Some adults recall receiving such lessons from their own parents and justify repeating them to their children as a way to toughen them up. Looking capable of taking care of oneself as a form of self-defense is a dominant theme among both street-oriented and decent adults who worry about the safety of their children. There is thus at times a convergence in their child-rearing practices, although the rationales behind them may differ.

Self-Image Based on "Juice"

By the time they are teenagers, most youths have either internalized the code of the streets or at least learned the need to comport themselves in accordance with its rules, which chiefly have to do with interpersonal communication. The code revolves around the presentation of self. Its basic requirement is the display of a certain predisposition to violence. Accordingly, one's bearing must send the unmistakable if sometimes subtle message to "the next person" in public that one is capable of violence and mayhem when the situation requires it, that one can take care of oneself. The nature of this communication is largely determined by the demands of the circumstances but can include facial expressions, gait, and verbal expressions—all of which are geared mainly to deterring aggression. Physical appearance, including clothes, jewelry, and grooming, also plays an important part in how a person is viewed; to be respected, it is important to have the right look.

Even so, there are no guarantees against challenges, because there are always people around looking for a fight to increase their share of respect—or "juice," as it is sometimes called on the street. Moreover, if a person is assaulted, it is important, not only in the eyes of his opponent but also in the eyes of his "running buddies," for him to avenge himself. Otherwise he risks being "tried" (challenged) or "moved on" by any number of others. To maintain his honor he must show he is not someone to be "messed with" or "dissed." In general, the person must "keep himself straight" by managing his position of respect among others; this involves in part his self-image, which is shaped by what he thinks others are thinking of him in relation to his peers.

Objects play an important and complicated role in establishing self-image. Jackets, sneakers, gold jewelry, reflect not just a person's taste, which tends to be tightly regulated among adolescents of all social classes, but also a willingness to possess things that may require defending. A boy wearing a fashionable, expensive jacket, for example, is vulnerable to attack by another who covets the jacket and either cannot afford to buy one or wants the added satisfaction of depriving someone else of his. However, if the boy forgoes the desirable jacket and wears one that isn't "hip," he runs the risk of being teased and possibly even assaulted as an unworthy person. To be allowed to hang with certain prestigious crowds, a boy must wear a different set of expensive clothes—sneakers and athletic suit—every day. Not to be able to do so might make him appear socially deficient. The youth comes to covet such items—especially when he sees easy prey wearing them.

In acquiring valued things, therefore, a person shores up his identity—but since it is an identity based on having things, it is highly precarious. This very precariousness gives a heightened sense of urgency to staying even with peers, with whom the person is actually competing. Young men and women who are able to command respect through their presentation of self—by allowing their possessions and their body language to speak for them—may not have to campaign for regard but may, rather, gain it by the force of their manner. Those who are unable to command respect in this way must actively campaign for it—and are thus particularly alive to slights.

One way of campaigning for status is by taking the possessions of others. In this context, seemingly ordinary objects can become trophies imbued with symbolic value that far exceeds their monetary worth. Possession of the trophy can symbolize the ability to violate somebody—to "get in his face," to take something of value from him, to "dis" him, and thus to enhance one's own worth by stealing someone else's. The trophy does not have to be something material. It can be another person's sense of honor, snatched away with a derogatory remark. It can be the outcome of a fight. It can be the imposition of a certain standard, such as a girl's getting herself recognized as the most beautiful. Material things, however, fit easily into the pattern. Sneakers, a pistol, even somebody else's girlfriend, can become a trophy. When a person can take something from another and then flaunt it, he gains a certain regard by being the owner, or the controller, of that thing. But this display of ownership can then provoke other people to challenge him. This game of who controls what is thus constantly being played out on inner-city streets, and the trophy—extrinsic or intrinsic, tangible or intangible—identifies the current winner.

An important aspect of this often violent give-and-take is its zero-sum quality. That is, the extent to which one person can raise himself up depends on his ability to put another person down. This underscores the alienation that permeates the inner-city ghetto community. There is a generalized sense that very little respect is to be had, and therefore everyone competes to get what affirmation he can of the little that is available. The craving for respect that results gives people thin skins. Shows of deference by others can be highly soothing, contributing to a sense of security, comfort, self-confidence, and self-respect. Transgressions by others which go unanswered diminish these feelings and are believed to encourage further transgressions. Hence one must be ever vigilant against the transgressions of others or even *appearing* as if transgressions will be tolerated. Among young people, whose sense of self-esteem is particularly vulnerable, there is an especially heightened concern with being disrespected. Many inner-city young men in particular crave respect to such a degree that they will risk their lives to attain and maintain it.

The issue of respect is thus closely tied to whether a person has an inclination to be violent, even as a victim. In the wider society people may not feel required to retaliate physically after an attack, even though they are aware that they have been degraded or taken advantage of. They may feel a great need to defend themselves *during* an attack, or to behave in such a way as to deter aggression (middle-class people certainly can and do become victims of street-oriented youths), but they are much more likely than street-oriented people to feel that they can walk away from a possible altercation with their self-esteem intact. Some people may even have the strength of character to flee, without any thought that their self-respect or esteem will be diminished.

In impoverished inner-city black communities, however, particularly among young males and perhaps increasingly among females, such flight would be extremely difficult. To run away would likely leave one's self-esteem in tatters. Hence people often feel constrained not only to stand up and at least attempt to resist during an assault but also to "pay back"—to seek revenge—after a successful assault on their person. This may include going to get a weapon or even getting relatives involved. Their very identity and self-respect, their honor, is often intricately tied up with the way they perform on the streets during and after such encounters. This outlook reflects the circumscribed opportunities of the inner-city poor. Generally people outside the ghetto have other ways of gaining status and regard, and thus do not feel so dependent on such physical displays. . . .

"Going for Bad"

In the most fearsome youths such a cavalier attitude toward death grows out of a very limited view of life. Many are uncertain about how long they are going to live and believe they could die violently at any time. They accept this fate; they live on the edge. Their manner conveys the message that nothing intimidates them; whatever turn the encounter takes, they maintain their attack—rather like a pit bull, whose spirit many such boys admire. The demonstration of such tenacity "shows heart" and earns their respect.

This fearlessness has implications for law enforcement. Many street-oriented boys are much more concerned about the threat of "justice" at the hands of a peer than at the hands of the police. Moreover, many feel not only that they have little to lose by going to prison but that they have something to gain. The toughening-up one experiences in prison can actually enhance one's reputation on the streets. Hence the system loses influence over the hard core who are without jobs, with little perceptible stake in the system. If mainstream society has done nothing *for* them, they counter by making sure it can do nothing *to* them.

At the same time, however, a competing view maintains that true nerve consists in backing down, walking away from a fight, and going on with one's business. One fights only in self-defense. This view emerges from the decent philosophy that life is precious, and it is an important part of the socialization process common in decent homes. It discourages violence as the primary means of resolving disputes and encourages youngsters to accept nonviolence and talk as confrontational strategies. But "if the deal goes down," self-defense is greatly encouraged. When there is enough positive support for this orientation, either in the home or among one's peers, then nonviolence has a chance to prevail. But it prevails at the cost of relinquishing a claim to being bad and tough, and therefore sets a young person up as at the very least alienated from street-oriented peers and quite possibly a target of derision or even violence.

Although the nonviolent orientation rarely overcomes the impulse to strike back in an encounter, it does introduce a certain confusion and so can prompt a measure of soul-searching, or even profound ambivalence. Did the person back down with his respect intact or did he back down only to be judged a "punk"—a person lacking manhood? Should he or she have acted? Should he or she have hit the other person in the mouth? These questions beset many young men and women during public confrontations. What is the "right" thing to do? In the quest for honor, respect, and local status—which few young people are uninterested in—common sense most often prevails, which leads many to opt for the tough approach, enacting their own particular versions of the display of nerve. The presentation of oneself as rough and tough is very often quite acceptable until one is tested. And then that presentation may help the person pass the test, because it will cause fewer questions to be asked about what he did and why. It is hard for a person to explain why he lost the fight or why he backed down. Hence many will strive to appear to "go for bad," while hoping they will never be tested. But when they are tested, the outcome of the situation may quickly be out of their hands, as they become wrapped up in the circumstances of the moment.

An Oppositional Culture

The attitudes of the wider society are deeply implicated in the code of the streets. Most people in inner-city communities are not totally invested in the code. But the significant minority of hard-core street youths who are have to maintain the code in order to establish reputations because they have—or feel they have—few other ways to assert themselves. For these young people the standards of the street code are the only game in town. The extent to which some children—particularly those who through upbringing have become most alienated and those lacking in strong and conventional social support—experience, feel, and internalize racist rejection and contempt from mainstream society may strongly encourage them to express contempt for the more conventional society in turn. In dealing with this contempt and rejection, some youngsters will consciously invest themselves and their considerable mental resources in what amounts to an oppositional culture to preserve themselves and their self-respect. Once they do, any respect they might be able to garner in the wider system pales in comparison with the respect available in the local system; thus they often lose interest in even attempting to negotiate the mainstream system.

At the same time, many less alienated young blacks have assumed a street-oriented demeanor as a way of expressing their blackness while really embracing a much more moderate way of life; they, too, want a nonviolent setting in which to live and raise a family. These decent people are trying hard to be part of the mainstream culture, but the racism, real and perceived, that they encounter helps to legitimate the oppositional culture. And so on occasion they adopt street behavior. In fact, depending on the demands of the situation, many people in the community slip back and forth between decent and street behavior.

A vicious cycle has thus been formed. The hopelessness and alienation many young inner-city black men and women feel, largely as a result of endemic joblessness and persistent racism, fuels the violence they engage in. This violence serves to confirm the negative feelings many whites and some middle-class blacks harbor toward the ghetto poor, further legitimating the oppositional culture and the code of the streets in the eyes of many poor young blacks. Unless the cycle is broken, attitudes on both sides will become increasingly entrenched, and the violence, which claims victims black and white, poor and affluent, will only escalate.

Questions

1. How would you define each of the following terms (used by Anderson in his article)?
   a. mayhem
   b. oppositional culture
   c. zero-sum

2. What factors of life on the street make it difficult for people to be "decent"?

3. In your judgment, are young men from more "middle-class" cultural settings at all preoccupied with earning respect? How do young men in middle-class culture earn the respect of others and prove themselves to be properly "manly"?

·13·

Separating the Men from the Girls:
The Gendered Language
of Televised Sports

Michael A. Messner, Margaret Carlisle Duncan, and Kerry Jensen

> When I was a kid, one of the most powerful insults ever tossed out on the base-ball field was "you throw like a girl." Given that girls and women are no longer strangers to the fields and coliseums where games are played, one would think that "throwing like a girl" would hardly be the insult it was a mere thirty years ago. The authors of this paper would agree, I think, but not wholeheartedly.

Feminist scholars have argued that in the twentieth century the institution of sport has provided men with a homosocial sphere of life through which they have bolstered the ideology of male superiority. Through the exclusion of women and the association of males with physical competence, strength, power, and even violence, sport has provided a basis through which men have sought to reconstitute an otherwise challenged masculine hegemony[1] (Bryson 1987; Hall 1988; Kidd 1987; Messner 1988; Theberge 1981; Whitson 1990).

But, starting with the 1972 passage of Title IX in the United States,[2] athletic participation of school-age girls increased dramatically. In 1971, only 294,015 girls participated in high school sports, compared with 3,666,917 boys. By the 1989–90 academic year, there were 1,858,659 girls participating in high school sports, compared with 3,398,192 boys.[3] Increased numerical participation in sports by girls and women has been accompanied by change in attitudes as well. A nationwide survey found large majorities of parents and children agreeing that "sports are no longer

---

[1] The standard dictionary defines hegemony as "dominance" or "leadership" but, as you might expect, the term has a special meaning in sociology. The concept was first invoked in sociology by the Italian Marxist scholar Antonio Gramsci to explain why working-class people accepted bourgeoisie (upper-class) norms and values—even though these norms and values clearly served the interests of the rich more than the interests of the poor. Hegemony has come to refer to the fact, then, that not only is a particular group (or nation) dominant, but that their dominance is perceived as legitimate. Ed.

"Separating the Men from the Girls: The Gendered Language of Televised Sports" by Michael A. Messner, Margaret Carlislie Duncan, and Kerry Jensen from *Gender & Society,* Vol. 7 (1), March 1993: pp. 121–137. Copyright © 1993 Sociologists for Women in Society. Reprinted by permission of Sage Publications, Inc.

[2] Title IX was a series of laws promulgated by the United States Congress under the heading of the Civil Rights Act of 1964. Title II, for example, prohibits discrimination on the basis of race, national origin, or religion in public accommodations; Title VII prohibits discrimination on the basis of race, national origin, religion, or sex in employment, and Title VII extended these prohibitions to housing. Title IX prohibited discrimination on the basis of sex in federally funded educational programs. Ed.

[3] These statistics are compiled yearly by the National Federation of State High School Associations in Kansas City, MO. The 1989–90 statistics were received via a phone interview with the federation. For a discussion of the implications of this continuing trend of increasing high school athletic participation by girls, see Sabo (1988).

103

for boys only" (Wilson Sporting Goods Co. and the Women's Sports Foundation 1988, 1). With increases in opportunities for female athletes, including expanded youth programs, better and earlier coaching, and increases in scholarships for college women athletes, some dramatic improvements in female athletic performance have resulted. In fact, the "muscle gap"—the degree of difference between male and female athletic performance in measurable sports like swimming and track and field—has closed considerably in the past 15 years (Crittenden 1979; K. Dyer 1983; Kidd 1990). Sport is still dominated by men at nearly all levels, and still serves to construct culturally dominant ideals of "exemplary masculinity" (Connell 1990, 93). But the dramatic increase in female athleticism in the past two decades directly challenges the assumed naturalness of the equation of men, muscles, and power. In short, the institution of sport has become a "contested terrain" of gender relations and ideologies (Birrell 1987–1988; Messner 1988).

Much of the continued salience of sport as an institutional site for the construction and legitimation of masculine power lies in its role as mass-mediated spectacle (Clarke and Clarke 1982; Hargreaves 1986; Willis 1982). There *has* been a boom in female athletic participation, but the sports media have been very slow to reflect it. Bryant's (1980) two-year content analysis of two newspapers revealed that only 4.4 percent of total column inches were devoted to coverage of women's sports. Graydon (1983) observed that, in the early 1980s, over

90 percent of sports reporting covered men's sports. Theberge and Cronk (1986) noted that work routines in newspaper sports departments and values of reporters tended to preclude adequate coverage of women's sports. Rintala and Birrell's (1984) analysis of *Young Athlete* magazine and Duncan and Sayaovong's (1990) examination of *Sports Illustrated for Kids* magazine revealed that visual images of male athletes in these magazines tend to outnumber those of female athletes by a roughly 2:1 ratio. Moreover, text and visual images tend to frame female and male athletes "as fundamentally and essentially different" and, thus, to support stereotypical notions of natural differences between the sexes (Duncan and Sayaovong 1990, 91). In a part of our study (not dealt with in this article), we examined four major metropolitan daily newspapers and found that, over a three-month period in 1990, 81 percent of all sports column inches were devoted exclusively to men's sports, 3.5 percent covered women's sports, and 15.5 percent covered both men's and women's sports or gender-neutral topics. We also examined six weeks of a leading television newscast and found that 92 percent of sports news time was devoted exclusively to men's sports, 5 percent covered women's sports, and 3 percent covered gender-neutral topics. This ignoring or underreporting of existing women's events contributes to the continuation of the invisibility of women athletes in the mass media.

Despite the paucity of coverage of women's sports by the media, there are some recent signs of increased coverage, especially on cable television (Eastman and Meyer 1989). If there is indeed a "window of opportunity" for increased coverage of women's sports on television, the question of *how* women's and men's sports are covered becomes crucial. To date, very few analyses of the quality of live, televised, play-by-play coverage of women's sports have been conducted. Studies of the 1970s and 1980s revealed that women athletes

AUTHORS' NOTE: *This research is based on a larger study of gender and sports media that was commissioned by the Amateur Athletic Foundation of Los Angeles. The authors gratefully acknowledge the assistance of Wayne Wilson of the foundation and Barrie Thorne, who commented on an earlier version of this article. We also thank Margaret Andersen and the Gender & Society reviewers for their constructive comments and suggestions.*
REPRINT REQUESTS: *Michael A. Messner, Department of Sociology, University of Southern California, Los Angeles, CA 90089-2539.*

(when they were reported on television at all) were likely to be overtly trivialized, infantilized, and sexualized (Boutilier and San Giovanni 1983; Duncan 1990; G. Dyer 1987; Felshin 1974). Duncan and Hasbrook (1988) analyzed the quality of verbal and visual coverage of women's basketball, surfing, and marathon and found that even excellent performances by women athletes were commonly framed "ambivalently" by sports commentators:

> We found ambivalence in positive portrayals stressing women's strength, skill, or expertise along with negative suggestions that trivialized the women's efforts or implied that they were unsuited to sport (i.e., that they were in some respect weak, inferior, or incapable, that the sports in which they participated were not *true* sports). (P. 18)

This ambivalent framing of women athletes, Duncan and Hasbrook argued, translates into a symbolic denial of power for women.

We were interested in comparing how live, play-by-play television sports commentators talk about women's sports and women athletes with how they talk about men's sports and men athletes. We constructed our research design, in part, from the now-vast feminist literature on gender and language. In short, this literature demonstrates that the ways in which men and women talk—and the ways in which we are talked about—are deeply gendered. For instance, a women secretary would likely use the formal "Mr.," along with the last name, when speaking to her male boss, whereas he would probably feel free to refer to her by her first name. This kind of language convention tends to (often subtly) mark gender difference (and, in the above example, social class difference as well) in ways that support and reinforce the power and privilege of "dominants" over "subordinates." The micropolitical realm of face-to-face interaction and language both reflects and constructs the macropolitical realm of unequal power relations between groups (Henley 1977, 1987; Lakoff 1975; Miller and Swift 1976; Schultz 1975; Spender 1980; Thorne, Kramarae, and Henley 1983).

Description of Research

We examined two sports for which televised coverage of women's and men's contests could be compared: basketball and tennis. For a number of years, women's tennis has been highly visible on television, but women's college basketball is only recently beginning to be televised (albeit mostly on cable TV, and often on late-night tape delay). We reasoned that a comparison of the more "established" televised sport of tennis with the relative "newcomer" of women's basketball might be revealing.

Live televised coverage of the 1989 women's and men's National Collegiate Athletic Association (NCAA) final four basketball tournaments was compared and analyzed. (It should be noted that we chose the "final four," rather than regular-season games because there are so few women's regular season games broadcast on television.) This amounted to three women's games and three men's games, including introductions or lead-ins and halftime shows. We also examined the four final days of televised coverage of the 1989 U.S. Open tennis tournament. Televised coverage consisted of four men's singles matches (two quarterfinals, one semifinal, and the final), three women's singles matches (two semifinals and the final), one men's doubles match (the final), two women's doubles matches (a semifinal and the final), and one mixed-doubles match (the final).

Three general questions guided our analysis: First, do commentators overtly trivialize or sexualize women's sports and individual women athletes in the ways that previous analysts have identified? Second, do sports commentators speak about women's and men's athletic contests differently? In particular, to what extent (if any) are women's and men's events verbally gender marked (e.g., "the *women's* national championship")? Third, do commentators speak of individual women and men athletes differently? For instance, are women athletes referred to as "girls" or as "women"? Are men athletes referred to as "boys," or as "men"?

First, we recorded the basketball games and tennis matches on videotape and conducted a pilot study of the tapes. The pilot study had two outcomes: First, the research design was fine-tuned, and a preliminary list of specific questions was constructed. Next, we developed standardized ways of analyzing the verbal commentary. Then, the research assistant viewed all of the tapes and compiled a detailed record of her observations. Next, all of the tapes were independently viewed and analyzed by one of the investigators, who then added her written analysis to that of the research assistant. Finally, the data were compiled and analyzed by the two investigators, using both sets of written descriptions of the tapes and by viewing portions of the tapes once again.

Our data revealed very little of the overtly sexist commentary that has been observed in past research. Women's sports and women athletes were not overtly trivialized in tennis or in basketball commentary. And, although camera angles at times may have subtly framed women athletes (especially in tennis) as sexual objects in ways that were not symmetrical with the ways men were framed, the verbal commentary did not frame women in this way. However, we did find two categories of difference in the verbal commentary: (1) gender marking and (2) a "hierarchy of naming" by gender and, to a certain extent, by race.

Women Marked as Other

In women's basketball, gender was constantly marked, both verbally and through the use of graphics. We were continually reminded that we were watching the *"Women's* final four," the NCAA *Women's* National Championship Game," that these were "some of the best *women's* college basketball teams," that coach Pat Summit "is a legend in *women's* basketball," that "this NCAA *women's* semifinal is brought to you by . . . ." Gender was also marked through the use of graphics in the women's games that CBS broadcasted, but not in the ESPN game. The CBS logo marked the women's championship game: "NCAA Women's National Championship," as did their graphics above game scores. ESPN's graphic did not mark gender: "NCAA Semifinal." As Table 1 indicates, over the course of the three women's games, there were 28 instances of graphic and 49 cases of verbal gender marking, for a total of 77 instances of gender marking. This meant that gender was being marked an average of 25.7 times per women's game.

During the women's games, when commentators were discussing the next day's men's games, the men's games were sometimes gender marked (e.g., "the *men's* championship game will be played tomorrow"). But, during the men's basketball games, we observed no instances of gender marking, either verbal or graphic. Men's games were always referred to as universal, both verbally and in on-screen graphic logos (e.g., "The NCAA National Championship Game," "The Final Four," etc.)

Table 1 Gender Marking in Basketball, Totals

	Verbal	Graphic	Total
Three women's games	49 (16.3)	28 (9.3)	77 (25.7)
Three men's games	0	0	0

NOTE: Numbers in parentheses represent the average per game.

Women's and men's tennis matches were verbally gender marked in a roughly equitable manner (e.g., "men's doubles finals," women's singles semifinals"). Verbal descriptions of athletes, however, revealed a tendency to gender mark women, not men. For instance, in the mixed-doubles match, the commentators stated several times that Rick Leach is "one of the best doubles players in the world," where Robyn White was referred to as one of "the most animated girls on the circuit." An instance of graphic gender marking in tennis that we found notable was the tendency by CBS to display a pink on-screen graphic for the women's matches and a blue on-screen graphic for the men's matches.

How might we interpret these observations? Stanley (1977) suggests that, although *asymmetrical* gender marking tends to mark women as "other," *symmetrical* gender marking is not necessarily oppressive. In fact, she argues that the move toward a totally gender-neutral language may serve to further render women invisible. This would probably be the case if the language of sports reporting and commentary became gender neutral. In fact, in certain cases (in the daily television program, for instance) gender marking is probably necessary to clarify what the viewer will be tuning in to watch. We observed this sort of gender marking in tennis, where women's and men's matches (although not always women and men *athletes*) were verbally gender marked in a roughly symmetrical manner. The rough symmetry of gender marking in tennis might be explained by the fact that the women's and men's tennis tournaments

were being played in the same venue, with coverage often cutting back and forth to women's, men's, and mixed-doubles matches. In this context, symmetrical gender marking probably provides a necessary sense of clarity for the viewers, although the pink (for women) and blue (for men) graphic on-screen logos tended to mark gender in a manner that reinforced conventional gender stereotypes.

In contrast, the women's and men's basketball games were played in different cities, on different nights. And our data revealed a dramatic asymmetry in the commentary: Women's games were verbally and graphically gender marked an average of 25.7 times per game, whereas men's games were never gender marked. We did not include gender-marked team names (e.g., Lady Techsters, Lady Tigers, Lady Volunteers) in these tabulations because we reasoned that team names are the responsibility of their respective universities, not the networks or commentators. Nevertheless, gender-marked team names have recently been criticized as "contributing to the maintenance of male dominance within college athletics by defining women athletes and women's athletic programs as second class and trivial" (Eitzen and Zinn 1989, 362). In several colleges and universities in recent years, faculty and students have attempted to change gender-marked women's team names (Eitzen and Baca Zinn 1990). In the three women's basketball games that we examined, team names were gender marked 53 times graphically and 49 times verbally (a total of 102 times). As Table 2 reveals, when we add these numbers

Table 2 Gender Marking in Basketball, including Gender-Marked Team Names

	Verbal	Graphic	Total
Three women's games	98 (32.7)	81 (27.0)	179 (59.7)
Three men's games	0	0	0

NOTE: Numbers in parentheses represents the average per game.

to our original tabulations, we see that the combination of on-screen graphics, verbal commentary, and team names and logos amounted to a constant barrage of gender marking in the women's games: Gender was marked in some fashion an average of 59.7 times per women's game. In contrast, the men's games were always simply referred to as "the national championship game," and so on. As a result, the men's games and tournament were presented as the norm, the universal, whereas the women's were continually marked as the other, derivative, and, by implication, inferior to the men's.

A Gendered Hierarchy of Naming

There were stark contrasts between how men athletes and women athletes were referred to by commentators. This was true both in tennis and in basketball. First, and as we had expected, women were commonly referred to as "girls," as "young ladies," and as "women." (Often the naming of women athletes was ambivalent. For instance, Steffi Graf was referred to as "the wonder girl of women's tennis.") In contrast, the male athletes, *never* referred to as "boys," were referred to as "men," "young men," or "young fellas." Second, when athletes were named, commentators used the first name only of the women far more commonly than for the men. This difference was most stark in tennis commentary, as revealed in Table 3.

In basketball, the degree of difference in the use of first names of women and men players was not as dramatic, but the pattern was similar. In the three women's basketball games,

we counted 31 incidents of women athletes being referred to by their first name only. This occurred 19 times in the men's games.

How do we interpret these differences in how commentators talk about male and female athletes? After these research findings were released at a national press conference, Diana Nyad, one of the USA Network tennis commentators, stated that the difference in first- and last-name use in women's and men's tennis commentary is not due to "sexism" but is simply a result of the fact that the women tennis players are more likely to be "teenaged girls," whereas the men players are likely to be older (Herbert 1990). This was an interesting response, given that in the tennis matches we examined in our study, the range of ages for the male players was 19–29, with the mean age 22.8, and the range of ages for the female players was 19–32, with the mean age 24.0. In the NCAA basketball tournaments, all of the female and male players were college students and roughly the same age. Clearly, actual age differences do not explain commentators' tendency to refer to women athletes as "girls," "young ladies," and by first name only.

Research has demonstrated that dominants (either by social class, age, occupational position, race, or gender) are more commonly referred to by their last names (often prefaced by titles such as *Mr.*). Dominants generally have license to refer to subordinates (younger people, employees, lower-class people, ethnic minorities, women, etc.) by their first names (Henley 1977; McConnell-Ginet 1978; Rubin 1981; Wolfson and Manes 1980). The practice of referring more "formally" to dominants

Table 3 First and Last Name Use in Tennis Commentary, Totals

	First Only	Last Only	First and Last
Women	304 (52.7)	166 (28.8)	107 (18.5)
Men	44 (7.8)	395 (69.8)	127 (22.4)

NOTE: Numbers in parentheses represent percentages.

and more "informally" (or "endearingly") to subordinates linguistically grants the former adult status, while marking the latter in an infantilizing way. And research suggests that these linguistic differences both reflect and (re)construct inequality. For instance, Brannon (1978) had 462 college students read a story describing a female's application for a high-level executive position, in which she was referred to either as a "girl" or as a "woman." Students' ratings of personality traits described the woman as more tough, brilliant, mature, and dignified, more qualified to be hired, and more deserving of a higher salary than the girl. Similarly, the term *lady* tends to "evoke a standard of propriety, correct behavior, and elegance" (Miller and Swift 1976), and "carries overtones recalling the age of chivalry, implying that women are helpless and cannot do things for themselves, "all of which are characteristics that are "decidedly unathletic" (Eitzen and Baca Zinn 1990, 5–6). It can be concluded that tennis commentators' tendency to call women athletes "girls" and "young ladies," and their utilization of the first name only of women athletes (52.7 percent of the time) far more commonly than men athletes (7.8 percent of the time) reflects the lower status of women athletes. Moreover, it is reasonable to speculate that this language is likely to be received by viewers in such a way that it reinforces any already-existing negative attitudes or ambivalences about women's sports and women athletes.

We can only speculate as to why the contrast in gendered patterns of naming was not as stark in basketball as it was in tennis. Perhaps, because female tennis players have traditionally been stereotyped in more conventionally "feminine" ways than other female athletes, there is a greater (probably unconscious) tendency for commentators to view them (and talk about them) in an infantilizing manner. Moreover, women tennis players are often participating in the same venue as the men (and in

the case of mixed doubles, in the very same *matches* with the men), and perhaps this contributes to an unconscious tendency to separate them verbally from the men by naming them differently. In contrast, female basketball players are participating in a traditionally defined "male" sport that requires a good deal of physically aggressive body contact. Perhaps, as a result, commentators are less likely to (again, probably unconsciously) view them and talk about them using conventionally feminine and infantilizing language. And because the women's basketball games are being constantly and thoroughly gender marked, both graphically and verbally, there is little chance that their games will be confused with those of the men. There may therefore be less of a tendency on the part of commentators to differentiate them verbally from the men in terms of how they are named.

In addition to the tendency to infantilize women linguistically while granting men athletes adult status, the quality of commentators' verbal attributions of strength and weakness, success and failure, for women's and men's events also tended to differ. In basketball, verbal attributions of strength to women were often stated in ambivalent language that undermined or neutralized the words conveying power and strength: "big girl," "she's tiny, she's small, but so effective under the boards," "her little jump hook," and so on. A difference in descriptions of basketball coaches was also noted. Joe Ciampi (male) "yells" at his team, whereas Pat Summit (female) was described twice in the Auburn versus Tennessee game as "screaming" off the bench. Men coaches were not described as screaming, a term that often implies lack of control, powerlessness, even hysteria.

In tennis, "confidence" was very frequently used to describe strength for women, but not so often for men. We speculated that confidence is considered a "given" for men, but an attribute for which women players must constantly strive. Even very strong descriptors, for women, were often framed ambivalently — "That young lady Graf is relentless" — or sexualized — "Sabatini has put together this first set with such naked aggression." And whereas, for women, spectacular shots were sometimes referred to as "lucky," for the men, there were constant references to the imposition of their wills on the games (and on opponents). In men's doubles, for example, "You can feel McEnroe imposing his will all over this court. I mean not just with Woodford but Flach and Seguso. He's just giving them messages by the way he's standing at the net, the way he kind of swaggers between points."

There was little ambivalence in the descriptions of men: These are "big" guys with "big" forehands, who play "big games." There was a constant suggestion of male power and agency in the commentary. Even descriptions of men's weaknesses were commonly framed in a language of agency.[4] He created his own error . . . ." Discussion of men's "nervousness" was often qualified to make it sound like strength and heroism. For instance, early in the match between Becker and Krickstein, the two commentators had this exchange: "They're both pretty nervous, and that's pretty normal." "Something would be wrong if they weren't." "It means you care." "Like Marines going into Iwo Jima saying they weren't nervous, something's a little fishy."

In both basketball and tennis, there were also qualitative differences in the ways that success and failure were discussed for women and men athletes. In fact, two formulas for success appeared to exist, one for men, the other for

women. Men appeared to succeed through a combination of talent, instinct, intelligence, size, strength, quickness, hard work, and risk taking. Women also appeared to succeed through talent, enterprise, hard work, and intelligence. But commonly cited along with these attributes were emotion, luck, togetherness, and family. Women were also more likely to be framed as failures due to some combination of nervousness, lack of confidence, lack of being "comfortable," lack of aggression, and lack of stamina. Men were far less often framed as failures — men appeared to miss shots and lose matches not so much because of their own individual shortcomings (nervousness, losing control, etc.) but because of the power, strength, and intelligence of their (male) *opponents*. This framing of failure suggests that it is the thoughts and actions of the male victor that wins games, rather than suggesting that the loser's lack of intelligence or ability is responsible for losing games. Men were framed as active agents in control of their destinies, women as reactive objects.

A Hierarchy of Naming by Gender and Race

It was not simply women athletes who were linguistically infantilized and framed ambivalently. Our research suggests that Black male basketball players shared some of this infantilization. Previous research revealed racial bias in televised commentary in men's sports. For instance, Rainville and McCormick (1977) found that white players received more praise and less criticism from football commentators than comparable Black players. And Jackson (1989) reported that white male football and basketball players were much more likely to be credited with "intelligence and hard work," whereas the successes of their Black male counterparts were more likely to be attributed to "natural athleticism." Our examination of basketball commentary occurred in the wake of

---

[4] If the outcome of a situation is up to you, then you have agency in that situation. In this case, the "language of agency" refers to language that describes what a person does if he or she has a choice or the power to make a difference in the situation. This use of "agency" appeared first in the work of the English sociologist Anthony Giddens, who argued that humans are not at the mercy of social structures but that humans have agency — that is, they choose to make use of social structures to initiate action.

widespread public discussion of Jackson's (1989) research. We observed what appeared to be a conscious effort on the part of commentators to cite both physical ability and intelligence when discussing successful Black and white male and female players. However, this often appeared to be an afterthought. For instance, a commentator would note of a star white player that "he has so much court intelligence . . . AND so much natural ability!" And a typical comment about a Black star player was "What a great athlete . . . AND he really plays the game intelligently!"

Although it appeared that television commentators were consciously attempting to do away with the "hard work/intelligence" (white) versus "natural athlete" (Black) dichotomy, we did find an indication of racial difference in the naming of male basketball players. In the three men's basketball games, in each of the cases in which men were referred to by their first names only, the commentators were referring to men of color (e.g., Rumeal [Robinson], Ramon [Ramos]). Although there were several "star" white male basketball players (e.g., Danny Ferry and Andrew Gaze) in these games, they were *never* referred to by their first names only.

These findings suggest that TV sports commentators are (again, probably unconsciously) utilizing a "hierarchy of naming": At the top of the linguistic hierarchy sit the always last-named white "men," followed by (sometimes) first-named Black "men," followed by (frequently) first-named "girls" and "young ladies." We found no racial differences in the ways that women athletes were named. We speculate that (at least within televised sports commentary) gender is the dominant defining feature of women athletes' shared subordinate status. In contrast, sports commentary tends to weave a taken-for-granted superordinate, adult masculine status around male athletes. Yet, in the case of male athletes of color, the commentary tends to (subtly and partially)

undermine their superordinate masculine status. This suggests, following the theory of gender stratification developed by Connell (1987) and applied to sport by Messner (1989), Messner and Sabo (1990), and Kidd (1987), that sports media reinforce the overall tendency of sport to be an institution that simultaneously (1) constructs and legitimizes men's overall power and privilege over women and (2) constructs and legitimizes heterosexual, white, middle-class men's power and privilege over subordinated and marginalized groups of men.

Conclusion

An individual who watches an athletic event constructs and derives various meanings from the activity. These meanings result from a process of interaction between the meanings that are built into the game itself (the formal rules and structure, as well as the history and accumulated mythology of the game), with the values, ideologies, and presuppositions that the viewer brings to the activity of watching. But viewing an athletic contest on television is not the same as watching a contest "live." Televised sport is an event that is mediated by the "framing" of the contest by commentators and technical people (Clarke and Clarke 1982; Duncan and Brummet 1987; Gitlin 1982; Gruneau 1989; Jhally 1989; Morse 1983; Wenner 1989). Thus any meanings that a television viewer constructs from the contest are likely to be profoundly affected by the framing of the contest (Altheide and Snow 1979; Antin 1982; Conrad 1982; Duncan and Hasbrook 1988; Fiske and Hartley 1978; Innis 1951; McLuhan 1964; Morse 1983).

Televised sports are live and largely unscripted, but the language that commentators use to frame the events tends to conform to certain linguistic conventions that are themselves a result of "a complex articulation of technical, organizational, economic, cultural, political, and social factors" (Jhally 1989, 84). In our study, the sex of the commentators did not appear to make a difference in how they linguistically framed gender. Both female and male commentators tended to gender mark and infantilize women athletes in roughly the same ways, and to the same extent.[5] As Gruneau (1989) has argued, although commentators are often aware of themselves as "story-tellers," they are not necessarily aware of the political and ideological ramifications of the linguistic conventions to which they — apparently unconsciously — conform.

Language is never neutral. An analysis of language reveals embedded social meanings, including overt and covert social biases, stereotypes, and inequities. There is an extensive body of literature that documents how language both reflects and reinforces gender inequalities (Baron 1986; Henley 1977, 1987; Lakoff 1975; Miller and Swift 1976, 1980; Schultz 1975; Spender 1980; Thorne, Kramarae, and Henley 1983; Van Den Bergh 1987). In a recent study of the gendered language of sport, sociologists Eitzen and Baca Zinn (1989) argue that

> [gendered] language places women and men within a system of differentiation and stratification. Language suggests how women and men

are to be evaluated. Language embodies negative and positive value stances and valuations related to how certain groups within society are appraised. Language in general is filled with biases about women and men. Specific linguistic conventions are sexist when they isolate or stereotype some aspect of an individual's nature or the nature of a group of individuals based on their sex. (P. 364)

The media — and sports media in particular — tend to reflect the social conventions of gender-biased language. In so doing, they reinforce the biased meanings built into language and, thus, contribute to the reconstruction of social inequities.

Newspaper editors and television programmers often argue that they are simply "giving the public what it wants." Programming decisions are clearly circumscribed by market realities, and, with few exceptions, men's athletic events tend to draw more spectators than women's. But one question that arises concerns the reciprocal effect of, on the one hand, public attitudes, values, and tastes, and, on the other hand, the quantity and quality of coverage of certain kinds of athletic events. What comes first: public "disinterest" in televised women's athletics or lack of quality coverage? Perhaps a more timely question now that women's sports are getting at least incrementally more coverage is, How do the ways that women's and men's sports are covered on television affect public interest in these events?

Our research on women's and men's tennis and basketball coverage indicated that commentators today are less likely than their predecessors to sexualize or trivialize women athletes overtly. However, the language used by commentators tends to mark women's sports and women athletes as other, infantilize women athletes, and frame their accomplishments negatively or ambivalently. Our research also suggests that Black male athletes share in some of the linguistic infantilization that is

---

[5]Women have only recently appeared on television as sports commentators and still represent a very small proportion of this profession. Thus, although some analysts have observed instances of women sports commentators resisting or objecting to sexist commentary by their male colleagues (Duncan and Hasbrook 1988), it is probably premature to expect them to have effected any significant change in the ways women's sports are reported. As Kanter (1977) argued, a significant proportion of any profession must be female before we might expect a dramatic change in the culture of that profession. Until many more women move into sports commentary, we can expect the few that do exist to remain marginalized and compartmentalized in ways that do not challenge the business-as-usual gendering of televised sports. But, as Yoder (1991) warns, increasing numbers of women (beyond tokenism) in traditionally male occupations often leads to a defensive backlash (sexual harassment, etc.) by men, some of which has already occurred in newspaper sports reporting.

commonly used to describe women athletes. As a result, the language of sports commentary tends to (often subtly) reconstruct gender and racial hierarchies.

Although subtle bias is no less dangerous than overt sexism, the decline of overtly sexist language suggests that some commentators are becoming more committed to presenting women's athletics fairly. For instance, women's basketball commentator Steve Physioc renamed "man-to-man defense" as "player-to-player" defense. This is an example of a conscious decision to replace androcentric language with language that is not gendered. Although Physioc did not do this consistently, the fact that he did it at all was an indication of his awareness of the gender biases built into the conventional language of sports. Critics might argue that changing language subverts the history or the "purity" of the game. But, in fact, terminology used to describe sports is constantly changing. For instance, in basketball, the part of the court nearest the basket that used to be called "the key" through the 1950s was renamed "the lane" in the 1960s and is more recently referred to as "the paint" or "the block." These changes have come about as a result of changes in the rules of the game, changes in the sizes and styles of players, and general changes in social values and mores. But language does not simply change as a reflection of changing social realities. Language also helps to construct social reality (Shute 1981; Van Den Bergh 1987). Thus the choice to use nonsexist language is a choice to affirm linguistically the right of women athletes to fair and equal treatment. Viewed in this context, Physioc's use of "player-to-player defense" can be viewed as a linguistic recognition that something significant has happened to basketball: It is no longer simply a men's game. There are women players out there, and the language used to report their games should reflect and endorse this fact.

References

Altheide, David L., and Robert P. Snow. 1979. *Media logic*. Beverly Hills, CA: Sage.

Antin, David. 1982. Video: The distinctive features of the medium. In *Television: The critical view*. 3d ed., edited by H. Newcomb. New York: Oxford University Press.

Baron, Dennis. 1986. *Grammar and gender*. New Haven, CT: Yale University Press.

Birrell, Susan. 1987–1988. The woman athlete's college experience: Knowns and unknowns. *Journal of Sport and Social Issues* 11:82–96.

Boutilier, Mary A., and Lucinda L. San Giovanni. 1983. *The sporting woman*. Champaign, IL: Human Kinetics.

Brannon, Robert. 1978. "The Consequences of Sexist Language." Paper presented at the American Psychological Association Meetings, Toronto.

Bryant, James. 1980. A two-year investigation of the female in sport as reported in the paper media. *Arena Review* 4:32–44.

Bryson, Lois. 1987. "Sport and the Maintenance of Masculine Hegemony." *Women's Studies International Forum* 10:349–60.

Clarke, Alan, and John Clarke. 1982. Highlights and Action Replays: Ideology, Sport, and the Media. In *Sport, Culture, and Ideology*, edited by Jennifer Hargreaves. London: Routledge & Kegan Paul.

Connell, R. W. 1987. *Gender and Power*. Stanford, CA: Stanford University Press.

————. 1990. "An Iron Man: the Body and Some Contradictions of Hegemonic Masculinity." In *Sport, Men, and the Gender Order: Critical Feminist Perspectives*, edited by Michael A. Messner and Donald F. Sabo. Champaign, IL: Human Kinetics.

Conrad, Peter. 1982. *Television: The Medium and Its Manners*. Boston: Routledge & Kegan Paul.

Crittenden, Ann. 1979. "Closing the Muscle Gap." In *Out of the Bleachers: Writings on Women and Sport*, edited by Stephanie L. Twin. Old Westbury, NY: Feminist Press.

Duncan, Margaret Carlisle. 1990. "Sports Photographs and Sexual Difference: Images of Women and Men in the 1984 and 1988 Olympic Games." *Sociology of Sport Journal* 7:22–43.

Duncan, Margaret Carlisle, and Barry Brummet. 1987. "The Mediation of Spectator Sport." *Research Quarterly for Exercise and Sport* 58:168–77.

Duncan, Margaret Carlisle, and Cynthia A. Hasbrook. 1988. "Denial of Power in Televised Women's Sports." *Sociology of Sport Journal* 5:1–21.

Duncan, Margaret Carlisle, and Amoun Sayaovong. 1990. "Photographic Images and Gender in *Sports Illustrated for Kids.*" *Play & Culture* 3:91–116.

Dyer, Gillian. 1987. "Women and Television: An Overview." In *Boxed in: Women and Television,* edited by Helen Bacher and Gillian Dyer. New York: Pandora Press.

Dyer, Kenneth. 1983. *Challenging the Men: The Social Biology of Female Sport Achievement.* St. Lucia: University of Queensland.

Eastman, Susan Tyler, and Timothy P. Meyer. 1989. "Sports Programming: Scheduling, Costs, and Competition." In *Media, Sports, and Society,* edited by Lawrence A. Wenner. Newbury Park, CA: Sage.

Eitzen, D. Stanley, and Maxine Baca Zinn. 1989. "The de-athleticization of Women: The Naming and Gender Marking of Collegiate Sport Teams." *Sociology of Sport Journal* 6:362–70.

_____. 1990. "Language and Gender Stratification: The Unequal Naming of Collegiate Athletic Teams by Gender and Resistance to Change." Paper presented at the International Sociological Association Meetings, Madrid, Spain, July 9–13.

Felshin, Jan. 1974. "The Social View." In *The American Woman in Sport,* edited by Eileen W. Gerber, Jan Felshin, Pearl Berlin, and Waneen Wyrick. Reading, MA: Addison-Wesley.

Fiske, John, and John Hartley. 1978. *Reading Television.* New York: Methuen.

Gitlin, Todd. 1982. "Prime Time Ideology: The Hegemonic Process in Television Entertainment." In *Television: The Critical View.* 3d ed., edited by H. Newcomb. New York: Oxford University Press.

Graydon, J. 1983. "But It's More Than a Game: It's an Institution." *Feminist Review* 13:5–16.

Gruneau, Richard. 1989. "Making Spectacle: A Case Study in Television Sports Production." In *Media, Sports, and Society,* edited by Lawrence A. Wenner. Newbury Park, CA: Sage.

Hall, M. Ann. 1988. "The Discourse on Gender and Sport: From Femininity to Feminism." *Sociology of Sport Journal* 5:330–40.

Hargreaves, Jennifer. 1986. "Where's the Virtue? Where's the Grace?" A discussion of the social production of gender through sport. *Theory, Culture and Society* 3:109–21.

Henley, Nancy M. 1977. *Body Politics: Power, Sex, and Nonverbal Communication.* Englewood Cliffs, NJ: Prentice-Hall.

_____. 1987. "This New Species That Seeks New Language: On Sexism in Language and Language Change". In *Women and Language in Transition,* edited by J. Penfield. Albany: State University of New York Press.

Herbert, Steven. 1990. "Study Charges Sexism in Women's Sports Coverage." *Los Angeles Times,* 30 August, F-2.

Innis, Harold A. 1951. *The Bias of Communication.* Toronto: University of Toronto Press.

Jackson, Derrick Z. 1989. "Sports Broadcasting: Calling the Plays in Black and White." *Boston Globe,* January 22, A-25, 28–29.

Jhally, Sat. 1989. "Cultural Studies and the Sports/Media Complex". In *Media, Sports, and Society,* edited by Lawrence A. Wenner. Newbury Park, CA: Sage.

Kanter, Rosabeth Moss. 1977. *Men and Women of the Corporation.* New York: Basic Books.

Kidd, Bruce. 1987. "Sports and Masculinity." In *Beyond Patriarchy: Essays by Men on Pleasure, Power, and Change,* edited by Michael Kaufman. Toronto: Oxford University Press.

_____. 1990. "The Men's Cultural Centre: Sports and the Dynamic of Women's Oppression/Men's Repression." In *Sport, Men, and the Gender Order: Critical Feminist perspectives,* edited by Michael A. Messner and Donald F. Sabo. Champaign, IL: Human Kinetics.

Lakoff, Robin. 1975. *Language and Woman's Place.* New York: Harper & Row.

McConnell-Ginet, Sally. 1978. "Address Forms in Sexual Politics." In *Women's Language and Style,* edited by Douglas Butturff and Edmund L. Epstein. Akron, OH: L&S Books.

McLuhan, Marshall. 1964. *Understanding Media: The Extensions of Man.* New York: Signet.

Messner, Michael A. 1988. "Sports and Male Domination: The Female Athlete as Contested Ideological Terrain." *Sociology of Sport Journal* 5:197–211.

_____. 1989. "Masculinities and Athletic Careers." *Gender & Society* 3:71–88.

Messner, Michael A., and Donald F. Sabo. 1990. " Toward a Critical Feminist Reappraisal of Sport, Men and the Gender Order." *In Sport, Men and the Gender Order: Critical Feminist Perspectives,* edited by Michael A. Messner and Donald F. Sabo. Champaign, IL: Human Kinetics.

Miller, Casey, and Kate Swift. 1976. *Words and Women: New Language in New Times.* Garden City, NY: Doubleday.

_____. 1980. *The Handbook of Nonsexist Writing.* New York: Lippincott & Crowell.

Morse, Margaret. 1983. "Sport on Television: Replay and Display." In *Regarding Television,* edited by E. Ann Kaplan. Los Angeles: American Film Institute/University Publications of America.

Rainville, Raymond E., and Edward McCormick. 1977. "Extent of Covert Prejudice in Pro Football Announcers' Speech." *Journalism Quarterly* 54:20–26.

Rintala, Jan, and Susan Birrell. 1984. "Fair Treatment for the Active Female: A Content Analysis of *Young Athlete* Magazine." *Sociology of Sport Journal* 1:231–50.

Rubin, Rebecca. 1981. "Ideal Traits and Terms of Address for Male and Female College Professors." *Journal of Personality and Social Psychology* 41:966–74.

Sabo, Donald. 1988. "Title IX and Athletics: Sex Equity in Schools." *Updating School Board Policies* 19 November, 1–3.

Schultz, Muriel. 1975. "The Semantic Derogation of Women." In *Language and Sex: Difference and Dominance,* edited by Barrie Thorne and Nancy Henley. Rowley, MA: Newbury House.

Shute, Sara. 1981. "Sexist Language and Sexism." In *Sexist Language: A Modern Philosophical Analysis,* edited by Mary Vetterling-Braggin. Totowa, NJ: Littlefield, Adams.

Spender, Dale. 1980. *Man made Language.* London: Routledge & Kegan Paul.

Stanley, Julia P. 1977. "Gender-marking in American English: Usage and Reference." In *Sexism and Language,* edited by Alleen Pace Nilsen et al. Urbana, IL: National Council of Teachers of English.

Theberge, Nancy. 1981. "A Critique of Critiques: Radical and Feminist Writings on Sport." *Social Forces* 60:387–94.

Theberge, Nancy, and Alan Cronk. 1986. "Work Routines in Newspaper Sports Departments and the Coverage of Women's Sports." *Sociology of Sport Journal* 3:195–203.

Thorne, Barrie, Cheris Kramarae, and Nancy Henley. 1983. "Language, Gender and Society: Opening a Second Decade of Research." In *Language, Gender and Society*, edited by Barrie Thorne, Cheris Kramarae, and Nancy Henley. Rowley, MA: Newbury House.

Van Den Bergh, N. 1987. "Renaming: Vehicle for Empowerment." In *Women and Language in Transition*, edited by J. Penfield. Albany: State University of New York Press.

Wenner, Lawrence A. 1989. "Media, Sports and Society: The Research Agenda." In *Media, Sports, and Society*, edited by Lawrence A. Wenner. Newbury Park, CA: Sage.

Whitson, David. 1990. "Sport in the Social Construction of Masculinity." In *Sport, Men, and the Gender Order: Critical Feminist Perspectives*, edited by Michael A. Messner and Donald F. Sabo. Champaign, IL: Human Kinetics.

Willis, Paul. 1982. "Women in Sport in Ideology." In *Sport, Culture, and Ideology*, edited by Jennifer Hargreaves. London: Routledge & Kegan Paul.

Wilson Sporting Goods Co. and the Women's Sports Foundation. 1988. The Wilson Report: Moms, Dads, Daughters and Sports. River Grove, IL. June.

Wolfson, Nessa, and Joan Manes. 1980. "Don't "Dear" Me!" In *Women and Language in Literature and Society*, edited by Sally McConnell-Ginet, Ruth Borker, and Nelly Furman. New York: Praeger.

Yoder, Janice D. 1991. "Rethinking Tokenism: Looking Beyond Numbers." *Gender & Society* 5: 178–92.

Questions

1. Explain what the following concepts mean
   a. *asymmetrical* versus *symmetrical* gender marking
   b. hierarchy of naming

2. Many social theorists believe that language not only serves as a vehicle for humans to describe what they think and see, but that it also shapes what they think and see. In your judgment, would Messner, Carlisle Duncan, and Jensen agree or disagree that language plays this dual role? Describe the best evidence you can find in the article to support your answer.

3. The authors of this article suggest that "subtle bias is no less dangerous than overt sexism." Do you agree or disagree? Why?

4. This article was published more than a decade ago and perhaps things have changed. Look at your school's newspaper as well as other local media. Is there asymmetrical or symmetrical gender marking? Is there evidence of a hierarchy of naming?

·14·

The Presentation of Self in Everyday Life

Erving Goffman

In this 1959 reading, Erving Goffman introduces what has come to be called the *dramaturgical* approach to the study of social interaction (so called because, in effect, it views social life as theater). Goffman's focus is on what happens when people are in the presence of others, on how they play their roles. As you will see, from Goffman's point of view, routine social interaction is a cooperative effort between the social actor and his or her audience. The actor may play a role, but frequently he or she must be helped along by the complicity of the audience.

When an individual enters the presence of others, they commonly seek to acquire information about him or to bring into play information about him already possessed. They will be interested in his general socio-economic status, his conception of self, his attitude toward them, his competence, his trustworthiness, etc. Although some of this information seems to be sought almost as an end in itself, there are usually quite practical reasons for acquiring it. Information about the individual helps to define the situation, enabling others to know in advance what he will expect of them and what they may expect of him. Informed in these ways, the others will know how best to act in order to call forth a desired response from him.

For those present, many sources of information become accessible and many carriers (or "sign-vehicles") become available for conveying this information. If unacquainted with the individual, observers can glean clues from his conduct and appearance which allow them to apply their previous experience with individuals roughly similar to the one before them or, more important, to apply untested stereotypes to him. They can also assume from past experience that only individuals of a particular kind are likely to be found in a given social setting. They can rely on what the individual says about himself or on documentary evidence he provides as to who and what he is. If they know, or know of, the individual by virtue of experience prior to the interaction, they can rely on assumptions as to the persistence and generality of psychological traits as a means of predicting his present and future behavior.

However, during the period in which the individual is in the immediate presence of the others, few events may occur which directly provide the others with the conclusive information they will need if they are to direct wisely their own activity. Many crucial facts lie beyond the time and place of interaction or lie concealed with it. For example, the "true" or "real" attitudes, beliefs, and emotions of the individual can be ascertained only indirectly, through his avowals or through what appears to be involuntary expressive behavior. Similarly, if the individual offers the others a product or service, they will often find that during the interaction there will be no time and place immediately available for eating the pudding that the proof can be found in. They will be forced to accept some events as conventional or natural signs of something not directly available to the senses. In other terms, the individual will have to act so that he intentionally or unintentionally *expresses* himself, and the others will in turn have to be *impressed* in some way by him (Ichheiser 1949, 6–7).

The expressiveness of the individual (and therefore his capacity to give impressions) appears to involve two radically different kinds of sign activity: the expression that he *gives*, and the expression that he *gives off*. The first involves verbal symbols or their substitutes which he uses admittedly and solely to convey the information that he and the others are known to attach to these symbols. This is communication in the traditional and narrow sense. The second involves a wide range of action that others can treat as symptomatic of the actor, the expectation being that the action was performed for reasons other than the information conveyed in this way. As we shall have to see, this distinction has only an initial validity. The individual does of course intentionally convey misinformation by means of both of these types of communication, the first involving deceit, the second feigning.

Taking communication in both its narrow and broad sense, one finds that when the individual is in the immediate presence of others, his activity will have a promissory character. The others are likely to find that they must accept the individual on faith, offering him a just return while he is present before them in exchange for something whose true value will not be established until after he has left their presence. (Of course, the others also live by inference in their dealings with the physical world, but it is only in the world of social interaction that the objects about which they make inferences will purposely facilitate and hinder this inferential process.) The security that they justifiably feel in making inferences about the individual will vary, of course, depending on such factors as the amount of information they already possess about him, but no amount of such past evidence can entirely obviate the necessity of acting on the basis of inferences. As William I. Thomas suggested:

> It is also highly important for us to realize that we do not as a matter of fact lead our lives, make our decisions, and reach our goals in everyday life either statistically or scientifically. We live in inference. I am, let us say, your guest. You do not know, you cannot determine scientifically, that I will not steal your money or your spoons. But inferentially I will not, and inferentially you have me as a guest. (quoted in Volkart 1951, 5)

Let us now turn from the others to the point of view of the individual who presents himself before them. He may wish them to think highly of him, or to think that he thinks highly of them, or to perceive how in fact he feels toward them, or to obtain no clear-cut impression; he may wish to ensure sufficient harmony so that the interaction can be sustained, or to defraud, get rid of, confuse, mislead, antagonize, or insult them. Regardless of the particular objective which the individual has in mind and of his motive for having this objective, it will be in his interests to control the conduct of the others, especially their responsive treatment of him. This control is achieved largely by influencing the definition of the situation which the others come to formulate, and he can influence this definition by expressing himself in such a way as to give them the kind of impression that will lead them to act voluntarily in accordance with his own plan. Thus, when an individual appears in the presence of others, there will usually be some reason for him to mobilize his activity so that it will convey an impression to others which it is in his interests to convey. Since a girl's dormitory mates will glean evidence of her popularity from the calls she receives on the phone, we can suspect that some girls will arrange for calls to be made, and Willard Waller's (n.d., 730) finding can be anticipated.

> It has been reported by many observers that a girl who is called to the telephone in the dormitories will often allow herself to be called several times, in order to give all the other girls ample opportunity to hear her paged.

Of the two kinds of communication—expressions given and expressions given off—this report will be primarily concerned with the latter, with the more theatrical and contextual kind, the non-verbal, presumably unintentional kind, whether this communication be purposely engineered or not. As an example of what we must try to examine, I would like to cite at length a novelistic incident in which Preedy, a vacationing Englishman, makes his first appearance on the beach of his summer hotel in Spain:

> But in any case he took care to avoid catching anyone's eye. First of all, he had to make it clear to those potential companions of his holiday that they were of no concern to him whatsoever. He stared through them, round them, over them—eyes lost in space. The beach might have been empty. If by chance a ball was thrown his way, he looked surprised; then let a smile of amusement lighten his face (Kindly Preedy), looked round dazed to see that there *were* people on the beach, tossed it back with a smile to himself and not a smile *at* the people, and then resumed carelessly his nonchalant survey of space.
>
> But it was time to institute a little parade, the parade of the Ideal Preedy. By devious handlings he gave any who wanted to look a chance to see the title of his book—a Spanish translation of Homer, classic thus, but not daring, cosmopolitan too—and then gathered together his beach-wrap and bag into a neat sand-resistant pile (Methodical and Sensible Preedy), rose slowly to stretch at ease his huge frame (Big-Cat Preedy), and tossed aside his sandals (Carefree Preedy, after all).
>
> The marriage of Preedy and the sea! There were alternative rituals. The first involved the stroll that turns into a run and a dive straight into the water, thereafter smoothing into a strong splashless crawl towards the horizon. But of course not really to the horizon. Quite suddenly he would turn on to his back and thrash great white splashes with his legs, somehow thus showing that he could have swum further had he wanted to, and then would stand up a quarter out of water for all to see who it was.
>
> The alternative course was simpler, it avoided the cold-water shock and it avoided the risk of appearing too high-spirited. The point was to appear to be so used to the sea, the Mediterranean, and this particular beach, that one might as well be in the sea as out of it. It involved a slow stroll down and into the edge of the water—not even noticing his toes were wet, land and water all the same to *him!*—with his eyes up at the sky gravely surveying portents, invisible to others, of the weather (Local Fisherman Preedy). (Samson 1956, 230–232)

The novelist means us to see that Preedy is improperly concerned with the extensive impressions he feels his sheer bodily action is giving off to those around him. We can malign Preedy further by assuming that he has acted merely in order to give a particular impression, that this is a false impression, and that the others present receive either no impression at all, or, worse still, the impression that Preedy is affectedly trying to cause them to receive this particular impression. But the important point for us here is that the kind of impression Preedy thinks he is making is in fact the kind of impression that others correctly and incorrectly glean from someone in their midst.

I have said that when an individual appears before others his actions will influence the definition of the situation which they come to have. Sometimes the individual will act in a thoroughly calculating manner, expressing himself in a given way solely in order to give the kind of impression to others that is likely to evoke from them a specific response he is concerned to obtain. Sometimes the individual will be calculating in his activity but be relatively unaware that this is the case. Sometimes he will intentionally and consciously express himself in a particular way, but chiefly because the tradition of his group or social status requires this kind of expression and not because of any particular response (other than vague acceptance or approval) that is likely to be evoked from those impressed by the expression. Sometimes the traditions of an individual's role will lead him to give a well-designed impression of a particular kind and yet he may be neither consciously nor unconsciously disposed to create such an impression. The others, in their turn, may be suitably impressed by the individual's efforts to convey something, or may misunderstand the situation and come to conclusions that are warranted neither by the individual's intent nor by the facts. In any case, in so far as the others act *as if* the individual had conveyed a particular impression, we may take a functional or pragmatic view and say that the individual has "effectively" projected a given definition of the situation and "effectively" fostered the understanding that a given state of affairs obtains.

There is one aspect of the others' response that bears special comment here. Knowing that the individual is likely to present himself in a light that is favorable to him, the others may divide what they witness into two parts: a part that is relatively easy for the individual to manipulate at will, being chiefly his verbal assertions, and a part in regard to which he seems to have little concern or control, being chiefly derived from the expressions he gives off. The others may then use what are considered to be the ungovernable aspects of his expressive behavior as a check upon the validity of what is conveyed by the governable aspects. In this a fundamental asymmetry is demonstrated in the communication process, the individual presumably being aware of only one stream of his communication, the witnesses of this stream and one other. For example, in Shetland Isle one crofter's wife, in serving native dishes to a visitor from the mainland of Britain, would listen with a polite smile to his polite claims of liking what he is eating; at the same time she would take note of the rapidity with which the visitor lifted his fork or spoon to his mouth, the eagerness with which he passed food into his mouth, and the gusto expressed in chewing the food, using these signs as a check on the stated feelings of the eater. The same woman, in order to discover what one acquaintance (A) "actually" thought of another acquaintance (B), would wait until B was in the presence of A but engaged in conversation with still another person (C). She would then covertly examine the facial expressions of A as he regarded B in conversation with C. Not being in conversation with B, and not being directly observed by him, A would sometimes relax usual constraints and tactful deceptions, and freely express what he was "actually" feeling about B. This Shetlander, in short, would observe the unobserved observer.

Now given the fact that others are likely to check up on the more controllable aspects of behavior by means of the less controllable, one can expect that sometimes the individual will try to exploit this very possibility, guiding the impression he makes through behavior felt to be reliably informing. For example, in gaining admission to a tight social circle, the participant observer may not only wear an accepting look while listening to an informant, but may also be careful to wear the same look when observing the informant talking to others; observers of the observer will then not as easily discover where he actually stands. A specific illustration may be cited from Shetland Isle. When a neighbor dropped in to have a cup of tea, he would ordinarily wear at least a hint of an expectant warm smile as he passed through the door into the cottage. Since lack of physical obstructions outside the cottage and lack of light within it usually made it possible to observe the visitor unobserved as he approached the house, islanders sometimes took pleasure in watching the visitor drop whatever expression he was manifesting and replace it with a sociable one just before reaching the door. However, some visitors, in appreciating that this examination was occurring, would blindly adopt a social face a long distance from the house, thus ensuring the projection of a constant image.

This kind of control upon the part of the individual reinstates the symmetry of the communication process, and sets the stage for a kind of information game—a potentially infinite cycle of concealment, discovery, false revelation, and rediscovery. It should be added that since the others are likely to be relatively unsuspicious of the presumably unguided aspect of the individual's conduct, he can gain much by controlling it. The others of course may sense that the individual is manipulating the presumably spontaneous aspects of his behavior, and seek in this very act of manipulation some shading of conduct that the individual has not managed to control. This again provides a check upon the individual's behavior, this time his presumably uncalculated behavior, thus re-establishing the asymmetry of the communication process. Here I would like only to add the suggestion that the arts of piercing an individual's effort at calculated unintentionality seem better developed than our capacity to manipulate our own behavior, so that regardless of how many steps have occurred in the information game, the witness is likely to have the advantage over the actor, and the initial asymmetry of the communication process is likely to be retained.

When we allow that the individual projects a definition of the situation when he appears before others, we must also see that the others, however passive their role may seem to be, will themselves effectively project a definition of the situation by virtue of their response to the individual and by virtue of any lines of action they initiate to him. Ordinarily the definitions of the situation projected by the several different participants are sufficiently attuned to one another so that open contradiction will not occur. I do not mean that there will be the kind of consensus that arises when each individual present candidly expresses what he really feels and honestly agrees with the expressed feelings of the others present. This kind of harmony is an optimistic ideal and in any case not necessary for the smooth working of society. Rather, each participant is expected to suppress his immediate heartfelt feelings, conveying a view of the situation which he feels the others will be able to find at least temporarily acceptable. The maintenance of this surface of agreement, this veneer of consensus, is facilitated by each participant concealing his own wants behind statements which assert values to which everyone present feels obliged to give lip service. Further, there is usually a kind of division of definitional labor. Each participant is allowed to establish the tentative official ruling regarding matters which are vital to him but not immediately important to others, e.g., the rationalizations and justifications by which he accounts for his past activity. In exchange for this courtesy he remains silent or non-committal on matters important to others but not immediately important to him. We have then a kind of interactional *modus vivendi*.[1] Together the participants contribute to a single over-all definition of the situation which involves not so much a

---

[1]*Modus vivendi* is Latin and can be literally translated as "a way of living." But generally it refers to "a way of acting" so that people who might not feel positively toward one another can nonetheless get along. —Ed.

real agreement as to what exists but rather a real agreement as to whose claims concerning what issues will be temporarily honored. Real agreement will also exist concerning the desirability of avoiding an open conflict of definitions of the situation.[2] I will refer to this level of agreement as a "working consensus." It is to be understood that the working consensus established in one interaction setting will be quite different in content from the working consensus established in a different type of setting. Thus, between two friends at lunch, a reciprocal show of affection, respect, and concern for the other is maintained. In service occupations, on the other hand, the specialist often maintains an image of disinterested involvement in the problem of the client, while the client responds with a show of respect for the competence and integrity of the specialist. Regardless of such differences in content, however, the general form of these working arrangements is the same.

In noting the tendency for a participant to accept the definitional claims made by the others present, we can appreciate the crucial importance of the information that the individual *initially* possesses or acquires concerning his fellow participants, for it is on the basis of this initial information that the individual starts to define the situation and starts to build up lines of responsive action. The individual's initial projection commits him to what he is proposing to be and requires him to drop all pretenses of being other things. As the interaction among the participants progresses, additions and modifications in this initial informational state will of course occur, but it is essential that these later developments be related without contradiction to, and even built up from, the initial positions taken by several participants. It would seem that an individual can more easily make a choice as to what line of treatment to demand from and extend to the others present at the beginning of an encounter than he can alter the line of treatment that is being pursued once the interaction is underway.

In everyday life, of course, there is a clear understanding that first impressions are important. Thus, the work adjustment of those in service occupations will often hinge upon a capacity to seize and hold the initiative in the service relation, a capacity that will require subtle aggressiveness on the part of the server when he is of lower socio-economic status than his client. W. F. Whyte (1946, 132–133) suggests the waitress as an example:

> The first point that stands out is that the waitress who bears up under pressure does not simply respond to her customers. She acts with some skill to control their behavior. The first question to ask when we look at the customer relationship is, "Does the waitress get the jump on the customers, or does the customer get the jump on the waitress?" The skilled waitress realizes the crucial nature of this question. . . .
>
> The skilled waitress tackles the customer with confidence and without hesitation. For example, she may find that a new customer has seated himself before she could clear off the dirty dishes and change the cloth. He is now leaning on the table studying the menu. She greets him, says, "May I change the cover, please?" and, without waiting for an answer, takes his menu away from him so that he moves back from the table, and she goes about her work. The relationship is handled politely but firmly, and there is never any question as to who is in charge.

When the interaction that is initiated by "first impressions" is itself merely the initial interaction in an extended series of interactions

---

[2] An interaction can be purposely set up as a time and place for voicing differences in opinion, but in such cases participants must be careful to agree not to disagree on the proper tone of voice, vocabulary, and degree of seriousness in which all arguments are to be phrased, and upon the mutual respect which disagreeing participants must carefully continue to express toward one another. This debaters' or academic definition of the situation may also be invoked suddenly and judiciously as a way of translating a serious conflict of views into one that can be handled within a framework acceptable to all present.

involving the same participants, we speak of "getting off on the right foot" and feel that it is crucial that we do so. Thus, one learns that some teachers take the following view:

> "You can't ever let them get the upper hand on you or you're through. So I start out tough. The first day I get a new class in, I let them know who's boss. . . . You've got to start off tough, then you can ease up as you go along. If you start out easy-going, when you try to get tough, they'll just look at you and laugh." (quoted in Becker n.d., 459)

Similarly, attendants in mental institutions may feel that if the new patient is sharply put in his place the first day on the ward and made to see who is boss, much future difficulty will be prevented (Taxel 1953).

Given the fact that the individual effectively projects a definition of the situation when he enters the presence of others, we can assume that events may occur within the interaction which contradict, discredit, or otherwise throw doubt upon this projection. When these disruptive events occur, the interaction itself may come to a confused and embarrassed halt. Some of the assumptions upon which the responses of the participants had been predicated become untenable, and the participants find themselves lodged in an interaction for which the situation has been wrongly defined and is now no longer defined. At such moments the individual whose presentation has been discredited may feel ashamed while the others present may feel hostile, and all the participants may come to feel ill at ease, nonplussed, out of countenance, embarrassed, experiencing the kind of anomy that is generated when the minute social system of face-to-face interaction breaks down.

In stressing the fact that the initial definition of the situation projected by an individual tends to provide a plan for the cooperative activity that follows—in stressing this action point of view—we must not overlook the crucial fact that any projected definition of the situation also has a distinctive moral character. It is this moral character of projections that will chiefly concern us in this report. Society is organized on the principle that any individual who possesses certain social characteristics has a moral right to expect that others will value and treat him in an appropriate way. Connected with this principle is a second, namely that an individual who implicitly or explicitly signifies that he has certain social characteristics ought in fact to be what he claims he is. In consequence, when an individual projects a definition of the situation and thereby makes an implicit or explicit claim to be a person of a particular kind, he automatically exerts a moral demand upon the others, obliging them to value and treat him in the manner that persons of his kind have a right to expect. He also implicitly forgoes all claims to be things he does not appear to be and hence forgoes the treatment that would be appropriate for such individuals. The others find, then, that the individual has informed them as to what is and as to what they *ought* to see as the "is."

One cannot judge the importance of definitional disruptions by the frequency with which they occur, for apparently they would occur more frequently were not constant precautions taken. We find that preventive practices are constantly employed to avoid these embarrassments and that corrective practices are constantly employed to compensate for discrediting occurrences that have not been successfully avoided. When the individual employs these strategies and tactics to protect his own projections, we may refer to them as "defensive practices"; when a participant employs them to save the definition of the situation projected by another, we speak of "protective practices" or "tact." Together, defensive and protective practices comprise the techniques employed to safeguard the impression fostered by an individual during his presence before others. It should be added that while we may be ready to see that no fostered impression would survive if defensive practices were not employed, we are less ready perhaps to see that few impressions could survive if those who received the impression did not exert tact in their reception of it.

In addition to the fact that precautions are taken to prevent disruption of projected definitions, we may also note that an intense interest in these disruptions comes to play a significant role in the social life of the group. Practical jokes and social games are played in which embarrassments which are to be taken unseriously are purposely engineered. Fantasies are created in which devastating exposures occur. Anecdotes from the past—real, embroidered, or fictitious—are told and retold, detailing disruptions which occurred, almost occurred, or occurred and were admirably resolved. There seems to be no grouping which does not have a ready supply of these games, reveries, and cautionary tales, to be used as a source of humor, a catharsis for anxieties, and a sanction for inducing individuals to be modest in their claims and reasonable in their projected expectations. The individual may tell himself through dreams of getting into impossible positions. Families tell of the time a guest got his dates mixed and arrived when neither the house nor anyone in it was ready for him. Journalists tell of times when an all-too-meaningful misprint occurred, and the paper's assumption of objectivity or decorum was humorously discredited. Public servants tell of times a client ridiculously misunderstood form instructions, giving answers which implied an unanticipated and bizarre definition of the situation (Blau n.d., 127–129). Seamen, whose home away from home is rigorously he-man, tell stories of coming back home and inadvertently asking mother to "pass the fucking butter" (Beattie 1950, 35). Diplomats tell of the time a nearsighted queen asked a republican ambassador about the health of his king (Ponsonby 1952, 46). . . .

It will be convenient to end this introduction with some definitions that are implied in what has gone before and required for what is to follow. For the purpose of this report, interaction (that is, face-to-face interaction) may be roughly defined as the reciprocal influence of individuals upon one another's actions when in one another's immediate physical presence. *An* interaction may be defined as all the interaction which occurs throughout any one occasion when a given set of individuals are in one another's continuous presence; the term "an encounter" would do as well. A "performance" may be defined as all the activity of a given participant on a given occasion which serves to influence in any way any of the other participants. Taking a particular participant and his performance as a basic point of reference, we may refer to those who contribute the other performances as the audience, observers, or co-participants. The pre-established pattern of action which is unfolded during a performance and which may be presented or played through on other occasions may be called a "part" or "routine." These situational terms can easily be related to conventional structural ones. When an individual or performer plays the same part to the same audience on different occasions, a social relationship is likely to arise. Defining social role as the enactment of rights and duties attached to a given status, we can say that a social role will involve one or more parts and that each of these different parts may be presented by the performer on a series of occasions to the same kinds of audience or to an audience of the same persons.

References

Beattie, Walter M., Jr. 1950. "The Merchant Seaman." Unpublished M. A. report, Department of Sociology, University of Chicago.

Becker, Howard S. n.d. "Social Class Variations in the Teacher–Pupil Relationship." *Journal of Educational Sociology* 25.

Blau, Peter. n.d. "Dynamics of Bureaucracy." Ph.D. dissertation, Department of Sociology, Columbia University.

Ichheiser, Gustav. 1949. "Misunderstandings in Human Relations." Supplement to *The American Journal of Sociology* 55 (September).

Ponsonby, Sir Frederick. 1952. *Recollections of Three Reigns.* New York: Dutton.

Sansom, William. 1956. *A Contest of Ladies.* London: Hogarth.

Taxel, Harold. 1953. "Authority Structure in a Mental Hospital Ward." Unpublished M.A. thesis, Department of Sociology, University of Chicago.

Volkart, E. H. (ed.). 1951. "Contributions of W. I. Thomas to Theory and Social Research." In *Social Behavior and Personality.* New York: Social Science Research Council.

Waller, Willard. n.d. "The Rating and Dating Complex." *American Sociological Review* 2.

Whyte, W. F. 1946. "When Workers and Customers Meet." Chap. 7 in W. F. Whyte (ed.), *Industry and Society.* New York: McGraw-Hill.

Questions

1. What is Goffman's distinction between expressions that one gives and expressions that one gives off?

2. Suppose you are about to visit your professor to ask a question about the upcoming exam. Besides information gathering, you would like to influence your professor's definition of the situation such that he or she infers that you are a smart student. How might you do this (in terms of both expressions you give and expressions you give off)?

   Now suppose you are preparing for a date that you've been looking forward to for several days. Your goal this time is to have fun and to influence your date's definition of the situation so that he or she infers that you are a cool person. How might you do this?

   Is there a difference between how you would act in each situation? Which is the "real" you?

3. Think of a time in which you exercised "tact." Using that situation as an example, how did you (as Goffman would say) employ this projective technique in order to save the definition of the situation projected by another?

·15·

The Pathology of Imprisonment

Philip G. Zimbardo

When I was a kid in school, I was very shy. I rarely volunteered answers to questions posed by my teachers, and I cringed whenever I was asked to do an arithmetic problem on the chalkboard. That wasn't the best way to fulfill my role as a student, but it was an acceptable way. Now I am a professor, and I am the one who not only asks questions but makes scholarly pronouncements that I expect everyone in the room to write down. My first-grade teacher, who regarded my shyness with despair, would be shocked to see that I actually seem to do these professorial things comfortably. Has my personality changed? Not really. I'm still shy. But the role expectations of a professor evoke a different side of me, one that's "outgoing" and even extroverted. As you will read in this 1972 article by Philip Zimbardo, roles—the social scripts that are attached to the statuses people occupy—are powerfully evocative. They can bring out parts of someone's "personality" that the individual never knew existed.

I was recently released from solitary confinement after being held therein for 37 months [months!]. A silent system was imposed upon me and to even whisper to the man in the next cell resulted in being beaten by guards, sprayed with chemical mace, blackjacked, stomped and thrown into a strip-cell naked to sleep on a concrete floor without bedding, covering, wash basin or even a toilet. The floor served as toilet and bed, and even there the silent system was enforced. To let a moan escape your lips because of the pain and discomfort . . . resulted in another beating. I spent not days, but months there during my 37 months in solitary. . . . I have filed every writ possible against the administrative acts of brutality. The state courts have all denied the petitions. Because of my refusal

to let the things die down and forget all that happened during my 37 months in solitary . . . I am the most hated prisoner in [this] penitentiary, and called a "hard-core incorrigible."

Maybe I am an incorrigible, but if true, it's because I would rather die than to accept being treated as less than a human being. I have never complained of my prison sentence as being unjustified except through legal means of appeals. I have never put a knife on a guard's throat and demanded my release. I know that thieves must be punished and I don't justify stealing, even though I am a thief myself. But now I don't think I will be a thief when I am released. No, I'm not rehabilitated. It's just that I no longer think of becoming wealthy by stealing. I now only think of killing—killing those who have beaten me and treated me as if I were a dog. I hope and pray for the sake of my own soul and future life of freedom that I am able to overcome the bitterness and hatred which eats daily at my soul, but I know to overcome it will not be easy.

This eloquent plea for prison reform — for humane treatment of human beings, for the basic dignity that is the right of every American — came to me secretly in a letter from a prisoner who cannot be identified because he is still in a state correctional institution. He sent it to me because he read of an experiment I recently conducted at Stanford University. In an attempt to understand just what it means psychologically to be a prisoner or a prison guard, Craig Haney, Curt Banks, Dave Jaffe and I created our own prison. We carefully screened over 70 volunteers who answered an ad in a Palo Alto city newspaper and ended up with about two dozen young men who were selected to be part of this study. They were mature, emotionally stable, normal, intelligent college students from middle-class homes throughout the United States and Canada. They appeared to represent the cream of the crop of this generation. None had any criminal record and all were relatively homogeneous on many dimensions initially.

Half were arbitrarily designated as prisoners by a flip of a coin, the others as guards. These were the roles they were to play in our simulated prison. The guards were made aware of the potential seriousness and danger of the situation and their own vulnerability. They made up their own formal rules for maintaining law, order and respect, and were generally free to improvise new ones during their eight-hour, three-man shifts. The prisoners were unexpectedly picked up at their homes by a city policeman in a squad car, searched, handcuffed, fingerprinted, booked at the Palo Alto station house and taken blindfolded to our jail. There they were stripped, deloused, put into a uniform, given a number and put into a cell with two other prisoners where they expected to live for the next two weeks. The pay was good ($15 a day) and their motivation was to make money.

We observed and recorded on videotape the events that occurred in the prison, and we interviewed and tested the prisoners and guards at various points throughout the study. Some of the videotapes of the actual encounters between the prisoners and guards were seen on the NBC News feature "Chronolog" on November 26, 1971.

At the end of only six days we had to close down our mock prison because what we saw was frightening. It was no longer apparent to most of the subjects (or to us) where reality ended and their roles began. The majority had indeed become prisoners or guards, no longer able to clearly differentiate between role playing and self. There were dramatic changes in virtually every aspect of their behavior, thinking and feeling. In less than a week the experience of imprisonment undid (temporarily) a lifetime of learning; human values were suspended, self-concepts were challenged and the ugliest, most base, pathological side of human nature surfaced. We were horrified because we saw some boys (guards) treat others as if they were despicable animals, taking pleasure in cruelty, while other boys (prisoners) became servile, dehumanized robots who thought only of escape, of their own individual survival and of their mounting hatred for the guards.

We had to release three prisoners in the first four days because they had such acute situational traumatic reactions as hysterical crying, confusion in thinking and severe depression. Others begged to be paroled, and all but three were willing to forfeit all the money they had earned if they could be paroled. By then (the fifth day) they had been so programmed to think of themselves as prisoners that when their request for parole was denied, they returned docilely to their cells. Now, had they been thinking as college students acting in an oppressive experiment, they would have quit once they no longer wanted the $15 a day we used as our only incentive. However, the reality was not quitting an experiment but "being paroled by the parole board from the Stanford County Jail." By the last days, the earlier solidarity among the prisoners (systematically broken by the guards) dissolved into "each man for himself." Finally, when one of their fellows was put in solitary confinement (a small closet) for refusing to eat, the prisoners were given a choice by one of the guards: give up their blankets and the incorrigible prisoner would be let out, or keep their blankets and he would be kept in all night. They voted to keep their blankets and to abandon their brother.

About a third of the guards became tyrannical in their arbitrary use of power, in enjoying their control over other people. They were corrupted by the power of their roles and became quite inventive in their techniques of breaking the spirit of the prisoners and making them feel they were worthless. Some of the guards merely did their jobs as tough but fair correctional officers, and several were good guards from the prisoners' point of view since they did them small favors and were friendly. However, no good guard ever interfered with a command by any of the bad guards; they never intervened on the side of the prisoners, they never told the others to ease off because it was only an experiment, and they never even came to me as prison superintendent or experimenter in charge to complain. In part, they were good because the others were bad; they needed the others to help establish their own egos in a positive light. In a sense, the good guards perpetuated the prison more than the other guards because their own needs to be liked prevented them from disobeying or violating the implicit guards' code. At the same time, the act of befriending the prisoners created a social reality which made the prisoners less likely to rebel.

By the end of the week the experiment had become a reality, as if it were a Pirandello[1]

play directed by Kafka[2] that just keeps going after the audience has left. The consultant for our prison, Carlo Prescott, an ex-convict with 16 years of imprisonment in California's jails, would get so depressed and furious each time he visited our prison, because of its psychological similarity to his experiences, that he would have to leave. A Catholic priest who was a former prison chaplain in Washington, D.C., talked to our prisoners after four days and said they were just like the other first-timers he had seen.

But in the end, I called off the experiment not because of the horror I saw out there in the prison yard, but because of the horror of realizing that *I* could have easily traded places with the most brutal guard or become the weakest prisoner full of hatred at being so powerless that I could not eat, sleep or go to the toilet without permission of the authorities. *I* could have become Calley at My Lai, George Jackson at San Quentin, one of the men at Attica or the prisoner quoted at the beginning of this article.

Individual behavior is largely under the control of social forces and environmental contingencies rather than personality traits, character, will power or other empirically unvalidated constructs. Thus we create an illusion of freedom by attributing more internal control to ourselves, to the individual, than actually exists. We thus underestimate the power and pervasiveness of situational controls over behavior because (a) they are often non-obvious and subtle, (b) we can often avoid entering situations where we might be so controlled, (c) we label as "weak" or "deviant" people in those

---

[1] Luigi Pirandello (1867–1936) was a Sicilian author. He won the 1934 Nobel Prize for literature. His fame is primarily owing to his grimly humorous plays dealing with the confusions of illusions and reality (for example, *Six Characters in Search of an Author*). —Ed.

[2] The writer Franz Kafka (1883–1924) was born in Prague of Jewish parents. In his novels and short stories, Kafka painted a world that was steeped in illusion and contradiction. His characters suffered from feelings of guilt, anxiety, and despair and an overwhelming sense of futility as they struggled to cope with rigid bureaucracies and totalitarian regimes. Today, similarly tortured visions of society are often referred to as "Kafkaesque." —Ed.

situations who do behave differently from how we believe we would.

Each of us carries around in our heads a favorable self-image in which we are essentially just, fair, humane and understanding. For example, we could not imagine inflicting pain on others without much provocation or hurting people who had done nothing to us, who in fact were even liked by us. However, there is a growing body of social psychological research which underscores the conclusion derived from this prison study. Many people, perhaps the majority, can be made to do almost anything when put into psychologically compelling situations—regardless of their morals, ethics, values, attitudes, beliefs or personal convictions. My colleague, Stanley Milgram, has shown that more than 60 percent of the population will deliver what they think is a series of painful electric shocks to another person even after the victim cries for mercy, begs them to stop and then apparently passes out. The subjects complained that they did not want to inflict more pain but blindly obeyed the command of the authority figure (the experimenter) who said that they must go on. In my own research on violence, I have seen mild-mannered coeds repeatedly give shocks (which they thought were causing pain) to another girl, a

stranger whom they had rated very favorably, simply by being made to feel anonymous and put in a situation where they were expected to engage in this activity.

Observers of these and similar experimental situations never predict their outcomes and estimate that it is unlikely that they themselves would behave similarly. They can be so confident only when they are outside the situation. However, since the majority of people in these studies do act in non-rational, non-obvious ways, it follows that the majority of observers would also succumb to the social psychological forces in the situation.

With regard to prisons, we can state that the mere act of assigning labels to people and putting them into a situation where those labels acquire validity and meaning is sufficient to elicit pathological behavior. This pathology is not predictable from any available diagnostic indicators we have in the social sciences, and is extreme enough to modify in very significant ways fundamental attitudes and behavior. The prison situation, as presently arranged, is guaranteed to generate severe enough pathological reactions in both guards and prisoners as to debase their humanity, lower their feelings of self-worth and make it difficult for them to be part of a society outside of their prison. . . .

Questions

1. What are the similarities between Zimbardo's findings and Milgram's (see reading 7)?

2. Zimbardo's experiment cemented sociologists' conviction that the roles people play have a lot of power to elicit particular behaviors from them. Sociologists refer to the process by which people take on socially constructed roles and carry them out as "role-taking." The men chosen to be prisoners and to be guards were, for all intents and purposes, the same until they took on their respective roles; it was taking on and

playing the roles that "changed" them (or elicited new behaviors from them).

Role-taking is a part of everyday life. When an individual reaches adulthood (or possibly sooner!), he or she may take the status and role of married person—husband or wife. As many women and men have found in recent decades, it is hard to change those roles to fit new understandings of, for example, gender roles. But sociologists are aware that all people, in all cases, do not simply take on conventional roles, that people do not simply do role-taking. In some cases, people adapt the roles to themselves rather than the other way around. Sociologists call that "role-making." It isn't easy; when you do not act the way people expect you to act, you can expect some sort of response— often, informal negative sanctions. Think of the young man who wishes, for example, to study ballet rather than football. He wants to make the role of young man fit his own proclivities.

Consider how you play the role of student. What things do you do that an observer would judge to be role-taking? What do you do that an observer would judge to be role-making?

·16·
Marked
Women in the Workplace

Deborah Tannen

As I discussed in chapter 8 in *The Practical Skeptic: Core Concepts in Sociology*, a status is a position in a group that an individual may occupy. Each status comes with a role—and a series of expectations about how the individual should carry out the role. But, as Deborah Tannen explains, even when people occupy the same status, the expectations that others have of them may differ depending on seemingly unrelated factors. In this 1994 essay, Tannen describes how some status incumbents are "marked" by virtue of their sex and how this makes a difference.

Some years ago I was at a small working conference of four women and eight men. Instead of concentrating on the discussion, I found myself looking at the three other women at the table, thinking how each had a different style and how each style was coherent.

One woman had dark brown hair in a classic style that was a cross between Cleopatra and Plain Jane. The severity of her straight hair was softened by wavy bangs and ends that turned under. Because she was beautiful, the effect was more Cleopatra than plain.

The second woman was older, full of dignity and composure. Her hair was cut in a fashionable style that left her with only one eye, thanks to a side part that let a curtain of hair fall across half her face. As she looked down to read her prepared paper, the hair robbed her of binocular vision and created a barrier between her and the listeners.

The third woman's hair was wild, a frosted blond avalanche falling over and beyond her shoulders. When she spoke, she frequently tossed her head, thus calling attention to her hair and away from her lecture.

Then there was makeup. The first woman wore facial cover that made her skin smooth and pale, a black line under each eye, and mascara that darkened her already dark lashes. The second wore only a light gloss on her lips and a hint of shadow on her eyes. The third had blue bands under her eyes, dark blue shadow, mascara, bright red lipstick, and rouge; her fingernails also flashed red.

I considered the clothes each woman had worn on the three days of the conference: In the first case, man-tailored suits in primary colors with solid-color blouses. In the second, casual but stylish black T-shirt, a floppy collarless jacket and baggy slacks or skirt in neutral colors. The third wore a sexy jumpsuit; tight sleeveless jersey and tight yellow slacks; a dress with gaping armholes and an indulged tendency to fall off one shoulder.

Shoes? The first woman wore string sandals with medium heels; the second, sensible, comfortable walking shoes; the third, pumps with spike heels. You can fill in the jewelry, scarves, shawls, sweaters—or lack of them.

As I amused myself finding patterns and coherence in these styles and choices, I suddenly wondered why I was scrutinizing only the women. I scanned the table to get a fix on the styles of the eight men. And then I knew why I wasn't studying them. The men's styles were unmarked.

The term "marked" is a staple of linguistic theory. It refers to the way language alters the base meaning of a word by adding something—a little linguistic addition that has no meaning on its own. The unmarked form of a word carries the meaning that goes without saying, what you think of when you're not thinking anything special.

The unmarked tense of verbs in English is the present—for example, *visit*. To indicate past, you have to mark the verb for "past" by adding *ed* to yield *visited*. For future, you add a word: *will visit*. Nouns are presumed to be singular until marked for plural. To convey the idea of more than one, we typically add something, usually *s* or *es*. More than one *visit* becomes *visits,* and one *dish* becomes two *dishes,* thanks to the plural marking.

The unmarked forms of most English words also convey "male." Being male is the unmarked case. We have endings, such as *ess* and *ette,* to mark words as female. Unfortunately, marking words for female also, by association, tends to mark them for frivolousness. Would you feel safe entrusting your life to a doctorette? This is why many poets and actors who happen to be female object to the marked forms "poetess" and "actress." Alfre Woodard, an Oscar nominee for Best Supporting Actress, says she identifies herself as an actor because "actresses worry about eyelashes and cellulite, and women who are actors worry about the characters we are playing." Any marked form can pick up extra meaning beyond what the marking is intended to denote. The extra meanings carried by gender markers reflect the traditional associations with the female gender: not quite serious, often sexual.

I was able to identify the styles and types of the women at the conference because each of us had to make decisions about hair, clothing, makeup and accessories, and each of those decisions carried meaning. Every style available to us was marked. Of course, the men in our group had to make decisions too, but their choices carried far less meaning. The men could have chosen styles that were marked, but they didn't have to, and in this group, none did. Unlike the women, they had the option of being unmarked.

I took account of the men's clothes. There could have been a cowboy shirt with string tie or a three-piece suit or a necklaced hippie in jeans. But there wasn't. All eight men wore brown or blue slacks and standard-style shirts of light colors.

No man wore sandals or boots; their shoes were dark, closed, comfortable, and flat. In short, unmarked.

Although no man wore makeup, you couldn't say the men didn't wear makeup in the sense that you could say a woman didn't wear makeup. For men, no makeup is unmarked.

I asked myself what style we women could have adopted that would have been unmarked, like the men's. The answer was: none. There is no unmarked woman.

There is no woman's hairstyle that could be called "standard," that says nothing about her. The range of women's hairstyles is staggering, but if a woman's hair has no particular style, this in itself is taken as a statement that she doesn't care how she looks—an eloquent message that can disqualify a woman for many positions.

Women have to choose between shoes that are comfortable and shoes that are deemed attractive. When our group had to make an unexpected trek, the woman who wore flat laced shoes arrived first. The last to arrive was the woman with spike heels, her shoes in her hand and a handful of men around her.

If a woman's clothes are tight or revealing (in other words, sexy), it sends a message—an intended one of wanting to be attractive but also a possibly unintended one of availability. But if her clothes are not sexy, that too sends a message, lent meaning by the knowledge that they could have been. In her book *Women Lawyers*, Mona Harrington quotes a woman who, despite being a partner in her firm, found herself slipping into this fault line when she got an unexpected call to go to court right away. As she headed out the door, a young (male) associate said to her, "Hadn't you better button your blouse?" She was caught completely off guard. "My blouse wasn't buttoned unusually low," the woman told Harrington. "And this was not a conservative guy. But he thought one more button was necessary for court." And here's the rub: "I started wondering if my authority was being undermined by one button."

A woman wearing bright colors calls attention to herself, but if she avoids bright colors, she has (as my choice of verb in this sentence suggests) avoided something. Heavy makeup calls attention to the wearer as someone who wants to be attractive. Light makeup tries to be attractive without being alluring. There are thousands of products from which makeup must be chosen and myriad ways of applying them. Yet no makeup at all is anything but unmarked. Some men even see it as a hostile refusal to please them. Women who ordinarily do not wear makeup can be surprised by the transforming effect of putting it on. In a book titled *Face Value*, my colleague Robin Lakoff noted the increased attention she got from men when she went forth from a television station still professionally made-up.

Women can't even fill out a form without telling stories about themselves. Most application forms now give four choices for titles. Men have one to choose—"Mr."—so their choice carries no meaning other than to say they are male. But women must choose among three, each of them marked. A woman who checks the box for "Mrs." or "Miss" communicates not only whether she has been married but also that she had conservative tastes in forms of address, and probably other conservative values as well. Checking "Ms." declines to let on about marriage (whereas "Mr." declines nothing since nothing was asked), but it also marks the woman who checks it on her form as either liberated or rebellious, depending on the attitudes and assumptions of the one making the judgment.

I sometimes try to duck these variously marked choices by giving my title as "Dr."—and thereby risk marking myself as either uppity (hence sarcastic responses like "Excuse *me!*") or an over-achiever (hence reactions of congratulatory surprise, like "Good for you!").

All married women's surnames are marked. If a woman takes her husband's name, she announces to the world that she is married and also that she is traditional in her values, according to some observers. To others it will indicate that she is less herself, more identified by her husband's identity. If she does not take her husband's name, this too is marked, seen as worthy of comment: She has *done* something; she has "kept her own name." Though a man can do exactly the same thing—and usually does—he is never said to have "kept his own name," because it never occurs to anyone that he might have given it up. For him, but not for her, using his own name is unmarked.

A married woman who wants to have her cake and eat it too may use her surname plus his. But this too announces that she is or has been married and often results in a tongue-tying string that makes life miserable for anyone who needs to alphabetize it. In a list (Harvey O'Donovan, Jonathan Feldman, Stephanie Woodbury McGillicutty), the woman's multiple name stands out. It is marked.

Pronouns conspire in this pattern as well. Grammar books tell us that "he" means "he or she" and that "she" is used only if a referent is specifically female. But this touting of "he" as the sex-indefinite pronoun is an innovation introduced into English by grammarians in the eighteenth and nineteenth centuries, according to Peter Mühlhäusler and Rom Harré in their book *Pronouns and People.* From at least about the year 1500, the correct sex-indefinite pronoun was "they," as it still is in casual spoken English. In other words, the female was declared by grammarians to be the marked case.

Looking at the men and women sitting around the conference table, I was amazed at how different our worlds were. Though men have to make choices too, and men's clothing styles may be less neutral now than they once were, nonetheless the parameters within which men must choose when dressing for work — the cut, fabric, or shade of jackets, shirts, and pants, and even the one area in which they are able to go a little wild, ties — are much narrower than the riotous range of colors and styles from which women must choose. For women, decisions about whether to wear a skirt, slacks, or a dress is only the start; the length of skirts can range from just above the floor to just below the hips, and the array of colors to choose from would make a rainbow look drab. But even this contrast in the range from which men and women must choose is irrelevant to the crucial point: A man can choose a style that will not attract attention or subject him to any particular interpretation, but a woman can't. Whatever she wears, whatever she calls herself, however she talks, will be fodder for interpretation about her character and competence. In a setting where most of the players are men, there is no unmarked woman.

This does not mean that men have complete freedom when it comes to dress. Quite the contrary — they have much less freedom than women have to express their personalities in their choice of fabrics, colors, styles, and jewelry. But the one freedom they have that women don't is the point of this discussion — the freedom to be unmarked.

That clothing is a metaphor for women's being marked was noticed by David Finkel, a journalist who wrote an article about women in Congress for *The Washington Post Magazine.* He used the contrast between women's and men's dress to open his article by describing the members coming through the doors to the floor of the U.S. House of Representatives:

> So many men, so many suits. Dark suits. Solid suits. Blue suits that look gray, gray suits that look blue. There's Tom Foley — he's in one, and Bob Michel, and Steny Hoyer, and Fred Grandy, and Dick Durbin, and dozens, make that hundreds, more.
>
> So many suits, so many white shirts. And dark ties. And five o'clock shadows. And short haircuts. And loosening jowls. And big, visible ears.
>
> So many, many men.
>
> . . .
>
> And still the members continue to pour through the doors — gray, grayer, grayest — until the moment when, emerging into this humidor, comes a surprise:
>
> The color red.
>
> It is Susan Molinari, a first-termer from New York . . .
>
> Now, turquoise. It is Barbara Boxer . . .
>
> Now, paisley. It is Jill Long . . .

Embroidering his color-of-clothing metaphor, Finkel, whose article appeared in May 1992, concluded, "Of the 435 members of the House of Representatives, 29 are women, which means that if Congress is a gray flannel suit, the women of Congress are no more than a handful of spots on the lapel."

When Is Sexism Realism?

If women are marked in our culture, their very presence in professional roles is, more often than not, marked. Many work settings, just like families, come with ready-made roles prescribed by gender, and the ones women are expected to fill are typically support roles. It was not long ago when medical offices and hospitals were peopled by men who were doctors and orderlies and women who were nurses and clerical workers, just as most offices were composed of men who ran the business and women who served them as receptionists, clerks, and secretaries. All members of Congress were men, and women found in the Capitol Building were aides and staff members. When a woman or man enters a setting in an atypical role, the expectation is always a backdrop to the scene.

All the freshmen women in Congress have had to contend with being mistaken for staff, even though they wear pins on their lapels identifying them as members. For her book *A Woman's Place*, Congresswoman Marjorie Margolies-Mezvinsky interviewed her female colleagues about their experiences. One congresswoman approached a security checkpoint with two congressmen when a guard stopped only her and told her to go through the metal detector. When Congresswoman Maria Cantwell needed to get into her office after hours, the guard wanted to know which member she worked for. But her press secretary, Larry West, has gone through the gate unthinkingly without being stopped. When Congresswoman Lynn Schenk attended a reception with a male aide, the host graciously held out his hand to the aide and said "Oh, Congressman Schenk."

You don't have to be in Congress to have experiences like that. A woman who owned her own business found that if she took any man along on business trips, regardless of whether he was her vice president or her assistant, people she met tended to address themselves to him, certain that he must be the one with power and she his helper. A double-bass player had a similar experience when she arrived for an audition with a male accompanist. The people who greeted them assumed she was the accompanist. A woman who heads a research firm and holds a doctorate finds she is frequently addressed as "Mrs.," while her assistant, who holds only a master's degree, is addressed as "Dr."

One evening after hours, I was working in my office at Georgetown University. Faculty offices in my building are lined up on both sides of a corridor, with cubicles in the corridor for secretaries and graduate-student assistants. Outside each office is a nameplate with the professor's title and last name. The quiet of the after-hours corridor was interrupted when a woman came to my door and asked if she could use my phone. I was surprised but glad to oblige, and explained that she had to dial "9." She made the call, thanked me, and left. A few minutes later, she reappeared and asked if I had any correction fluid. Again surprised, but still happy to be of help, I looked in my desk drawer but had to disappoint her: Since my typewriter was self-correcting, I had none. My patience began to waver, but my puzzlement was banished when the woman bounded into my office for the third and final time to ask if I was Dr. Murphy's secretary, in which case she would like to leave with me the paper she was turning in to him.

I doubt this woman would have imposed on my time and space to use my telephone and borrow correction fluid if she had known I was a professor, even though I would not have minded had she done so. At least she would probably have been more deferential in intruding. And the experience certainly gave me a taste of how hard it must be for receptionists to get any work done, as everyone regards them as perpetually interruptible. But what amused and amazed me was that my being female had overridden so many clues to my position: My office was along the wall, it was fully enclosed like all faculty offices, my name and title were on the door, and I was working after five, the hour when offices close and secretaries go home. But all these clues were nothing next to the master clue of gender: In the university environment, she expected that professors were men and women were secretaries. Statistics were on her side: Of the eighteen members of my department at the time, sixteen were men; of the five members of Dr. Murphy's department, four were men. So she was simply trusting the world to be as she knew it was.

It is not particularly ironic or surprising that the student who mistook me for a secretary was female. Women are no less prone to assume that people will adhere to the norm than are men. And this includes women who themselves are exceptions. A woman physician who works in a specialty in which few of her colleagues are female told me of her annoyance when she telephones a colleague, identifies herself as "Dr. Jones calling for Dr. Smith," and is told by Dr. Smith's receptionist, "I'll go get Dr. Smith while you put Dr. Jones on the line." But this same woman catches herself referring to her patients' general practitioners as "he," even though she ought to know better than anyone that a physician could be a woman.

Children seem to pick up norms as surely as adults do. A woman who was not only a doctor but a professor at a medical school was surprised when her five-year-old said to her, "You're not a doctor, Mommy. You're a nurse." Intent on impressing her daughter, she said, "Yes, I am a doctor. In fact, I teach other doctors how to be doctors." The little girl thought about this as she incorporated the knowledge into her worldview. "Oh," she said. "But you only teach women doctors." (Conversely, male nurses must deal with being mistaken for doctors, and men who work as assistants must deal with being mistaken for their boss.)

Another of my favorite stories in this mode is about my colleague who made a plane reservation for herself and replied to the question "Is that Mrs. or Miss?" by giving her title: "It's Dr." So the agent asked, "Will the doctor be needing a rental car when he arrives?" Her attempt to reframe her answer to avoid revealing her marital status resulted in the agent reframing her as a secretary.

I relate these stories not to argue that sexism is rampant and that we should all try to bear in mind that roles are changing, although I believe these statements to be true. I am inclined to be indulgent of such errors, even though I am made uncomfortable when they happen to me, because I myself have been guilty of them. I recall an occasion when I gave a talk to a gathering of women physicians, and then signed books. The woman who organized the signing told me to save one book because she had met a doctor in the elevator who couldn't make it to the talk but asked to have a book signed nonetheless. I was pleased to oblige and asked, pen poised, to whom I should sign the book—and was surprised when I heard a woman's name. Even though I had just spent the evening with a room full of doctors who were all women, in my mind "a doctor" had called up the image of a man.

So long as women are a minority of professional ranks, we cannot be surprised if people assume the world is as it is. I mention these stories to give a sense of what the world is like for people who are exceptions to expectations—every moment they live in the unexpected role, they must struggle against others' assumptions that do not apply to them, much like gay men and lesbians with regard to their sexual orientation, and, as Ellis Cose documents in his book *The Rage of a Privileged Class,* much like middle-class black professionals in most American settings.

One particular burden of this pattern for a woman in a position of authority is that she must deal with incursions on her time, as others make automatic assumptions that her time is more expendable, although she also may benefit from hearing more information because people find her "approachable." There is a sense in which every woman is seen as a receptionist—available to give information and help, perennially interruptible. A woman surgeon complained that although she has very good relations with the nurses in her hospital, they simply do not wait on her the way they wait on her male colleagues. (The very fact that I must say "woman surgeon" and "male nurse" reflects this dilemma: All surgeons are presumed male, all nurses presumed female, unless proven otherwise. In other words, the unmarked surgeon is male, the unmarked nurse female.)

Questions

1. Tannen asserts that "any marked form [of a word] can pick up extra meaning beyond what the marking is intended to denote." Consider the terms *waitress* and *waiter*. Do these words suggest anything other than a woman who waits on tables and a man who waits on tables?

2. Tannen suggests that in the business world, women do not have the freedom to be "unmarked." Is this true only in the business world? What about among college students? Do female college students have more or less freedom to be unmarked than women in the business world? How about men?

3. Assume that there are three types of jobs in our society: those whose incumbents are expected to be men, those whose incumbents are expected to be women, and those for whom there are no expectations about the sex of incumbents. Try to list a half dozen examples for each category. How difficult is this task?

   Look at your three lists. What do the jobs within each list have in common with one another?

·17·

"Getting" and "Making" a Tip

Greta Foff Paules

In this 1991 article, Greta Foff Paules, who received a Ph.D. in cultural anthropology from Princeton University, takes us into the world of the waitress. If you've never waited on tables, you might naturally assume that waitresses (and waiters, for that matter) are there to serve the customers. But as Paules discovered through participant observation, there is a lot more to the customer–waitress relationship than meets the eye. You decide who has what kind of power in this relationship.

The waitress can't help feeling a sense of personal failure and public censure when she is "stiffed."

— William F. Whyte, "When Workers and Customers Meet"

They're rude, they're ignorant, they're obnoxious, they're inconsiderate. . . . Half of these people don't deserve to come out and eat, let alone try and tip a waitress.

— Route waitress

Making a Tip at Route

A common feature of past research is that the worker's control over the tipping system is evaluated in terms of her efforts to con, coerce, compel, or otherwise manipulate a customer into relinquishing a bigger tip. Because these efforts have for the most part proven futile, the worker has been seen as having little defense against the financial vicissitudes of the tipping system. What these studies have overlooked is

that an employee can increase her tip income by controlling the number as well as the size of tips she receives. This oversight has arisen from the tendency of researchers to concentrate narrowly on the relationship between server and served, while failing to take into account the broader organizational context in which this relationship takes place.

Like service workers observed in earlier studies, waitresses at Route strive to boost the amount of individual gratuities by rendering special services and being especially friendly. As one waitress put it, "I'll sell you the world if you're in my station." In general though, waitresses at Route Restaurant seek to boost their tip income, not by increasing the amount of individual gratuities, but by increasing the number of customers they serve. They accomplish this (a) by securing the largest or busiest stations and working the most lucrative shifts; (b) by "turning" their tables quickly; and (c) by controlling the flow of customers within the restaurant.

Technically, stations at Route are assigned on a rotating basis so that all waitresses, including rookies, work fast and slow stations equally. Station assignments are listed on the work schedule that is posted in the office window where it can be examined by all workers on all shifts, precluding the possibility of blatant favoritism or discrimination. Yet a number of methods exist whereby experienced waitresses are able to circumvent the formal rotation system and secure the more lucrative stations for themselves. A waitress can trade assignments with a rookie who is uncertain of her ability to handle a fast station; she can volunteer to take over a large station when a *call-out*[1] necessitates reorganization of station assignments; or she can establish herself as the only waitress capable of handling a particularly large or chaotic station. Changes in station assignments tend not to be formally recorded, so inconsistencies in the rotation system often do not show up on the schedule. Waitresses on the same shift may notice of course that a co-worker has managed to avoid an especially slow station for many days, or has somehow ended up in the busiest station two weekends in a row, but the waitresses' code of noninterference . . . inhibits them from openly objecting to such irregularities.

A waitress can also increase her tip income by working the more lucrative shifts. Because day is the busiest and therefore most profitable shift at Route, it attracts experienced, professional waitresses who are most concerned and best able to maximize their tip earnings. There are exceptions: some competent, senior-ranking waitresses are unable to work during the day due to time constraints of family or second jobs. Others choose not to work during the day despite the potential monetary rewards, because they are unwilling to endure the intensely competitive atmosphere for which day shift is infamous.

The acutely competitive environment that characterizes day shift arises from the aggregate striving of each waitress to maximize her tip income by serving the greatest possible number of customers. Two strategies are enlisted to this end. First, each waitress attempts to *turn* her tables as quickly as possible. Briefly stated, this means she takes the order, delivers the food, clears and resets a table, and begins serving the next party as rapidly as customer lingering and the speed of the kitchen allow. A seven-year veteran of Route describes the strategy and its rewards:

> What I do is I prebus my tables. When the people get up and go all I got is glasses and cups, pull off, wipe, set, and I do the table turnover. But see that's from day shift. See the girls on graveyard . . . don't understand the more times you turn that table the more money you make. You could have three tables and still make a hundred dollars. If you turn them tables.

As the waitress indicates, a large part of turning tables involves getting the table cleared and set for the next customer. During a rush, swing and grave waitresses tend to leave dirty tables standing, partly because they are less experienced and therefore less efficient, partly to avoid being given parties, or *sat,* when they are already behind. In contrast, day waitresses assign high priority to keeping their tables cleared and ready for customers. The difference in method reflects increased skill and growing awareness of and concern with money-making strategies.

A waitress can further increase her customer count by controlling the flow of customers within the restaurant. Ideally the hostess or manager running the front house rotates customers among stations, just as stations are rotated among waitresses. Each waitress is given, or *sat,* one party at a time in turn so that all waitresses have comparable customer counts at the close of a shift. When no hostess is on duty, or both she and the manager are detained and customers are waiting to be seated, waitresses will typically seat incoming parties.

[1]A call-out (which more logically might be termed a "call-in") occurs when an employee calls in sick or with some other reason why he or she can't make it to work that day. —Ed.

Whether or not a formal hostess is on duty, day waitresses are notorious for bypassing the rotation system by racing to the door and directing incoming customers to their own tables. A sense of the urgency with which this strategy is pursued is conveyed in the comment of one five-year veteran, "They'll run you down to get that person at the door, to seat them in their station." The competition for customers is so intense during the day that some waitresses claim they cannot afford to leave the floor (even to use the restroom) lest they return to find a co-worker's station filled at their expense. "In the daytime, honey," remarks an eight-year Route waitress, "in the daytime it's like pulling teeth. You got to stay on the floor to survive. To survive." It is in part because they do not want to lose customers and tips to their co-workers that waitresses do not take formal breaks. Instead, they rest and eat between waiting tables or during lulls in business, returning to the floor intermittently to check on parties in progress and seat customers in their stations.

The fast pace and chaotic nature of restaurant work provide a cover for the waitress's aggressive pursuit of customers, since it is difficult for other servers to monitor closely the allocation of parties in the bustle and confusion of a rush. Still, it is not uncommon for waitresses to grumble to management and co-workers if they notice an obvious imbalance in customer distribution. Here again, the waitress refrains from directly criticizing her fellow servers, voicing her displeasure by commenting on the paucity of customers in her own station, rather than the overabundance of customers in the stations of certain co-waitresses. In response to these grumblings, other waitresses may moderate somewhat their efforts to appropriate new parties, and management may make a special effort to seat the disgruntled server favorably.

A waitress can also exert pressure on the manager or hostess to keep her station filled.

She may, for instance, threaten to leave if she is not seated enough customers.

> I said, "Innes [a manager], I'm in [station] one and two. If one and two is not filled at all times from now until three, I'm getting my coat, my pocketbook, and I'm leaving." And one and two was filled, and I made ninety-five dollars.

Alternatively, she can make it more convenient for the manager or hostess to seat her rather than her co-workers, either by keeping her tables open (as described), or by taking extra tables. If customers are waiting to be seated, a waitress may offer to pick up parties in a station that is closed or, occasionally, to pick up parties in another waitress's station. In attempting either strategy, but especially the latter, the waitress must be adept not only at waiting tables, but in interpersonal restaurant politics. Autonomy and possession are of central concern to waitresses, and a waitress who offers to pick up tables outside her station must select her words carefully if she is to avoid being accused of invading her co-workers' territory. Accordingly, she may choose to present her bid for extra parties as an offer to help—the manager, another waitress, the restaurant, customers—rather than as a request.

The waitress who seeks to increase her tip income by maximizing the number of customers she serves may endeavor to cut her losses by refusing to serve parties that have stiffed her in the past. If she is a low-ranking waitress, her refusal is likely to be overturned by the manager. If she is an experienced and valuable waitress, the manager may ask someone else to take the party, assure the waitress he will take care of her (that is, pad the bill and give her the difference), or even pick up the party himself. Though the practice is far from common, a waitress may go so far as to demand a tip from a customer who has been known to stiff in the past.

> This party of two guys come in and they order thirty to forty dollars worth of food . . . and

they stiff us. Every time. So Kaddie told them, "If you don't tip us, we're not going to wait on you." They said, "We'll tip you." So Kaddie waited on them, and they tipped her. The next night they came in, I waited on them and they didn't tip me. The third time they came in [the manager] put them in my station and I told [the manager] straight up, "I'm not waiting on them. . . ." So he made Hailey pick them up. And they stiffed Hailey. So when they came in the next night . . . [they] said, "Are you going to give us a table?" I said, "You going to tip me? I'm not going to wait on you. You got all that money, you sell all that crack on the streets and you come here and you can't even leave me a couple of bucks?" . . . So they left me a dollar. So when they come in Tuesday night, I'm telling them a dollar ain't enough.

The tactics employed by waitresses, and particularly day-shift waitresses, to increase their customer count and thereby boost their tip earnings have earned them a resounding notoriety among their less competitive co-workers. Day (and some swing) waitresses are described as "money hungry," "sneaky little bitches," "self-centered," "aggressive," "back-stabbing bitches," and "cutthroats over tables." The following remarks of two Route waitresses, however, indicate that those who employ these tactics see them as defensive, not aggressive measures. A sense of the waitress's preoccupation with autonomy and with protecting what is hers also emerges from these comments.

> You have to be like that. Because if you don't be like that, people step on you. You know, like as far as getting customers. I mean, you know, I'm sorry everybody says I'm greedy. I guess that's why I've survived this long at Route. Cause I am greedy. . . . *I want what's mine,* and if it comes down to me cleaning your table or my table, I'm going to clean my table. Because see I went through all that stage where I would do your table. To be fair. And you would walk home with seventy dollars, and I'd have twenty-five, cause I was being fair all night. (emphasis added)

> If the customer comes in the door and I'm there getting that door, don't expect me to cover your backside while you in the back smoking a cigarette and I'm here working for myself. You're not out there working for me. . . . When I go to the door and get the customers, when I keep my tables clean and your tables are dirty, and you wonder why you only got one person . . . then that's just tough shit. . . . You're damn right my station is filled. *I'm not here for you.* (emphasis added)

Whether the waitress who keeps her station filled with customers is acting aggressively or defensively, her tactics are effective. It is commonly accepted that determined day waitresses make better money than less competitive co-workers even when working swing or grave. Moreover Nera, the waitress most infamous for her relentless use of "money-hungry tactics," is at the same time most famous for her consistently high daily takes. While other waitresses jingle change in their aprons, Nera is forced to store wads of bills in her shoes and in paper bags to prevent tips from overflowing her pockets. She claims to make a minimum of five hundred dollars a week in tip earnings; her record for one day's work exceeds two hundred dollars and is undoubtedly the record for the restaurant.

Inverting the Symbolism of Tipping

It may already be apparent that the waitress views the customer—not as a master to pamper and appease—but as a substance to be processed as quickly and in as large a quantity as possible. The difference in perspective is expressed in the objectifying terminology of waitresses: a customer or party is referred to as a *table,* or by table number, as *table five* or simply *five;* serving successive parties at a table is referred to as *turning the table;* taking an order is also known as *picking up a table;* and to serve water, coffee, or other beverages is to *water, coffee,* or *beverage* a table, number, or customer. Even personal acquaintances assume the status of inanimate matter, or tip-bearing plants, in the language of the server:

> I got my fifth-grade teacher [as a customer] one time. . . . I kept her coffeed. I kept her boyfriend coked all night. Sodaed. . . . And I kept them filled up.

If the customer is perceived as material that is processed, the goal of this processing is the production or extraction of a finished product: the tip. This image too is conveyed in the language of the floor. A waitress may comment that she "got a good tip" or "gets good tips," but she is more likely to say that she "made" or "makes good tips." She may also say that she "got five bucks out of" a customer, or complain that some customers "don't want to give up on" their money. She may accuse a waitress who stays over into her shift of "tapping on" her money, or warn an aspiring waitress against family restaurants on the grounds that "there's no money in there." In all these comments (and all are actual), the waitress might as easily be talking about mining for coal or drilling for oil as serving customers.

Predictably, the waitress's view of the customer as substance to be processed influences her perception of the meaning of tips, and especially substandard tips. At Route, low tips and stiffs are not interpreted as a negative reflection on the waitress's personal qualities or social status. Rather, they are felt to reveal the refractory nature or poor quality of the raw material from which the tip is extracted, produced, or fashioned. In less metaphorical terms, a low tip or stiff is thought to reflect the negative qualities and low status of the customer who is too cheap, too poor, too ignorant, or too coarse to leave an appropriate gratuity. In this context, it is interesting to note that *stiff,* the term used in restaurants to refer to incidents of nontipping or to someone who does not tip, has also been used to refer to a wastrel or penniless man, a hobo, tramp, vagabond, deadbeat, and a moocher (Wentworth and Flexner 1975).

Evidence that waitresses assign blame for poor tips to the tipper is found in their reaction to being undertipped or stiffed. Rather than breaking down in tears and lamenting her "personal failure," the Route waitress responds to a stiff by announcing the event to her co-workers and managers in a tone of angry disbelief. Co-workers and managers echo the waitress's indignation and typically ask her to identify the party (by table number and physical description), or if she has already done so, to be more specific. This identification is crucial for it allows sympathizers to join the waitress in analyzing the cause of the stiff, which is assumed a priori[2] to arise from some shortcoming of the party, not the waitress. The waitress and her co-workers may conclude that the customers in question were rude, troublemakers, or bums, or they may explain their behavior by identifying them as members of a particular category of customers. It might be revealed, for instance, that the offending party was a church group: church groups are invariably tightfisted. It might be resolved that the offenders were senior citizens, Southerners, or businesspeople: all well-known cheapskates. If the customers were European, the stiff will be attributed to ignorance of the American tipping system; if they were young, to immaturity; if they had children, to lack of funds.

These classifications and their attendant explanations are neither fixed nor trustworthy. New categories are invented to explain otherwise puzzling incidents, and all categories are subject to exception. Though undependable as predictive devices, customer typologies serve a crucial function: they divert blame for stiffs and low tips from the waitress to the characteristics

---

[2]*A priori* is Latin for "from what comes before," or reasoning from what is already known. —Ed.

of the customer. It is for this reason that it is "important" for workers to distinguish between different categories of customers, despite the fact that such distinctions are based on "unreliable verbal and appearance clues." In fact, it is precisely the unreliability, or more appropriately the flexibility, of customer typologies that makes them valuable to waitresses. When categories can be constructed and dissolved on demand, there is no danger that an incident will fall outside the existing system of classification and hence be inexplicable.

While waitresses view the customer as something to be processed and the tip as the product of this processing, they are aware that the public does not share their understanding of the waitress–diner–tip relationship. Waitresses at Route recognize that many customers perceive them as needy creatures willing to commit great feats of service and absorb high doses of abuse in their anxiety to secure a favorable gratuity or protect their jobs. They are also aware that some customers leave small tips with the intent to insult the server and that others undertip on the assumption that for a Route waitress even fifty cents will be appreciated. One waitress indicated that prior to being employed in a restaurant, she herself subscribed to the stereotype of the down-and-out waitress "because you see stuff on television, you see these wives or single ladies who waitress and they live in slummy apartments or slummy houses and they dress in rags." It is these images of neediness and desperation, which run so strongly against the waitress's perception of herself and her position, that she attacks when strained relations erupt into open conflict.

> Five rowdy black guys walked in the door and they went to seat themselves at table seven. I said, "Excuse me. You all got to wait to be seated." "We ain't got to do *shit*. We here to eat. . . . " So they went and sat down. And I turned around and just looked at them. And they said, "Well, I hope you ain't our waitress,

cause you blew your tip. Cause you ain't getting nothing from us." And I turned around and I said, "You need it more than I do, baby."

This waitress's desire to confront the customer's assumption of her destitution is widely shared among service workers whose status as tipped employees marks them as needy in the eyes of their customers. Davis (1959, 162–163) reports that among cabdrivers "a forever repeated story is of the annoyed driver, who, after a grueling trip with a Lady Shopper, hands the coin back, telling her, 'Lady, keep your lousy dime. You need it more than I do.'" Mars and Nicod (1984, 75) report a hotel waitress's claim that "if she had served a large family with children for one or two weeks, and then was given a 10p piece,[3] she would give the money back, saying, 'It's all right, thank you, I've got enough change for my bus fare home.'" In an incident I observed (not at Route), a waitress followed two male customers out of a restaurant calling, "Excuse me! You forgot this!" and holding up the coins they had left as a tip. The customers appeared embarrassed, motioned for her to keep the money, and continued down the sidewalk. The waitress, now standing in the outdoor seating area of the restaurant and observed by curious diners, threw the money after the retreating men and returned to her work. Episodes such as these allow the worker to repudiate openly the evaluation of her financial status that is implied in an offensively small gratuity, and permit her to articulate her own understanding of what a small tip says and about whom. If customers can only afford to leave a dime, or feel a 10p piece is adequate compensation for two weeks' service, they must be very hard up or very ignorant indeed.

---

[3]Until it converts to the Eurodollar, the British monetary unit is the pound sterling (£). One pound is worth about $1.65 in U.S. currency. There are 100 pence to the pound. So, 10p (pronounced "10 pea") is worth about 17 cents. —Ed.

In the following incident the waitress interjects a denial of her neediness into an altercation that is not related to tipping, demonstrating that the customer's perception of her financial status is a prominent and persistent concern for her.

> She [a customer] wanted a California Burger with mayonnaise. And when I got the mayonnaise, the mayonnaise had a little brown on it. . . . So this girl said to me, she said, "What the fuck is this you giving me?" And I turned around, I thought, "Maybe she's talking to somebody else in the booth with her." And I turned around and I said, "Excuse me?" She said, "You hear what I said. I said, 'What the fuck are you giving me?'" And I turned around, I said, "I don't know if you're referring your information to *me*," I said, "but if you're referring your information to *me*," I said, "I don't *need* your bullshit." I said, "I'm not going to even take it. . . . Furthermore, I could care less if you eat or *don't* eat. . . . And you see this?" And I took her check and I ripped it apart. . . . And I took the California Burger and I says, "You don't have a problem anymore now, right?" She went up to the manager. And she says, "That black waitress"—I says, "Oh. By the way, what is my name? I don't have a name, [using the words] 'that black waitress'. . . . My name happens to be Nera. . . . That's N-E-R-A. . . . And I don't need your bullshit, sweetheart. . . . People like you I can walk on, because you don't know how to talk to human beings." And I said, "I don't need you. I don't need your quarters. I don't need your nickels. I don't need your dimes. So if you want service, be my guest. Don't you *ever* sit in my station, cause I won't wait on you." The manager said, "Nera, please. Would you wait in the back?" I said, "No. I don't take back seats no more for nobody."

In each of these cases, the waitress challenges the customer's definition of the relationship in which tipping occurs. By speaking out, by confronting the customer, she demonstrates that she is not subservient or in fear of losing her job; that she is not compelled by financial need or a sense of social hierarchy to accept abuse from customers; that she does not, in Nera's words, "take back seats no more for nobody." At the same time, she reverses the symbolic force of the low tip, converting a statement on her social status or work skills into a statement on the tipper's cheapness or lack of savoir faire.[4] . . .

References

Davis, Fred. 1959. "The Cabdriver and His Fare: Facets of a Fleeting Relationship." *American Journal of Sociology* 65(2): 158–165.

Mars, Gerald, and Michael Nicod. 1984. *The World of Waiters*. London: Allen & Unwin.

Wentworth, Harold, and Stuart Berg Flexner (eds. and comps.). 1975. *Dictionary of American Slang*. 2nd supplemental ed. New York: Crowell.

---

[4]*Savoir faire* is French and means literally "knowing how to do." Generally the phrase is used to mean "a knowledge of how to get around in the world," or simply, tact. —Ed.

Questions

1. You've just been out to dinner at a nice restaurant. Your waitress presented you with a tab for $72.50. Assuming the service was fine, how much did you tip her? How much do you think she might have expected? Where did you learn the appropriate amount to tip?

2. Have you ever tried to send a "message" to a waitperson by leaving no tip or a very small one? What was that message? Whether you've ever sent such a message, based on what you've read in Paules's article, do you think the message was received?

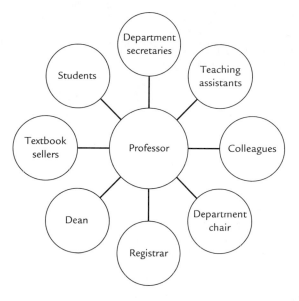

Professor's Role Set

3. One of the techniques for understanding how people interact within a social structure is to look at "role sets" — that is, the set of statuses with which one interacts in carrying out one's role. In the accompanying diagram, I've sketched my role set as a professor. Try your hand at this by sketching the role set of the waitress.

   Generally, people within a particular role set have a similar understanding of one another's role — that is, their rights and duties as incumbents in a particular status. As Paules tells it, however, the customer has a different understanding of the waitress's role than the waitress does. To what sorts of complications might this lead? What would be the effect on the relationship if both customer and waitress understood the waitress's role from the waitress's point of view? From the customer's point of view?

·18·

Handling the Stigma of Handling the Dead

Morticians and Funeral Directors

William E. Thompson

As William Thompson observes in his 1991 article on the funeral profession, an individual's occupational status—and the role attached to that status—is central to his or her identity. How, then, do people who do work that others find *repugnant* manage things such that they themselves do not feel repugnant?

In a complex, industrialized society a person's occupation or profession is central to his or her personal and social identity. As Pavalko (1988) pointed out, two strangers are quite " . . . likely to 'break the ice' by indicating the kind of work they do." As a result, individuals often make a number of initial judgments about others based on preconceived notions about particular occupations.

This study examines how morticians and funeral directors handle the stigma associated with their work. Historically, stigma has been attached to those responsible for caring for the dead, and the job typically was assigned to the lower classes (e.g., the Eta of Japan and the Untouchables in India),[1] and in some cases, those who handled the dead were forbidden from touching the living (Bendann 1930; Kearl 1989; Murray 1969). Today, the stigma has grown to new and potentially more threatening proportions for those engaged in the profession, for during the twentieth century Americans have become preoccupied with the denial of death (Becker 1973; Charmaz 1980; Fulton 1961; Jackson 1980; Kearl 1989; Momeyer 1988; Sudnow 1967).[2] As Stephenson (1985, 223) noted, "In a society which seeks to deny the reality of death, the

---

[1]The Eta were a people of Japan who—like the scheduled castes (or untouchables) of India—were regarded as ritually polluted. The distinction between Eta and non-Eta was officially outlawed in Japan in the nineteenth century, just as the distinction between the scheduled castes and others was outlawed in India in the mid-twentieth century. In both countries, however, the distinction continues informally.—Ed.

[2]The wholesale denial of death in contemporary American society has been seriously questioned by some. For example, Parsons and Lidz (1967) eloquently refuted the "denial of death" thesis, indicating that "American society has institutionalized a broadly stable, though flexible and changing, orientation to death that is fundamentally not a 'denial' but a mode of acceptance appropriate to our primary cultural patterns of activism" (134). In a later article Parsons, Fox, and Lidz (1972, 368) argued that "what is often interpreted as 'denial' is in reality a kind of 'apathy.'" They insist that, in a religious sense, death must be viewed as "a reciprocal gift to God, the consummatory reciprocation of the gift of life" (451). Others counter, however, that death and funerals have become increasingly secularized and that although constantly confronted with the realities of death, most Americans choose to ignore and deny it as much as possible.

funeral director is a living symbol of this dreaded subject."

Two major problems faced by members of the funeral industry are that they make their living by doing work considered taboo by most Americans and that they are viewed as profiting from death and grief—a fact from which they must continually attempt to divert public attention. The "7-billion-dollar-a-year American funeral industry" has received much criticism over the past 2 decades and widespread complaints have led to "congressional hearings, new trade practices rules from the Federal Trade Commission, and undercover sting operations by various consumer groups" (Kearl 1989, 271). Those in the funeral business were further stigmatized when it was revealed that 58% of the funeral homes studied by the FTC had committed at least one billing abuse against their bereaved clients, and public testimony revealed "horror stories" of inflated charges for funeral services neither required nor requested (Kearl 1989, 278).

Morticians and funeral directors are fully aware of the stigma associated with their work, so they continually strive to enhance their public image and promote their social credibility. They must work to shift the emphasis of their work from the dead to the living, and away from sales and toward service. As Aries (1976, 99) noted:

> In order to sell death, it had to be made friendly . . . since 1885 . . . [funeral directors have] presented themselves not as simple sellers of services, but as "doctors of grief" who have a mission . . . [which] consists in aiding the mourning survivors to return to normalcy.

Couched within the general theoretical framework of symbolic interactionism, there are a variety of symbolic and dramaturgical methods[3] whereby morticians and funeral

directors attempt to redefine their occupations and minimize and/or neutralize negative attitudes toward them and what they do.

Method

This study reflects over 2 years of qualitative fieldwork as outlined by Schatzman and Strauss (1973), Spradley (1979) and Berg (1989). Extensive ethnographic interviews were conducted during 1987–1989 with 19 morticians and funeral directors in four states: Kansas, Missouri, Oklahoma, and Texas. The funeral homes included both privately owned businesses and branches of large franchise operations. They were located in communities ranging from less than 1,000 population to cities of over 1 million people.

First contacts were made by telephone, and appointments were made to tour the funeral homes and meet with the directors and morticians. Initial taped interviews ranged from $1\frac{1}{2}$ to a little over 4 hours in duration. In all but two cases, follow-up interviews were used to obtain additional information about the individuals and their work.

Rather than limiting questions to a standardized interview schedule, the researcher soon discovered that, as with most ethnographic fieldwork (Berg, 1989; Spradley 1979), interviewees were much more comfortable and provided more information during casual conversation. Consequently, the structured portion of the interview focused primarily on demographic data, educational credentials, how they decided to enter the profession, how they felt about their jobs, and how they handled the stigma associated with their work. The questions were open-ended, and answers to one question invariably led to a variety of spontaneous follow-up questions.

Respondents

Interviewees included people from different age groups, both sexes, and both whites and

---

[3]You may recall that the concept of dramaturgical was introduced at the beginning of reading 14—it developed from the line of sociological analysis followed by Erving Goffman. —Ed.

nonwhites. There were 16 males and 3 females interviewed for this study, ranging in age from 26 to 64 years. Most of the respondents were between their late 30s and early 50s. Fourteen of the males were both morticians (licensed embalmers) and licensed funeral directors. The other two males were licensed embalmers who were employed in funeral homes, but were not licensed funeral directors. None of the females had been trained or licensed to embalm. Two of the females were licensed funeral directors, and the other woman was neither licensed as an embalmer nor funeral director. She was married to a man who was licensed to do both, and she simply helped out around the funeral home—usually answering the phone and helping with bookkeeping. All the women admitted, however, that they often helped out in the embalming room and in making funeral arrangements.

Seventeen of the people interviewed were white. The other two were African American brothers who jointly owned and operated a funeral home located in a city of approximately 150,000 people. Only one was a licensed funeral director and licensed embalmer. They candidly admitted, however, that they both worked in the embalming room and arranged funeral services.

With only one exception, all of the morticians and funeral directors interviewed were more than willing to talk about their occupations. They were aware that the author was conducting research, and several of them commented that the funeral industry was much maligned and stigmatized, and they were anxious to get an opportunity to "set the record straight," or "tell their side of the story" about their jobs. As the interviews progressed, however, the author was struck by the candor with which most of the interviewees responded to questions and provided additional information. Only one of the funeral directors, a single 50-year-old white male, was reluctant to talk about his work, refused to be taped, and was extremely guarded throughout the interview.

He attempted to answer as many questions as possible with short, cryptic responses, and on several occasions became quite defensive and asked: "Why did you ask that?" and "What are you going to do with this information?" Despite his defensiveness, his answers indicated that his experiences as a mortician and funeral director were very similar to the others interviewed. In fact, his reticence about answering some of the questions served to underscore the fact that he believed there was a great deal of stigma attached to his work and he wanted to be careful not to add to it (a point he made verbally during the interview).

Occupational Stigma

Erving Goffman (1963) defined *stigma* as any attribute that sets people apart and discredits them or disqualifies them from full social acceptance. This paper explores what happens when people are discredited (stigmatized) because of the work they perform, and how they attempt to reduce or eliminate the stigma.

People are most likely to be stigmatized because of their work if it is viewed as deviant by other members of society. George Ritzer (1977) cited three criteria, any one of which can cause an occupation to be considered deviant: (a) if it is illegal, (b) if it is considered immoral, and (c) if it is considered improper.

The first category of occupations, those that are illegal, has been widely studied by sociologists. Even a cursory list of studies on organized crime, prostitution, shoplifting, counterfeiting, confidence swindling, professional thievery, and other illegal occupations would be voluminous. The second category of deviant occupations is less straightforward than the first. Although many occupations that are considered immoral also have been made illegal (e.g., prostitution), there is much less agreement on the morality of occupations than on their legality.

The final category is a fascinating one, and perhaps the most ripe for sociological investigation. It includes those jobs that may not be considered "a proper or fitting occupation by society" (Polsky 1969, 32). In any society there are certain jobs that most people prefer not to do. These jobs often require little or no training, pay very little, rank low in occupational prestige, and involve "dirty work" (Garson 1975; Hughes 1971). As Hughes (1971, 344) pointed out:

> . . . the delegation of dirty work to someone else is common among humans. Many cleanliness taboos . . . depend for their practice upon success in delegating the tabooed activity to someone else.

Although the occupations of mortician and funeral director do not fit neatly into any of Ritzer's three categories, preparing the dead for funerals, burial, and/or cremation can be characterized as "dirty work." The stigma associated with these occupations is not so much that they are literally unclean, although embalming can be rather messy. It is, however, no more so than surgery—a highly prestigious profession. Rather, they are figuratively unclean because they violate social taboos against handling the dead.

THE STIGMA OF HANDLING THE DEAD

Ritualistic disposal of dead human bodies is a cultural universal (Bendann 1930; Habenstein and Lamers 1960; Huntington and Metcalf 1979). These ceremonies ". . . manifest the collective image of death—what the larger society thinks and feels about death" (Stephenson 1985). In American society, death is surrounded by mystery and taboos. David Sudnow (1967) pointed out that Americans shun the idea that death is a natural process begun at birth; instead, they view death as a very brief process or an act.

Until the turn of the century, in this country, people died at home and friends and family members prepared the bodies for burial (Lesy 1987). As medical knowledge and technology progressed and became more specialized, more

and more deaths occurred outside the home— usually in hospitals. Death became something to be handled by a select group of highly trained professionals—doctors, nurses, and hospital staff. As fewer people witnessed death firsthand, it became surrounded with more mystery, and physically handling the dead became the domain of only a few.

Members or friends of the family relinquished their role in preparing bodies for disposal to an *undertaker*, ". . . a special person who would 'undertake' responsibility for the care and burial of the dead" (Amos 1983, 2). From the beginning, stigma was associated with funerary occupations because they were "linked to the American death orientation whereby the industry is the cultural scapegoat for failed immortality" (Kearl 1989, 278).

To counter this stigma, undertakers (later to be called morticians) initially emphasized the scientific aspects of their work. Embalming and preparation for burial were presented as highly technical skills that required scientific knowledge and sophisticated training. Most states began licensing embalmers around the end of the nineteenth century (Amos 1983). These licensed embalmers did not enjoy the prestige accorded to the medical profession, however, and almost immediately were surrounded by mystery and viewed as unusual, if not downright weird. They were not family members or friends of the deceased faced with the unsavory but necessary responsibility for disposing of a loved one's body, but strangers who *chose* to work with dead bodies—for compensation. Although most welcomed the opportunity to relinquish this chore, they also viewed those who willingly assumed it with some skepticism and even disdain. Having failed to gain the desired prestige associated with the scientific aspects of embalming, and realizing that emphasizing embalming only served to increase what was perhaps the most stigmatizing aspect of their work (handling the dead), morticians shifted the focus away from their work on the dead body to their work with the living by emphasizing their roles as funeral directors and bereavement counselors.

In contemporary American society, those who routinely handle the dead have entered what Michael Lesy calls the "forbidden zone." Lesy (1987, 5) points out:

> In some cultures, the dead are ritually unclean and those who touch them must be ritually cleansed. In America, those who deal with the dead have social identities that shift back and forth like stationary objects that seem to move from left to right and back again as one eye is opened and the other is closed. Sometimes they look like pariahs and deviants, sometimes like charlatans. Other times they look like heroes or even adepts, initiates, and priests. Those who deal with death work at an intersection of opposites, tainted by the suffering and decay of the body, transfigured by the plight of the self and the destiny of the soul. The world never considers anyone who routinely deals with death to be "pure." . . .

Sudnow (1967, 51–64) underscored the negative attitudes toward people who work with the dead in describing how those who work in a morgue, for example, are "death-tainted" and work very hard to rid themselves of the social stigma associated with their jobs. Morticians and funeral directors cannot escape from this "taint of death" and they must constantly work to "counteract the stigma" directed at them and their occupations (Charmaz 1980, 182). Warner (1959, 315) described the funeral director as "a private enterpriser who will do the ritually unclean and physically distasteful work of disposing of the dead in a manner satisfying to the living, at a price which they can pay." Fulton (1961) echoed this definition when he wrote, "In a word, the funeral director, by virtue of his close association with death, and by the 'relative' attitude he takes toward all funerals is, in a religious sense, 'unclean'" (322).

Are morticians and funeral directors really that stigmatized? After all, they generally are well-known and respected members of their communities. In small communities and even many large cities, local funeral homes have been owned and operated by the same family for several generations. These people usually are members of civic organizations, have substantial incomes, and live in nice homes and drive nice automobiles. Most often they are viewed as successful business people. On the other hand, their work is surrounded by mystery, taboos, and stigma, and they often are viewed as cold, detached, and downright morbid for doing it. All the respondents in this study openly acknowledged that stigma was associated with their work. Some indicated that they thought the stigma primarily came from the "misconception" that they were "getting rich" off other people's grief; others believed it simply came from working with the dead. Clearly these two aspects of their work—handling the dead and profiting from death and grief—emerged as the two most stigmatizing features of the funeral industry according to respondents. Pine (1975) noted that funeral directors cannot escape the "contamination by death," and contended:

> . . . people view individuals in such work as different . . . because they feel that they themselves could never do it and that there must be something "strange" about those who voluntarily choose to do it. (38)

Kathy Charmaz (1980, 174–206) discussed the stigma experienced by morticians, funeral directors, and others involved in "death work," and the negative impact that working with the dead can have on self-image. It is important from their perspective, she notes, that "who they are should not be defined by what they do" (174). This idea was confirmed by all the respondents in this study in one way or another. As one funeral director/embalmer noted, "I don't want to be thought of as somebody who likes working with the *dead*—that's morbid—I enjoy what I do because I like working with the *living*."

Managing Stigma

Erving Goffman wrote the most systematic analysis of how individuals manage a "spoiled" social identity in his classic work, *Stigma* (1963). He described several techniques, such as "passing," "dividing the social world," "mutual aid," "physical distance," "disclosure," and "covering," employed by the *discredited* and *discreditable* to manage information and conceal their stigmatizing attributes (41–104). Although these techniques work well for the physically scarred, blind, stammerers, bald, drug addicted, ex-convicts, and many other stigmatized categories of people, they are less likely to be used by morticians and funeral directors.

Except perhaps when on vacation, it is important for funeral directors to be known and recognized in their communities and to be associated with their work. Consequently, most of the morticians and funeral directors studied relied on other strategies for reducing the stigma associated with their work. Paramount among these strategies were symbolic redefinition of their work, role distance, professionalism, emphasizing service, and enjoying socioeconomic status over occupational prestige. This was much less true for licensed embalmers who worked for funeral directors, especially in chain-owned funeral homes in large cities. In those cases the author found that many embalmers concealed their occupation from their neighbors and others with whom they were not intimately acquainted, by using the techniques of information control discussed by Goffman (1963).

SYMBOLIC REDEFINITION

A rose by any other name may smell as sweet, but death work by almost any other name does not sound quite as harsh. One of the ways in which morticians and funeral directors handle the stigma of their occupations is through symbolically negating as much of it as possible.

Language is the most important symbol used by human beings, and Woods and Delisle (1978, 98) revealed how sympathy cards avoid the use of the terms "dead" and "death" by substituting less harsh words such as "loss," "time of sorrow," and "hour of sadness." This technique is also used by morticians and funeral directors to reduce the stigma associated with their work.

Words that are most closely associated with death are rarely used, and the most harsh terms are replaced with less ominous ones. The term *death* is almost never used by funeral directors; rather, they talk of "passing on," "meeting an untimely end," or "eternal slumber." There are no *corpses* or *dead bodies*; they are referred to as "remains," "the deceased," "loved one," or more frequently, by name (e.g., "Mr. Jones"). Use of the term *body* is almost uniformly avoided around the family. Viewing rooms (where the embalmed body is displayed in the casket) usually are given serene names such as "the sunset room," "the eternal slumber room," or, in one case, "the guest room."[4] Thus, when friends or family arrive to view the body, they are likely to be told that "Mr. Jones is lying in repose in the eternal slumber room." This language contrasts sharply with that used by morticians and funeral directors in "backstage" areas (Goffman 1959, 112)[5] such as the embalming room where drowning victims often are called "floaters," burn victims are called "crispy critters," and others are simply referred to as "bodies" (Turner and Edgley 1976).

All the respondents indicated that there was less stigma attached to the term *funeral director* than *mortician* or *embalmer*, underscoring the

---

[4]In this case the denial of death was symbolically enhanced by having the embalmed body lying in bed, as if asleep. The funeral director indicated that this room was used when families had not yet decided on a casket, thus allowing for viewing of the body in what he called a "natural, peaceful surrounding."

[5]In keeping with his dramaturgical perspective, Goffman divided social settings between "front stage" (where the actor would interact with the audience) and "backstage" (where the audience was prohibited). – Ed.

notion that much of the stigma they experienced was attached to physically handling the dead. Consequently, when asked what they do for a living, those who acknowledge that they are in the funeral business (several indicated that they often do not) referred to themselves as "funeral directors" even if all they did was the embalming. *Embalming* is referred to as "preservation" or "restoration," and in order to be licensed, one must have studied "mortuary arts" or "mortuary science." Embalming no longer takes place in an *embalming room,* but in a "preparation room," or in some cases the "operating room."

Coffins are now "caskets," which are transported in "funeral coaches" (not *hearses*) to their "final resting place" rather than to the *cemetery* or worse yet, *graveyard,* for their "interment" rather than *burial.* Thus, linguistically, the symbolic redefinition is complete, with death verbally redefined during every phase, and the stigma associated with it markedly reduced.

All the morticians and funeral directors in this study emphasized the importance of using the "appropriate" terms in referring to their work. Knowledge of the stigma attached to certain words was readily acknowledged, and all indicated that the earlier terminology was stigma-laden, especially the term "undertaker," which they believed conjured up negative images in the mind of the public. For example, a 29-year-old male funeral director indicated that his father still insisted on calling himself an "undertaker." "He just hasn't caught up with the twentieth century," the son remarked. Interestingly, when asked why he did not refer to himself as an undertaker, he replied, "It just sounds so old-fashioned [pause] plus, it sounds so morbid." As Pine (1975) noted, the special argot of the funeral industry performs an important function in reducing the stigma associated with the work and allows funeral directors to achieve role distance.

In addition to using language to symbolically redefine their occupations, funeral directors carefully attempt to shift the focus of their work away from the care of the dead (especially handling the body), and redefine it primarily in terms of caring for the living. The dead are de-emphasized as most of the funeral ritual is orchestrated for the benefit of the friends and family of the deceased (Turner and Edgley 1976). By redefining themselves as "grief therapists" or "bereavement counselors," their primary duties are associated with making funeral arrangements, directing the services, and consoling the family in their time of need.

ROLE DISTANCE

Because a person's sense of self is so strongly linked to occupation, it is common practice for people in undesirable or stigmatized occupations to practice role distance (e.g., Garson 1975; Pavalko 1988; Ritzer 1977; Terkel 1974; Thompson 1983). Although the specific role-distancing techniques vary across different occupations and among different individuals within an occupation, they share the common function of allowing individuals to violate some of the role expectations associated with the occupation, and to express their individuality within the confines of the occupational role. Although the funeral directors and morticians in this study used a variety of role-distancing techniques, three common patterns emerged: emotional detachment, humor, and countering the stereotype.

Emotional Detachment   One of the ways that morticians and funeral directors overcome their socialization regarding death taboos and the stigma associated with handling the dead is to detach themselves from the body work. Charmaz (1980) pointed out that a common technique used by coroners and funeral directors to minimize the stigma associated with death work is to routinize the work as much as possible. When embalming, morticians focus on the technical aspects of the job rather than thinking about the person they are working on. One mortician explained:

When I'm in the preparation room I never think about *who* I'm working on, I only think about what has to be done next. When I picked up the body, it was a person. When I get done, clean and dress the body, and place it in the casket, it becomes a person again. But in here it's just something to be worked on. I treat it like a mechanic treats an automobile engine—with respect, but there's no emotion involved. It's just a job that has to be done.

Another mortician described his emotional detachment in the embalming room:

You can't think too much about this process [embalming], or it'll really get to you. For example, one time we brought in this little girl. She was about four years old—the same age as my youngest daughter at the time. She had been killed in a wreck; had gone through the windshield; was really a mess. At first, I wasn't sure I could do that one—all I could think of was my little girl. But when I got her in the prep room, my whole attitude changed. I know this probably sounds cold, and hard I guess, but suddenly I began to think of the challenge involved. This was gonna be an open-casket service, and while the body was in pretty good shape, the head and face were practically gone. This was gonna take a lot of reconstruction. Also, the veins are so small on children that you have to be a lot more careful. Anyway, I got so caught up in the job, that I totally forgot about working on a little girl. I was in the room with her about six hours when ___ ___ [his wife] came in and reminded me that we had dinner plans that night. I washed up and went out to dinner and had a great time. Later that night, I went right back to work on her without even thinking about it. It wasn't until the next day when my wife was dressing the body, and I came in, and she was crying, that it hit me. I looked at the little girl, and I began crying. We both just stood there crying and hugging. My wife kept saying "I know this was tough for you," and "yesterday must have been tough." I felt sorta guilty, because I knew what she meant, and it should've

been tough for me, real tough, emotionally, but it wasn't. The only "tough" part had been the actual work, especially the reconstruction—I had totally cut off the emotional part. It sometimes makes you wonder. Am I really just good at this, or am I losing something. I don't know. All I know is, if I'd thought about the little girl the way I did that next day, I never could have done her. It's just part of this job—you gotta just do what has to be done. If you think about it much, you'll never make it in this business.

Humor   Many funeral directors and morticians use humor to detach themselves emotionally from their work.[6] The humor, of course, must be carefully hidden from friends and relatives of the deceased, and takes place in backstage areas such as the embalming room, or in professional group settings such as at funeral directors' conventions.

The humor varies from impromptu comments while working on the body to standard jokes[7] told over and over again. Not unexpectedly, all the respondents indicated a strong distaste for necrophilia jokes. One respondent commented, "I can think of nothing less funny—the jokes are sick, and have done a lot of damage to the image of our profession."

Humor is an effective technique of diffusing the stigma associated with handling a dead body, however, and when more than one person is present in the embalming room, it is common for a certain amount of banter to take place, and jokes or comments are often

---

[6]This is a common practice among medical students who are notorious for using "cadaver jokes" and pranks to help overcome the taboos associated with death and to ease the tension experienced when dissecting cadavers (Hafferty 1986, 1988; Knight 1973).

[7]The author asked each respondent to tell his/her favorite joke about the occupation. One respondent was very indignant and said he hated all the jokes about the profession. All the others, however, quickly launched into what amounted to almost an amateur comedy routine. The author routinely heard several of the same jokes time and time again. Clearly, the most popular was several variations on the theme of burying someone in a rented tuxedo.

made about the amount of body fat or the overendowment, or lack thereof, of certain body parts. For example, one mortician indicated that a common remark made about males with small genitalia is, "Well, at least he won't be missed."

As with any occupation, levels of humor varied among the respondents. During an interview one of the funeral directors spoke of some of the difficulties in advertising the business, indicating that because of attitudes toward death and the funeral business, he had to be sure that his newspaper advertisements did not offend anyone. He reached into his desk drawer and pulled out a pad with several "fake ads" written on it. They included:

*"Shake and Bake Special –
Cremation with No Embalming"
"Business Is Slow, Somebody's Gotta Go"
"Try Our Layaway Plan – Best in the Business"
"Count on Us, We'll Be the Last to Let You Down"
"People Are Dying to Use Our Services"
"Pay Now, Die Later"
"The Buck Really Does Stop Here"*

He indicated that he and one of his friends had started making up these fake ads and slogans when they were doing their mortuary internships. Over the years, they occasionally corresponded by mail and saw each other at conventions, and they would always try to be one up on the other with the best ad. He said, "Hey, in this business, you have to look for your laughs where you can find them." Garson (1975, 210) refers to a line from a song from *Mary Poppins*, "In every job that must be done, there is an element of fun."

Countering the Stereotype   Morticians and funeral directors are painfully aware of the common negative stereotype of people in their occupations. The women in this study were much less concerned about the stereotype, perhaps because simply being female shattered the stereotype anyway. The men, however, not

only acknowledged that they were well aware of the public's stereotypical image of them, but also indicated that they made every effort *not* to conform to it.

One funeral director, for instance, said:

People think we're cold, unfriendly, and unfeeling. I always make it a point to be just the opposite. Naturally, when I'm dealing with a family I must be reserved and show the proper decorum, but when I am out socially, I always try to be very upbeat—very alive. No matter how tired I am, I try not to show it.

Another indicated that he absolutely never wore gray or black suits. Instead, he wore navy blue and usually with a small pinstripe. "I might be mistaken for the minister or a lawyer," he said, "but rarely for an undertaker."

The word "cold," which often is associated with death, came up in a number of interviews. One funeral director was so concerned about the stereotype of being "cold," that he kept a handwarmer in the drawer of his desk. He said, "My hands tend to be cold and clammy. It's just a physical trait of mine, but there's no way that I'm going to shake someone's hand and let them walk away thinking how cold it was." Even on the warmest of days, he indicated that during services, he carried the handwarmer in his right-hand coat pocket so that he could warm his hand before shaking hands with or touching someone.

Although everyone interviewed indicated that he or she violated the public stereotype, each one expressed a feeling of being atypical. In other words, although they believed that they did not conform to the stereotype, they felt that many of their colleagues did. One funeral director was wearing jeans, a short-sleeved sweatshirt and a pair of running shoes during the interview. He had just finished mowing the lawn at the funeral home. "Look at me," he said, "Do I look like a funeral director? Hell, _____ [the funeral director across the street] wears a suit and tie to mow his grass!—or, at least he would if he didn't hire it done."[8]

Others insisted that very few funeral directors conform to the public stereotype when out of public view, but feel compelled to conform to it when handling funeral arrangements, because it is an occupational role requirement. "I always try to be warm and upbeat," one remarked, "But, let's face it, when I'm working with a family, they're experiencing a lot of grief—I have to respect that, and act accordingly." Another indicated that he always lowered his voice when talking with family and friends of the deceased, and that it had become such a habit, that he found himself speaking softly almost all the time. "One of the occupational hazards, I guess," he remarked.

The importance of countering the negative stereotype was evident, when time after time, persons being interviewed would pause and ask "I'm not what you expected, am I?" or something similar. It seemed very important for them to be reassured that they did not fit the stereotype of funeral director or mortician.

PROFESSIONALISM

Another method used by morticians and funeral directors to reduce occupational stigma is to emphasize professionalism. Amos (1983, 3) described embalming as:

. . . an example of a vocation in transition from an occupation to a profession. Until mid-nineteenth century, embalming was not considered a profession and this is still an issue debated in some circles today.

Most morticians readily admit that embalming is a very simple process and can be learned very easily. In all but two of the funeral homes studied, the interviewees admitted that people who were not licensed embalmers often helped with the embalming process. In one case, in which the funeral home was owned and operated by two brothers, one of the brothers was a licensed funeral director and licensed embalmer. The other brother had dropped out of high school and helped their father with the funeral business while his brother went to school to meet the educational requirements for licensure. The licensed brother said:

By the time I got out of school and finished my apprenticeship, _____ [his brother] had been helping Dad embalm for over three years—and he was damned good at it. So when I joined the business, Dad thought it was best if I concentrated on handling the funeral arrangements and pre-service needs. After Dad died, I was the only licensed embalmer, so "officially" I do it all—all the embalming and the funeral arrangements. But, to tell you the truth, I only embalm every now and then when we have several to do, 'cause _____ usually handles most of it. He's one of the best—I'd match him against any in the business.

Despite the relative simplicity of the embalming process and the open admission by morticians and funeral directors that "almost anyone could do it with a little practice," most states require licensure and certification for embalming. The four states represented in this study (Kansas, Oklahoma, Missouri, and Texas) have similar requirements for becoming a licensed certified embalmer. They include a minimum of 60 college hours with a core of general college courses (English, mathematics, social studies, etc.) plus 1 year of courses in the "mortuary sciences," or "mortuary arts." These consist of several courses in physiology and biology, and a 1-year apprenticeship under a licensed embalmer. To become a licensed funeral director requires the passing of a state board examination, which primarily requires a knowledge of state laws related to

[8]In many communities (especially small towns) rival funeral homes are located in close proximity, often across the street, or within a block of one another. A colleague, Michael Stein at the University of Missouri, St. Louis, suggests this is not unlike the clustering of other "stigmatized places," such as adult bookstores or adult movie theaters.

burial, cremation, disposal of the body, and insurance.

All the respondents in this study who were licensed and certified embalmers and funeral directors exceeded the minimum educational requirements. In fact, all but one of them had a college degree, and three had advanced degrees. The most common degree held was a Bachelor of Science in mortuary sciences. Two of the males had degrees in business (one held the MBA degree), one male had a Bachelor's degree with a major in biology and had attended one year of medical school, one male had a degree in geology, and one had a degree in music. One of the women had a Bachelor's degree in English; another held a degree in business; and one woman had a degree in nursing. Although the general consensus among them was that an individual did not need a college education to become a good embalmer, they all stressed the importance of a college education for being a successful funeral director. Most thought that some basic courses in business, psychology, death and dying, and "bereavement counseling" were valuable preparation for the field. Also, most of the funeral directors were licensed insurance agents, which allowed them to sell burial policies.

Other evidence of the professionalization of the funeral industry includes state, regional, and national professional organizations that hold annual conventions and sponsor other professional activities; professional journals; state, regional, and national governing and regulating boards; and a professional code of ethics. Although the funeral industry is highly competitive, like most other professions, its members demonstrate a strong sense of cohesiveness and in-group identification.

Reduction of stigma is not the sole purpose for professionalization among funeral directors and morticians, as other benefits are reaped from the process. Nevertheless, as Charmaz (1980, 182) noted, membership in the professional organizations of coroners and funeral directors is one of the most effective ways to "counteract the stigma conferred upon them." One of the married couples in this study indicated that it was reassuring to attend national conventions where they met and interacted with other people in the funeral industry because it helps to "reassure us that we're not weird." The wife went on to say:

> A lot of people ask us how we can stand to be in this business—especially _____ because he does all of the embalming. They act like we must be strange or something. When we go to the conventions and meet with all of the other people there who are just like us—people who like helping other people—I feel *normal* again.

All these elements of professionalization—educational requirements, exams, boards, organizations, codes of ethics, and the rest—lend an air of credibility and dignity to the funeral business while diminishing the stigma associated with it. Although the requirements for licensure and certification are not highly exclusive, they still represent forms of boundary maintenance, and demand a certain level of commitment from those who enter the field. Thus, professionalization helped in the transition of the funeral business from a vocation that can be pursued by virtually anyone to a profession that can be entered only by those with the appropriate qualifications. As Pine (1975, 28) indicated:

> Because professionalization is highly respected in American society, the word "profession" tends to be used as a symbol by occupations seeking to improve or enhance the lay public's conception of that occupation, and funeral directing is no exception. To some extent, this appears to be because the funeral director hopes to overcome the stigma of "doing death work."

"By claiming professional status, funeral directors claim prestige and simultaneously seek to minimize the stigma they experience for being death workers involved in 'dirty work'" (Charmaz 1980, 192).

THE SHROUD OF SERVICE

One of the most obvious ways in which morticians and funeral directors neutralize the stigma associated with their work is to wrap themselves in a "shroud of service." All the respondents emphasized their service role over all other aspects of their jobs. Although their services were not legally required in any of the four states included in this study, all the respondents insisted that people desperately *needed* them.[9] As one funeral director summarized, "Service, that's what we're all about—we're there when people need us the most."

Unlike the humorous fantasy ads mentioned earlier, actual advertisements in the funeral industry focus on service. Typical ads for the companies in this study read:

"Our Family Serving Yours for Over 60 Years"
"Serving the Community for Four Generations"
"Thoughtful Service in Your Time of Need"

The emphasis on service, especially on "grief counseling" and "bereavement therapy," shifts the focus away from the two most stigmatizing elements of funeral work: the handling and preparation of the body, which already has been discussed at length; and retail sales, which are widely interpreted as profiting from other people's grief. Many of the funeral directors indicated that they believed the major reason for negative public feelings toward their occupation was not only that they handled dead bodies, but the fact that they made their living off the dead, or at least, off the grief of the living.[10]

_____

[9]In Kansas, Missouri, Oklahoma, and Texas, as in most states, bodies do not have to be embalmed or cremated if a legal death certificate is obtained and the body is disposed of within 24 hours.

[10]Several studies have focused on how unscrupulous members of the funeral industry capitalize on the grief of their customers to reap enormous profits from the sale of caskets, vaults, burial clothing, grave markers, and a variety of unnecessary and often unwanted "services" (e.g., see Consumers' Union 1977; Fulton 1961; Harmer 1963; Mitford 1963).

All admitted that much of their profit came from the sale of caskets and vaults, where markup is usually a minimum of 100%, and often 400–500%, but all played down this aspect of their work. The Federal Trade Commission requires that funeral directors provide their customers with itemized lists of all charges. The author was provided with price lists for all merchandise and services by all the funeral directors in this study. When asked to estimate the "average price" of one of their funerals, respondents' answers ranged from $3,000 to $4,000. Typically, the casket accounted for approximately half of the total expense. Respondents indicated that less than 5% of their business involved cremations, but that even then they often encouraged the purchase of a casket. One said, "A lot of people ask about cremation, because they think it's cheaper, but I usually sell them caskets even for cremation; then, if you add the cost of cremation and urn, cremation becomes more profitable than burial."

Despite this denial of the retail aspects of the job, trade journals provide numerous helpful hints on the best techniques for displaying and selling caskets, and great care is given to this process. In all the funeral homes visited, one person was charged with the primary responsibility for helping with "casket selection." In smaller family-operated funeral homes, this person usually was the funeral director's wife. In the large chain-owned companies, it was one of the "associate funeral directors." In either case, the person was a skilled salesperson.

Nevertheless, the sales pitch is wrapped in the shroud of service. During each interview, the author asked to be shown the "selection room," and to be treated as if he were there to select a casket for a loved one. All the funeral directors willingly complied, and most treated the author as if he actually were there to select a casket. Interestingly, most perceived this as an actual sales opportunity, and mentioned their "pre-need selection service" and said that if the author had not already made such arrangements, they would gladly assist him with the process. The words "sell," "sales," "buy," and "purchase," were carefully avoided. Also, although by law the price for each casket must be displayed separately, most funeral homes also displayed a "package price" that included the casket and "full services." If purchased separately, the casket was always more expensive than if it was included in the package of services. This gave the impression that a much more expensive casket could be purchased for less money if bought as part of a service package. It also implied that the services provided by the firm were of more value than the merchandise.

The funeral directors rationalized the high costs of merchandise and funerals by emphasizing that they were a small price to pay for the services performed. One insisted, "We don't sell merchandise, we sell service!" Another asked, "What is peace of mind worth?" and another, "How do you put a price on relieving grief?"

Another rationalization for the high prices was the amount of work involved in arranging and conducting funeral services. When asked about the negative aspects of their jobs, most emphasized the hard work and long hours involved.[11] In fact, all but two of the interviewees said that they did not want their children to follow in their footsteps, because the work was largely misunderstood (stigmatized), too hard, the hours too long, and "the income not nearly as high as most people think."

In addition to emphasizing the service aspect of their work, funeral directors also tend to join a number of local philanthropic and service organizations (Pine 1975, 40). Although many businessmen find that joining such organizations is advantageous for making contacts, Stephenson (1985, 223) contended that the

small-town funeral director "may be able to counter the stigma of his or her occupation by being active in the community, thereby counteracting some of the negative images associated with the job of funeral directing."

SOCIOECONOMIC STATUS VERSUS OCCUPATIONAL PRESTIGE

Ritzer (1977, 9) pointed out that some jobs suffer from "occupational status insecurity." This clearly is the case with morticians and funeral directors. They are members of an occupation wrought with "social stigma . . . an occupational group which is extremely sensitive to public criticism, and which works hard to enhance its position in society" (Stephenson 1985, 225).

It seems that what funeral directors lack in occupational prestige, they make up for in socioeconomic status. Although interviewees were very candid about the number of funerals they performed every year and the average costs per funeral, most were reluctant to disclose their annual incomes. One exception was a 37-year-old funeral home owner, funeral director, and licensed embalmer in a community of approximately 25,000 who indicated that in the previous year he had handled 211 funerals and had a gross income of just under $750,000. After deducting overhead (three licensed embalmers on staff, a receptionist, a gardener, a student employee, insurance costs, etc.), he estimated his net income to have been "close to $250,000." He quickly added, however, that he worked long hours, had his 5-day vacation cut to two (because of a "funeral call that he had to handle personally") and despite his relatively high income (probably one of the two or three highest incomes in the community), he felt morally, socially, and professionally obligated to hide his wealth in the community. "I have to walk a fine line," he said, "I can live in a nice home, drive a nice car, and wear nice suits, because people know that I

---

[11]One funeral director estimated that he spent approximately 125 hours on each funeral, and performed on the average of 100 funerals a year. By his estimate, if he worked 24 hours per day, he would have to work 561 days in a year!

am a successful businessman—but, I have to be careful not to flaunt it."

One of the ways he reconciled this dilemma was by enjoying "the finer things in life" outside the community. He owned a condominium in Vail where he took ski trips and kept his sports car. He also said that none of his friends or neighbors there knew that he was in the funeral business. In fact, when they inquired about his occupation, he told them he was in insurance (which technically was true because he also was a licensed insurance agent who sold burial policies). When asked why he did not disclose his true occupational identity, he responded:

> When I tell people what I really do, they initially seem "put off," even repulsed. I have literally had people jerk their hands back during a handshake when somebody introduces me and then tells them what I do for a living. Later, many of them become very curious and ask a lot of questions. If you tell people you sell insurance, they usually let the subject drop.

Although almost all the funeral directors in this study lived what they characterized as fairly "conservative lifestyles," most also indicated that they enjoyed many of the material things that their jobs afforded them. One couple rationalized their recent purchase of a very expensive sailboat (which both contended they "really couldn't afford"), by saying, "Hey, if anybody knows that you can't take it with you, it's us—we figured we might as well enjoy it while we can." Another commented, "Most of the people in this community would never want to do what I do, but most of them would like to have my income."

Summary and Conclusion

A person's occupation is an integral component of his or her personal and social identity. This study describes and analyzes how people in the funeral industry attempt to reduce and neutralize the stigma associated with their occupations. Morticians and funeral directors are particularly stigmatized, not only because they perform work that few others would be willing to do (preparing dead bodies for burial), but also because they profit from death. Consequently, members of the funeral industry consciously work at stigma reduction.

Paramount among their strategies are symbolically redefining their work. This especially involves avoiding all language that reminds their customer of death, the body, and retail sales; morticians and funeral directors emphasize the need for their professional services of relieving family grief and bereavement counseling. They also practice role distance, emphasize their professionalism, wrap themselves in a "shroud of service," and enjoy their relatively high socioeconomic status rather than lament their lower occupational prestige.

Stephenson (1985, 231) pointed out an interesting paradox:

> In spite of our current preoccupation with death, we have given it a taboo status that implies a great deal of underlying fear and anxiety. Anything that will ease our fears is used to protect us from death. We give millions of dollars to fight disease, we occupy our spare time with staying physically fit, and we blunt death's awful impact with the use of the skills of the funeral director. While critics may consider such activities as barbaric or in bad taste, they are certainly in harmony with the basic values of American society.

Morticians and funeral directors are in a precarious social situation. They perform work that the majority of society believes is needed (Kastenbaum and Aisenberg 1973), and although their services are not legally required, they are socially demanded. Yet, their occupations place them in a paradoxical position of performing duties deemed by larger society as "necessary," but "undesirable." Try as they may, they cannot fully escape the stigma associated with their work.

All but two of the people in this study indicated that if they had it all to do over again, they would choose the same occupation. Yet, only one indicated that he hoped his children pursued the funeral business. And, even he commented, " . . . but, they need to understand that it's hard work, and largely unappreciated." All agreed that one of their major tasks was handling the stigma of handling the dead.

Handling the dead will not become any more glamorous in the future, and that aspect of the mortician's work probably will continue to be stigmatized. However, if Americans become more comfortable with death and their own mortality, it also is likely that emphasizing morticians' roles as bereavement counselors will no longer be sufficient to redefine their work. If that is indeed the case, how will morticians and funeral directors symbolically redefine their work in the future to neutralize the stigma associated with handling the dead and profiting from grief? This research suggests that there is a growing tendency for funeral directors to emphasize their roles as "pre-need counselors." Since death is inevitable, and an aged population is more likely to recognize that, funeral directors may even more prominently tout themselves as akin to financial planners who can help in the advance planning and preparation of funeral arrangements. This could be important in neutralizing the two most stigmatizing attributes of their work. First, like previous strategies, it de-emphasizes the body work; secondly, and perhaps more importantly, it may alleviate some of the stigma associated with profiting from death and grief because they would be viewed as helping people to prepare for funeral needs in advance so that they might create a "hedge" against inflation and make important financial decisions at a time when they are not grief-stricken. Future research on the funeral industry should focus on this emerging role.

References

Amos, E. P. 1983. *Kansas Funeral Profession Through the Years.* Topeka: Kansas Funeral Directors' Association.

Aries, P. 1976. *Western Attitudes Toward Death: From the Middle Ages to the Present.* Trans. P. M. Ranum. Baltimore: Johns Hopkins University Press, p. 99.

Becker, E. 1973. *The Denial of Death.* New York: Free Press.

Bendann, E. 1930. *Death Customs: An Analytical Study of Burial Rites.* New York: Knopf.

Berg, B. L. 1989. *Qualitative Research Methods for the Social Sciences.* Boston: Allyn & Bacon.

Charmaz, K. 1980. *The Social Reality of Death: Death in Contemporary America.* Reading, MA: Addison-Wesley.

Consumers' Union. 1977. *Funerals: Consumers' Last Rights.* New York: Norton.

Fulton, R. 1961. "The Clergyman and the Funeral Director: A Study in Role Conflict." *Social Forces* 39: 317–323.

Garson, B. 1975. *All the Livelong Day: The Meaning and Demeaning of Routine Work.* Garden City, NY: Doubleday.

Goffman, E. 1959. *The Presentation of Self in Everyday Life.* Garden City, NY: Anchor Doubleday.

_____. 1963. *Stigma: Notes on the Management of Spoiled Identity.* Englewood Cliffs, NJ: Prentice-Hall.

Habenstein, R. W., and W. M. Lamers. 1960. *Funeral Customs the World Over.* Milwaukee: Bulfin.

Hafferty, F. W. 1986. "Cadaver Story Humor." Paper presented at the annual meeting of the Midwest Sociological Society, Des Moines, IA.

_____. 1988. "Cadaver Stories and the Emotional Socialization of Medical Students." *Journal of Health and Social Behavior* 29: 344–356.

Harmer, R. M. 1963. *The High Cost of Dying.* New York: Collier.

Hughes, E. C. 1979. *The Sociological Eye: Selected Papers.* Chicago: Aldine-Atherton.

Huntington, R., and P. Metcalf. 1979. *Celebrations of Death.* Cambridge: Cambridge University Press.

Jackson, C. O. 1980. "Death Shall Have No Dominion: The Passing of the World of the Dead in America." Pp. 47–55 in R. A. Kalish (ed.), *Death and Dying: Views from Many Cultures.* Farmingdale, NY: Baywood.

Kastenbaum, R., and R. Aisenberg. 1972. *The Psychology of Death.* New York: Springer.

Kearl, M. C. 1989. *Endings: A Sociology of Death and Dying.* New York: Oxford University Press.

Knight, J. A. 1973. *Doctor to Be: Coping with the Trials and Triumphs of Medical School.* New York: Appleton-Century-Crofts.

Lesy, M. 1987. *The Forbidden Zone.* New York: Farrar, Straus & Giroux.

Mitford, J. 1963. *The American Way of Death.* New York: Simon & Schuster.

Momeyer, R. W. 1988. *Confronting Death.* Bloomington: Indiana University Press.

Murray, M. A. 1969. *The Splendor That Was Egypt,* rev. ed. New York: Praeger.

Parsons, T., and V. M. Lidz. 1967. "Death in American Society." Pp. 133–170 in E. Shneidman (ed.), *Essays in Self-Destruction.* New York: Science House.

Parsons, T., R. C. Fox, and V. M. Lidz. 1972. "The 'Gift of Life' and Its Reciprocation." *Social Research* 39: 367–415.

Pavalko, R. M. 1988. *Sociology of Occupations and Professions,* 2nd ed. Itasca, IL: Peacock.

Pine, V. R. 1975. *Caretaker of the Dead: The American Funeral Director.* New York: Irvington.

Polsky, N. 1969. *Hustlers, Beats and Others.* Garden City, NY: Anchor.

Ritzer, G. 1977. *Working: Conflict and Change,* 2nd ed. Englewood Cliffs, NJ: Prentice-Hall.

Schatzman, L., and A. L. Strauss. 1973. *Field Research: Strategies for a Natural Sociology.* Englewood Cliffs, NJ: Prentice-Hall.

Spradley, J. P. 1979. *The Ethnographic Interview.* New York: Holt, Rinehart & Winston.

Stephenson, J. S. 1985. *Death, Grief, and Mourning: Individual and Social Realities.* New York: Free Press.

Sudnow, D. 1967. *Passing On: The Social Organization of Dying.* Englewood Cliffs, NJ: Prentice-Hall.

Terkel, S. 1974. *Working: People Talk About What They Do All Day and How They Feel About What They Do.* New York: Pantheon.

Thompson, W. E. 1983. "Hanging Tongues: A Sociological Encounter with the Assembly Line." *Qualitative Sociology* 6 (Fall): 215–237.

Turner, R. E., and D. Edgley. 1976. "Death as Theater: A Dramaturgical Analysis of the American Funeral." *Sociology and Social Research* 60 (July): 377–392.

Warner, W. L. 1959. *The Living and the Dead.* New Haven, CT: Yale University Press.

Wass, H., F. M. Berardo, and R. A. Neimeyer. 1988. "The Funeral in Contemporary Society." In H. Wass, F. M. Berardo, and R. A. Neimeyer (eds.), *Dying: Facing the Facts,* 2nd ed. New York: Hemisphere.

Woods, A. S., and R. G. Delisle. 1978. "The Treatment of Death in Sympathy Cards." Pp. 95–103 in C. Winick (ed.), *Deviance and Mass Media.* Beverly Hills, CA: Sage.

Questions

1. Thompson makes use of Goffman's concept of the back stage to explain how things work in the funeral home. Can you think of other settings that are divided between front and back stage?

2. Recall Goffman's notion of the "definition of the situation." What sort of definition of the situation do funeral workers want to create for their clients and potential clients—the live ones, that is?

3. What techniques do funeral workers utilize as they attempt to manage the stigma of their jobs? How successful are these techniques?

4. Thompson's review of the literature on death suggested that there is some dispute about whether Americans are in "denial" about death. How might this issue be studied empirically?

5. In your town's "yellow pages," what sorts of ads do funeral homes publish? How do these compare with the ones cited by Thompson?

·19·

The Rest Room and Equal Opportunity *

Harvey Molotch

On the face of it, this article is about the degree to which Western society provides men and women with equal opportunities to pee. Now, while few would argue that having a place to pee is a trivial matter, this would hardly seem to be a topic worthy of inclusion in a book of sociological readings. If you read this article carefully, however, you will discover that Professor Molotch is making a larger point: Structure affects behavior as well as opportunities. Yes, people make choices, but their choices are influenced by pre-existing social arrangements. And, given all of the relevant facts, structures that seem equal may not be.

At the risk of appearing disrespectful, let me say that the best way to understand equal opportunity is to use the public toilet. Sometimes a gross approach can best clarify a subtle issue. Through the example of how society is organized to provide men and women with the capacity to relieve themselves, we can understand what it takes, as a more general matter, to provide members of different social groups with authentic equal opportunity.

In many public buildings, the amount of floor area dedicated for the men's room and the women's room is the same. The prevailing public bathroom doctrine in the U.S. is one of segregation among the genders, but with equality the guiding ideology. In some jurisdictions, this square footage equality is enshrined in law.

Such an arrangement follows the dictum that equality can be achieved only by policies that are "gender-blind" (or "color-blind" or "ethnic-blind") in the allocation of a public resource. To give less to women (or blacks or Hispanics) would be discrimination; to give more would be "reverse discrimination." Women and men have the same proportion of a building to use as rest rooms. Presumably this should provide members of both genders with equal opportunity for dealing with their bodily needs in a timely and convenient way.

The trouble with this sort of equality is that, being blind, it fails to recognize differences between men as a group and women as a group. These differences are not amenable to easy change. Part of women's demand for bathrooms cannot exist for men because only women menstruate. Women make trips to the rest room to secure hygienic and socially appropriate adaptations to this physical fact. And because men's physiology suits them for the use of urinals, a large number of men can be

"The Rest Room and Equal Opportunity." by Harvey Molotch from *Sociological Forum*, Vol. 3, No. 1: pp. 128–132. Copyright © 1988. Reprinted with kind permission from Springer Science and Business Media.

*Encouragement and assistance was provided by Howard Becker, Gayle Binion, and Beth Schneider.

serviced by a relatively small physical space. Women in our society use toilets to urinate, and toilets require a larger area than urinals. By creating men's and women's rooms of the same size, society guarantees that *individual* women will be worse off than individual men. By distributing a resource equally, an unequal result is structurally guaranteed.

The consequences are easily visible at intermission time whenever men and women congregate in theater lobbies. When the house is full, the women form a waiting line in front of the bathroom while the men do their business without delay. Women experience discomfort and are excluded from conversations that occur under more salutary conditions elsewhere in the lobby. If toward the rear of the line, women may experience anxiety that they will miss the curtain rise. Indeed, they may arrive too late to be seated for the opening scene, dance routine, or orchestral movement. Their late arrival is easily taken by others (particularly men) as evidence of characterological slowness or preoccupation with primping and powder room gossip. All these difficulties are built into the structure of the situation. Equality of square feet to the genders delivers women special burdens of physical discomfort, social disadvantage, psychological anxiety, compromised access to the full product (the performance), and public ridicule.

An obvious solution, one I'll call the "liberal" policy, is to make women's rooms larger than men's. Women's bathrooms need to be big enough to get women in and out as quickly as men's bathrooms get men in and out. No more and no less. A little applied sociological research in various types of settings would establish the appropriate ratios needed to accomplish such gender equality.

An alternative solution, one I'll call "conservative," would be for women to change the way they do things, rather than for society to change the structuring of rest room space. There is no need to overturn the principle of equality of square footage among the genders. Instead, women need to use their allotted square footage more efficiently. If women truly want to relieve themselves as efficiently as men, they can take some initiative. Options do exist short of biological alteration. While women may not be capable of adapting to urinals, they could relieve themselves by squatting over a common trough. This would save some space—perhaps enough to achieve efficiency parity with men. Women are not physically bound to use up so many square feet. It is a cultural issue, and in this case the problem derives from a faulty element of women's culture. It is not physiologically given that each woman should have her own cubicle, much less her own toilet, or that she should sit rather than squat.

This joins the issue well. Should women be forced to change or should the burden be placed on men who may have to give up some of their own square footage so that women might have more? The response from the liberal camp is that even if women's spatial needs are cultural, these needs should be recognized and indulged. Cultural notions of privacy and modes of using toilets were not arrived at by women in isolation from men. Men's conceptions of "decency"—at least as much as women's—encourage women to be physically modest and demure. Men's recurring violence toward women encourages bathroom segregation in the first instance because segregation makes it easier for potential assailants to be spotted as "out of place." Providing women with latched cubicles provides a further bit of security in a world made less secure by men. Thus, prescriptions of dignity and protections from assault come from the common culture produced by women and men. Whatever their origins, these cultural imperatives have become a real force and are sustained by continuing pressures on women's lives. Until this common culture is itself transformed, U.S. women cannot become as efficient as Tiwi women in their capacity to urinate in public settings, regardless of the efficiency advantages. On the other hand, altering the spatial allocations for men's and women's bathrooms is relatively simple and inexpensive.

It becomes harder to be a liberal as the weight of cultural imperative seems to lighten. Suppose, for example, that *a part* of the reason for the line in front of the ladies' room is, in fact, a tendency for women to primp longer than men or to gossip among one another at the sinks (although the lines in front of *toilet stalls* would belie such an assumption). Should vanity and sociability be subsidized at the expense of the larger community? But here again, the culture that men and women have produced in common becomes relevant. Perhaps women "take a powder" to escape the oppression of men, using the rest room as a refuge from social conditions imposed by the dominant gender? Perhaps the need to look lovely, every moment and in every way, is created by men's need to display a public companion whose make-up is flawless, whose head has every hair in place, and whose body is perfectly scented. Women are driven to decorate themselves as men's commodities and the consequence is bathroom demand. Should men pay for this "service" through sacrificing their own square footage or should women adjust by waiting in line and climbing all over one another for a patch of the vanity mirror?

Again it turns on who should change what. The conservative answer might be for women to give up primping, but that would fly in the face of the demand (also championed by conservatives) that women's cultural role is to be beautiful for their men. Although not because they wished to increase rest room efficiency, radical feminists have argued that women should ease up on their beauty treatments, precisely because it ratifies their subservience to men and deflects them from success in occupational and other realms. But again the liberal view holds appeal: at least until the transition to feminism, the *existing cultural arrangement* necessitates an asymmetric distribution of space to provide equality of opportunity among the genders.

As the issues become subtle, reasonable people come to disagree on who should do what and what community expense should be incurred to achieve parity. Such controversy stems from the effort to provide equal opportunity for individuals by taking into account differences among groups. The same problem arises no matter what the issue and no matter what the group. If people commonly get their job leads by word-of-mouth through friends and neighbors, then black people—excluded from the neighborhoods of employers and of those employed in expanding job sectors—will be at a labor market disadvantage. Black people's chronically higher unemployment rate stands as evidence of disadvantage: their longer queue for jobs is analogous to the longer line in front of the women's rest room. Blacks can be told to work harder, to use their meager resources more efficiently, to rearrange their lives and cultures to better their job qualifications. Alternatively, their present plight can be understood as *structural*—stemming from a history of enslavement, Jim Crow segregation, and white prejudice that now results in concrete arrangements that hinder individual life changes. One must be color-sighted, rather than color-blind, to deal with these differences. But this is no reverse racism: it rests on perception of social structural locations, not upon inherent inferiority attributed to group membership. Such government mandated policies as open job-searches, ethnic hiring targets, and preference for minority vendors and subcontractors can counteract structural biases that hold down opportunities of women, blacks, and other minorities. Affirmative action programs should be conceived as compensatory efforts to overcome such structured disadvantage (although the legal interpretation of the statutes is usually drawn more narrowly).

Equality is not a matter of arithmetic division, but of social accounting. Figuring out what is equal treatment necessitates—in every instance—a sociological analysis of exactly how it is that structures operate on people's lives. Besides rejecting the conservatives' penchant for blaming the victim, liberal policies need a concrete analytic basis that goes beyond good-hearted sympathy for the downtrodden. As in the rest room case, we need to specify how current patterns of "equal" treatment of groups yield unequal opportunities to individuals. We then should determine exactly what it would take (e.g., square feet to gender ratios) to redress the inequality.

Besides careful analysis, equality also involves a decision as to who is going to change and in what way. These decisions will often take from some and give to others. Thus we have the two-pronged essence of action on behalf of equal opportunity: sociological analysis and political struggle.

Questions

1. Briefly summarize the author's point: Under what circumstances does equality of space to pee not mean equality of opportunity to pee? Do you agree or disagree with his analysis?

2. At one point, Professor Molotch offers two possibilities for creating more equality between men and women. One of these options he labels as "liberal"; the other he labels as "conservative." Summarize (briefly) each option. Which option seems (to you) to be more fair? Why?

3. Here's a difficult question: Why does the author use the labels "liberal" and "conservative" to describe the options for change?

·20·
Hidden Lessons

Myra Sadker and David Sadker

Myra and David Sadker are frequently asked how they found their mutual interest in gender bias in education, the subject of this 1994 article. They reply that it came to them when they were in graduate school where, as wife and husband, they were enrolled in the same program: "We attended the same classes, prepared the same assignments, read the same books—and realized that we were getting two very different educations." The turning point, they explain, came in a meeting of students and professors in the program.

> About fifty participants, almost all men, were discussing civil rights for minorities in education. One male voice after another joined in the discussion until Myra made a suggestion and waited for a reaction. But the men kept right on talking. "Perhaps they didn't hear me," she thought, so she tried again. But the discussion rambled on as if she had not uttered a word. Then a loud, deep voice boomed out, the kind of powerful voice that causes eyes to look skyward searching for Charlton Heston to bring down the tablets. All eyes turned to six-foot Mike from Utah as he slowly repeated Myra's idea. The talking stopped, there was complete silence, and then the room exploded with praise. "That's what we've been looking for! Great idea!"
>
> As a result of Myra's good idea that was attributed to Mike, a professor assigned the task of writing grant proposals to improve education for minorities. We worked together and signed our names as coauthors. The faculty member began the next meeting with this announcement: "There's one paper that stands out," he said. "I'd like to talk with you about David's proposal. He has some ideas I think we can pursue." There was enthusiasm for our proposal, our ideas, but "our" had become "David's." "I wrote it, too," Myra said lightly so as not to appear petty. The faculty member looked surprised and concerned. "Of course when we say David, we mean you, too. You know that, don't you?"

Sitting in the same classroom, reading the same textbook, listening to the same teacher, boys and girls receive very different educations.

From grade school through graduate school female students are more likely to be invisible members of classrooms. Teachers interact with males more frequently, ask them better questions, and give them more precise and helpful feedback. Over the course of years the uneven distribution of teacher time, energy, attention, and talent, with boys getting the lion's share, takes its toll on girls. Since gender bias is not a noisy problem, most people are unaware of the secret sexist lessons and the quiet losses they engender.

Girls are the majority of our nation's schoolchildren, yet they are second-class educational citizens. The problems they face—loss of self-esteem, decline in achievement, and elimination of career options—are at the heart of the educational process. Until educational sexism is eradicated, more than half our children will be shortchanged and their gifts lost to society.

Award-winning author Susan Faludi discovered that backlash "is most powerful when it goes private, when it lodges inside a woman's mind and turns her vision inward, until she imagines the pressure is all in her head, until she begins to enforce the backlash too—on herself" (Faludi 1991). Psychological backlash internalized by adult women is a frightening concept, but what is even more terrifying is a curriculum of sexist school lessons becoming secret mind games played against female children, our daughters, tomorrow's women.

After almost two decades of research grants and thousands of hours of classroom observation, we remain amazed at the stubborn persistence of these hidden sexist lessons. When we began our investigation of gender bias, we looked first in the classrooms of one of Washington, D.C.'s elite and expensive private schools. Uncertain of exactly what to look for, we wrote nothing down; we just observed. The classroom was a whirlwind of activity, so fast paced we could easily miss the quick but vital phrase or gesture, the insidious incident, the tiny inequity that held a world of meaning. As we watched, we had to push ourselves beyond the blind spots of socialization and gradually focus on the nature of the interaction between teacher and student. On the second day we saw our first example of sexism, a quick, jarring flash within the hectic pace of the school day:

Two second graders are kneeling beside a large box. They whisper excitedly to each other as they pull out wooden blocks, colored balls, counting sticks. So absorbed are these two small children in examining and sorting the materials, they are visibly startled by the teacher's impatient voice as she hovers over them. "Ann! Julia! Get your cotton-pickin' hands out of the math box. Move over so the boys can get in there and do their work."

Isolated here on the page of a book, this incident is not difficult to interpret. It becomes even more disturbing if you think of it with the teacher making a racial distinction. Picture Ann and Julia as African American children moved away so white children can gain access to the math materials. If Ann and Julia's parents had observed this exchange, they might justifiably wonder whether their tuition dollars were well spent. But few parents actually watch teachers in action, and fewer still have learned to interpret the meaning behind fast-paced classroom events.

The incident unsettles, but it must be considered within the context of numerous interactions this harried teacher had that day. While she talked to the two girls, she was also keeping a wary eye on fourteen other active children. Unless you actually shadowed the teacher, stood right next to her as we did, you might not have seen or heard the event. After all, it lasted only a few seconds.

It took us almost a year to develop an observation system that would register the hundreds of daily classroom interactions, teasing out the gender bias embedded in them. Trained raters coded classrooms in math, reading, English, and social studies. They observed students from different racial and ethnic backgrounds. They saw lessons taught by women and by men, by teachers of different races. In short, they analyzed America's classrooms. By the end of the year we had thousands of observation sheets, and after another year of statistical analysis, we discovered a syntax of sexism so elusive that most teachers and students were completely unaware of its influence (Sadker, Sadker, and Klein 1991).[1]

Recently a producer of NBC's "Dateline" contacted us to learn more about our discovery that girls don't receive their fair share of education. Jane Pauley, the show's anchorwoman, wanted to visit classrooms, capture these covert sexist lessons on videotape, and expose them before a television audience. The task was to extricate sound bites of sexism from a fifth-grade classroom where the teacher, chosen to be the subject of the exposé, was aware she was being scrutinized for sex bias.

"Dateline" had been taping in her class for two days when we received a concerned phone call. "This is a fair teacher," the producer said. "How can we show sexism on our show when there's no gender bias in this teacher's class?" We drove to the NBC studio in Washington, D.C., and found two "Dateline" staffers, intelligent women concerned about fair treatment in school, sitting on the floor in a darkened room staring at the videotape of a fifth-grade class. "We've been playing this over and over. The teacher is terrific. There's no bias in her teaching. Come watch."

After about twenty minutes of viewing, we realized it was a case of déjà vu: The episodal sexist themes and recurring incidents were all too familiar. The teacher was terrific, but she was more effective for half of the students than she was for the other. She was, in fact, a classic example of the hundreds of skillful well-intentioned professionals we have seen who inadvertently teach boys better than girls.

We had forgotten how difficult it was to recognize subtle sexism before you learn how to look. It was as if the "Dateline" staff members were wearing blinders. We halted the tape,

pointed out the sexist behaviors, related them to incidents in our research, and played the tape again. There is a classic "aha!" effect in education when people finally "get it." Once the hidden lessons of unconscious bias are understood, classrooms never look the same again to the trained observer.

Much of the unintentional gender bias in that fifth-grade class could not be shown in the short time allowed by television, but the sound bites of sexism were also there. "Dateline" chose to show a segregated math group: boys sitting on the teacher's right side and girls on her left. After giving the math book to a girl to hold open at the page of examples, the teacher turned her back to the girls and focused on the boys, teaching them actively and directly. Occasionally she turned to the girls' side, but only to read the examples in the book. This teacher, although aware that she was being observed for sexism, had unwittingly transformed the girls into passive spectators, an audience for the boys. All but one, that is: The girl holding the math book had become a prop.

"Dateline" also showed a lively discussion in the school library. With both girls' hands and boys' hands waving for attention, the librarian chose boy after boy to speak. In one interaction she peered through the forest of girls' hands waving directly in front of her to acknowledge the raised hand of a boy in the back of the room. Startled by the teacher's attention, the boy muttered, "I was just stretching."

The next day we discussed the show with future teachers, our students at The American University. They were bewildered. "Those teachers really were sexist. They didn't mean to be, but they were. How could that happen — with the cameras and everyone watching?" When we took those students into classrooms to discover the hidden lessons for themselves, they began to understand. It is difficult to detect sexism unless you know precisely how to observe. And if a lifetime of socialization makes it difficult to spot gender bias even

---

[1]Our first study, which analyzed gender bias in elementary and secondary classrooms, lasted more than three years and was funded by the National Institute of Education. The report submitted to the government was Myra Sadker and David Sadker, *Year 3: Final Report: Promoting Effectiveness in Classroom Instruction,* Washington, DC: National Institute of Education, 1984.

when you're looking for it, how much harder it is to avoid the traps when you are the one doing the teaching.

Among Schoolchildren

Subtle sexism is visible to only the most astute readers of *Among Schoolchildren,* Tracy Kidder's chronicle of real-life educator Chris Zajac. A thirty-four-year-old teacher in Mt. Holyoke, Massachusetts, Mrs. Zajac is a no-nonsense veteran of the classroom. She does not allow her fifth-grade students to misbehave, forget to do their homework, or give up without trying their hardest. Underlying her strict exterior is a woman who cares about schoolchildren. Our students admired her dedication and respected her as a good human being, and it took several readings and discussions before they discovered her inadvertent gender bias. Then came the questions: Does Mrs. Zajac work harder teaching boys than girls? Does she know there is sex bias in her classroom?

These questions probably do not occur to most readers of *Among Schoolchildren* and might jolt both Chris Zajac and the author who so meticulously described the classroom. Here's how Tracy Kidder begins the story of a year in the life of this New England teacher:

"Mrs. Zajac wasn't born yesterday. She knows you didn't do your best work on this paper, Clarence. Don't you remember Mrs. Zajac saying that if you didn't do your best, she'd make you do it over? As for you, Claude, God forbid that you should ever need brain surgery. But Mrs. Zajac hopes that if you do, the doctor won't open up your head and walk off saying he's almost done, as you said when Mrs. Zajac asked you for your penmanship, which, by the way, looks like who did it and ran. Felipe, the reason you have hiccups is, your mouth is always open and the wind rushes in. You're in fifth grade now. So, Felipe, put a lock on it. Zip it up. Then go get a drink of water. Mrs. Zajac means business, Robert. The sooner you realize she never said everybody in the room has to do the work except

for Robert, the sooner you'll get along with her. And . . . Clarence. Mrs. Zajac knows you didn't try. You don't just hand in junk to Mrs. Zajac. She's been teaching an awful lot of years. She didn't fall off the turnip cart yesterday. She told you she was an old-lady teacher." (Kidder 1989)

Swiftly, adroitly, Kidder introduces the main characters in the classroom—Clarence, Claude, Felipe, Robert, and back to Clarence, the boy in whom Mrs. Zajac invests most. But where are the girls?

As our students analyzed the book and actually examined who Mrs. Zajac was speaking to, they saw that page after page she spent time with the boys—disciplining them, struggling to help them understand, teaching them with all the energy and talent she could muster. In contrast, the pages that showed Mrs. Zajac working with girls were few and far between.

When we ask teachers at our workshops why they spend more time helping boys, they say, "Because boys need it more" or "Boys have trouble reading, writing, doing math. They can't even sit still. They need me more." In *Among Schoolchildren,* Chris Zajac feels that way, too. Kidder describes how she allows boys to take her over because she thinks they need her.

So teachers of good intention, such as Chris Zajac, respond to boys and teach them more actively, but their time and attention are not limitless. While the teachers are spending time with boys, the girls are being ignored and shortchanged. The only girl clearly realized in *Among Schoolchildren* is Judith, a child who is so alert that she has a vast English vocabulary even though her parents speak only Spanish. But while Judith is a girl of brilliant potential, she rarely reaps the benefit of Mrs. Zajac's active teaching attention. In fact, rather than trouble her teacher and claim time and attention for herself, Judith helps Mrs. Zajac, freeing her to work with the more demanding boys. Mrs. Zajac knows she isn't giving this talented girl what she needs and deserves: "If only I had more time," she thinks as she looks at Judith.

On a field trip to Old Sturbridge Village, the children have segregated themselves by sex on the bus, with the boys claiming the back. In a moment of quiet reflection, Chris realizes that in her classroom "the boys rarely give her a chance to spend much time with her girls." She changes her seat, joins the girls, and sings jump rope songs with them for the remainder of the trip.

But her time spent with the girls is short-lived—the length of the day-long field trip—and her recognition of the gender gap in time and attention is brief: a paragraph-long flash of understanding in a book of more than three hundred pages. On the whole, Chris Zajac does not invest her talent in girls. But nurturing children is not unlike tending a garden: Neglect, even when benign, is withering; time and attention bear fruit. Mrs. Zajac and other caring teachers across the country are unaware of the full impact of uneven treatment. They do not realize the high academic and emotional price many girls pay for being too good.

Drawn from years of research, the episodes that follow demonstrate the sexist lessons taught daily in America's classrooms.[2] Pulled out of the numerous incidents in a school day, these inequities become enlarged, as if observed through a magnifying glass, so we can see clearly how they extinguish learning and shatter self-esteem. Imagine yourself in a sixth-grade science class like the one we observed in Maryland.

The teacher is writing a list of inventors and their discoveries on the board:

Elias Howe	sewing machine
Robert Fulton	steamboat
Thomas A. Edison	light bulb
James Otis	elevator
Alexander Graham Bell	telephone
Cyrus McCormick	reaper
Eli Whitney	cotton gin
Orville and Wilbur Wright	airplane

A girl raises her hand and asks, "It looks like all the inventors were men. Didn't women invent anything?" The teacher does not add any female inventors to the list, nor does he discuss new scholarship recognizing the involvement of women in inventions such as the cotton gin. He does not explain how hard it was in times past for women to obtain patents in their own names, and therefore we may never know how many female inventors are excluded from the pages of our history books.[3] Instead he grins, winks, and says, "Sweetheart, don't worry

---

[2]These episodes are drawn primarily from our three-year study of sex bias in elementary and secondary classrooms. They are also taken from classroom observations conducted as we supervised student teachers at The American University and as we consulted with schools around the country and assessed their classrooms for gender bias.

[3]We may never know how many women inventors are excluded from the pages of history books, but we do know the names of some. For example, Russell Conwell (1843–1925) published accounts of the role played by women in several important inventions:

> Who was it that invented the sewing machine? If I would go to school tomorrow and ask your children, they would say "Elias Howe." He was in the Civil War with me, and often in my tent, and I often heard him say that he worked fourteen years to get up that sewing machine. But his wife [Elizabeth J. Ames Howe] made up her mind one day that they would starve to death if there wasn't something or other invented pretty soon, and so in two hours she invented the sewing machine. Of course he took out the patent in his name. Men always do that. (296)

Conwell also published an interview with Cyrus McCormick, "in which the inventor admitted that after he and his father had tried to create the reaper and failed 'a West Virginia woman . . . took a lot of shears and nailed them together on the edge of a board [with one blade of each pair loose]. Then she wired them so that when she pulled the wire one way it closed them, and . . . the other way it opened them. And there she had the principle of the mowing machine. If you look at the mowing-machine, you will see that it is nothing but a lot of shears'" (80).

Eli Whitney (whom history records as the inventor of the cotton gin, the machine that revolutionized life in the southern United States) admitted that the idea for the gin was given him by Catherine Littlefield Green. While working on the gin Whitney was living in her home. Although he tended to underplay her contribution in public, Whitney paid her a share of his royalties for the machine (82–83). [See Autumn Stanley, *Mothers and Daughters of Invention: Notes for a Revised History of Technology*, New Brunswick, NJ: Rutgers University Press, 1993. —Ed.]

about it. It's the same with famous writers and painters. It's the man's job to create things and the woman's job to look beautiful so she can inspire him." Several boys laugh. A few clown around by flexing their muscles as they exclaim, "Yes!" One girl rolls her eyes toward the ceiling and shakes her head in disgust. The incident lasts less than a minute, and the discussion of male inventors continues.

We sometimes ask our students at The American University to list twenty famous women from American history. There are only a few restrictions. They cannot include figures from sports or entertainment. Presidents' wives are not allowed unless they are clearly famous in their own right. Most students cannot do it. The seeds of their ignorance were sown in their earliest years of schooling.

In the 1970s, analyses of best-selling history books showed a biological oddity, a nation with only founding fathers (Trecker 1971). More space was given to the six-shooter than to the women's suffrage movement. In fact, the typical history text gave only two sentences to enfranchising half the population. Science texts continued the picture of a one-gender world, with the exception of Marie Curie who was permitted to stand behind her husband and peer over his shoulder as he looked into a microscope. Today's history and science texts are better — but not much (Weitzman and Rizzo 1976).

At our workshops we ask teachers and parents to tell or write about any sexism they have seen in their schools. We have been collecting their stories for years (Trecker 1971). A Utah teacher told us: "Last year I had my U.S. history classes write biographies about famous Americans. When I collected all one hundred and fifty, I was dismayed to find only five on women. When I asked my kids why, they said they didn't know any famous women. When I examined their textbook more closely, I saw there were few females in it.

And there were even fewer books on famous American women in our school library."

Teachers add to textbook bias when they produce sexist materials of their own. One parent described her efforts to stop a teacher-made worksheet that perpetuated stereotypes of yesteryear:

> A few years ago my daughter came home upset over her grade. When I looked at her paper, I got more angry than she was. At the top of the worksheet were the faces of a man and a woman. At the bottom were different objects — nails, a saw, a sewing needle, thread, a hammer, a screwdriver, a broom. The directions said to draw a line from the man to the objects that belong to him and a line from the woman to the objects that go with her. In our house my husband does the cooking and I do the repair work, so you can imagine what the lines on my daughter's paper looked like. There was a huge red F in the middle of her worksheet. I called the teacher right away. She was very understanding and assured me the F wouldn't count. A small victory, I thought, and forgot about it.
>
> This year my son is in her class. Guess what he brought home last week. Same worksheet — same F. Nothing had changed at all.

When girls do not see themselves in the pages of textbooks, when teachers do not point out or confront the omissions, our daughters learn that to be female is to be an absent partner in the development of our nation. And when teachers add their stereotypes to the curriculum bias in books, the message becomes even more damaging.

In a 1992 survey in *Glamour,* 74 percent of those responding said that they had "a teacher who was biased against females or paid more attention to the boys." Math class was selected as the place where inequities were most likely to occur. Fifty-eight percent picked it as their most sexist subject. Physical education was second, and science came in third, selected by 47 percent of the respondents (*Glamour* 1992). Women at our workshops recall remarks made by math and science teachers that years later still leave them upset and angry:

> In my A.P. physics class in high school in 1984 there were only three girls and twenty-seven boys. The three girls, myself included, consistently scored at the top end of the scale. On one test I earned a 98. The next closest boy earned an 88. The teacher handed the tests back saying, "Boys, you are failing. These three pretty cookies are outscoring you guys on every test." He told the boys it was embarrassing for them to be beaten by a girl. He always referred to us (the girls) as "Cookie" or made our names sound very cutesy!

Sometimes the humiliating lessons come not from school policies, teachers, or books but from boys, the very individuals that adolescent girls most want to impress:

> The New England high school was having an assembly during the last period on Friday, and the auditorium was packed with more than a thousand students, who were restless as they listened to announcements. A heavy, awkward tenth grader made her way across the stage to reach the microphone located in the center. As she walked, several male students made loud barking noises to signify she was a dog. Others oinked like pigs. Later a slender long-haired senior walked to the mike; she was greeted by catcalls and whistles. Nobody attempted to stop the demeaning and hurtful public evaluation of the appearance of these teenage girls.

Tolerated under the assumptions that "boys will be boys" and hormone levels are high in high school, sexual harassment is a way of life in America's schools. While teachers and administrators look the other way, sexually denigrating comments, pinching, touching, and propositioning happen daily. Sensitive and insecure about their appearance, some girls are so intimidated they suffer in silence. Others fight back only to find this heightens the harassment. Many girls don't even realize they have a right to protest. And when they do come

forward, bringing school sexual harassment into the open, it is often dealt with quickly and nervously; it is swept under the rug, turned aside, or even turned against the girl who had the courage to complain. A teacher at a workshop in Indiana told us: "In our school a girl was pinched on the derriere by two boys and verbally harassed. When she reported the incident to the principal, she was told that her dress was inappropriate and that she had asked for it."

Intimidating comments and offensive sexual jokes are even more common in college and sometimes are even made public as part of a classroom lecture and discussion. A female faculty member, teaching at a university that was historically all male, told us about one of the most popular teachers on campus, an economics professor:

> He would show slides illustrating an economic theory and insert women in bikinis in the middle "to keep the students interested."[4] He illustrated different phases of the economic cycle by showing a slide of a woman's breast and pointed out how far away from the nipple each phase was. When a number of female students complained, the local newspaper supported the professor and criticized the "ultrasensitive coeds." That semester the university gave the professor the Teacher of the Year award.

Although sexually harassing remarks, stories, and jokes occur only occasionally in classrooms, female silence is the norm. During our two-year study of colleges, our raters found that girls grow quieter as they grow older. In coeducational classes, college women are even less likely to participate in discussions than elementary and secondary school girls. In the typical college classroom, 45 percent of students do not speak; the majority of these voiceless students are women.

---

[4]One wonders just which group of students he was concerned about here. —Ed.

Breaking the Sound Barrier

Women who have spent years learning the lessons of silence in elementary, secondary, and college classrooms have trouble regaining their voices. In our workshops we often set up a role play to demonstrate classroom sex bias. Four volunteers, two women and two men, are asked to pretend to be students in a middle school social studies lesson. They have no script; their only direction is to take a piece of paper with them as David, playing the part of the social studies teacher, ushers them to four chairs in front of the room. He tells the audience that he will condense all the research on sexism in the classroom into a ten-minute lesson, so the bias will look blatant, even overwhelming. The job of the parents and teachers in the audience is to detect the different forms of egregious sexism. He begins the lesson.

"Today we're going to discuss the chapter in your book, 'The Gathering Clouds of War,' about the American Revolution. But first I'd like you to take out your homework so I can check it." David walks over to Sarah, the first student in the line of four. (In real life she is an English teacher at the local high school.)

"Let's see your paper, Sarah." He pauses to look it over. "Questions three and seven are not correct." Sarah looks concerned.

David moves to Peggy (who is a communications professor at a state college). "Oh, Peggy, Peggy, Peggy!" She looks up as everyone stares. David holds up Peggy's paper. "Would you all look at this. It is sooo neat. You print just like a typewriter. This is the kind of paper I like to put on the bulletin board for open school night." Peggy looks down, smiles, blushes, looks up wide-eyed, and bats her eyelashes. She is not faking or exaggerating these behaviors. Before our eyes she has returned to childhood as the stereotypical good girl with pretty penmanship. The lessons have been well learned.

Next David stops by Tony (who is a vocational education teacher) and looks at the blank paper he is holding. "Tony, you've missed questions three, seven, and eleven. I think you would do better on your assignments if you used the bold headings to guide your reading. I know you can get this if you try harder." Tony nods earnestly as David moves to Roy. Sarah, who missed questions three and seven, looks perplexed.

David scans Roy's paper and hands it back. "Roy, where's your homework?"

Roy (a college physics teacher) stammers, "Here it is," and again offers the blank paper that served as homework for the others in the role play.

"Roy, that's not your history homework. That's science." Roy still looks puzzled. "Trust me, Roy," David says. "No matter what you come up with, it won't be history homework. Now, where is it?"

"The dog ate it," Roy mutters, getting the picture and falling into the bad boy role.

Next David discusses revolutionary battles, military tactics, and male leaders—George Washington, John and Samuel Adams, Paul Revere, Benjamin Franklin, Thomas Jefferson, and more. He calls on Roy and Tony more than twenty times each. When they don't know the answer, he probes, jokes, challenges, offers hints. He calls on Sarah only twice. She misses both her questions because David gives her less than half a second to speak. After effusively praising Peggy's pretty paper, David never calls on her again. As the lesson progresses, Sarah's face takes on a sad, almost vacant expression. Peggy keeps on smiling.

When the scene of blatant sexism is over, many in the audience want to know how the two women felt.

"That was me all through school," Peggy blurts out. "I did very well. My work was neat. I was always prepared. I would have the right answer if someone had called on me. But they never did."

"Why did you watch the two males get all the attention?" we ask. "If you weren't called on, why didn't you call out?"

"I tried. I just couldn't do it."

"Why? You weren't wearing a muzzle. The men were calling out."

"I know. I felt terrible. It reminded me of all those years in school when I wanted to say something but couldn't."

"What about you, Sarah?" we ask. "Why didn't you just shout out an answer?"

"It never occurred to me to do it," Sarah says, then pauses. "No, that's not true. I thought about it, but I didn't want to be out there where I might get laughed at or ridiculed."

David has taught this role play class hundreds and hundreds of times in workshops in big cities and small towns all across the United States. Each time he demonstrates sex bias by blatantly and offensively ignoring female students, and almost always the adult women, put back into the role of twelve-year-olds, sit and say nothing; once again they become the nice girls watching the boys in action. Inside they may feel sad or furious or relieved, but like Sarah and Peggy, they remain silent.

When women try to get into classroom interaction, they rarely act directly. Instead they doodle, write letters, pass notes, and wait for the teacher to notice them. In a California workshop one parent who was playing the part of a student developed an elaborate pantomime. She reached into her large purse, pulled out a file, and began to do her nails. When that failed to attract David's attention, she brought out a brush, makeup, and a mirror. But David continued to ignore her, talking only with the two males.

"I was so mad I wanted to hit you," the woman fumed at the end of the role play when she was invited to express her feelings.

"What did you do to show your anger?" David asked.

"I didn't do anything." Then she paused, realizing the passive-aggressive but ultimately powerless strategy she had pursued. "No, I did do something—my nails," she said sadly.

After hundreds of these role plays, we are still astonished at how quickly the veneer of adulthood melts away. Grown women and men replay behavior they learned as children at school. The role plays are always revealing—funny, sad, and sometimes they even have a troubling twist.

At a workshop for college students at a large university in the Midwest, one of the young women ignored in the role play did not exhibit the usual behavior of silence or passive hostility. Instead, in the middle of the workshop in front of her classmates, she began to sob. She explained later in private that as one of only a few girls in the university's agricultural program, she had been either ignored or harassed. That week in an overenrolled course an instructor had announced, "There are too many students in this class. Everyone with ovaries—out!"

"What did you do?"

"What could I do? I left. Later I told my adviser about it. He was sympathetic but said if there was no room, I should consider another major."

Silent Losses

Each time a girl opens a book and reads a womanless history, she learns she is worth less. Each time the teacher passes over a girl to elicit the ideas and opinions of boys, that girl is conditioned to be silent and to defer. As teachers use their expertise to question, praise, probe, clarify, and correct boys, they help these male students sharpen ideas, refine their thinking, gain their voice, and achieve more. When female students are offered the leftovers of teacher time and attention, morsels of amorphous feedback, they achieve less.

Then girls and women learn to speak softly or not at all; to submerge honest feelings, withhold opinions, and defer to boys; to avoid math and science as male domains; to value neatness and quiet more than assertiveness and creativity; to emphasize appearance and hide intelligence. Through this curriculum in sexism they are turned into educational spectators instead of players; but education is not a spectator sport.

When blatantly sexual or sexist remarks become an accepted part of classroom conversation, female students are degraded. Sexual harassment in business and the military now causes shock waves and legal suits. Sexual harassment in schools is dismissed as normal and unavoidable "boys will be boys" behavior; but by being targeted, girls are being intimidated and caused to feel like members of an inferior class.

Like a thief in school, sexist lessons subvert education, twisting it into a system of socialization that robs potential. Consider this record of silent, devastating losses (Sadker, Sadker, and Klein 1991):

- In the early grades girls are ahead of or equal to boys on almost every standardized measure of achievement and psychological well-being. By the time they graduate from high school or college, they have fallen back. Girls enter school ahead but leave behind.

- In high school, girls score lower on the SAT and ACT tests, which are critical for college admission. The greatest gender gap is in the crucial areas of science and math.

- Girls score far lower on College Board Achievement tests, which are required by most of the highly selective colleges.

- Boys are much more likely to be awarded state and national college scholarships.

- The gap does not narrow in college. Women score lower on all sections of the Graduate Record Exam, which is necessary to enter many graduate programs.

- Women also trail on most tests needed to enter professional schools: The GMAT for business school, the LSAT for law school, and the MCAT for medical school.

- From elementary school through higher education, female students receive less active instruction, both in the quantity and in the quality of teacher time and attention.

In addition to the loss of academic achievement, girls suffer other difficulties:

- Eating disorders among girls in middle and secondary schools and in college are rampant and increasing.

- Incidents of school-based sexual harassment are now reported with alarming frequency.

- One in ten teenage girls becomes pregnant each year. Unlike boys, when girls drop out, they usually stay out.

- As girls go through school, their self-esteem plummets, and the danger of depression increases.

- Economic penalties follow women after graduation. Careers that have a high percentage of female workers, such as teaching and nursing, are poorly paid. And even when women work in the same jobs as men, they earn less money. Most of America's poor live in households that are headed by women.

If the cure for cancer is forming in the mind of one of our daughters, it is less likely to become a reality than if it is forming in the mind of one of our sons. Until this changes, everybody loses.

References

Faludi, Susan. 1991. *Backlash: The Undeclared War Against American Women*. New York: Crown.

Glamour. 1992. "This Is What You Thought: Were Any of Your Teachers Biased Against Females?" August, p. 157.

Kidder, Tracy. 1989. *Among Schoolchildren*. Boston: Houghton Mifflin.

Sadker, Myra, David Sadker, and Susan Klein. 1991. "The Issue of Gender in Elementary and Secondary Education." In Gerald Grant (ed.), *Review of Research in Education,* Vol 17. Washington, DC: American Educational Research Association.

Trecker, Janice Law. 1971. "Women in U.S. History High School Textbooks." *Social Education* 35: 249–260.

Weitzman, Lenore, and Diane Rizzo. 1976. *Biased Textbooks: Image of Males and Females in Elementary School Textbooks.* Washington, DC: Resource Center on Sex Roles in Education.

Questions

1. Consider the exercise that the Sadkers said they routinely gave their students—to list twenty famous women from American history ("not including figures from sports or entertainment. Presidents' wives are not allowed unless they are clearly famous in their own right"). Can you do better on this assignment than the Sadkers' students did? Why or why not?

2. On various occasions, I have assigned the Sadkers' book to students in my introductory sociology classes. Regardless of their gender, students most commonly respond by denying that any similar sorts of things happened in their schools. After extensive discussion, however, many students (especially women students) can recall some incidents of sexism they encountered.

   Why is sexism in the schools so difficult for people to notice? Is it because there is no sexism in schools? How would the Sadkers respond to questions about why sexism is hard to spot?

·21·
Elite Boarding Schools
Curricula as Cultural Capital

Peter W. Cookson, Jr., and Caroline Hodges Persell

Legend has it that in 1936, Ernest Hemingway (1899–1961), while having lunch with a couple of colleagues, remarked that he was "getting to know the rich." One of his companions responded quickly: "The only difference between the rich and other people is that the rich have more money." But is money the only difference between the rich and everyone else? Based on their study of boarding schools, these authors suggest in this 1985 article that there is more to fitting in with the high and mighty than a healthy bank account. To get ahead in our society takes certain kinds of "cultural capital." The term *cultural capital* was introduced by a French sociologist, Pierre Bourdieu, and it is used to refer to the kinds of skills and knowledge—including ways of speaking, manners, and social skills—that are peculiar to each social class in a society.

Borrowing from the British, early American headmasters and teachers advocated a boarding school curriculum that was classical, conservative, and disciplined. It wasn't until the latter part of the nineteenth century that such "soft" subjects as English, history, and mathematics were given a place beside Latin, Greek, rhetoric, and logic in the syllabus. It was the early schoolmasters' belief that young minds, especially boys' minds, if left to their own devices, were undisciplined, even anarchic. The only reliable antidote to mental flabbiness was a rigorous, regular regime of mental calisthenics. A boy who could not flawlessly recite long Latin passages was required to increase his

mental workouts. Classical languages were to the mind that cold showers were to the body: tonics against waywardness.

Girls, with some exceptions, were not thought of as needing much mental preparation for their future roles as wives and mothers. Their heads were best left uncluttered by thought; too much book learning could give a girl ideas about independence. Besides, the great majority of them were not going on to college, where even more classical languages were required.

As an intellectual status symbol, the classical curriculum helped distinguish gentlemen from virtually everyone else and thus defined the difference between an "educated" man and an untutored one, as well as the difference between high culture and popular culture. Such a division is critical to exclude nonmembers from groups seeking status. For a long time a classical curriculum was the only path to admission to a university, as Harvard and many others required candidates to demonstrate proficiency in Latin and Greek (Levine 1980). Thus, the curriculum of boarding schools has long served both social and practical functions.

Culture, much like real estate or stocks, can be considered a form of capital. As the French scholars Pierre Bourdieu and Jean-Claude Passeron (1977) have indicated, the accumulation of cultural capital can be used to reinforce class differences. Cultural capital is socially created: what constitutes the "best in Western civilization" is not arrived at by happenstance, nor was it decided upon by public election. The more deeply embedded the values, the more likely they will be perceived as value free and universal.

Thus curriculum is the nursery of culture and the classical curriculum is the cradle of high culture. The definition of what is a classical course of study has evolved, of course, since the nineteenth century. Greek and Latin are no longer required subjects in most schools—electives abound. But the disciplined and trained mind is still the major objective of the boarding school curriculum.

> The Groton curriculum is predicated on the belief that certain qualities of mind are of major importance: precise and articulate communication; the ability to compute accurately and to reason quantitatively; a grasp of scientific approaches to problem-solving; an understanding of the cultural, social, scientific, and political background of Western civilization; and the ability to reason carefully and logically and to think imaginatively and sensitively. Consequently the School puts considerable emphasis on language, mathematics, science, history, and the arts. (*Groton School* 1981–82, 15)

The contrast between the relatively lean curricula of many public schools and the abundant courses offered by boarding schools is apparent. In catalogues of the boarding school's academic requirements, courses are usually grouped by subject matter, and at the larger schools course listings and descriptions can go on for several dozen pages. Far from sounding dreary, the courses described in most catalogues are designed to whet the intellectual appetite. Elective subjects in particular have intriguing titles such as "Hemingway: The Man and His Work," "Varieties of the Poetic Experience," "Effecting Political Change," "Rendezvous with Armageddon," and for those with a scientific bent, "Vertebrate Zoology" and "Mammalian Anatomy and Physiology."

Boarding school students are urged to read deeply and widely. A term course on modern American literature may include works from as many as ten authors, ranging from William Faulkner to Jack Kerouac. Almost all schools offer a course in Shakespeare in which six or seven plays will be read.

In history, original works are far more likely to be assigned than excerpts from a textbook. A course on the Presidency at one school included the following required readings: Rossiter, *The American Presidency;* Hofstadter, *The American Political Tradition;* Hargrove, *Presidential Leadership;* Schlesinger, *A Thousand Days;* Kearns, *Lyndon Johnson and the American Dream;* and White, *Breach of Faith.* Courses often use a college-level text, such as Garraty's *The American Nation* or Palmer's *A History of the Modern World.* Economic history is taught as well—in one school we observed a discussion of the interplay between politics and the depression of 1837—and the idea that there are multiple viewpoints in history is stressed. It is little wonder that many prep school graduates find their first year of college relatively easy.

An advanced-placement English class uses a collection of *The Canterbury Tales* by Geoffrey Chaucer that includes the original middle English on the left page and a modern English translation on the right. An advanced third-year French course includes three or four novels as well as two books of grammar and readings. Even social science courses require a great deal of reading. In a course called "An Introduction to Human Behavior," students are assigned eleven texts including works from B. F. Skinner, Sigmund Freud, Erich Fromm, Jean Piaget, and Rollo May.

Diploma requirements usually include 4 years of English, 3 years of math, 3 years in one foreign language, 2 years of history or social science, 2 years of laboratory science, and 1 year of art. Many schools require a year of philosophy or religion and also may have such noncredit diploma requirements as 4 years of physical education, a library skills course, introduction to computers, and a seminar on human sexuality. On average, American public high-school seniors take one year less English and math, and more than a year less foreign language than boarding school students (Coleman, Hoffer, and Kilgore 1982, 90). Moreover, in the past two decades there has been a historical decline in the number of academic subjects taken by students in the public schools (Adelman 1983).

Because success on the Scholastic Aptitude Test is so critical for admission to a selective college, it is not uncommon for schools to offer English review classes that are specifically designed to help students prepare for the tests. Most schools also offer tutorials and remedial opportunities for students who are weak in a particular subject. For foreign students there is often a course in English as a second language.

As the arts will be part of the future roles of boarding school students, the music, art, and theater programs at many schools are enriching, with special courses such as "The Sound and Sense of Music," "Advanced Drawing," and "The Creative Eye in Film." Student art work is usually on display, and almost every school will produce several full-length plays each year, for example, *Arsenic and Old Lace, A Thurber Carnival, Dracula,* and *The Mousetrap.*

Music is a cherished tradition in many boarding schools, in keeping with their British ancestry. The long-standing "Songs" at Harrow, made famous because Winston Churchill liked

to return to them for solace during World War II, are a remarkable display of school solidarity. All 750 boys participate, wearing identical morning coats with tails. Every seat is filled in the circular, sharply tiered replica of Shakespeare's Globe Theater as the boys rise in unison, their voices resonating in the rotunda.

The belief that a well-rounded education includes some "hands-on" experience and travel runs deep in the prep view of learning. Virtually every boarding school provides opportunities for their students to study and work off campus. As volunteers, Taft students, for instance, can "tutor on a one-to-one basis in inner-city schools in Waterbury, act as teachers' helpers in Waterbury Public Schools and work with retarded children at Southbury Training School." They can also work in convalescent homes, hospitals, and day-care centers, and act as "apprentices to veterinarians and help with Girl Scout troops" (*Taft* 1981–82, 21). At the Ethel Walker School in Connecticut, girls can go on whale watches, trips to the theater, or work in the office of a local politician. The Madeira School in Virginia has a co-curriculum program requiring students to spend every Wednesday participating in volunteer or internship situations.

Generally speaking, the schools that take the position that manual labor and firsthand experience are good for the soul as well as the mind and body, are more progressive in orientation than other schools. At the Putney School every student has to take a tour of duty at the cow barn, starting at 5:30 A.M. In their own words, "Putney's work program is ambitious. We grow much of our own food, mill our own lumber, pick up our own trash, and have a large part in building our buildings. . . . Stoves won't heat until wood is cut and split" (*The Putney School* 1982, 3).

Various styles of student-built structures dot the campus of the Colorado Rocky Mountain School, and at the tiny Midland School in California, there is no service staff, except for one cook. When the water pump breaks, faculty and students fix it, and when buildings are to be built, faculty and students pitch in. "We choose to live simply, to distinguish between our needs and our wants, to do without many of the comforts which often obscure the significant things in life" (*Midland School* 1983, 1). The creed of self-reliance is reenacted every day at Midland. When a trustee offered to buy the school a swimming pool, he was turned down. Lounging around a pool is not part of the Midland philosophy.

Travel is very much part of the prep way of life and is continued right through the school year. Not only are semesters or a year abroad (usually in France or Spain) offered, but at some of the smaller schools, everyone goes on an extensive field trip. Every March at the Verde Valley School in Arizona the students travel to "Hope, Navajo and Zuni reservations, to small villages in northern Mexico, to isolated Spanish-American communities in northern New Mexico and to ethnic neighborhoods of Southwestern cities. They live with native families, attend and teach in schools, work on ranches, and participate in the lives of the host families and their communities" (*Verde Valley School* 1982–83, 9). Not all boarding schools, of course, place such a high value on rubbing shoulders with the outside world. At most of the academies, entrepreneurial, and girls schools the emphasis is on service rather than sharing.

While boarding schools may vary in their general philosophy, the actual curricula do not widely differ. The pressures exerted on prep schools to get their students into good colleges mean that virtually all students must study the same core subjects. Although not quick to embrace educational innovation, many boarding schools have added computers to their curricula. This has no doubt been encouraged by announcements by a number of Ivy League and other elite colleges that they want their future applicants to be "computer literate." While people at most boarding schools, or anywhere else for that matter, are not quite sure what is meant by computer literate, they are trying to provide well-equipped computer rooms and teachers who can move their students toward computer proficiency.

For students who have particular interests that cannot be met by the formal curriculum, almost all schools offer independent study, which gives students and teachers at boarding schools a great deal of intellectual flexibility. At Groton, for example, independent study can cover a diverse set of topics including listening to the works of Wagner, conducting a scientific experiment, or studying a special aspect of history.

The boarding school curriculum offers students an abundant buffet of regular course work, electives, volunteer opportunities, travel, and independent study, from which to choose a course of study. By encouraging students to treat academic work as an exciting challenge rather than just a job to be done, the prep schools not only pass on culture but increase their students' competitive edge in the scramble for admission to selective colleges.

The Importance of Sports

Even the most diligent student cannot sit in classrooms all day, and because the prep philosophy emphasizes the whole person, boarding schools offer an impressive array of extracurricular activities, the most important of which is athletics. At progressive schools, the competitive nature of sport is deemphasized. The "afternoon out-of-door program" at Putney, for example, allows for a wide variety of outdoor activities that are noncompetitive; in fact, "skiing is the ideal sport for Putney as one may ski chiefly to enjoy himself, the air, the snow" (*The Putney School* 1982, 15).

Putney's sense that sport should be part of a communion with nature is not shared by most other schools, however. At most prep schools sport is about competition, and even more important, about winning. An athletically powerful prep school will field varsity, junior varsity, and third-string teams in most major sports. A typical coed or boys school will offer football, soccer, cross-country, water polo, ice hockey, swimming, squash, basketball, wrestling, winter track, gymnastics, tennis, golf, baseball, track, and lacrosse. For the faint-hearted there are alternative activities such as modern dance, cycling, tai chi, yoga, ballet, and for the hopelessly unathletic, a "fitness" class. A truly traditional prep school will also have a crew like their English forbears at Eton and Harrow. Certain schools have retained such British games as "Fives," but most stop short of the mayhem masquerading as a game called rugby.

Prep teams compete with college freshmen teams, other prep teams, and occasionally with public schools, although public school competitors are picked with care. Not only is there the possible problem of humiliation on the field, there is the even more explosive problem of fraternization in the stands when prep meets townie. Some schools, known as "jock" schools, act essentially as farm teams for Ivy League colleges, consistently providing them with athletes who have been polished by the prep experience. Many prep schools take public high-school graduates for a post-graduate year, as a way of adding some size and weight to their football teams.

Prep girls also love sports; they participate as much as the boys, often in the same sports, and with as much vigor. A girls' field hockey game between Exeter and Andover is as intense as when the varsity football teams clash. Horse-back riding at girls schools is still popular; a number of the girls go on to ride in the show or hunt circuit. Unlike many of the girls in public schools, the boarding-school girl is discouraged from being a spectator. Loafing is considered to be almost as bad for girls as it is for boys.

During the school year the halls of nearly all prep schools are decorated with either bulletins of sporting outcomes or posters urging victory in some upcoming game. Pep rallies are common, as are assemblies when awards are given and the competitive spirit is eulogized. Often the whole school will be bussed to an opponent's campus if the game is considered to be crucial or if the rivalry is long-standing.

Alumni return to see games, and there are frequent contests between alumni and varsity teams. Because preps retain the love of fitness and sports, it is not uncommon for the old warriors to give the young warriors a thrashing. Similarly, the prep life also invariably includes ritual competitions between, say, the girls field hockey team and a pick-up faculty team.

Nowhere is the spirit of victory more pronounced than on the ice of the hockey rink. Few public schools can afford a hockey rink so prep schools can attract the best players without much competition. Some prep schools import a few Canadians each year to fill out the roster. Speed, strength, endurance, and fearlessness are the qualities that produce winning hockey, and more than one freshman team from an Ivy League college has found itself out-skated by a prep team. Whatever else may be, in Holden Caulfield's term, "phony" about prep schools, sports are for real. This emphasis on sport is not without its critics. At the Harrow School in London, the new headmaster, who was an all-England rugby player, has begun a program to reward artistic and musical prowess as well as athletic and academic skills.

The athletic facilities at prep schools are impressive, and at the larger schools, lavish. Acres and acres of playing fields, scores of tennis courts, one or more gyms, a hockey rink, a golf course, swimming pools, squash courts, workout rooms—all can be found on many prep school campuses. Generally, the facilities are extremely well maintained. The equipment most preps use is the best, as are the uniforms. One boy described how "when your gym clothes get dirty, you simply turn them in at the locker room for a fresh set." The cost of all this, of course, is extraordinary, but considered necessary, because excellence in sport is part of the definition of a gentleman or gentlewoman.

The pressure for athletic success is intense on many campuses, and a student's, as well as a school's, social standing can ride on the narrow margin between victory and defeat. Perhaps because of this, schools generally take great pains to play schools of their own size and social eliteness. A study of who plays whom among prep schools reveals that schools will travel great distances, at considerable expense, to play other prep schools whose students and traditions are similar to their own.

Extracurriculars and Preparation for Life

Not all prep school extracurricular activities require sweating, however. Like public school students, preps can work on the school newspaper, yearbook, help to organize a dance, or be part of a blood donor drive, and are much more likely than their public school counterparts to be involved in such activities. For example, one in three boarding school students are involved in student government compared to one in five public school students, and two in five are involved in the school newspaper or yearbook compared to one in five. This evidence is consistent with other research. Coleman, Hoffer, and Kilgore (1982) found that private school students participate more in extracurricular activities than do public school students. The fact that more boarding school students than public school students are involved in activities provides additional opportunities for them to practice their verbal, interpersonal, and leadership skills.

The catalogue of clubs at prep schools is nearly endless. The opportunity for students to develop special nonacademic interests is one of the qualities of life at prep schools that distinguishes them from many public schools. Special interest clubs for chess, sailing, bowling, or gun clubs are popular at boys schools. One elite boys school has a "war games" club. As the boys at this school are feverishly calculating their country's next strategic arms move, the girls in a Connecticut school are attending a meeting of Amnesty International. Girls, in general, tend to spend their off hours studying the gentler arts such as gourmet cooking and art history. One girls school has a club with a permanent service mission to the governor's office.

At some schools, students can learn printing, metalwork, or woodworking. The shop for the latter at Groton is amply equipped and much of the work turned out by the students is professional quality. The less traditional schools offer clubs for vegetarian cooking, weaving, quilting, folk music, and—in subtle juxtaposition to the Connecticut girls school—international cooking. At western schools, the horse still reigns supreme and many students spend endless hours riding, training, cleaning, and loving their own horse, or a horse they have leased from the school.

With the prep emphasis on music, choirs, glee clubs, madrigals, chamber music groups, as well as informal ensembles, are all given places to practice. Most schools also have individual practice rooms, and like athletic teams, many prep musicians travel to other schools for concerts and performances.

Some schools offer a five-week "Winterim," during which students and faculty propose and organize a variety of off- and on-campus activities and studies. Such a program breaks the monotony of the usual class routine in the middle of winter, a season teachers repeatedly told us was the worst time at boarding school. It also enables students and faculty to explore new areas or interests in a safe way, that is, without grades.

In prep schools there is a perceived need for students to exercise authority as apprentice leaders early in their educational careers. The tradition of delegating real authority to students has British roots, where head boys and prefects have real power within the public schools. Head boys can discipline other boys by setting punishments and are treated by headmaster and housemasters alike as a part of the administration. In the United States, student power is generally more limited, although at the progressive schools students can be quite involved in the administrative decision-making process.

Virtually all prep schools have a student government. The formal structure of government usually includes a student body president, vice president, treasurer, secretary, class presidents, and dorm prefects, representatives, or "whips," as they are called at one school. Clubs also have presidents and there are always committees to be headed. Some schools have student-faculty senates and in schools like Wooster, in Connecticut, students are expected to play a major part in the disciplinary system. An ambitious student can obtain a great deal of experience in committee work, developing transferable skills for later leadership positions in finance, law, management, or politics.

The office of student body president or head prefect is used by the administration primarily as an extension of the official school culture, and most of the students who fill these offices are quite good at advancing the school's best public relations face. A successful student body president, like a good head, is artful in developing an easy leadership style, which is useful because he or she is in a structural political dilemma. Elected by the students but responsible to the school administration, the student politician is a classic go-between, always running the danger of being seen as "selling out" by students and as "uncooperative" by the administration. Occasionally students rebel against too much pandering to the administration and elect a rebel leader, who makes it his or her business to be a thorn in the side of the administration. A number of heads and deans of students watch elections closely, because if

elections go "badly" it could mean a difficult year for them.

The actual content of real power varies by school. At some, authority is more apparent than real; at others, student power can affect important school decisions. At Putney, the "Big Committee" is composed of the school director, student leaders, and teachers. The powers of the Big Committee are laid out in the school's constitution, and students at Putney have real input into the decision-making process. At the Thacher School in California, the Student Leadership Council, which is composed of the school chairman, presidents of the three lower classes, and head prefects, is not only responsible for student activities and events, but also grants funds to groups who petition for special allocations. The power of the purse is learned early in the life of a prep school student. At the Westtown School in Pennsylvania, the student council arrives at decisions not by voting yea or nay, "but by following the Quaker custom of arriving at a 'sense of the meeting'" (*Westtown School* 1982–83, 25).

Not all students, of course, participate in school politics; it may well be that many of the students most admired by their peers never run, or never would run, for a political position. The guerrilla leaders who emerge and flourish in the student underlife—or counterculture—may have far greater real power than the "superschoolies" that tend to get elected to public office.

In most coeducational schools, boys tend to monopolize positions of power. The highest offices are generally held by boys; girls are found in the vice presidential and secretarial positions. Politics can be important to prep families and we suspect that a number of prep boys arrive at boarding school with a good supply of political ambition. One of the reasons advanced in support of all-girls schools is that girls can gain important leadership experience there.

Some schools try to capture what they see as the best aspects of single-sex and coed schools.

They do this by having boys and girls elect distinct school leaders, by having certain customs, places, and events that they share only with members of their own sex, and by having classes, certain other activities, and social events be coeducational. These schools, often called co-ordinate schools, see themselves as offering the chance to form strong single-sex bonds, to build self-confidence in adolescents, and to provide experience in working and relating to members of both sexes. Girls at coed schools more generally are likely to say they think in ten years they will find the social skills they learned to be the most valuable part of their boarding-school experience.

Learning by Example

Part of the social learning students obtain is exposure to significant public personalities. Virtually all the schools have guest speaker programs in which well-known people can be seen and heard. Some of the speakers that have appeared at Miss Porter's School in the last several years include Alex Haley, author; Russell Baker, humorist; Arthur Miller, playwright; and Dick Gregory, comedian. At the boys schools there is a tendency to invite men who are successful in politics and journalism. Recent speakers at the Hill School include James A. Baker III, Secretary of the Treasury (Hill class of 1948); James Reston, columnist; Frank Borman, astronaut and president of Eastern Airlines; and William Proxmire, United States senator (Hill class of 1934).

Inviting successful alumni to return for talks is one of the ways boarding schools can pass on a sense of the school's efficacy. Throughout the year panels, assemblies, and forums are organized for these occasions. Often the alumni speakers will also have informal sessions with students, visit classrooms, and stay for lunch, tea, or supper.

In keeping with cultural environment of prep schools, especially the select 16 schools,

professional musicians, actors, and dancers are regularly invited to perform. Art and sculpture exhibits are common and some schools, such as Andover and Exeter, have permanent art galleries. The art at prep schools is generally either original works by artists such as Toulouse-Lautrec, Matisse, or Daumier, or the work of established contemporary artists such as Frank Stella, who graduated from Andover. At a large school there may be so much cultural activity that it is unnecessary to leave campus for any kind of high cultural event.

Those who come to elite boarding schools to talk or perform are the makers of culture. For adolescents seeking to be the best, these successful individuals give them a sense of importance and empowerment. All around them are the symbols of their special importance—in Groton's main hallway hangs a personal letter from Ronald Reagan to the headmaster, reminding the students that Groton "boasts a former President of the United States and some of America's finest statesmen." Five or six books a year will be published by a school's alumni; Exeter in particular has many alumni authors, including James Agee, Nathaniel G. Benchley, John Knowles, Dwight Macdonald, Jr., Arthur M. Schlesinger, Jr., Sloan Wilson, and Gore Vidal. Roger L. Stevens, Alan Jay Lerner, and Edward Albee are all Choate-Rosemary Hall alumni, adding luster to a theater program that trains many professional actresses and actors. A student at an elite school is part of a world where success is expected, and celebrity and power are part of the unfolding of life. Not every school is as culturally rich as the elite eastern prep schools, but in the main, most schools work hard to develop an appreciation for high culture. At the Orme School in Arizona, a week is set aside each year in which the whole school participates in looking at art, watching art being made, and making art.

Nowhere is the drive for athletic, cultural, and academic excellence more apparent than in the awards, honors, and prizes that are given to outstanding teams or students at the end of each year. Sporting trophies are often large silver cups with the names of annual champions engraved on several sides. At some schools the triumphs have come with enough regularity to warrant building several hundred yards of glass casing to hold the dozens of medals, trophies, and other mementos that are the victors' spoils. Pictures of past winning teams, looking directly into the camera, seem frozen in time.

Academic prizes tend to be slightly less flashy but no less important. Much like British schoolmasters, American schoolmasters believe in rewarding excellence, so most schools give a number of cultural, service, and academic prizes at the end of each year. There is usually at least one prize in each academic discipline, as well as prizes for overall achievement and effort. There are service prizes for dedicated volunteers, as well as debating and creative writing prizes. Almost all schools have cum laude and other honor societies.

Sitting through a graduation ceremony at a boarding school can be an endurance test—some schools give so many prizes that one could fly from New York to Boston and back in the time it takes to go from the classics prize to the prize for the best woodworking or weaving project. But of course, the greatest prize of all is graduation, and more than a few schools chisel, paint, etch, or carve the names of the graduates into wood, stone, or metal to immortalize their passage from the total institution into the world.

References

Adelman, Clifford. 1983. *Devaluation, Diffusion and the College Connection: A Study of High School Transcripts, 1964–1981.* Washington, DC: National Commission on Excellence in Education.

Bourdieu, Pierre, and Jean-Claude Passeron. 1977. *Reproduction: In Education, Society and Culture.* Beverly Hills, CA: Sage.

Coleman, James S., Thomas Hoffer, and Sally Kilgore. 1982. *High School Achievement.* New York: Basic Books.

Levine, Steven B. 1980. "The Rise of American Boarding Schools and the Development of a National Upper Class." *Social Problems* 28: 63–94.

Question

1. In American society it is commonly assumed that whether or not people succeed is determined by the degree to which they work hard to develop their talents. Still, it seems likely that some people have the advantage. In the competition to succeed, what advantages do students who attend boarding school seem to have? How important will these advantages be in the competition for success in the world of adults?

   Then, think more generally: What kinds of advantages do students who attend public schools in middle-class neighborhoods have over students who attend public schools in the poor neighborhoods? How important are these advantages?

·22·
The Nurture and Admonition of the Lord
Raising Children

Nancy Tatom Ammerman

This 1987 article is an excerpt from the book *Bible Believers: Fundamentalists in the Modern World.* Professor Ammerman explores how Fundamentalists attempt to integrate church, school, and family life. As Ammerman observes, what sets Fundamentalists apart from most other Christians is their belief in the Bible as literal truth. You will see that membership in the Southside Gospel Church is not a Sunday-only thing, but a fact whose influence reaches nearly all aspects of everyday life.

Train up a child in the way he should go; and when he is old, he will not depart from it.

— Proverbs 22:6

Children, obey your parents in the Lord, for this is right. . . . And, ye fathers, provoke not your children to wrath, but bring them up in the nurture and admonition of the Lord.

— Ephesians 6:1, 4

Southside members not only want to reach the lost in their community but also want to make sure that the lost in their own homes come to salvation. Although Christian homes may exist in part to extend the shelter of the church into everyday life, their most important function in the minds of believers is bringing children into the world and raising them "in the nurture and admonition of the Lord." While providing a shelter for adult believers, Christian homes also provide the primary means for introducing young believers to Fundamentalism. Parents who take the task seriously find that the goals that guide their nurturing are shaped by the Fundamentalist world of which they are a part. As Bonnie Towles put it, "I hope to see my children grow up to surrender their lives to the Lord."

The Nurture of the Church

In part, children learn about "surrendering their lives to the Lord" by participating with their families in the church. Adults find that church offers activities and relationships that replace the attractions of the world, and they are eager for their children to have the same opportunities. From the time they are dedicated as babies, the children of Southside's faithful members become "church kids." As one mother put it, "These kids, all they've ever known is church!" The people of the church become a kind of extended family, with relationships that carry over into weekday activities. Church kids become best friends with each other and help each other to learn the ways of the faith. They go to church together on Sunday, to AWANA[1] on Wednesday night, to Vacation Bible School in the summer, and to any other activity the church plans. And, like their parents, Southside's children do "church work" at home, memorizing next Sunday's Bible verse, inviting a friend to church, and the like.

One of the most important things church kids learn from all this activity is that the Bible is a part of everything. They begin to memorize its verses before they can read, and they know the names and order of all sixty-six books about as soon as they know their home address. Both at church and at home, they hear Bible stories instead of fairy tales and learn more about Mary and Joseph than about Dick and Jane. By the time they are six or seven, they are as likely to have a favorite Bible verse as to have a favorite color, to be able to tell a Bible story as to be able to recite a nursery rhyme, to be able to sing a hymn as any other song. The people and places of the Bible simply become a part of the everyday world of Southside's children.

Church kids also learn about faith in subtle ways. They learn to think about life as a battle by singing about being in "the Lord's army" and by constantly engaging in competition. From Sunday School to Junior Church to AWANA, Southside's kids learn to be adept at fighting hard to win, and they learn to expect rewards for their actions. Prizes and trophies and ribbons are tangible reminders of the everlasting rewards God's children can expect in

heaven when they do their best for him. They also learn that one of the surest ways to be rewarded is to be obedient. There are rules to be obeyed at home and at church and authorities in each place to enforce those rules.

Church kids learn too that what a person is allowed to do depends on who that person is: Members are not pastors; children are not parents; and girls are not boys. God made each with a special and different plan for how to live. For instance, from the earliest ages, there are separate activities, different styles of dress, and divergent expectations for boys and girls, building and reinforcing the idea that God made the sexes to be different.

Southside also introduces its children to the world of Fundamentalism by offering them an alternative set of heroes. For church kids, foreign missionaries are as heroic as Luke Skywalker or Mr. T may be to other children. They begin to learn about missionaries as soon as they are old enough to understand what is happening at church. They see slides of exotic lands and hear stories of terrible evil being overcome by the gospel. They write letters to missionaries in Sunday School and send them gifts at Christmas. They may even make their own faith promise and have a missions piggy bank. Southside's kids know that preachers and missionaries have "surrendered their lives to the Lord" and that no other vocational choice would make their parents prouder of them. Church kids dream of being missionaries no less than other children dream of being Olympic athletes or "president of the world." Sometimes youthful dreams come true but always they shape the present and the future.

Once church kids reach their teens, the task of providing alternative dreams and plausible explanations becomes more difficult. The church realizes that teens are especially susceptible to the influences of worldly friends and activities, and it counterattacks with a vigorous youth program. The church hopes to keep its teens so busy that they have little time for

---

[1]Elsewhere, Ammerman explains that "the name is an acronym based on II Timothy 2:15—Approved Workmen Are Not Ashamed. It is a club for children from kindergarten through junior high, complete with uniforms, a flag, and scoutlike awards for achievements in Bible knowledge and church attendance" (35–36).—Ed.

outside friends or activities. To keep youngsters away from secular social activities, they plan an event of their own, for instance, at the same time youth might otherwise attend a school dance. Because the youth group is fairly large, there are plenty of available friends and potential dates. When they need a sympathetic adult ear, Southside's youth minister is there to be a positive role model and confidant.

In addition, the church invests its youth with the adult responsibility of witnessing to their unsaved peers. Trying to convince a friend can be an experiment in owning the Fundamentalist identity. Those who learn well the lessons of witnessing and separation are able to establish for themselves an identity that includes both being Christians and being in the world. The church also encourages its youth to try on identities as teachers, preachers, and missionaries. . . . Among the activities sponsored by Word of Life Bible Clubs is Teens Involved, in which youth try their hands at preaching (for boys) and story telling (for girls and boys). When teens are older, they may even have an opportunity to spend a summer working with a foreign missionary on the field. Southside works hard to make the Fundamentalist way of life attractive to its youth and to give them opportunities to establish their identities within its boundaries.

The activities and relationships, ideals and goals that the church provides mold the lives and thinking of children even more than of adults. They simply have fewer alternatives to compare with what Southside offers them, especially if they are from a home where both parents are believers. As we saw with bus kids, the church cannot succeed alone. It is most influential as an extension of the home. Children with unsaved parents must balance the church's ideas against everything else they experience. But church kids with saved parents receive consistent information about how life is to be lived, consistent models of what is good.

The Nurture of the Home

Church kids with church parents rarely step outside the sheltering canopy of the faith. Competing ideas and ways of life are as foreign to them as the native customs they see in missionary slides. Southside's parents see the church's responsibility as an extension of theirs, neither effort being complete without the other. Mary Danner, for instance, reflected on raising her children.

> When you have a little one, you think, "How do I want to raise her?" So she was raised in the church. The church became her second home. She loved Sunday School. We worshiped together. I remember when we first started, we used a little folder of verses. They we had family devotions, time to pray together. For our children, church was always a place they wanted to be. . . . Children have a way of knowing something that is real and right with you, something you really believe in and are not just saying.

The church and its families work together to make sure that children know that Fundamentalism is what is "real and right."

The homes in which Southside members raise their children are guided by the ideas and expectations of their religious world. Above all, they are characterized by discipline, respect, and obedience. Southside's children learn about rules both at home and at church. We have already heard parents talk about discipline and about not watching television; but most church kids also have rules about how they can dress, where they can go, and, most importantly, with whom they can play. The mother of a five-year-old said that her son is always required to be within her sight and is not allowed to play at other neighborhood homes because the other families are not Christians. Ann Lazzaro has teenaged children, but they have similar restrictions: "We always know where they are; they are with Christians. If they do go with someone who is unsaved, it is either in our home or with their parents. But our boys are told, they know to lead their friends to the Lord, and we are thankful. Well, Stanleyville is quite a town. We never have to tell them; they know from reading God's word that they are to be separate."

As Ann pointed out, her sons know not only the rules but the reasons for the rules. Another parent observed that his neighbors are always amazed when they see his teenaged children going to church, even when he and his wife are away. The children who grow up in Southside's fold are likely to emerge from adolescence firmly entrenched in a Fundamentalist world. Their development has been shaped by Fundamentalist norms no less than the development of a child in any other culture is shaped by its norms. . . . [E]ach of the predictable stages of childhood is encountered in ways that prepare the child for full participation in his or her particular adult society.

In the early stages of childhood, for instance, church kids learn about initiative and guilt: "Occasionally I would have one that when you went to wake them up didn't want to go today. And I never hollered at them or pushed them. I just simply said, 'Well, you know the Lord has been very good to us.' And I reminded them of all the answers to our prayers and the things he had done, and then I would just walk out. . . . They always got up and went." Guilt and obligation are recurring themes at Southside, but what is interesting here is that as young children go through the natural process of acquiring a conscience, their religious culture is supplying them the substance over which they are to feel guilty: not going to church, forgetting to read the Bible, disobeying, or playing with an unsaved child. Sometimes they are spanked when they step out of line, but external control is soon replaced by firm internal discipline.

All children come to internalize their parents' demands, but at Southside that process is made all the more dramatic by the constant presence of a heavenly father in addition to the earthly one. . . . The idea that sin inevitably produces suffering takes root first in the punishment children receive from their earthly fathers. The more sure and swift the punishment—or reward—the more firmly children become convinced that neither sin nor righteousness will be overlooked by their heavenly father. At church, as well as at home, children learn that God is like a father, and they come to expect him to be a tangible presence in their lives. One four-year-old was so sure that Jesus was "in his heart" that he was afraid Jesus might get dizzy from all his jumping around. The boy might not yet quite understand, but he is already learning that Jesus sees everything he does. Good deeds please Jesus, and bad deeds make Jesus sad. By the same process that a conscience is formed, an omniscient (potentially punitive) God becomes the overseer of the conscience. Long after they become adults, these children will still explain their misfortunes as God "disciplining" them, punishing them for stepping out of line.

As the conscience takes shape and the child's desires become internally regulated, attention can be turned to substantive matters. Each culture must teach its offspring necessary skills, and Southside is no exception. Among the most important skills to be learned are the use of the Bible, how to be separated, and how to witness. We have already noted that the church and the home work together to teach children about the Bible. As they participate in all the Bible activities of the church and family, they learn more about scripture than many seminary students know. If church kids also go to the Academy, they have additional Bible lessons every day. As they learn to locate and memorize scripture, they come to understand that the Bible can provide answers for whatever questions they might have.

One of the most important reasons to learn about the Bible is to be able to use it in witnessing. Southside's children not only come to accept the faith at an early age but also learn that witnessing is the most important activity for even a young Christian. By the time they are teens, church kids are expected to be fully responsible for spreading the gospel among their peers, but they often start to practice much earlier. The mother of a first-grader proudly told about her daughter's efforts.

> Stephanie went over on Sunday — it was so cute — and she sat them all down, the three kids. She said, "If you don't do this, you're going to hell." And she said, "If you want to come to heaven and see me up there . . . ." And then she said, "I'll start a prayer, and you just say what I say." She got the three kids to say the prayer after her. . . . She was real excited, and she said, "I think I'm a missionary, Mom!"

Bonnie gave a similar account of her second-grade daughter's activities: "That little girl that is with Sarah now is Jewish. Sarah led her to the Lord, but her family, of course, won't let her come to church or anything." By witnessing to their playmates, Southside's children become firmly committed to a Fundamentalist identity and practice the skills necessary to sustain that commitment. . . .

Children at Southside also establish their skills and identity by learning to abide by the rules of separation and to explain those rules to nonbelievers. Some of the rules are common to believing and nonbelieving families alike: Don't hit other children. Don't steal. Be polite. Don't use curse words. Other rules are unique to a Fundamentalist household: Turn off bad programs and bad commercials on television. Don't go to the movies. Don't dance. These are rules that must be explained to even the best of nonbelieving parents. Southside parents know that when their children are with outsiders, the children are not always able to resist the temptation of living by the outsiders' more lenient rules. Nevertheless, parents work hard to teach their children what to expect and how to "take a stand." Bonnie has taught her children well and was especially proud when they could even explain why they would not participate in a camp square dance: "We walked up,

and all the other kids were out on the dance floor, and my two were sitting in chairs. And my cousin came over to me, and she said, 'Sarah told me she can't dance because she's a Christian. Is that true?' And I said, 'Yeah, that's true.'" In the midst of learning the other necessary skills for adult survival, Southside children are also learning that they have special rules "because they are Christians."

One of the rules they learn, both overtly and subtly, is that families are supposed to divide their labor by sex. They learn the ideal standards for Christian families — priestly fathers, full-time mothers, and daily family devotions — and they watch as their parents work toward that goal. They probably also learn, though, that their mothers do far more than anyone admits. They know that mother provides part of the family's resources, subtly guides the family's decision making, and is likely to be the more enthusiastic teacher of religious values. Sometimes children thus learn at home how to make practical compromises between the Bible and the modern world. Even when ideals do not quite match reality, however, Southside children learn at home to experience and justify a Fundamentalist way of life.

The Nurture of the School

If Southside children also attend the Academy, they learn the lessons of the Fundamentalist life even more thoroughly. They are able to spend all their youthful energy learning the ways of the faith and are protected from almost every conceivable evil influence.

Learning the rules and skills of Fundamentalist culture at an academy is a relatively new phenomenon. Until recently, it was enough for Fundamentalist children to learn their religious skills at church and at home, leaving it to the public schools to provide general knowledge. For a variety of reasons, that arrangement has become unsatisfactory, and "Christian academies" are being started all over the country. These schools emphasize basic verbal and mathematical skills, as well as preparing children for using the Bible, witnessing, and living a separated life. At an academy, children learn about biblical rules and a disciplined life at the same time they are learning their multiplication tables.

Southside Christian Academy was founded in 1974, soon after the present pastor arrived. It began with six grades and gradually added junior and senior high. The pastor's dream is to build a complete new church complex, including a sanctuary and buildings for the school. The people of the church are busy raising money toward that goal; but in the meanwhile the elementary school occupies the lower two floors and the high school the upper floor of an old elementary school building that is owned by the town of Valley View. The nursery school meets in the church building, about two miles away. There are about fifty nursery schoolers, one hundred elementary pupils, and seventy secondary students. About two-thirds of these are children of church members, while the rest come from the community. During the 1979–1980 school year, there was one class for kindergarten and first grade, one for second and third grade, another for advanced third graders and fourth grade, and one each for fifth and sixth grades. Classes averaged about twenty pupils.

All the elementary teachers are women and are described as "committed, born-again Christians" who are also well qualified to teach. Many on the school staff are also members of the church staff. The pastor serves as superintendent and leads chapel every day, while his wife teaches English, French, and speech in the secondary school. The youth minister helps with choir, Bible, and physical education; and his wife teaches the kindergarten/first-grade class. The second-grade teacher doubles as elementary supervisor, and the headmaster and high school principal each also teach in the secondary school. There are ten full-time and three

part-time staff members in the combined elementary and secondary schools. Despite the small staff, however, the school is approved by the state board of education, so that credits can be transferred to the public school system.

Financially, the Academy requires sacrifice from everyone. Its teachers work at low salaries. Parents must pay tuition and are called on for additional gifts and for labor. In addition, the church has provided underwriting funds in nearly every year of the school's operation. When the Academy has a need, parents and other church members give their time, energy, and money. For most the sacrifice is worth it. They are eager to maintain the Academy as a part of the ministry of the church and of the proper upbringing of their children.

The new headmaster at the Academy uses the idea of a triangle to talk about what children need. His school is one side of the triangle, the other sides being the church and home. Each is equally important and depends on the others. His idea is echoed by other Southside members. Bonnie sees the Academy as especially important because her children's father is not saved: "I think the main thing I wanted for them—because Sam isn't saved—I wanted them to have a complete circle, a complete picture, as far as—I don't know how to explain it. In other words, I didn't want them to think that salvation and the love of the Lord and living a Christian life was just my opinion. I wanted Sunday School and home and school. I wanted them to see as many Christians living a Christian life as they could. I wanted as much influence in their life as possible." Similarly, Janet Slavin sees the Academy as a way of choosing the influences in her daughter's life: "I think she is going to have less options thrown at her in a Christian school than if she was in a public school, where there might be a few more things that she might have to choose about. I would rather control her environment as much as possible while she is young, until she is old enough to be let go."

Almost everyone who supports the Academy sees it as a place with a "good Christian atmosphere," the sort of environment parents can trust. There children encounter ideas and behavior that are consistent with the Fundamentalist world view they experience at home and at church. Children are educated within the bounds of the world they call Christian.

In part, schools like Southside's have been started in response to perceived deterioration in the public schools. Even Southside parents who do not send their children to the Academy agree that schools are pretty bad these days. That is one of the things most often cited as evidence of the world's deplorable condition. At the most basic level, parents fear for their children's safety in schools they see as lawless. They also think their children are not getting a good education and that there are no good models for teaching children how to learn and how to behave. As Howard Otto said, "Linda doesn't really have a clear idea of what would be happening or what she would be doing if she weren't at Southside. But as far as I'm concerned, from seeing some of it, the public system is so bad . . . that I can't conceive of placing my daughters on the altar of sacrifice to offer them up to the public school system. They're treasures, God-given treasures."

Parents also worry that their children will pick up the bad habits of public school children. One mother, who works part-time in a public school, talked about how glad she is that her own daughter is at the Academy: "She has the whole atmosphere, you know, good Christians. You don't have to be worried that the kids are going to start swearing; and believe me, during the lunch program, they think nothing of saying it to the adults. I don't have to worry about all that."

That woman's sister touched on an even more important advantage of the Academy: "I think it is something that we missed out on. We always felt like we were different." When Southside children maintain their standards in the midst of a public school, they risk feeling different, having no real friends. At the Academy, they can feel normal and make friends with others who think and act just as they do. . . .

For whatever reason, then, public schools are seen as undisciplined environments and potentially bad influences for Christian children. Equally important, the public schools are seen as repositories of knowledge that is contrary to Fundamentalist ways of thinking. Believers have long known that they could not trust secular colleges, but now they do not trust elementary and secondary schools either. They see public school children being taught false ideas not only about biology but also about government, economics, history, geology, astronomy, physics, and other sciences. About the only safe things to be learned are reading, writing, and arithmetic; and most schools do not seem to be doing a good job of that.

The changes believers perceive are not entirely imaginary. As recently as the early 1960s, evolution had barely entered the classroom, but religious observances were fairly common. Now the case is reversed. Since 1963, schools have become careful about supporting religious activities; and since Sputnik science education has been restructured and now includes evolution as an overarching theoretical framework. Evolution does, in fact, permeate virtually all the physical and social sciences. Schools assume that everything can be explained by human reason and can be changed for the better by human initiative. This is the "secular humanism" against which Fundamentalists rail. Its prevalence has prompted both their efforts to again ban the teaching of evolution (or at least to give creationism equal time) and their decision simply to give up and start their own schools.

The establishment of separate schools implies that the public schools were equipping Fundamentalist children with a set of skills unsuited to the culture of their parents. This is a familiar problem for minority cultures, but it is a problem not often resolved in favor of the minority. Public schools have historically served the purpose of assimilation. Parents may have grieved that their children were losing the ability to speak in the native tongue, but they rejoiced that those offspring would be able to function in the new land. Even Catholic and Hebrew schools have not sought to challenge the basic assumptions of the larger society about the kind of knowledge that is necessary. Perhaps the schools closest to Fundamentalist schools are those supported by the Amish. . . . Academies are not just teaching religion in addition to other knowledge, not just teaching in a strict, well-mannered environment. They are seeking to make all knowledge conform to their understanding of the Bible. The Bible is to be the "hub of the educational wheel" (Academy *Handbook*, p. 9). The members of Southside correctly perceive that other schools are not willing to entertain Fundamentalist views as plausible, and they have responded by enlarging their own territory to include the social function of education.

Ironically, at the same time that believers are protecting their children from the ideas and behavior of decadent public schools, they may be depriving those children of the skills necessary for living outside the boundaries of Fundamentalist institutions. Many of Southside's members worry about that possibility. They are afraid that Academy graduates will be trained only "for the Lord's work." They fear that those who emerge to face the secular world of work will be totally unable to handle the challenge: "I am realistic. I mean we are different in that we have this personal commitment and beliefs, but we still have to coexist side by side with those in the world, and if you don't know what is out there, it is a pretty wild jungle, if you are seventeen or eighteen and start facing it. It can throw you."

Some parents speak to the problems out of their own successful experience in sending children to public schools: "In the Christian school, kids are not exposed to negative things of life. They are more protected. In public school, they are more exposed, but I think that if they have a good basis in the home, it shouldn't shatter them. It didn't my children. . . . They have an opportunity to prove themselves, to share what they have received." Mary reflected similar ideas: "It's hard never to be in your community. It's through our children that we made many contacts for witness."

A few Southside members also worry about other ways in which the Academy narrows the experience of its students. The Academy has no room for exceptional students of any kind. Everyone must conform to one set of standards. Emotionally disturbed children, those with physical or mental handicaps, and those who have had academic or behavior problems in other schools are not permitted to enroll at the Academy "if their condition were to hold back the progress of the entire class" (*Handbook*, p. 11). Ann lamented that her son, who is a slow learner, was not able to make it at the Academy: "I wish he could be there, but it is just too limited over there, it is just too small. They don't have the facilities to offer all of the subjects." The problem is largely one of size and facilities, but it is also one of protecting the Christian environment. As a result, everyone is the same: well behaved, moderately bright, physically normal, middle class, and white.

Southside Christian Academy, then, creates an environment where Fundamentalist ideas and behavior are normal. The *Handbook* says that "the school will endeavor to provide an atmosphere that is conducive to the best Christian living" (p. 9). When that theoretical goal hits the practical reality of the classroom, it finds concrete form in rules, emphasis on traditional skills, and the presence of Bible study in all the subjects. This biblical, traditional, regulated structure is the everyday world in which the consciousness of Southside's youth is shaped.

The first thing everybody mentions about the Academy—pro or con—is that it has strict rules; and they are right. Rules against lying, cheating, stealing, swearing, and the use of alcohol or drugs would be expected at any school. At the Academy, the rules go far beyond such obvious offenses. Students are expected to be respectful, to have a good attitude, not to "gripe," and to be courteous. They are also expected to maintain Christian standards when they are away from school because their behavior might "harm the testimony of the school" (*Handbook*, p. 14). If they disobey or act in any way unbecoming a Christian, they are subject to detention, suspension, or expulsion. They may be spanked by teachers or administrators, or their parents may be called in for a conference. The Academy strives toward self-discipline in its students, but adults emphasize that those who do not exhibit self-discipline will be disciplined (that is, punished) by others.

Southside Academy also has rules about how Christians should dress and groom themselves. Girls of all ages must always wear dresses, although culottes are allowed for physical education, and slacks may be worn under a dress in cold weather. Make-up, hair styles, stockings, blouses, and everything else about their appearance must be modest and "becoming to a Christian girl" (*Handbook*, p. 16). Little girls are allowed to wear short skirts, but by the time they reach junior high, their skirts must touch the floor when they are kneeling. For boys, the rule of thumb is "neat and conservative." Jeans are not allowed, belts are required, and shirts must be buttoned and tucked in. T-shirts, sandals, and facial hair are forbidden. And, in all cases, the "judgment of the Administration will be final" (p. 17).

As with all the rules of the Fundamentalist life, these dress rules can be defended from the Bible. For instance, the Academy *Handbook* states, "Hair (for boys) should be clean and groomed at least two fingers' width above the brows. It must not come down over the ears or shirt collar" (p. 16). This rule is enforced with periodic hair checks for all junior and senior high boys. One day, nearly half the boys failed the check and were told that they could not go to the Friday basketball game if they did not get haircuts. There was considerable grumbling, and one of the boys summoned the courage to ask why long hair was so bad. The teacher pointed them to 1 Corinthians 11:14, which asserts that it is a shame for a man to have long hair. When someone else complained that his hair was not really long, the teacher went back to the seventh verse of that same chapter, which says that a man should not "cover his head." The teacher explained that if the ears and forehead are covered, a boy is on his way toward a "covered head." Finally another student made what he thought would be a winning argument: "But, didn't Jesus have long hair?" The teacher was indignant and cautioned the students that the pictures they see of Jesus are just representations painted by sinful men. The Bible teaches that long hair is a sin and also teaches that Jesus never sinned; Jesus, therefore, could not have had long hair. Case closed.

This group of teenagers had just learned a rather complicated explanation for a minor rule. More importantly, they had been reminded again that the Bible is their ultimate authority, the source for all their explanations. Yet it is also possible that for some of them the seeds of doubt were sown. They may have heard that Fundamentalist explanations do not always make sense of the world as they see it.

Not surprisingly, Southside Christian Academy also worries about "proper Christian conduct with the opposite sex" (*Handbook*, p. 14). It does not so much discourage the formation of relationships (hoping, after all, that its children will marry Christians), but it seeks to prevent those relationships from becoming either serious or actively sexual. It discourages steady dating out of a feeling that teens are too young to be ready to marry. It seeks to protect the "purity" of those future marriages by prohibiting any physical contact at school and forbidding couples to arrive or leave alone in a car. Pairs may sit together at school, and they may ride in cars with a set of parents, but they are strictly forbidden any public display of their affection or any opportunity for the private expression of it.

All these rules have little overtly to do with education, but the same structure of rules and discipline shapes what is learned in the class-room. Students learn not only what to wear and how to behave but also where to put their names on a paper and how many sharpened pencils to have on their desks. In the elementary school, students have a carefully structured routine. They know when they must line up, stand beside their seats, or sit quietly. Each subject and activity comes in a predictable order, and whenever they have extra time, there are "seat-work" assignments on the board. Students who fail to do their homework or to bring required equipment to class are given demerits as quickly as they would be for being disrespectful or wearing inappropriate clothing.

How well the rule keeping is integrated into the learning process varies greatly from class to class. Some teachers seem to be able to maintain an acceptable level of discipline with only occasional reminders, while others spend a good deal of time supervising the details of their pupils' behavior. In each classroom, however, students are expected to do their school-work with the same kind of self-discipline that governs the rest of their behavior. They are expected to work hard and do well. As the sign in the second-grade classroom says, "It is a sin to do less than your best."

This emphasis on hard work and discipline is the traditional Protestant work ethic, which has historically dominated American society and education. It is part of what the people at Southside mean when they say that they want their children to have a good, old-fashioned education. They also mean that they want the Bible and the flag to be honored in every class-room. We have already seen that the Bible is very present at the Academy, with daily Bible classes and chapel. Biblical ideas are also likely to appear on spelling tests, in biology lessons, and in government or history classes. History, in fact, is called American Christian History. Each detail of the past is understood in light of this nation's special calling to spread the gospel.

The United States, by this telling of the story, is meant to be a Christian nation, and, at Southside Academy, capitalism and democracy are as essential to that identity as is conservative religion. Government and Economics is taught as one subject and consists of learning how to defend the American way. J. Edgar Hoover's *Masters of Deceit* (1957) is one of the texts. Students in Rudiments, another high school requirement, are taught to develop a self-disciplined, loyal, patriotic character. Although as good Christians these students would never subvert duly elected authorities, they do not support their country "right or wrong." Rather, they are taught to work toward keeping the United States the kind of Christian nation God established it to be. As one parent described the ideal nation, "It would be Fundamental, just the way the whole country was built—with Fundamental, Bible-believing Christians, like when America was really great."

Besides teaching a work ethic, emphasizing patriotism, and requiring study of the Bible, the Academy is traditional in subtle ways. The learning process reflects Fundamentalists' Baconian view of the universe. For them, knowledge is a fixed body of facts, all of which have their origin with God and can be found in one form or another in the Bible. The learner's task is to uncover the facts and to appropriate them. Students at the Academy, therefore, spend a great deal of their time copying, memorizing, and reciting. They faithfully reproduce in their notebooks what the teacher has written on the board. They are tested on what they can remember and recite. Even in the high school, there is no attempt to move toward creative, critical, or integrative thinking. Biology students memorize the parts of plants and animals—not to discover relationships among various species or to understand the adaptive features of some plant or animal but to add to their store of knowledge about God's unique creations. When speech students learn how to conduct a debate or discussion, they learn a list of rules. It is not the place of human beings to criticize or to create new knowledge. The way in which these students learn equips them for a world where tradition is more valued than change.

The education Southside's pupils receive, then, is both structurally and substantively different from that offered in the public schools. At the elementary level, the skills that are emphasized enable Academy students to do as well as or better than public school students their age. They are, for instance, required to read regularly with and to their parents. Their school and home environment emphasizes the value of learning basic skills and the unacceptability of failure or sloppiness. Although the school does not have the material resources of books, machines, and highly paid staff that have come to be equated with a quality education, it does have a solid elementary program. Students emerge with a vast knowledge of the Bible and with good basic language and number skills.

At the high school level, the lack of equipment and personnel becomes more of a problem. The entire staff of the junior and senior high is four full-time teachers, part-time help from the headmaster, pastor, and youth minister, plus a study-hall aide. Science equipment consists of one microscope. Typing classes have two ancient machines. There is no facility for teaching home economics or shop or instrumental music. As a result, students have almost no choice of electives or of which course to take to fulfill a requirement or of teachers. There is only one government course,

one chemistry course, and one English course, and one teacher for each. With only twenty-six junior high and forty-three senior high school students, even the range of available friends is limited. Many parents would echo one of Jim Forester's reasons for withdrawing his daughter: "I don't think the education she was getting was worth the sacrifice and the turmoil it was causing." Even Academy administrators admit that the high school does not offer everything it should.

If one of the primary tasks of adolescence is "trying on" available roles and settling on a comfortable identity, Southside Academy's teens face a far less bewildering time than their secular peers. They have few roles from which to choose, a limited number of models to observe, and a narrow range of knowledge about the world with which to make their choices. If they remain at the Academy through graduation, these adolescents are likely to commit themselves to identities firmly within Fundamentalist boundaries, in part because their present and future alternatives have been so effectively controlled.

Where Nurture Fails

Not every Fundamentalist child grows up to be a Fundamentalist. The best available national data hint that "sectarians" are less likely to keep their children in the fold than any other denominational group (Hadaway 1978; Roof and Hadaway 1977). Although few people who grow up as sectarians drop out of religion entirely, at least 40 percent switch to other denominations by adulthood. Of the thirty-three families I interviewed who had teenaged or adult children, fifteen had at least one child who was raised in the church but about whose salvation the families were now worried. Of the parents who responded to the Sunday morning survey, 15 percent of those with teens reported that their children do not attend with them. One mother, who has two grown children in the church and two who are not, talked about her feelings of helplessness: "It is very frustrating to have your children grown and to know that they are not Christian. Pastor is always saying 'Get your house in order,' and there is nothing that we would like better, but it doesn't work that way. . . . [Our son] is too far away and too old." Many of Southside's youth drop out of church when they are old enough to say "no" to their parents. Some eventually return to another church or denomination, but many leave organized religion entirely.

What happens? With a system of socialization as all-encompassing as Southside's, how do so many children escape? Because I do not have systematic data on these dropouts, my conclusions must be tentative. I wish, however, to suggest a possible explanation. Just as relationships and activities inside the church's fellowship support the ideas of believers, so strong attachments outside the church may make Fundamentalist ideas implausible even (or perhaps especially) for those who have never known anything else.

The teen years are a time when most children experiment, and Southside's youth are no exception. If they have an opportunity to choose, they may select friends of whom their parents do not approve or participate in activities their parents would condemn. Sometimes youthful experiments turn into adult careers; other times they are but passing fancies. The difference has a good deal to do with the strength and nature of the relationships that are formed along the way.

When theorists explain juvenile delinquency, for instance, they ask about the relationships in which a young person is involved and the behavior that is considered normative within those groups (for example, Sutherland and Cressey 1978). For Fundamentalist youth, leaving the church may be analogous to juvenile delinquency. It may be possible to explain who leaves by asking similar questions. Those

who leave may be those who spend more time, more often, with doubters, and less time, of poorer quality, with those who believe. Dropouts either develop close relationships with outsiders or have deteriorating relationships with insiders or both.

Sometimes the influence of the outside world comes from inside the home: Nearly one-third of the families I interviewed who had "wayward" children were families where the father was not saved. In such homes, the ways of the world are always present as an alternative. Just as often, the outsider is a friend from the neighborhood or from school. The mother we heard earlier mentioned that her son had had a "friend who was strongly antireligious," and she suspected that had something to do with her son's disaffection. By the time children reach their teens, it becomes difficult to isolate them from friends and romances that can draw them away from Fundamentalism.

That same young man also had "some teachers at church that turned him off." Sometimes the reason for leaving is more push than pull. Some youth come to dislike and rebel against specific people in the church, including their parents. In Dudley's (1978) study of students in Seventh Day Adventist academies, the strongest predictor of rebellion was poor relationships with parents and school officials. Sorting out the causal direction is difficult after the fact. Some children may turn away from Fundamentalism because they are angry with their parents, and others may develop poor relationships with their parents because of their irreligious ideas and activities. In either case, without strong, positive bonds with people inside Fundamentalism, Southside's teens are likely to drift away. If they have the opportunity, they may well choose another religion or no religion at all.

Southside's nurture of its children is designed to make the Fundamentalist identity the only plausible choice. But ironically the very thoroughness of their efforts at socialization may sometimes backfire. Sometimes the problem is that once outside the sheltering canopy, young adults have no internal controls to guide them back to the fold. That is a possibility about which one woman voiced concern: "Sometimes there are kids that are brought up in Christian schools, Christian homes, Christian this and that, and sometimes they learn to act like a Christian before they actually really accept Christ. They even know how to get up and pray, but sometimes they don't have a personal relationship with Christ at all. They just know how to act." She would have said such youth needed to be converted, but the only true "conversion" possible for someone brought up in Fundamentalism is to leave. Indeed, upon achieving some distance from the all-encompassing faith of their childhoods, many Fundamentalist youth find it inadequate to meet the demands of the world they now live in. Rather than leaving religion entirely, many "convert" to other denominations and become among the most committed leaders of the same liberal churches they grew up disparaging.

In many cases, the church's efforts are simply not enough to counter the definitions of reality and standards of behavior that exist outside of Fundamentalism. As Fundamentalist ideas and lifestyles diverge increasingly from those in the larger culture, it is becoming more necessary for parents to limit their children's opportunities to choose, to isolate them from the people and activities of the world. As we have seen, it used to be sufficient to keep youth out of secular colleges; now they must be kept from public elementary and secondary schools as well. Some parents are able to counter successfully the influences of a secular education, but few children can pass through twelve years of public schooling without modifying the beliefs with which they have been raised. Some children are able to maintain their conviction that everything outside Fundamentalism is inherently evil, but others begin to encounter people, ideas, and activities they simply cannot bring themselves to condemn. In neighborhoods and in school, children are likely to find the outside world not nearly so offensive as they had been warned it was. If parents, in cooperation with the church and the Academy, are able to isolate their children from such positive experiences with the world, those children are less likely to stray. But the opportunities for failure are legion.

References

Dudley, R. L. 1978. "Alienation from Religion in Adolescents from Fundamentalist Religious Homes." *Journal for the Scientific Study of Religion* 17: 389–398.

Hadaway, C. K. 1978. "Denomination Switching and Membership Growth." *Sociological Analysis* 39: 321–337.

Roof, W. C., and C. K. Hadaway. 1977. "Shifts in Religious Preference in the Mid-Seventies." *Journal for the Scientific Study of Religion* 16: 409–412.

Sutherland, E. H., and D. R. Cressey. 1978. *Criminology,* 10th ed. Philadelphia: Lippincott.

Questions

1. Sociologist Peter Berger once wrote that "an individual's nomos [sense and understanding the world] is constructed with significant others. . . . The world begins to shake in the very instant that its sustaining conversation begins to falter." What Berger meant was that one's beliefs about the nature of the world come about as a result of interactions with others, and should those interactions and conversations end, individuals would lose their hold on their beliefs and their entire understanding of the world.

Because the Fundamentalists' "nomos" is quite unlike that of most people in our society, it seems as if they must take more precautions to guard against conversation with others. What evidence do you see in Ammerman's article that members of Southside take such precautions? What sorts of precautions?

2. Ammerman says that "the very thoroughness of their [the church members'] efforts at socialization many sometimes backfire."

What did she mean by this? What causes their efforts to backfire?

3. In reading 21, the concept of cultural capital was introduced. What kinds of cultural capital are acquired by the children whose parents belong to Southside? In your judgment, how suited is this cultural capital to life in society at large?

·23·

New Families
Modern Couples as New Pioneers

Philip Cowan and Carolyn Pape Cowan

Is the American family in decline? Using data from their own as well as others' research, Philip Cowan and Carolyn Pape Cowan explore in this 1998 article the problems faced by modern husbands and wives once they decide to start a family. Their findings suggest that we must rethink the whole idea of "family values" and decide just what sort of family we hope to promote in our society.

Mark and Abby met when they went to work for a young, ambitious candidate who was campaigning in a presidential primary. Over the course of an exhilarating summer, they debated endlessly about values and tactics. At summer's end they parted, returned to college, and proceeded to forge their individual academic and work careers. When they met again several years later at a political function, Mark was employed in the public relations department of a large company and Abby was about to graduate from law school. Their argumentative, passionate discussions about the need for political and social change gradually expanded to the more personal, intimate discussions that lovers have.

They began to plan a future together. Mark moved into Abby's apartment. Abby secured a job in a small law firm. Excited about their jobs and their flourishing relationship, they talked about making a long-term commitment and soon decided to marry. After the wedding, although their future plans were based on a strong desire to have children, they were uncertain about when to start a family. Mark raised the issue tentatively, but felt he did not have enough job security to take the big step. Abby was fearful of not being taken seriously if she became a mother too soon after joining her law firm.

Several years passed. Mark was now eager to have children. Abby, struggling with competing desires to have a baby *and* to move ahead in her professional life, was still hesitant. Their conversations about having a baby seemed to go nowhere but were dramatically interrupted when they suddenly discovered that their birth control method had failed: Abby was unmistakably pregnant. Somewhat surprised by their own reactions, Mark and Abby found that they were relieved to have the timing decision taken out of their hands. Feeling readier than they anticipated, they became increasingly excited as they shared the news with their parents, friends, and coworkers.

Most chapters in this book focus on high-risk families, a category in which some observers include all families that deviate from the traditional two-parent, nonteenage, father-at-work–mother-at-home "norm." The increasing prevalence of these families has been cited by David Popenoe (1993), David Blankenhorn (1990), and others as strong evidence that American families are currently in a state of decline. In the debate over the state of contemporary family life, the family decline theorists imply that traditional families are faring well. This view ignores clear evidence of the pervasive stresses and vulnerabilities that are affecting most families these days — even those with two mature, relatively advantaged parents.

In the absence of this evidence, it appears as if children and parents in traditional two-parent families do not face the kinds of problems that require the attention of family policymakers. We will show that Abby and Mark's life, along with those of many modern couples forming new families, is less ideal and more subject to distress than family observers and policymakers realize. Using data from our own and others' studies of partners becoming parents, we will illustrate how the normal process of becoming a family *in this culture, at this time* sets in motion a chain of potential stressors that function as risks that stimulate moderate to severe distress for a substantial number of parents. Results of a number of recent longitudinal[1] studies make clear that if the parents' distress is not addressed, the quality of their marriages and their relationships with their children are more likely to be compromised. In turn, conflictful or disengaged family relationships during the family's formative years foreshadow later problems for the children when they reach the preschool and elementary school years. This means that substantial numbers of new two-parent families in the United States do not fit the picture of the ideal family portrayed in the family decline debate.

---

[1]Longitudinal studies follow their subjects over time, unlike "cross-sectional" studies that may ask questions or observe at a single point in time. — Ed.

In what follows we (1) summarize the changing historical context that makes life for many modern parents more difficult than it used to be; (2) explore the premises underlying the current debate about family decline; (3) describe how conditions associated with the transition to parenthood create risks that increase the probability of individual, marital, and family distress; and (4) discuss the implications of this family strain for American family policy. We argue that systematic information about the early years of family life is critical to social policy debates in two ways: first, to show how existing laws and regulations can be harmful to young families, and second, to provide information about promising interventions with the potential to strengthen family relationships during the early childrearing years.

Historical Context: Changing Families in a Changing World

From the historical perspective of the past two centuries, couples like Mark and Abby are unprecedented. They are a modern, middle-class couple attempting to create a different kind of family than those of their parents and grandparents. Strained economic conditions and the shifting ideology about appropriate roles for mothers and fathers pose new challenges for these new pioneers whose journey will lead them through unfamiliar terrain. With no maps to pinpoint the risks and hardships, contemporary men and women must forge new trails on their own.

Based on our work with couples starting families over the past twenty years, we believe that the process of becoming a family is more difficult now than it used to be. Because of the dearth of systematic study of these issues, it is impossible to locate hard evidence that modern parents face more challenges than parents of the past. Nonetheless, a brief survey of the changing context of family life in North America suggests that the transition to parenthood presents different and more confusing challenges for modern couples creating families than it did for parents in earlier times.

LESS SUPPORT = MORE ISOLATION

While 75 percent of American families lived in rural settings in 1850, 75 percent were living in urban or suburban environments in 1979. Increasingly, new families are created far from grandparents, kin, and friends with babies the same age, leaving parents without the support of those who could share their experiences of the ups and down of parenthood. Most modern parents bring babies home to isolated dwellings where their neighbors are strangers. Many women who stay home to care for their babies find themselves virtually alone in the neighborhood during this major transition, a time when we know that inadequate social support poses a risk to their own and their babies' well-being.

MORE CHOICE = MORE AMBIGUITY

Compared with the experiences of their parents and grandparents, couples today have more choice about whether and when to bring children into their lives. In addition to the fact that about 10 percent of couples now choose not to have children, partners who do become parents are older and have smaller families — only one or two children, compared to the average of three, forty years ago. The reduction in family size tends to make each child seem especially precious, and the decision about whether and when to become parents even more momentous. Modern birth control methods give couples more control over the timing of a pregnancy, in spite of the fact that many methods fail with some regularity, as they did for Mark and Abby. Although the legal and moral issues surrounding abortion are hotly debated, modern couples have a choice about whether to become parents, even after conception begins.

Once the baby is born, there are more choices for modern couples. Will the mother return to work or school, which most were involved in before giving birth, and if so, how soon and for how many hours? Whereas only 18 percent of women with a child under six were employed outside the home in 1960, more than 50 percent of women with a child *under one* were working at least part time in 1990. Will the father take an active role in daily child care, and if so, how much? Although having these new choices is regarded by many as a benefit of modern life, choosing from among alternatives with such far-reaching consequences creates confusion and uncertainty for both men and women — which itself can lead to tension within the couple.

NEW EXPECTATIONS FOR MARRIAGE = NEW EMOTIONAL BURDENS

Mark and Abby, like many other modern couples, have different expectations for marriage then their forebears. In earlier decades, couples expected marriage to be a working partnership in which men and women played unequal but clearly defined roles in terms of family and work, especially once they had children. Many modern couples are trying to create more egalitarian relationships in which men and women have more similar and often interchangeable family work roles.

The dramatic increase of women in the labor force has challenged old definitions of what men and women are expected to do inside and outside the family. As women have taken on a major role of contributing to family income, there has been a shift in *ideology* about fathers' greater participation in housework and child care, although the *realities* of men's and women's division of family labor have lagged behind. Despite the fact that modern fathers are a little more involved in daily family activities than their fathers were, studies in every industrialized country reveal that women continue to carry the major share of the burden of family work and care of the children, even when both partners are employed full time. In a detailed qualitative study, Arlie Hochschild (1989) notes that working mothers come home to a "second shift." She describes vividly couples' struggle with contradictions between the values of egalitarianism and traditionalism, and between egalitarian ideology and the constraints of modern family life.

As husbands and wives struggle with these issues, they often become adversaries. At the same time, they expect their partners to be their major suppliers of emotional warmth and support. These demanding expectations for marriage as a haven from the stresses of the larger world come naturally to modern partners, but this comfort zone is difficult to create, given current economic and psychological realities and the absence of helpful models from the past. The difficulty of the task is further compounded by the fact that when contemporary couples feel stressed by trying to work and nurture their children, they feel torn by what they hear from advocates of a "simpler," more traditional version of family life. In sum, we see Abby and Mark as new pioneers because they are creating a new version of family life in an era of greater challenges and fewer supports, increased and confusing choices about work and family arrangements, ambiguities about men's and women's proper roles, and demanding expectations of themselves to be both knowledgeable and nurturing partners and parents.

Political Context: Does Family Change Mean Family Decline?

A number of writers have concluded that the historical family changes we described have weakened the institution of the family. One of the main spokespersons for this point of view, David Popenoe, interprets the trends as documenting a "retreat from the traditional nuclear family in terms of a lifelong, sexually exclusive unit, with a separate-sphere division of labor between husbands and wives." He asserts, "Nuclear units are losing ground to single-parent families, serial and stepfamilies, and unmarried and homosexual couples." The main problem in contemporary family life, he argues, is a shift in which familism as a cultural value has lost ground to other values such as individualism, self-focus, and egalitarianism.

Family decline theorists are especially critical of single-parent families whether created by divorce or out-of-wedlock childbirth. They assume that two-parent families of the past functioned with a central concern for children that led to putting children's needs first. They characterize parents who have children under other arrangements as putting themselves first, and they claim that children are suffering as a result.

The primary index for evaluating the family decline is the well-being of children. Family decline theorists repeatedly cite statistics suggesting that fewer children are being born, and that a higher proportion of them are living with permissive, disengaged, self-focused parents who ignore their physical and emotional needs. Increasing numbers of children show signs of mental illness, behavior problems, and social deviance. The remedy suggested? A social movement and social policies to promote "family values" that emphasize nuclear families with two married, monogamous parents who want to have children and are willing to devote themselves to caring for them. These are the families we have been studying.

Based on the work of following couples starting families over the past twenty years, we suggest that there is a serious problem with the suggested remedy, which ignores the extent of distress and dysfunction in this idealized family form. We will show that in a surprisingly high proportion of couples, the arrival of the first child is accompanied by increased levels of tension, conflict, distress, and divorce, not because the parents are self-centered but because it is inherently difficult in today's world to juggle the economic and emotional needs of all family members, even for couples in relatively "low-risk" circumstances. The need to pay more attention to the underside of the traditional family myth is heightened by the fact that we can now (1) identify in advance those couples most likely to have problems as they make the transition to parenthood, and (2) intervene to reduce the prevalence and intensity of these problems. Our concern with the state of contemporary families leads us to suggest remedies that would involve active support to enable parents to provide nurturance and stability for their children, rather than exhortations that they change their values about family life.

Real Life Context: Normal Risks Associated with Becoming a Family

To illustrate the short-term impact of becoming parents, let us take a brief look at Mark and Abby four days after they bring their daughter, Lizzie, home from the hospital.

It is 3 A.M. Lizzie is crying lustily. Mark had promised that he would get up and bring the baby to Abby when she woke, but he hasn't stirred. After nudging him several times, Abby gives up and pads across the room to Lizzie's cradle. She carries her daughter to a rocking chair and starts to feed her. Abby's nipples are sore and she hasn't yet been able to relax while nursing. Lizzie soon stops sucking and falls asleep. Abby broods silently, the quiet broken only by the rhythmic squeak of the rocker. She is angry at Mark for objecting to her suggestion that her parents come to help. She fumes, thinking about his romantic image of the three of them as a cozy family. "Well, Lizzie and I are cozy all right, but

where is Mr. Romantic now?" Abby is also preoccupied with worry. She is intrigued and drawn to Lizzie but because she hasn't experienced the "powerful surge of love" that she thinks "all mothers" feel, she worries that something is wrong with her. She is also anxious because she told her boss that she'd be back to work shortly, but she simply doesn't know how she will manage. She considers talking to her best friend, Adrienne, but Adrienne probably wouldn't understand because she doesn't have a child.

Hearing what he interprets as Abby's angry rocking, Mark groggily prepares his defense about why he failed to wake up when the baby did. Suddenly, recalling that Abby "barked" at him when he hadn't remembered to stop at the market and pharmacy on the way home from work, he pretends to be asleep. He becomes preoccupied with thoughts about the pile of work he will face at the office in the morning.

We can seen how two well-meaning, thoughtful people have been caught up in changes and reactions that neither has anticipated or feels able to control. Based on our experience with new parent couples, we imagine that, if asked, Abby and Mark would say that these issues arousing their resentment are minor; in fact, they feel foolish about being so upset about them. Yet studies of new parents suggest that the stage is set for a snowball effect in which these minor discontents can grow into more troubling distress in the next year or two. What are the consequences of this early disenchantment? Will Mark and Abby be able to prevent it from triggering more serious negative outcomes for them or for the baby?

To answer these questions about the millions of couples who become first-time parents each year, we draw on the results of our own longitudinal study of the transition to parenthood and those of several other investigators who also followed men and women from late pregnancy into the early years of life with a first child. The samples in these studies were remarkably similar: the average age of first-time expectant fathers was about thirty years, of expectant mothers approximately one year younger. Most investigators studied urban couples, but a few included rural families. Although the participants' economic level varied from study to study, most fell on the continuum from working class, through lower-middle, to upper-middle class. In 1995 we reviewed more than twenty longitudinal studies of this period of family life; we included two in Germany by Engfer (1998) and Schneewind (1983) and one in England by Clulow (1982), and found that results in all but two reveal an elevated risk for the marriages of couples becoming parents.

We talk about this major normative transition in the life of a couple in terms of risk, conflict, and distress for the relationship because we find that the effects of the transition to parenthood create disequilibrium in each of five major domains of family life: (1) the parents' sense of self; (2) parent-grandparent relationships; (3) the parent-child relationships; (4) relationships with friends and work; and (5) the state of the marriage. . . .

PARENTS' SENSE OF SELF

Henry, aged 32, was doing well in his job at a large computer store. Along with Mei-Lin, his wife of four years, he was looking forward to the birth of his first child. Indeed, the first week or two found Henry lost in a euphoric haze. But as he came out of the clouds and went back to work, Henry began to be distracted by new worries. As his coworkers kept reminding him, he's a father now. He certainly feels like a different person, though he's not quite sure what a new father is supposed to be doing. Rather hesitantly, he confessed his sense of confusion to Mei-Lin, who appeared visibly relieved. "I've been feeling so fragmented," she told him. "It's been difficult to hold on to my sense of *me*. I'm a wife, a daughter, a friend, and a teacher, but the Mother part seems to have taken over my whole being."

Having a child forces a redistribution of the energy directed to various aspects of parents' identity. We asked expectant parents to describe themselves by making a list of the main aspects of themselves, such as son, daughter, friend, worker, and to divide a circle we called *The Pie* into pieces representing how large each aspect of self feels. Men and women filled out *The Pie* again six and eighteen months after their babies were born. As partners became parents, the size of the slice labeled *parent* increased markedly until it occupied almost one-third of the identity of mothers of eighteen-month-olds. Although men's *parent* slice also expanded, their sense of self as father occupied only one-third the "space" of their wives'. For both women and men, the *partner* or *lover* part of their identities got "squeezed" as the *parent* aspect of self expanded. . . .

RELATIONSHIPS WITH PARENTS AND IN-LAWS

Sandra, one of the younger mothers in our study, talked with us about her fear of repeating the pattern from her mother's life. Her mother gave birth at sixteen, and told her children repeatedly that she was too young to raise a family. "Here I am with a beautiful little girl, and I'm worrying about whether I'm really grown up enough to raise her." At the same time, Sandra's husband, Daryl, who was beaten by his stepfather, is having flashbacks about how helpless he felt at those times: "I'm trying to maintain the confidence I felt when Sandra and I decided to start our family, but sometimes I get scared that I'm not going to be able to avoid being the kind of father I grew up with."

. . . There is considerable evidence that having a baby stimulates men's and women's feelings of vulnerability and loss associated with their childhoods, and that these issues play a role in their emerging sense of self as parents. There is also evidence that negative relationship patterns tend to be repeated across the generations, despite parents' efforts to avoid them; so Sandra and Daryl have good reason to be concerned. However, studies showing that a strong, positive couple relationship can provide a buffer against negative parent-child interactions suggest that the repetition of negative cycles is not inevitable.

We found that the birth of a first child increases the likelihood of contact between the generations, often with unanticipated consequences. Occasionally, renewed contact allows the expectant parents to put years of estrangement behind them if their parents are receptive to renewed contact. More often, increased contact between the generations stimulates old and new conflicts—within each partner, between the partners, and between the generations. To take one example: Abby wants her mother to come once the baby is born but Mark has a picture of beginning family life on their own. Tensions between them around this issue can escalate regardless of which decision they make. If Abby's parents do visit, Mark may have difficulty establishing his place with the baby. Even if Abby's parents come to help, she and Mark may find that the grandparents need looking after too. It may be weeks before Mark and Abby have a private conversation. If the grandparents do not respond or are not invited, painful feelings between the generations are likely to ensue.

THE PARENT-CHILD RELATIONSHIP

Few parents have had adequate experience in looking after children to feel confident immediately about coping with the needs of a first baby.

> Tyson and Martha have been arguing, it seems, for days. Eddie, their six-month-old, has long crying spells every day and into the night. As soon as she hears him, Martha moves to pick him up. When he is home, Tyson objects, reasoning that this just spoils Eddie and doesn't let him learn how to soothe himself. Martha responds that Eddie wouldn't be crying if something weren't wrong, but she worries that Tyson might be right; after all, she's never looked after a six-month-old for more than an evening of baby-sitting. Although Tyson continues to voice his objections, he worries that if Martha is right, *his* plan may not be the best for his son either.

To make matters more complicated, just as couples develop strategies that seem effective, their baby enters a new developmental phase that calls for new reactions and routines. What makes the new challenges difficult to resolve is that each parent has a set of ideas and expectations about how parents should respond to a child, most based on experience in their families of origin. Meshing both parents' views of how to resolve basic questions about child rearing proves to be a more complex and emotionally draining task than most couples had anticipated.

WORK AND FRIENDS

Dilemmas about partners' work outside the home are particularly salient during a couple's transition to parenthood.

> Both Hector and Isabel have decided that Isabel should stay home for at least the first year after having the baby. One morning, as Isabel is washing out Jose's diapers and hoping the phone will ring, she breaks into tears. Life is not as she imagined it. She misses her friends at work. She misses Hector, who is working harder now to provide for his family than he was before Jose was born. She misses her parents and sisters who live far away in Mexico. She feels strongly that she wants to be with her child full time, and that she should be grateful that Hector's income makes this possible, but she feels so unhappy right now. This feeling adds to her realization that she has always contributed half of their family income, but now she has to ask Hector for household money, which leaves her feeling vulnerable and dependent.

Maria is highly invested in her budding career as an investment counselor, making more money than her husband, Emilio. One morning, as she faces the mountain of unread files on her desk and thinks of Lara at the child care center almost ready to take her first steps, Maria bursts into tears. She feels confident that she and Emilio have found excellent child care for Lara, and reminds herself that research has suggested that when mothers work outside the home, their daughters develop more competence than daughters of mothers who stay home. Nevertheless, she feels bereft, missing milestones that happen only once in a child's life.

We have focused on the women in both families because, given current societal arrangements, the initial impact of the struggle to balance work and family falls more heavily on mothers. If the couple decides that one parent will stay home to be the primary caretaker of the child, it is almost always the mother who does so. As we have noted, in contemporary America, about 50 percent of mothers of very young children remain at home after having a baby and half return to work within the first year. Both alternatives have some costs and some benefits. If mothers like Isabel want to be home with their young children, and the family can afford this arrangement, they have the opportunity to participate fully in the early day-to-day life of their children. This usually has benefits for parents and children. Nevertheless, most mothers who stay home face limited opportunities to accomplish work that leads them to feel competent, and staying home deprives them of emotional support that coworkers and friends can provide, the kinds of support that play a significant role in how parents fare in the early postpartum years.[2] This leaves women like Isabel at risk for feeling lonely and isolated from friends and family. By contrast, women like Maria who return to work are able to maintain

a network of adults to work with and talk with. They may feel better about themselves and "on track" as far as their work is concerned, but many become preoccupied with worry about their children's well-being, particularly in this age of costly but less than ideal day care. Furthermore, once they get home, they enter a "second shift" in which they do the bulk of the housework and child care.

We do not mean to imply that all the work-family conflicts surrounding the transition to parenthood are experienced by women. Many modern fathers feel torn about how to juggle work and family life, move ahead on the job, and be more involved with their children than their fathers were with them. Rather than receive a reduction in workload, men tend to work longer hours once they become fathers, mainly because they take their role as provider even more seriously now that they have a child. In talking to more than 100 fathers in our ongoing studies, we have become convinced that the common picture of men as resisting the responsibilities and workload involved in family life is seriously in error. We have become painfully aware of the formidable obstacles that bar men from assuming more active roles as fathers and husbands.

First, parents, bosses, and friends often discourage men's active involvement in the care of their children ("How come you're home in the middle of the day?" "Are you really serious about your work here?" "She's got you babysitting again, huh?"). Second, the economic realities in which men's pay exceeds women's make it less viable for men to take family time off. Third, by virtue of the way males and females are socialized, men rarely get practice in looking after children and are given very little support for learning by trial and error with their new babies.

In the groups that we conducted for expectant and new parents, to which parents brought their babies after they were born, we saw and heard many versions of the following: we are

---

[2]Postpartum means "after the birth" of a child. — Ed.

discussing wives' tendency to reach for the baby, on the assumption that their husbands will not respond. Cindi describes an incident last week when little Samantha began to cry. Cindi waited. Her husband, Martin, picked up Samantha gingerly, groped for a bottle, and awkwardly started to feed her. Then, according to Martin, within about sixty seconds, Cindi suggested that Martin give Samantha's head more support and prop the bottle in a different way so that the milk would flow without creating air bubbles. Martin quickly decided to hand the baby back to "the expert" and slipped into the next room "to get some work done."

The challenge to juggle the demands of work, family, and friendship presents different kinds of stressors for men and women, which propels the spouses even farther into separate worlds. When wives stay at home, they wait eagerly for their husbands to return, hoping the men will go "on duty" with the child, especially on difficult days. This leaves tired husbands who need to unwind facing wives who long to talk to an adult who will respond intelligibly to them. When both parents work outside the family, they must coordinate schedules, arrange child care, and decide how to manage when their child is ill. Parents' stress from these dilemmas about child care and lack of rest often spill over into the workday — and their work stress, in turn, gets carried back into the family atmosphere.

THE MARRIAGE

It should be clearer now why we say that the normal changes associated with becoming a family increase the risk that husbands and wives will experience increased marital dissatisfaction and strain after they become parents. Mark and Abby, and the other couples we have described briefly, have been through changes in their sense of themselves and in their relationships with their parents. They have struggled with uncertainties and disagreements about how to provide the best care for their child. Regardless of whether one parent stays home full or part time or both work full days outside the home, they have limited time and energy to meet conflicting demands from their parents, bosses, friends, child, and each other, and little support from outside the family to guide them on this complex journey into uncharted territory. In almost every published study of the transition conducted over the last four decades, men's and women's marital satisfaction declined. Belsky and Rovine (1990) found that from 30 percent to 59 percent of the participants in their Pennsylvania study showed a decline between pregnancy and nine months postpartum, depending on which measure of the marriage they examined. In our study of California parents, 45 percent of the men and 58 percent of the women showed declining satisfaction with marriage between pregnancy and eighteen months postpartum. The scores of approximately 15 percent of the new parents moved from below to above the clinical cutoff that indicates serious marital problems, whereas only 4 percent moved from above to below the cutoff.

Why should this optimistic time of life pose so many challenges for couples? One key issue for couples becoming parents has been treated as a surefire formula for humor in situation comedies — husband-wife battles over the "who does what?" of housework, child care, and decision making. Our own study shows clearly that, regardless of how equally family work is divided before having a baby, or of how equally husbands and wives *expect* to divide the care of the baby, the roles men and women assume tend to be gender-linked, with wives doing more family work than they had done before becoming a parent and substantially more housework and baby care than their husbands do. Furthermore, the greater the discrepancy between women's predicted and actual division of family tasks with their spouses, the more symptoms of depression they report. The more traditional the arrangements—that is, the less husbands are responsible for family work—the greater fathers' *and* mothers' postpartum dissatisfaction with their overall marriage.

Although theories of life stress generally assume that *any* change is stressful, we found no correlation between sheer *amount* of change in the five aspects of family life and parents' difficulties adapting to parenthood. In general, parenthood was followed by increasing discrepancies between husbands' and wives' perceptions of family life and their descriptions of their actual family and work roles. Couples in which the partners showed the greatest increase in those discrepancies—more often those with increasingly traditional role arrangements—described increasing conflict as a couple and greater declines in marital satisfaction.

These findings suggest that whereas family decline theorists are looking at statistics about contemporary families through 1950 lenses, actual families are responding to the realities of life in the 1990s. Given historical shifts in men's and women's ideas about family roles and present economic realities, it is not realistic to expect them to simply reverse trends by adopting more traditional values and practices. Contemporary families in which the parents' arrangements are at the more traditional end of the spectrum are *less* satisfied with themselves, with their relationships as couples, and with their role as parents, than those at the more egalitarian end. . . .

Policy Implications

We return briefly to the family values debate to examine the policy implications of promoting traditional family arrangements [and] of altering workplace policies. . . .

THE POTENTIAL CONSEQUENCES OF PROMOTING TRADITIONAL FAMILY ARRANGEMENTS

What are the implications of the argument that families and children would benefit by a return to traditional family arrangements? We are aware that existing data are not adequate to provide a full test of the family values argument, but we believe that some systematic information on this point is better than none. At first glance, it may seem as if studies support the arguments of those proposing that "the family" is in decline. We have documented the fact that a substantial number of new two-parent families are experiencing problems of adjustment—parents' depression, troubled marriages, intergenerational strain, and stress in juggling the demands of work and family. Nevertheless, there is little in the transition to parenthood research to support the idea that parents' distress is attributable to a decline in their family-oriented *values*. First, the populations studied here are two-parent, married, nonteenage, lower-middle- to upper-middle-class families, who do not represent the "variants" in family form that most writers associate with declining quality of family life.

Second, threaded throughout the writings on family decline is the erroneous assumption that because these changes in the family have been occurring at the same time as increases in negative outcomes for children, the changes are the *cause* of the problems. These claims are not buttressed by systematic data establishing the direction of causal influence. For example, it is well accepted (but still debated) that children's adaptation is poorer in the period after their parents' divorce. Nevertheless, some studies suggest that it is the unresolved conflict between parents prior to and after the divorce, rather than the divorce itself, that accounts for most of the debilitating effects on the children.

Third, we find the attack on family egalitarianism puzzling when the fact is that, despite the increase in egalitarian ideology, modern couples move toward more traditional family role arrangements as they become parents— despite their intention to do otherwise. Our key point here is that increased traditionality of family and work roles in families of the 1980s and 1990s tends to be associated with *more* individual and marital distress for parents. Furthermore, we find that when fathers have little involvement in household and child care tasks, both parents are less responsive and less able to provide the structure necessary for their children to accomplish new and challenging tasks in our project playroom. Finally, when we ask teachers how all of the children in their classrooms are faring at school, it is the children of these parents who are less academically competent and more socially isolated. There is, then, a body of evidence suggesting that a return to strictly traditional family arrangements may not have the positive consequences that the proponents of "family values" claim they will.

FAMILY AND WORKPLACE POLICY

Current discussions about policies for reducing the tensions experienced by parents of young children tend to be polarized around two alternatives: (1) Encourage more mothers to stay home and thereby reduce their stress in juggling family and work; (2) Make the workplace more flexible and "family friendly" for both parents through parental leave policies, flextime, and child care provided or subsidized by the workplace. There is no body of systematic empirical research that supports the conclusion that when mothers work outside the home, their children or husbands suffer negative consequences. In fact, our own data and others' suggest that (1) children, especially girls, benefit from the model their working mothers provide as productive workers, and (2) mothers of

young children who return to work are less depressed than mothers who stay home full time. Thus it is not at all clear that a policy designed to persuade contemporary mothers of young children to stay at home would have the desired effects, particularly given the potential for depression and the loss of one parent's wages in single paycheck families. Unless governments are prepared, as they are in Sweden and Germany, for example, to hold parents' jobs and provide *paid* leave to replace lost wages, a stay-at-home *policy* seems too costly for the family on both economic and psychological grounds.

We believe that the issue should not be framed in terms of policies to support single-worker *or* dual-worker families, but rather in terms of support for the well-being of all family members. This goal could entail financial support for families with very young children so that parents could choose to do full-time or substantial part-time child care themselves *or* to have support to return to work. . . .

What about the alternative of increasing workplace flexibility? Studies of families making the transition to parenthood suggest that this alternative may be especially attractive and helpful when children are young, if it is accompanied by substantial increases in the availability of high-quality child care to reduce the stress of locating adequate care or making do with less than ideal caretakers. Adults and children tend to adapt well when both parents work *if both parents support that alternative.* Therefore, policies that support paid family leave along with flexible work arrangements could enable families to choose arrangements that make most sense for their particular situation. . . .

Like writers describing "family decline," we are concerned about the strength and hardiness of two-parent families. Unlike those who advocate that parents adopt more traditional family values, we recommend that policies to address family health and well-being allow for the creation of programs and services for families in diverse family arrangements, with the goal of enhancing the development and well-being of all children. We recognize that with economic resources already stretched very thin, this is not an auspicious time to recommend additional collective funding of family services. Yet research suggests that without intervention, there is a risk that the vulnerabilities and problems of the parents will spill over into the lives of their children, thus increasing the probability of the transmission of the kinds of intergenerational problems that erode the quality of family life and compromise children's chances of optimal development. This will be very costly in the long run.

We left Mark and Abby, and a number of other couples, in a state of animated suspension. Many of them were feeling somewhat irritable and disappointed, though not ready to give up on their dreams of creating nurturing families. These couples provide a challenge—that the information they have offered through their participation in scores of systematic family studies in many locales will be taken seriously, and that their voices will play a role in helping our society decide how to allocate limited economic and social resources for the families that need them.

References

Belsky, J., and M. Rovine. 1990. "Patterns of Marital Change Across the Transition to Parenthood." *Journal of Marriage and the Family* 52: 109–123.

Blankenhorn, D., S. Bayme, and J. B. Eishtain (eds.). 1990. *Rebuilding the Nest: A New Commitment to the American Family.* Milwaukee, WI: Family Service America.

Clulow, C. F. 1982. *To Have and to Hold: Marriage, the First Baby and Preparing Couples for Parenthood.* Aberdeen, Scotland: Aberdeen University Press.

Engfer, A. 1988. "The Interrelatedness of Marriage and the Mother-Child Relationship." Pp. 104–118 in R. A. Hinde and J. Stevenson-Hinde (eds.), *Relationships Within Families: Mutual Influences.* Cambridge, England: Cambridge University Press.

Hochschild, A. R. 1989. *The Second Shift: Working Parents and the Revolution at Home.* New York: Viking Penguin.

Popenoe, D. 1993. "American Family Decline, 1960–1990." *Journal of Marriage and the Family* 55: 527–541.

Schneewind, K. A. 1983. "Konsequenzen der Erstelternschaft" [Consequences of the Transition to Parenthood: An Overview"]. *Psychologie in Erzienhung und Unterricht* 30: 161–172.

Questions

1. List the five major domains of family life that, according to the authors, are most influenced by the arrival of the first child. For you, which of these domains would be the most important? Why?

2. Why is the transition to parenthood more confusing for today's couples than it was for their parents?

3. Why do the authors of this article conclude that emphasizing traditional family values is wrong and might even be harmful? Do you agree with their conclusion? Why or why not?

·24·
Anybody's Son Will Do

Gwynne Dyer

Ordinary people would be loathe to do the sorts of things that soldiers may be called upon to do—but societies seem to need soldiers. As Dyer explains in this chapter excerpted from his 1985 book *War*, the means of socializing men out of the civilian role and into the soldier/killer role has become institutionalized as a result of centuries of experience.

. . . All soldiers belong to the same profession, no matter what country they serve, and it makes them different from everybody else. They have to be different, for their job is ultimately about killing and dying, and those things are not a natural vocation for any human being. Yet all soldiers are born civilians. The method for turning young men into soldiers—people who kill other people and expose themselves to death—is basic training. It's essentially the same all over the world, and it always has been, because young men everywhere are pretty much alike.

Human beings are fairly malleable, especially when they are young, and in every young man there are attitudes for any army to work with: the inherited values and postures, more or less dimly recalled, of the tribal warriors who were once the model for every young boy to emulate. Civilization did not involve a sudden clean break in the way people behave, but merely the progressive distortion and redirection of all the ways in which people in the old tribal societies used to behave, and modern definitions of maleness still contain a great deal of the old warrior ethic. The anarchic machismo of the primitive warrior is not what modern armies really need in their soldiers, but it does provide them with promising raw material for the transformation they must work in their recruits.

Just how this transformation is wrought varies from time to time and from country to country. In totally militarized societies—ancient Sparta, the samurai class of medieval Japan, the areas controlled by organizations like the Eritrean People's Liberation Front today[1]—it begins at puberty or before, when the young boy is immersed in a disciplined society in which only the military values are allowed to penetrate. In more sophisticated modern societies, the process is briefer and more concentrated, and the way it works is much more visible. It is, essentially, a conversion process in an almost religious sense—and as in all conversion phenomena, the emotions are far more important than the specific ideas. . . .

> When I was going to school, we used to have to recite the Pledge of Allegiance every day. They don't do that now. You know, we've got kids that come in here now, when they first get here, they don't know the Pledge of Allegiance to the

[1]Eritrea, an Italian colony from 1885 to 1941, was annexed by Ethiopia in 1962. After a 30-year civil war, Eritrea gained its independence in 1992. —Ed.

flag. And that's something—that's like a cardinal sin. . . . My daughter will know that stuff by the time she's three; she's two now and she's working on it. . . . You know, you've got to have your basics, the groundwork where you can start to build a child's brain from. . . .

—USMC drill instructors,
Parris Island recruit training depot, 1981

That is what the rhetoric of military patriotism sounds like, in every country and at every level—and it is virtually irrelevant so far as the actual job of soldiering is concerned. Soldiers are not just robots; they are ordinary human beings with national and personal loyalties, and many of them do feel the need for some patriotic or ideological justification for what they do. But which nation, which ideology, does not matter: men will fight as well and die as bravely for the Khmer Rouge as for "God, King, and Country." Soldiers are the instruments of politicians and priests, ideologues and strategists, who may have high national or moral purposes in mind, but the men down in the trenches fight for more basic motives. The closer you get to the front line, the fewer abstract nouns you hear.

Armies know this. It is their business to get men to fight, and they have had a long time to work out the best way of doing it. All of them pay lip service to the symbols and slogans of their political masters, though the amount of time they must devote to this activity varies from country to country. It is less in the United States than in the Soviet Union, and it is still less in a country like Israel, which actually fights frequent wars. Nor should it be thought that the armies are hypocritical—most of their members really do believe in their particular national symbols and slogans. But their secret is that they know these are not the things that sustain men in combat.

What really enables men to fight is their own self-respect, and a special kind of love that has nothing to do with sex or idealism. Very few men have died in battle, when the

moment actually arrived, for the United States of America or for the sacred cause of Communism, or even for their homes and families; if they had any choice in the matter at all, they chose to die for each other and for their own vision of themselves. . . .

The way armies produce this sense of brotherhood in a peacetime environment is basic training: a feat of psychological manipulation on the grand scale which has been so consistently successful and so universal that we fail to notice it as remarkable. In countries where the army must extract its recruits in their late teens, whether voluntarily or by conscription, from a civilian environment that does not share the military values, basic training involves a brief but intense period of indoctrination whose purpose is not really to teach the recruits basic military skills, but rather to change their values and their loyalties. "I guess you could say we brainwash them a little bit," admitted a U.S. Marine drill instructor, "but you know they're good people." . . .

It's easier if you catch them young. You can train older men to be soldiers; it's done in every major war. But you can never get them to believe that they like it, which is the major reason armies try to get their recruits before they are twenty. There are other reasons too, of course, like the physical fitness, lack of dependents, and economic dispensability of teenagers, that make armies prefer them, but the most important qualities teenagers bring to basic training are enthusiasm and naiveté. Many of them actively want the discipline and the closely structured environment that the armed forces will provide, so there is no need for the recruiters to deceive the kids about what will happen to them after they join.

There is discipline. There is drill. . . . When you are relying on your mates and they are relying on you, there's no room for slackness or sloppiness. If you're not prepared to accept the rules, you're better off where you are.

—British army recruiting advertisement, 1976

People are not born soldiers, they become soldiers. . . . And it should not begin at the moment when a new recruit is enlisted into the ranks, but rather much earlier, at the time of the first signs of maturity, during the time of adolescent dreams.

—*Red Star* (Soviet army newspaper), 1973

Young civilians who have volunteered and have been accepted by the Marine Corps[2] arrive at Parris Island, the Corps's East Coast facility for basic training, in a state of considerable excitement and apprehension: most are aware that they are about to undergo an extraordinary and very difficult experience. But they do not make their own way to the base; rather, they trickle in to Charleston airport on various flights throughout the day on which their training platoon is due to form, and are held there, in a state of suppressed but mounting nervous tension, until late in the evening. When the buses finally come to carry them the seventy-six miles to Parris Island, it is often after midnight—and this is not an administrative oversight. The shock treatment they are about to receive will work most efficiently if they are worn out and somewhat disoriented when they arrive.

The basic training organization is a machine, processing several thousand young men every month, and every facet and gear of it has been designed with the sole purpose of turning civilians into Marines as efficiently as possible. Provided it can have total control over their bodies and their environment for approximately three months, it can practically guarantee converts. Parris Island provides that controlled environment, and the recruits do not set foot outside it again until they graduate as Marine privates eleven weeks later.

They're allowed to call home, so long as it doesn't get out of hand—every three weeks or so they can call home and make sure everything's all right, if they haven't gotten a letter or there's a particular set of circumstances. If it's a case of an emergency call coming in, then they're allowed to accept that call; if not, one of my staff will take the message. . . .

In some cases I'll get calls from parents who haven't quite gotten adjusted to the idea that their son had cut the strings—and in a lot of cases that's what they're doing. The military provides them with an opportunity to leave home but they're still in a rather secure environment.

—Captain Brassington, USMC

For the young recruits, basic training is the closest thing their society can offer to a formal rite of passage,[3] and the institution probably stands in an unbroken line of descent from the lengthy ordeals by which young males in precivilized groups were initiated into the adult community of warriors. But in civilized societies it is a highly functional institution whose product is not anarchic warriors, but trained soldiers.

Basic training is not really about teaching people skills; it's about changing them, so that they can do things they wouldn't have dreamt of otherwise. It works by applying enormous physical and mental pressure to men who have been isolated from their normal civilian environment and placed in one where the only right way to think and behave is the way the Marine Corps wants them to. The key word the men who run the machine use to describe this process is *motivation*.

I can motivate a recruit and in third phase, if I tell him to jump off the third deck, he'll jump off the third deck. Like I said before, it's a captive audience and I can train that guy; I can get him to do anything I want him to do. . . . They're good kids and they're out to do the

---

[2]Something you might not know if you have no military experience and don't watch war movies or attend the ballet is that the word *corps* is pronounced "core" (from the Latin *corpus*, meaning "body").—Ed.

[3]The concept of rite of passage (or *rites de passage*) is discussed in *The Practical Skeptic*, chapter 10.—Ed.

right thing. We get some bad kids, but you know, we weed those out. But as far as motivation—here, we can motivate them to do anything you want, in recruit training.
—USMC drill instructor, Parris Island

The first three days the raw recruits spend at Parris Island are actually relatively easy, though they are hustled and shouted at continuously. It is during this time that they are documented and inoculated, receive uniforms, and learn the basic orders of drill that will enable young Americans (who are not very accustomed to this aspect of life) to do everything simultaneously in large groups. But the most important thing that happens in "forming" is the surrender of the recruits' own clothes, their hair—all the physical evidence of their individual civilian identities.

During a period of only seventy-two hours, in which they are allowed little sleep, the recruits lay aside their former lives in a series of hasty rituals (like being shaven to the scalp) whose symbolic significance is quite clear to them even though they are quite deliberately given absolutely no time for reflection, or any hint that they might have the option of turning back from their commitment. The men in charge of them know how delicate a tightrope they are walking, though, because at this stage the recruits are still newly caught civilians who have not yet made their ultimate inward submission to the discipline of the Corps.

> Forming Day One makes me nervous. You've got a whole new mob of recruits, you know, sixty or seventy depending, and they don't know anything. You don't know what kind of a reaction you're going to get from the stress you're going to lay on them, and it just worries me the first day.
>
> Things could happen, I'm not going to lie to you. Something might happen. A recruit might decide he doesn't want any part of this stuff and maybe take a poke at you or something like that. In a situation like that it's going to be a spur-of-the-moment thing and that worries me.
> —USMC drill instructor

But it rarely happens. The frantic bustle of forming is designed to give the recruit no time to think about resisting what is happening to him. And so the recruits emerge from their initiation into the system, stripped of their civilian clothes, shorn of their hair, and deprived of whatever confidence in their own identity they may previously have had as eighteen-year-olds, like so many blanks ready to have the Marine identity impressed upon them.

The first stage in any conversion process is the destruction of an individual's former beliefs and confidence, and his reduction to a position of helplessness and need. It isn't really as drastic as all that, of course, for three days cannot cancel out eighteen years; the inner thoughts and the basic character are not erased. But the recruits have already learned that the only acceptable behavior is to repress any unorthodox thoughts and to mimic the character the Marine Corps wants. Nor are they, on the whole, reluctant to do so, for they *want* to be Marines. From the moment they arrive at Parris Island, the vague notion that has been passed down for a thousand generations that masculinity means being a warrior becomes an explicit article of faith, relentlessly preached: to be a man means to be a Marine.

There are very few eighteen-year-old boys who do not have highly romanticized ideas of what it means to be a man, so the Marine Corps has plenty of buttons to push. And it starts pushing them on the first day of real training: the officer in charge of the formation appears before them for the first time, in full dress uniform with medals, and tells them how to become men.

> The United States Marine Corps has 205 years of illustrious history to speak for itself. You have made the most important decision in your life . . . by signing your name, your life, your pledge to the Government of the United States, and even more importantly, to the United States Marine Corps—a brotherhood, an elite unit. In 10.3 weeks you are going to become a

member of that history, those traditions, this organization—if you have what it takes.

All of you want to do that by virtue of your signing your name as a man. The Marine Corps says that we build men. Well, I'll go a little bit further. We develop the tools that you have— and everybody has those tools to a certain extent right now. We're going to give you the blueprints, and we are going to show you how to build a Marine. *You've* got to build a Marine—you understand?

—Captain Pingree, USMC

The recruits, gazing at him with awe and adoration, shout in unison, "Yes sir!" just as they have been taught. They do it willingly, because they are volunteers—but even conscripts tend to have the romantic fervor of volunteers if they are only eighteen years old. Basic training, whatever its hardships, is a quick way to become a man among men, with an undeniable status, and beyond the initial consent to undergo it, it doesn't even require any decisions.

I had just dropped out of high school and I wasn't doing much on the street except hanging out, as most teenagers would be doing. So they gave me an opportunity—a recruiter picked me up, gave me a good line, and said that I could make it in the Marines, that I have a future ahead of me. And since I was living with my parents, I figured that I could start my own life here and grow up a little.

—USMC recruit, 1982

I like the hand-to-hand combat and . . . things like that. It's a little rough going on me, and since I have a small frame I would like to become deadly, as I would put it. I like to have them words, especially the way they've been teaching me here.

—USMC recruit (from Brooklyn), Parris Island, 1982

The training, when it starts, seems impossibly demanding physically for most of the recruits—and then it gets harder week by week. There is a constant barrage of abuse and insults aimed at the recruits, with the deliberate

purpose of breaking down their pride and so destroying their ability to resist the transformation of values and attitudes that the Corps intends them to undergo. At the same time the demands for constant alertness and for instant obedience are continuously stepped up, and the standards by which the dress and behavior of the recruits are judged become steadily more unforgiving. But it is all carefully calculated by the men who run the machine, who think and talk in terms of the stress they are placing on the recruits: "We take so many c.c.'s of stress and we administer it to each man—they should be a little bit scared and they should be unsure, but they're adjusting." The aim is to keep the training arduous but just within most of the recruits' capability to withstand. One of the most striking achievements of the drill instructors is to create and maintain the illusion that basic training is an extraordinary challenge, one that will set those who graduate apart from others, when in fact almost everyone can succeed.

There has been some preliminary weeding out of potential recruits even before they begin training, to eliminate the obviously unsuitable minority, and some people do "fail" basic training and get sent home, at least in peacetime. The standards of acceptable performance in the U.S. armed forces, for example, tend to rise and fall in inverse proportion to the number and quality of recruits available to fill the forces to the authorized manpower levels. (In 1980, about 15 percent of Marine recruits did not graduate from basic training.) But there are very few young men who cannot be turned into passable soldiers if the forces are willing to invest enough effort in it.

Not even physical violence is necessary to effect the transformation, though it has been used by most armies at most times.

It's not what it was fifteen years ago down here. The Marine Corps still occupies the position of a tool which the society uses when it feels like that is a resort that they have to fall to. Our society changes as all societies do, and our society felt that through enlightened training methods we could still produce the same product—and when you examine it, they're right. . . . Our 100 c.c.'s of stress is really all we need, not two gallons of it, which is what used to be.[4] . . . In some cases with some of the younger drill instructors it was more an initiation than it was an acute test, and so we introduced extra officers and we select our drill instructors to "fine-tune" it.

—Captain Brassington, USMC

There is, indeed, a good deal of fine-tuning in the roles that the men in charge of training any specific group of recruits assume. At the simplest level, there is a sort of "good cop—bad cop" manipulation of the recruits' attitudes toward those applying the stress. The three younger drill instructors with a particular serial are quite close to them in age and unremittingly harsh in their demands for ever higher performance, but the senior drill instructor, a man almost old enough to be their father, plays a more benevolent and understanding part and is available for individual counseling. And generally offstage, but always looming in the background, is the company commander, an impossibly austere and almost godlike personage.

At least these are the images conveyed to the recruits, although of course all these men cooperate closely with an identical goal in view. It works: in the end they become not just role models and authority figures, but the focus of the recruits' developing loyalty to the organization.

I imagine there's some fear, especially in the beginning, because they don't know what to expect. . . . I think they hate you at first, at least for a week or two, but it turns to respect. . . . They're seeking discipline, they're seeking someone to take charge, 'cause at home they never got it. . . . They're looking to be told what to do and then someone is standing there enforcing what they tell them to do, and it's kind of like the father-and-son game, all the way through. They form a fatherly image of the DI[5] whether they want to or not.

—Sergeant Carrington, USMC

Just the sheer physical exercise, administered in massive doses, soon has the recruits feeling stronger and more competent than ever before. Inspections, often several times daily, quickly build up their ability to wear the uniform and carry themselves like real Marines, which is a considerable source of pride. The inspections also help to set up the pattern in the recruits of unquestioning submission to military authority: standing stock-still, staring straight ahead, while somebody else examines you closely for faults is about as extreme a ritual act of submission as you can make with your clothes on.

But they are not submitting themselves merely to the abusive sergeant making unpleasant remarks about the hair in their nostrils. All around them are deliberate reminders—the flags and insignia displayed on parade, the military music, the marching formations and drill instructors' cadenced calls—of the idealized organization, the "brotherhood" to which they will be admitted as full members if they submit and conform. Nowhere in the armed forces are the military courtesies so elaborately observed, the staffs' uniforms so immaculate (some DIs change several times a day), and the ritual aspects of military life so highly visible as on a basic training establishment.

Even the seeming inanity of close-order drill has a practical role in the conversion process. It has been over a century since mass formations of men were of any use on the battlefield, but every army in the world still drills its troops, especially during basic training, because marching

---

[4]As a point of information, there are 4 c.c.'s in a teaspoon.—Ed.

[5]Drill instructor.—Ed.

in formation, with every man moving his body in the same way at the same moment, is a direct physical way of learning two things a soldier must believe: that orders have to be obeyed automatically and instantly, and that you are no longer an individual, but part of a group.

The recruits' total identification with the other members of their unit is the most important lesson of all, and everything possible is done to foster it. They spend almost every waking moment together—a recruit alone is an anomaly to be looked into at once—and during most of that time they are enduring shared hardships. They also undergo collective punishments, often for the misdeed or omission of a single individual (talking in the ranks, a bed not swept under during barracks inspection), which is a highly effective way of suppressing any tendencies toward individualism. And, of course, the DIs place relentless emphasis on competition with other "serials" in training: there may be something infinitely pathetic to outsiders about a marching group of anonymous recruits chanting, "Lift your heads and hold them high, 3313 is a-passin' by," but it doesn't seem like that to the men in the ranks.

Nothing is quite so effective in building up a group's morale and solidarity, though, as a steady diet of small triumphs. Quite early in basic training, the recruits begin to do things that seem, at first sight, quite dangerous: descend by ropes from fifty-foot towers, cross yawning gaps hand-over-hand on high wires (known as the Slide for Life, of course), and the like. The common denominator is that these activities are daunting but not really dangerous: the ropes will prevent anyone from falling to his death off the rappelling tower, and there is a pond of just the right depth—deep enough to cushion a falling man, but not deep enough that he is likely to drown—under the Slide for Life. The goal is not to kill recruits, but to build up their confidence as individuals and as a group by allowing them to overcome apparently frightening obstacles.

You have an enemy here at Parris Island. The enemy that you're going to have at Parris Island is in every one of us. It's in the form of cowardice. The most rewarding experience you're going to have in recruit training is standing on line every evening, and you'll be able to look into each other's eyes, and you'll be able to say to each other with your eyes: "By God, we've made it one more day! We've defeated the coward."

—Captain Pingree, USMC

Number on deck, sir, forty-five . . . highly motivated, truly dedicated, rompin', stompin', bloodthirsty, kill-crazy United States Marine Corps recruits, SIR!

—Marine chant, Parris Island, 1982

If somebody does fail a particular test, he tends to be alone, for the hurdles are deliberately set low enough that most recruits can clear them if they try. In any large group of people there is usually a goat: someone whose intelligence or manner or lack of physical stamina marks him for failure and contempt. The competent drill instructor, without deliberately setting up this unfortunate individual for disgrace, will use his failure to strengthen the solidarity and confidence of the rest. When one hapless young man fell off the Slide for Life into the pond, for example, his drill instructor shouted the usual invective—"Well, get out of the water. Don't contaminate it all day"—and then delivered the payoff line: "Go back and change your clothes. You're useless to your unit now."

"Useless to your unit" is the key phrase, and all the recruits know that what it means is "useless *in battle*." The Marine drill instructors at Parris Island know exactly what they are doing to the recruits, and why. They are not rear-echelon people filling comfortable jobs, but the most dedicated and intelligent NCOs[6] the Marine Corps can find: even now, many of them have combat experience. The Corps has a clear-eyed understanding of precisely what

---

[6]Noncommissioned officers.—Ed.

it is training its recruits for—combat—and it ensures that those who do the training keep that objective constantly in sight.

The DIs "stress" the recruits, feed them their daily ration of synthetic triumphs over apparent obstacles, and bear in mind all the time that the goal is to instill the foundations for the instinctive, selfless reactions and the fierce group loyalty that is what the recruits will need if they ever see combat. They are arch-manipulators, fully conscious of it, and utterly unashamed. These kids have signed up as Marines, and they could well see combat; this is the way they have to think if they want to live. . . .

Combat is the ultimate reality that Marines—or any other soldiers, under any flag—have to deal with. Physical fitness, weapons training, battle drills, are all indispensable elements of basic training, and it is absolutely essential that the recruits learn the attitudes of group loyalty and interdependency which will be their sole hope of survival and success in combat. The training inculcates or fosters all of those things, and even by the halfway point in the eleven-week course, the recruits are generally responding with enthusiasm to their tasks.

But there is nothing in all this (except the weapons drill) that would not be found in the training camp of a professional football team. What sets soldiers apart is their willingness to kill. But it is not a willingness that comes easily to most men—even young men who have been provided with uniforms, guns, and official approval to kill those whom their government has designated as enemies. They will, it is true, fall very readily into the stereotypes of the tribal warrior group. Indeed, most of them have had at least a glancing acquaintance in their early teens with gangs (more or less violent, depending on, among other things, the neighborhood), the modern relic of that ancient institution.

And in many ways what basic training produces is the uniformed equivalent of a modern street gang: a bunch of tough, confident kids full of bloodthirsty talk. But gangs don't actually kill each other in large numbers. If they behaved the way armies do, you'd need trucks to clean the bodies off the streets every morning. They're held back by the civilian belief—the normal human belief—that killing another person is an awesome act with huge consequences.

There is aggression in all of us—men, women, children, babies. Armies don't have to create it, and they can't even increase it. But most of us learn to put limits on our aggression, especially physical aggression, as we grow up. . . .

There is such a thing as a "natural soldier": the kind of man who derives his greatest satisfaction from male companionship, from excitement, and from the conquering of physical and psychological obstacles. He doesn't necessarily want to kill people as such, but he will have no objections if it occurs within a moral framework that gives him a justification—like war—and if it is the price of gaining admission to the kind of environment he craves. Whether such men are born or made, I do not know, but most of them end up in armies (and many move on again to become mercenaries, because regular army life in peacetime is too routine and boring).

But armies are not full of such men. They are so rare that they form only a modest fraction even of small professional armies, mostly congregating in the commando-type special forces. In large conscript armies they virtually disappear beneath the weight of numbers of more ordinary men. And it is these ordinary men, who do not like combat at all, that the armies must persuade to kill. Until only a generation ago, they did not even realize how bad a job they were doing.

Armies had always assumed that, given the proper rifle training, the average man would kill in combat with no further incentive than the knowledge that it was the only way to defend his own life. After all, there are no historical records of Roman legionnaires refusing to use their swords, or Marlborough's infantrymen[7] refusing to fire their muskets against the enemy. But then dispersion hit the battlefield, removing each rifleman from the direct observation of his companions—and when U.S. Army Colonel S. L. A. Marshall finally took the trouble to inquire into what they were doing in 1943–45, he found that on average only 15 percent of trained combat riflemen fired their weapons at all in battle. The rest did not flee, but they would not kill—even when their own position was under attack and their lives were in immediate danger.

> The thing is simply this, that out of an average one hundred men along the line of fire during the period of an encounter, only fifteen men on average would take any part with the weapons. This was true whether the action was spread over a day, or two days or three. . . . In the most aggressive infantry companies, under the most intense local pressure, the figure rarely rose above 25% of total strength from the opening to the close of an action.
>
> —Col. S. L. A. Marshall

Marshall conducted both individual interviews and mass interviews with over four hundred infantry companies, both in Europe and in the Central Pacific, immediately after they had been in close combat with German or Japanese troops, and the results were the same each time. They were, moreover, as astonishing to the company officers and the troops themselves as they were to Marshall; each man who hadn't fired his rifle thought he had been alone in his defection from duty.

Even more indicative of what was going on was the fact that almost all the crew-served weapons had been fired. Every man had been trained to kill and knew it was his duty to kill, and so long as he was in the presence of other soldiers who could see his actions, he went ahead and did it. But the great majority of the riflemen, each unobserved by the others in his individual foxhole, had chosen not to kill, even though it increased the likelihood of his own death. . . .

But the question naturally arises: if the great majority of men are not instinctive killers, and if most military killing these days is in any case done by weapons operating from a distance at which the question of killing scarcely troubles the operators—then why is combat an exclusively male occupation? The great majority of women, everyone would agree, are not instinctive killers either, but so what? If the remote circumstances in which the killing is done or the deliberate conditioning supplied by the military enable most men to kill, why should it be any different for women?

My own guess would be that it probably wouldn't be different; it just hasn't been tried very extensively. But it is an important question, because it has to do with the causes and possible cure of war. If men fight wars because that is an intrinsic part of the male character, then nothing can abolish the institution of warfare short of abolishing the male half of the human race (or at least, as one feminist suggested, disfranchising it for a hundred years).

If, on the other hand, wars are a means of allocating power between civilized human groups, in which the actual soldiers have always been male simply because men were more suited to it by their greater physical strength and their freedom from the burden of childbearing, then what we are discussing is not Original Sin, but simply a mode of social behavior. The fact that almost every living male for thousands of generations has imbibed some of the warrior mystique is no proof of a genetic predisposition to be warlike. The cultural continuity is quite enough to transmit such attitudes, and men were specialized in the hunting and warrior functions for the same physical reasons long before civilized war was invented.

---

[7]John Churchill (1650–1722), first Duke of Marlborough, British general, supreme commander of the British forces in the War of the Spanish Succession. —Ed.

It was undoubtedly men, the "hunting" specialists, who invented civilized war, just as it was probably women, specializing in the "gathering" part of the primitive economy, who invented agriculture. That has no necessary relevance today: we all eat vegetables, and we can all die in war. It is a more serious allegation against males to say that all existing forms of political power have been shaped predominantly by men, so that even if wars are about power and not about the darker side of the masculine psyche, war is still a male problem. That has unquestionably been true through all of history (although it remains to be proven that women exercising power respond very differently to its temptations and obsessions). But there is no need to settle that argument: if war and masculinity are not inseparable, then we have already moved onto negotiable ground. For the forms of political power, unlike psyches, are always negotiable.

Unfortunately there is little direct support for this optimistic hypothesis in the prevailing current of opinion among soldiers generally, where war and maleness are indeed seen as inseparable. To say that the combat branches of the armed forces are sexist is like remarking that gravity generally pulls downward, and nowhere is the contempt for women greater than at a recruit training base like Parris Island. The DIs are quite ruthless in exploiting every prejudice and pushing every button that will persuade the recruits to accept the value system they are selling, and one of those buttons (quite a large one) is the conviction of young males—or at least the desire to be convinced—that they are superior to young females. (After all, even recruits want to feel superior to somebody, and it certainly isn't going to be anybody in their immediate vicinity at Parris Island.)

When it's all boys together, especially among the younger men, Marine Corps slang for any woman who isn't the wife, mother, or daughter of anyone present is "Suzie." It is short for "Suzie Rottencrotch"—and Suzie crops up a lot in basic training. Even when the topic of instruction is hand and arm signals in combat.

> Privates, if you don't have a little Suzie now, maybe you're going to find one when you get home. You bet. You'll find the first cheap slut you can get back home. What do you mean, "No"? You're a Marine, you're going to do it.
>
> If we get home with little Suzie . . . we're in a nice companionship with little Suzie and here you are getting hot and heavy and then you're getting ready to go down there and make that dive, privates, and Suzie says . . . Suzie says it's the wrong time of the month. Privates, if you don't want to get back home and indulge in this little adventure, you can show your girlfriend the hand and arm signal for "close it up."
>
> And you want her to close up those nasty little thighs of hers, do you not, privates? The hand and arm signal: the arms are laterally shoulder height, the fingers are extended, and the palms are facing toward the front. This is the starting position for "close it up" [tighten up the formation]: just like closing it up, bring the arms together just like that.
>
> Privates, in addition, I want you to dedicate all this training to one very special person. Can anyone tell me who that is, privates?
>
> (Voice) The Senior Drill Instructor, sir?
>
> No, not your Senior Drill Instructor. You're going to dedicate all this training, privates, to your enemy . . . to your enemy. To your enemy: the reason being, so *he* can die for *his* country. So who are we going to dedicate all this training to, privates?
>
> —lecture on hand and arm signals, Parris Island, 1982

And they shouted enthusiastically: "The enemy, sir! The enemy, sir!" It would not be instantly clear to the disinterested observer from Mars, however, why these spotty-faced male eighteen-year-olds are uniquely qualified to kill the enemy, while their equally spotty-faced female counterparts get to admire them from afar (or so the supposition goes), and get called Suzie Rottencrotch for their trouble.

Interestingly, it isn't entirely clear either to the senior military and civilian officials whose responsibility it is to keep the organization filled up with warm bodies capable of doing the job. Women are not employed in combat roles in the regular armed forces of any country (though increasing numbers of women have been admitted to the noncombat military jobs in the course of this century). But in the last decade the final barrier has come under serious consideration. It was, unsurprisingly, in the United States, where the problems of getting enough recruits for the all-volunteer armed forces converged with the changes of attitude flowing from the women's liberation movement, that the first serious proposals to send women into combat were entertained, during the latter years of the Carter administration.

> There is no question but that women could do a lot of things in the military. So could men in wheelchairs. But you couldn't expect the services to want a whole company of people in wheelchairs.
>
> —Gen. Lewis B. Hershey,
> former director, Selective Service System, 1978

> If for no other reason than because women are the bearers of children, they should not be in combat. Imagine your daughter as a ground soldier sleeping in the fields and expected to do all the things that soldiers do. It represents to me an absolute horror.
>
> —Gen. Jacqueline Cochran, U.S. Air Force

Despite the anguished cries of military conservatives, both male and female, the reaction of younger officers in the combat branches (all male, of course) was cautious but not entirely negative. The more intelligent ones dismissed at once arguments about strength and stamina—the average American woman, one pointed out, is bigger than the average Vietnamese man—and were as little impressed by the alleged special problems arising from the fact that female soldiers may become pregnant. In the noncombat branches, the army loses less time from its women soldiers due to pregnancy than it loses from desertion, drug abuse, and alcoholism in its male soldiers.

More important, few of the male officers involved in the experimental programs giving combat training to women recruits in the late 1970s had any doubt that the women would function effectively in combat. Neither did the women themselves. Despite their lack of the traditional male notions about the warrior stereotype, the training did its job. As one female trainee remarked: "I don't like the idea of killing anything . . . [and] I may not at this moment go into combat. But knowing that I can fire as well as I can fire now, knowing that today, I'd go in. I believe in my country . . . I'd fight to keep it."

The one major reservation the male officers training the "infantrywomen" had was about how the presence of women in combat would affect the men. The basic combat unit, a small group of men bound together by strong male ties of loyalty and trust, was a time-tested system that worked, and they were reluctant to tamper with it by adding an additional, unknown factor to the equation.

In the end a more conservative administration canceled the idea of introducing women to American combat units, and it may be some years yet before there are female soldiers in the infantry of any regular army. But it is manifestly sheer social conservatism that is retarding this development. Hundreds of thousands, if not millions, of women have fought in combat as irregular infantry in the past half-century, from the Yugoslav and Soviet partisans of World War II to Nicaragua in 1978–79. They performed quite satisfactorily, and so did the mixed units of which they were members. There are numerous differences of detail between guerrilla and regular army units, but none of them is of the sort to suggest that women would not fight just as well in a regular infantry battalion, or that the battalion would function less well if women were present.

The point of all this is not that women should be allowed (or indeed compelled) to take their fair share of the risks in combat. It is rather that war has moved a very long way from its undeniably warrior male origins, and that human behavior, male or female, is extremely malleable. Combat of the sort we know today, even at the infantryman's level — let alone the fighter pilot's — simply could not occur unless military organizations put immense effort into reshaping the behavior of individuals to fit their unusual and exacting requirements. The military institution, for all its imposing presence, is a highly artificial structure that is maintained only by constant endeavor. And if ordinary people's behavior is malleable in the direction the armed forces require, it is equally open to change in other directions. . . .

Questions

1. Why did Dyer title his article "*Anybody's* Son Will Do"?

2. "To be a man means to be a Marine" — or so recruits are taught. In what ways does the success of basic training seem to rely on the additional idea that if one cannot perform as a Marine, one is no better than a woman? How might the presence of female Marines in boot camp complicate the job of socializing males into their soldier role?

3. Erving Goffman (1961) defined "total institution" as "a place of residence and work where a large number of like-situated individuals, cut off from the wider society for an appreciable period of time, together lead an enclosed, formally administered round of life." Imagine that you've been put in charge of creating a total institution that has the goal of radically changing people's behavior. Military boot camp is one of the most successful types of total institutions. Based on what you've learned from Dyer's description of the way this total institution resocializes men, what sorts of procedures would you institute in your total institution to help ensure its success? For example, what sorts of things would you do to your "recruits" when they first arrive at your total institution?

·25·

Suspended Identity
Identity Transformation in a Maximum Security Prison

Thomas J. Schmid and Richard S. Jones

Schmid and Jones look closely at the resocialization process that new prison inmates undergo—but from the point of view of the prisoner and his concerns about his identity. As you read this 1991 article, consider how experiences in this sort of total institution differ from those undergone by men in boot camp.

A prison sentence constitutes a "massive assault" on the identity of those imprisoned (Berger 1963, 100–101). This assault is especially severe on first-time inmates, and we might expect radical identity changes to ensue from their imprisonment. At the same time, a prisoner's awareness of the challenge to his identity affords some measure of protection against it. As part of an ethnographic analysis of the prison experiences of first-time, short-term inmates, this article presents an identity transformation model that differs both from the gradual transformation processes that characterize most adult identity changes and from such radical transformation processes as brainwashing or conversion.

Data for the study are derived principally from ten months of participant observation at a maximum security prison for men in the upper

midwest of the United States. One of the authors was an inmate serving a felony sentence for one year and one day, while the other participated in the study as an outside observer. Relying on traditional ethnographic data collection and analysis techniques, this approach offered us general observations of hundreds of prisoners, and extensive fieldnotes that were based on repeated, often daily, contacts with about fifty inmates, as well as on personal relationships established with a smaller number of inmates. We subsequently returned to the prison to conduct focused interviews with other prisoners; using information provided by prison officials, we were able to identify and interview twenty additional first-time inmates who were serving sentences of two years or less. See Schmid and Jones (1987) for further description of this study.

Three interrelated research questions guided our analysis: How do first-time, short-term inmates define the prison world, and how do their definitions change during their prison careers? How do these inmates adapt to the prison world, and how do their adaptation strategies change during their prison careers?

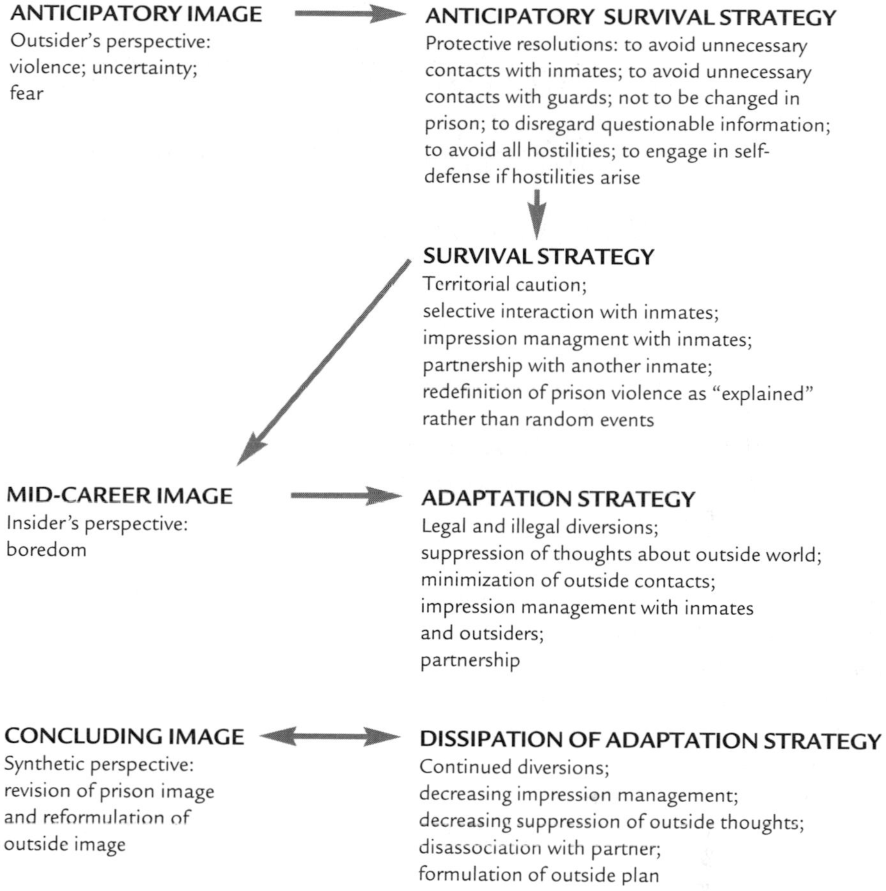

ANTICIPATORY IMAGE → ANTICIPATORY SURVIVAL STRATEGY

ANTICIPATORY IMAGE
Outsider's perspective:
violence; uncertainty;
fear

ANTICIPATORY SURVIVAL STRATEGY
Protective resolutions: to avoid unnecessary
contacts with inmates; to avoid unnecessary
contacts with guards; not to be changed in
prison; to disregard questionable information;
to avoid all hostilities; to engage in self-
defense if hostilities arise

SURVIVAL STRATEGY
Territorial caution;
selective interaction with inmates;
impression managment with inmates;
partnership with another inmate;
redefinition of prison violence as "explained"
rather than random events

MID-CAREER IMAGE
Insider's perspective:
boredom

ADAPTATION STRATEGY
Legal and illegal diversions;
suppression of thoughts about outside world;
minimization of outside contacts;
impression management with inmates
and outsiders;
partnership

CONCLUDING IMAGE
Synthetic perspective:
revision of prison image
and reformulation of
outside image

DISSIPATION OF ADAPTATION STRATEGY
Continued diversions;
decreasing impression management;
decreasing suppression of outside thoughts;
disassociation with partner;
formulation of outside plan

Figure 1 Prison Images and Strategies of New Inmates

How do their self-definitions change during their prison careers? Our analyses of the first two questions are presented in detail elsewhere (Schmid and Jones 1987, 1990); an abbreviated outline of these analyses, to which we will allude throughout this article, is presented in Figure 1. The identity transformation model presented here, based on our analysis of the third question, is outlined in Figure 2.

Preprison Identity

Our data suggest that the inmates we studied have little in common before their arrival at prison, except their conventionality. Although convicted of felonies, most do not possess "criminal" identities (cf. Irwin 1970, 29–34). They begin their sentences with only a vague, incomplete image (Boulding 1961) of what prison is like, but an image that nonetheless stands in contrast to how they view their own social worlds. Their prison image is dominated by the theme of violence: they see prison inmates as violent, hostile, alien human beings, with whom they have nothing in common. They have several specific fears about what will happen to them in prison, including fears of assault, rape, and death. They are also concerned about their identities, fearing that—if they survive prison at all—they are in danger

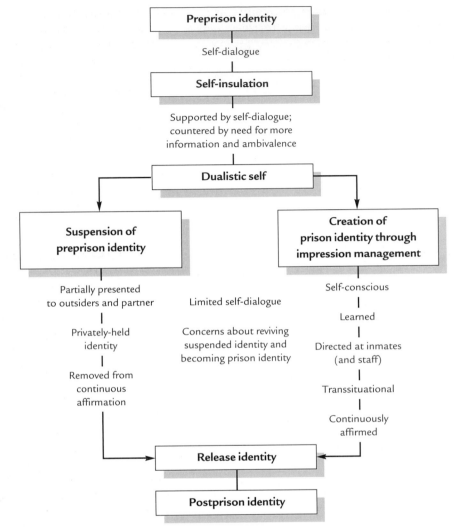

Figure 2 *Suspended Identity Dialectic*

of changing in prison, either through the intentional efforts of rehabilitation personnel or through the unavoidable hardening effects of the prison environment. Acting on this imagery (Blumer 1969) — or, more precisely, on the inconsonance of their self-images with this prison image — they develop an anticipatory survival strategy (see Figure 1) that consists primarily of protective resolutions: a resolve to avoid all hostilities; a resolve to avoid all nonessential contacts with inmates and guards; a resolve to defend themselves in any way possible; and a resolve not to change, or to be changed, in prison.

A felon's image and strategy are formulated through a running self-dialogue, a heightened state of reflexive awareness (Lewis 1979) through which he ruminates about his past behavior and motives, and imaginatively projects himself into the prison world. This self-dialogue begins shortly after his arrest, continues intermittently during his trial or court hearings, and becomes especially intense at the time of his transfer to prison.

> You start taking a review—it's almost like your life is passing before your eyes. You wonder how in the heck you got to this point and, you know, what are—what's your family gonna think about it—your friends, all the talk, and how are you going to deal with that—and the kids, you know, how are they gonna react to it? . . . All those things run through your head. . . . The total loss of control—the first time in my life that some other people were controlling my life.
>
> • • •
>
> My first night in the joint was spent mainly on kicking myself in the butt for putting myself in the joint. It was a very emotional evening. I thought a lot about all my friends and family, the good-byes, the things we did the last couple of months, how good they had been to me, sticking by me. I also thought about my fears: Am I going to go crazy? Will I end up fighting for my life? How am I going to survive in here for a year? Will I change? Will things be the same when I get out?

His self-dialogue is also typically the most extensive self-assessment he has ever conducted; thus, at the same time that he is resolving not to change, he is also initiating the kind of introspective analysis that is essential to any identity transformation process.

Self-Insulation

A felon's self-dialogue continues during the initial weeks and months of his sentence, and it remains a solitary activity, each inmate struggling to come to grips with the inconsonance of his established (preprison) identity and his present predicament. Despite the differences in their preprison identities, however, inmates now share a common situation that affects their identities. With few exceptions, their self-dialogues involve feelings of vulnerability,

discontinuity, and differentiation from other inmates, emotions that reflect both the degradations and deprivations of institutional life (cf. Garfinkel 1956; Goffman 1961; and Sykes 1958) and their continuing outsiders' perspective on the prison world. These feelings are obviously the result of everything that has happened to the inmates, but they are something else as well: they are the conditions in which every first-time, short-term inmate finds himself. They might even be called the common attributes of the inmates' selves-in-prison, for the irrelevance of their preprison identities within the prison world reduces their self-definitions, temporarily, to the level of pure emotion. These feelings, and a consequent emphasis on the "physical self" (Zurcher 1977, 176), also constitute the essential motivation for the inmates' self-insulation strategies.[1]

An inmate cannot remain wholly insulated within the prison world, for a number of reasons. He simply spends too much of his time in the presence of others to avoid all interaction with them. He also recognizes that his prison image is based on incomplete and inadequate information, and that he must interact with others in order to acquire first-hand information about the prison world. His behavior in prison, moreover, is guided not only by his prison image but by a fundamental ambivalence he feels about his situation, resulting from his marginality between the prison and outside social worlds (Schmid and Jones 1987). His ambivalence has several manifestations

---

[1]There are four principal components to the survival strategies of the inmates we studied, in the early months of their prison sentences. "Selective interaction" and "territorial caution" are essentially precautionary guidelines that allow inmates to increase their understanding of the prison world while minimizing danger to themselves. "Partnership" is a special friendship bond between two inmates, typically based on common backgrounds and interests (including a shared uncertainty about prison life) and strengthened by the inmates' mutual exploration of a hostile prison world. The fourth component of their strategies, impression management, is discussed in subsequent sections of this article.

throughout his prison career, but the most important is his conflicting desires for self-insulation and for human communication.

Managing a Dualistic Self

An inmate is able to express both directions of his ambivalence (and to address his need for more information about the prison) by drawing a distinction between his "true" identity (i.e., his outside, preprison identity) and a "false" identity he creates for the prison world. For most of a new inmate's prison career, his preprison identity remains a "subjective" or "personal" identity while his prison identity serves as his "objective" or "social" basis for interaction in prison (see Goffman 1963; Weigert 1986). This bifurcation of his self (Figure 2) is not a conscious decision made at a single point in time, but it does represent two conscious and interdependent identity-preservation tactics, formulated through self-dialogue and refined through tentative interaction with others.

First, after coming to believe that he cannot "be himself" in prison because he would be too vulnerable, he decides to "suspend" his preprison identity for the duration of his sentence. He retains his resolve not to let prison change him, protecting himself by choosing not to reveal himself (his "true" self) to others. Expressions of a suspension of identity emerged repeatedly and consistently in both the fieldwork and interview phases of our research through such statements as

> I was reserved. . . . I wouldn't be very communicative, you know. I'd try to keep conversation to a minimum. . . . I wasn't interested in getting close to anybody . . . or asking a lot of questions. You know, try to cut the conversation short . . . go my own way back to my cell or go to the library or do something.
>
> • • •
>
> I didn't want nobody to know too much about me. That was part of the act.

An inmate's decision to suspend his preprison identity emanates directly from his feelings of vulnerability, discontinuity and differentiation from other inmates. These emotions foster something like a "proto-sociological attitude" (Weigert, 1986, 173; see also Zurcher 1977), in which new inmates find it necessary to step outside their taken-for-granted preprison identities. Rather than viewing these identities and the everyday life experience in which they are grounded as social constructions, however, inmates see the *prison* world as an artificial construction, and judge their "naturally occurring" preprison identities to be out of place within this construction. By attempting to suspend his preprison identity for the time that he spends in prison, an inmate believes that he will again "be his old self" after his release.

While he is in confinement, an inmate's decision to suspend his identity leaves him with little or no basis for interaction. His second identity tactic, then, is the creation of an identity that allows him to interact, however cautiously, with others. This tactic consists of his increasingly sophisticated impression management skills (Goffman 1959;[2] Schlenker 1980), which are initially designed simply to hide his vulnerability, but which gradually evolve into an alternative identity felt to be more suitable to the prison world. The character of the presented identity is remarkably similar from inmate to inmate:

> Well, I learned that you can't act like—you can't get the attitude where you are better than they are. Even where you might be better than them, you can't strut around like you are. Basically, you can't stick out. You don't stare at people and things like that. I knew a lot of these things from talking to people and I figured them out by myself. I sat down and

---

[2] Recall from reading 14 Goffman's concepts of expressions given and expressions given off—these are important components of impression management.—Ed.

figured out just what kind of attitude I'm going to have to take.

• • •

Most people out here learn to be tough, whether they can back it up or not. If you don't learn to be tough, you will definitely pay for it. This toughness can be demonstrated through a mean look, tough language, or an extremely big build. . . . One important thing is never to let your guard down.

An inmate's prison identity, as an inauthentic presentation of self, is not in itself a form of identity transformation but is rather a form of identity construction. His prison identity is simply who he must pretend to be while he is in prison. It is a false identity created for survival in an artificial world. But this identity nonetheless emerges in the same manner as any other identity: it is learned from others, and it must be presented to, negotiated with, and validated by others. A new inmate arrives at prison with a general image of what prisoners are like, and he begins to flesh out this image from the day of his arrival, warily observing others just as they are observing him. Through watching others, through eavesdropping, through cautious conversation and selective interaction, a new inmate refines his understanding of what maximum security prisoners look like, how they talk, how they move, how they act. Despite his belief that he is different from these other prisoners, he knows that he cannot appear to be too different from them, if he is to hide his vulnerability. His initial image of other prisoners, his early observations, and his concern over how he appears to others thus provide a foundation for the identity he gradually creates through impression management.

Impression management skills, of course, are not exclusive to the prison world; a new inmate, like anyone else, has had experience in presenting a "front" to others, and he draws upon his experience in the creation of his prison identity. He has undoubtedly even had experience in projecting the very attributes—strength,

stoicism, aplomb—required by his prison identity. Impression management in prison differs, however, in the totality with which it governs interactions and in the perceived costs of failure: humiliation, assault, or death. For these reasons the entire impression management process becomes a more highly conscious endeavor. When presenting himself before others, a new inmate pays close attention to such minute details of his front as eye contact, posture, and manner of walking:

I finally got out of orientation. I was going out with the main population, going down to get my meals and things. The main thing is not to stare at a bunch of people, you know. I tried to just look ahead, you know, not stare at people. 'Cause I didn't really know; I just had to learn a little at a time.

• • •

The way you look seems to be very important. The feeling is you shouldn't smile, that a frown is much more appropriate. The eyes are very important. You should never look away; it is considered a sign of weakness. Either stare straight ahead, look around, or look the person dead in the eyes. The way you walk is important. You shouldn't walk too fast; they might think you were scared and in a hurry to get away.

To create an appropriate embodiment (Stone 1962; Weigert 1986) of their prison identities, some new inmates devote long hours to weightlifting or other body-building exercises, and virtually all of them relinquish their civilian clothes—which might express their preprison identities—in favor of the standard issue clothing that most inmates wear. Whenever a new inmate is open to the view of other inmates, in fact, he is likely to relinquish most overt symbols of his individuality, in favor of a standard issue "prison inmate" appearance.

By acting self-consciously, of course, a new inmate runs the risk of exposing the fact that he *is* acting. But he sees no alternative to playing his part better; he cannot "not act" because that too would expose the vulnerability of his "true" identity. He thus sees every new prison experience, every new territory that he is allowed to explore, as a test of his impression management skills. Every nonconfrontive encounter with another inmate symbolizes his success at these skills, but it is also a social validation of his prison identity. Eventually he comes to see that many, perhaps most, inmates are engaging in the same kind of inauthentic presentations of self (cf. Glaser and Strauss 1964). Their identities are as "false" as his, and their validations of his identity may be equally false. But he realizes that he is powerless to change this state of affairs, and that he must continue to present his prison identity for as long as he remains in prison.

A first-time inmate enters prison as an outsider, and it is from an outsider's perspective that he initially creates his prison identity. In contrast to this suspended preprison identity, his prison identity is a *shared* identity, because it is modeled on his observations of other inmates. Like those of more experienced prisoners, his prison identity is tied directly to the social role of "prison inmate" (cf. Scheff 1970; Solomon 1970); because he is an outsider, however, his prison identity is also severely limited by his narrow understanding of that role. It is based on an outsider's stereotype of who a maximum security inmate is and what he acts like. It is, nonetheless, a *structural* identity (Weigert 1968), created to address his outsider's institutional problems of social isolation and inadequate information about the prison world.

By the middle of his sentence, a new inmate comes to adopt what is essentially an insider's perspective on the prison world. His prison image has evolved to the point where it is dominated by the theme of boredom rather than violence. (The possibility of violence is still acknowledged and feared, but those violent incidents that do occur have been redefined as the consequences of prison norm violations rather than as random predatory acts; see Schmid and Jones 1990.) His survival strategy, although still extant, has been supplemented by such general adaptation techniques as legal and illegal diversionary activities and conscious efforts to suppress his thoughts about the outside world (Figure 1). His impression management tactics have become second nature rather than self-conscious, as he routinely interacts with others in terms of his prison identity.

An inmate's suspension of his preprison identity, of course, is never absolute, and the separation between his suspended identity and his prison identity is never complete. He continues to interact with his visitors at least partially in terms of his preprison identity, and he is likely to have acquired at least one inmate "partner" with whom he interacts in terms of his preprison as well as his prison identity. During times of introspection, however—which take place less frequently but do not disappear—he generally continues to think of himself as being the same person he was before he came to prison. But it is also during these periods of self-dialogue that he begins to have doubts about his ability to revive his suspended identity.

> That's what I worry about a lot. Because I didn't want to change. . . . I'm still fighting it, 'cause from what I understood, before, I wasn't that bad—I wasn't even violent. But I have people say stuff to me now, before I used to say "O.k., o.k."—but now it seems like I got to eye them back, you know.
>
> • • •
>
> I don't know, but I may be losing touch with the outside. I am feeling real strange during visits, very uncomfortable. I just can't seem to be myself, although I am not really sure what myself is all about. My mind really seems to be glued to the inside of these walls. I can't even really comprehend the outside. I haven't even been here three months, and I feel like I'm starting to lose it. Maybe I'm just paranoid. But during these visits I really feel like I'm acting.

I'm groping for the right words, always trying to keep the conversation going. Maybe I'm just trying to present a picture that will relieve the minds of my visitors, I just don't know.

• • •

I realized that strength is going to be an important factor whether I'm going to turn into a cold person or whether I'm going to keep my humanitarian point of view. I know it is going to be an internal war. It's going to take a lot of energy to do that. . . . I just keep telling myself that you gotta do it and sometimes you get to the point where you don't care anymore. You just kinda lose it and you get so full of hate, so full of frustration, it gets wound up in your head a lot.

At this point, both the inmate's suspended preprison identity and his created prison identity are part of his "performance consciousness" (Schechner 1985), although they are not given equal value. His preprison identity is grounded primarily in the memory of his biography (Weigert 1986) rather than in self-performance. His concern, during the middle of his sentence, is that he has become so accustomed to dealing with others in terms of his prison identity—that he has been presenting and receiving affirmation of this identity for so long—that it is becoming his "true" identity.[3]

An inmate's fear that he is becoming the character he has been presenting is not unfounded. All of his interactions within the prison world indicate the strong likelihood of a

[3]Clemmer (1958, 299) has defined "prisonization" as the "taking on in greater or less degree of the folkways, mores, customs, and general culture of the penitentiary." Yet new inmates begin to "take on" these things almost immediately, as part of the impression they are attempting to present to other inmates. Thus, we would argue instead that prisonization (meaning assimilation to the prison world) begins to occur for these inmates when their prison identities become second nature—when their expressions of prison norms and customs are no longer based on self-conscious acting. A new inmate's identity concerns, during the middle of his sentence, are essentially a recognition of this assimilation.

"role-person merger" (Turner 1978). An inmate views his presentation of his prison identity as a necessary expression of his inmate status. Unlike situational identities presented through impression management in the outside world, performance of the inmate role is transsitutional and continuous. For a new inmate, prison consists almost exclusively of front regions, in which he must remain in character. As long as he is in the maximum security institution, he remains in at least partial view of the audience for which his prison identity is intended: other prison inmates. Moreover, because the stakes of his performance are so high, there is little room for self-mockery or other forms of role distance (Coser 1966; Ungar 1984) from his prison identity, and there is little possibility that an inmate's performance will be "punctured" (Adler and Adler 1989) by his partner or other prison acquaintances. And because his presentation of his prison identity is continuous, he also receives continuous affirmation of his identity from others—affirmation that becomes more significant in light of the fact that he also remains removed from day-to-day reaffirmation of his preprison identity by his associates in the outside world. The inauthenticity of the process is beside the point: Stone's (1962, 93) observation that "one's identity is established when others *place* him as a social object by assigning him the same words of identity that he appropriates for himself or *announces*" remains sound even when both the announcements and the placements are recognized as false.

Standing against these various forms of support for an inmate's prison identity are the inmate's resolve not to be changed in prison, the fact that his sentence is relatively brief (though many new inmates lose sight of this brevity during the middle of their careers) and the limited reaffirmation of his preprison identity that he receives from outsiders and from his partner. These are not insubstantial resources, but nor do they guarantee an inmate's future ability to discard his prison identity and revive the one he has suspended.

Identity Dialectic

When an inmate's concerns about his identity first emerge, there is little that he can do about them. He recognizes that he has no choice but to present his prison identity so, following the insider's perspective he has now adopted, he consciously attempts to suppress his concerns. Eventually, however, he must begin to consider seriously his capacity to revive his suspended identity: his identity concerns, and his belief that he must deal with them, become particularly acute if he is transferred to the minimum security unit of the prison for the final months of his sentence.[4] At the conclusion of his prison career, an inmate shifts back toward an outsider's perspective on the prison world (see Figure 1); this shift involves the dissipation of his maximum security adaptation strategy, further revision of his prison image, reconstruction of an image of the outside world, and the initial development of an outside plan.[5] The inmate's efforts to revive his suspended identity are part of his shift in perspectives.

It is primarily through a renewed self-dialogue that the inmate struggles to revive his suspended identity—a struggle that amounts to a dialectic between his suspended identity and his prison identity. Through self-dialogue he recognizes, and tries to confront, the extent to which these two identities really do differ. He again tries to differentiate himself from maximum security inmates.

> There seems to be a concern with the inmates here to be able to distinguish . . . themselves from the other inmates. That is—they feel they are above the others. . . . Although they may associate with each other, it still seems important to degrade the majority here.

And he does have some success in freeing himself from his prison identity.

> Well, I think I am starting to soften up a little bit. I believe the identity I picked up in the prison is starting to leave me now that I have left the world of the [maximum security] joint. I find myself becoming more and more involved with the happenings of the outside world. I am even getting anxious to go out and see the sights, just to get away from this place.

But he recognizes that he *has* changed in prison, and that these changes run deeper than the mask he has been presenting to others. He has not returned to his "old self" simply because his impression management skills are used less frequently in minimum security. He raises the question—though he cannot answer it—of how permanent these changes are. He wonders how much his family and friends will see him as having changed. As stated by one of our interview respondents:

> I know I've changed a little bit. I just want to realize how the people I know are going to see it, because they [will] be able to see it more than I can see it. . . . Sometimes I just want to go somewhere and hide.

He speculates about how much the outside world—especially his own network of outside relationships—has changed in his absence. (It is his life, not those of his family and friends, that has been suspended during his prison sentence; he knows that changes have occurred

---

[4]Not all prisoners participate in this unit; inmates must apply for transfer to the unit, and their acceptance depends both on the crimes for which they were sentenced and staff evaluation of their potential for success in the unit. Our analysis focuses on those inmates who are transferred.

[5]There are three features of the minimum security unit that facilitate this shift in perspectives: a more open physical and social environment; the fact that the unit lies just outside the prison wall (so that an inmate who is transferred is also physically removed from the maximum security prison); and greater opportunity for direct contact with the outside world, through greater access to telephones, an unrestricted visitor list, unrestricted visiting hours and, eventually, weekend furloughs.

in the outside world, and he suspects that some of these changes may have been withheld from him, intentionally or otherwise.) He has questions, if not serious doubts, about his ability to "make it" on the outside, especially concerning his relationships with others; he knows, in any case, that he cannot simply return to the outside world as if nothing has happened. Above all, he repeatedly confronts the question of who he is, and who he will be in the outside world.

An inmate's struggle with these questions, like his self-dialogue at the beginning of his prison career, is necessarily a solitary activity. The identity he claims at the time of his release, in contrast to his prison identity, cannot be learned from other inmates. Also like his earlier periods of self-dialogue, the questions he considers are not approached in a rational systematic manner. The process is more one of rumination—of pondering one question until another replaces it, and then contemplating the new question until it is replaced by still another, or suppressed from his thoughts. There is, then, no final resolution to any of the inmate's identity questions. Each inmate confronts these questions in his own way, and each arrives at his own understanding of who he is, based on this unfinished, unresolved self-dialogue. In every case, however, an inmate's release identity is a synthesis of his suspended preprison identity and his prison identity.[6]

Postprison Identity

Because each inmate's release identity is the outcome of his own identity dialectic, we cannot provide a profile of the "typical" release identity. But our data do allow us to specify

some of the conditions that affect this outcome. Reaffirmations of his preprison identity by outsiders—visits and furloughs during which others interact with him as if he has not changed—provide powerful support for his efforts to revive his suspended identity. These efforts are also promoted by an inmate's recollection of his preprison identity (i.e., his attempts, through self-dialogue, to assess who he was before he came to prison), by his desire to abandon his prison identity, and by his general shift back toward an outsider's perspective. But there are also several factors that favor his prison identity, including his continued use of diversionary activities; his continued periodic efforts to suppress thoughts about the outside world; his continued ability to use prison impression management skills; and his continuing sense of injustice about the treatment he has received. Strained or cautious interactions with outsiders, or unfulfilled furlough expectations, inhibit the revival of his preprison identity. And he faces direct, experiential evidence that he has changed: when a minimum security resident recognizes that he is now completely unaffected by reports of violent incidents in maximum security, he acknowledges that he is no longer the same person that he was when he entered prison. Turner (1978, 1) has suggested three criteria for role-person merger: "failure of role compartmentalization, resistance to abandoning a role in the face of advantageous alternative roles, and the acquisition of role-appropriate attitudes"; at the time of their release from prison, the inmates we studied had already accrued some experience with each of these criteria.

Just as we cannot define a typical release identity, we cannot predict these inmates' future, postprison identities, not only because we have restricted our analysis to their prison experiences but because each inmate's future identity is inherently unpredictable. What effect an ex-inmate's prison experience has on his identity depends on how he, in interaction

---

[6]This is an important parallel with our analysis of the inmate's changing prison definitions: his concluding prison image is a synthesis of the image he formulates before coming to prison and the image he holds at the middle of his prison career; see Schmid and Jones, 1990.

with others, defines this experience. Some of
the men we have studied will be returned to
prison in the future; others will not. But all will
have been changed by their prison experiences. They entered the prison world fearing
for their lives; they depart with the knowledge
that they have survived. On the one hand,
these men are undoubtedly stronger persons
by virtue of this accomplishment. On the other
hand, the same tactics that enabled them to
survive the prison world can be called upon,
appropriately or not, in difficult situations in
the outside world. To the extent that these men
draw upon their prison survival tactics to cope
with the hardships of the outside world—to
the extent that their prison behavior becomes a
meaningful part of their "role repertoire"
(Turner 1978) in their everyday lives—their
prison identities will have become inseparable
from their "true" identities. . . .

References

Adler, Patricia A., and Peter Adler. 1989. "The Glo-
ried Self: The Aggrandizement and the Construction of Self." *Social Psychology Quarterly* 52:
299–310.

Berger, Peter L. 1963. *Invitation to Sociology: A Hu-
manistic Perspective.* Garden City, NY: Doubleday
Anchor Books.

Blumer, Herbert. 1972. "Action vs. Interaction: Review of *Relations in Public* by Erving Goffman."
Transaction 9: 50–53.

Boulding, Kenneth. 1961. *The Image.* Ann Arbor:
University of Michigan Press.

Clemmer, Donald. 1958. *The Prison Community.*
New York: Holt, Rinehart & Winston.

Coser, R. 1966. "Role Distance, Sociological Ambivalence and Traditional Status Systems."
American Journal of Sociology 72: 173–187.

Goffman, Erving. 1961. *Asylums.* Garden City, NY:
Doubleday Anchor Books.

———. 1959. *The Presentation of Self in Everyday Life.*
Garden City, NY: Doubleday Anchor Books.

———. 1963. *Stigma: Notes on the Management of Spoiled
Identity.* Englewood Cliffs, NJ: Prentice-Hall.

Irwin, John. 1970. *The Felon.* Englewood Cliffs, NJ:
Prentice-Hall.

Lewis, David J. 1979. "A Social Behaviorist Interpretation of the Median I." *American Journal of
Sociology* 84: 261–287.

Schechner, Richard. 1985. *Between Theater and Anthropology.* Philadelphia: University of Pennsylvania
Press.

Scheff, Thomas. 1970. "On the Concepts of Identity
and Social Relationships." Pp. 193–207 in
T. Shibutani (ed.), *Human Nature and Collective
Behavior.* Englewood Cliffs, NJ: Prentice-Hall.

Schlenker, B. 1980. *Impression Management: The Self
Concept, Social Identity and Interpersonal Relations.*
Belmont, CA: Wadsworth.

Schmid, Thomas, and Richard Jones. 1987. "Ambivalent Actions: Prison Adaptation Strategies
of New Inmates." American Society of Criminology, annual meetings, Montreal, Quebec.

Schmid, Thomas, and Richard Jones. 1990. "Experi-
ential Orientations to the Prison Experience:
The Case of First-Time, Short-Term Inmates."
Pp. 189–210 in Gale Miller and James A. Holstein
(eds.), *Perspectives on Social Problems.* Greenwich,
CT: JAI Press.

Solomon, David N. 1970. "Role and Self-
Conception: Adaptation and Change in Occupa-
tions." Pp. 286–300 in T. Shibutani (ed.), *Human
Nature and Collective Behavior.* Englewood Cliffs,
NJ: Prentice-Hall.

Stone, Gregory P. 1962. "Appearance and the
Self." Pp. 86–118 in Arnold Rose (ed.), *Human
Behavior and Social Processes.* Boston: Houghton
Mifflin.

Sykes, Gresham. 1958. *The Society of Captives: A
Study of a Maximum Security Prison.* Princeton,
NJ: Princeton University Press.

Turner, Ralph H. 1978. "The Role and the Person."
American Journal of Sociology 84: 1–23.

Ungar, Sheldon. 1984. "Self-Mockery: An Alternative Form of Self-Presentation." *Symbolic Interaction* 7: 121–133.

Weigert, Andrew J. 1986. "The Social Production of
Identity: Metatheoretical Foundations." *Sociological Quarterly* 27: 165–183.

Zurcher, Louis A. 1977. *The Mutable Self.* Beverly
Hills, CA: Sage.

Questions

1. Define the following terms, as used by Schmid and Jones in the article.
   a. rumination
   b. inauthentic presentation of self
   c. performance consciousness
   d. identity dialectic
   e. proto-sociological attitude

2. How do Schmid and Jones distinguish between "identity transformation" and "identity construction"?

3. In what ways, if any, do you think prison might have a different effect on women's identity than on men's identity? Explain.

4. Identify the parallels between identity transformation in prison and the implicit identity transformation undergone by kids as they are introduced to street culture (as described by Anderson in reading 12).

·26·

Not Just Bodies: Strategies for Desexualizing the Physical Examination of Patients

Patti A. Giuffre and Christine L. Williams

The role of a health care practitioner requires one to maintain what sociologist Talcott Parsons called "affective neutrality": one must keep a tight grip on one's affect (emotions). At no time is the need for affective neutrality more important than during the physical exam. Patients are comforted by their belief that the sight of a naked body is routine to physicians and nurses; they trust that not only will their health care practitioner not comment on the size or shape of their body parts, but that he or she does not even notice them except in medically relevant ways. As Giuffre and Williams point out, however, affective neutrality does not come easily to practitioners.

Physicians and nurses routinely examine naked bodies and discuss intimate, sexual issues with their patients. Yet, these health care professionals are expected to avoid or deny personal sexual feelings and ignore the expression of any sexual desire from their patients. How do they do it? That is, how do they desexualize the physical exam?

Health care professionals are guided in this task in several ways. First, formal organizational policies and professional ethics govern doctors' and nurses' interactions with patients. Health care providers are usually prohibited from engaging in sexual relationships with patients, particularly when patients are under their direct care. Second, the medical school curriculum socializes students to desexualize the human body. Medical students are trained to hide their feelings and avoid emotional involvement with their patients. Students are taught to use scientific, biomedical language for the human body, rather than colloquial terms, which may encourage students to approach the human body in a less personal, more abstract way. Medical students often devise their own strategies for managing inappropriate feelings, for example, engaging in sick humor with other students and mentally transforming their patients into inanimate objects.

Interaction rituals also may help to desexualize the physical examination of patients.

"Not Just Bodies: Strategies for Desexualizing the Physical Examination of Patients" by Patti A. Giuffre and Christine L. Williams from *Gender & Society*, Vol. 14 (3), June 2000: pp. 457–482. Copyright © 2000 Sociologists for Women in Society. Reprinted by permission of Sage Publications, Inc.

AUTHORS' NOTE: *We would like to thank Kirsten Dellinger, Dana Britton, Martin Button, Ellen Slaten, Edith Elwood, Beth Schneider, and the reviewers for comments on this article. We would also like to thank Teresa Sullivan, Ronald Angel, Charles Bonjean, Sue Hoppe, and Janice Beyer, who supervised the original research.*

For example, some physicians engage in casual conversation with the fully clothed patient prior to the actual exam, leave the room and allow the nurse to enter and instruct the patient about the exam, insist on the presence of a nurse to chaperone the exam, or use draping sheets to expose only specific parts of the body. By adhering closely to scripted performances such as these, physicians may be better able to control the interaction and repress the arousal of sexual feelings and interpretations.

Because social definitions of appropriate—and inappropriate—sexual behavior are linked to gender, it is likely that men and women use different desexualization strategies, but researchers have yet to examine this possibility. In this article, we address the following questions: Do male and female health care professionals rely on different strategies for desexualizing the physical exam? Are male and female patients subjected to different strategies? Are there differences in how doctors and nurses examine the bodies of male and female patients?

To address these questions, we conducted in-depth interviews with nurses and physicians who routinely conduct physical examinations of patients. Our overall goal is to investigate how the enactment of the physical examination is based on, and reproduces assumptions about, gender differences. We do not make claims about the average or typical behavior of men and women (an impossible goal in a qualitative study such as this). Rather, we describe and analyze the gendered meanings in the logic used by men and women health care providers who are trying to desexualize the physical examination of their patients. How does the gender of the doctor or nurse, and the gender of their patients, figure into their choices of which strategies to use? We are less interested in the effectiveness of these strategies and more interested in understanding what logic compels male and female health care providers to use different strategies. We also seek to understand why nurses and physicians might choose different

strategies for desexualizing the physical exam of male and female patients.

Method

Semistructured in-depth interviews were conducted with 36 nurses (licensed vocational nurses and registered nurses) and 34 doctors, most of whom were employed in one teaching hospital. To protect the anonymity of the respondents and to generate a more racially diverse sample, doctors and nurses from two surrounding cities who did not work in this teaching hospital were also interviewed. Four of the nurses were faculty members at the nursing school; the others were hospital staff nurses. The sample of doctors includes men and women from a variety of clinical specialties, including family practice, several surgical specialties, and internal medicine. Excluded were specialties that did not require physical examinations of patients while they are partially or fully unclothed, such as psychiatry and ophthalmology.

Only one respondent (a physician) said during the interview that he was gay. Several nurses and physicians noted that it was difficult for their gay and lesbian coworkers to be "out" in the hospital with patients and among colleagues.

The sample was generated by using "snowball" techniques. An original list of contacts was obtained from colleagues in the teaching hospital and through personal acquaintances. This group were sent letters describing the study and inviting their participation. At the close of each interview, respondents were asked for names of other doctors or nurses who might be willing to be interviewed, who were also sent letters. In total, 81 letters were sent. Fifty-four of the 81 people who received letters agreed to do the interview. (Two people refused to participate, and 27 never responded to the letter.) An additional 16 respondents were contacted by telephone or in person, and all agreed to participate, making the total response rate 72 percent.

Findings

With few exceptions, the men and women in this study reported that they were uncomfortable performing physical examinations in the early part of their training but that they became more comfortable as they progressed through their careers. Several physicians and nurses noted that they "see 20 patients a day and everybody looks the same" and that they "have been doing this for so long" that they never get uncomfortable. All of the respondents, however, had developed strategies to desexualize the physical exam so that their patients would not interpret the interaction as sexual and to repress any feelings of sexual attraction that they might have toward their patients.

Three of the strategies mentioned were general ones, used by both men and women health care providers, regardless of the patient's characteristics. To make patients feel more comfortable, some doctors and nurses engaged them in casual conversation or nonsexual joking ("Try on our designer gown"). Some physicians insisted on meeting their patients fully clothed prior to the exam to decrease patients' feelings of vulnerability. Finally, two physicians mentioned using medical terms instead of colloquial terms, which helped to define the interaction as a scientific, diagnostic encounter instead of a sexual and personal one.

However, six strategies were used more selectively. The respondent either indicated that there was a special condition for the use of these strategies or the strategy emerged from the analysis as one that was mentioned primarily by men or women. In the discussion that follows, we describe each of these "gendered strategies" and explore the organizational logic and individual interests that underlie them.

USING A CHAPERONE

Nineteen physicians (13 men and 6 women) and two nurses (both men) insisted on the presence of a chaperone during physical exams. Two of the women used chaperones for both male and female patients, but all of the others who mentioned this strategy used chaperones only for their female patients. And with only one exception, the chaperone was always a woman.

The men and women who mentioned this strategy used it for a variety of reasons. Some believed that having a chaperone present helped to comfort their female patients:

> I always use chaperones for gynecological examinations and breast examinations. Part of it is a medical-legal issue, and part of it is that it's a big comfort to the patient. There's been a situation where I've only had a male nurse, and I won't or I guess I can't use a male nurse for chaperones with female patients . . . I don't think women would be comfortable with two men in the room. A female needs to be physically present. (Latino family practitioner)

Why are only female patients offered the comfort of a female chaperone? When directly asked, most physicians could not explain why they did not use chaperones for male patients, noting that they "have just never thought about it." One of the four male physicians who did not use chaperones explained that his reason was because all of his patients were men, and "male patients are comfortable with a male physician." Another doctor explained why she did not use chaperones with men:

> I can't have a woman in the room with me when I'm examining a man. Plus I think it would be worse to have another guy in there for the guy . . . I just think it's embarrassing enough for him already. I think it would be even more embarrassing if there was another guy in there. . . . I have male help, so theoretically I could have someone else in there with

me but it would be embarrassing for them.
(white female physician in internal medicine)

This physician believes that her physical presence during the exam is "embarrassing enough" to male patients; adding a chaperone to the scene potentially would worsen his embarrassment.

Thus, female patients are protected by chaperones, but men must be protected from chaperones. Men's vulnerability during the physical exam is defined differently from women's. Perhaps, as Cassell (1998) argues, the comfort provided by a female surgeon's body elicits feelings of childish dependency. While such feelings may be considered acceptable in female patients, they may be considered emasculating in male patients. A woman physically examining a man may be "embarrassing enough" because this is an affront to a man's sense of mastery and self-control. The presence of a witness to this emasculation—either a man or a woman—could exacerbate his feelings of powerlessness.

A second interpretation of this asymmetry is that in our society women are more readily defined as victims than men are; thus, female patients are considered to be in greater need of a chaperone to comfort and protect them. In a male doctor/female patient situation, the female chaperone equalizes the female power of the weaker member of the encounter (the female patient). The presence of the second man as a chaperone would be more threatening and could lead to suggestions of multiple men abusing a woman. In contrast, a man is assumed to have sufficient resources to protect himself, and this appears to be true even when he is a patient in a doctor-patient encounter. The presence of a chaperone would tip the scales in favor of the physician's power and thus make the male patient a potential "victim." Using any chaperone might also imply that any given man is unable to protect himself, which could be interpreted as an affront to his masculinity. Thus, the

gender differences in the use of chaperones reflect assumptions about the relative power and powerlessness of men and women in social interactions.

Some health care providers claim that they use chaperones for *their* protection and not their patients. Respondents mentioned three ways that chaperones protected them. First, chaperones provide legal protection in cases where patients falsely accuse doctors of sexual misconduct. One male physician referred to chaperones as "cheap insurance" against such charges. This rationale for using chaperones was given by both male and female physicians, as well as by two male nurses. Because "sexual allegations usually come from women," as one female doctor put it, most believed they only needed this legal protection from female patients.

The women who used chaperones did not articulate any fears about false accusations from lesbian patients in particular, but this may have been a contributing factor in their practice. A nurse claimed that a complaint of sexual misconduct from a lesbian patient about a female physician prompted some women in the teaching hospital to start using chaperones for their female patients. On the other hand, female physicians may feel the need to protect themselves from accusations that they harbor lesbian desires toward their patients. Although none of these female doctors articulated this concern, it is commonly assumed that women in nontraditional occupations are lesbian, and granted the intimate nature of their work, some may feel especially vulnerable to such charges.

A second form of protection provided by chaperones is protection from sexual advances by patients. This rationale was mentioned by one female doctor, a urologist, which is a specialty composed of only 2 percent women (Randolph, Seidman, and Pasko 1996). She claimed that many men, especially her Hispanic patients, are often embarrassed to be treated by her because they are "really macho" and uneasy with women "in a position of authority." She discussed a variety of strategies she uses to make her male patients feel comfortable during invasive procedures such as the rectal exam, but she did not mention chaperones until she was asked (in a follow-up question), "Has a male patient ever tried to fondle you or anything?" In direct response, she said, "I have a chaperone in the room with me any time I examine a patient. Male or female. I have a male chaperone with men, and a female with women." The context of the interview suggests that her purpose for using a chaperone is physical protection from sexual harassment or assault.

Several other female health care providers we interviewed experienced sexual harassment by patients, but they did not use chaperones to protect themselves. This urologist was unique in using this strategy. Instead, as we will discuss later, female doctors and nurses typically relied on more informal strategies for dealing with the problem of sexual harassment and assault from patients.

The third form of protection that chaperones offer, according to the respondents, is protection from the doctor's own sexual feelings. Four men in this study gave this rationale for using a chaperone. A surgeon explained,

> One time I had a patient . . . [and] there were times I couldn't even examine her. I don't know if she and I were flirting with each other. It really unsettled me. She was gorgeous. I knew then that if I ever got in that situation again, I needed to use a chaperone. A chaperone not for her comfort but for mine. (white male orthopedic surgeon)

For this physician the presence of a chaperone helps him control his own sexual desires.

Some female health care professionals admitted that they sometimes experienced unwanted sexual feelings when examining an attractive man, but they never used chaperones to control themselves or diffuse this sexual tension. The women who were interviewed seemed more concerned about controlling their male patients' sexual desire. Several respondents perceive that men are expected to act on their sexual desires and women are not. One nurse suggested that this social expectation limits the roles of male nurses:

> Younger teenage girls, I would rather just female nurses take care of them. I think we kind of discourage male nurses from taking care of teenage girls. You don't want anybody to get the wrong idea. Teenage boys are very uncomfortable with me, so I try to distract them, talk to them, try to make them more comfortable. (Latina nurse)

Although this nurse admits that teenage boys may be uncomfortable with her, she does not believe that a man should be called in to replace her because this discomfort is unlikely to result in the "wrong idea," that is, that the nurse is not in control of her sexual feelings and might sexually assault the boys. However, this is the assumption made of male nurses, and it is compelling enough for her to dissuade men from administering care to teenage girls. Again, this asymmetry reflects certain hegemonic beliefs regarding gender and sexuality. Just as women are more likely to be cast in the role of "victim," so are men likely to be seen as sexual aggressors. These beliefs are internalized by some health care providers and institutionalized in the patterns of chaperone use.

Nurses typically do not have the organizational authority to call in a chaperone, but as the above example illustrates, on occasion a male or a female nurse may be specifically requested to administer certain invasive procedures. One nurse recalled that in her training, women were not allowed to catheterize male patients. Today this rule is no longer in place, but occasionally male patients will request a male nurse for this procedure. This practice seems intended to lessen the discomfort and embarrassment of the patient, more than to protect them from sexual assault by female nurses. She said, "If a male patient wants a male, that's fine. Some male patients are hesitant about anyone catheterizing them. They feel their pride. They feel embarrassed. They usually feel okay if men do it" (white female nurse). On the other hand, some male patients prefer female nurses to perform such intimate procedures because they are uncomfortable with men. One nurse claimed that "some men are homophobic. They think their male nurses are homosexual" and thus prefer female nurses. Again, the unstated assumption is that men will act on their sexual desires; women will not.

Using a chaperone is a complex gendered strategy for desexualizing the physical exam. According to the organization's logic, female patients are comforted by the presence of a female chaperone, but male patients are likely to be embarrassed by one. Some doctors and nurses consider chaperones necessary when examining female patients to protect them from false accusations of sexual misconduct, but they assume that male patients will not falsely accuse them: Male patients are perceived to be better able to protect themselves from such misconduct. One doctor uses a chaperone to protect her from sexual harassment or assault from her patients. Some male doctors use chaperones to help them control their sexual feelings toward their female patients. Male nurses are almost never chosen as chaperones; in fact, some male nurses are expected to use chaperones (or to refrain from performing certain procedures altogether) for the same reasons that male physicians use chaperones. It is critical in most instances that the chaperone is a woman: A man in this role might make female patients feel even more victimized and vulnerable, and might be emasculating for male patients.

This complex strategy to desexualize the physical exam is grounded on assumptions about men's and women's sexuality. Men are sexually powerful; women are sexually vulnerable. Women's bodies are comforting and soothing, but they also elicit feelings of childish vulnerability, which is an acceptable feeling in women but not in men. Men act on their sexual desires; women do not. These gender and sex stereotypes are bolstered through the organizational practice of using chaperones to desexualize the physical exam.

OBJECTIFYING THE PATIENT

Eight of the physicians and nurses reported that viewing their patients as something other than a person helped them to cope with the sexual nature of their work. This finding is consistent with previous research indicating that medical students and residents deal with uncomfortable feelings about patient nudity and examinations by objectifying their patient's bodies. Smith and Kleinman (1989) noted that students referred to examining patients as analogous to "looking under the hood of a car." The medical curriculum encourages students to dehumanize their patients' bodies because it focuses on the biological disease process and its cure ("lung in room 5") (Todd 1989). In contrast, the nursing school curriculum with its focus on "caring" and not "curing" emphasizes a more humane and holistic approach to treating patients. Fisher (1995) suggests that the nursing profession's focus on empathy discourages nurses from dehumanizing their patients in an extreme manner.

We found that both men and women objectify patients, but we noticed that the men and women interviewed used different metaphors in the process. The four women who mentioned using this strategy referred to their patients as "just another body" and did so for male and female patients. The four men who mentioned using this strategy referred to their patient as something other than a human being, usually a car. Moreover, these men only used this strategy with female patients.

A white female nurse described her training:

[The nursing faculty] tried to tell us like, "Don't think about it. Treat it like just another body." Usually, you've already messed with cadavers by the time you get to the hospital. So it's just another body. The hardest thing is trying to convince your patients of that . . . that it doesn't bother you.

Because she dissected cadavers in nursing school, this nurse was better able to view her patients as "just another body" and thus desexualize her own view of the patient. And according to a physician:

I'm never uncomfortable now. . . . You forget that students get uncomfortable. It's almost humorous, when you see how uncomfortable they are and you remember how uncomfortable it was at first. I tell them that it is just a body. If you get embarrassed, then your patient is going to be embarrassed. . . . If you're a professional, then they'll think it's a matter of course. (white female neurologist)

Many women provide care for their children and other relatives. If women routinely manage bodies in their personal lives, they may be more comfortable than men examining naked bodies in their professional lives, without thinking of them in a sexual way. One nurse explained that she thought of her patients as family members to make herself more comfortable with the physical exam:

I've never been nervous. My husband sometimes asks me about it. I tell him, "I can't even tell you what size a man was. I don't look at their bodies in that way." . . . You focus on a certain part of their body, and it's just a body. Nothing else. They stressed in school that we should preserve dignity and privacy. Treat the patient like they were one of your family members. Put yourself in their place. (African American female nurse)

While this nurse refers to her patients as "just a body," she also empathizes with them, thinking of them as family members. Referring to patients as bodies does not seem to imply that these women lose compassion or empathy for their patients as human beings.

In contrast, the four male practitioners who claimed to dehumanize their patients as a strategy to desexualize the physical exam compared them to machines, and they did so only for their female patients. For example, a nurse said that examining female patients was no different from "checking the oil." Similarly, a physician described examining female patients:

When you're doing an examination, the genital examination, it's so routine and mundane. . . . You're looking at the body and trying to identify other things that are going on, like a pathology. . . . Sometimes I use the analogy of the car. . . . What you're focusing on is under the hood. You step back and say, "This is a nice car." But I'm not looking at the car. I'm checking the spark plugs. . . . It's part of my job. They are there because their car is misfiring. . . . You're not looking at it on a personal level or a sexual excitement level . . . it's not a turn on. (Latino physician in family practice)

This physician is not uncomfortable examining female patients because he is not looking at their bodies for his own personal sexual enjoyment. From his point of view, examining a patient "on a personal level" might provoke "sexual excitement." Thinking of his female patients as inanimate objects enables him to desexualize the exam.

Some physicians report they are most uncomfortable examining people they know. Having a personal relationship with someone clouds professional judgment according to one physician: "It's harder to take care of patients you know very well, and they're in a dangerous situation. I still treat them, but I'm more nervous about it compared to patients who I've just met" (white male cardiologist).

In the operating room, the patient may be more anonymous, and even unconscious, making the encounter less personal and unsettling for this physician. Having a personal relationship with a patient who is being examined is more difficult for him. This contrasts with the nurse, quoted above, who attributed family status to her patients to ensure the top quality of care.

Similarly, some physicians said they managed to maintain their composure around nude patients when the patient is passively lying down on an examination table, but they are more vulnerable to embarrassment if the patient is not so passive:

> I can walk into an exam room and see a lady in the wide-open-legs position, and examine her, and do a breast exam and pelvic exam, and that doesn't bother me at all. That's so clinical. But if I walk in, and you're getting dressed or undressed, I lose it. I get flabbergasted. I turn red and I have to walk out. That's the weird thing. I can see you totally buck naked and it doesn't bother me, but if you're getting dressed or undressed, that's it. . . . It's like when you're undressed and you have a gown on, and you're on the table, you're an auto engine. You're not really, but . . . I'm here to do a job, to make a diagnosis and do a treatment, and there are certain things I have to look for so it becomes mechanical. (white male urologist)

This physician is less able to dehumanize his patients like "an auto engine" when he sees female patients in a stage of dressing. Witnessing the transition between the clothed and the unclothed states disturbs his fantasy that the human being is an inanimate machine. Three other male physicians and nurses reported that they were only uncomfortable during physical exams if they saw a female patient dressing or undressing. None of the women reported that this made them uncomfortable.

The men who were interviewed only mentioned this strategy when describing exams of female patients. They did not describe dehumanizing their male patients in this way, perhaps because these heterosexual men only fear sexual arousal with their female patients. They may not have to dehumanize their male

patients as cars because they perceive no danger of sexual attraction.

Dehumanization seems to help these health care professionals deal with the sexual nature of their work. This strategy sheds new light on complaints that doctors do not care enough about their patients. Health care professionals are taught that they should have some level of detachment to deal rationally with their patients' problems. For some physicians and nurses, objectifying their patients might also help them to cope with the sexual nature of their work. Our interviews suggest further that this may be a gendered strategy, with men more likely than women to feel the need to distance themselves from their female patients to provide a high level of care.

EMPATHIZING WITH THE PATIENT AND PROTECTING PRIVACY

Some health care providers used the opposite strategy to objectification: to diffuse sexual tension and to make their patients feel more comfortable during the physical exam, they said they empathized with them. Some said that this empathy was combined with their efforts to protect the patient's privacy, by draping or covering the patient, exposing only the small area in need of attention, or drawing privacy curtains around the patient's bed. We combined empathy and protecting privacy in tallying up the strategies since the rationale given by the respondents was similar in both cases. In sum, 6 men and 27 women reported using one or both of these strategies to desexualize the physical exam.

For example, to make her patients feel more comfortable during the exam, one nurse follows these guidelines:

> First, explain what's going to happen and that privacy will be maintained as much as possible. The door will be shut and the curtains will be

drawn or whatever. Let them know that you understand how uncomfortable it can be. Empathize. (white female nurse)

This practice of empathizing with the patient, and protecting their privacy, seems more characteristic of nursing than medicine. Seven of the physicians and 15 of the nurses said that they always covered their patients.

Whereas several nurses explained that they were taught in nursing school to empathize with their patients' needs for privacy, the opposite lesson was stressed in the medical training of some of the physicians who were interviewed. One doctor reported that a former professor required students to physically examine him in front of the class:

He tried to show that there's nothing to be uncomfortable about during the exam. Every year it escalated, and it got to the point where he completely disrobed and insisted that all parts of the exam be performed on him in front of this huge group of people. I don't know how effective it was. I thought it was embarrassing. (white male internist)

Students even administered a rectal exam on this professor in front of the class. In contrast to nursing education, which stresses patient dignity and privacy, the goal here seems to be to desensitize medical students and to disregard the personal and physical boundaries of patients.

Other physicians mentioned aspects of their education that seem intended to violate their own physical integrity and sense of personal boundaries. One medical student intern described a former professor who forced some of the male students to be physically examined in front of the class, an experience he described as sexual harassment. Female students were not called upon to submit to these public examinations; the organization almost certainly would have considered that an illegal and harmful practice. At the medical school where most of this study was conducted, students had been

required to conduct full examinations of each other, but when the students collectively rebelled against this practice, the school changed to its current practice of employing people from the community to help students practice their exam skills.

Nurses also are required to examine each other in training and even to give each other bed baths, but unlike these examples from medical schools, nursing students are explicitly taught how to conduct these invasive procedures while maintaining personal boundaries. One nurse recalled how she was taught to "be gentle and handle conversation carefully":

Conversation shouldn't be about what you see on their body. It should be about the weather or the game that was on last night, or finding something in common with your patient. You should be able to converse with all people, from the retired professional to the laborer who can't read. I feel like we were trained well. (white female nurse)

In this way, sensitivity to the patients' needs for privacy and dignity is emphasized as part of the standard nursing curriculum.

In contrast, some doctors are subjected to insensitivity training. One doctor recalled being shown "desensitization tapes" as preparation for dealing with patients' sexuality:

You're not supposed to be judgmental [as a doctor]. They showed us a bunch of tapes, like on sexual counseling. It's supposed to desensitize us to sexual things and to help us acknowledge our own sexual feelings and deal with them. They were generally kind of like gross porno-like films. Not porno films, but everybody made a lot of fun of them. In medical school, some people were offended by them, by the nudity in them. So they began showing them at night. Of course, the students were still uncomfortable. There were still jokes, but everybody was uncomfortable watching naked people and sexual acts. This was stuff we had never seen outside of porno films. (white female gynecologist)

Empathy and modesty, which are values built into nursing education, appear to be actively suppressed in physician education. This difference reflects a gendered organizational logic: Since most nursing students are women, and until recently, women have been vastly underrepresented among medical students, the expectations of appropriate professional behavior that are embedded in physician and nurse education reflect and reinforce gender stereotypes. To be a good nurse/woman means to be empathetic and modest; to be a good physician/man means to be unflappable, detached, and powerful. The hidden curriculum of health care education is thus a gendered and, to some extent, sexualized curriculum.

JOKING ABOUT SEX

Joking about sex might seem incongruent with attempts to desexualize interactions with patients, but eight men and women engaged in sexual banter with their patients as a strategy to make themselves or the patient more comfortable with intimate topics, such as the sexual history. The interviews indicate, however, that this strategy was used selectively: With a few exceptions, the men and women interviewed only joked with opposite-sex patients or older patients.

A male urologist said he occasionally jokes about sex with his female patients:

> There is innuendo. Like yesterday there was a 23-year-old girl in, who had recurrent urinary tract infections. . . . It seemed to be with her new partner that she got a lot of infections . . . I said, "Well, what you're going to need to do is take an antibiotic tablet after you have intercourse . . . every time after you have intercourse. For some women, that means you have to take one everyday." She looked at me and said, "Everyday?" I said, "There was a time in my life where I would have had to take one everyday. It didn't last very long but. . . ." So that's about as risqué as it gets. . . . Men are more uncomfortable being messed with, with

their bodies than women. Women pretty much recognize that they have to go get a pap smear, and when they've had babies, everyone is sticking their fingers up there. So women, from an early age are pretty much, for lack of a better word, resigned to it. Men . . . don't like it. You know, we see a lot of men for impotence. . . . That's . . . getting into intimate details, broaching subjects that . . . many men find very difficult to talk about . . . there's not that much joking with the men. . . . When they're talking about difficulty getting an erection, I don't think they want a locker room discussion. (white male urologist)

While he is cautious about engaging in sexual banter with women, he assumes that women are more comfortable joking about these personal matters. He perceives men's exams and histories as more sensitive than women's. He therefore avoids sexual joking with men; he does not think the examining room is the proper context for a "locker room discussion." Because the joking that does take place in locker rooms and other all-male contexts typically involves the ritual exchange of sexual insults—about sexual practices, the women they date, and the size of a man's penis (Lyman 1987)—it is inappropriate in the examining room, where the unclothed patient is in an especially passive and vulnerable position, unable to return the banter or to maintain his composure. Moreover, in the context of the exam, any sexual innuendo made to another man might be interpreted as sexual harassment.

The other physicians who mentioned this strategy engaged in joking with patients of the opposite sex to make patients more comfortable. A female general surgeon describes how she occasionally jokes about sex:

> I remember one time . . . this guy had a hernia. . . . His wife was with him. He had been coming to see us for several weeks, once a week, so we kind of had a relationship going. I walked in the room and said, "Drop your pants." He said, "Oh, I love it when women talk dirty." We all stood around laughing. It's

not something you would do with everybody, but I felt comfortable in this situation. I think most patients respond well to humor, when they know it's humor. (white female surgeon)

Joking about sex with this patient seems to diffuse any hint of sexual interest. Their sexual banter plays on the absurdity of sexual interest between a female doctor and a male patient, thus dispelling any concerns the patient's wife might have.

This function of sexual humor was most apparent when some of the men and women discussed ways to avoid false allegations. A female nurse described how she avoided false allegations from patients:

> Well, really I don't worry because I use a lot of joking and kidding and get to know my patients a little bit before I have to do anything to them. I have a patient now, and the first thing this guy said was, "You just want to peek at me, don't you? You just want to take a look at me?" I said, "Sure, that's going to be the thrill of my day. I've seen 9 million of these things honey." (white female nurse)

This nurse uses joking to assure her male patient that this exam is not intended to have sexual overtones, even though he initiates the banter. These interviews suggest that joking about sex is a way to let the patient know that the physician or nurse is not sexually attracted to them, and that any hint of sexual attraction is both outrageous and taboo. As Fine (1976, 135) observes, sexual joking often functions this way: "By describing behavior considered sexually improper (and thus comical), [sexual humor] reveals by implication the correct forms of sexual interaction."

Men and women also engaged in sexual joking with older patients. A male nurse described how he made older patients more comfortable during physical exams:

> I joke about sex with some of the male patients. Once in a while I might say something to a female. . . . One woman that we're rendering care to right now is 93 years old. When you go to visit her, the first thing she wants to know is why hasn't she died. . . . One day I said, "I think it's because you need to find a man. You haven't done that yet." She laughed, but I don't think I would go more than that. With male patients, we joke pretty openly. Like a diabetic patient in his middle seventies, who also had a little bit of cancer of the prostate, asked me if he should be involved in sex. . . . He wanted to know about protection with respect to AIDS. . . . Well, I seriously doubt he was going to get any, pardon my language (laughs). . . . With younger males, it's easy. I even joke with homosexuals a little bit, but not about homosexuals. I tell homosexuals heterosexual jokes. They know I'm straight pretty soon. (white male nurse)

This nurse engages in sexual joking with older patients and some young men as a way to set them at ease. But significantly, the strategy is used very selectively. He makes the ageist assumption that joking with older patients is safe because these individuals are neither active sexually nor do they have sexual interests. This reaffirms the hegemonic belief that only young people are sexual. His joking with young men appears to be a strategy designed to let them know that he is straight. Male nurses often face stereotypes that they are gay (Williams 1995), and this may be one way to dispel this suspicion among his patients.

Sexual banter with patients is a strategy that might fail if the patient is gay or lesbian, and the physician or nurse is heterosexual. Stevens (1996) conducted a study of lesbians' experiences with physicians during physical exams and found that physicians engaged in sexual innuendo with the respondents. The respondents noted that physicians seemed uncomfortable and unsure how to proceed if they "came out" during the physical examination. For example, one woman noted that her physician "didn't seem to know how to make conversation with a female client except through heterosexual jokes" (Stevens 1996, 34). Stevens' research suggests that joking about sex was based on the assumption of heterosexuality of the doctor and patient, and it might be used more often in heterosocial encounters in the intimate context of the physical exam.

Joking reaffirms the legitimacy and normalcy of some sexual behaviors, and the taboo nature of others. But it does this by inverting the normal and the taboo. Often what makes a joke funny is the absurdity and impossibility of the situations it describes. Thus, some of the health care workers who were interviewed felt comfortable joking about sex with opposite-sex patients and elderly patients. By pointing out what is absurd, it affirms what is normal and expected. Sexual joking is also a means through which men establish intimacy, although typically this involves challenging each other's masculinity and sexual prowess. Male joking of this type requires that participants appear invulnerable to these attacks (Lyman 1987), a situation impossible to maintain in the context of a medical examination. Consequently, this type of joking is absent from the accounts of our respondents, except in the case of the male nurse who uses joking to demonstrate his heterosexuality to his male patients. Finally, joking can decrease the social distance between patients and their health care providers, and hence it can be used to help comfort and empathize with patients. Even so, it is used selectively, often only with elderly patients, reflecting the ageist assumption that old people are asexual. Several health care providers did acknowledge that sexual joking is potentially dangerous in heterosocial encounters in the examining room because of its sexualized overtones: Consequently, most of the doctors and nurses interviewed said they assiduously avoid any such joking because they fear it will be misconstrued as a sexual interest.

THREATENING THE PATIENT

Four female physicians and nurses encountered problems desexualizing the physical examination of their patients because they experienced unwanted sexual advances from male patients. To control such patients, they threatened to physically or verbally punish them. Some men also reported sexual harassment from patients, but they never threatened them to control their behaviors. Seven physicians (5 of them were women) and 11 nurses (9 of them women) said they experienced sexual harassment from patients, ranging from male patients who attempted to fondle or grab them, to engage in sexual innuendo, and/or to expose themselves. Some of these behaviors were experienced as threatening; others were seen as "nothing to get upset about" and "a part of the job."

Recent studies indicate that sexual harassment affects many women in the health care industry. Phillips and Schneider (1993) found that 75 percent of female doctors surveyed reported sexual harassment from patients, most of whom were male. Grieco (1987) found that 76 percent of nurses surveyed experienced sexual harassment from both physicians and patients. Foner's (1994) study of a nursing home indicates that some female health care workers actually may be required to tolerate these behaviors as part of their jobs.

A nurse described her experience of sexual harassment:

> I had a patient try to pull me into bed with him. I hit him. . . . I reached down to take his pulse, and he yanked my hand. I had a foreigner grab my hand and shove it down his pants. . . . At first I thought, "Well, He's just a foreigner. He can't speak English. He's used to having women serve all of his needs." He wasn't speaking so I assumed that he didn't speak English. He was pretty dark. I thought he was Middle Eastern. He took my hand like he was trying to tell me something. So I was saying, "What's the matter? What are you trying to tell me?" He grabbed my hand, pulled it down his pants and he had a hard-on. That was very scary . . . I got very angry. I yelled at him, "I don't care if you speak English or not! You don't do that again! I'll tie you to the bed!" I went back and got mad at the other nurses for

not telling me about him. They were like, "Whoops. We forgot he did that to young women." I said, "He's done this before?!" They said, "You can give him up if you want to." I said, "No. I can handle it." He would say, "Will you help me?" I said, "Nope. Don't you touch me." I was rude. (white female nurse)

The fact that her coworkers "forgot" to tell her that this patient sexually harassed other women suggests that sexual harassment is a routine and expected part of their job, which is managed through informal "warnings" about patients who instigate unwanted sexual advances. To desexualize the exam and control this patient, she gets "rude" and threatens to tie his hands.

None of the physicians or nurses interviewed had received formal or informal training about handling unwanted sexual advances from patients. The women who were interviewed had to devise their own strategies to control behaviors of male patients. According to one nurse:

Oh yeah. [Sexual harassment from male patients] happens all the time. Oh yeah (laughs). . . . Last week, this one guy exposed himself to me every time I walked in the room, or he'd grab himself and leer at me. I've had them proposition me, grab my boobs, my butt. It's been a wild time (laughs). . . . The guy who was exposing himself and grabbing himself just had an infected left hand. There was nothing wrong up here [points to her forehead] . . . I said to him, "Are you having trouble keeping your gown down, buddy?" I talk to them real stern. With my size, they tend to do what I say. . . I've had to report a couple of guys who wouldn't keep their hands to themselves. I went to their doctor. The doctors are always real supportive about that. I tell them, "I'm having trouble with this guy," and the doctor goes in and says, "That's not acceptable. You leave the nurses alone." (white female nurse)

Even though she feels protected because of her size (she is more than six feet tall), ultimately

this nurse must call on physicians to control the unacceptable sexual behavior of some of her patients. Three other nurses noted that they threaten to call the police if male patients "got out of hand." This strategy thus perpetuates gendered beliefs about women (nurses) as victims and men (police/doctors) as protectors.

One female physician changed specialties from internal medicine to obstetrics-gynecology to avoid sexual harassment by male patients:

When I was in internal medicine—I remember one guy in the ER had a heart attack. I was listening to his heart beating and he reaches around and grabs my butt. I said, "I don't think you understand. You have had a heart attack. I'm your doctor. If I were you, I don't think I'd piss me off." He was drunk as a skunk. Out dancing with a woman who wasn't his wife. I said, "Would you like for me to call your wife and explain the situation to your family? Okay. We understand each other." . . . I was [in] internal medicine for about four months. I found [the male patients] unpleasant and went into ob-gyn. (white female physician in obstetrics-gynecology)

In order to control the sexual behavior of her patient, this physician had to assert her professional status and threaten to expose his sexual infidelity to his family. After she changed specialties to obstetrics-gynecology, she treated only female patients. In this way, sexual harassment may contribute to internal occupational segregation in the health care professions. In fact, research shows that women in professional, nontraditional occupations suffer high rates of sexual harassment, often the "hostile work environment" type that punishes women for entering traditionally male environments (DiTomaso 1989); Konrad and Gutek 1986; Schultz 1998).

Physicians are often criticized today for their domineering and controlling attitudes toward patients. Our study suggests that for at least some female physicians, asserting power may be a means to overcome sexual harassment. According to Phillips and Schneider (1993, 1939),

At a time when physicians are criticized for magnifying the inevitable differences in power that separate them from their patients, it is ironic that female doctors see the reinforcement of a physician's power as a means of protection. Despite this power, female doctors are treated primarily as women, not as physicians, by many of their male patients. The vulnerability inherent in their sex seems in many cases to override their power as doctors, leaving female physicians open to sexual harassment.

Female physicians and nurses may be forced to draw on their institutional power and authority to desexualize the physical exam, in response to unwanted sexual advances from their male patients.

LOOKING PROFESSIONAL

Four female nurses and doctors in this study attempted to control the sexual desires of their patients and diffuse the sexual meanings of the physical exam by emphasizing their professionalism. This was usually accomplished by dressing in a particular way:

> The way you dress is important. I think it's really important for women. I don't go to work with tight pants or short skirts. I wear business attire so the patient gets the idea that you're there to take care of them and nothing else. It's also important how the other people in the clinic dress. We have the nurses dress in scrubs or uniforms, and the secretaries also don't dress like they're going out to the disco (laughs). (Latina internist)

The importance of dressing to suppress sexual feelings was also emphasized by this physician:

> Some female physicians have their hair all made up, and lots of makeup and they look like a Barbie doll. I like to dress nicely but I don't wear excessive jewelry. I don't wear excessive makeup. I'm not too ornate. I don't try to look like a Barbie doll because I can see where it would be difficult for the patient to keep in mind that you're their physician, you

know? (Asian American female in general medicine)

The conventional markers of femininity (styled hair, makeup, jewelry) are incompatible with "looking professional" because they sexualize the female health care provider and thus potentially arouse sexual feelings in patients. It is telling that none of the male health care providers mentioned the importance of dress for controlling patients' sexuality. Men may have an easier time than women looking the part of a professional. According to Dellinger and Williams (1997), the fact that men do not have to strategize their appearance reinforces the idea that women are the ones who bring "gender" and "sexuality" to the workplace.

Certain institutional practices exacerbate the problems women face "looking professional." Three of the female surgeons who occasionally worked at the same hospital mentioned that they were unhappy with the uniforms made available to them there. Two types of scrub suits were worn in the operating room: the typical green scrubs, which they preferred, and flowery scrubs with longer sleeves and tops intended to be worn by the female nurses. These physicians did not like the flowery scrubs because they claimed it was harder to do surgery in them, and because they did not want to be mistaken for nurses, yet they were typically the only type available in the women's changing room (which was shared by doctors and nurses). The administration ignored their complaints that the flowery scrubs undermined their efforts to look professional and garner the respect they felt they deserved. One said she often had to go into the doctors' dressing room (which was used by men only) to retrieve a set of green scrubs to wear:

> In some hospitals that don't have separate female surgeons' dressing rooms, there are no male scrubs available. So I just knock on the door to the male dressing room, and I walk in and get some scrubs. If there's men in there and they're naked, I don't care. I just walk in. I say,

"If you don't like me doing this, then complain to so-and-so, and get us a female physicians' dressing room." But they don't care. The men don't care. It's kind of a joke. They kind of laugh about it. It's another form of insidious discrimination . . . to not provide female physicians with the same clothes that they provide the male physicians. (white female urologist)

In addition to having the right clothes, having the right body shape also helps to "look professional," according to another physician. When asked if she had ever been sexually harassed, she said,

Younger guys have said something suggestive over the years but it's never been a big problem [for me]. Again, I think it helps that I am tall with dark hair. I think there are ways of being friendly, yet clearly professional, and that's hard to teach. I know some women have had more of a problem. I'm not very buxom either, and I think that makes a difference. I really think these things are things that women have no control over, but they make a huge difference. There are also clothes I wouldn't wear to see patients, like no short skirts. I dress conservatively. It shouldn't make a difference, but it does. (white female internist)

Women's bodies arouse sexual feelings, according to this physician, making it more difficult for women to achieve professional recognition. Some women's bodies may be especially incompatible with professional status. This is another example of how organizations are gendered and sexualized: The image of professionalism in the hospital is a masculine one. Women's bodies must be desexualized to achieve the same level of respect that men are accorded automatically. Having the wrong kind of body can be a formidable impediment to success.

Conclusion

Health care professionals are expected to manage their personal feelings during the physical examination of patients. This article describes how physicians and nurses control their own sexual feelings and the sexual behaviors of their patients. The men and women interviewed devised strategies to desexualize the exam, several of which were used selectively, depending on the gender and other characteristics of the patient and the health care worker. The interviews with doctors and nurses indicate that the choice to use certain strategies is shaped by, and reinforces, stereotypes about gender and sexuality.

The findings in this article are based on a small, nonrandom sample; hence, it is difficult to generalize to the entire population of doctors and nurses. Health care practitioners in other settings, such as private practices, may manage sexuality differently, compared with the physicians and nurses in teaching hospitals. The management of sexuality may also be specialty specific. Surgeons, pediatricians, urologists, and family practitioners may desexualize the exam differently.

This study suggests that desexualizing the exam is a gendered process. Men and women confront different obstacles to desexualizing the physical examination of patients. Male physicians and nurses are subject to assumptions that they are out of control of their sexuality. The use of female chaperones during their examination of female patients is based, in part, on this belief. Some men actually do fear sexual arousal, especially in their gynecological examinations of young, attractive women. Some men are also uncomfortable when they examine women they know or when they witness female patients undressing. Having a personal relationship with women is conflated with sexual meanings for some. Some endeavor to dehumanize their patient as a car to help them control their physical attraction.

In contrast, the women who were interviewed were less concerned about controlling their own sexual desire and more concerned about controlling the sexual desire of their male patients. Many of the female physicians and nurses in this study reported that sexual harassment from patients was "a part of their job." To protect themselves from sexual harassment, the female health care providers changed specialties, threatened their male patients, and dressed in ways to minimize their femininity and sexual attractiveness.

It is interesting how stereotypes about male and female patients' behavior provoke different institutional responses. Some doctors (both men and women) and male nurses fear that female patients will falsely accuse them of sexual assault, so they take measures to protect their reputations, including the institutionalized use of female chaperones. On the other hand, some female health care providers (both doctors and nurses) fear that they will be sexually harassed or assaulted by their male patients. But chaperones typically are not used to prevent these behaviors because chaperones might "embarrass" the male patient. Consequently, female health care providers must devise personal solutions to this problem without institutionalized support.

The professions of medicine and nursing, like many occupations, are profoundly gendered. Doctors are assumed to possess characteristics conventionally associated with masculinity (mastery, control, objectivity), while nurses are expected to display putatively feminine characteristics (empathy, modesty). The different training they receive in professional schools bolsters these expectations, with physicians focused on "curing" the disease and nurses learning to "care" for the whole patient. These gendered expectations are reflected in the strategies that men/doctors and women/nurses use to desexualize the exam. Women/nurses manage the relationship (empathize/protect privacy) between the provider and the patient, reflecting women's widely emphasized interactional and communication skills. The men/doctors do not stress managing the relationship; they just bring in another person (the chaperone) to control and to monitor the

situation. Because female doctors and male nurses have to negotiate conflicting sets of gender expectations, they use some strategies not common to their professional colleagues of the opposite sex. Thus, female doctors stress the importance of looking professional, and male nurses sometimes call in chaperones.

This study of desexualization strategies reveals how gender is embedded in the informal organization and daily interactions with patients in the hospital. It is difficult to imagine how an embodied procedure such as a physical exam could ever escape gendered meanings. But recognizing how cultural assumptions about gender and sexuality shape this experience is a critical first step toward eventually reconfiguring those expectations in more just and liberating ways.

References

Cassell, J. 1998. The Woman in the Surgeon's Body. Cambridge, MA: Harvard University Press.

Dellinger, K. A., and C. L. Williams, 1997. "Makeup at Work: Negotiating Appearance Rules in the Workplace." Gender & Society 11:151–77.

DiTomaso, N. 1989. "Sexuality in the Workplace: Discrimination and Harassment." In The Sexuality of Organization, edited by J. Hearn, D. L. Sheppard, P. Tancred-Sheriff, and G. Burrell. London: Sage.

Fine, G. A. 1976. "Obscene Joking Across Cultures." Journal of Communication 26:134–40.

Fisher, S. 1995. Nursing Wounds: Nurse Practitioners/ Doctors/Women Patients/and the Negotiation of Meaning. New Brunswick, NJ: Rutgers University Press.

Foner, N. 1994. The Caregiving Dilemma: Work in an American Nursing Home. Berkeley: University of California Press.

Grieco, A. 1987. "Scope and Nature of Sexual Harassment in Nursing." Journal of Sex Research 23:261–66.

Konrad, A. M., and B. A. Gutek. 1986. "Impact of Work Experiences on Attitudes Toward Sexual Harassment." Administrative Science Quarterly 31:422–38.

Lyman, P. 1987. "The Fraternal Bond as a Joking Relationship: A Case Study of the Role of Sexist Jokes in Male Group Bonding." In *Changing Men: New Directions in Research on Men and Masculinity,* ed., M. S. Kimmel. Newbury Park, CA: Sage.

Phillips, S. P., and M. S. Schneider. 1993. "Sexual Harassment of Doctors by Patients." *New England Journal of Medicine* 329: 1936–39.

Randolph, L., B. Seidman, and T. Pasko. 1996. *Physician Characteristics and Distribution in the U.S.* Chicago: American Medical Association.

Schultz, V. 1998. "Reconceptualizing Sexual Harassment." *Yale Law Journal* 107: 1683–1805.

Smith, A. C., and S. Kleinman. 1989. "Managing Emotions in Medical School: Students' Contact with the Living and the Dead." *Social Psychology Quarterly* 52: 56–69.

Stevens, P. E. 1996. Lesbians and doctors: Experiences of solidarity and domination in health care settings. *Gender & Society* 10:24–41.

Todd, A. D. 1989. *Intimate Adversaries: Cultural Conflict Between Doctors and Women Patients.* Philadelphia: University of Pennsylvania Press.

Williams, C. L. 1995. *Still a Man's World: Men Who Do "Women's Work."* Berkeley: University of California Press.

Questions

1. What do the authors mean when they say that the physical exam must be "desexualized"?

2. According to professors Giuffre and Williams, desexualizing physical exams is done in a gendered way. What strategies are primarily employed by women practitioners? What strategies are primarily employed by male practitioners?

3. The authors argue that "female patients are protected by chaperones, but men must be protected from chaperones." What do they mean?

4. This article focuses mostly on what practitioners do to desexualize physical exams. In your experience, what role does the patient play in desexualizing physical exams? Is the patient's response gendered? (That is, do men play their role as patients during the physical exam differently than women do?)

·27·

The Normality of Crime

Émile Durkheim

The following excerpt is from Émile Durkheim's 1895 essay *Rules of the Sociological Method*. The excerpt is brief but (like much of what people wrote in the nineteenth century) fairly complex. Durkheim begins by pointing out that crime—or acts that offend the collective conscience—is normal in every society. In other words, every society can expect some of its members occasionally to do things that offend that society's shared values and beliefs. According to Durkheim's analysis, the only way to completely do away with murder, for example, would be for every single person in the society to develop intense respect for all other members. If that happened, Durkheim points out, then the crime of murder might disappear, but previously minor offenses would then seem more serious. In a society of saints, he says, the crime of murder would not be a problem, but perhaps the "crime" of insulting others would be.

Here we are, then, in the presence of a conclusion in appearance quite paradoxical. Let us make no mistake. To classify crime among the phenomena of normal sociology is not to say merely that it is an inevitable, although regrettable phenomenon, due to the incorrigible wickedness of men; it is to affirm that it is a factor in public health, an integral part of all healthy societies. This result is, at first glance, surprising enough to have puzzled even ourselves for a long time. Once this first surprise has been overcome, however, it is not difficult to find reasons explaining this normality and at the same time confirming it.

In the first place crime is normal because a society exempt from it is utterly impossible. Crime, we have shown elsewhere, consists of an act that offends certain very strong collective sentiments. In a society in which criminal acts are no longer committed, the sentiments they offend would have to be found without exception in all individual consciousnesses, and they must be found to exist with the same degree as sentiments contrary to them. Assuming that this condition could actually be realized, crime would not thereby disappear; it would only change its form, for the very cause which would thus dry up the sources of criminality would immediately open up new ones.

Indeed, for the collective sentiments which are protected by the penal law[1] of a people at a specific moment of its history to take possession of the public conscience or for them to acquire a

---

[1]Penal law is criminal law.—Ed.

stronger hold where they have an insufficient grip, they must acquire an intensity greater than that which they had hitherto had. The community as a whole must experience them more vividly, for it can acquire from no other source the greater force necessary to control these individuals who formerly were the most refractory. For murderers to disappear, the horror of bloodshed must become greater in those social strata from which murderers are recruited; but, first it must become greater throughout the entire society. Moreover, the very absence of crime would directly contribute to produce this horror; because any sentiment seems much more respectable when it is always and uniformly respected.

One easily overlooks the consideration that these strong states of the common consciousness cannot be thus reinforced without reinforcing at the same time the more feeble states, whose violation previously gave birth to mere infraction of convention—since the weaker ones are only the prolongation, the attenuated form, of the stronger. Thus robbery and simple bad taste injure the same single altruistic sentiment, the respect for that which is another's. However, this same sentiment is less grievously offended by bad taste than by robbery; and since, in addition, the average consciousness has not sufficient intensity to react keenly to the bad taste, it is treated with greater tolerance. That is why the person guilty of bad taste is merely blamed, whereas the thief is punished. But, if

this sentiment grows stronger, to the point of silencing in all consciousnesses the inclination which disposes man to steal, he will become more sensitive to the offenses which, until then, touched him but lightly. He will react against them, then, with more energy; they will be the object of greater opprobrium, which will transform certain of them from the simple moral faults that they were and give them the quality of crimes. For example, improper contracts, or contracts improperly executed, which only incur public blame or civil damages, will become offenses in law.

Imagine a society of saints, a perfect cloister of exemplary individuals. Crimes, properly so called, will there be unknown; but faults which appear venial to the layman will create there the same scandal that the ordinary offense does in ordinary consciousnesses. If, then, this society has the power to judge and punish, it will define these acts as criminal and will treat them as such. For the same reason, the perfect and upright man judges his smallest failings with a severity that the majority reserve for acts more truly in the nature of an offense. Formerly, acts of violence against persons were more frequent than they are today, because respect for individual dignity was less strong. As this has increased, these crimes have become more rare; and also, many acts violating this sentiment have been introduced into the penal law which were not included there in primitive times. . . .

Questions

1. Durkheim argues that crime is "normal." What does he mean by this?

2. Does Durkheim believe that it is either possible or desirable for a society to exist in which there is no crime? Why or why not?

·28·

The Saints and the Roughnecks

William J. Chambliss

Robert K. Merton was inspired by the "Thomas theorem"—the notion (from W. I. Thomas) that if people "define situations as real, they are real in their consequences." Merton observed that Thomas was pointing out that people "not only respond to the objective features of a situation" but to the "meaning this situation has for them." One implication of the Thomas theorem was something that Merton called the "self-fulfilling prophecy": "The self-fulfilling prophecy is, in the beginning, a *false* definition of the situation evoking a new behavior which makes the originally false conception come *true*." For example, if a rumor circulates that the town bank is about to fail, that rumor, even if initially false, can come true simply because it's there. That is, the rumor may worry people sufficiently that they hurry to the bank and withdraw their funds. Ultimately, the bank *does* fail. Then, the rumormonger can say, "See, I told you the bank was going to fail."[1]

The following 1972 article by William Chambliss explores some of the ways in which public definitions of a situation come into being with respect to two small groups of high school kids. As you read this article, look for examples of how the ways in which people define the situation have real consequences for the people involved.

Eight promising young men—children of good, stable, white upper-middle-class families, active in school affairs, good pre-college students—were some of the most delinquent boys at Hanibal High School. While community residents and parents knew that these boys occasionally sowed a few wild oats, they were totally unaware that sowing wild oats completely occupied the daily routine of these young men. The Saints were constantly occupied with truancy, drinking, wild driving, petty theft and vandalism. Yet not one was officially arrested for any misdeed during the two years I observed them.

This record was particularly surprising in light of my observations during the same two years of another gang of Hanibal High School students, six lower-class white boys known as the Roughnecks. The Roughnecks were constantly in trouble with police and community even though their rate of delinquency was about equal with that of the Saints. What was the cause of this disparity? the result? The following consideration of the activities, social class and community perceptions of both gangs may provide some answers.

[1]From Robert Merton, *Social Theory and Social Structure* (New York: Free Press, 1968), p. 477.—Ed.

"The Saints and the Roughnecks" by William J. Chambliss from *Society*, November/December 1972. Copyright © 1972 by Transaction Publishers. Reproduced with permission of Transaction Publishers via Copyright Clearance Center.

The Saints from Monday to Friday

The Saints' principal daily concern was with getting out of school as early as possible. The boys managed to get out of school with minimum danger that they would be accused of playing hookey through an elaborate procedure for obtaining "legitimate" release from class. The most common procedure was for one boy to obtain the release of another by fabricating a meeting of some committee, program or recognized club. Charles might raise his hand in his 9:00 chemistry class and asked to be excused — a euphemism for going to the bathroom. Charles would go to Ed's math class and inform the teacher that Ed was needed for a 9:30 rehearsal of the drama club play. The math teacher would recognize Ed and Charles as "good students" involved in numerous school activities and would permit Ed to leave at 9:30. Charles would return to his class, and Ed would go to Tom's English class to obtain his release. Tom would engineer Charles' escape. The strategy would continue until as many of the Saints as possible were freed. After a stealthy trip to the car (which had been parked in a strategic spot), the boys were off for a day of fun.

Over the two years I observed the Saints, this pattern was repeated nearly every day. There were variations on the theme, but in one form or another, the boys used this procedure for getting out of class and then off the school grounds. Rarely did all eight of the Saints manage to leave school at the same time. The average number avoiding school on the days I observed them was five.

Having escaped from the concrete corridors the boys usually went either to a pool hall on the other (lower-class) side of town or to a cafe in the suburbs. Both places were out of the way of people the boys were likely to know (family or school officials), and both provided a source of entertainment. The pool hall entertainment was the generally rough atmosphere, the occasional hustler, the sometimes drunk

proprietor and, of course, the game of pool. The cafe's entertainment was provided by the owner. The boys would "accidentally" knock a glass on the floor or spill cola on the counter — not all the time, but enough to be sporting. They would also bend spoons, put salt in sugar bowls and generally tease whoever was working in the cafe. The owner had opened the cafe recently and was dependent on the boys' business which was, in fact, substantial since between the horsing around and the teasing they bought food and drinks.

The Saints on Weekends

On weekends the automobile was even more critical than during the week, for on weekends the Saints went to Big Town — a large city with a population of over a million 25 miles from Hanibal. Every Friday and Saturday night most of the Saints would meet between 8:00 and 8:30 and would go into Big Town. Big Town activities included drinking heavily in taverns or nightclubs, driving drunkenly through the streets, and committing acts of vandalism and playing pranks.

By midnight on Fridays and Saturdays the Saints were usually thoroughly high, and one or two of them were often so drunk they had to be carried to the cars. Then the boys drove around town, calling obscenities to women and girls; occasionally trying (unsuccessfully so far as I could tell) to pick girls up; and driving recklessly through red lights and at high speeds with their lights out. Occasionally they played "chicken." One boy would climb out the back window of the car and across the roof to the driver's side of the car while the car was moving at high speed (between 40 and 50 miles an hour); then the driver would move over and the boy who had just crawled across the car roof would take the driver's seat.

Searching for "fair game" for a prank was the boys' principal activity after they left the tavern. The boys would drive alongside a foot patrolman and ask directions to some street. If the policeman leaned on the car in the course of answering the question, the driver would speed away, causing him to lose his balance. The Saints were careful to play this prank only in an area where they were not going to spend much time and where they could quickly disappear around a corner to avoid having their license plate number taken.

Construction sites and road repair areas were the special province of the Saints' mischief. A soon-to-be-repaired hole in the road inevitably invited the Saints to remove lanterns and wooden barricades and put them in the car, leaving the hole unprotected. The boys would find a safe vantage point and wait for an unsuspecting motorist to drive into the hole. Often, though not always, the boys would go up to the motorist and commiserate with him about the dreadful way the city protected its citizenry.

Leaving the scene of the open hole and the motorist, the boys would then go searching for an appropriate place to erect the stolen barricade. An "appropriate place" was often a spot on a highway near a curve in the road where the barricade would not be seen by an oncoming motorist. The boys would wait to watch an unsuspecting motorist attempt to stop and (usually) crash into the wooden barricade. With saintly bearing the boys might offer help and understanding.

A stolen lantern might well find its way onto the back of a police car or hang from a street lamp. Once a lantern served as a prop for a reenactment of the "midnight ride of Paul Revere" until the "play," which was taking place at 2:00 AM in the center of a main street of Big Town, was interrupted by a police car several blocks away. The boys ran, leaving the lanterns on the street, and managed to avoid being apprehended.

Abandoned houses, especially if they were located in out-of-the-way places, were fair game for destruction and spontaneous vandalism. The boys would break windows, remove furniture to the yard and tear it apart, urinate on the walls and scrawl obscenities inside.

Through all the pranks, drinking and reckless driving the boys managed miraculously to avoid being stopped by police. Only twice in two years was I aware that they had been stopped by a Big City policeman. Once was for speeding (which they did every time they drove whether they were drunk or sober), and the driver managed to convince the policeman that it was simply an error. The second time they were stopped they had just left a nightclub and were walking through an alley. Aaron stopped to urinate and the boys began making obscene remarks. A foot patrolman came into the alley, lectured the boys and sent them home. Before the boys got to the car one began talking in a loud voice again. The policeman, who had followed them down the alley, arrested this boy for disturbing the peace and took him to the police station where the other Saints gathered. After paying a $5.00 fine, and with the assurance that there would be no permanent record of the arrest, the boy was released.

The boys had a spirit of frivolity and fun about their escapades. They did not view what they were engaged in as "delinquency," though it surely was by any reasonable definition of that word. They simply viewed themselves as having a little fun and who, they would ask, was really hurt by it? The answer had to be no one, although this fact remains one of the most difficult things to explain about the gang's behavior. Unlikely though it seems, in two years of drinking, driving, carousing and vandalism no one was seriously injured as a result of the Saints' activities.

The Saints in School

The Saints were highly successful in school. The average grade for the group was "B," with two of the boys having close to a straight "A" average. Almost all of the boys were popular and many of them held offices in the school.

One of the boys was vice president of the student body one year. Six of the boys played on athletic teams.

At the end of their senior year, the student body selected ten seniors for special recognition as the "school wheels"; four of the ten were Saints. Teachers and school officials saw no problem with any of these boys and anticipated that they would all "make something of themselves."

How the boys managed to maintain this impression is surprising in view of their actual behavior while in school. Their technique for covering truancy was so successful that teachers did not even realize that the boys were absent from school much of the time. Occasionally, of course, the system would backfire and then the boy was on his own. A boy who was caught would be most contrite, would plead guilty and ask for mercy. He inevitably got the mercy he sought.

Cheating on examinations was rampant, even to the point of orally communicating answers to exams as well as looking at one another's papers. Since none of the group studied, and since they were primarily dependent on one another for help, it is surprising that grades were so high. Teachers contributed to the deception in their admitted inclination to give these boys (and presumably others like them) the benefit of the doubt. When asked how the boys did in school, and when pressed on specific examinations, teachers might admit that they were disappointed in John's performance, but would quickly add that they "knew that he was capable of doing better," so John was given a higher grade than he had actually earned. How often this happened is impossible to know. During the time that I observed the group, I never saw any of the boys take homework home. Teachers may have been "understanding" very regularly.

One exception to the gang's generally good performance was Jerry, who had a "C" average in his junior year, experienced disaster the next year and failed to graduate. Jerry had always been a little more nonchalant than the others about the liberties he took in school. Rather than wait for someone to come get him from class, he would offer his own excuse and leave. Although he probably did not miss any more classes than most of the others in the group, he did not take the requisite pains to cover his absences. Jerry was the only Saint whom I ever heard talk back to a teacher. Although teachers often called him a "cut up" or a "smart kid," they never referred to him as a troublemaker or as a kid headed for trouble. It seems likely, then, that Jerry's failure his senior year and his mediocre performance his junior year were consequences of his not playing the game the proper way (possibly because he was disturbed by his parents' divorce). His teachers regarded him as "immature" and not quite ready to get out of high school.

The Police and the Saints

The local police saw the Saints as good boys who were among the leaders of the youth in the community. Rarely, the boys might be stopped in town for speeding or for running a stop sign. When this happened the boys were always polite, contrite and pled for mercy. As in school, they received the mercy they asked for. None ever received a ticket or was taken into the precinct by the local police.

The situation in Big City, where the boys engaged in most of their delinquency, was only slightly different. The police there did not know the boys at all, although occasionally the boys were stopped by a patrolman. Once they were caught taking a lantern from a construction site. Another time they were stopped for running a stop sign, and on several occasions they were stopped for speeding. Their behavior was as before: contrite, polite and penitent. The urban police, like the local police, accepted their demeanor as sincere. More important, the urban police were convinced that these were good boys just out for a lark.

The Roughnecks

Hanibal townspeople never perceived the Saints' high level of delinquency. The Saints were good boys who just went in for an occasional prank. After all, they were well dressed, well mannered and had nice cars. The Roughnecks were a different story. Although the two gangs of boys were the same age, and both groups engaged in an equal amount of wild-oat sowing, everyone agreed that the not-so-well-dressed, not-so-well-mannered, not-so-rich boys were heading for trouble. Townspeople would say, "You can see the gang members at the drugstore, night after night, leaning against the storefront (sometimes drunk) or slouching around inside buying cokes, reading magazines, and probably stealing old Mr. Wall blind. When they are outside and girls walk by, even respectable girls, these boys make suggestive remarks. Sometimes their remarks are downright lewd."

From the community's viewpoint, the real indication that these kids were in for trouble was that they were constantly involved with the police. Some of them had been picked up for stealing, mostly small stuff, of course, "but still it's stealing small stuff that leads to big time crimes." "Too bad," people said. "Too bad that these boys couldn't behave like the other kids in town; stay out of trouble, be polite to adults, and look to their future."

The community's impression of the degree to which this group of six boys (ranging in age from 16 to 19) engaged in delinquency was somewhat distorted. In some ways the gang was more delinquent than the community thought; in other ways they were less.

The fighting activities of the group were fairly readily and accurately perceived by almost everyone. At least once a month, the boys would get into some sort of fight, although most fights were scraps between members of the group or involved only one member of the group and some peripheral hanger-on. Only three times in the period of observation did the group fight together: once against a gang from across town, once against two blacks and once against a group of boys from another school. For the first two fights the group went out "looking for trouble"—and they found it both times. The third fight followed a football game and began spontaneously with an argument on the football field between one of the Roughnecks and a member of the opposition's football team.

Jack had a particular propensity for fighting and was involved in most of the brawls. He was a prime mover of the escalation of arguments into fights.

More serious than fighting, had the community been aware of it, was theft. Although almost everyone was aware that the boys occasionally stole things, they did not realize the extent of the activity. Petty stealing was a frequent event for the Roughnecks. Sometimes they stole as a group and coordinated their efforts; other times they stole in pairs. Rarely did they steal alone.

The thefts ranged from very small things like paperback books, comics and ballpoint pens to expensive items like watches. The nature of the thefts varied from time to time. The gang would go through a period of systematically shoplifting items from automobiles or school lockers. Types of thievery varied with the whim of the gang. Some forms of thievery were more profitable than others, but all thefts were for profit, not just thrills.

Roughnecks siphoned gasoline from cars as often as they had access to an automobile, which was not very often. Unlike the Saints, who owned their own cars, the Roughnecks would have to borrow their parents' cars, an event which occurred only eight or nine times a year. The boys claimed to have stolen cars for joy rides from time to time.

Ron committed the most serious of the group's offenses. With an unidentified associate the boy attempted to burglarize a gasoline station. Although this station had been robbed twice previously in the same month, Ron denied any involvement in either of the other thefts. When Ron and his accomplice approached the station, the owner was hiding in the bushes beside the station. He fired both barrels of a double-barreled shotgun at the boys. Ron was severely injured; the other boy ran away and was never caught. Though he remained in critical condition for several months, Ron finally recovered and served six months of the following year in reform school. Upon release from reform school, Ron was put back a grade in school, and began running around with a different gang of boys. The Roughnecks considered the new gang less delinquent than themselves, and during the following year Ron had no more trouble with the police.

The Roughnecks, then, engaged mainly in three types of delinquency: theft, drinking and fighting. Although community members perceived that this gang of kids was delinquent, they mistakenly believed that their illegal activities were primarily drinking, fighting and being a nuisance to passersby. Drinking was limited among the gang members, although it did occur, and theft was much more prevalent than anyone realized.

Drinking would doubtless have been more prevalent had the boys had ready access to liquor. Since they rarely had automobiles at their disposal, they could not travel very far, and the bars in town would not serve them. Most of the boys had little money, and this, too, inhibited their purchase of alcohol. Their major source of liquor was a local drunk who would buy them a fifth if they would give him enough extra to buy himself a pint of whiskey or a bottle of wine.

The community's perception of drinking as prevalent stemmed from the fact that it was the most obvious delinquency the boys engaged in.

When one of the boys had been drinking, even a casual observer seeing him on the corner would suspect that he was high.

There was a high level of mutual distrust and dislike between the Roughnecks and the police. The boys felt very strongly that the police were unfair and corrupt. Some evidence existed that the boys were correct in their perception.

The main source of the boys' dislike for the police undoubtedly stemmed from the fact that the police would sporadically harass the group. From the standpoint of the boys, these acts of occasional enforcement of the law were whimsical and uncalled for. It made no sense to them, for example, that the police would come to the corner occasionally and threaten them with arrest for loitering when the night before the boys had been out siphoning gasoline from cars and the police had been nowhere in sight. To the boys, the police were stupid on the one hand, for not being where they should have been and catching the boys in a serious offense, and unfair on the other hand, for trumping up "loitering" charges against them.

From the viewpoint of the police, the situation was quite different. They knew, with all the confidence necessary to be a policeman, that these boys were engaged in criminal activities. They knew this partly from occasionally catching them, mostly from circumstantial evidence ("the boys were around when those tires were slashed"), and partly because the police shared the view of the community in general that this was a bad bunch of boys. The best the police could hope to do was to be sensitive to the fact that these boys were engaged in illegal acts and arrest them whenever there was some evidence that they had been involved. Whether or not the boys had in fact committed a particular act in a particular way was not especially important. The police had a broader view: their job was to stamp out these kids' crimes; the tactics were not as important as the end result.

Over the period that the group was under observation, each member was arrested at least once. Several of the boys were arrested a number of times and spent at least one night in jail. While most were never taken to court, two of the boys were sentenced to six months' incarceration in boys' schools.

The Roughnecks in School

The Roughnecks' behavior in school was not particularly disruptive. During school hours they did not all hang around together, but tended instead to spend most of their time with one or two other members of the gang who were their special buddies. Although every member of the gang attempted to avoid school as much as possible, they were not particularly successful and most of them attended school with surprising regularity. They considered school a burden—something to be gotten through with a minimum of conflict. If they were "bugged" by a particular teacher, it could lead to trouble. One of the boys, Al, once threatened to beat up a teacher and, according to the other boys, the teacher hid under a desk to escape him.

Teachers saw the boys the way the general community did, as heading for trouble, as being uninterested in making something of themselves. Some were also seen as being incapable of meeting the academic standards of the school. Most of the teachers expressed concern for this group of boys and were willing to pass them despite poor performance, in the belief that failing them would only aggravate the problem.

The group of boys had a grade point average just slightly above "C". No one in the group failed either grade, and no one had better than a "C" average. They were consistent in their achievement or, at least, the teachers were consistent in their perception of the boys' achievement.

Two of the boys were good football players. Herb was acknowledged to be the best player in the school and Jack was almost as good. Both boys were criticized for their failure to abide by training rules, for refusing to come to practice as often as they should, and for not playing their best during practice. What they lacked in sportsmanship they made up for in skill, apparently, and played every game no matter how poorly they had performed in practice or how many practice sessions they had missed.

Two Questions

Why did the community, the school and the police react to the Saints as though they were good, upstanding, nondelinquent youths with bright futures but to the Roughnecks as though they were tough, young criminals who were headed for trouble? Why did the Roughnecks and the Saints in fact have quite different careers after high school—careers which, by and large, lived up to the expectations of the community?

The most obvious explanation for the differences in the community's and law enforcement agencies' reactions to the two gangs is that one group of boys was "more delinquent" than the other. Which group *was* more delinquent? The answer to this question will determine in part how we explain the differential responses to these groups by the members of the community and, particularly, by law enforcement and school officials.

In sheer number of illegal acts, the Saints were the more delinquent. They were truant from school for at least part of the day almost every day of the week. In addition, their drinking and vandalism occurred with surprising regularity. The Roughnecks, in contrast, engaged sporadically in delinquent episodes. While these episodes were frequent, they certainly did not occur on a daily or even a weekly basis.

The difference in frequency of offenses was probably caused by the Roughnecks' inability to obtain liquor and to manipulate legitimate excuses from school. Since the Roughnecks had less money than the Saints, and teachers carefully supervised their school activities, the Roughnecks' hearts may have been as black as the Saints', but their misdeeds were not nearly as frequent.

There are really no clear-cut criteria by which to measure qualitative differences in antisocial behavior. The most important dimension of the difference is generally referred to as the "seriousness" of the offenses.

If seriousness encompasses the relative economic costs of delinquent acts, then some assessment can be made. The Roughnecks probably stole an average of about $5.00 worth of goods a week. Some weeks the figure was considerably higher, but these times must be balanced against long periods when almost nothing was stolen.

The Saints were more continuously engaged in delinquency but their acts were not for the most part costly to property. Only their vandalism and occasional theft of gasoline would so qualify. Perhaps once or twice a month they would siphon a tankful of gas. The other costly items were street signs, construction lanterns and the like. All of these acts combined probably did not quite average $5.00 a week, partly because much of the stolen equipment was abandoned and presumably could be recovered. The difference in cost of stolen property between the two groups was trivial, but the Roughnecks probably had a slightly more expensive set of activities than did the Saints.

Another meaning of seriousness is the potential threat of physical harm to members of the community and to the boys themselves. The Roughnecks were more prone to physical violence; they not only welcomed an opportunity to fight; they went seeking it. In addition, they fought among themselves frequently. Although the fighting never included deadly weapons, it was still a menace, however minor, to the physical safety of those involved.

The Saints never fought. They avoided physical conflict both inside and outside the group. At the same time, though, the Saints frequently endangered their own and other people's lives. They did so almost every time they drove a car, especially if they had been drinking. Sober, their driving was risky; under the influence of alcohol it was horrendous. In addition, the Saints endangered the lives of others with their pranks. Street excavations left unmarked were a very serious hazard.

Evaluating the relative seriousness of the two gangs' activities is difficult. The community reacted as though the behavior of the Roughnecks was a problem, and they reacted as though the behavior of the Saints was not. But the members of the community were ignorant of the array of delinquent acts that characterized the Saints' behavior. Although concerned citizens were unaware of much of the Roughnecks' behavior as well, they were much better informed about the Roughnecks' involvement in delinquency than they were about the Saints'.

Visibility

Differential treatment of the two gangs results in part because one gang was infinitely more visible than the other. This differential visibility was a direct function of the economic standing of the families. The Saints had access to automobiles and were able to remove themselves from the sight of the community. In as routine a decision as to where to go to have a milkshake after school, the Saints stayed away from the mainstream of community life. Lacking transportation, the Roughnecks could not make it to the edge of town. The center of town was the only practical place for them to meet since their homes were scattered throughout the town and any noncentral meeting place put an undue hardship on some members. Through necessity the Roughnecks congregated in a crowded area where everyone in the community passed frequently, including teachers and law enforcement officers. They could easily see the Roughnecks hanging around the drugstore.

The Roughnecks, of course, made themselves even more visible by making remarks to passersby and by occasionally getting into fights on the corner. Meanwhile, just as regularly, the Saints were either at the cafe on one edge of town or in the pool hall at the other edge of town. Without any particular realization that they were making themselves inconspicuous, the Saints were able to hide their time-wasting. Not only were they removed from the mainstream of traffic, but they were almost always inside a building.

On their escapades the Saints were also relatively invisible, since they left Hanibal and travelled to Big City. Here, too, they were mobile, roaming the city, rarely going to the same area twice.

Demeanor

To the notion of visibility must be added the difference in the responses of group members to outside intervention with their activities. If one of the Saints was confronted with an accusing policeman, even if he felt he was truly innocent of a wrongdoing, his demeanor was apologetic and penitent. A Roughneck's attitude was almost the polar opposite. When confronted with a threatening adult authority, even one who tried to be pleasant, the Roughneck's hostility and disdain were clearly observable. Sometimes he might attempt to put up a veneer of respect, but it was thin and was not accepted as sincere by the authority.

School was no different from the community at large. The Saints could manipulate the system by feigning compliance with the school norms. The availability of cars at school meant that once free from the immediate sight of the teacher, the boys could disappear rapidly. And this escape was well enough planned that no administrator or teacher was nearby when the boys left. A Roughneck who wished to escape for a few hours was in a bind. If it were possible to get free from class, downtown was still a mile away, and even if he arrived there, he was still very visible. Truancy for the Roughnecks meant almost certain detection, while the Saints enjoyed almost complete immunity from sanctions.

Bias

Community members were not aware of the transgressions of the Saints. Even if the Saints had been less discreet, their favorite delinquencies would have been perceived as less serious than those of the Roughnecks.

In the eyes of the police and school officials, a boy who drinks in an alley and stands intoxicated on the street corner is committing a more serious offense than is a boy who drinks to inebriation in a nightclub or a tavern and drives around afterwards in a car. Similarly, a boy who steals a wallet from a store will be viewed as having committed a more serious offense than a boy who steals a lantern from a construction site.

Perceptual bias also operates with respect to the demeanor of the boys in the two groups when they are confronted by adults. It is not simply that adults dislike the posture affected by boys of the Roughneck ilk; more important is the conviction that the posture adopted by the Roughnecks is an indication of their devotion and commitment to deviance as a way of life. The posture becomes a cue, just as the type of the offense is a cue, to the degree to which the known transgressions are indicators of the youths' potential for other problems.

Visibility, demeanor and bias are surface variables which explain the day-to-day operations of the police. Why do these surface variables operate as they do? Why did the police choose to disregard the Saints' delinquencies while breathing down the backs of the Roughnecks?

The answer lies in the class structure of American society and the control of legal institutions by those at the top of the class structure. Obviously, no representative of the upper class drew up the operational chart for the police which led them to look in the ghettoes and on streetcorners—which led them to see the demeanor of lower-class youth as troublesome and that of upper-middle-class youth as tolerable. Rather, the procedures simply developed from experience—experience with irate and influential upper-middle-class parents insisting that their son's vandalism was simply a prank and his drunkenness only a momentary "sowing of wild oats"—experience with cooperative or indifferent, powerless, lower-class parents who acquiesced to the law's definition of their son's behavior.

Adult Careers of the Saints and the Roughnecks

The community's confidence in the potential of the Saints and the Roughnecks apparently was justified. If anything, the community members underestimated the degree to which these youngsters would turn out "good" or "bad."

Seven of the eight members of the Saints went on to college immediately after high school. Five of the boys graduated from college in four years. The sixth one finished college after two years in the army, and the seventh spent fours years in the air force before returning to college and receiving a B.A. degree. Of these seven college graduates, three went on for advanced degrees. One finished law school and is now active in state politics, one finished medical school and is practicing near Hanibal, and one boy is now working for a Ph.D. The other four college graduates entered submanagerial, managerial or executive training positions with larger firms.

The only Saint who did not complete college was Jerry. Jerry had failed to graduate from high school with the other Saints. During his second senior year, after the other Saints had gone on to college, Jerry began to hang around with what several teachers described as a "rough crowd"—the gang that was heir apparent to the Roughnecks. At the end of his second senior year, when he did graduate from high school, Jerry took a job as a used-car salesman, got married and quickly had a child. Although he made several abortive attempts to go to college by attending night school, when I last saw him (ten years after high school) Jerry was unemployed and had been living on unemployment for almost a year. His wife worked as a waitress.

Some of the Roughnecks have lived up to community expectations. A number of them were headed for trouble. A few were not.

Jack and Herb were the athletes among the Roughnecks and their athletic prowess paid off handsomely. Both boys received unsolicited athletic scholarships to college. After Herb received his scholarship (near the end of his senior year), he apparently did an about-face. His demeanor became very similar to that of the Saints. Although he remained a member in good standing of the Roughnecks, he stopped participating in most activities and did not hang on the corner as often.

Jack did not change. If anything, he became more prone to fighting. He even made excuses for accepting the scholarship. He told the gang members that the school had guaranteed him a "C" average if he would come to play football—an idea that seems far-fetched, even in this day of highly competitive recruiting.

During the summer after graduation from high school, Jack attempted suicide by jumping from a tall building. The jump would certainly have killed most people trying it, but Jack survived. He entered college in the fall and played four years of football. He and Herb graduated in four years, and both are teaching and coaching in high schools. They are married and have stable families. If anything, Jack appears to have a more prestigious position in the community than does Herb, though both are well respected and secure in their positions.

Two of the boys never finished high school. Tommy left at the end of his junior year and went to another state. That summer he was arrested and placed on probation on a manslaughter charge. Three years later he was arrested for murder; he pleaded guilty to second degree murder and is serving a 30-year sentence in the state penitentiary.

Al, the other boy who did not finish high school, also left the state in his senior year. He is serving a life sentence in a state penitentiary for first degree murder.

Wes is a small-time gambler. He finished high school and "bummed around." After several years he made contact with a bookmaker who employed him as runner. Later he acquired his own area and has been working it ever since. His position among the bookmakers is almost identical to the position he had in the gang; he is always around but no one is really aware of him. He makes no trouble and he does not get into any. Steady, reliable, capable of keeping his mouth closed, he plays the game by the rules, even though the game is an illegal one.

That leaves only Ron. Some of his former friends reported that they had heard he was "driving a truck up north," but no one could provide any concrete information.

Reinforcement

The community responded to the Roughnecks as boys in trouble, and the boys agreed with that perception. Their pattern of deviancy was reinforced, and breaking away from it became increasingly unlikely. Once the boys acquired an image of themselves as deviants, they selected new friends who affirmed that self-image. As that self-conception became more firmly entrenched, they also became willing to try new and more extreme deviances. With their growing alienation came freer expression of disrespect and hostility for representatives of the legitimate society. This disrespect increased the community's negativism, perpetuating the entire process of commitment to deviance. Lack of a commitment to deviance works the same way. In either case, the process will perpetuate itself unless some event (like a scholarship to college or a sudden failure) external to the established relationship intervenes. For two of the Roughnecks (Herb and Jack), receiving college athletic scholarships created new relations and culminated in a break with the established pattern of deviance. In the case of one of the Saints (Jerry), his parents' divorce and his failing to graduate from high school changed some of his other relations. Being held back in school for a year and losing his place among the Saints had sufficient impact on Jerry to alter his self-image and virtually to assure that he would not go on to college as his peers did. Although the experiments of life can rarely be reversed, it seems likely in view of the behavior of the other boys who did not enjoy this special treatment by the school that Jerry, too, would have "become something" had he graduated as anticipated. For Herb and Jack outside intervention worked to their advantage; for Jerry it was his undoing.

Selective perception and labelling—finding, processing and punishing some kinds of criminality and not others—means that visible, poor, nonmobile, outspoken, undiplomatic "tough" kids will be noticed, whether their actions are seriously delinquent or not. Other kids, who have established a reputation for being bright (even though underachieving), disciplined and involved in respectable activities, who are mobile and monied, will be invisible when they deviate from sanctioned activities. They'll sow their wild oats—perhaps even wider and thicker than their lower-class cohorts—but they won't be noticed. When it's time to leave adolescence most will follow the expected path, settling into the ways of the middle class, remembering fondly the delinquent but unnoticed fling of their youth. The Roughnecks and others like them may turn around, too. It is more likely that their noticeable deviance will have been so reinforced by police and community that their lives will be effectively channelled into careers consistent with their adolescent background.

Questions

1. Why were the Saints seen as good boys and the Roughnecks seen as bad boys?

2. The conventional wisdom is that criminals are different from noncriminals, that bad things are done by bad people. To what extent does the information presented in Chambliss's article contradict the conventional wisdom?

3. In what specific way did differences in social class (for example, economic resources and cultural capital) contribute to the community's different treatment of and regard for the Saints and the Roughnecks?

4. What evidence do you find in this article that supports Merton's ideas about the self-fulfilling prophecy? What evidence seems to contradict it?

·29·

On Being Sane in Insane Places

D. L. Rosenhan

Although the following selection was written by a professor of psychology and law at Stanford University, it seems that everyone who publishes a reader for introductory sociology students includes this 1973 article (obviously, including me). There's a reason. Rosenhan's exploration of what happens to sane people in mental hospitals contains some important lessons about the impact of people's definition of the situation—especially the impact of the definitions of people in authority.

If sanity and insanity exist, how shall we know them?

The question is neither capricious nor itself insane. However much we may be personally convinced that we can tell the normal from the abnormal, the evidence is simply not compelling. It is commonplace, for example, to read about murder trials wherein eminent psychiatrists for the defense are contradicted by equally eminent psychiatrists for the prosecution on the matter of the defendant's sanity. More generally, there are a great deal of conflicting data on the reliability, utility, and meaning of such terms as "sanity," "insanity," "mental illness," and "schizophrenia." Finally, as early as 1934, Benedict suggested that normality and abnormality are not universal. What is viewed as normal in one culture may be seen as quite aberrant in another. Thus, notions of normality and abnormality may not be quite as accurate as people believe they are.

To raise questions regarding normality and abnormality is in no way to question the fact that some behaviors are deviant or odd. Murder

is deviant. So, too, are hallucinations. Nor does raising such questions deny the existence of the personal anguish that is often associated with "mental illness." Anxiety and depression exist. Psychological suffering exists. But normality and abnormality, sanity and insanity, and the diagnoses that flow from them may be less substantive than many believe them to be.

At its heart, the question of whether the sane can be distinguished from the insane (and whether degrees of insanity can be distinguished from each other) is a simple matter: do the salient characteristics that lead to diagnoses reside in the patients themselves or in the environments and contexts in which observers find them? From Bleuler[1] through the

---

[1] Paul Eugen Bleuler (1857–1939) was a Swiss psychiatrist who, in 1911, introduced the term *schizophrenia* (from the Greek *shizo*, "split or cleave," and *phren*, "mind") to refer to a form of dementia (madness). Today, schizophrenia refers to a general pathology characterized by disturbance of thinking, mood, and behavior (including inappropriate emotional responses and lack of empathy), and sometimes hallucinations and delusions. It is thought to afflict more than 2 million Americans, and "about half of the available hospital beds for the mentally ill (or about one-quarter of available beds in all U.S. hospitals) are occupied by patients diagnosed as schizophrenic" (Philip M. Groves and George V. Rebec, *Introduction to Biological Psychology*. [Dubuque, IA: Brown, 1988], p. 479). —Ed.

formulators of the recently revised *Diagnostic and Statistical Manual* of the American Psychiatric Association, the belief has been strong that patients present symptoms, that those symptoms can be categorized, and, implicitly, that the sane are distinguishable from the insane. More recently, however, this belief has been questioned. Based in part on theoretical and anthropological considerations, but also on philosophical, legal, and therapeutic ones, the view has grown that psychological categorization of mental illness is useless at best and downright harmful, misleading, and pejorative at worst. Psychiatric diagnoses, in this view, are in the minds of the observers and are not valid summaries of characteristics displayed by the observed.

Gains can be made in deciding which of these is more nearly accurate by getting normal people (that is, people who do not have, and have never suffered, symptoms of serious psychiatric disorders) admitted to psychiatric hospitals and then determining whether they were discovered to be sane and, if so, how. If the sanity of such pseudopatients were always detected, there would be prima facie[2] evidence that a sane individual can be distinguished from the insane context in which he is found. Normality (and presumably abnormality) is distinct enough that it can be recognized wherever it occurs, for it is carried within the person. If, on the other hand, the sanity of the pseudopatients were never discovered, serious difficulties would arise for those who support traditional modes of psychiatric diagnosis. Given that the hospital staff was not incompetent, that the pseudopatient had been behaving as sanely as he had been outside of the hospital, and that it had never been previously suggested that he belonged in a psychiatric hospital, such an unlikely outcome would support the view that psychiatric diagnosis betrays little about the patient but much about the environment in which an observer finds him.

This article describes such an experiment. Eight sane people gained secret admission to 12 different hospitals. . . .

Pseudopatients and Their Settings

The eight pseudopatients were a varied group. One was a psychology graduate student in his 20's. The remaining seven were older and "established." Among them were three psychologists, a pediatrician, a psychiatrist, a painter, and a housewife. Three pseudopatients were women, five were men. All of them employed pseudonyms, lest their alleged diagnoses embarrass them later. Those who were in mental health professions alleged another occupation in order to avoid the special attentions that might be accorded by staff, as a matter of courtesy or caution, to ailing colleagues. With the exception of myself (I was the first pseudopatient and my presence was known to the hospital administrator and chief psychologist and, so far as I can tell, to them alone), the presence of pseudopatients and the nature of the research program was not known to the hospital staffs.

The settings were similarly varied. In order to generalize the findings, admission into a variety of hospitals was sought. The 12 hospitals in the sample were located in five different states on the East and West coasts. Some were old and shabby, some were quite new. Some were research-oriented, others not. Some had good staff–patient ratios, others were quite understaffed. Only one was a strictly private hospital. All of the others were supported by state or federal funds or, in one instance, by university funds.

After calling the hospital for an appointment, the pseudopatient arrived at the admissions office complaining that he had been

---

[2]*Prima facie*, from the Latin, means "at first sight." Prima facie evidence of something is regarded as apparently valid evidence.—Ed.

hearing voices. Asked what the voices said, he replied that they were often unclear, but as far as he could tell they said "empty," "hollow," and "thud." The voices were unfamiliar and were of the same sex as the pseudopatient. The choice of these symptoms was occasioned by their apparent similarity to existential symptoms. Such symptoms are alleged to arise from painful concerns about the perceived meaninglessness of one's life. It is as if the hallucinating person were saying, "My life is empty and hollow." The choice of these symptoms was also determined by the *absence* of a single report of existential psychoses in the literature.

Beyond alleging the symptoms and falsifying name, vocation, and employment, no further alterations of person, history, or circumstances were made. The significant events of the pseudopatient's life history were presented as they had actually occurred. Relationships with parents and siblings, with spouse and children, with people at work and in school, consistent with the aforementioned exceptions, were described as they were or had been. Frustrations and upsets were described along with joys and satisfactions. These facts are important to remember. If anything, they strongly biased the subsequent results in favor of detecting sanity, since none of their histories or current behaviors were seriously pathological in any way.

Immediately upon admission to the psychiatric ward, the pseudopatient ceased simulating *any* symptoms of abnormality. In some cases, there was a brief period of mild nervousness and anxiety, since none of the pseudopatients really believed that they would be admitted so easily. Indeed, their shared fear was that they would be immediately exposed as frauds and greatly embarrassed. Moreover, many of them had never visited a psychiatric ward; even those who had, nevertheless had some genuine fears about what might happen to them. Their nervousness, then, was quite appropriate to the novelty of the hospital setting, and it abated rapidly.

Apart from that short-lived nervousness, the pseudopatient behaved on the ward as he "normally" behaved. The pseudopatient spoke to patients and staff as he might ordinarily. Because there is uncommonly little to do on a psychiatric ward, he attempted to engage others in conversation. When asked by staff how he was feeling, he indicated that he was fine, that he no longer experienced symptoms. He responded to instructions from attendants, to calls for medication (which was not swallowed),[3] and to dining-hall instructions. Beyond such activities as were available to him on the admissions ward, he spent his time writing down his observations about the ward, its patients, and the staff. Initially these notes were written "secretly," but as it soon became clear that no one much cared, they were subsequently written on standard tablets of paper in such public places as the dayroom. No secret was made of these activities.

The pseudopatient, very much as a true psychiatric patient, entered a hospital with no foreknowledge of when he would be discharged. Each was told that he would have to get out by his own devices, essentially by convincing the staff that he was sane. The psychological stresses associated with hospitalization were considerable, and all but one of the pseudopatients desired to be discharged almost immediately after being admitted. They were, therefore, motivated not only to behave

---

[3]In part of the article not included in this excerpt, Rosenhan notes that over the course of their hospitalization, "the pseudopatients were administered nearly 2100 pills, including Elavil, Stelazine, Compazine, and Thorazine, to name a few. (That such a variety of medications should have been administered to patients presenting identical symptoms is itself worthy of note.) Only two were swallowed. The rest were either pocketed or deposited in the toilet. The pseudopatients were not alone in this. Although I have no precise records on how many patients rejected their medications, the pseudopatients frequently found the medications of other patients in the toilets before they deposited their own. As long as they were cooperative, their behavior and the pseudopatients' own in this matter, as in other important matters, went unnoticed throughout." —Ed.

sanely, but to be paragons of cooperation. That their behavior was in no way disruptive is confirmed by nursing reports, which have been obtained on most of the patients. These reports uniformly indicate that the patients were "friendly," "cooperative," and "exhibited no abnormal indications."

The Normal Are Not Detectably Sane

Despite their public "show" of sanity, the pseudopatients were never detected. Admitted, except in one case, with a diagnosis of schizophrenia, each was discharged with a diagnosis of schizophrenia "in remission." The label "in remission" should in no way be dismissed as a formality, for at no time during any hospitalization had any question been raised about any pseudopatient's simulation. Nor are there any indications in the hospital records that the pseudopatient's status was suspect. Rather, the evidence is strong that, once labeled schizophrenic, the pseudopatient was stuck with that label. If the pseudopatient was to be discharged, he must naturally be "in remission"; but he was not sane, nor, in the institution's view, had he ever been sane.

The uniform failure to recognize sanity cannot be attributed to the quality of the hospitals, for, although there were considerable variations among them, several are considered excellent. Nor can it be alleged that there was simply not enough time to observe the pseudopatients. Length of hospitalization ranged from 7 to 52 days, with an average of 19 days. The pseudopatients were not, in fact, carefully observed, but this failure clearly speaks more to traditions within psychiatric hospitals than to lack of opportunity.

Finally, it cannot be said that the failure to recognize the pseudopatients' sanity was due to the fact that they were not behaving sanely. While there was clearly some tension present in all of them, their daily visitors could detect no serious behavioral consequences—nor, indeed, could other patients. It was quite common for the patients to "detect" the pseudopatients' sanity. During the first three hospitalizations, when accurate counts were kept, 35 of a total of 118 patients on the admissions ward voiced their suspicions, some vigorously. "You're not crazy. You're a journalist, or a professor [referring to the continual note-taking]. You're checking up on the hospital." While most of the patients were reassured by the pseudopatient's insistence that he had been sick before he came in but was fine now, some continued to believe that the pseudopatient was sane throughout his hospitalization. The fact that the patients often recognized normality when staff did not raises important questions.

Failure to detect sanity during the course of hospitalization may be due to the fact that physicians . . . are more inclined to call a healthy person sick (a false positive) than a sick person healthy (a false negative). The reasons for this are not hard to find: it is clearly more dangerous to misdiagnose illness than health. Better to err on the side of caution, to suspect illness even among the healthy.

But what holds for medicine does not hold equally well for psychiatry. Medical illnesses, while unfortunate, are not commonly pejorative. Psychiatric diagnoses, on the contrary, carry with them personal, legal, and social stigmas. It was therefore important to see whether the tendency toward diagnosing the sane insane could be reversed. The following experiment was arranged at a research and teaching hospital whose staff had heard these findings but doubted that such an error could occur in their hospital. The staff was informed that at some time during the following 3 months, one or more pseudopatients would attempt to be admitted into the psychiatric hospital. Each staff member was asked to rate each patient who presented himself at admissions or on the ward according to the likelihood that the patient was a pseudopatient. A 10-point scale was used, with a 1 and 2 reflecting high confidence that the patient was a pseudopatient.

Judgments were obtained on 193 patients who were admitted for psychiatric treatment. All staff who had had sustained contact with or primary responsibility for the patient—attendants, nurses, psychiatrists, physicians, and psychologists—were asked to make judgments. Forty-one patients were alleged, with high confidence, to be pseudopatients by at least one member of the staff. Twenty-three were considered suspect by at least one psychiatrist. Nineteen were suspected by one psychiatrist *and* one other staff member. Actually, no genuine pseudopatient (at least from my group) presented himself during this period.

The experiment is instructive. It indicates that the tendency to designate sane people as insane can be reversed when the stakes (in this case, prestige and diagnostic acumen) are high. But what can be said of the 19 people who were suspected of being "sane" by one psychiatrist and another staff member? Were these people truly "sane," or was it rather the case that in the course of avoiding the false positive error the staff tended to make more errors of the false negative sort—calling the crazy "sane"? There is no way of knowing. But one thing is certain: any diagnostic process that lends itself so readily to massive errors of this sort cannot be a very reliable one.

The Stickiness of Psychodiagnostic Labels

Beyond the tendency to call the healthy sick—a tendency that accounts better for diagnostic behavior on admission than it does for such behavior after a lengthy period of exposure—the data speak to the massive role of labeling in psychiatric assessment. Having once been labeled schizophrenic, there is nothing the pseudopatient can do to overcome the tag. The tag profoundly colors others' perceptions of him and his behavior.

From one viewpoint, these data are hardly surprising, for it has long been known that elements are given meaning by the context in which they occur. Gestalt psychology made this point vigorously, and Asch demonstrated that there are "central" personality traits (such as "warm" versus "cold") which are so powerful that they markedly color the meaning of other information in forming an impression of a given personality. "Insane," "schizophrenic," "manic-depressive," and "crazy" are probably among the most powerful of such central traits. Once a person is designated abnormal, all of his other behaviors and characteristics are colored by that label. Indeed, that label is so powerful that many of the pseudopatients' normal behaviors were overlooked entirely or profoundly misinterpreted. Some examples may clarify this issue.

Earlier I indicated that there were no changes in the pseudopatient's personal history and current status beyond those of name, employment, and, where necessary, vocation. Otherwise, a veridical description of personal history and circumstances was offered. Those circumstances were not psychotic. How were they made consonant with the diagnosis of psychosis? Or were those diagnoses modified in such a way as to bring them into accord with the circumstances of the pseudopatient's life, as described by him?

As far as I can determine, diagnoses were in no way affected by the relative health of the circumstances of a pseudopatient's life. Rather, the reverse occurred: the perception of his circumstances was shaped entirely by the diagnosis. A clear example of such translation is found in the case of a pseudopatient who had had a close relationship with his mother but was rather remote from his father during his early childhood. During adolescence and beyond, however, his father became a close friend, while his relationship with his mother cooled. His present relationship with his wife was characteristically close and warm. Apart from occasional angry exchanges, friction was minimal. The children had rarely been spanked. Surely there is nothing especially pathological about such a history. Indeed, many readers may see a similar pattern in their own experiences with no markedly deleterious consequences. Observe, however, how such a history was translated in the psychopathological context, this from the case summary prepared after the patient was discharged.

> This white 39-year-old male . . . manifests a long history of considerable ambivalence in close relationships, which begins in early childhood. A warm relationship with his mother cools during his adolescence. A distant relationship to his father is described as becoming very intense. Affective[4] stability is absent. His attempts to control emotionality with his wife and children are punctuated by angry outbursts and, in the case of the children, spankings. And while he says that he has several good friends, one senses considerable ambivalence embedded in those relationships also. . . .

The facts of the case were unintentionally distorted by the staff to achieve consistency with a popular theory of the dynamics of a schizophrenic reaction. Nothing of an ambivalent nature had been described in relations with parents, spouse, or friends. To the extent that ambivalence could be inferred, it was probably not greater than is found in all human relationships. It is true the pseudopatient's relationships with his parents changed over time, but in the ordinary context that would hardly be remarkable — indeed, it might very well be expected. Clearly, the meaning ascribed to his verbalizations (that is, ambivalence, affective instability) was determined by the diagnosis: schizophrenia. An entirely different meaning would have been ascribed if it were known that the man was "normal."

All pseudopatients took extensive notes publicly. Under ordinary circumstances, such behavior would have raised questions in the minds of observers, as, in fact, it did among patients. Indeed, it seemed so certain that the notes would elicit suspicion that elaborate precautions were taken to remove them from the ward each day. But the precautions proved needless. The closest any staff member came to questioning these notes occurred when one pseudopatient asked his physician what kind of medication he was receiving and began to write down the response. "You needn't write it," he was told gently. "If you have trouble remembering, just ask me again."

If no questions were asked of the pseudopatients, how was their writing interpreted? Nursing records for three patients indicate that the writing was seen as an aspect of their pathological behavior. "Patient engages in writing behavior" was the daily nursing comment on one of the pseudopatients who was never questioned about his writing. Given that the patient is in the hospital, he must be psychologically disturbed. And given that he is disturbed, continuous writing must be a behavioral manifestation of that disturbance, perhaps a subset of the compulsive behaviors that are sometimes correlated with schizophrenia.

One tacit characteristic of psychiatric diagnosis is that it locates the sources of aberration within the individual and only rarely within the complex of stimuli that surrounds him. Consequently, behaviors that are stimulated by the environment are commonly misattributed to the patient's disorder. For example, one kindly nurse found a pseudopatient pacing the long hospital corridors. "Nervous, Mr. X?" she asked. "No, bored," he said.

The notes kept by pseudopatients are full of patient behaviors that were misinterpreted by well-intentioned staff. Often enough, a patient would go "berserk" because he had, wittingly or unwittingly, been mistreated by, say, an attendant. A nurse coming upon the scene

---

[4]*Affective* means "emotional." —Ed.

would rarely inquire even cursorily into the environmental stimuli of the patient's behavior. Rather, she assumed that his upset derived from his pathology, not from his present interactions with other staff members. Occasionally, the staff might assume that the patient's family (especially when they had recently visited) or other patients had stimulated the outburst. But never were the staff found to assume that one of themselves or the structure of the hospital had anything to do with a patient's behavior. One psychiatrist pointed to a group of patients who were sitting outside the cafeteria entrance half an hour before lunchtime. To a group of young residents he indicated that such behavior was characteristic of the oral-acquisitive nature of the syndrome. It seemed not to occur to him that there were very few things to anticipate in a psychiatric hospital besides eating.

A psychiatric label has a life and an influence of its own. Once the impression has been formed that the patient is schizophrenic, the expectation is that he will continue to be schizophrenic. When a sufficient amount of time has passed, during which the patient has done nothing bizarre, he is considered to be in remission and available for discharge. But the label endures beyond discharge, with the unconfirmed expectation that he will behave as a schizophrenic again. Such labels, conferred by mental health professionals, are as influential on the patient as they are on his relatives and friends, and it should not surprise anyone that the diagnosis acts on all of them as a self-fulfilling prophecy.[5] Eventually, the patient himself accepts the diagnosis, with all of its surplus meanings and expectations, and behaves accordingly.

The inferences to be made from these matters are quite simple. Much as Zigler and Phillips have demonstrated that there is enormous

overlap in the symptoms presented by patients who have been variously diagnosed, so there is enormous overlap in the behaviors of the sane and the insane. The sane are not "sane" all of the time. We lose our tempers "for no good reason." We are occasionally depressed or anxious, again for no good reason. And we may find it difficult to get along with one or another person—again for no reason that we can specify. Similarly, the insane are not always insane. Indeed, it was the impression of the pseudopatients while living with them that they were sane for long periods of time—that the bizarre behaviors upon which their diagnoses were allegedly predicated constituted only a small fraction of their total behavior. . . .

The Consequences of Labeling and Depersonalization

Whenever the ratio of what is known to what needs to be known approaches zero, we tend to invent "knowledge" and assume that we understand more than we actually do. We seem unable to acknowledge that we simply don't know. The needs for diagnosis and remediation of behavioral and emotional problems are enormous. But rather than acknowledge that we are just embarking on understanding, we continue to label patients "schizophrenic," "manic-depressive," and "insane," as if in those words we had captured the essence of understanding. The facts of the matter are that we have known for a long time that diagnoses are often not useful or reliable, but we have nevertheless continued to use them. We now know that we cannot distinguish insanity from sanity. It is depressing to consider how that information will be used.

Not merely depressing, but frightening. How many people, one wonders, are sane but not recognized as such in our psychiatric institutions? How many have been needlessly stripped of their privileges of citizenship, from

---

[5]See the introductory notes to reading 28, "The Saints and the Roughnecks," for an explanation of this concept. — Ed.

the right to vote and drive to that of handling their own accounts? How many have feigned insanity in order to avoid the criminal consequences of their behavior, and, conversely, how many would rather stand trial than live interminably in a psychiatric hospital—but are wrongly thought to be mentally ill? How many have been stigmatized by well-intentioned, but nevertheless erroneous, diagnoses? On the last point, recall again that a false positive error in psychiatric diagnosis does not have the same consequences it does in medical diagnosis. A diagnosis of cancer that has been found to be in error is cause for celebration. But psychiatric diagnoses are rarely found to be in error. The label sticks, a mark of inadequacy forever. . . .

Questions

1. With which of the following statements would Rosenhan agree, and why?
   a. In this study, the symptoms observed by the psychiatric staff led to the diagnosis.
   b. In this study, the diagnosis led to the symptoms observed by the psychiatric staff.

2. What might be the significance of the fact that many *patients* managed to detect pseudopatients while none of the staff did?

3. Why does a false diagnosis of mental illness generally have more serious repercussions than a false diagnosis of physical illness?

Fraternities and Collegiate Rape Culture
Why Are Some Fraternities More Dangerous Places for Women?

A. Ayres Boswell and Joan Z. Spade

In the mid-1980s, social scientific researchers began to identify college fraternities as places where women were in special jeopardy of being raped. In 1985, for example, Julie Ehrhart and Bernice Sandler published a study titled "Campus Gang Rape: Party Games?" (in the Association of American Colleges, *Project on the Status and Education of Women*). In 1989, Patricia Martin and Robert Hummer published their study, "Fraternities and Rape on Campus," in which they concluded that "the organization and membership of fraternities contribute heavily to coercive and often violent sex. . . . Brotherhood norms require 'sticking together' regardless of right or wrong; thus rape episodes are unlikely to be stopped or reported to outsiders, even when witnesses disapprove" (*Gender and Society*, December). In 1990, anthropologist Peggy Reeves Sanday published *Fraternity Gang Rape: Sex, Brotherhood, and Privilege on Campus*, in which she described her research finding that in many fraternities, gang rape was practiced as a "male bonding ritual."

The conclusion was building that fraternities were places in which a "rape culture" prevailed. In their 1996 study, A. Ayres Boswell and Joan Spade report that although fraternities can be dangerous places for women, some are more dangerous than others. Their findings bolster the sociological theory that it is not the members of the fraternity, but rather the social structure of the fraternity, that makes the difference.

Date rape and acquaintance rape on college campuses are topics of concern to both researchers and college administrators. Some estimate that 60 to 80 percent of rapes are date or acquaintance rape (Koss et al. 1988). Further, 1 out of 4 college women say they were raped or experienced an attempted rape, and 1 out of 12 college men say they forced a woman to have sexual intercourse against her will (Koss, Gidycz, and Wisniewski 1985).

"Fraternities and Collegiate Rape Culture: Why Are Some Fraternities More Dangerous Places for Women?" by A. Ayres Boswell and Joan Z. Spade from *Gender & Society*, Vol. 10 (2), April 1996: pp. 133–147. Copyright © 1996 by Sage Publications, Inc. Reprinted by permission of Sage Publications, Inc.

Although considerable attention focuses on the incidence of rape, we know relatively little about the context or the *rape culture* surrounding date and acquaintance rape. Rape culture is a set of values and beliefs that provide an environment conducive to rape (Buchwald, Fletcher, and Roth 1993; Herman 1984). The term applies to a generic culture surrounding and promoting rape, not the specific settings in which rape is likely to occur. We believe that the specific settings also are important in defining relationships between men and women.

Some have argued that fraternities are places where rape is likely to occur on college campuses (Martin and Hummer 1989; O'Sullivan 1993; Sanday 1990) and that the students most likely to accept rape myths and be more sexually aggressive are more likely to live in fraternities and sororities, consume higher doses of alcohol and drugs, and place a higher value on social life at college (Gwartney-Gibbs and Stockard 1989; Kalof and Cargill 1991). Others suggest that sexual aggression is learned in settings such as fraternities and is not part of predispositions or preexisting attitudes (Boeringer, Shehan, and Akers 1991). To prevent further incidences of rape on college campuses, we need to understand what it is about fraternities in particular and college life in general that may contribute to the maintenance of a rape culture on college campuses.

Our approach is to identify the social contexts that link fraternities to campus rape and promote a rape culture. Instead of assuming that all fraternities provide an environment conducive to rape, we compare the interactions of men and women at fraternities identified on campus as being especially *dangerous* places for women, where the likelihood of rape is high, to those seen as *safer* places, where the perceived probability of rape occurring is lower. Prior to collecting data for our study, we found that most women students identified some fraternities as having more sexually aggressive members and a higher probability of

rape. These women also considered other fraternities as relatively safe houses, where a woman could go and get drunk if she wanted to and feel secure that the fraternity men would not take advantage of her. We compared parties at houses identified as high-risk and low-risk houses as well as at two local bars frequented by college students. Our analysis provides an opportunity to examine situations and contexts that hinder or facilitate positive social relations between undergraduate men and women.

The abusive attitudes toward women that some fraternities perpetuate exist within a general culture where rape is intertwined in traditional gender scripts. Men are viewed as initiators of sex and women as either passive partners or active resisters, preventing men from touching their bodies (LaPlante, McCormick, and Brannigan 1980). Rape culture is based on the assumptions that men are aggressive and dominant whereas women are passive and acquiescent (Buchwald et al. 1993; Herman 1984). What occurs on college campuses is an extension of the portrayal of domination and aggression of men over women that exemplifies the double standard of sexual behavior in U.S. society (Barthel 1988; Kimmel 1993).

Sexually active men are positively reinforced by being referred to as "studs," whereas women who are sexually active or report enjoying sex are derogatorily labeled as "sluts" (Herman 1984; O'Sullivan 1993). These gender scripts are embodied in rape myths and stereotypes such as "She really wanted it; she just said no because she didn't want me to think she was a bad girl" (Burke, Stets, and Pirog-Good 1989; Jenkins and Dambrot 1987; Lisak and Roth 1988; Malamuth 1986; Muehlenhard and Linton 1987; Peterson and Franzese 1987). Because men's sexuality is seen as more natural, acceptable, and uncontrollable than women's sexuality, many men and women excuse acquaintance rape by affirming that men cannot control their natural urges (Miller and Marshall 1987).

Whereas some researchers explain these attitudes toward sexuality and rape using an individual or a psychological interpretation, we argue that rape has a social basis, one in which both men and women create and re-create masculine and feminine identities and relations. Based on the assumption that rape is part of the social construction of gender, we examine how men and women "do gender" on a college campus (West and Zimmerman 1987). We focus on fraternities because they have been identified as settings that encourage rape (Sanday 1990). By comparing fraternities that are viewed by women as places where there is a high risk of rape to those where women believe there is a low risk of rape as well as two local commercial bars, we seek to identify characteristics that make some social settings more likely places for the occurrence of rape.

Method

We observed social interactions between men and women at a private coeducational school in which a high percentage (49.4 percent) of students affiliate with Greek organizations. The university has an undergraduate population of approximately 4,500 students, just more than one third of whom are women; the students are primarily from upper-middle-class families. The school, which admitted only men until 1971, is highly competitive academically.

We used a variety of data collection approaches: observations of interactions between men and women at fraternity parties and bars, formal interviews, and informal conversations. The first author, a former undergraduate at this school and a graduate student at the time of the study, collected the data. She knew about the social life at the school and had established rapport and trust between herself and undergraduate students as a teaching assistant in a human sexuality course.

The process of identifying high- and low-risk fraternity houses followed Hunter's (1953) reputational approach. In our study, 40 women students identified fraternities that they considered to be high risk, or to have more sexually aggressive members and higher incidence of rape, as well as fraternities that they considered to be safe houses. The women represented all four years of undergraduate college and different living groups (sororities, residence halls, and off-campus housing). Observations focused on the four fraternities named most often by these women as high-risk houses and the four identified as low-risk houses.

Throughout the spring semester, the first author observed at two fraternity parties each weekend at two different houses (fraternities could have parties only on weekends at this campus). She also observed students' interactions in two popular university bars on weeknights to provide a comparison of students' behavior in non-Greek settings. The first local bar at which she observed was popular with seniors and older students; the second bar was popular with first-, second-, and third-year undergraduates because the management did not strictly enforce drinking age laws in this bar.

The observer focused on the social context as well as interaction among participants at each setting. In terms of social context, she observed the following: ratio of men to women, physical setting such as the party decor and theme, use and control of alcohol and level of intoxication, and explicit and implicit norms. She noted interactions between men and women (i.e., physical contact, conversational style, use of jokes) and the relations among men (i.e., their treatment of pledges and other men at fraternity parties). Other than the observer, no one knew the identity of the high- or low-risk fraternities. Although this may have introduced bias into the data collection, students on this campus who read this article before it was submitted for publication commented on how accurately the social scene is described.

In addition, 50 individuals were interviewed including men from the selected fraternities, women who attended those parties, men not affiliated with fraternities, and self-identified rape victims known to the first author. The first author approached men and women by telephone or on campus and asked them to participate in interviews. The interviews included open-ended questions about gender relations on campus, attitudes about date rape, and their own experiences on campus.

To assess whether self-selection was a factor in determining the classification of the fraternity, we compared high-risk houses to low-risk houses on several characteristics. In terms of status on campus, the high- and low-risk houses we studied attracted about the same number of pledges; however, many of the high-risk houses had more members. There was no difference in grade point averages for the two types of houses. In fact, the highest and lowest grade point averages were found in the high-risk category. Although both high- and low-risk fraternities participated in sports, brothers in the low-risk houses tended to play intramural sports whereas brothers in the high-risk houses were more likely to be varsity athletes. The high-risk houses may be more aggressive, as they had a slightly larger number of disciplinary incidents and their reports were more severe, often with physical harm to others and damage to property. Further, in year-end reports, there was more property damage in the high-risk houses. Last, more of the low-risk houses participated in a campus rape-prevention program. In summary, both high- and low-risk fraternities seem to be equally attractive to freshmen men on this campus, and differences between the eight fraternities we studied were not great; however, the high-risk houses had a slightly larger number of reports of aggression and physical destruction in the houses and the low-risk houses were more likely to participate in a rape-prevention program.

Results

THE SETTINGS

Fraternity Parties   We observed several differences in the quality of the interaction of men and women at parties at high-risk fraternities compared to those at low-risk houses. A typical party at a low-risk house included an equal number of women and men. The social atmosphere was friendly, with considerable interaction between women and men. Men and women danced in groups and in couples, with many of the couples kissing and displaying affection toward each other. Brothers explained that, because many of the men in these houses had girlfriends, it was normal to see couples kissing on the dance floor. Coed groups engaged in conversations at many of these houses, with women and men engaging in friendly exchanges, giving the impression that they knew each other well. Almost no cursing and yelling was observed at parties in low-risk houses; when pushing occurred, the participants apologized. Respect for women extended to the women's bathrooms, which were clean and well supplied.

At high-risk houses, parties typically had skewed gender ratios, sometimes involving more men and other times involving more women. Gender segregation also was evident at these parties, with the men on one side of a room or in the bar drinking while women gathered in another area. Men treated women differently in the high-risk houses. The women's bathrooms in the high-risk houses were filthy, including clogged toilets and vomit in the sinks. When a brother was told of the mess in the bathroom at a high-risk house, he replied, "Good, maybe some of these beer wenches will leave so there will be more beer for us."

Men attending parties at high-risk houses treated women less respectfully, engaging in jokes, conversations, and behaviors that degraded women. Men made a display of assessing women's bodies and rated them with thumbs up or thumbs down for the other men in the sight of the women. One man attending a party at a high-risk fraternity said to another, "Did you know that this week is Women's Awareness Week? I guess that means we get to abuse them more this week." Men behaved more crudely at parties at high-risk houses. At one party, a brother dropped his pants, including his underwear, while dancing in front of several women. Another brother slid across the dance floor completely naked.

The atmosphere at parties in high-risk fraternities was less friendly overall. With the exception of greetings, men and women rarely smiled or laughed and spoke to each other less often than was the case at parties in low-risk houses. The few one-on-one conversations between women and men appeared to be strictly flirtatious (lots of eye contact, touching, and very close talking). It was rare to see a group of men and women together talking. Men were openly hostile, which made the high-risk parties seem almost threatening at times. For example, there was a lot of touching, pushing, profanity, and name calling, some done by women.

Students at parties at the high-risk houses seemed self-conscious and aware of the presence of members of the opposite sex, an awareness that was sexually charged. Dancing early in the evening was usually between women. Close to midnight, the sex ratio began to balance out with the arrival of more men or more women. Couples began to dance together but in a sexual way (close dancing with lots of pelvic thrusts). Men tried to pick up women using lines such as "Want to see my fish tank?" and "Let's go upstairs so that we can talk; I can't hear what you're saying in here."

Although many of the same people who attended high-risk parties also attended low-risk parties, their behavior changed as they moved from setting to setting. Group norms differed across contexts as well. At a party that was held jointly at a low-risk house with a high-risk fraternity, the ambience was that of a party at a high-risk fraternity with heavier drinking, less dancing, and fewer conversations between women and men. The men from both high- and low-risk fraternities were very aggressive; a fight broke out, and there was pushing and shoving on the dance floor and in general.

As others have found, fraternity brothers at high-risk houses on this campus told about routinely discussing their sexual exploits at breakfast the morning after parties and sometimes at house meetings (cf. Martin and Hummer 1989; O'Sullivan 1993; Sanday 1990). During these sessions, the brothers we interviewed said that men bragged about what they did the night before with stories of sexual conquests often told by the same men, usually sophomores. The women involved in these exploits were women they did not know or knew but did not respect, or *faceless victims*. Men usually treated girlfriends with respect and did not talk about them in these storytelling sessions. Men from low-risk houses, however, did not describe similar sessions in their houses.

The Bar Scene   The bar atmosphere and social context differed from those of fraternity parties. The music was not as loud, and both bars had places to sit and have conversations. At all fraternity parties, it was difficult to maintain conversations with loud music playing and no place to sit. The volume of music at parties at high-risk fraternities was even louder than it was at low-risk houses, making it virtually impossible to have conversations. In general, students in the local bars behaved in the same way that students did at parties in low-risk houses with conversations typical, most occurring between men and women.

The first bar, frequented by older students, had live entertainment every night of the week. Some nights were more crowded than others, and the atmosphere was friendly, relaxed, and conducive to conversation. People laughed and smiled and behaved politely toward each other. The ratio of men to women was fairly equal, with students congregating in mostly coed groups. Conversation flowed freely and people listened to each other.

Although the women and men at the first bar also were at parties at low- and high-risk fraternities, their behavior at the bar included none of the blatant sexual or intoxicated behaviors observed at some of these parties. As the evenings wore on, the number of one-on-one conversations between men and women increased and conversations shifted from small talk to topics such as war and AIDS. Conversations did not revolve around picking up another person, and most people left the bar with same-sex friends or in coed groups.

The second bar was less popular with older students. Younger students, often under the legal drinking age, went there to drink, sometimes after leaving campus parties. This bar was much smaller and usually not as crowded as the first bar. The atmosphere was more mellow and relaxed than it was at the fraternity parties. People went there to hang out and talk to each other.

On a couple of occasions, however, the atmosphere at the second bar became similar to that of a party at a high-risk fraternity. As the number of people in the bar increased, they removed chairs and tables, leaving no place to sit and talk. The music also was turned up louder, drowning out conversation. With no place to dance or sit, most people stood around but could not maintain conversations because of the noise and crowds. Interactions between women and men consisted mostly of flirting. Alcohol consumption also was greater than it was on the less crowded nights, and the number of visibly drunk people increased. The more people drank, the more conversation and socializing broke down. The only differences between this setting and that of a party at a high-risk house were that brothers no longer controlled the territory and bedrooms were not available upstairs.

GENDER RELATIONS

Relations between women and men are shaped by the contexts in which they meet and interact. As is the case on other college campuses, *hooking up* has replaced dating on this campus, and fraternities are places where many students hook up. Hooking up is a loosely applied term on college campuses that had different meaning for men and women on this campus.

Most men defined hooking up similarly. One man said it was something that happens

> when you are really drunk and meet up with a woman you sort of know, or possibly don't know at all and don't care about. You go home with her with the intention of getting as much sexual, physical pleasure as she'll give you, which can range anywhere from kissing to intercourse, without any strings attached.

The exception to this rule is when men hook up with women they admire. Men said they are less likely to press for sexual activity with someone they know and like because they want the relationship to continue and be based on respect.

Women's version of hooking up differed. Women said they hook up only with men they cared about and described hooking up as kissing and petting but not sexual intercourse. Many women said that hooking up was disappointing because they wanted longer-term relationships. First-year women students realized quickly that hook-ups were usually one-night stands with no strings attached, but many continued to hook up because they had few opportunities to develop relationships with men on campus. One first-year woman said that "70 percent of hook-ups never talk again and try to avoid one another; 26 percent may actually hear from them or talk to them again, and 4 percent may actually go on a date, which can lead to a relationship." Another first-year woman said, "It was fun in the beginning. You get a lot of attention and kiss a lot of boys and think this is what college is about, but it gets tiresome fast."

Whereas first-year women get tired of the hook-up scene early on, many men do not become bored with it until their junior or senior year. As one upperclassman said, "The whole game of hooking up became really meaningless and tiresome for me during my second semester of my sophomore year, but most of my friends didn't get bored with it until the following year."

In contrast to hooking up, students also described monogamous relationships with steady partners. Some type of commitment was expected, but most people did not anticipate marriage. The term *seeing each other* was applied when people were sexually involved but free to date other people. This type of relationship involved less commitment than did one of boyfriend/girlfriend but was not considered to be a hook-up.

The general consensus of women and men interviewed on this campus was that the Greek system, called "the hill," set the scene for gender relations. The predominance of Greek membership and subsequent living arrangements segregated men and women. During the week, little interaction occurred between women and men after their first year in college because students in fraternities or sororities live and dine in separate quarters. In addition, may non-Greek upper-class students move off campus into apartments. Therefore, students see each other in classes or in the library, but there is no place where students can just hang out together.

Both men and women said that fraternities dominate campus social life, a situation that everyone felt limited opportunities for meaningful interactions. One senior Greek man said,

This environment is horrible and so unhealthy for good male and female relationships and interactions to occur. It is so segregated and male dominated. . . . It is our party, with our rules and our beer. We are allowing these women and

other men to come to our party. Men can feel superior in their domain.

Comments from a senior woman reinforced his views: "Men are dominant; they are the kings of the campus. It is their environment that they allow us to enter; therefore, we have to abide by their rules." A junior woman described fraternity parties as

good for meeting acquaintances but almost impossible to really get to know anyone. The environment is so superficial, probably because there are so many social cliques due to the Greek system. Also, the music is too loud and the people are too drunk to attempt to have a real conversation anyway.

Some students claim that fraternities even control the dating relationships of their members. One senior woman said, "Guys dictate how dating occurs on this campus, whether it's cool, who it's with, how much time can be spent with the girlfriend and with the brothers." Couples either left campus for an evening or hung out separately with their own same-gender friends at fraternity parties, finally getting together with each other at about 2 A.M. Couples rarely went together to fraternity parties. Some men felt that a girlfriend was just a replacement for a hook-up. According to one junior man, "Basically a girlfriend is someone you go to at 2 A.M. after you've hung out with the guys. She is the sexual outlet that the guys can't provide you with."

Some fraternity brothers pressure each other to limit their time with and commitment to their girlfriends. One senior man said, "The hill [fraternities] and girlfriends don't mix." A brother described a constant battle between girlfriends and brothers over who the guy is going out with for the night, with the brothers usually winning. Brothers teased men with girlfriends with remarks such as "whipped" or "where's the ball and chain?" A brother from a high-risk house said that few brothers at his house had girlfriends; some did, but it was uncommon. One man said that from the minute he was a pledge he knew he would probably never have a girlfriend on this campus because "it was just not the norm in my house. No one has girlfriends; the guys have too much fun with [each other]."

The pressure on men to limit their commitment to girlfriends, however, was not true of all fraternities or of all men on campus. Couples attended low-risk fraternity parties together, and men in the low-risk houses went out on dates more often. A man in one low-risk house said that about 70 percent of the members of his house were involved in relationships with women, including the pledges (who were sophomores).

TREATMENT OF WOMEN

Not all men held negative attitudes toward women that are typical of a rape culture, and not all social contexts promoted the negative treatment of women. When men were asked whether they treated the women on campus with respect, the most common response was "On an individual basis, yes, but when you have a group of men together, no." Men said that, when together in groups with other men, they sensed a pressure to be disrespectful toward women. A first-year man's perception of the treatment of women was that "they are treated with more respect to their faces, but behind closed doors, with a group of men present, respect for women is not an issue." One senior man stated, "In general, college-aged men don't treat women their age with respect because 90 percent of them think of women as merely a means to sex." Women reinforced this perception. A first-year woman stated, "Men here are more interested in hooking up and drinking beer than they are in getting to know women as real people." Another woman said, "Men here use and abuse women."

Characteristic of rape culture, a double standard of sexual behavior for men versus women was prevalent on this campus. As one Greek senior man stated, "Women who sleep around are sluts and get bad reputations; men who do are champions and get a pat on the back from their brothers." Women also supported a double standard for sexual behavior by criticizing sexually active women. A first-year woman spoke out against women who are sexually active: "I think some girls here make it difficult for the men to respect women as a whole."

One concrete example of demeaning sexually active women on this campus is the "walk of shame." Fraternity brothers come out on the porches of their houses the night after parties and heckle women walking by. It is assumed that these women spent the night at fraternity houses and that the men they were with did not care enough about them to drive them home. Although sororities now reside in former fraternity houses, this practice continues and sometimes the victims of hecklings are sorority women on their way to study in the library.

A junior man in a high-risk fraternity described another ritual of disrespect toward women called "chatter." When an unknown woman sleeps over at the house, the brothers yell degrading remarks out the window at her as she leaves the next morning such as "Fuck that bitch" and "Who is that slut?" He said that sometimes brothers harass the brothers whose girlfriends stay over instead of heckling those women.

Fraternity men most often mistreated women they did not know personally. Men and women alike reported incidents in which brothers observed other brothers having sex with unknown women or women they knew only casually. A sophomore woman's experience exemplifies this anonymous state: "I don't mind if 10 guys were watching or it was videotaped. That's expected on this campus. It's the fact that he didn't apologize or even offer to drive me home that really upset me." Descriptions of sexual encounters involved the satisfaction of men by nameless women. A brother in a high-risk fraternity described a similar occurrence:

> A brother of mine was hooking up upstairs with an unattractive woman who had been pursuing him all night. He told some brothers to go outside the window and watch. Well, one thing led to another and they were almost completely naked when the woman noticed the brothers outside. She was then unwilling to go any further, so the brother went outside and yelled at the other brothers and then closed the shades. I don't know if he scored or not, because the woman was pretty upset. But he did win the award for hooking up with the ugliest chick that weekend.

ATTITUDES TOWARD RAPE

The sexually charged environment of college campuses raises many questions about cultures that facilitate the rape of women. How women and men define their sexual behavior is important legally as well as interpersonally. We asked students how they defined rape and had them compare it to the following legal definition: the perpetration of an act of sexual intercourse with a female against her will and consent, whether her will is overcome by force or fear resulting from the threat of force, or by drugs or intoxicants; or when, because of mental deficiency, she is incapable of exercising rational judgment. (Brownmiller 1975, 368)

When presented with this legal definition, most women interviewed recognized it as well as the complexities involved in applying it. A first-year woman said, "If a girl is drunk and the guy knows it and the girl says, 'Yes, I want to have sex,' and they do, that is still rape because the girl can't make a conscious, rational decision under the influence of alcohol." Some women disagreed. Another first-year woman stated, "I don't think it is fair that the guy gets blamed when both people involved are drunk."

The typical definition men gave for rape was "when a guy jumps out of the bushes and forces himself sexually onto a girl." When asked what date rape was, the most common answer was "when one person has sex with another person who did not consent." Many men said, however, that "date rape is when a woman wakes up the next morning and regrets having sex." Some men said that date rape was too gray an area to define. "Consent is a fine line," said a Greek senior man student. For the most part, the men we spoke with argued that rape did not occur on this campus. One Greek sophomore man said, "I think it is ridiculous that someone here would rape someone." A first-year man stated, "I have a problem with the word rape. It sounds so criminal, and we are not criminals; we are sane people."

Whether aware of the legal definitions of rape, most men resisted the idea that a woman who is intoxicated is unable to consent to sex. A Greek junior man said, "Men should not be responsible for women's drunkenness." One first-year man said, "If that is the legal definition of rape, then it happens all the time on this campus." A senior man said, "I don't care whether alcohol is involved or not; that is not rape. Rapists are people that have something seriously wrong with them." A first-year man even claimed that when women get drunk, they invite sex. He said, "Girls get so drunk here and then come on to us. What are we supposed to do? We are only human."

Discussion and Conclusion

These findings describe the physical and normative aspects of one college campus as they relate to attitudes about and relations between men and women. Our findings suggest that an explanation emphasizing rape culture also must focus on those characteristics of the social setting that play a role in defining heterosexual relationships on college campuses (Kalof and Cargill 1991). The degradation of women as portrayed in rape culture was not found in all fraternities on this campus. Both group norms and individual behavior changed as students went from one place to another. Although individual men are the ones who rape, we found that some settings are more likely places for rape than are others. Our findings suggest that rape cannot be seen only as an isolated act and blamed on individual behavior and proclivities, whether it be alcohol consumption or attitudes. We also must consider characteristics of the settings that promote the behaviors that reinforce a rape culture.

Relations between women and men at parties in low-risk fraternities varied considerably from those in high-risk houses. Peer pressure and situational norms influenced women as well as men. Although many men in high- and low-risk houses shared similar views and attitudes about the Greek system, women on this campus, and date rape, their behaviors at fraternity parties were quite different.

Women who are at highest risk of rape are women whom fraternity brothers did not know. These women are faceless victims, nameless acquaintances—not friends. Men said their responsibility to such persons and the level of guilt they feel later if the hook-ups end in sexual intercourse are much lower if they hook up with women they do not know. In high-risk houses, brothers treated women as subordinates and kept them at a distance. Men in high-risk houses actively discouraged ongoing heterosexual relationships, routinely degraded women, and participated more fully in the hook-up scene; thus, the probability that women would become faceless victims was higher in these houses. The flirtatious nature of the parties indicated that women go to these parties looking for available men, but finding boyfriends or relationships was difficult at parties in high-risk houses. However,

in the low-risk houses, where more men had long-term relationships, the women were not strangers and were less likely to become faceless victims.

The social scene on this campus, and on most others, offers women and men few other options to socialize. Although there may be no such thing as a completely safe fraternity party for women, parties at low-risk houses and commercial bars encouraged men and women to get to know each other better and decreased the probability that women would become faceless victims. Although both men and women found the social scene on this campus demeaning, neither demanded different settings for socializing, and attendance at fraternity parties is a common form of entertainment.

These findings suggest that a more conducive environment for conversation can promote more positive interactions between men and women. Simple changes would provide the opportunity for men and women to interact in meaningful ways, such as adding places to sit and lowering the volume of music at fraternity parties or having parties in neutral locations, where men are not in control. The typical party room in fraternity houses includes a place to dance but not to sit and talk. The music often is loud, making it difficult, if not impossible, to carry on conversations; however, there were more conversations at the low-risk parties, where there also was more respect shown toward women. Although the number of brothers who had steady girlfriends in the low-risk houses as compared to those in the high-risk houses may explain the differences, we found that commercial bars also provided a context for interaction between men and women. At the bars, students sat and talked and conversations between men and women flowed freely, resulting in deep discussion and fewer hookups.

Alcohol consumption was a major focus of social events here and intensified attitudes and orientations of a rape culture. Although pressure to drink was evident at all fraternity parties and at both bars, drinking dominated high-risk fraternity parties, at which nonalcoholic beverages usually were not available and people chugged beers and became visibly drunk. A rape culture is strengthened by rules that permit alcohol only at fraternity parties. Under this system, men control the parties and dominate the men as well as the women who attend. As college administrators crack down on fraternities and alcohol on campus, however, the same behaviors and norms may transfer to other places such as parties in apartments or private homes where administrators have much less control. At commercial bars, interaction and socialization with others were as important as drinking, with the exception of the nights when the bar frequented by under-class students became crowded. Although one solution is to offer nonalcoholic social activities, such events receive little support on this campus. Either these alternative events lacked the prestige of the fraternity parties or the alcohol was seen as necessary to unwind, or both.

In many ways, the fraternities on this campus determined the settings in which men and women interacted. As others before us have found, pressures for conformity to the norms and values exist at both high-risk and low-risk houses (Kalof and Cargill 1991; Martin and Hummer 1989; Sanday 1990). The desire to be accepted is not unique to this campus or the Greek system (Holland and Eisenhart 1990; Horowitz 1988; Moffat 1989). The degree of conformity required by Greeks may be greater than that required in most social groups, with considerable pressure to adopt and maintain the image of their houses. The fraternity system intensifies the "groupthink syndrome" (Janis 1972) by solidifying the identity of the in-group and creating an us/them atmosphere. Within the fraternity culture, brothers are highly regarded and women are viewed as outsiders. For men in high-risk fraternities, women threatened their brotherhood;

therefore, brothers discouraged relationships and harassed those who treated women as equals or with respect. The pressure to be one of the guys and hang out with the guys strengthens a rape culture on college campus by demeaning women and encouraging the segregation of men and women.

Students on this campus were aware of the contexts in which they operated and the choices available to them. They recognized that, in their interactions, they created differences between men and women that are not natural, essential, or biological (West and Zimmerman 1987). Not all men and women accepted the demeaning treatment of women, but they continued to participate in behaviors that supported aspects of a rape culture. Many women participated in the hook-up scene even after they had been humiliated and hurt because they had few other means of initiating contact with men on campus. Men and women alike played out this scene, recognizing its injustices in many cases but being unable to change the course of their behaviors.

Although this research provides some clues to gender relations on college campuses, it raises many questions. Why do men and women participate in activities that support a rape culture when they see its injustices? What would happen if alcohol were not controlled by groups of men who admit that they disrespect women when they get together? What can be done to give men and women on college campuses more opportunities to interact responsibly and get to know each other better? These questions should be studied on other campuses with a focus on the social settings in which the incidence of rape and the attitudes that support a rape culture exist. Fraternities are social contexts that may or may not foster a rape culture.

Our findings indicate that a rape culture exists in some fraternities, especially those we identified as high-risk houses. College administrators are responding to this situation by providing counseling and educational programs that increase awareness of date rape including campaigns such as "No means no." These strategies are important in changing attitudes, values, and behaviors; however, changing individuals is not enough. The structure of campus life and the impact of that structure on gender relations on campus are highly determinative. To eliminate campus rape culture, student leaders and administrators must examine the situations in which women and men meet and restructure these settings to provide opportunities for respectful interaction. Change may not require abolishing fraternities; rather, it may require promoting settings that facilitate positive gender relations.

References

Barthel, D. 1988. *Putting on Appearances: Gender and Advertising.* Philadelphia: Temple University Press.

Boeringer, S. B., C. L. Shehan, and R. L. Akers. 1991. "Social Contexts and Social Learning in Sexual Coercion and Aggression: Assessing the Contribution of Fraternity Membership." *Family Relations* 40: 58–64.

Brownmiller, S. 1975. *Against Our Will: Men, Women and Rape.* New York: Simon & Schuster.

Buchwald, E., P. R. Fletcher, and M. Roth (eds.). 1993. *Transforming a Rape Culture.* Minneapolis, MN: Milkweed Editions.

Burke, P., J. E. Stets, and M. A. Pirog-Good. 1989. "Gender Identity, Self-Esteem, Physical Abuse and Sexual Abuse in Dating Relationships." In M. A. Pirog-Good and J. E. Stets (eds.), *Violence in Dating Relationships: Emerging Social Issues.* New York: Praeger.

Gwartney-Gibbs, P., and J. Stockard. 1989. "Courtship Aggression and Mixed-Sex Peer Groups." In M. A. Pirog-Good and J. E. Stets (eds.), *Violence in Dating Relationships: Emerging Social Issues.* New York: Praeger.

Herman, D. 1984. "The Rape Culture." In J. Freeman (ed.), *Women: A Feminist Perspective.* Mountain View, CA: Mayfield.

Holland, D. C., and M. A. Eisenhart. 1990. *Educated in Romance: Women, Achievement, and College Culture.* Chicago: University of Chicago Press.

Horowitz, H. L. 1988. *Campus Life; Undergraduate Cultures from the End of the 18th Century to the Present.* Chicago: University of Chicago Press.

Hunter, F. 1953. *Community Power Structure.* Chapel Hill: University of North Carolina Press.

Janis, I. L. 1972. *Victims of Groupthink.* Boston: Houghton Mifflin.

Jenkins, M. J., and F. H. Dambrot. 1987. "The Attribution of Date Rape: Observer's Attitudes and Sexual Experiences and the Dating Situation." *Journal of Applied Social Psychology* 17: 875–895.

Kalof, L., and T. Cargill. 1991. "Fraternity and Sorority Membership and Gender Dominance Attitudes." *Sex Roles* 25: 417–423.

Kimmel, M. S. 1993. "Clarence, William, Iron Mike, Tailhook, Senator Packwood, Spur Posse, Magic . . . and Us." In E. Buchwald, P. R. Fletcher, and M. Roth (eds.), *Transforming a Rape Culture.* Minneapolis, MN: Milkweed Editions.

Koss, M. P., T. E. Dinero, C. A. Seibel, and S. L. Cox. 1988. "Stranger and Acquaintance Rape: Are There Differences in the Victim's Experience?" *Psychology of Women Quarterly* 12: 1–24.

Koss, M. P., C. A. Gidycz, and N. Wisniewski. 1985. "The Scope of Rape: Incidence and Prevalence of Sexual Aggression and Victimization in a National Sample of Higher Education Students." *Journal of Consulting and Clinical Psychology* 55: 162–170.

LaPlante, M. N., N. McCormick, and G. G. Brannigan. 1980. "Living the Sexual Script: College Students' Views of Influence in Sexual Encounters." *Journal of Sex Research* 16: 338–355.

Lisak, D., and S. Roth. 1988. "Motivational Factors in Nonincarcerated Sexually Aggressive Men." *Journal of Personality and Social Psychology* 55: 795–802.

Malamuth, N. 1986. "Predictors of Naturalistic Sexual Aggression." *Journal of Personality and Social Psychology* 50: 953–962.

Martin, P. Y., and R. Hummer. 1989. "Fraternities and Rape on Campus." *Gender and Society* 3: 457–473.

Miller, B., and J. C. Marshall. 1987. "Coercive Sex on the University Campus." *Journal of College Student Personnel* 28: 38–47.

Moffat, M. 1989. *Coming of Age in New Jersey: College Life in American Culture.* New Brunswick, NJ: Rutgers University Press.

Muehlenhard, C. L., and M. A. Linton. 1987. "Date Rape and Sexual Aggression in Dating Situations: Incidence and Risk Factors." *Journal of Counseling Psychology* 34: 186–196.

O'Sullivan, C. 1993. "Fraternities and the Rape Culture." In E. Buchwald, P. R. Fletcher, and M. Roth (eds.), *Transforming a Rape Culture.* Minneapolis, MN: Milkweed Editions.

Peterson, S. A., and B. Franzese. 1987. "Correlates of College Men's Sexual Abuse of Women." *Journal of College Student Personnel* 28: 223–228.

Sanday, P. R. 1990. *Fraternity Gang Rape: Sex, Brotherhood, and Privilege on Campus.* New York: New York University Press.

West, C., and D. Zimmerman. 1987. "Doing Gender." *Gender and Society* 1: 125–151.

Questions

1. In your judgment, what sorts of questions would allow a researcher to obtain reliable and valid information about people's (men's and women's) attitudes toward acquaintance rape?

2. What are the elements of a rape culture?

3. On the campus that Boswell and Spade studied, students distinguished between different types of relationships: "hooking up," "seeing each other," and "committed." (And men and women defined hooking up differently.) Are similar distinctions made on the campuses with which you are familiar?

4. When Boswell and Spade asked men whether they treated the women on campus with respect, the most common response was "on an individual basis, yes, but when you have a group of men together, no." In your judgment, what might account for the difference?

5. Boswell and Spade conclude that "some settings are more likely places for rape than are others." How do the types of settings that are more likely places for rape differ from those that are less likely places for rape? Explain.

6. Most researchers focus their analysis on the negative impact of rape cultures on women. What are the possible negative consequences of a rape culture on men?

7. Imagine that you've been asked to write a booklet for young college women titled "How to Be Safe from Rape on This Campus." What would you include in the booklet?

·31·

Situational Ethics and College Student Cheating

Emily E. LaBeff, Robert E. Clark, Valerie J. Haines, and George M. Diekhoff

In this 1990 article Professor LaBeff and her colleagues explore the ways in which students who have cheated avoid guilt by finding excuses for their wrongdoing. In other words, the authors explore how students "neutralize" their actions.

Introduction

Studies have shown that cheating in college is epidemic, and some analysts of this problem estimate that fifty percent of college students may engage in such behavior. . . . Such studies have examined demographic and social characteristics of students such as age, sex, academic standing, major, classification, extracurricular activity, level of test anxiety, degree of sanctioned threat, and internal social control. Each of these factors has been found to be related, to some extent, to cheating although the relationship of these factors varies considerably from study to study. . . .

In our freshman classes, we often informally ask students to discuss whether they have cheated in college and, if so, how. Some students have almost bragged about which of their methods have proven most effective including writing notes on shoes and caps and

on the backs of calculators. Rolling up a tiny cheat sheet into a pen cap was mentioned. And one student said he had "incredibly gifted eyes" which allowed him to see the answers of a smart student four rows in front of him. One female student talked about rummaging through the dumpsters at night close to final examination time looking for test dittos. She did find at least one examination. A sorority member informed us that two of her term papers in her freshman year were sent from a sister chapter of the sorority at another university, retyped and submitted to the course professor. Further, many of these students saw nothing wrong with what they were doing, although they verbally agreed with the statement that cheating was unethical.

It appears that students hold qualified guidelines for behavior which are situationally determined. As such, the concept of situational ethics might well describe this college cheating in that rules for behavior may not be considered rigid but depend on the circumstances involved (Norris and Dodder 1979, 545). Joseph Fletcher, in his well-known philosophical treatise, *Situation Ethics: The New Morality* (1966), argues that this position is based on the notion

"Situational Ethics and College Student Cheating" by Emily E. LaBeff, Robert E. Clark, Valerie J. Haines, and George M. Diekhoff from *Sociological Inquiry*, Vol. 60, No. 2, May 1990: pp. 190–197. Copyright © 1990 The University of Texas Press. Reprinted by permission of Blackwell Publishing.

that any action may be considered good or bad depending on the social circumstances. In other words, what is wrong in most situations might be considered right or acceptable if the end is defined as appropriate. This concept focuses on contextual appropriateness, not necessarily what is good or right, but what is viewed as fitting, given the circumstances. Central to this process is the idea that situations alter cases, thus altering the rules and principles guiding behavior (Edwards 1967).

Of particular relevance to the present study is the work of Gresham Sykes and David Matza (1957) who first developed the concept of neutralization to explain delinquent behavior. Neutralization theory in the study of delinquency expresses the process of situationally defining deviant behavior. In this view, deviance is based upon ". . . an unrecognized extension of defenses to crimes, in the form of justifications . . . seen as valid by the delinquent but not by . . . society at large" (Sykes and Matza 1957, 666). Through neutralization individuals justify violation of accepted behavior. This provides protection ". . . from self blame and the blame of others . . ." (Sykes and Matza 1957, 666). They do this before, during, and after the act. Such techniques of neutralization are separated into five categories: denial of responsibility, condemnation of condemners, appeal to higher loyalties, denial of victim, and denial of injury. In each case, individuals profess a conviction about a particular law but argue that special circumstances exist which cause them to violate the rules in a particular instance. However, in recent research, only Liska (1978) and Haines et al. (1986) found neutralization to be an important factor in college student cheating.

Methodology

The present analysis is based on a larger project conducted during the 1983–1984 academic year when a 49-item questionnaire about cheating

was administered to students at a small southwestern university. The student body (N = 4950) was evenly distributed throughout the university's programs with a disproportionate number (27%) majoring in business administration. In order to achieve a representative sample from a cross-section of the university student body, the questionnaire was administered to students enrolled in courses classified as a part of the university's core curriculum. Freshmen and sophomores were overrepresented (84% of the sample versus 60% of the university population). Females were also overrepresented (62% of the sample versus 55% of the university population).

There are obvious disadvantages associated with the use of self-administered questionnaires for data-gathering purposes. One such problem is the acceptance of student responses without benefit of contest. To maximize the return rate, questionnaires were administered during regularly scheduled class periods. Participation was on a voluntary basis. In order to establish the validity of responses, students were guaranteed anonymity. Students were also instructed to limit their responses regarding whether they had cheated to the current academic year.

. . . The present analysis is intended to assess the narrative responses to the incidence of cheating in three forms, namely on major examinations, quizzes, and class assignments, as well as the perceptions of and attitudes held by students toward cheating and the effectiveness of deterrents to cheating. Students recorded their experiences in their own words. Most students (87%) responded to the open-ended portion of the questionnaire.

Results

Of the 380 undergraduate students who participated in the spring survey, 54% indicated they had cheated during the previous six-month period. Students were requested to indicate whether cheating involved examination, weekly quizzes, and/or homework assignments. Much cheating took the form of looking on someone else's paper, copying homework, and either buying term papers or getting friends to write papers for them. Only five of the 205 students who admitted cheating reported being caught by the professor. However, 7% (n = 27) of the students reported cheating more than five times during the preceding six-month period. Twenty percent (n = 76) indicated that most students openly approved of cheating. Only seventeen students reported they would inform the instructor if they saw another student cheating. Many students, especially older students, indicated they felt resentment toward cheaters, but most also noted that they would not do anything about it (i.e., inform the instructor).

To more fully explore the ways in which students neutralize their behavior, narrative data from admitted student cheaters were examined (n = 149). The narrative responses were easily classified into three of the five techniques described by Sykes and Matza (1957).

DENIAL OF RESPONSIBILITY

Denial of responsibility was the most often identified response. This technique involves a declaration by the offenders that, in light of circumstances beyond their control, they cannot be held accountable for their actions. Rather than identifying the behavior as "accidental," they attribute wrongdoing to the influence of outside forces. In some instances, students expressed an inability to withstand peer pressure to cheat. Responses show a recognition of cheating as an unacceptable behavior, implying that under different circumstances cheating would not have occurred. One student commented:

> I was working forty plus hours a week and we had a lot to read for that day. I just couldn't get it all in. . . . I'm not saying cheating is okay, sometimes you just have to.

Another student explained her behavior in the following statement:

> . . . I had the flu the week before . . . had to miss several classes so I had no way of knowing what was going to be on the exam. My grades were good up to that point and I hadn't cheated. . . . I just couldn't risk it.

It is noteworthy that these statements indicate the recognition that cheating is wrong under normal circumstances.

Other responses demonstrate the attempt by students to succeed through legitimate means (e.g., taking notes and studying) only to experience failure. Accordingly, they were left with no alternative but to cheat. One student commented:

> . . . even though I've studied in the past, I've failed the exam so I cheated on my last test hoping to bring a better grade.

Another student explained his behavior in the following manner:

> I studied for the exam and I studied hard but the material on the test was different from what I expected. . . . I had to make a good grade.

In some accounts, students present a unique approach to the denial of responsibility. Upon entering the examination setting, these students had no intention of cheating, but the opportunity presented itself. The following statement by one student provides a clear illustration of this point:

> . . . I was taking the test and someone in another part of the room was telling someone else an answer. I heard it and just couldn't not write it down.

Although viewing such behavior as dishonest, the blame for any wrongdoing is quickly transferred to those who provide the answers. Another student justified her action in the following manner:

> . . . I didn't mean to cheat but once you get the right answer it's hard, no impossible, not to.

How could you ignore an answer that you knew was right?

In addition, some students reported accidentally seeing other students' test papers. In such instances, the cheaters chastised classmates for not covering up their answer sheets. As one student wrote, such temptation simply cannot be overcome:

> I studied hard for the exam and needed an A. I just happened to look up and there was my neighbor's paper uncovered. I found myself checking my answers against his through the whole test.

APPEAL TO HIGHER LOYALTIES

Conflict also arises between peer group expectations and the normative expectations of the larger society. When this occurs, the individual may choose to sacrifice responsibility, thereby maintaining the interest of peers. Such allegiance allows these individuals to supersede moral obligations when special circumstances arise.

Students who invoke this technique of neutralization frequently described their behavior as an attempt to help another. One student stated:

> I only cheated because my friend had been sick and she needed help. . . . it (cheating) wouldn't have happened any other time.

Another student denied any wrongdoing on her part as the following statement illustrates:

> I personally have never cheated. I've had friends who asked for help so I let them see my test. Maybe some would consider that to be cheating.

These students recognize the act of cheating is wrong. However, their statements also suggest that in some situations cheating can be overlooked. Loyalty to a friend in need takes precedence over honesty in the classroom. Another student described his situation in the following manner:

> I was tutoring this girl but she just couldn't understand the material. . . . I felt I had to help her on the test.

CONDEMNATION OF CONDEMNERS

Cheaters using this technique of neutralization attempt to shift attention from their own actions to the actions of others, most often authority figures. By criticizing those in authority as being unfair or unethical, the behavior of the offender seems less consequential by comparison. Therefore, dishonest behavior occurs in reaction to the perceived dishonesty of the authority figure. Students who utilize this technique wrote about uncaring, unprofessional instructors with negative attitudes who were negligent in their behavior. These incidents were said to be a precursor to their cheating behavior. The following response illustrates this view:

> The teachers here are boring and I dislike this school. The majority of teachers here don't care about the students and are rude when you ask them for help.

In other instances, students cite unfair teaching practices which they perceive to be the reason for their behavior. One student stated:

> Major exams are very important to your grade and it seems that the majority of instructors make up the exams to try and trick you instead of testing your knowledge.

In this case, the instructor is thought to engage in a deliberate attempt to fail the students by making the examinations difficult. Also within this category were student accounts which frequently express a complaint of being overworked. As one student wrote:

> One instructor assigns more work than anyone could possibly handle . . . at least I know I can't, so sometimes cheating is the answer.

Another student described his situation as follows:

> Sometimes it seems like these instructors get together and plan to make it difficult. . . . I had three major tests in one day and very little time to study. . . .

Although less frequently mentioned, perceived parental pressure also serves as a neutralizing factor for dishonesty. One student stated:

> During my early years at school my parents constantly pressured me for good grades. . . . They would have withheld money if grades were bad.

Another student blamed the larger society for his cheating:

> In America, we're taught that results aren't achieved through beneficial means, but through the easiest means.

Another stated:

> Ted Kennedy has been a modeling example for many of us. . . . This society teaches us to survive, to rationalize. . . . It is built on injustice and expediency.

This student went on to say that he cheated throughout a difficult science course so he could spend more time studying for major courses which he enjoyed.

DENIAL OF INJURY AND DENIAL OF THE VICTIM

Denial of injury and denial of the victim do not appear in the student accounts of their cheating. In denial of injury, the wrongdoer states that no one was harmed or implies that accusations of injury are grossly exaggerated. In the second case, denial of the victim, those who violate norms often portray their targets as legitimate. Due to certain factors such as the societal role, personal characteristics, or lifestyle of the victim, the wrongdoer felt the victim "had it coming."

It is unlikely that students will either deny injury or deny the victim since there are no real targets in cheating. However, attempts to deny injury are possible when the one who is cheating argues that cheating is a personal matter rather than a public one. It is also possible that some students are cognizant of the effect their cheating activities have upon the educational system as a whole and, therefore, choose to neutralize their behavior in ways which allow them to focus on the act rather than the consequences of cheating. By observing their actions from a myopic viewpoint, such students avoid the larger issues of morality.

Conclusion

The purpose of this report was to analyze student responses to cheating in their college coursework. Using Sykes and Matza's model of techniques neutralization, we found that students rationalized their cheating behavior and do so without challenging the norm of honesty. Student responses fit three of the five techniques of neutralization. The most common technique is a denial of responsibility. Second, students tend to "condemn the condemners," blaming faculty and testing procedures. Finally, students "appeal to higher loyalties" by arguing that it is more important to help a friend than to avoid cheating. The use of these techniques of neutralization conveys the message that students recognize and accept cheating as an undesirable behavior which, nonetheless, can be excused under certain circumstances. Such findings reflect the prevalence of situational ethics.

The situation appears to be one in which students are not caught and disciplined by instructors. Additionally, students who cheat do not concern themselves with overt negative sanctions from other students. In some groups, cheating is planned, expected, and often rewarded in that students may receive better grades. That leaves a student's ethical, internalized control as a barrier to cheating. However, the neutralizing attitude allows students to sidestep issues of ethics and guilt by placing the blame for their behavior elsewhere. Neutralization allows them to state their belief that in general cheating is wrong, but in some special circumstances cheating is acceptable, even necessary.

Given such widespread acceptance of cheating in the university setting, it may be useful to further test the salience of neutralization and other such factors in more diverse university environments. This study is limited to a small state university. It is important also to extend the research to a wider range of institutions including prestigious private colleges, large state universities, and church-related schools.

Cross-cultural studies of cheating may also prove useful for identifying broader social and cultural forces which underlie situational ethics and cheating behavior. In this regard, the process involved in learning neutralizing attitudes could be integrated with work in the field of deviance in order to expand our understanding of the rule breakers along a continuum of minor to major forms of deviance.

References

Edwards, Paul. 1967. *The Encyclopedia of Philosophy,* Vol. 3, edited by Paul Edwards. New York: Macmillan Company and Free Press.

Fletcher, Joseph. 1966. *Situation Ethics: The New Morality.* Philadelphia: The Westminster Press.

Haines, Valerie J., George Diekhoff, Emily LaBeff, and Robert Clark. 1986. "College Cheating: Immaturity, Lack of Commitment, and the Neutralizing Attitude." *Research in Higher Education* 25: 342–354.

Liska, Allen. 1978. "Deviant Involvement, Associations, and Attitudes: Specifying the Underlying Causal Structures." *Sociology and Social Research* 63: 73–88.

Norris, Terry D., and Richard A. Dodder. 1979. "A Behavioral Continuum Synthesizing Neutralization Theory, Situational Ethics and Juvenile Delinquency." *Adolescence* 55: 545–555.

Sykes, Gresham, and David Matza. 1957. "Techniques of Neutralization: A Theory of Delinquency." *American Sociological Review* 22: 664–670.

Questions

1. Explain what the authors mean by "neutralization."

2. List the five major categories of neutralization techniques. According to LaBeff and her colleagues, what do these techniques have in common?

3. Review the kinds of excuses given by student cheaters in this study. Then, assume that you are a college professor who has just caught some students cheating. Which kinds of excuses would seem the most compelling to you? Would any of these lead you to treat the students' behavior as acceptable (i.e., not take any action against them for cheating)? Which kinds of excuses would seem the most lame to you? Why?

·32·

Denying the Guilty Mind
Accounting for Involvement in a White-Collar Crime

Michael L. Benson

In this 1985 article, Michael Benson reports on the results of conversations he had with thirty men convicted of white-collar crime. The term *white-collar crime* was coined by criminologist Edwin Sutherland in 1949 to refer to any "crime committed by a person of respectability and high social status in the course of his occupation."

Benson encouraged each convict to talk about how he felt about his involvement with the justice system. One interesting finding: None of the men said he felt he was a "criminal."

Denying the Guilty Mind

Adjudication as a criminal is, to use Garfinkel's (1956) classic term, a degradation ceremony.[1] The focus of this article is on how offenders attempt to defeat the success of this ceremony and deny their own criminality through the use of accounts. However, in the interest of showing in as much detail as possible all sides of the experience undergone by these offenders, it is necessary to treat first the guilt and inner anguish that is felt by many white-collar offenders even though they deny being criminals. This is best accomplished by beginning with a description of a unique feature of the prosecution of white-collar crimes.

In white-collar criminal cases, the issue is likely to be *why* something was done, rather than *who* did it (Edelhertz 1970, 47). There is often relatively little disagreement as to what happened. In the words of one Assistant U.S. Attorney interviewed for the study:

> If you actually had a movie playing, neither side would dispute that a person moved in this way and handled this piece of paper, etc. What it comes down to is, did they have the criminal intent?

If the prosecution is to proceed past the investigatory stages, the prosecutor must infer from the pattern of events that conscious criminal intent was present and believe that sufficient evidence exists to convince a jury of this interpretation of the situation. As Katz (1979, 445–446) has noted, making this inference can be difficult because of the way in which white-collar illegalities are integrated into ordinary

---

[1] A degradation ceremony is a public ritual in which the individual is stripped of his or her identity as a member of respectable society and formally labeled as an outsider or even as something less than human. — Ed.

"Denying the Guilty Mind: Accounting for Involvement in a White-Collar Crime" by Michael L. Benson from *Criminology*, Vol. 23, No. 4, 1985: pp. 590–599. Reprinted by permission of the American Society of Criminology.

occupational routines. Thus, prosecutors in conducting trials, grand jury hearings, or plea negotiations spend a great deal of effort establishing that the defendant did indeed have the necessary criminal intent. By concentrating on the offender's motives, the prosecutor attacks the very essence of the white-collar offender's public and personal image as an upstanding member of the community. The offender is portrayed as someone with a guilty mind.

Not surprisingly, therefore, the most consistent and recurrent pattern in the interviews, though not present in all of them, was denial of criminal intent, as opposed to the outright denial of any criminal behavior whatsoever. Most offenders acknowledged that their behavior probably could be construed as falling within the conduct proscribed by statute, but they uniformly denied that their actions were motivated by a guilty mind. This is not to say, however, that offenders *felt* no guilt or shame as a result of conviction. On the contrary, indictment, prosecution, and conviction provoke a variety of emotions among offenders.

The enormous reality of the offender's lived emotion (Denzin 1984) in admitting guilt is perhaps best illustrated by one offender's description of his feelings during the hearing at which he pled guilty.

> You know (the plea's) what really hurt. I didn't even know I had feet. I felt numb. My head was just floating. There was no feeling, except a state of suspended animation. . . . For a brief moment, I almost hesitated. I almost said not guilty. If I had been alone, I would have fought, but my family. . . .

The traumatic nature of this moment lies, in part, in the offender's feeling that only one aspect of his life is being considered. From the offender's point of view his crime represents only one small part of his life. It does not typify his inner self, and to judge him solely on the basis of this one event seems an atrocious injustice to the offender.

For some the memory of the event is so painful that they want to obliterate it entirely, as the two following quotations illustrate.

> I want quiet. I want to forget. I want to cut with the past.

> I've already divorced myself from the problem. I don't even want to hear the names of certain people ever again. It brings me pain.

For others, rage rather than embarrassment seemed to be the dominant emotion.

> I never really felt any embarrassment over the whole thing. I felt rage and it wasn't false or self-serving. It was really (something) to see this thing in action and recognize what the whole legal system has come to through its development, and the abuse of the grand jury system and the abuse of the indictment system. . . .

The role of the news media in the process of punishment and stigmatization should not be overlooked. All offenders whose cases were reported on by the news media were either embarrassed or embittered or both by the public exposure.

> The only one I am bitter at is the newspapers, as many people are. They are unfair because you can't get even. They can say things that are untrue, and let me say this to you. They wrote an article on me that was so blasphemous, that was so horrible. They painted me as an insidious miserable creature, wringing out the last penny. . . .

Offenders whose cases were not reported on by the news media expressed relief at having avoided that kind of embarrassment, sometimes saying that greater publicity would have been worse than any sentence they could have received.

In court, defense lawyers are fond of presenting white-collar offenders as having suffered enough by virtue of the humiliation of public adjudication as criminals. On the other hand, prosecutors present them as cavalier individuals who arrogantly ignore the law and brush off its weak efforts to stigmatize them as criminals. Neither of these stereotypes is entirely accurate. The subjective effects of conviction on white-collar offenders are varied and complex. One suspects that this is true of all offenders, not only white-collar offenders.

The emotional responses of offenders to conviction have not been the subject of extensive research. However, insofar as an individual's emotional response to adjudication may influence the deterrent or crime-reinforcing impact of punishment on him or her, further study might reveal why some offenders stop their criminal behavior while others go on to careers in crime (Casper 1978, 80).

Although the offenders displayed a variety of different emotions with respect to their experiences, they were nearly unanimous in denying basic criminality. To see how white-collar offenders justify and excuse their crimes, we turn to their accounts. The small number of cases rules out the use of any elaborate classification techniques. Nonetheless, it is useful to group offenders by offense when presenting their interpretations.

ANTITRUST VIOLATORS[2]

Four of the offenders have been convicted of antitrust violations, all in the same case involving the building and contracting industry. Four major themes characterized their accounts. First, antitrust offenders focused on the everyday character and historical continuity of their offenses.

> It was a way of doing business before we even got into the business. So it was like why do you brush your teeth in the morning or something. . . . It was part of the everyday. . . . It was a method of survival.

[2]Antitrust laws date back to the end of the nineteenth century. They are intended to promote fair business practices. For example, it is a violation of antitrust laws for business leaders to get together (or "collude") to fix consumer prices at artificially high levels. — Ed.

The offenders argued that they were merely following established and necessary industry practices. These practices were presented as being necessary for the well-being of the industry as a whole, not to mention their own companies. Further, they argued that cooperation among competitors was either allowed or actively promoted by the government in other industries and professions.

The second theme emphasized by the offenders was the characterization of their actions as blameless. They admitted talking to competitors and admitted submitting intentionally noncompetitive bids. However, they presented these practices as being done not for the purpose of rigging prices nor to make exorbitant profits. Rather, the everyday practices of the industry required them to occasionally submit bids on projects they really did not want to have. To avoid the effort and expense of preparing full-fledged bids, they would call a competitor to get a price to use. Such a situation might arise, for example, when a company already had enough work for the time being, but was asked by a valued customer to submit a bid anyway.

> All you want to do is show a bid, so that in some cases it was for as small a reason as getting your deposit back on the plans and specs. So you just simply have no interest in getting the job and just call to see if you can find someone to give you a price to use, so that you didn't have to go through the expense of an entire bid preparation. Now that is looked on very unfavorably, and it is a technical violation, but it was strictly an opportunity to keep your name in front of a desired customer. Or you may find yourself in a situation where somebody is doing work for a customer, has done work for many, many years and is totally acceptable, totally fair. There is no problem. But suddenly they (the customer) get an idea that they ought to have a few tentative figures, and you're called in, and you are in a moral dilemma. There's really no reason for you to attempt to compete in that circumstance. And so there was a way to back out.

Managed in this way, an action that appears on the surface to be a straightforward and conscious violation of antitrust regulations becomes merely a harmless business practice that happens to be a "technical violation." The offender can then refer to his personal history to verify his claim that, despite technical violations, he is in reality a law-abiding person. In the words of one offender, "Having been in the business for 33 years, you don't just automatically become a criminal overnight."

Third, offenders were very critical of the motives and tactics of prosecutors. Prosecutors were accused of being motivated solely by the opportunity for personal advancement presented by winning a big case. Further, they were accused of employing prosecution selectively and using tactics that allowed the most culpable offenders to go free. The Department of Justice was painted as using antitrust prosecutions for political purposes.

The fourth theme emphasized by the antitrust offenders involved a comparison between their crimes and the crimes of street criminals. Antitrust offenses differ in their mechanics from street crimes in that they are not committed in one place and at one time. Rather, they are spatially and temporally diffuse and are intermingled with legitimate behavior. In addition, the victims of antitrust offenses tend not to be identifiable individuals, as is the case with most street crimes. These characteristics are used by antitrust violators to contrast their own behavior with that of common stereotypes of criminality. Real crimes are pictured as discrete events that have beginnings and ends and involve individuals who directly and purposely victimize someone else in a particular place and at a particular time.

> It certainly wasn't a premeditated type of thing in our cases as far as I can see. . . . To me it's different than—and I sitting down and we plan, well, we're going to rob this bank tomorrow and premeditatedly go in there. . . . That wasn't the case at all. . . . It wasn't like sitting down

and planning I'm going to rob this bank type of thing. . . . It was just a common everyday way of doing business and surviving.

A consistent thread running through all of the interviews was the necessity for antitrust-like practices, given the realities of the business world. Offenders seemed to define the situation in such a manner that two sets of rules could be seen to apply. On the one hand, there are the legislatively determined rules—laws—which govern how one is to conduct one's business affairs. On the other hand, there is a higher set of rules based on the concepts of profit and survival, which are taken to define what it means to be in business in a capitalistic society. These rules do not just regulate behavior; rather, they constitute or create the behavior in question. If one is not trying to make a profit or trying to keep one's business going, then one is not really "in business." Following Searle (1969, 33–41), the former type of rule can be called a regulative rule and the latter type a constitutive rule. In certain situations, one may have to violate a regulative rule in order to conform to the more basic constitutive rule of the activity in which one is engaged.

This point can best be illustrated through the use of an analogy involving competitive games. Trying to win is a constitutive rule of competitive games in the sense that if one is not trying to win, one is not really playing the game. In competitive games, situations may arise where a player deliberately breaks the rules even though he knows or expects he will be caught. In the game of basketball, for example, a player may deliberately foul an opponent to prevent him from making a sure basket. In this instance, one would understand that the fouler was trying to win by gambling that the opponent would not make the free throws. The player violates the rule against fouling in order to follow the higher rule of trying to win.

Trying to make a profit or survive in business can be thought of as a constitutive rule of capitalist economies. The laws that govern *how* one is allowed to make a profit are regulative rules, which can understandably be subordinated to the rules of trying to survive and profit. From the offender's point of view, he is doing what businessmen in our society are supposed to do — that is, stay in business and make a profit. Thus, an individual who violates society's laws or regulations in certain situations may actually conceive of himself as thereby acting more in accord with the central ethos of his society than if he had been a strict observer of its law. One might suggest, following Denzin (1977), that for businessmen in the building and contracting industry, an informal structure exists below the articulated legal structure, one which frequently supersedes the legal structure. The informal structure may define as moral and "legal" certain actions that the formal legal structure defines as immoral and "illegal."

TAX VIOLATORS

Six of the offenders interviewed were convicted of income tax violations. Like antitrust violators, tax violators can rely upon the complexity of the tax laws and an historical tradition in which cheating on taxes is not really criminal. Tax offenders would claim that everybody cheats somehow on their taxes and present themselves as victims of an unlucky break, because they got caught.

> Everybody cheats on their income tax, 95% of the people. Even if it's for ten dollars it's the same principle. I didn't cheat. I just didn't know how to report it.

The widespread belief that cheating on taxes is endemic helps to lend credence to the offender's claim to have been singled out and to be no more guilty than most people.

Tax offenders were more likely to have acted as individuals rather than as part of a group and, as a result, were more prone to account for their offenses by referring to them

as either mistakes or the product of special circumstances. Violations were presented as simple errors which resulted from ignorance and poor recordkeeping. Deliberate intention to steal from the government for personal benefit was denied.

> I didn't take the money. I have no bank account to show for all this money, where all this money is at that I was supposed to have. They never found the money, ever. There is no Swiss bank account, believe me.

> My records were strictly one big mess. That's all it was. If only I had an accountant, this wouldn't even of happened. No way in God's creation would this ever have happened.

Other offenders would justify their actions by admitting that they were wrong while painting their motives as altruistic rather than criminal. Criminality was denied because they did not set out to deliberately cheat the government for their own personal gain. Like the antitrust offenders discussed above, one tax violator distinguished between his own crime and the crimes of real criminals.

> I'm not a criminal. That is, I'm not a criminal from the standpoint of taking a gun and doing this and that. I'm a criminal from the standpoint of making a mistake, a serious mistake. . . . The thing that really got me involved in it is my feeling for the employees here, certain employees that are my right hand. In order to save them a certain amount of taxes and things like that, I'd extend money to them in cash, and the money came from these sources that I took it from. You know, cash sales and things of that nature, but practically all of it was turned over to the employees, because of my feeling for them.

All of the tax violators pointed out that they had no intention of deliberately victimizing the government. None of them denied the legitimacy of the tax laws, nor did they claim that they cheated because the government is not representative of the people (Conklin 1977, 99). Rather, as a result of ignorance or for altruistic reasons, they made decisions which turned out to be criminal when viewed from the perspective of the law. While they acknowledged the technical criminality of their actions, they tried to show that what they did was not criminally motivated.

VIOLATIONS OF FINANCIAL TRUST

Four offenders were involved in violations of financial trust. Three were banking officers who embezzled or misapplied funds, and the fourth was a union official who embezzled from a union pension fund.[3] Perhaps because embezzlement is one crime in this sample that can be considered *mala in se*, these offenders were much more forthright about their crimes. Like the other offenders, the embezzlers would not go so far as to say "I am a criminal," but they did say "What I did was wrong, was criminal, and I knew it was." Thus, the embezzlers were unusual in that they explicitly admitted responsibility for their crimes. . . .

Unlike tax evasion, which can be excused by reference to the complex nature of tax regulations or antitrust violations, which can be justified as for the good of the organization as a whole, embezzlement requires deliberate action on the part of the offender and is almost inevitably committed for personal reasons. The crime of embezzlement, therefore, cannot be accounted for by using the same techniques that tax violators or antitrust violators do. The act itself can only be explained by showing that one was under extraordinary circumstances which explain one's uncharacteristic behavior. Three of the offenders referred explicitly to extraordinary circumstances and

presented the offense as an aberration in their life history. For example, one offender described his situation in this manner:

> As a kid, I never even—you know kids will sometimes shoplift from the dime store—I never even did that. I had never stolen a thing in my life and that was what was so unbelievable about the whole thing, but there were some psychological and personal questions that I wasn't dealing with very well. I wasn't terribly happily married. I was married to a very strong-willed woman and it just wasn't working out.

The offender in this instance goes on to explain how, in an effort to impress his wife, he lived beyond his means and fell into debt.

A structural characteristic of embezzlement also helps the offender demonstrate his essential lack of criminality. Embezzlement is integrated into ordinary occupational routines. The illegal action does not stand out clearly against the surrounding set of legal actions. Rather, there is a high degree of surface correspondence, the offender must exercise some restraint when committing his crime. The embezzler must be discreet in his stealing; he cannot take all of the money available to him without at the same time revealing crime. Once exposed, the offender can point to this restraint on his part as evidence that he is not really a criminal. That is, he can compare what happened with what could have happened in order to show how much more serious the offense could have been if he was really a criminal at heart.

> What I could have done if I had truly had a devious criminal mind and perhaps if I had been a little smarter—and I am not saying that with any degree of pride or any degree of modesty whatever, [as] it's being smarter in a bad, an evil way—I could have pulled this off on a grander scale and I might still be doing it.

Even though the offender is forthright about admitting his guilt, he makes a distinction

---

[3]Embezzlement is not just theft. Embezzlement is theft from someone who has entrusted his or her money or property to you.—Ed.

between himself and someone with a truly "devious criminal mind."

Contrary to Cressey's (1953, 57–66) findings, none of the embezzlers claimed that their offenses were justified because they were underpaid or badly treated by their employers. Rather, attention was focused on the unusual circumstances surrounding the offense and its atypical character when compared to the rest of the offender's life. This strategy is for the most part determined by the mechanics and organizational format of the offense itself. Embezzlement occurs within the organization but not for the organization. It cannot be committed accidentally or out of ignorance. It can be accounted for only by showing that the actor "was not himself" at the time of the offense or was under such extraordinary circumstances that embezzlement was an understandable response to an unfortunate situation. This may explain the finding that embezzlers tend to produce accounts that are viewed as more sufficient by the justice system than those produced by other offenders (Rothman and Gandossy 1982). The only plausible option open to a convicted embezzler trying to explain his offense is to admit responsibility while justifying the action, an approach that apparently strikes a responsive chord with judges.

FRAUD AND FALSE STATEMENTS

Ten offenders were convicted of some form of fraud or false statements charge. Unlike embezzlers, tax violators, or antitrust violators, these offenders were much more likely to deny committing any crime at all. Seven of the ten claimed that they, personally, were innocent of any crime, although each admitted that fraud had occurred. Typically, they claimed to have been set up by associates and to have been wrongfully convicted by the U.S. Attorney handling the case. One might call this the scapegoat strategy. Rather than admitting technical wrongdoing and then justifying or excusing it, the offender attempts to paint himself as a victim by shifting the blame entirely to another party. Prosecutors were presented as being either ignorant or politically motivated.

The outright denial of any crime whatsoever is unusual compared to the other types of offenders studied here. It may result from the nature of the crime of fraud. By definition, fraud involves a conscious attempt on the part of one or more persons to mislead others. While it is theoretically possible to accidentally violate the antitrust and tax laws, or to violate them for altruistic reasons, it is difficult to imagine how one could accidentally mislead someone else for his or her own good. Furthermore, in many instances, fraud is an aggressively acquisitive crime. The offender develops a scheme to bilk other people out of money or property, and does this not because of some personal problem but because the scheme is an easy way to get rich. Stock swindles, fraudulent loan scams, and so on are often so large and complicated that they cannot possibly be excused as foolish and desperate solutions to personal problems. Thus, those involved in large-scale frauds do not have the option open to most embezzlers of presenting themselves as persons responding defensively to difficult personal circumstances.

Furthermore, because fraud involves a deliberate attempt to mislead another, the offender who fails to remove himself from the scheme runs the risk of being shown to have a guilty mind. That is, he is shown to possess the most essential element of modern conceptions of criminality: an intent to harm another. His inner self would in this case be exposed as something other than what it has been presented as, and all of his previous actions would be subject to reinterpretation in light of his new perspective. For this reason, defrauders are most prone to denying any crime at all. The cooperative and conspiratorial nature of many fraudulent schemes makes it possible to put the blame on someone else and to present oneself as a scapegoat. Typically, this is done by claiming to have been duped by others.

Two illustrations of this strategy are presented below.

> I figured I wasn't guilty, so it wouldn't be that hard to disprove it, until, as I say, I went to court and all of a sudden they start bringing in these guys out of the woodwork implicating me that I never saw. Lot of it could be proved that I never saw.

> Inwardly, I personally felt that the only crime that I committed was not telling on these guys. Not that I deliberately, intentionally committed a crime against the system. My only crime was that I should have had the guts to tell on these guys, what they were doing, rather than putting up with it and then trying to gradually get out of the system without hurting them or without them thinking I was going to snitch on them.

Of the three offenders who admitted committing crimes, two acted alone and the third acted with only one other person. Their accounts were similar to the others presented earlier and tended to focus on either the harmless nature of their violations or on the unusual circumstances that drove them to commit their crimes. One claimed that his violations were only technical and that no one besides himself had been harmed.

> First of all, no money was stolen or anything of that nature. The bank didn't lose any money. . . . What I did was a technical violation. I made a mistake. There's no question about that, but the bank lost no money.

Another offender who directly admitted his guilt was involved in a check-kiting scheme. In a manner similar to embezzlers, he argued that his actions were motivated by exceptional circumstances.

> I was faced with the choice of all of a sudden, and I mean now, closing the doors or doing something else to keep that business open. . . . I'm not going to tell you that this wouldn't have

happened if I'd had time to think it over, because I think it probably would have. You're sitting there with a dying patient. You are going to try to keep him alive.

In the other fraud cases more individuals were involved, and it was possible and perhaps necessary for each offender to claim that he was not really the culprit.

Discussion: Offenses, Accounts, and Degradation Ceremonies

The investigation, prosecution, and conviction of a white-collar offender involves him in a very undesirable status passage (Glaser and Strauss 1971). The entire process can be viewed as a long and drawn-out degradation ceremony with the prosecutor as the chief denouncer and the offender's family and friends as the chief witnesses. The offender is moved from the status of law-abiding citizen to that of convicted felon. Accounts are developed to defeat the process of identity transformation that is the object of a degradation ceremony. They represent the offender's attempt to diminish the effect of his legal transformation and to prevent its becoming a publicly validated label. It can be suggested that the accounts developed by white-collar offenders take the forms that they do for two reasons: (1) the forms are required to defeat the success of the degradation ceremony, and (2) the specific forms used are the ones available given the mechanics, history, and organizational context of the offenses.

Three general patterns in accounting strategies stand out in the data. Each can be characterized by the subject matter on which it focuses: the event (offense), the perpetrator (offender), or the denouncer (prosecutor). These are the natural subjects of accounts in that to be successful, a degradation ceremony requires each of these elements to be presented in a particular manner (Garfinkel 1956). If an account giver can undermine the presentation of one or more of the elements, then the effect of the ceremony can be reduced. Although there are overlaps in the accounting strategies used by the various types of offenders, and while any given offender may use more than one strategy, it appears that accounting strategies and offenses correlate. . . .

References

Casper, Jonathan D. 1978. *Criminal Courts: The Defendant's Perspective*. Washington, DC: U.S. Department of Justice.

Conklin, John E. 1977. *Illegal But Not Criminal: Business Crime in America*. Englewood Cliffs, NJ: Prentice-Hall.

Cressey, Donald. 1953. *Other People's Money*. New York: Free Press.

Denzin, Norman K. 1977. "Notes on the Criminogenic Hypothesis: A Case Study of the American Liquor Industry." *American Sociological Review* 42: 905–920.

Denzin, Norman K. 1984. *On Understanding Emotion*. San Francisco: Jossey-Bass.

Edelhertz, Herbert. 1970. *The Nature, Impact, and Prosecution of White Collar Crime*. Washington, DC: U.S. Government Printing Office.

Garfinkel, Harold. 1956. "Conditions of Successful Degradation Ceremonies." *American Journal of Sociology* 61: 420–424.

Glazer, Barney G., and Anselm L. Strauss. 1971. *Status Passage*. Chicago: Aldine.

Katz, Jack. 1979. "Legality and Equality: Plea Bargaining in the Prosecution of White-Collar Crimes." *Law and Society Review* 13: 431–460.

Rothman, Martin, and Robert F. Gandossy. 1982. "Sad Tales: The Accounts of White-Collar Defendants and the Decision to Sanction." *Pacific Sociological Review* 4: 449–473.

Searle, John R. 1969. *Speech Acts*. Cambridge: Cambridge University Press.

Questions

1. Look back at the list of "techniques of neutralization" that you made in response to the first question following reading 31 about student cheating. Which of the explanations offered by white-collar criminals interviewed by Benson used any of the techniques of neutralization?

2. A single white-collar criminal may steal as much money as a whole host of burglars. Why, then, do white-collar offenders deny that they are as bad as street criminals? In your judgment, who is more criminal—the thief who steals $50 from a convenience store or the thief who steals $100,000 from an insurance company?

3. Consider the student cheater who says that "cheating is the only way to get through all the ridiculous demands that teachers place on us" and the insurance executive who says that "breaking the law is the only way to do business in this country." What, if anything, do they have in common?

·33·
The Land of Opportunity

James Loewen

Many of us who teach sociology in U.S. colleges are frequently puzzled and even stunned by students' reactions to the subject of social inequality. If we blithely explain the extent and consequences of social inequality in the United States, we find our students regarding us as if we are sadly misinformed or (less charitably) have simply gone mad: "What do you mean America is not the land of equal opportunity?" Sometimes students' responses are downright hostile.

Still, if there is one thing sociologists know, it is that there is a great deal of inequality in the United States. The question is: Why does this fact come as such a big surprise to students? Perhaps James Loewen has the answer. He says that students graduate from high school as "terrible sociologists." As you will read in this 1995 piece, he puts part of the blame for this situation on the content of those social studies and history texts to which students were subjected in elementary, middle, and high school. Loewen is confident that he is right. He explains:

> For several years I have been lugging around twelve [history] textbooks, taking them seriously as works of history and ideology, studying what they say and don't say, and trying to figure out why. I chose the twelve as representing the range of textbooks available for history courses. . . . These twelve textbooks have been my window into the world of what high school students carry home, read, memorize, and forget. In addition, I have spent many hours observing high school history classes in Mississippi, Vermont, and the Washington, DC, metropolitan area, and more hours interviewing high school history teachers.

High school students have eyes, ears, and television sets (all too many have their own TV sets), so they know a lot about relative privilege in America. They measure their family's social position against that of other families, and their community's position against other communities. Middle-class students, especially, know little about how the American class structure works, however, and nothing at all about how it has changed over time. These students do not leave high school merely ignorant of the workings of the class structure; they come out as terrible sociologists. "Why are people poor?" I have asked first-year college students. Or, if their own class position is one of relative privilege, "Why is your family well off?" The answers I've received, to characterize them charitably, are half-formed and naive.

The students blame the poor for not being successful. They have no understanding of the ways that opportunity is not equal in America and no notion that social structure pushes people around, influencing the ideas they hold and the lives they fashion.

High school history textbooks can take some of the credit for this state of affairs. Some textbooks cover certain high points of labor history, such as the 1894 Pullman strike near Chicago that President Cleveland broke with federal troops,[1] or the 1911 Triangle Shirtwaist fire that killed 146 women in New York City,[2] but the most recent event mentioned in most books is the Taft-Hartley Act of fifty years ago.[3] No book mentions the Hormel meat-packers' strike in the mid-1980s or the air traffic controllers' strike broken by President Reagan. Nor do textbooks describe any continuing issues facing labor, such as the growth of multinational corporations and their exporting of jobs overseas. With such omissions, textbooks authors can construe labor history as something that happened long ago, like slavery, and that, like slavery, was corrected long ago. It logically follows that unions appear anachronistic. The idea that they might be necessary in order for workers to have a voice in the workplace goes unstated.

---

[1] The trouble started when George M. Pullman, owner of the Pullman Palace Car Company, refused even to discuss his employees' grievances (for example, deep wage cuts) with them. The workers' cause was taken up by the American Railway Union, which started a boycott against all Pullman train cars. Because Pullman cars were used on nearly every train running, the boycott brought the entire U.S. rail system to a standstill. President Cleveland called in federal troops to break the strike (Cleveland justified his intervention by claiming that the boycott was interfering with the U.S. mail).—Ed.

[2] The fire broke out on Saturday, March 25. Smoke was first seen on the eighth floor of the building where some 500 people—mostly female—were working. Escape was nearly impossible because the owners of the factory had locked the doors in order to keep their employees at work. Many women and girls jumped to their deaths from the windows of the building rather than face death in fire.—Ed.

[3] The Taft-Hartley Act of 1947 placed serious restrictions on union activities, including the requirement that union leaders swear under oath that they weren't communists.—Ed.

Textbooks' treatments of events in labor history are never anchored in any analysis of social class. This amounts to delivering the footnotes instead of the lecture! Six of the dozen high school American history textbooks I examined contain no index listing at all for "social class," "social stratification," "class structure," "income distribution," "inequality," or any conceivably related topic. Not one book lists "upper class," "working class," or "lower class." Two of the textbooks list "middle class," but only to assure students that America is a middle-class country. "Except for slaves, most of the colonists were members of the 'middling ranks,'" says *Land of Promise,* and nails home the point that we are a middle-class country by asking students to "Describe three 'middle-class' values that united free Americans of all classes." Several of the textbooks note the explosion of middle-class suburbs after World War II. Talking about the middle class is hardly equivalent to discussing social stratification, however; in fact, as Gregory Mantsios (1988) has pointed out, "such references appear to be acceptable precisely because they mute class differences."

Stressing how middle-class we all are is particularly problematic today, because the proportion of households earning between 75 percent and 125 percent of the median income has fallen steadily since 1967. The Reagan-Bush administrations accelerated this shrinkage of the middle class, and most families who left its ranks fell rather than rose. This is the kind of historical trend one would think history books would take as appropriate subject matter, but only four of the twelve books in my sample provide any analysis of social stratification in the United States. Even these fragmentary analyses are set mostly in colonial America. *Land of Promise* lives up to its reassuring title by heading its discussion of social class "Social Mobility." "One great difference between colonial and European society was that the colonists had more social mobility," echoes *The American Tradition.* "In contrast with contemporary Europe, eighteenth-century America was a shining land of equality and opportunity—with the notorious exception of slavery," chimes in *The American Pageant*. Although *The Challenge of Freedom* identifies three social classes—upper, middle, and lower—among whites in colonial society, compared to Europe "there was greater *social mobility*."

Never mind that the most violent class conflicts in American history—Bacon's Rebellion and Shays's Rebellion[4]—took place in and just after colonial times. Textbooks still say that colonial society was relatively classless and marked by upward mobility. And things have gotten rosier since. "By 1815," *The Challenge of Freedom* assures us, two classes had withered away and "America was a country of middle class people and of middle class goals." This book returns repeatedly, at intervals of every fifty years or so, to the theme of how open opportunity is in America. "In the years after 1945, *social mobility*—movement from one social class to another—became more widespread in America," *Challenge* concludes. "This meant that people had a better chance to move upward in society." The stress on upward mobility is striking. There is almost nothing in any of these textbooks about class inequalities or barriers of any kind to social mobility. "What conditions made it possible for poor white immigrants to become richer in the colonies?" *Land of Promise* asks. "What conditions made/make it difficult?" goes unasked. Textbook authors thus present an America in which, as preachers were fond of saying in the nineteenth century, men start from "humble origins" and attain "the most elevated positions."

---

[4]Bacon's Rebellion (1676) involved a bloody dispute between settlers and colonial authorities. The settlers' complaints included the fact that the authorities were not providing protection against hostile Native Americans. Shays's Rebellion (1786–1787) resulted from the refusal of Massachusetts legislators to assist debt-ridden farmers who were facing foreclosures.—Ed.

Social class is probably the single most important variable in society. From womb to tomb, it correlates with almost all other social characteristics of people that we can measure. Affluent expectant mothers are more likely to get prenatal care, receive current medical advice, and enjoy general health, fitness, and nutrition. Many poor and working-class mothers-to-be first contact the medical profession in the last month, sometimes the last hours, of their pregnancies. Rich babies come out healthier and weighing more than poor babies. The infants go home to very different situations. Poor babies are more likely to have high levels of poisonous lead in their environments and their bodies. Rich babies get more time and verbal interaction with their parents and higher quality day care when not with their parents. When they enter kindergarten, and through the twelve years that follow, rich children benefit from suburban schools that spend two to three times as much money per student as schools in inner cities or impoverished rural areas. Poor children are taught in classes that are often 50 percent larger than the classes of affluent children. Differences such as these help account for the higher school-dropout rate among poor children.

Even when poor children are fortunate enough to attend the same school as rich children, they encounter teachers who expect only children of affluent families to know the right answers. Social science research shows that teachers are often surprised and even distressed when poor children excel. Teachers and counselors believe they can predict who is "college material." Since many working-class children give off the wrong signals, even in first grade, they end up in the "general education" track in high school. "If you are the child of low-income parents, the chances are good that you will receive limited and often careless attention from adults in your high school," in the words of Theodore Sizer's best-selling study of American high schools, *Horace's Compromise*. "If you are the child of upper-middle-income parents, the chances are good that you will receive substantial and careful attention" (quoted in Karp 1985, 73). Researcher Reba Page (1987) has provided vivid accounts of how high school American history courses use rote learning to turn off lower-class students. Thus schools have put into practice Woodrow Wilson's recommendation: "We want one class of persons to have a liberal education, and we want another class of persons, a very much larger class of necessity in every society, to forgo the privilege of a liberal education[5] and fit themselves to perform specific difficult manual tasks" (quoted in Lapham 1991).

As if this unequal home and school life were not enough, rich teenagers then enroll in the Princeton Review or other coaching sessions for the Scholastic Aptitude Test. Even without coaching, affluent children are advantaged because their background is similar to that of the test-makers, so they are comfortable with the vocabulary and subtle subcultural assumptions of the test. To no one's surprise, social class correlates strongly with SAT scores.

All these are among the reasons why social class predicts the rate of college attendance and the type of college chosen more effectively than does any other factor, including intellectual ability, however measured. After college, most affluent children get white-collar jobs, most working-class children get blue-collar jobs, and the class differences continue. As adults, rich people are more likely to have hired an attorney and to be a member of formal organizations that increase their civic power. Poor people are more likely to watch TV. Because affluent families can save some money while poor families must spend what they make, wealth differences are ten times larger than income differences. Therefore most poor and

working-class families cannot accumulate the down payment required to buy a house, which in turn shuts them out from our most important tax shelter, the writeoff of home mortgage interest. Working-class parents cannot afford to live in elite subdivisions or hire high-quality day care, so the process of educational inequality replicates itself in the next generation. Finally, affluent Americans also have longer life expectancies than lower- and working-class people, the largest single cause of which is better access to health care. Echoing the results of Helen Keller's study of blindness, research has determined that poor health is not distributed randomly about the social structure but is concentrated in the lower class. Social Security then becomes a huge transfer system, using monies contributed by all Americans to pay benefits disproportionately to longer-lived affluent Americans.

Ultimately, social class determines how people think about social class. When asked if poverty in America is the fault of the poor or the fault of the system, 57 percent of business leaders blamed the poor; just 9 percent blamed the system. Labor leaders showed sharply reversed choices: only 15 percent said the poor were at fault while 56 percent blamed the system. (Some replied "don't know" or chose a middle position.) The largest single difference between our two main political parties lies in how their members think about social class: 55 percent of Republicans blamed the poor for their poverty, while only 13 percent blamed the system for it; 68 percent of Democrats, on the other hand, blamed the system, while only 5 percent blamed the poor (Verba and Orren 1985, 72–75).

Few of these statements are news, I know, which is why I have not documented most of them, but the majority of high school students do not know or understand these ideas. Moreover, the processes have changed over time, for the class structure in America today is not the same as it was in 1890, let alone in colonial

---

[5]"Liberal education," by definition, is education suited for the free (or liberated) citizen. The contrasting form of education is not "conservative education," but "vocational training." — Ed.

America. Yet in *Land of Promise,* for example, social class goes unmentioned after 1670.

Many teachers compound the problem by avoiding talking about social class. Recent interviews with teachers "revealed that they had a much broader knowledge of the economy, both academically and experientially, than they admitted in class." Teachers "expressed fear that students might find out about the injustices and inadequacies of their economic and political institutions" (McNeil 1983, 116). . . .

Historically, social class is intertwined with all kinds of events and processes in our past. Our governing system was established by rich men, following theories that emphasized government as a bulwark of the propertied class. Although rich himself, James Madison worried about social inequality and wrote *The Federalist* #10 to explain how the proposed government would not succumb to the influence of the affluent. Madison did not fully succeed, according to Edward Pessen, who examined the social-class backgrounds of all American presidents through Reagan. Pessen found that more than 40 percent hailed from the upper class, mostly from the upper fringes of that elite group, and another 15 percent originated in families located between the upper and upper-middle classes. More than 25 percent came from a solid upper-middle-class background, leaving just six presidents, or 15 percent, to come from the middle and lower-middle classes and just one, Andrew Johnson, representing any part of the lower class. For good reason, Pessen (1984) titled his book *The Log Cabin Myth.* While it was sad when the great ship *Titanic* went down, as the old song refrain goes, it was saddest for the lower classes: among women, only 4 of 143 first-class passengers were lost, while 15 of 93 second-class passengers drowned, along with 81 of 179 third-class women and girls. The crew ordered third-class passengers to remain below deck, holding some of them there at gunpoint (Hollingshead and Redlich 1958).

More recently, social class played a major role in determining who fought in the Vietnam War: sons of the affluent won educational and medical deferments through most of the conflict (Baskir and Strauss 1986). Textbooks and teachers ignore all this.

Teachers may avoid social class out of a laudable desire not to embarrass their charges. If so, their concern is misguided. When my students from nonaffluent backgrounds learn about the class system, they find the experience liberating. Once they see the social processes that have helped keep their families poor, they can let go of their negative self-image about being poor. If to understand is to pardon, for working-class children to understand how stratification works is to pardon *themselves* and their families. Knowledge of the social-class system also reduces the tendency of Americans from other social classes to blame the victim for being poor. Pedagogically, stratification provides a gripping learning experience. Students are fascinated to discover how the upper class wields disproportionate power relating to everything from energy bills in Congress to zoning decisions in small towns.

Consider a white ninth-grade student taking American history in a predominantly middle-class town in Vermont. Her father tapes Sheetrock, earning an income that in slow construction seasons leaves the family quite poor. Her mother helps out by driving a school bus part-time, in addition to taking care of her two younger siblings. The girl lives with her family in a small house, a winterized former summer cabin, while most of her classmates live in large suburban homes. How is this girl to understand her poverty? Since history textbooks present the American past as 390 years of progress and portray our society as a land of opportunity in which folks get what they deserve and deserve what they get, the failures of working-class Americans to transcend their class origin inevitably get laid at their own doorsteps.

Within the white working-class community the girl will probably find few resources—teachers, church parishioners, family members—who can tell her of heroes or struggles among people of her background, for, except in pockets of continuing class conflict, the working class usually forgets its own history. More than any other group, white working-class students believe that they deserve their low status. A subculture of shame results. This negative self-image is foremost among what Richard Sennett and Jonathan Cobb have called "the hidden injuries of class" (1972). Several years ago, two students of mine provided a demonstration: they drove around Burlington, Vermont, in a big, nearly new, shiny black American car (probably a Lexus would be more appropriate today) and then in a battered ten-year-old subcompact. In each vehicle, when they reached a stoplight and it turned green, they waited until they were honked at before driving on. Motorists averaged less than seven seconds to honk at them in the subcompact, but in the luxury car the students enjoyed 13.2 seconds before anyone honked. Besides providing a good reason to buy a luxury car, this experiment shows how Americans unconsciously grant respect to the educated and successful. Since motorists of all social stations honked at the subcompact more readily, working-class drivers were in a sense disrespecting themselves while deferring to their betters. The biting quip "If you're so smart, why aren't you rich?" conveys the injury done to the self-image of the poor when the idea that America is a meritocracy goes unchallenged in school.

Part of the problem is that American history textbooks describe American education itself as meritocratic. A huge body of research confirms that education is dominated by the class structure and operates to replicate that structure in the next generation. Meanwhile, history textbooks blithely tell of such federal largesse to education as the Elementary and Secondary Education Act, passed under President Lyndon Johnson. Not one textbook offers any data on or analysis of inequality within educational institutions. None mentions how school districts in low-income areas labor under financial constraints so shocking that Jonathan Kozol (1991) calls them "savage inequalities." No textbook ever suggests that students might research the history of their own school and the population it serves. The only two textbooks that relate education to the class system at all see it as a remedy! Schooling "was a key to upward mobility in postwar America," in the words of *The Challenge of Freedom*.

The tendency of teachers and textbooks to avoid social class as if it were a dirty little secret only reinforces the reluctance of working-class families to talk about it. Paul Cowan has told of interviewing the children of Italian immigrant workers involved in the famous 1912 Lawrence, Massachusetts, mill strike. He spoke with the daughter of one of the Lawrence workers who testified at a Washington congressional hearing investigating the strike. The worker, Camella Teoli, then thirteen years old, had been scalped by a cotton-twisting machine just before the strike and had been hospitalized for several months. Her testimony "became front-page news all over America." But Teoli's daughter, interviewed in 1976 after her mother's death, could not help Cowan. Her mother had told her nothing of the incident, nothing of her trip to Washington, nothing about her impact on America's conscience—even though almost every day, the daughter "had combed her mother's hair into a bun that disguised the bald spot" (Gutman 1987, 386–390). A professional of working-class origin told me a similar story about being ashamed of her uncle "for being a steelworker." A certain defensiveness is built into working-class culture; even its successful acts of working-class resistance, like the Lawrence strike, necessarily presuppose lower status and income, hence connote a certain inferiority. If the larger community is so good, as textbooks tell us it is, then celebrating or even passing on the memory of conflict with it seems somehow disloyal.

Textbooks do present immigrant history. Around the turn of the century immigrants dominated the American urban working class, even in cities as distant from seacoasts as Des Moines and Louisville. When more than 70 percent of the white population was native stock, less than 10 percent of the urban working class was (Gutman 1987, 386–390). But when textbooks tell the immigrant story, they emphasize Joseph Pulitzer, Andrew Carnegie, and their ilk—immigrants who made supergood. Several textbooks apply the phrases *rags to riches* or *land of opportunity* to the immigrant experience. Such legendary successes were achieved, to be sure, but they were the exceptions, not the rule. Ninety-five percent of the executives and financiers in America around the turn of the century came from upper-class or upper-middle-class backgrounds. Fewer than 3 percent started as poor immigrants or farm children. Throughout the nineteenth century, just 2 percent of American industrialists came from working-class origins (Miller 1962, 326–328). By concentrating on the inspiring exceptions, textbooks present immigrant history as another heartening confirmation of America as the land of unparalleled opportunity.

Again and again, textbooks emphasize how America has differed from Europe in having less class stratification and more economic and social mobility. This is another aspect of the archetype of American exceptionalism: our society has been uniquely fair. It would never occur to historians in, say, France or Australia, to claim that their society was exceptionally equalitarian. Does this treatment of the United States prepare students for reality? It certainly does not accurately describe our country today. Social scientists have on many occasions compared the degree of economic equality in the United States with that in other industrial nations. Depending on the measure used, the United States has ranked sixth of six, seventh

of seven, ninth of twelve, or fourteenth of fourteen (Verba and Orren 1985, 10). In the United States the richest fifth of the population earns eleven times as much income as the poorest fifth, one of the highest ratios in the industrialized world; in Great Britain the ratio is seven to one, in Japan just four to one (Mantsios 1988, 59). In Japan the average chief executive officer in an automobile-manufacturing firm makes 20 times as much as the average worker in an automobile assembly plant; in the United States he (and it is not she) makes 192 times as much (*Harper's* 1990, 19). The Jeffersonian conceit of a nation of independent farmers and merchants is also long gone: only one working American in thirteen is self-employed, compared to one in eight in Western Europe (*Harper's* 1993, 19). Thus not only do we have far fewer independent entrepreneurs compared to two hundred years ago, we have fewer compared to Europe today.

Since textbooks claim that colonial America was radically less stratified than Europe, they should tell their readers when inequality set in. It surely was not a recent development. By 1910 the top 1 percent of the United States population received more than a third of all personal income, while the bottom fifth got less than one-eighth (Tyack and Hansot 1981). This level of inequality was on a par with that in Germany or Great Britain (Williamson and Lindert 1980). If textbooks acknowledged inequality, then they could describe the changes in our class structure over time, which would introduce their students to fascinating historical debate.

For example, some historians argue that wealth in colonial society was more equally distributed than it is today and that economic inequality increased during the presidency of Andrew Jackson—a period known, ironically, as the age of the common man. Others believe that the flowering of the large corporation in the late nineteenth century made the class structure more rigid. Walter Dean Burnham, has argued that the Republican presidential victory in 1896

(McKinley over Bryan) brought about a sweeping political realignment that changed "a fairly democratic regime into a rather broadly based oligarchy,"[6] so by the 1920s business controlled public policy (1965, 23–25). Clearly the gap between rich and poor, like the distance between blacks and whites, was greater at the end of the Progressive Era in 1920 than at its beginning around 1890 (Schwartz 1991, 94). The story is not all one of increasing stratification, for between the depression and the end of World War II income and wealth in America gradually became more equal. Distributions of income then remained reasonably constant until President Reagan took office in 1981, when inequality began to grow. Still other scholars think that little change has occurred since the Revolution. Lee Soltow (1989), for example, finds "surprising inequality of wealth and income" in America in 1798. At least for Boston, Stephan Thernstrom (1973) concludes that inequalities in life chances owing to social class show an eerie continuity. All this is part of American history. But it is not part of American history as taught in high school.

To social scientists, the level of inequality is a portentous thing to know about a society. When we rank countries by this variable, we find Scandinavian nations at the top, the most equal, and agricultural societies like Colombia and India near the bottom. The policies of the Reagan and Bush administrations, which openly favored the rich, abetted a trend already in motion, causing inequality to increase measurably between 1981 and 1992. For the United States to move perceptibly toward Colombia in social inequality is a development of no small import (Danziger and Gottschalf 1993; Kohn 1990; Macrobert 1984). Surely high school students would be interested to learn that in 1950 physicians made two and a half times what unionized industrial workers made but now make six

times as much. Surely they need to understand that top managers of clothing firms, who used to earn fifty times what their American employees made, now make 1,500 times what their Malaysian workers earn. Surely it is wrong for our history textbooks and teachers to withhold the historical information that might prompt and inform discussion of these trends.

Why might they commit such a blunder? First and foremost, publisher censorship of textbook authors. "You always run the risk, if you talk about social class, of being labeled Marxist," the editor for social studies and history at one of the biggest publishing houses told me. This editor communicates the taboo, formally or subtly, to every writer she works with, and she implied that most other editors do too.

Publisher pressure derives in part from textbook adoption boards and committees in states and school districts. These are subject in turn to pressure from organized groups and individuals who appear before them. Perhaps the most robust such lobby is Educational Research Analysts, led by Mel Gabler of Texas. Gabler's stable of right-wing critics regards even alleging that a textbook contains some class analysis as a devastating criticism. As one writer has put it, "Formulating issues in terms of class is unacceptable, perhaps even un-American" (Mantsios 1988). Fear of not winning adoption in Texas is a prime source of publisher angst, and might help explain why *Life and Liberty* limits its social-class analysis to colonial times in *England!* By contrast, "the colonies were places of great opportunity," even back then. Some Texans cannot easily be placated, however. Deborah L. Brezina, a Gabler ally, complained to the Texas textbook board that *Life and Liberty* describes America "as an unjust society," unfair to lower economic groups, and therefore should not be approved. Such pressure is hardly new. Harold Rugg's *Introduction to Problems of American Culture* and his popular history textbook, written during the depression, included some

[6]*Oligarchy* means "rule by a few"—as opposed to *aristocracy*, which means, technically, "rule by the best few."—Ed.

class analysis. In the early 1940s, according to Frances FitzGerald, the National Association of Manufacturers attacked Rugg's books, partly for this feature, and "brought to an end" social and economic analysis in American history textbooks (1979).

More often the influence of the upper class is less direct. The most potent rationale for class privilege in American history has been Social Darwinism,[7] an archetype that still has great power in American culture. The notion that people rise and fall in a survival of the fittest may not conform to the data on intergenerational mobility in the United States, but that has hardly caused the archetype to fade away from American education, particularly from American history classes (Tyack and Hansot 1981). Facts that do not fit with the archetype, such as the entire literature of social stratification, simply get left out. . . .

But isn't it nice simply to believe that America is equal? Maybe the "land of opportunity" archetype is an empowering myth— maybe believing in it might even help make it come true. For if students *think* the sky is the limit, they may reach for the sky, while if they don't, they won't.

The analogy of gender points to the problem with this line of thought. How could high school girls understand their place in American history if their textbooks told them that, from colonial America to the present, women have had equal opportunity for upward mobility and political participation? How could they then explain why no woman has been president? Girls would have to infer, perhaps unconsciously, that it has been their own gender's fault, a conclusion that is hardly empowering.

Textbooks do tell how women were denied the right to vote in many states until 1920 and faced other barriers to upward mobility.

Textbooks also tell of barriers confronting racial minorities. The final question *Land of Promise* asks students following its "Social Mobility" section is "What social barriers prevented blacks, Indians, and women from competing on an equal basis with white male colonists?" After its passage extolling upward mobility, *The Challenge of Freedom* notes, "Not all people, however, enjoyed equal rights or an equal chance to improve their way of life," and goes on to address the issues of sexism and racism. But neither here nor anywhere else do *Promise* or *Challenge* (or most other textbooks) hint that opportunity might not be equal today for white Americans of the lower and working classes. Perhaps as a result, even business leaders and Republicans, the respondents statistically most likely to engage in what sociologists call "blaming the victim," blame the social system rather than African Americans for black poverty and blame the system rather than women for the latter's unequal achievement in the workplace. In sum, affluent Americans, like their textbooks, are willing to credit racial discrimination as the cause of poverty among blacks and Indians and sex discrimination as the cause of women's inequality but don't see class discrimination as the cause of poverty in general (Verba and Orren 1985, 72–75).

More than math or science, more even than American literature, courses in American history hold the promise of telling high school students how they and their parents, their communities, and their society came to be as they are. One way things are is unequal by social class. Although poor and working-class children usually cannot identify the cause of their alienation, history often turns them off because it justifies rather than explains the present. When these students react by dropping out, intellectually if not physically, their poor school performance helps convince them as well as their peers in the faster tracks that the system is meritocratic and that they themselves lack merit. In the end, the absence of social-class analysis in

---

[7]For a discussion of this concept, see chapter 1 in *The Practical Skeptic: Core Concepts in Sociology.* — Ed.

American history courses amounts to one more way that education in America is rigged against the working class.

References

Baskir, L., and W. Strauss. 1986. *Chance and Circumstance.* New York: Random House.

Bowles, S., and H. Gintis. 1976. *Schooling in Capitalist America.* New York: Basic Books.

Brezina, D. L. 1993. "Critique of *Life and Liberty*," distributed by Mel Gabler's Educational Research Analysts.

Burnham, W. D. 1965. "The Changing Shape of the American Political University." *American Political Science Review* 59: 23–25.

Danziger, S., and P. Gottschalf. 1993. *Uneven Tides.* New York: Sage.

FitzGerald, F. 1979. *America Revised.* New York: Vintage Books.

Gutman, H. 1987. *Power and Culture.* New York: Pantheon Books.

Harper's. 1990. "Index" (citing data from the United Automobile Workers; Chrysler Corp; "Notice of Annual Meeting of Stockholders"). April 1.

Harper's. 1993. "Index" (citing the Organization for Economic Cooperation and Development). January 19.

Hollingshead, A., and F. C. Redlich. 1958. *Social Class and Mental Illness.* New York: Wiley.

Karp, Walter. 1985. "Why Johnny Can't Think." *Harper's,* June, p. 73.

Kohn, A. 1990. *You Know What They Say. . . .* New York: HarperCollins.

Kozol, J. 1991. *Savage Inequalities.* New York: Crown.

Lapham, Lewis. 1991. "Notebook." *Harper's,* July, p. 10.

Macrobert, A. 1984. "The Unfairness of It All." *Vermont Vanguard Press,* September 30, pp. 12–13.

Mantsios, Gregory. 1988. "Class in America: Myths and Realities." In Paula S. Rothenberg (ed.), *Racism and Sexism: An Integrated Study.* New York: St. Martin's Press.

McNeil, Linda. 1983. "Teaching and Classroom Control." In M. W. Apple and L. Weis (eds.), *Ideology and Practice in Schooling.* Philadelphia: Temple University Press.

Miller, W. 1962. "American Historians and the Business Elite." In W. Miller (ed.), *Men in Business.* New York: Harper & Row.

Page, Reba. 1987. *The Lower-track Students' View of Curriculum.* Washington, DC: American Education Research Association.

Pessen, E. 1984. *The Log Cabin Myth.* New Haven, CT: Yale University Press.

Schwartz, B. 1991. "The Reconstruction of Abraham Lincoln," in D. Middleton and D. Edwards (eds.), *Collective Remembering.* London: Sage.

Sennett, R., and J. Cobb. 1972. *The Hidden Injuries of Class.* New York: Knopf.

Soltow, L. 1989. *Distribution of Wealth and Income in the United States in 1798.* Pittsburgh: University of Pittsburgh Press.

Thernstrom, S. 1973. *The Other Bostonians.* Cambridge, MA: Harvard University Press.

Tyack, D., and E. Hansot. 1981. "Conflict and Consensus in American Public Education." *Daedalus* 110: 11–12.

Verba, S., and G. Orren. 1985. *Equality in America.* Cambridge, MA: Harvard University Press.

Williamson and Lindert. 1980. *American Inequality: A Macroeconomic History.* New York: Academic Press.

Questions

1. Loewen asserts that high school students graduate as "terrible sociologists." To what extent do you agree or disagree with this assessment? Why?

2. Assuming that Loewen is correct about the "mythical" quality of the information given in high school history textbooks, what might be the function of these myths in American society? What might be the dysfunctions?

·34·

Some Principles of Stratification
A Critical Analysis

Melvin M. Tumin

I recall that as a college sophomore taking sociology, one of our reading assignments was "Some Principles of Stratification," by Kingsley Davis and Wilbert Moore. Their argument (simply put) was that people who had higher social class and status positions did so because they deserve it, owing to the fact that higher-status occupations were (1) more important to society and (2) more difficult to fulfill. It wasn't an easy article to read, but I became enthralled with it; I found Davis and Moore's account of social stratification to be utterly compelling. Suddenly, everything (about stratification, anyway) made sense to me.

My next moment of epiphany led to a great deal of intellectual development. It happened when I came across the following 1953 paper by Melvin Tumin. As Tumin makes clear, the Davis and Moore thesis contains some serious errors in logic. As I reflect back on this now, I suppose my response to Davis and Moore proves that I was one of those "terrible sociologists" to whom Loewen referred in reading 33.

The fact of social inequality in human society is marked by its ubiquity and its antiquity. Every known society, past and present, distributes its scarce and demanded goods and services unequally. And there are attached to the positions which command unequal amounts of such goods and services certain highly morally toned evaluations of their importance for the society.

The ubiquity and the antiquity of such inequality has given rise to the assumption that there must be something both inevitable and positively functional about social arrangements.

Clearly, the truth or falsity of such an assumption is a strategic question for any general theory of social organization. It is therefore most curious that the basic premises and implications of the assumption have only been most casually explored by American sociologists.

The most systematic treatment is to be found in the well-known article by Kingsley Davis and Wilbert Moore, entitled "Some Principles of Stratification." More than twelve years have passed since its publication, and though it is one of the very few treatments of stratification on a high level of generalization, it is difficult to locate a single systematic analysis of its reasoning. It will be the principal concern of this paper to present the beginnings of such an analysis.

The central argument advanced by Davis and Moore can be stated in a number of sequential propositions, as follows:

1. Certain positions in any society are functionally more important than others, and require special skills for their performance.

2. Only a limited number of individuals in any society have the talents which can be trained into the skills appropriate to these positions.

3. The conversion of talents into skills involves a training period during which sacrifices of one kind or another are made by those undergoing the training.

4. In order to induce the talented persons to undergo these sacrifices and acquire the training, their future positions must carry an inducement value in the form of differential, i.e., privileged and disproportionate access to the scarce and desired rewards which the society has to offer.

5. These scarce and desired goods consist of the rights and perquisites attached to, or built into, the positions, and can be classified into those things which contribute to (a) sustenance and comfort, (b) humor and diversion, (c) self-respect and ego expansion.

6. This differential access to the basic rewards of the society has as a consequence the differentiation of the prestige and esteem which various strata acquire. This may be said, along with the rights and perquisites, to constitute institutionalized social inequality, i.e., stratification.

7. Therefore, social inequality among different strata in the amounts of scarce and desired goods, and the amounts of prestige and esteem which they receive, is both positively functional and inevitable in any society.

Let us take these propositions and examine them *seriatim*.[1]

1. *Certain positions in any society are more functionally important than others and require special skills for their performance.*

The key term here is "functionally important." The functionalist theory of social organization is by no means clear and explicit about this term. The minimum common referent is to something known as the "survival value" of a social structure. This concept immediately involves a number of perplexing questions. Among these are (a) the issue of minimum vs. maximum survival, and the possible empirical referents which can be given to those terms; (b) whether such a proposition is a useless tautology since any *status quo* at any given moment is nothing more and nothing less than everything present in the *status quo*. In these terms, all acts and structures must be judged positively functional in that they constitute essential portions of the *status quo*; (c) what kind of calculus of functionality exists which will enable us, at this point in our development, to add and subtract long and short range consequences, with their mixed qualities, and arrive at some summative judgment regarding the rating an act or structure should receive on a scale of greater or lesser functionality? At best, we tend to make primarily intuitive judgments. Often enough, these judgments involve the use of value-laden criteria, or, at least, criteria which are chosen in preference to others not for any sociologically systematic reasons but by reason of certain implicit value preferences.

Thus, to judge that the engineers in a factory are functionally more important to the factory than the unskilled workmen involves a notion regarding the dispensability of the unskilled workmen, or their replaceability, relative to that of the engineers. But this is not a process of

[1]*Seriatim* is Latin for "in series." — Ed.

choice with infinite time dimensions. For at some point along the line one must face the problem of adequate motivation for *all* workers at all levels of skill in the factory. In the long run, *some* labor force of unskilled workmen is as important and as indispensable to the factory as *some* labor force of engineers. Often enough, the labor force situation is such that this fact is brought home sharply to the entrepreneur in the short run rather than in the long run.

Moreover, the judgment as to the relative indispensability and replaceability of a particular segment of skills in the population involves a prior judgment about the bargaining-power of that segment. But this power is itself a culturally shaped *consequence* of the existing system of rating, rather than something inevitable in the nature of social organization. At least the contrary of this has never been demonstrated, but only assumed.

A generalized theory of social stratification must recognize that the prevailing system of inducements and rewards is only one of many variants in the whole range of possible systems of motivation which, at least theoretically, are capable of working in human society. It is quite conceivable, of course, that a system of norms could be institutionalized in which the idea of threatened withdrawal of services, except under the most extreme circumstances, would be considered as absolute moral anathema. In such a case, the whole notion of relative functionality, as advanced by Davis and Moore, would have to be radically revised.

2. *Only a limited number of individuals in any society have the talents which can be trained into the skills appropriate to these positions (i.e., the more functionally important positions).*

The truth of this proposition depends at least in part on the truth of proposition 1 above. It is, therefore, subject to all the limitations indicated above. But for the moment, let us assume the validity of the first proposition and concentrate on the question of the rarity of appropriate talent.

If all that is meant is that in every society there is a *range* of talent, and that some members of any society are by nature more talented than others, no sensible contradiction can be offered, but a question must be raised here regarding the amount of sound knowledge present in any society concerning the presence of talent in the population.

For, in every society there is some demonstrable ignorance regarding the amount of talent present in the population. *And the more rigidly stratified a society is, the less chance does that society have of discovering any new facts about the talents of its members.* Smoothly working and stable systems of stratification, wherever found, tend to build-in obstacles to the further exploration of the range of available talent. This is especially true in those societies where the opportunity to discover talent in any one generation varies with the differential resources of the parent generation. Where, for instance, access to education depends upon the wealth of one's parents, and where wealth is differentially distributed, large segments of the population are likely to be deprived of the chance even to *discover* what are their talents.

Whether or not differential rewards and opportunities are functional in any one generation, it is clear that if those differentials are allowed to be socially inherited by the next generation, then, the stratification system is specifically dysfunctional for the discovery of talents in the next generation. In this fashion, systems of social stratification tend to limit the chances available to maximize the efficiency of discovery, recruitment and training of "functionally important talent."

Additionally, the unequal distribution of rewards in one generation tends to result in the unequal distribution of motivation in the succeeding generation. Since motivation to succeed is clearly an important element in the entire process of education, the unequal distribution of motivation tends to set limits on the possible extensions of the educational system, and hence, upon the efficient recruitment and training of the widest body of skills available in the population.[2]

Lastly, in this context, it may be asserted that there is some noticeable tendency for elites to restrict further access to their privileged positions, once they have sufficient power to enforce such restrictions. This is especially true in a culture where it is possible for an elite to contrive a high demand and a proportionately higher reward for its work by restricting the numbers of the elite available to do the work. The recruitment and training of doctors in modern United States is at least partly a case in point.

Here, then, are three ways, among others which could be cited, in which stratification systems, once operative, tend to reduce the survival value of a society by limiting the search, recruitment and training of functionally important personnel far more sharply than the facts of available talent would appear to justify. It is only when there is genuinely equal access to recruitment and training for all potentially talented persons that differential rewards can conceivably be justified as functional. And stratification systems are apparently *inherently antagonistic* to the development of such full equality of opportunity.

3. *The conversion of talents into skills involves a training period during which sacrifices of one kind or another are made by those undergoing the training.*

Davis and Moore introduce here a concept, "sacrifice," which comes closer than any of the rest of their vocabulary of analysis to being a direct reflection of the rationalizations, offered by the more fortunate members of a society, of

the rightness of their occupancy of privileged positions. It is the least critically thought-out concept in the repertoire, and can also be shown to be least supported by the actual facts.

In our present society, for example, what are the sacrifices which talented persons undergo in the training period? The possibly serious losses involve the surrender of earning power and the cost of the training. The latter is generally borne by the parents of the talented youth undergoing training, and not by the trainees themselves. But this cost tends to be paid out of income which the parents were able to earn generally by virtue of *their* privileged positions in the hierarchy of stratification. That is to say, the parents' ability to pay for the training of their children is part of the differential *reward* they, the parents, received for their privileged positions in the society. And to charge this sum up against sacrifices made by the youth is falsely to perpetuate a bill or a debt already paid by the society to the parents.

So far as the sacrifice of earning power by the trainees themselves is concerned, the loss may be measured relative to what they might have earned had they gone into the labor market instead of into advanced training for the "important" skills. There are several ways to judge this. One way is to take all the average earnings of age peers who did go into the labor market for a period equal to the average length of the training period. The total income, so calculated, roughly equals an amount which the elite can, on the average, earn back in the first decade of professional work, over and above the earnings of his age peers who are not trained. Ten years is probably the maximum amount needed to equalize the differential. There remains, on the average, twenty years of work during each of which the skilled person then goes on to earn far more than his unskilled age peers. And, what is often forgotten, there is then still another ten- or fifteen-year period during which the skilled person continues to work and earn when his unskilled age peer is either totally or

---

[2]In the United States, for instance, we are only now becoming aware of the amount of productivity we, as a society, lose by allocating inferior opportunities and rewards, and hence, inferior motivation, to our Negro population. The actual amount of loss is difficult to specify precisely. Some rough estimate can be made, however, on the assumption that there is present in the Negro population about the same range of talent that is found in the White population.

partially out of the labor market by virtue of the attrition of his strength and capabilities.

One might say that the first ten years of differential pay is perhaps justified, in order to regain for the trained person what he lost during his training period. But it is difficult to imagine what would justify continuing such differential rewards beyond that period.

Another and probably sounder way to measure how much is lost during the training period is to compare the per capita income available to the trainee with the per capita income of the age peer on the untrained labor market during the so-called sacrificial period. If one takes into account the earlier marriage of untrained persons, and the earlier acquisition of family dependents, it is highly dubious that the per capita income of the wage worker is significantly larger than that of the trainee. Even assuming, for the moment, that there is a difference, the amount is by no means sufficient to justify a lifetime of continuing differentials.

What tends to be completely overlooked, in addition, are the psychic and spiritual rewards which are available to the elite trainees by comparison with their age peers in the labor force. There is, first, the much higher prestige enjoyed by the college student and the professional-school student as compared with persons in shops and offices. There is, second, the extremely highly valued privilege of having greater opportunity for self-development. There is, third, all the psychic gain involved in being allowed to delay the assumption of adult responsibilities such as earning a living and supporting a family. There is, fourth, the access to leisure and freedom of a kind not likely to be experienced by the persons already at work.

If these are never taken into account as rewards of the training period it is not because they are not concretely present, but because the emphasis in American concepts of reward is almost exclusively placed on the material returns of positions. The emphases on enjoyment, entertainment, ego enhancement, prestige and esteem are introduced only when the differentials in these which accrue to the skilled positions need to be justified. If these other rewards were taken into account, it would be much more difficult to demonstrate that the training period, as presently operative, is really sacrificial. Indeed, it might turn out to be the case that even at this point in their careers, the elite trainees were being differentially rewarded relative to their age peers in the labor force.

All of the foregoing concerns the quality of the training period under our present system of motivation and rewards. Whatever may turn out to be the factual case about the present system—and the factual case is moot—the more important theoretical question concerns the assumption that the training period under *any* system must be sacrificial.

There seem to be no good theoretical grounds for insisting on this assumption. For, while under any system certain costs will be involved in training persons for skilled positions, these costs could easily be assumed by the society-at-large. Under these circumstances, there would be no need to compensate anyone in terms of differential rewards once the skilled positions were staffed. In short, there would be no need or justification for stratifying social positions on *these* grounds.

4. *In order to induce the talented persons to undergo these sacrifices and acquire the training, their future positions must carry an inducement value in the form of differential, i.e., privileged and disproportionate access to the scarce and desired rewards which the society has to offer.*

Let us assume, for the purposes of the discussion, that the training period is sacrificial and the talent is rare in every conceivable human society. There is still the basic problem as to whether the allocation of differential rewards in scarce and desired goods and services is the only or the most efficient way of recruiting the appropriate talent to these positions.

For there are a number of alternative motivational schemes whose efficiency and adequacy ought at least to be considered in this context. What can be said, for instance, on behalf of the motivation which De Man called "joy in work," Veblen termed "instinct for workmanship" and which we latterly have come to identify as "intrinsic work satisfaction"? Or, to what extent could the motivation of "social duty" be institutionalized in such a fashion that self interest and social interest come closely to coincide? Or, how much prospective confidence can be placed in the possibilities of institutionalizing "social service" as a widespread motivation for seeking one's appropriate position and fulfilling it conscientiously?

Are not these types of motivations, we may ask, likely to prove most appropriate for precisely the "most functionally important positions"? Especially in a mass industrial society, where the vast majority of positions become standardized and routinized, it is the skilled jobs which are likely to retain most of the quality of "intrinsic job satisfaction" and be most readily identifiable as socially serviceable. Is it indeed impossible then to build these motivations into the socialization pattern to which we expose our talented youth?

To deny that such motivations could be institutionalized would be to overclaim our present knowledge. In part, also, such a claim would seem to derive from an assumption that what has not been institutionalized yet in human affairs is incapable of institutionalization. Admittedly, historical experience affords us evidence we cannot afford to ignore. But such evidence cannot legitimately be used to deny absolutely the possibility of heretofore untried alternatives. Social innovation is as important a feature of human societies as social stability.

On the basis of these observations, it seems that Davis and Moore have stated the case much too strongly when they insist that a "functionally important position" which requires skills that are scarce, "must command great prestige, high salary, ample leisure, and the like," if the appropriate talents are to be attracted to the position. Here, clearly, the authors are postulating the unavoidability of very specific types of rewards and, by implication, denying the possibility of others.

5. *These scarce and desired goods consist of rights and perquisites attached to, or built into, the positions and can be classified into those things which contribute to (a) sustenance and comfort; (b) humor and diversion; (c) self-respect and ego expansion.*

6. *This differential access to the basic rewards of the society has as a consequence the differentiation of the prestige and esteem which various strata acquire. This may be said, along with the rights and perquisites, to constitute institutionalized social inequality, i.e., stratification.*

With the classification of the rewards offered by Davis and Moore there need be little argument. Some question must be raised, however, as to whether any reward system, built into a general stratification system, must allocate equal amounts of all three types of reward in order to function effectively, or whether one type of reward may be emphasized to the virtual neglect of others. This raises the further question regarding which type of emphasis is likely to prove most effective as a differential inducer. Nothing in the known facts about human motivation impels us to favor one type of reward over the other, or to insist that all three types of reward must be built into the positions in comparable amounts if the position is to have an inducement value.

It is well known, of course, that societies differ considerably in the kinds of rewards they emphasize in their efforts to maintain a reasonable balance between responsibility and reward. There are, for instance, numerous societies in which the conspicuous display of differential economic advantage is considered extremely bad taste. In short, our present knowledge commends to us the possibility of considerable plasticity in the way in which different types of rewards can be structured into a functioning society. This is to say, it cannot yet be demonstrated that it is *unavoidable* that differential prestige and esteem shall accrue to positions which command differential rewards in power and property.

What does seem to be unavoidable is that differential prestige shall be given to those in any society who conform to the normative order as against those who deviate from that order in a way judged immoral and detrimental. On the assumption that the continuity of a society depends on the continuity and stability of its normative order, some such distinction between conformists and deviants seems inescapable.

It also seems to be unavoidable that in any society, no matter how literate its tradition, the older, wiser and more experienced individuals who are charged with the enculturation and socialization of the young must have more power than the young, on the assumption that the task of effective socialization demands such differential power.

But this differentiation in prestige between the conformist and the deviant is by no means the same distinction as that between strata of individuals each of which operates *within* the normative order, and is composed of adults. The *latter* distinction, in the form of differentiated rewards and prestige between social strata is what Davis and Moore, and most sociologists, consider the structure of a stratification system. The *former* distinctions have nothing necessarily to do with the workings of such a system nor with the efficiency of motivation and recruitment of functionally important personnel.

Nor does the differentiation of power between young and old necessarily create differentially valued strata. For no society rates its young as less morally worthy than its older persons, no matter how much differential power the older ones may temporarily enjoy.

7. *Therefore, social inequality among different strata in the amounts of scarce and desired goods, and the amounts of prestige and esteem which they receive, is both positively functional and inevitable in any society.*

If the objections which have heretofore been raised are taken as reasonable, then it may be stated that the only items which any society *must* distribute unequally are the power and property necessary for the performance of different tasks. If such differential power and property are viewed by all as commensurate with the differential responsibilities, and if they are culturally defined as *resources* and not as rewards, then, no differentials in prestige and esteem need follow.

Historically, the evidence seems to be that every time power and property are distributed unequally, no matter what the cultural definition, prestige and esteem differentiations have tended to result as well. Historically, however, no systematic effort has ever been made, under propitious circumstances, to develop the tradition that each man is as socially worthy as all other men so long as he performs his appropriate tasks conscientiously. While such a tradition seems utterly utopian, no known facts in psychological or social science have yet demonstrated its impossibility or its dysfunctionality for the continuity of a society. The achievement of a full institutionalization of such a tradition seems far too remote to contemplate. Some successive approximations at such a tradition, however, are not out of the range of prospective social innovation.

What, then, of the "positive functionality" of social stratification? Are there other, negative, functions of institutionalized social inequality which can be identified, if only tentatively? Some such dysfunctions of stratification have already been suggested in the body of this paper. Along with others they may now be stated, in the form of provisional assertions, as follows:

1. Social stratification systems function to limit the possibility of discovery of the full range of talent available in a society. This results from the fact of unequal access to appropriate motivation, channels of recruitment and centers of training.

2. In foreshortening the range of available talent, social stratification systems function to set limits upon the possibility of expanding the productive resources of the society, at least relative to what might be the case under conditions of greater equality of opportunity.

3. Social stratification systems function to provide the elite with the political power necessary to procure acceptance and dominance of an ideology which rationalizes the *status quo,* whatever it may be, as "logical," "natural" and "morally right." In this manner, social stratification systems function as essentially conservative influences in the societies in which they are found.

4. Social stratification systems function to distribute favorable self-images unequally throughout a population. To the extent that such favorable self-images are requisite to the development of the creative potential inherent in men, to that extent stratification systems function to limit the development of this creative potential.

5. To the extent that inequalities in social rewards cannot be made fully acceptable to the less privileged in a society, social stratification systems function to encourage hostility, suspicion and distrust among the various segments of a society and thus to limit the possibilities of extensive social integration.

6. To the extent that the sense of significant membership in a society depends on one's place on the prestige ladder of the society, social stratification systems function to distribute unequally the sense of significant membership in the population.

7. To the extent that loyalty to a society depends on a sense of significant membership in the society, social stratification systems function to distribute loyalty unequally in the population.

8. To the extent that participation and apathy depend upon the sense of significant membership in the society, social stratification systems function to distribute the motivation to participate unequally in a population. . . .

Reference

Davis, Kingsley, and Wilbert Moore. 1945. "Some Principles of Stratification." *American Sociological Review* 10: 242–249.

Questions

1. In your own words, how would you summarize Davis's and Moore's theory of stratification? How about Tumin's response to Davis's and Moore's theory?

2. How would Davis and Moore account for the fact that physicians earn more than, say, truck drivers? Explain.

3. How would Davis and Moore account for the fact that male physicians earn more than, say, female physicians? Explain.

4. Why does Tumin argue that "the more rigidly stratified a society is, the less chance does that society have of discovering any new facts about the talents of its members"? Do you agree or disagree with Tumin on this point? Explain.

·35·

Nickel and *Dimed*
On (Not) Getting By in America

Barbara Ehrenreich

This article, published in 1999, eventually became the first chapter in Ehrenreich's book by the same title; it's an interesting but thoroughly depressing account of what it takes to survive on the proceeds of a minimum wage job. In the introduction to her book, Ehrenreich stresses the fact that her experience represented the *best* case scenario: "A person with every advantage that ethnicity and education, health and motivation can confer attempting, in a time of exuberant prosperity, to survive in the economy's lowest depths."

At the beginning of June 1998 I leave behind everything that normally soothes the ego and sustains the body — home, career, companion, reputation, ATM card — for a plunge into the low-wage workforce. There, I become another, occupationally much diminished "Barbara Ehrenreich" — depicted on job-application forms as a divorced homemaker whose sole work experience consists of housekeeping in a few private homes. I am terrified, at the beginning, of being unmasked for what I am: a middle-class journalist setting out to explore the world that welfare mothers are entering, at the rate of approximately 50,000 a month, as welfare reform kicks in. Happily, though, my fears turn out to be entirely unwarranted: during a month of poverty and toil, my name goes unnoticed and for the most part unuttered. In this parallel universe where my father never got out of the mines and I never got through college, I am "baby," "honey," "blondie," and, most commonly, "girl."

My first task is to find a place to live. I figure that if I can earn $7 an hour — which, from the want ads, seems doable — I can afford to spend $500 on rent, or maybe, with severe economies, $600. In the Key West area, where I live, this pretty much confines me to flophouses and trailer homes — like the one, a pleasing fifteen-minute drive from town, that has no air-conditioning, no screens, no fans, no television, and, by way of diversion, only the challenge of evading the landlord's Doberman pinscher. The big problem with this place, though, is the rent, which at $675 a month is well beyond my reach. All right, Key West is expensive. But so is New York City, or the Bay Area, or Jackson Hole, or Telluride, or Boston, or any other place where tourists and the wealthy compete for living space with the people who clean their toilets and fry their hash browns.[1] Still, it is a shock to

---

[1] According to the Department of Housing and Urban Development, the "fair-market rent" for an efficiency is $551 here in Monroe County, Florida. A comparable rent in the five boroughs of New York City is $704; in San Francisco, $713; and in the heart of Silicon Valley, $808. The fair-market rent for an area is defined as the amount that would be needed to pay rent plus utilities for "privately owned, decent, safe, and sanitary rental housing of a modest (non-luxury) nature with suitable amenities."

realize that "trailer trash" has become, for me, a demographic category to aspire to.

So I decide to make the common trade-off between affordability and convenience, and go for a $500-a-month efficiency thirty miles up a two-lane highway from the employment opportunities of Key West, meaning forty-five minutes if there's no road construction and I don't get caught behind some sun-dazed Canadian tourists. I hate the drive, along a roadside studded with white crosses commemorating the more effective head-on collisions, but it's a sweet little place—a cabin, more or less, set in the swampy back yard of the converted mobile home where my landlord, an affable TV repairman, lives with his bartender girlfriend.

No, this is a purely objective, scientific sort of mission. The humanitarian rationale for welfare reform—as opposed to the more punitive and stingy impulses that may actually have motivated it—is that work will lift poor women out of poverty while simultaneously inflating their self-esteem and hence their future value in the labor market. Thus, whatever the hassles involved in finding child care, transportation, etc., the transition from welfare to work will end happily, in greater prosperity for all. Now there are many problems with this comforting prediction, such as the fact that the economy will inevitably undergo a downturn, eliminating many jobs. Even without a downturn, the influx of a million former welfare recipients into the low-wage labor market could depress wages by as much as 11.9 percent, according to the Economic Policy Institute (EPI) in Washington, D.C.

But is it really possible to make a living on the kinds of jobs currently available to unskilled people? Mathematically, the answer is no, as can be shown by taking $6 to $7 an hour, perhaps subtracting a dollar or two an hour for child care, multiplying by 160 hours a month, and comparing the result to the prevailing rents. According to the National Coalition for the Homeless, for example, in 1998 it took, on average nationwide, an hourly wage of $8.89 to afford a one-bedroom apartment, and the Preamble Center for Public Policy estimates that the odds against a typical welfare recipient's landing a job at such a "living wage" are about 97 to 1. If these numbers are right, low-wage work is not a solution to poverty and possibly not even to homelessness.

It may seem excessive to put this proposition to an experimental test. As certain family members keep unhelpfully reminding me, the viability of low-wage work could be tested, after a fashion, without ever leaving my study. I could just pay myself $7 an hour for eight hours a day, charge myself for room and board, and total up the numbers after a month. Why leave the people and work that I love? But I am an experimental scientist by training. In that business, you don't just sit at a desk and theorize; you plunge into the everyday chaos of nature, where surprises lurk in the most mundane measurements. Maybe, when I got into it, I would discover some hidden economies in the world of the low-wage worker. After all, if 30 percent of the workforce toils for less than $8 an hour, according to the EPI, they may have found some tricks as yet unknown to me. Maybe—who knows?—I would even be able to detect in myself the bracing psychological effects of getting out of the house, as promised by the welfare wonks at places like the Heritage Foundation. Or, on the other hand, maybe there would be unexpected costs—physical, mental, or financial—to throw off all my calculations. Ideally, I should do this with two small children in tow, that being the welfare average, but mine are grown and no one is willing to lend me theirs for a month-long vacation in penury. So this is not the perfect experiment, just a test of the best possible case: an unencumbered woman, smart and even strong, attempting to live more or less off the land.

On the morning of my first full day of job searching, I take a red pen to the want ads, which are auspiciously numerous. Everyone in Key West's booming "hospitality industry" seems to be looking for someone like me — trainable, flexible, and with suitably humble expectations as to pay. I know I possess certain traits that might be advantageous — I'm white and, I like to think, well-spoken and poised — but I decide on two rules: One, I cannot use any skills derived from my education or usual work — not that there are a lot of want ads for satirical essayists anyway. Two, I have to take the best-paid job that is offered me and of course do my best to hold it; no Marxist rants or sneaking off to read novels in the ladies' room. In addition, I rule out various occupations for one reason or another: Hotel front-desk clerk, for example, which to my surprise is regarded as unskilled and pays around $7 an hour, gets eliminated because it involves standing in one spot for eight hours a day. Waitressing is similarly something I'd like to avoid, because I remember it leaving me bone tired when I was eighteen, and I'm decades of varicosities and back pain beyond that now. Telemarketing, one of the first refuges of the suddenly indigent, can be dismissed on grounds of personality. This leaves certain supermarket jobs, such as deli clerk, or house-keeping in Key West's thousands of hotel and guest rooms. House-keeping is especially appealing, for reasons both atavistic and practical: it's what my mother did before I came along, and it can't be too different from what I've been doing part-time, in my own home, all my life.

So I put on what I take to be a respectful-looking outfit of ironed Bermuda shorts and scooped-neck T-shirt and set out for a tour of the local hotels and supermarkets. Best Western, Econo Lodge, and HoJo's all let me fill out application forms, and these are, to my relief, interested in little more than whether I am a legal resident of the United States and have committed any felonies. My next stop is Winn-Dixie, the supermarket, which turns out to have a particularly onerous application process, featuring a fifteen-minute "interview" by computer since, apparently, no human on the premises is deemed capable of representing the corporate point of view. I am conducted to a large room decorated with posters illustrating how to look "professional" (it helps to be white and, if female, permed) and warning of the slick promises that union organizers might try to tempt me with. The interview is multiple choice: Do I have anything, such as child-care problems, that might make it hard for me to get to work on time? Do I think safety on the job is the responsibility of management? Then, popping up cunningly out of the blue: How many dollars' worth of stolen goods have I purchased in the last year? Would I turn in a fellow employee if I caught him stealing? Finally, "Are you an honest person?"

Apparently, I ace the interview, because I am told that all I have to do is show up in some doctor's office tomorrow for a urine test. This seems to be a fairly general rule: if you want to stack Cheerio boxes or vacuum hotel rooms in chemically fascist America, you have to be willing to squat down and pee in front of some health worker (who has no doubt had to do the same thing herself). The wages Winn-Dixie is offering — $6 and a couple of dimes to start with — are not enough, I decide, to compensate for this indignity.[2]

---

[2]According to the *Monthly Labor Review* (November 1996), 28 percent of work sites surveyed in the service industry conduct drug tests (corporate workplaces have much higher rates), and the incidence of testing has risen markedly since the Eighties. The rate of testing is highest in the South (56 percent of work sites polled), with the Midwest in second place (50 percent). The drug most likely to be detected — marijuana, which can be detected in urine for weeks — is also the most innocuous, while heroin and cocaine are generally undetectable three days after use. Prospective employees sometimes try to cheat the tests by consuming excessive amounts of liquids and taking diuretics and even masking substances available through the Internet.

I lunch at Wendy's where $4.99 gets you unlimited refills at the Mexican part of the Superbar, a comforting surfeit of refried beans and "cheese sauce." A teenage employee, seeing me studying the want ads, kindly offers me an application form, which I fill out, though here, too, the pay is just $6 and change an hour. Then it's off for a round of the locally owned inns and guesthouses. At "The Palms," let's call it, a bouncy manager actually takes me around to see the rooms and meet the existing housekeepers, who, I note with satisfaction, look pretty much like me—faded ex-hippie types in shorts with long hair pulled back in braids. Mostly, though, no one speaks to me or even looks at me except to proffer an application form. At my last stop, a palatial B&B, I wait twenty minutes to meet "Max," only to be told that there are no jobs now but there should be one soon, since "nobody lasts more than a couple weeks." (Because none of the people I talked to knew I was a reporter, I have changed their names to protect their privacy and, in some cases perhaps, their jobs.)

Three days go by like this, and, to my chagrin, no one out of the approximately twenty places I've applied calls me for an interview. I had been vain enough to worry about coming across as too educated for the jobs I sought, but no one even seems interested in finding out how overqualified I am. Only later will I realize that the want ads are not a reliable measure of the actual jobs available at any particular time. They are, as I should have guessed from Max's comment, the employers' insurance policy against the relentless turnover of the low-wage workforce. Most of the big hotels run ads almost continually, just to build a supply of applicants to replace the current workers as they drift away or are fired, so finding a job is just a matter of being at the right place at the right time and flexible enough to take whatever is being offered that day. This finally happens to me at a one of the big discount hotel chains, where I go, as usual, for housekeeping and am sent, instead, to try out as a waitress at the attached "family restaurant," a dismal spot with a counter and about thirty tables that looks out on a parking garage and features such tempting fare as "Pollish [sic] sausage and BBQ sauce" on 95-degree days. Phillip, the dapper young West Indian who introduces himself as the manager, interviews me with about as much enthusiasm as if he were a clerk processing me for Medicare, the principal questions being what shifts can I work and when can I start. I mutter something about being woefully out of practice as a waitress, but he's already on to the uniform: I'm to show up tomorrow wearing black slacks and black shoes; he'll provide the rust-colored polo shirt with HEARTHSIDE embroidered on it, though I might want to wear my own shirt to get to work, ha ha. At the word "tomorrow," something between fear and indignation rises in my chest. I want to say, "Thank you for your time, sir, but this is just an experiment, you know, not my actual life."

So begins my career at the Hearthside, I shall call it, one small profit center within a global discount hotel chain, where for two weeks I work from 2:00 P.M. till 10:00 P.M. for $2.43 an hour plus tips.[3] In some futile bid for gentility, the management has barred employees from using the front door, so my first day I enter through the kitchen, where a red-faced man with shoulder-length blond hair is throwing frozen steaks against the wall and yelling, "Fuck this shit!" "That's just Jack," explains Gail, the wiry middle-aged waitress who is assigned to train me. "He's on the rag again"—a condition occasioned, in this instance, by the

---

[3]According to the Fair Labor Standards Act, employers are not required to pay "tipped employees," such as restaurant servers, more than $2.13 an hour in direct wages. However, if the sum of tips plus $2.13 an hour falls below the minimum wage, or $5.15 an hour, the employer is required to make up the difference. This fact was not mentioned by managers or otherwise publicized at either of the restaurants where I worked.

fact that the cook on the morning shift had forgotten to thaw out the steaks. For the next eight hours, I run after the agile Gail, absorbing bits of instruction along with fragments of personal tragedy. All food must be trayed, and the reason she's so tired today is that she woke up in a cold sweat thinking of her boyfriend, who killed himself recently in an upstate prison. No refills on lemonade. And the reason he was in prison is that a few DUIs caught up with him, that's all, could have happened to anyone. Carry the creamers to the table in a monkey bowl, never in your hand. And after he was gone she spent several months living in her truck, peeing in a plastic pee bottle and reading by candlelight at night, but you can't live in a truck in the summer, since you need to have the windows down, which means anything can get in, from mosquitoes on up.

At least Gail puts to rest any fears I had of appearing overqualified. From the first day on, I find that of all the things I have left behind, such as home and identity, what I miss the most is competence. Not that I have ever felt utterly competent in the writing business, in which one day's success augurs nothing at all for the next. But in my writing life, I at least have some notion of procedure: do the research, make the outline, rough out a draft, etc. As a server, though, I am beset by requests like bees: more iced tea here, ketchup over there, a to-go box for table fourteen, and where are the high chairs, anyway? Of the twenty-seven tables, up to six are usually mine at any time, though on slow afternoons or if Gail is off, I sometimes have the whole place to myself. There is the touch-screen computer-ordering system to master, which is, I suppose, meant to minimize server-cook contact, but in practice requires constant verbal fine-tuning: "That's gravy on the mashed, okay? None on the meatloaf," and so forth—while the cook scowls as if I were inventing these refinements just to torment him. Plus, something I had forgotten in the years since I was eighteen: about a third of a server's job is "side work" that's invisible to customers— sweeping, scrubbing, slicing, refilling, and restocking. If it isn't all done, every little bit of it, you're going to face the 6:00 P.M. dinner rush defenseless and probably go down in flames. I screw up dozens of times at the beginning, sustained in my shame entirely by Gail's support—"It's okay, baby, everyone does that sometime"—because, to my total surprise and despite the scientific detachment I am doing my best to maintain, I care.

The whole thing would be a lot easier if I could just skate through it as Lily Tomlin in one of her waitress skits, but I was raised by the absurd Booker T. Washingtonian precept that says: If you're going to do something, do it well. In fact, "well" isn't good enough by half. Do it better than anyone has ever done it before. Or so said my father, who must have known what he was talking about because he managed to pull himself, and us with him, up from the mile-deep copper mines of Butte to the leafy suburbs of the Northeast, ascending from boilermakers to martinis before booze beat out ambition. As in most endeavors I have encountered in my life, doing it "better than anyone" is not a reasonable goal. Still, when I wake up at 4:00 A.M. in my own cold sweat, I am not thinking about the writing deadlines I'm neglecting; I'm thinking about the table whose order I screwed up so that one of the boys didn't get his kiddie meal until the rest of the family had moved on to their Key Lime pies. That's the other powerful motivation I hadn't expected—the customers, or "patients," as I can't help thinking of them on account of the mysterious vulnerability that seems to have left them temporarily unable to feed themselves. After a few days at the Hearthside, I feel the service ethic kick in like a shot of oxytocin, the nurturance hormone. The plurality of my customers are hard-working locals—truck drivers, construction workers, even house-keepers from the attached hotel—and I want them to have the closest to a "fine dining" experience that the grubby circumstances will allow. No "you guys" for me; everyone over twelve is "sir" or "ma'am." I ply them with iced tea and coffee refills; I return, mid-meal, to inquire how everything is; I doll up their salads with chopped raw mushrooms, summer squash slices, or whatever bits of produce I can find that have survived their sojourn in the cold-storage room mold-free.

Sometimes I play with the fantasy that I am a princess who, in penance for some tiny transgression, has undertaken to feed each of her subjects by hand. But the non-princesses working with me are just as indulgent, even when this means flouting management rules — concerning, for example, the number of croutons that can go on a salad (six). "Put on all you want," Gail whispers, "as long as Stu isn't looking." She dips into her own tip money to buy biscuits and gravy for an out-of-work mechanic who's used up all his money on dental surgery, inspiring me to pick up the tab for his milk and pie. Maybe the same high levels of agape can be found throughout the "hospitality industry." I remember the poster decorating one of the apartments I looked at, which said "If you seek happiness for yourself you will never find it. Only when you seek happiness for others will it come to you," or words to that effect — an odd sentiment, it seemed to me at the time, to find in the dank one-room basement apartment of a bellhop at the Best Western. At the Hearthside, we utilize whatever bits of autonomy we have to ply our customers with the illicit calories that signal our love. It is our job as servers to assemble the salads and desserts, pouring the dressings and squirting the whipped cream. We also control the number of butter patties our customers get and the amount of sour cream on their baked potatoes. So if you wonder why Americans are so obese, consider the fact that waitresses both express their humanity and earn their tips through the covert distribution of fats.

Ten days into it, this is beginning to look like a livable lifestyle. I like Gail, who is "looking at fifty" but moves so fast she can alight in one place and then another without apparently being anywhere between them. I clown around with Lionel, the teenage Haitian busboy, and catch a few fragments of conversation with Joan, the svelte fortyish hostess and militant feminist who is the only one of us who dares to tell Jack to shut the fuck up. I even warm up to Jack when, on a slow night and to make up for a particularly unwarranted attack on my abilities, or so I imagine, he tells me about his glory days as a young man at "coronary school" — or do you say "culinary"? — in Brooklyn, where he dated a knock-out Puerto Rican chick and learned everything there is to know about food. I finish up at 10:00 or 10:30, depending on how much side work I've been able to get done during the shift, and cruise home to the tapes I snatched up at random when I left my real home — Marianne Faithfull, Tracy Chapman, Enigma, King Sunny Ade, the Violent Femmes — just drained enough for the music to set my cranium resonating but hardly dead. Midnight snack is Wheat Thins and Monterey Jack, accompanied by cheap white wine on ice and whatever AMC has to offer. To bed by 1:30 or 2:00, up at 9:00 or 10:00, read for an hour while my uniform whirls around in the landlord's washing machine, and then it's another eight hours spent following Mao's central instruction, as laid out in the Little Red Book, which was: Serve the people.

I could drift along like this, in some dreamy proletarian idyll, except for two things. One is management. If I have kept this subject on the margins thus far it is because I still flinch to think that I spent all those weeks under the surveillance of men (and later women) whose job it was to monitor my behavior for signs of sloth, theft, drug abuse, or worse. Not that managers and especially "assistant managers" in low-wage settings like this are exactly the class enemy. In the restaurant business, they are mostly former cooks or servers, still capable of pinch-hitting in the kitchen or on the floor, just as in hotels they are likely to be former clerks, and paid a salary of only about $400 a week. But everyone knows they have crossed over to the other side, which is, crudely put, corporate as opposed to human. Cooks want to prepare tasty meals; servers want to serve them graciously; but managers are there for only one reason—to make sure that money is made for some theoretical entity that exists far away in Chicago or New York, if a corporation can be said to have a physical existence at all. Reflecting on her career, Gail tells me ruefully that she had sworn, years ago, never to work for a corporation again. "They don't cut you no slack. You give and you give, and they take."

Managers can sit—for hours at a time if they want—but it's their job to see that no one else ever does, even when there's nothing to do, and this is why, for servers, slow times can be as exhausting as rushes. You start dragging out each little chore, because if the manager on duty catches you in an idle moment, he will give you something far nastier to do. So I wipe, I clean, I consolidate ketchup bottles and recheck the cheesecake supply, even tour the tables to make sure the customer evaluation forms are all standing perkily in their places—wondering all the time how many calories I burn in these strictly theatrical exercises. When, on a particularly dead afternoon, Stu finds me glancing at a *USA Today* a customer has left behind, he assigns me to vacuum the entire floor with the broken vacuum cleaner that has a handle only two feet long, and the only way to do that without incurring orthopedic damage is to proceed from spot to spot on your knees.

On my first Friday at the Hearthside there is a "mandatory meeting for all restaurant employees," which I attend, eager for insight into our overall marketing strategy and the niche (your basic Ohio cuisine with a tropical twist?) we aim to inhabit. But there is no "we" at this meeting. Phillip, our top manager except for an occasional "consultant" sent out by corporate headquarters, opens it with a sneer: "The break room—it's disgusting. Butts in the ashtrays, newspapers lying around, crumbs." This windowless little room, which also houses the time clock for the entire hotel, is where we stash our bags and civilian clothes and take our half-hour meal breaks. But a break room is not a right, he tells us. It can be taken away. We should also know that the lockers in the break room and whatever is in them can be searched at any time. Then comes gossip; there has been gossip; gossip (which seems to mean employees talking among themselves) must stop. Off-duty employees are henceforth barred from eating at the restaurant, because "other servers gather around them and gossip." When Phillip has exhausted his agenda of rebukes, Joan complains about the condition of the ladies' room and I throw in my two bits about the vacuum cleaner. But I don't see any backup coming from my fellow servers, each of whom has subsided into her own personal funk; Gail, my role model, stares sorrowfully at a point six inches from her nose. The meeting ends when Andy, one of the cooks, gets up, muttering about breaking up his day off for this almighty bullshit.

Just four days later we are suddenly summoned into the kitchen at 3:30 P.M., even though there are live tables on the floor. We all—about ten of us—stand around Phillip, who announces grimly that there has been a report of some "drug activity" on the night shift and that, as a result, we are now to be a "drug-free" workplace, meaning that all new hires will be tested, as will possibly current employees on a random basis. I am glad that this part of the kitchen is so dark, because I find myself blushing as hard as if I had been caught toking up in the ladies' room myself: I haven't been treated this way—lined up in the corridor, threatened with locker searches, peppered with carelessly aimed accusations—since junior high school.

Back on the floor, Joan cracks, "Next they'll be telling us we can't have sex on the job." When I ask Stu what happened to inspire the crackdown, he just mutters about "management decisions" and takes the opportunity to upbraid Gail and me for being too generous with the rolls. From now on there's to be only one per customer, and it goes out with the dinner, not with the salad. He's also been riding the cooks, prompting Andy to come out of the kitchen and observe—with the serenity of a man whose customary implement is a butcher knife—that "Stu has a death wish today."

Later in the evening, the gossip crystallizes around the theory that Stu is himself the drug culprit, that he uses the restaurant phone to order up marijuana and sends one of the late servers out to fetch it for him. The server was caught, and she may have ratted Stu out or at least said enough to cast some suspicion on him, thus accounting for his pissy behavior. Who knows? Lionel, the busboy, entertains us for the rest of the shift by standing just behind Stu's back and sucking deliriously on an imaginary joint.

The other problem, in addition to the less-than-nurturing management style, is that this job shows no sign of being financially viable. You might imagine, from a comfortable distance, that people who live, year in and year out, on $6 to $10 an hour have discovered some survival stratagems unknown to the middle class. But no. It's not hard to get my co-workers to talk about their living situations, because housing, in almost every case, is the principal source of disruption in their lives, the first thing they fill you in on when they arrive for their shifts. After a week, I have compiled the following survey:

- Gail is sharing a room in a well-known downtown flophouse for which she and a roommate pay about $250 a week. Her roommate, a male friend, has begun hitting on her, driving her nuts, but the rent would be impossible alone.

- Claude, the Haitian cook, is desperate to get out of the two-room apartment he shares with his girlfriend and two other, unrelated, people. As far as I can determine, the other Haitian men (most of whom only speak Creole) live in similarly crowded situations.

- Annette, a twenty-year-old server who is six months pregnant and has been abandoned by her boyfriend, lives with her mother, a postal clerk.

- Marianne and her boyfriend are paying $170 a week for a one-person trailer.

- Jack, who is, at $10 an hour, the wealthiest of us, lives in the trailer he owns, paying only the $400-a-month lot fee.

- The other white cook, Andy, lives on his dry-docked boat, which, as far as I can tell from his loving descriptions, can't be more than twenty feet long. He offers to take me out on it, once it's repaired, but the offer comes with inquiries as to my marital status, so I do not follow up on it.

- Tina and her husband are paying $60 a night for a double room in a Days Inn. This is because they have no car and the Days Inn is within walking distance of the Hearthside. When Marianne, one of the breakfast servers, is tossed out of her trailer for subletting (which is against the trailer-park rules), she leaves her boyfriend and moves in with Tina and her husband.

- Joan, who had fooled me with her numerous and tasteful outfits (hostesses wear their own clothes), lives in a van she parks behind a shopping center at night and showers in Tina's motel room. The clothes are from thrift shops.[4]

---

[4] I could find no statistics on the number of employed people living in cars or vans, but according to the National Coalition for the Homeless's 1997 report "Myths and Facts About Homelessness," nearly one in five homeless people (in twenty-nine cities across the nation) is employed in a full- or part-time job.

It strikes me, in my middle-class solipsism, that there is gross improvidence in some of these arrangements.[5] When Gail and I are wrapping silverware in napkins—the only task for which we are permitted to sit—she tells me she is thinking of escaping from her roommate by moving into the Days Inn herself. I am astounded: How can she even think of paying between $40 and $60 a day? But if I was afraid of sounding like a social worker, I come out just sounding like a fool. She squints at me in disbelief, "And where am I supposed to get a month's rent and a month's deposit for an apartment?" I'd been feeling pretty smug about my $500 efficiency, but of course it was made possible only by the $1,300 I had allotted myself for start-up costs when I began my low-wage life: $1,000 for the first month's rent and deposit, $100 for initial groceries and cash in my pocket, $200 stuffed away for emergencies. In poverty, as in certain propositions in physics, starting conditions are everything.

There are no secret economies that nourish the poor; on the contrary, there are a host of special costs. If you can't put up the two months' rent you need to secure an apartment, you end up paying through the nose for a room by the week. If you have only a room, with a hot plate at best, you can't save by cooking up huge lentil stews that can be frozen for the week ahead. You eat fast food, or the hot dogs and styrofoam cups of soup that can be microwaved in a convenience store. If you have no money for health insurance—and the Hearthside's niggardly plan kicks in only after three months—you go without routine care or prescription drugs and end up paying the price. Gail, for example, was

fine until she ran out of money for estrogen pills. She is supposed to be on the company plan by now, but they claim to have lost her application form and need to begin the paperwork all over again. So she spends $9 per migraine pill to control the headaches she wouldn't have, she insists, if her estrogen supplements were covered. Similarly, Marianne's boyfriend lost his job as a roofer because he missed so much time after getting a cut on his foot for which he couldn't afford the prescribed antibiotic.

My own situation, when I sit down to assess it after two weeks of work, would not be much better if this were my actual life. The seductive thing about waitressing is that you don't have to wait for payday to feel a few bills in your pocket, and my tips usually cover meals and gas, plus something left over to stuff into the kitchen drawer I use as a bank. But as the tourist business slows in the summer heat, I sometimes leave work with only $20 in tips (the gross is higher, but servers share about 15 percent of their tips with the busboys and bartenders). With wages included, this amounts to about the minimum wage of $5.15 an hour. Although the sum in the drawer is piling up, at the present rate of accumulation it will be more than a hundred dollars short of my rent when the end of the month comes around. Nor can I see any expenses to cut. True, I haven't gone the lentil-stew route yet, but that's because I don't have a large cooking pot, pot holders, or a ladle to stir with (which cost about $30 at Kmart, less at thrift stores), not to mention onions, carrots, and the indispensable bay leaf. I do make my lunch almost every day—usually some slow-burning, high-protein combo like frozen chicken patties with melted cheese on top and canned pinto beans on the side. Dinner is at the Hearthside, which offers its employees a choice of BLT, fish sandwich, or hamburger for only $2. The burger lasts longest, especially if it's heaped with gut-puckering jalapeños, but by midnight my stomach is growling again.

[5]Solipsism is a tricky concept—even if you are a philosophy major. It comes from the Latin *solus* (alone) and *ipse* (self), literally it means "only-oneself-ism." The extreme form of solipsism holds that there is no reality outside of one's mind. In this case, Ehrenreich is using the term loosely to suggest that her thinking was limited to the middle-class reasoning that holds it is improvident to spend $1200–$1800 a month for a motel room as long as there are apartments to be had for half that amount.

So unless I want to start using my car as a residence, I have to find a second, or alternative, job. I call all the hotels where I filled out housekeeping applications weeks ago—the Hyatt, Holiday Inn, Econo Lodge, HoJo's, Best Western, plus a half dozen or so locally run guesthouses. Nothing. Then I start making the rounds again, wasting whole mornings waiting for some assistant manager to show up, even dipping into places so creepy that the front-desk clerk greets you from behind bulletproof glass and sells pints of liquor over the counter. But either someone has exposed my real-life housekeeping habits—which are, shall we say, mellow—or I am at the wrong end of some infallible ethnic equation: most, but by no means all, of the working housekeepers I see on my job searches are African Americans, Spanish-speaking, or immigrants from the Central European post-Communist world, whereas servers are almost invariably white and mono-lingually English-speaking. When I finally get a positive response, I have been identified once again as server material. Jerry's, which is part of a well-known national family restaurant chain and physically attached here to another budget hotel chain, is ready to use me at once. The prospect is both exciting and terrifying, because, with about the same number of tables and counter seats, Jerry's attracts three or four times the volume of customers as the gloomy old Hearthside.

Picture a fat person's hell, and I don't mean a place with no food. Instead there is everything you might eat if eating had no bodily consequences—cheese fries, chicken-fried steaks, fudge-laden desserts—only here every bite must be paid for, one way or another, in human discomfort. The kitchen is a cavern, a stomach leading to the lower intestine that is the garbage and dishwashing area, from which issue bizarre smells combining the edible and the offal: creamy carrion, pizza barf, and that unique and enigmatic Jerry's scent—citrus fart. The floor is slick with spills, forcing us to walk through the kitchen with tiny steps, like Susan McDougal in leg irons. Sinks everywhere are clogged with scraps of lettuce, decomposing lemon wedges, waterlogged toast crusts. Put your hand down on any counter and you risk being stuck to it by the film of ancient syrup spills, and this is unfortunate, because hands are utensils here, used for scooping up lettuce onto salad plates, lifting out pie slices, and even moving hash browns from one plate to another. The regulation poster in the single unisex restroom admonishes us to wash our hands thoroughly and even offers instructions for doing so, but there is always some vital substance missing—soap, paper towels, toilet paper—and I never find all three at once. You learn to stuff your pockets with napkins before going in there; and too bad about the customers, who must eat, though they don't realize this, almost literally out of our hands.

The break room typifies the whole situation: there is none, because there are no breaks at Jerry's. For six to eight hours in a row, you never sit except to pee. Actually, there are three folding chairs at a table immediately adjacent to the bathroom, but hardly anyone ever sits here, in the very rectum of the gastro-architectural system. Rather, the function of the peritoilet area is to house the ashtrays in which servers and dishwashers leave their cigarettes burning at all times, like votive candles, so that they don't have to waste time lighting up again when they dash back for a puff. Almost everyone smokes as if his or her pulmonary well-being depended on it—the multinational mélange of cooks, the Czech dishwashers, the servers, who are all American natives—creating an atmosphere in which oxygen is only an occasional pollutant. My first morning at Jerry's, when the hypoglycemic shakes set in, I complain to one of my fellow servers that I don't understand how she can go so long without food. "Well, I don't understand how you can go so long without a cigarette," she responds in a tone of reproach—because work is what you do for others; smoking is what you do for yourself. I don't know why the anti-smoking crusaders have never grasped the element of defiant self-nurturance that makes the habit so endearing to its victims—as if, in the American workplace, the only thing people have to call their own is the tumors they are nourishing and the spare moments they devote to feeding them.

Now, the Industrial Revolution is not an easy transition, especially when you have to zip through it in just a couple of days. I have gone from craft work straight into the factory, from the air-conditioned morgue of the Hearthside directly into the flames. Customers arrive in human waves, sometimes disgorged fifty at a time from their tour buses, peckish and whiny. Instead of two "girls" on the floor at once, there can be as many as six of us running around in our brilliant pink-and-orange Hawaiian shirts. Conversations, either with customers or fellow employees, seldom last more than twenty seconds at a time. On my first day, in fact, I am hurt by my sister servers' coldness. My mentor for the day is an emotionally uninflected twenty-three-year-old, and the others, who gossip a little among themselves about the real reason someone is out sick today and the size of the bail bond someone else has had to pay, ignore me completely. On my second day, I find out why. "Well, it's good to see you again," one of them says in greeting. "Hardly anyone comes back after the first day." I feel powerfully vindicated—a survivor—but it would take a long time, probably months, before I could hope to be accepted into this sorority.

I start out with the beautiful, heroic idea of handling the two jobs at once, and for two days I almost do it: the breakfast/lunch shift at Jerry's, which goes till 2:00 P.M., arriving at the Hearthside at 2:10 P.M., and attempting to hold out until 10:00 P.M. In the ten minutes between jobs, I pick up a spicy chicken sandwich at the Wendy's drive-through window, gobble it

down in the car, and change from khaki slacks to black, from Hawaiian to rust polo. There is a problem, though. When during the 3:00 P.M. to 4:00 P.M. dead time I finally sit down to wrap silver, my flesh seems to bond to the seat. I try to refuel with a purloined cup of soup, as I've seen Gail and Joan do dozens of times, but a manager catches me and hisses "No eating!" though there's not a customer around to be offended by the sight of food making contact with a server's lips. So I tell Gail I'm going to quit, and she hugs me and says she might just follow me to Jerry's herself.

But the chances of this are minuscule. She has left the flophouse and her annoying roommate and is back to living in her beat-up old truck. But guess what? she reports to me excitedly later that evening: Phillip has given her permission to park overnight in the hotel parking lot, as long as she keeps out of sight, and the parking lot should be totally safe, since it's patrolled by a hotel security guard! With the Hearthside offering benefits like that, how could anyone think of leaving?

Gail would have triumphed at Jerry's, I'm sure, but for me it's a crash course in exhaustion management. Years ago, the kindly fry cook who trained me to waitress at a Los Angeles truck stop used to say: Never make an unnecessary trip; if you don't have to walk fast, walk slow; if you don't have to walk, stand. But at Jerry's the effort of distinguishing necessary from unnecessary and urgent from whenever would itself be too much of an energy drain. The only thing to do is to treat each shift as a one-time-only emergency: you've got fifty starving people out there, lying scattered on the battlefield, so get out there and feed them! Forget that you will have to do this again tomorrow, forget that you will have to be alert enough to dodge the drunks on the drive home tonight—just burn, burn, burn! Ideally, at some point you enter what servers call "a rhythm" and psychologists term a "flow state," in which signals pass from the sense organs directly to the muscles, bypassing the cerebral cortex, and a Zen-like emptiness sets in. A male server from the Hearthside's morning shift tells me about the time he "pulled a triple"—three shifts in a row, all the way around the clock—and then got off and had a drink and met this girl, and maybe he shouldn't tell me this, but they had sex right then and there, and it was like, beautiful.

But there's another capacity of the neuro-muscular system, which is pain. I start tossing back drugstore-brand ibuprofen pills as if they were vitamin C, four before each shift, because an old mouse-related repetitive-stress injury in my upper back has come back to full-spasm strength, thanks to the tray carrying. In my ordinary life, this level of disability might justify a day of ice packs and stretching. Here I comfort myself with the Aleve commercial in which the cute blue-collar guy asks: If you quit after working four hours, what would your boss say? And the not-so-cute blue-collar guy, who's lugging a metal beam on his back, answers: He'd fire me, that's what. But fortunately, the commercial tells us, we workers can exert the same kind of authority over our painkillers that our bosses exert over us. If Tylenol doesn't want to work for more than four hours, you just fire its ass and switch to Aleve.

Management at Jerry's is generally calmer and more "professional" than at the Hearthside, with two exceptions. One is Joy, a plump, blowsy woman in her early thirties, who once kindly devoted several minutes to instructing me in the correct one-handed method of carrying trays but whose moods change disconcertingly from shift to shift and even within one. Then there's B.J., a.k.a. B.J.-the-bitch, whose contribution is to stand by the kitchen counter and yell, "Nita, your order's up, move it!" or, "Barbara, didn't you see you've got another table out there? Come on, girl!" Among other things, she is hated for having replaced the whipped-cream squirt cans with big plastic whipped-cream-filled baggies that have to be squeezed with both hands—because,

reportedly, she saw or thought she saw employees trying to inhale the propellant gas from the squirt cans, in the hope that it might be nitrous oxide. On my third night, she pulls me aside abruptly and brings her face so close that it looks as if she's planning to butt me with her forehead. But instead of saying, "You're fired," she says, "You're doing fine." The only trouble is I'm spending time chatting with customers: "That's how they're getting you." Furthermore I am letting them "run me," which means harassment by sequential demands: you bring the ketchup and they decide they want extra Thousand Island; you bring that and they announce they now need a side of fries; and so on into distraction. Finally she tells me not to take her wrong. She tries to say things in a nice way, but you get into a mode, you know, because everything has to move so fast.[6]

I mumble thanks for the advice, feeling like I've just been stripped naked by the crazed enforcer of some ancient sumptuary law.[7] No chatting for you, girl. No fancy service ethic allowed for the serfs. Chatting with customers is for the beautiful young college-educated servers in the downtown carpaccio joints, the kids who can make $70 to $100 a night. What had I been thinking? My job is to move orders from tables to kitchen and then trays from kitchen to tables. Customers are, in fact, the

[6]In *Workers in a Lean World: Unions in the International Economy* (Verso, 1997), Kim Moody cites studies finding an increase in stress-related workplace injuries and illness between the mid-1980s and the early 1990s. He argues that rising stress levels reflect a new system of "management by stress," in which workers in a variety of industries are being squeezed to extract maximum productivity, to the detriment of their health.

[7]Sumptuary laws (from Latin *sumptus,* or expense, and *sumere,* or to take, use, or consume) were quite common in England, European countries, and even colonial American through the seventeenth century. Sumptuary laws prohibited consumers from spending their money "foolishly" to purchase luxury or extravagent clothing, food, and so forth. The Constitution of the United States would seem to forbid sumptuary laws except in cases where the government seeks to protect the health of its citizens. Many regard the prohibition of alcohol sales in the early twentieth century as the last real example of a sumptuary law in the United states.

major obstacle to the smooth transformation of information into food and food into money—they are, in short, the enemy. And the painful thing is that I'm beginning to see it this way myself. There are the traditional asshole types—frat boys who down multiple Buds and then make a fuss because the steaks are so emaciated and the fries so sparse—as well as the variously impaired—due to age, diabetes, or literacy issues—who require patient nutritional counseling. The worst, for some reason, are the Visible Christians—like the ten-person table, all jolly and sanctified after Sunday-night service, who run me mercilessly and then leave me $1 on a $92 bill. Or the guy with the crucifixion T-shirt (SOMEONE TO LOOK UP TO) who complains that his baked potato is too hard and his iced tea too icy (I cheerfully fix both) and leaves no tip. As a general rule, people wearing crosses or WWJD? (What Would Jèsus Do?) buttons look at us disapprovingly no matter what we do, as if they were confusing waitressing with Mary Magdalene's original profession.

I make friends, over time, with the other "girls" who work my shift: Nita, the tattooed twenty-something who taunts us by going around saying brightly, "Have we started making money yet?" Ellen, whose teenage son cooks on the graveyard shift and who once managed a restaurant in Massachusetts but won't try out for management here because she prefers being a "common worker" and not "ordering people around." Easy-going fiftyish Lucy, with the raucous laugh, who limps toward the end of the shift because of something that has gone wrong with her leg, the exact nature of which cannot be determined without health insurance. We talk about the usual girl things—men, children, and the sinister allure of Jerry's chocolate peanut-butter cream pie—though no one, I notice, ever brings up anything potentially expensive, like shopping or movies. As at the Hearthside, the only recreation ever referred to is partying, which requires little more than some beer, a joint, and

a few close friends. Still, no one here is homeless, or cops to it anyway, thanks usually to a working husband or boyfriend. All in all, we form a reliable mutual-support group: If one of us is feeling sick or overwhelmed, another one will "bev" a table or even carry trays for her. If one of us is off sneaking a cigarette or a pee,[8] the others will do their best to conceal her absence from the enforcers of corporate rationality.

But my saving human connection—my oxytocin receptor, as it were—is George, the nineteen-year-old, fresh-off-the-boat Czech dishwasher. We get to talking when he asks me, tortuously, how much cigarettes cost at Jerry's. I do my best to explain that they cost over a dollar more here than at a regular store and suggest that he just take one from the half-filled packs that are always lying around on the break table. But that would be unthinkable. Except for the one tiny earring signaling his allegiance to some vaguely alternative point of view, George is a perfect straight arrow—crew-cut, hardworking, and hungry for eye contact. "Czech Republic," I ask, "or Slovakia?" and he seems delighted that I know the difference. "Václav Havel," I try. "Velvet Revolution, Frank Zappa?" "Yes, yes, 1989," he says, and I realize we are talking about history.

I make the decision to move closer to Key West. First, because of the drive. Second and third, also because of the drive: gas is eating up

---

[8]Until April 1998, there was no federally mandated right to bathroom breaks. According to Marc Linder and Ingrid Nygaard, authors of *Void Where Prohibited: Rest Breaks and the Right to Urinate on Company Time* (Cornell University Press, 1997), "The right to rest and void at work is not high on the list of social or political causes supported by professional or executive employees, who enjoy personal workplace liberties that millions of factory workers can only daydream about. . . . While we were dismayed to discover that workers lacked an acknowledged legal right to void at work, [the workers] were amazed by outsiders' naive belief that their employers would permit them to perform this basic bodily function when necessary. . . . A factory worker, not allowed a break for six-hour stretches, voided into pads worn inside her uniform; and a kindergarten teacher in a school without aides had to take all twenty children with her to the bathroom and line them up outside the stall door when she voided."

$4 to $5 a day, and although Jerry's is as high-volume as you can get, the tips average only 10 percent, and not just for a newbie like me. Between the base pay of $2.15 an hour and the obligation to share tips with the busboys and dishwashers, we're averaging only about $7.50 an hour. Then there is the $30 I had to spend on the regulation tan slacks worn by Jerry's servers—a setback it could take weeks to absorb. (I had combed the town's two downscale department stores hoping for something cheaper but decided in the end that these marked-down Dockers, originally $49, were more likely to survive a daily washing.) Of my fellow servers, everyone who lacks a working husband or boyfriend seems to have a second job: Nita does something at a computer eight hours a day; another welds. Without the forty-five-minute commute, I can picture myself working two jobs and having the time to shower between them.

So I take the $500 deposit I have coming from my landlord, the $400 I have earned toward the next month's rent, plus the $200 reserved for emergencies, and use the $1,100 to pay the rent and deposit on trailer number 46 in the Overseas Trailer Park, a mile from the cluster of budget hotels that constitute Key West's version of an industrial park. Number 46 is about eight feet in width and shaped like a barbell inside, with a narrow region—because of the sink and the stove—separating the bedroom from what might optimistically be called the "living" area, with its two-person table and half-sized couch. The bathroom is so small my knees rub against the shower stall when I sit on the toilet, and you can't just leap out of the bed, you have to climb down to the foot of it in order to find a patch of floor space to stand on. Outside, I am within a few yards of a liquor store, a bar that advertises "free beer tomorrow," a convenience store, and a Burger King—but no supermarket or, alas, laundromat. By reputation, the Overseas park is a nest of crime and crack, and I am hoping at least

for some vibrant, multicultural street life. But desolation rules night and day, except for a thin stream of pedestrian traffic heading for their jobs at the Sheraton or 7-Eleven. There are not exactly people here but what amounts to canned labor, being preserved from the heat between shifts.

In line with my reduced living conditions, a new form of ugliness arises at Jerry's. The next day, when I go for straws, for the first time I find the dry-storage room locked. Ted, the portly assistant manager who opens it for me, explains that he caught one of the dishwashers attempting to steal something, and, unfortunately, the miscreant will be with us until a replacement can be found—hence the locked door. I neglect to ask what he had been trying to steal, but Ted tells me who he is—the kid with the buzz cut and the earring. You know, he's back there right now.

I wish I could say I rushed back and confronted George to get his side of the story. I wish I could say I stood up to Ted and insisted that George be given a translator and allowed to defend himself, or announced that I'd find a lawyer who'd handle the case pro bono. The mystery to me is that there's not much worth stealing in the dry-storage room, at least not in any fenceable quantity: "Is Gyorgi here, and am having 200—maybe 250—ketchup packets. What do you say?" My guess is that he had taken—if he had taken anything at all—some Saltines or a can of cherry-pie mix, and that the motive for taking it was hunger.

So why didn't I intervene? Certainly not because I was held back by the kind of moral paralysis that can pass as journalistic objectivity. On the contrary, something new—something loathsome and servile—had infected me, along with the kitchen odors that I could still sniff on my bra when I finally undressed at night. In real life I am moderately brave, but plenty of brave people shed their courage in concentration camps, and maybe something similar goes on in the infinitely more congenial milieu of the low-wage American workplace. Maybe, in a month or two more at Jerry's, I might have regained my crusading spirit. Then again, in a month or two I might have turned into a different person altogether—say, the kind of person who would have turned George in.

But this is not something I am slated to find out. When my month-long plunge into poverty is almost over, I finally land my dream job—housekeeping. I do this by walking into the personnel office of the only place I figure I might have some credibility, the hotel attached to Jerry's, and confiding urgently that I have to have a second job if I am to pay my rent and, no, it couldn't be front-desk clerk. "All right," the personnel lady fairly spits, "So it's house-keeping," and she marches me back to meet Maria, the housekeeping manager, a tiny, fre-netic Hispanic woman who greets me as "babe" and hands me a pamphlet emphasizing the need for a positive attitude. The hours are nine in the morning till whenever, the pay is $6.10 an hour, and there's one week of vacation a year. I don't have to ask about health insurance once I meet Carlotta, the middle-aged African American woman who will be training me. Carla, as she tells me to call her, is missing all of her top front teeth.

On that first day of housekeeping and last day of my entire project—although I don't yet know it's the last—Carla is in a foul mood. We have been given nineteen rooms to clean, most of them "checkouts," as opposed to "stay-overs," that require the whole enchilada of bed-stripping, vacuuming, and bathroom-scrubbing. When one of the rooms that had been listed as a stay-over turns out to be a checkout, Carla calls Maria to complain, but of course to no avail. "So make up the mother-fucker," Carla orders me, and I do the beds while she sloshes around the bathroom. For four hours without a break I strip and remake beds, taking about four and a half minutes per queen-sized bed, which I could get down to three if there were any reason to. We try to

avoid vacuuming by picking up the larger specks by hand, but often there is nothing to do but drag the monstrous vacuum cleaner—it weighs about thirty pounds—off our cart and try to wrestle it around the floor. Sometimes Carla hands me the squirt bottle of "BAM" (an acronym for something that begins, ominously, with "butyric"; the rest has been worn off the label) and lets me do the bathrooms. No service ethic challenges me here to new heights of per-formance. I just concentrate on removing the public hairs from the bathtubs, or at least the dark ones that I can see.

I had looked forward to the breaking-and-entering aspect of cleaning the stay-overs, the chance to examine the secret, physical existence of strangers. But the contents of the rooms are always banal and surprisingly neat—zipped up shaving kits, shoes lined up against the wall (there are no closets), flyers for snorkeling trips, maybe an empty wine bottle or two. It is the TV that keeps us going, from *Jerry* to *Sally* to *Hawaii Five*-O and then on to the soaps. If there's some-thing especially arresting, like "Won't Take No for Answer" on *Jerry*, we sit down on the edge of a bed and giggle for a moment as if this were a pajama party instead of a terminally dead-end job. The soaps are the best, and Carla turns the volume up full blast so that she won't miss any-thing from the bathroom or while the vacuum is on. In room 503, Marcia confronts Jeff about Lauren. In 505, Lauren taunts poor cuckolded Marcia. In 511, Helen offers Amanda $10,000 to stop seeing Eric, prompting Carla to emerge from the bathroom to study Amanda's troubled face. "You take it, girl," she advises. "I would for sure."

The tourists' rooms that we clean and, be-yond them, the far more expensively appointed interiors in the soaps, begin after a while to merge. We have entered a better world—a world of comfort where every day is a day off, waiting to be filled up with sexual intrigue. We, however, are only gatecrashers in this fantasy, forced to pay for our presence with backaches and perpetual thirst. The mirrors, and there are far too many of them in hotel rooms, contain the kind of person you would normally find pushing a shopping cart down a city street—bedraggled, dressed in a damp hotel polo shirt two sizes too large, and with sweat dribbling down her chin like drool. I am enormously relieved when Carla announces a half-hour meal break, but my appetite fades when I see that the bag of hot-dog rolls she has been carrying around on our cart is not trash salvaged from a checkout but what she has brought for her lunch.

When I request permission to leave at about 3:30, another housekeeper warns me that no one has so far succeeded in combining housekeeping at the hotel with serving at Jerry's: "Some kid did it once for five days, and you're no kid." With that helpful information in mind, I rush back to number 46, down four Advils (the name brand this time), shower, stooping to fit into the stall, and attempt to compose myself for the oncoming shift. So much for what Marx termed the "reproduction of labor power," meaning the things a worker has to do just so she'll be ready to work again. The only unforeseen obstacle to the smooth transition from job to job is that my tan Jerry's slacks, which had looked reasonably clean by 40-watt bulb last night when I handwashed my Hawaiian shirt, prove by daylight to be mottled with ketchup and ranch-dressing stains. I spend most of my hour-long break between jobs attempting to remove the edible portions with a sponge and then drying the slacks over the hood of my car in the sun.

I can do this two-job thing, is my theory, if I can drink enough caffeine and avoid getting distracted by George's ever more obvious suffering.[9] The first few days after-being caught he

seemed not to understand the trouble he was in, and our chirpy little conversations had continued. But the last couple of shifts he's been listless and unshaven, and tonight he looks like the ghost we all know him to be, with dark half-moons hanging from his eyes. At one point, when I am briefly immobilized by the task of filling little paper cups with sour cream for baked potatoes, he comes over and looks as if he'd like to explore the limits of our shared vocabulary, but I am called to the floor for a table. I resolve to give him all my tips that night and to hell with the experiment in low-wage money management. At eight, Ellen and I grab a snack together standing at the mephitic[10] end of the kitchen counter, but I can only manage two or three mozzarella sticks and lunch had been a mere handful of McNuggets. I am not tired at all, I assure myself, though it may be that there is simply no more "I" left to do the tiredness monitoring. What I would see, if I were more alert to the situation, is that the forces of destruction are already massing against me. There is only one cook on duty, a young man named Jesus ("Hay-Sue," that is) and he is new to the job. And there is Joy, who shows up to take over in the middle of the shift, wearing high heels and a long, clingy white dress and fuming as if she'd just been stood up in some cocktail bar.

Then it comes, the perfect storm. Four of my tables fill up at once. Four tables is nothing for me now, but only so long as they are obligingly staggered. As I bev table 27, tables 25, 28, and 24 are watching enviously. As I bev 25, 24 glowers because their bevs haven't even been ordered. Twenty-eight is four yuppyish types, meaning everything on the side and agonizing instructions as to the chicken Caesars. Twenty-five is a middle-aged black couple, who complain, with some justice, that the iced tea

[9]In 1996, the number of persons holding two or more jobs averaged 7.8 million, or 6.2 percent of the workforce. It was about the same rate for men and for women (6.1 versus 6.2), though the kinds of jobs differ by gender. About two thirds of multiple jobholders work one job full-time and the other part-time. Only a heroic minority—4 percent of men and 2 percent of women—work two full-time jobs simultaneously. (From John F. Stinson Jr., "New Data on Multiple Jobholding Available from the CPS," in the *Monthly Labor Review,* March 1997.)

[10]I confess, I have never encountered the word "mephitic" in anything written later than the nineteenth century. A thing is mephitic if it has an offensive or noxious smell (hence, the term "mephitic weasel" was once used to refer to what we call skunks).

isn't fresh and the tabletop is sticky. But table 24 is the meteorological event of the century: ten British tourists who seem to have made the decision to absorb the American experience entirely by mouth. Here everyone has at least two drinks—iced tea and milk shake, Michelob and water (with lemon slice, please)—and a huge promiscuous orgy of breakfast specials, mozzarella sticks, chicken strips, quesadillas, burgers with cheese and without, sides of hash browns with cheddar, with onions, with gravy, seasoned fries, plain fries, banana splits. Poor Jesus! Poor me! Because when I arrive with their first tray of food—after three prior trips just to refill bevs—Princess Di refuses to eat her chicken strips with her pancake-and-sausage special, since, as she now reveals, the strips were meant to be an appetizer. Maybe the others would have accepted their meals, but Di, who is deep into her third Michelob, insists that everything else go back while they work on their "starters." Meanwhile, the yuppies are waving me down for more decaf and the black couple looks ready to summon the NAACP.

Much of what happened next is lost in the fog of war. Jesus starts going under. The little printer on the counter in front of him is spewing out orders faster than he can rip them off, much less produce the meals. Even the invincible Ellen is ashen from stress. I bring table 24 their reheated main courses, which they immediately reject as either too cold or fossilized by the microwave. When I return to the kitchen with their trays (three trays in three trips), Joy confronts me with arms akimbo: "What is this?" She means the food—the plates of rejected pancakes, hash browns in assorted flavors, toasts, burgers, sausages, eggs. "Uh, scrambled with cheddar," I try, "and that's . . ." "NO," she screams in my face. "Is it a traditional, a super-scramble, an eye-opener?" I pretend to study my check for a clue, but entropy has been up to its tricks, not only on the plates but in my head, and I have to admit that the original order is beyond reconstruction. "You don't know an eye-opener from a traditional?"

she demands in outrage. All I know, in fact, is that my legs have lost interest in the current venture and have announced their intention to fold. I am saved by a yuppie (mercifully not one of mine) who chooses this moment to charge into the kitchen to bellow that his food is twenty-five minutes late. Joy screams at him to get the hell out of her kitchen, please, and then turns on Jesus in a fury, hurling an empty tray across the room for emphasis.

I leave. I don't walk out, I just leave. I don't finish my side work or pick up my credit-card tips, if any, at the cash register or, of course, ask Joy's permission to go. And the surprising thing is that you can walk out without permission, that the door opens, that the thick tropical night air parts to let me pass, that my car is still parked where I left it. There is no vindication in this exit, no fuck-you surge of relief, just an overwhelming, dank sense of failure pressing down on me and the entire parking lot. I had gone into this venture in the spirit of science, to test a mathematical propositions, but somewhere along the line, in the tunnel vision imposed by long shifts and relentless concentration, it became a test of myself, and clearly I have failed. Not only had I flamed out as a housekeeper/server, I had even forgotten to give George my tips, and, for reasons perhaps best known to hardworking, generous people like Gail and Ellen, this hurts. I don't cry, but I am in a position to realize, for the first time in many years, that the tear ducts are still there, and still capable of doing their job.

When I moved out of the trailer park, I gave the key to number 46 to Gail and arranged for my deposit to be transferred to her. She told me that Joan is still living in her van and that Stu had been fired from the Hearthside. I never found out what happened to George.

In one month, I had earned approximately $1,040 and spent $517 on food, gas, toiletries, laundry, phone, and utilities. If I had remained in my $500 efficiency, I would have been able to pay the rent and have $22 left over (which is $78 less than the cash I had in my pocket at the start of the month). During this time I bought no clothing except for the required slacks and no prescription drugs or medical care (I did finally buy some vitamin B to compensate for the lack of vegetables in my diet). Perhaps I could have saved a little on food if I had gotten to a supermarket more often, instead of convenience stores, but it should be noted that I lost almost four pounds in four weeks, on a diet weighted heavily toward burgers and fries.

How former welfare recipients and single mothers will (and do) survive in the low-wage workforce, I cannot imagine. Maybe they will figure out how to condense their lives—including child-raising, laundry, romance, and meals—into the couple of hours between full-time jobs. Maybe they will take up residence in their vehicles, if they have one. All I know is that I couldn't hold two jobs and I couldn't make enough money to live on with one. And I had advantages unthinkable to many of the long-term poor—health, stamina, a working car, and no children to care for and support. Certainly nothing in my experience contradicts the conclusion of Kathryn Edin and Laura Lein, in their recent book *Making Ends Meet:*

How Single Mothers Survive Welfare and Low-Wage Work, that low-wage work actually involves more hardship and deprivation than life at the mercy of the welfare state. In the coming months and years, economic conditions for the working poor are bound to worsen, even without the almost inevitable recession. As mentioned earlier, the influx of former welfare recipients into the low-skilled workforce will have a depressing effect on both wages and the number of jobs available. A general economic downturn will only enhance these effects, and the working poor will of course be facing it without the slight, but nonetheless often saving, protection of welfare as a backup.

The thinking behind welfare reform was that even the humblest jobs are morally uplifting and psychologically buoying. In reality they are likely to be fraught with insult and stress. But I did discover one redeeming feature of the most abject low-wage work—the camaraderie of people who are, in almost all cases, far too smart and funny and caring for the work they do and the wages they're paid. The hope, of course, is that someday these people will come to know what they're worth, and take appropriate action.

Questions

1. Compare Ehrenreich's story of life as a waitress to the Paules' account (reading # 17) of being a waitress. Given that both studied similar subjects, one would expect there to be several similarities. However, did you spot important differences? Paules interviewed women working as waitresses while Ehrenreich lived the life. To what extent might this difference in methods explain the differences in their findings?

2. Imagine that tomorrow you had to postpone finishing college and survive in the "real world." How difficult would it be for you to put together enough money to get started out there? (Consider such things as transportation, housing [including first and last months' rent and security deposit] the cost of uniforms, etc.) (If your instructor assigns you to answer this question on paper and turn it in, take care not to reveal any details that are too personal!) Do you think that your parents or others would be happy to help you get started? What do you think happens to people whose relatives can't (or won't) help them out financially?

·36·

The Job Ghetto

Katherine Newman and Chauncy Lennon

One of my students expressed the conventional "wisdom" this way: "If people want to bad enough, they can get a job and make something of themselves. It might not be a great job, but at least it's a job. No one has to be poor in this society." In this 1995 article, Katherine Newman and Chauncy Lennon challenge such widely held assumptions about the availability of employment in our society.

To fix the welfare mess, conservatives say, we should stop making life on the dole so comfortable, cut benefits, and force overindulged welfare moms to go out and find honest jobs. Unskilled foreigners can find work, so why can't AFDC[1] recipients? With unemployment rates down, these expectations sound reasonable, particularly to middle-class Americans with stagnating incomes. The premise that jobs are available for those willing to take them is a great comfort to politicians with budget axes in hand and to conservative commentators calling on them to slash benefits. After all, they can claim they're not really casting poor women and children into the streets; they're just upholding the American work ethic.

But can just any warm body find a job? For the past two years, we have studied the low-wage labor market in Harlem, focusing on minimum-wage jobs in the fast-food industry, which are typical of the employment opportunities many reformers have in mind for welfare recipients. After all, these jobs presumably demand little skill, education, or prior work experience—or so the public believes.

The fast-food industry is growing more rapidly than almost any other service business and now employs more than 2.3 million workers. One in 15 Americans working today found their first job at McDonald's—not including Burger King and the rest. As a gateway to employment, fast-food establishments are gaining on the armed forces, which have long functioned as a national job-training factory. No wonder the average citizen believes these jobs are wide open! Yet, in inner cities, the picture looks different. With manufacturing gone, fast-food jobs have become the object of fierce competition.

Downward Pressures

Between 1992 and 1994, we tracked the work histories of 200 people working in fast-food restaurants in central Harlem, where according to official data about 18 percent of the population are unemployed and about 40 percent live below the poverty line. These numbers are typical of the communities where many long-term recipients of public assistance will have to look for work if their benefits are cut off. Some 29 percent of the households in Harlem receive public assistance.

---

[1] Aid to Families with Dependent Children, a form of welfare. —Ed.

Although the 200 workers in our study receive only the minimum wage, they are actually the victors in an intense competition to find work in a community with relatively few jobs to offer. At the restaurants where they work, the ratio of applicants to hires is approximately 14 to 1. Among those people who applied but were rejected for fast-food work in early 1993, 73 percent had not found work of any kind a year later, despite considerable effort. Even the youngest job hunters in our study (16- to 18-year-olds) had applied for four or five positions before they came looking for these fast-food jobs. The oldest applicants (over 25) had applied for an average of seven or eight jobs.

The oversupply of job seekers causes a creeping credentialism in the ghetto's low-wage service industries. Older workers in their twenties, who are more often high school graduates, now dominate jobs once taken by school dropouts or other young people first starting out. Long-term welfare recipients will have a tough time beating out their competition even for these low-wage jobs. They will be joining an inner-city labor market that is already saturated with better educated and more experienced workers who are preferred by employers.

Winners and Losers

We tracked nearly 100 people who applied for these minimum-wage jobs but were turned down, and compared them to the fortunate ones who got jobs. The comparison is instructive. Even in Harlem, African Americans are at a disadvantage in hiring compared to Latinos and others. Employers, including black employers, favor applicants who are not African American. Blacks are not shut out of the low-wage labor market; indeed, they represent about 70 percent of the new hires in these jobs. But they are rejected at a much higher rate than applicants from other ethnic groups with the same educational qualifications.

Employers also seem to favor job applicants who commute from more distant neighborhoods. The rejection rate for local applicants is higher than the rate for similarly educated individuals who live farther away. This pattern holds even for people of the same race, sex, and age. Other studies in the warehouse and dockyard industries report the same results. These findings suggest that residents of poor neighborhoods such as central Harlem are at a distinct disadvantage in finding minimum-wage jobs near home.

Mothers of young children face particular problems if they can't find jobs close to home. The costs and logistical complexities of commuting (and paying for longer child care hours to accommodate it) are a big burden.

In searching for jobs, "who you know" makes a big difference. Friends and family members who already have jobs help people get work even in the fast-food industry; those isolated from such networks are less likely to get hired. Personal contacts have long been recognized as crucial for getting higher-skilled employment. This research suggests that contacts are important at the bottom of the job ladder, too.

Native-born applicants are at a disadvantage compared to legal immigrants in securing entry-level work. In fact, even though central Harlem residents are nearly all African American, recent immigrants have a higher probability of being hired for Harlem's fast-food jobs than anyone else. Interviews with employers suggest that they believe immigrants are easier to manage in part because they come from countries where $4.25 an hour represents a king's ransom. Whether or not employers are right about the tractability of immigrants, such attitudes make it harder for the native-born to obtain low-wage jobs.

The people who succeed in getting these minimum-wage jobs are not new to the labor market. More than half of the new hires over the age of 18 found their first jobs when they were younger than 15 years of age. Even the people rejected for the minimum-wage positions had some prior job experience. Half of them also began working before they were 15 years old. Welfare recipients with no prior job experience, or no recent job experience, are going to be at a disadvantage in the competition.

"They Expect Too Much"

One explanation often advanced for low employment in poor communities is that the poor have unrealistic expectations. In this view, they are reluctant to seek (or take) jobs that fall below a "reservation wage," which is supposedly far above the minimum. We asked job seekers who were refused these entry-level jobs what they were hoping for and what wages they would accept. Their desires were modest: $4.59 per hour on average, which is quite close to the minimum wage. The younger the jobseeker, the lower was the expectation.

These job seekers were willing to accept even more modest wages. On average the lowest they would take was $4.17 per hour, which is less than the minimum level legally permitted for adult workers. It is striking that many applicants previously had higher salaries; the average wage for the best job they had ever held was $6.79 per hour. Many of central Harlem's job hunters are suffering from downward mobility, falling into the minimum-wage market even though they have done better in the past.

Comparing job seekers to jobholders shows the intensity of employment competition in the inner city, but it doesn't tell us how welfare recipients will fare. What assets do welfare recipients bring to the competition compared to other job hunters? The news is grim.

Nationally, one-third of the long-term welfare recipients have received high school diplomas. Recently hired fast-food workers in central Harlem have completed high school at a higher rate—54 percent. Almost 40 percent of welfare recipients have not held jobs in the year preceding their enrollment in welfare. Yet even the central Harlem applicants rejected for fast-food jobs have had more job experience. They have held an average of more than three jobs before applying for these positions.

In short, it is simply not the case that anyone who wants a low-wage job can get one. As is true for almost any glutted labor market, there is a queue of applicants, and employers can be fairly choosy. When conservatives point to the success of immigrants as proof that jobs are available for welfare moms, they are ignoring the realities of the inner city. Ethnic minorities of all kinds are already locked into a fierce struggle for scarce opportunities at the bottom.

When they go looking for jobs, welfare recipients go to the back of a long line. Policymakers should neither fool nor comfort themselves with the notion that welfare mothers can simply go out and get jobs. Investment in public employment and tax incentives for private employers will be needed on a massive scale if anything like that rosy scenario is to come about. Even then, the competitive hurdles facing the very poor will be high and many better-qualified people will be out there looking to leap over them.

Questions

1. According to Newman and Lennon's research, what sorts of factors distinguish jobholders and job seekers in Harlem?

2. How likely do Newman and Lennon think it is that welfare moms will be able to get off welfare and find jobs in the near future? Explain.

·37·
Racism

Joe R. Feagin

If ever there comes a time that I want absolute silence in my classroom, I will simply announce, "Today, we are going to talk about racism."

It is hard to talk about race, let alone racism, in a public setting. White students confide that black students are "too sensitive" and "will think I'm a racist if I say anything." Black students mostly just say that white students "just don't get it," and "don't *want* to get it."

In his book, *Racist America: Roots, Current Realities, and Future Reparations*, Professor Feagin, one of today's most respected sociologists, offers us insight into why conversations about racism are so difficult. Whites and blacks, he has found, have very different understandings of the importance of race in U.S. society. Blacks experience racist behavior in schoolrooms, on the streets, in shops, at work, and even in health care settings. As Feagin notes, "being black in U.S. society means always having to be prepared for antiblack actions by whites — in most places and at most times of the day, week, month, or year." For black men and women, racism is an unfortunately large part of the present.

On the other hand, as far as most whites are concerned, "racism is a thing of the past"; thus, "black Americans who complain of it are paranoid or confused. There is a common saying among whites that a black person is 'playing the race card,' a comment generally used to suggest that person is making an illegitimate demand [or complaint] because antiblack racism is no longer thought of as a serious obstacle in the United States."

What follows is an excerpt from *Racist America,* in which Feagin explores the disjunction between race as it's seen by white and black Americans.

Soon after the 1960s civil rights movement declined in intensity, most whites were moving toward the view that racial discrimination is no longer an important problem for the nation. In a 1976 survey, for example, most (71 percent) whites agreed that "blacks and other minorities no longer face unfair employment conditions. In fact they are favored in many training and job programs." A meager 12 percent of whites agreed with the statement that "discrimination affects all black people. The only way to handle it is for blacks to organize together and demand rights for all." In a 1980 survey respondents were asked, "How much discrimination do you feel there is against blacks and other minorities in any area of life that limits their chances to get ahead?" Just over half of

Excerpts from *Racist America: Roots, Current Realities, and Future Reparations* by Joe R. Feagin. Copyright © 2000 by Routledge. Reproduced by permission of Routledge/Taylor & Francis Books, Inc.

blacks replied "a lot," compared to only a quarter of whites. In these surveys only a minority of whites viewed discrimination as a major hurdle (Kluegel & Smith 1986).

In more recent surveys, black and white Americans still differ dramatically in how they view discrimination. A 1990 NORC survey question asked why blacks have worse jobs, income, and housing than whites. Choosing among alternative explanations, two-thirds of black respondents said that it was "mainly due to discrimination," compared to only 35 percent of whites. Similarly, in a mid-1990s Pennsylvania survey researchers found that eight in ten black respondents thought inequality in jobs, housing, and income stemmed mostly from discrimination, while the majority of whites viewed this inequality as resulting from blacks' lack of motivation. Respondents were asked whether the quality of life for black Americans had gotten better in the last decade. Nearly six in ten whites said it had gotten better, compared to less than a third of black respondents (Smith 1996). Recent national polls have shown the same pattern. A 1997 ABC/*Washington Post* poll found that only 17 percent of the white respondents felt there was a lot of racial discrimination, compared to nearly half the blacks polled. In addition, several other surveys have found that on questions dealing with specific institutional areas such as housing, education, and jobs less than a majority of whites believe that blacks currently face discrimination (Blendon et al. 1986).

Several recent surveys have found that many whites think blacks are as well off as or are better off than whites in regard to education, health care, and jobs. For example, a Massachusetts survey found a majority of the white respondents saying that African Americans, Asian Americans, and Latino Americans now have *equality* in life chances with whites (Lehigh 1998). However, government statistical data indicate that such views are very much in error. Perhaps because of erroneous or misleading media reports, most whites do not understand just how much worse off blacks actually are than whites in most areas of political and economic life (Feagin & Feagin 1999).

"I AM NOT A RACIST": DENYING INDIVIDUAL RACISM

Clearly, a majority of whites do not see the United States as a nation that has a problem of serious and widespread racial discrimination. Apparently, most whites also do not view themselves as significantly racist in thought or action, often asserting "I am not a racist." In recent years many whites have also made such statements as "my family never owned slaves" or "my family did not segregate lunch counters." Many will say to black Americans something like, "Slavery happened hundreds of years ago—get over it." They do not know, or pretend they do not, that official slavery ended less than 140 years or so prior to their statements. In addition, whites making such assertions usually do not admit that they and their families have benefited greatly from slavery, segregation, and present-day discrimination.[1]

Many whites seem to mix negative views of black Americans with images of white innocence, thereby giving specific expression to elements of a broader racial ideology. Take this example of a white college student's reply to a question about her first experience with black Americans, in this case children: "I switched from a private school which had no blacks to a

---

[1] Elsewhere in his book, Feagin observes that "slaveholders were not the only beneficiaries of the slavery system; those who bought and sold products of plantations were also major beneficiaries. This latter group included merchants and consumers in many nations. In addition, many white workers in Britain and other parts of Europe owed their livelihood directly or indirectly to the slaves and plantation products. It seems unlikely that British and other European economic development would have occurred when it did without the very substantial capital generated by the slavery system" (51).

public school, and I was thrown in the middle of a bunch of apes, no I'm just kidding. . . . And I don't know, my parents have always instilled in me that blacks aren't equal, because we are from [the Deep South]." In her interview she continues in this vein, making several negative comments about African Americans. Then at the end of her interview, she adds, "I don't consider myself racist. I, when I think of the word racist, I think of KKK, people in white robes burning black people on crosses and stuff, or I think of the Skinheads or some exaggerated form of racism" (Feagin & Vera 1995). We see here the imaging of the white self in positive terms.

It seems that most whites can assert that they are "not racist" because they see racism as something that *other* whites do. That is, they know other whites who are much more racist in thought or action than they are, and thus they see themselves as already beyond that racism. Jerome Culp has said, "To many white people, not being racist means having less racial animosity than their parents (something almost all can at least claim); having less racial animosity than someone they know (something all can claim); or not belonging to a white supremacist group. . . . For many white people, unless they believe overwhelmingly in the inferiority of black people, they are not collaborators with racism and are not racist" (Culp 1993). As we saw in white views of athletes and actors on "The Cosby Show," many whites hold some more or less positive images of selected black men or women. However, these usually superficial positive views reduce the ability of whites to see their own culpability in personal and institutional racism. Indeed, many a white person has a false consciousness that occurs when a white "believes he or she is identifying with a person of color, but in fact is doing so only in a slight, superficial way" (Delgado 1996). It is possible to hold that black Americans can be good entertainers,

musicians, or sports figures, yet also believe that most are inferior to whites in character, morality, or intelligence.[2]

Historical changes in racism have also been misperceived by whites. When the legal segregation era came to an end with the passage of civil rights laws in the 1960s, most whites apparently concluded that serious racism was being rapidly extinguished. Today, most whites, like the young woman interviewed above, seem to view what racism remains as a matter of isolated Klan-type bigotry and not as a system of racism cutting across U.S. institutions. As a result, they do not see their own racism. Moreover, the level at which racist attitudes are held can vary in degree of consciousness. Psychologist Patricia Devine has suggested that whites who reject overtly prejudiced views can still hold less consciously prejudiced thoughts that stem from prior socialization. For many whites this attitudinal racism is a persisting bad habit that keeps coming up in everyday thought and behavior. One reason for this is the fact that human beings are characterized by automatic information processing, which involves the unintentional activation of previously socialized attitudes such as racist stereotypes and prejudices (Devine 1989). Racist

---

[2] Feagin introduced the racist stereotype of lazy black men and women earlier in the book and argued that it persists today: "A recent NORC national survey asked whites to evaluate on a scale just how work-oriented blacks are. Only a small percentage, 16 percent, ranked blacks at the hardworking end; just under half put blacks at the lazy end of the spectrum. . . . Notions of laziness are so strong as to overcome countering evidence. Researchers Justin Lewis and Sut Jhally had white subjects watch 'The Cosby Show,' a popular television show from the 1980s and 1990s that is still seen in reruns across the globe. Whites generally like the black Huxtable family portrayed on the show, yet many processed the images in a way that fit in with preexisting attitudes. They saw the success of the Huxtables as evidence that any black person could succeed if he or she would just work harder. As Lewis and Jhally concluded about white views, "The Huxtables proved that black people can succeed; yet in so doing they also prove the inferiority of black people in general (who have, in comparison with whites, failed)" (111).

attitudes can thus be conscious, half-conscious, or even subconscious.

White Views on Government Action Against Discrimination

If antiblack discrimination is no longer regarded as a serious problem, then it is not surprising that most whites see less need, or no need, for strong antidiscrimination efforts by governments. From this perspective blacks pressing for continuing or enhanced antidiscrimination programs, such as aggressive affirmative action, are seen as making illegitimate demands. David Wellman has suggested that "the concrete problem facing white people is how to come to grips with the demands made by blacks while at the same time *avoiding* the possibility of institutional change and reorganization that might affect them" (Wellman 1977).

SYMBOLIC AND LAISSEZ-FAIRE RACISM

Some researchers have described a contemporary white perspective called *symbolic racism.* Whites often combine the notion of declining or eradicated blatant racism with the idea that blacks are making illegitimate demands for societal changes. As these researchers see the current situation, a majority of whites have shifted away from old-fashioned racist ideas and have accepted modest desegregation while strongly resisting aggressive government action for large-scale desegregation. This symbolic racism is grounded in white resistance to substantial changes in the status quo. Central to white concerns is a fear whites have of losing status and power because of black attempts to bring change. Deep-lying antiblack views—especially views of blacks violating traditional American work values—are still present, but white resentment of pressures for substantial change is central to the current racist ideology (Sears 1988).

This symbolic racism perspective has been criticized by some scholars as playing down old-fashioned racism, when the latter still exists among whites and is directly connected to negative views of programs to eradicate discrimination.

Lawrence Bobo, James Kluegel, and Ryan Smith have suggested a more historical approach. Since the 1950s, and shaped by structural changes in the society, they say white attitudes have shifted from an accent on strict segregation and overt bigotry to "laissez-faire racism,"[3] by which they mean whites' continuing stereotyping of blacks and blaming of blacks for their problems. Most ordinary whites have given up a commitment to compulsory racial segregation. Yet, they still strive to maintain white privilege and position. Survey data since the 1960s indicate a substantial discrepancy between white views on the *principle* of desegregation versus whites views on the *implementation* of desegregation by government. While surveys in the mid-1960s indicated that nearly two-thirds of whites accepted integrated schooling in principle, just 38 percent accepted a role for government in pressing for more integration. By the mid-1980s white support for the principle of school integration had grown to 93 percent, while endorsement of government intervention had declined to 26 percent (Bobo et al. 1997). The survey data indicate similar discrepancies in white views of job and housing integration. Acceptance of the principle of racial integration does not mean that whites wish to see government intervene aggressively, or to personally have more contact with blacks. Whites maintain a positive sense of self and

---

[3]*Laissez-faire* (French, "let alone, don't interfere"). Laissez-faire capitalism thus is based on the premise that capitalism will work best if the government doesn't interfere by regulating. By extension, laissez-faire racism is racism that will continue and even flourish as long as the government does not attempt to push antiracist laws and policies (e.g., affirmative action).—Ed.

their claims to greater privileges and resources while fending off what whites see as illegitimate black demands for a fair share of those resources.

VIEWS ON AFFIRMATIVE ACTION

Affirmative action is a major example of a remedial program to deal with racial discrimination. Yet most whites, including most white leaders, have been opposed to *aggressive* affirmative action since at least the 1970s. In one 1977 survey of mostly white and male local and national leaders in business, farming, unions, the media, and academia, *most* were overwhelmingly opposed to affirmative-action quotas for black Americans in school admissions and jobs. Only 10 to 22 percent of the several leadership groups favored strong remedial quotas (Verba & Orren 1985). In addition, the overwhelming majority of these elites thought that equality of opportunity, not equality of results, was the best way to eradicate disparities. The white public seems to share this view.

Earlier we noted mid-1970s surveys suggesting that the white majority views blacks as no longer facing serious job discrimination and expresses opposition to an expanded effort for civil rights. Recent data show the same pattern: more than half of whites do not believe that government or private agencies should be making aggressive remedial efforts on behalf of black Americans or other Americans of color. In an ABC News/*Washington Post* survey only a quarter of whites thought minorities should receive some preferences in jobs and college admissions (Ladd 1995). And a late-1990s Gallup poll found that 70 percent of Republicans, a heavily white group, felt the federal government should not make special efforts to help Americans of color, because they should help themselves (Blendon et al. 1986). A majority of whites took the same position in a late-1990s survey in Massachusetts (Lehigh 1998). Most national surveys have shown the same pattern

of white opposition to strong programs with special preferences or quotas as a means of aggressively remedying past discrimination. (Milder remedial programs may sometimes be acceptable.) Indeed, today many whites believe that they are likely to be the victims of governmental policies helping black Americans. One recent Pennsylvania survey asked a question as to how likely it would be that a white worker might lose a job or a promotion to a less qualified black worker. Most black respondents (57 percent) thought this was unlikely, while most whites (80 percent) thought it was likely (Smith 1996). National polls using such a question have gotten similar responses: The majority of whites seem convinced that antiwhite discrimination is now commonplace.

White elites have periodically expended substantial effort to shape the public's views of remedial programs. Researcher Robert Entman has examined trends in mass media reports of the controversy over affirmative action that recurred periodically in the 1980s and 1990s. He found significant peaking in media attention to affirmative action during the years 1987, 1991, and 1995—years that preceded presidential elections. This pattern suggests elite manipulation of the affirmative action issue for political purposes. The media elites and their white-collar employees tended to present the issue of affirmative action in white-framed ways or in terms of national controversy, using such phrases as the "tide of white anger" or the "growing white backlash." Entman concludes that "journalists, it seems, built their frame on claims by elite sources with an interest in promoting the impression of white arousal, filtered through the conflict norm that shapes story construction" (Entman 1997). The media attention accelerated concerns about affirmative action in the white public.

Related to opposition to strong affirmative action programs is the old individualistic ethic, especially the blame-the-victim version. Today, as in the past, many whites comment about the problems of blacks with such statements as, "Why can't they be like us?" The notion here is that if "they" will work harder and improve their personal and family values, then the normal assimilation processes will enable them to have greater socioeconomic mobility. One recent survey asked whether respondents agreed with this statement: "The Irish, Italians, and many other groups overcame prejudice and worked their way up, African Americans and other minorities should do the same without any special help from the government." Most whites (69 percent) agreed (Blendon et al. 1986). Most seem to perceive the black experience in terms of an individualistic mobility model. Black Americans, from this viewpoint, are little different from white immigrant groups, such as the southern and eastern European immigrants of the early 1900s. Like those immigrants, who are seen as having encountered discrimination, black Americans should be able to work themselves up the social ladder. If they do not make it, it is mostly their own fault.

Imaging the White Self

The racist ideas and attitudes of white Americans encompass *much more* than their antiblack views. Among these racist attitudes are positive views of white superiority and merit. Generally, the broad white-racist ideology sees white history as meritorious. Indeed, in the United States, group merit and individual merit are judged by standards created by the white majority. In chapter 3 we noted the images of white superiority and virtue in many Hollywood films. From the first years of moviemaking to the present, when racial matters have been portrayed, whites as a group have almost always been portrayed as morally superior, intellectually superior, or otherwise meritorious. In these movies—including more recent television movies—there may be a few white individuals who are racist bigots, but the society as a whole is not portrayed as racist. Some white person is

typically a central hero, even in movies mostly about black Americans (for example, *Glory*).

Among elites and in the general public, whites have developed numerous sincere fictions that reproduce aspects of the broad racist ideology at an everyday level. Such fictions may describe whites as "not racist" and as "good people" even as the same whites take part in racist actions or express racist ideas. This moral privileging of whiteness may be conscious or it can be half-conscious or unconscious. Ruth Frankenberg found evidence of this unconsciousness in her research on white women: whiteness, she noted, is "difficult for white people to name. . . . Those who are securely housed within its borders usually do not examine it" (Frankenberg 1993). The sense of whiteness is often hidden deeply in individual psyches and practices. Being white, one might say, means rarely or never having to think about it. Whiteness is the national norm, and thus the white majority's views, practices, and culture are generally seen as normal.

Examining commentaries on racial inequality written by white students, Joyce King found that most were "unaware of how their own subjective identities reflect an uncritical identification with the existing social order." Only one student out of fifty-seven linked persisting racial inequality to the larger system of racial oppression (King 1991). Thus, while whites get many substantial advantages from systemic racism, they do pay a subtle and hidden price. This may include a lack of conscious awareness about certain critical aspects of social reality. Many have an uncritical mind that accepts the existing racial order with little questioning.

Perhaps most amazing is that a majority of whites today do not see the centuries of slavery and segregation as bringing whites substantial socioeconomic benefit. One survey found that nearly two-thirds of white respondents did *not* think that whites as a group had benefited from past and present discrimination against black Americans. Nor did they think whites should take significant action to remedy continuing discrimination (Blendon et al. 1991). Moreover, as we have seen, many whites have asserted their innocence with a torrent of comments such as "my family never owned slaves." This white guiltlessness is professed at all class levels, even by presidential candidates. Clearly, much work has gone into reframing the American history of racial oppression so that white Americans can appear blameless for the brutality and carnage they and their ancestors created.

Fostering and Learning Racist Attitudes

THE ROLE OF ELITES

[Elsewhere in this book] we examined how elites have fostered a racist ideology rationalizing the realities of unjust impoverishment and enrichment. This effort is a major source of the racist ideology and its associated attitudes that are held in the nonelite part of the white population. Through various means the white elites have manipulated ordinary white Americans to accept the racist ideology and its component parts. Moreover, after the elements of an era's racist ideology and structural arrangements are in place, ordinary whites need less manipulation, for they generally understand what is in their group interest. Indeed, groups of ordinary people often generate new permutations on old racist ideas, innovations that in their turn reinforce and reproduce the racist ideology.

The often hidden power of the elite works through propagating the racist ideology and its associated beliefs and images by means of the mass media and the educational system, as well as in workplaces and churches. Increasingly, the mass media are as important as family or school in creating and propagating racist images and attitudes. When blacks encounter whites in a broad array of contemporary settings, they often meet negative beliefs about their abilities, values, and orientations. Racial barriers persist today because a substantial majority of whites harbor antiblack sentiments, images, and beliefs and because a large minority are very negative in their perspectives. When most whites interact with black Americans at work, in restaurants, on the street, at school, or in the media they tend to think about the latter, either consciously or unconsciously, in terms of racist stereotypes inherited from the past and constantly reiterated and reinforced in the present.

The translation of antiblack attitudes into actual discrimination is shaped not only by these attitudes but also by subjective norms, such as what other people might think, and by perceived behavioral controls, such as what the response to discrimination will be. Most discrimination is thereby contextualized. Routinized discrimination in housing, employment, politics, and public accommodations is carried out by whites acting alone or in groups. Whites are usually implementing shared racist attitudes and norms of their families and other important social networks. The social norms guiding discrimination can be formal or legal, but most today are unwritten and informal. Moreover, much antiblack action is not sporadic but is carried out repeatedly and routinely by numerous dominant-group members influenced by the norms of their social networks. Whites have the power to discriminate as individuals, but much of their power to harm comes from membership in traditionally white networks and organizations.

EVERYDAY RACISM: SUBTLE, COVERT, AND BLATANT

The character of discrimination varies. Whites may actively persecute blacks, or they may engage in an array of avoidance behaviors. Discrimination can be self-consciously motivated, or it can be half-conscious or unconscious and deeply imbedded in an actor's core beliefs. At the level of everyday interaction with black

Americans, most whites can create racial tensions and barriers even without conscious awareness they are doing so. Examples of this include when white men lock their car doors as a black man walks by on the street or when white women step out or pull their purses close to them when a black man comes into an elevator they are on.[4] Stereotyped images of black men as criminals probably motivate this and similar types of defensive action. Such practices represent, according to Philomena Essed, the "integration of racism into everyday situations" (Essed 1991). Systemic racism is thus a system of oppression made up of many thousands of everyday acts of mistreatment of black Americans by white Americans, incidents that range from the subtle and hard to observe to the blatant and easy to notice. These acts of mistreatment can be nonverbal or verbal, nonviolent or violent. Moreover, many racist actions that crash in on everyday life are, from the victim's viewpoint, unpredictable and sporadic. Such actions are commonplace, recurring, and cumulative in their negative impact. They are, as one retired black American in her eighties put it, "little murders" that happen every day (Feagin & Sikes 1994).

In a specific setting, such as an employment setting, a white person in authority may select another white person over an equally or better qualified black person because of a preconceived notion that whites are more competent or because of discomfort with people perceived as somehow different. This latter type of subtle discrimination includes, in John Calmore's words, "the unconscious failure to extend to a minority the same recognition of humanity, and hence the same sympathy and care, given as a matter of course to one's own group." The selectivity results "often unconsciously—from our tendency to sympathize most readily with those who seem most like ourselves" (Calmore 1989). Yet oppression is not less serious because it is more subtle.

The racist system is made even more complex by its reinforcement in many other aspects of the everyday behavior of white Americans. When whites make racist comments to other whites, or when they think or say racist things when watching television by themselves or with their families, they also reinforce and maintain the white-racist system, even though no blacks are present. Racism is systemic because it infiltrates most aspects of life.

WHO DOES THE DISCRIMINATING?

Antiblack discrimination comes from all levels and categories of white Americans. Most whites are involved in some way in creating, reinforcing, or maintaining, the racist reality of U.S. society. Depending on the situation and the opportunity to discriminate, very large numbers of whites can and do discriminate. Judging from housing audit studies[5], perhaps half of all whites are inclined to discriminate in some fashion, whether subtly or blatantly, in situations where they have housing to rent or sell to black individuals or families. It may well be that whites discriminate at similarly high levels in other major institutional arenas.

---

[4]Elsewhere in the book, Professor Feagin notes the irony of this situation: "Federal surveys of white victims of violent crime have found that about 17 percent of these attackers are black, while about three-quarters are white. Most violent crime affecting whites is carried out by *white* criminals. Yet most whites do not take similar precautions when they are in the presence of those whites—disproportionately white men—who perpetrate most of the violent crime suffered by whites. The reason for this is that they do not see themselves as being in the presence of someone likely to commit a violent crime when they are around those socially defined as white" (114).

---

[5]Audit studies are used to test the degree to which discrimination exists in a particular social arena. In a housing audit study, a white couple and a black couple might (separately) visit rental agencies to inquire about the availability of rentals. If antiblack discrimination exists, the study will show that black couples were more likely to be told that no appropriate rentals are currently available, whereas the white couple may discover that several rentals just happen to be available.   Ed.

There are actively antiracist whites scattered across the nation. They consistently and regularly speak out against white racism, even to the point of risking personal injury, friendships, and jobs. However, in regard to racist practice, most whites seem to fall into three other categories of action. One large group of whites regularly engage in overtly racist behavior; some of these whites are greatly consumed by their racist hatreds, as can be seen in lynchings and hate crimes. A second, much larger, group of whites discriminate against blacks in a variety of ways, as the occasion arises, but they frequently discriminate in less overt or more subtle ways and may often not be consciously aware of their discrimination. A third group of whites are consistently bystanders, engaging in less direct discrimination but knowingly providing support for those who do. Whites in the latter two groups often reject the type of blatant discrimination in which some in the first group engage, and may speak out against it, even as they themselves are engaging in more subtle or covert types of discrimination. Most whites in these three groups routinely think in white-oriented terms when choosing mates, neighborhoods, schools, and business partners. The racist system is thereby reinforced in daily interactions among whites. A sense of white superiority, however dim, seems to be part of the consciousness of most whites, including those who are relatively liberal on racial matters.

Interestingly, when issues of racism are discussed in the mass media, it is often working-class whites, the Archie Bunkers of television fame, who get tagged as the serious racists by the news and other media programs. Blue-collar violence against black Americans often does get significant news attention. Yet elite and middle-class whites are less frequently the focus of attention in media discussions of racial problems, and media discussions of discrimination that do involve a few middle class or elite discriminators usually avoid making connections to broader issues of systemic racism.

Indeed, most elite and middle class whites vigorously deny that they are racist.

The portrait of discriminatory practice that emerges from research is quite different. Judging from hundreds of interviews that I and my colleagues have conducted with black and white Americans over the last decade, as well as from numerous other field studies of discrimination in housing, employment, and public accommodations, the majority of whites who do the serious discriminating are those with some power to bring harm, such as white employers, managers, teachers, social workers, real estate agents, lenders, landlords and apartment managers, and police officers (Feagin & Sikes 1994; Feagin, Vera & Imani 1996; St. Jean & Feagin 1998). Middle-income and upper-income men and women are heavily implicated in racial oppression, though it is likely that in most major institutional areas, such as corporate promotions and urban policing, white men account for the lion's share of discriminatory actions. Generally speaking, these middle-income and upper-income whites are the ones in a position to most significantly affect black lives. Certainly, whites with less social or economic power also discriminate against black Americans in all income categories. Blue-collar employees frequently harass black workers in the workplace, and blue-collar bigots may yell racist epithets or hurl beer cans at a black man, woman, or child on the street. And working-class whites do seem to predominate as perpetrators in violent attacks on blacks in public places.

Given the right circumstances, most whites in all income groups have the ability to put black Americans "in their place," to frustrate or sabotage their lives for racist reasons. However, the patterns of discrimination vary. Many in the employer class, for instance, may be most interested in the exploitation of black workers, whose lowest-paid members constitute a reserve army of workers. In contrast, those in the white working and middle classes may be more concerned about housing or educational competition with black Americans, and they appear to be the most likely to discriminate in these latter areas.

Facing Lifetimes of Racial Discrimination

Whether subtle, covert, or blatant, racist practices are commonplace and recurring in a great variety of settings, ranging from public accommodations to educational facilities, business arenas, workplaces, and neighborhoods. How frequent is the discrimination faced by black Americans? What forms does this discrimination take? We do not yet have full answers to these questions, but recent surveys are helpful.

Researchers Nancy Krieger and Stephen Sidney gave some 2,000 black respondents a list of seven settings, such as the workplace, where one can face discrimination. Seventy percent of the female and 84 percent of the male respondents reported encountering discrimination in at least one area. The majority reported discrimination in at least three settings (Krieger & Sidney 1996). Similarly, a survey in the Detroit area asked black respondents about facing discrimination in six situations. Thirty-two percent reported discrimination recently in at least one of the situations, and four in ten reported facing at least one form of discrimination frequently (Formen, Williams, & Jackson 1997). In addition, a recent Gallup survey inquired of black respondents if they had experienced discrimination in five areas (work, dining out, shopping, with police, in public transportation) during the last month. Just under half reported discrimination in one or more of these areas, including 70 percent of black men under the age of 35 (Gallup 1977). Many black Americans frequently face racist barriers in an array of societal arenas.

Even these substantial data are likely to be serious underestimates of the frequency of racist obstacles. Short survey questions do not explore the great range of discrimination faced by black Americans in everyday life. Indeed, survey research on the black experience with discrimination is relatively recent and remarkably limited. Survey questions are usually brief and customarily deal with only a few of the many types of racial mistreatment in the society. Indeed, a few survey researchers have suggested that more detailed questioning would reveal a more substantial portrait of discrimination (Siegelman & Welch 1991).

There are other reasons why the existing survey data do not adequately describe the reality of everyday racism. Most black and white Americans are taught as children to focus on individual reasons for personal barriers or failures. Most are taught that blaming others, however legitimate that may seem, is generally not appropriate. The reasoning behind such socialization seems to be that a system-blame orientation makes a person seem weak to those she or he respects. Some black Americans who suffer from discrimination may thus feel that talking too much about racist barriers suggests that they as individuals are not capable of dealing with these difficulties. However, this reluctance to report to survey researchers some of the discrimination they experience does not mean that the discrimination is not harmful in the respondent's life.

In addition, the terminology used in most surveys leads to underestimates. The term "discrimination" itself is used by some black Americans only for very serious abuse by whites. Lesser forms of mistreatment, because they are so commonplace, may not be characterized as discrimination. For example, a young black college professor recently explained to me that he does not ordinarily think of certain everyday examples of differential treatment—such as white cashiers not putting money in his hand because they do not want to touch a black person—as "racial discrimination." It is the more serious incidents of racism that he would recall if asked a question by a pollster about having encountered racial discrimination recently. Racial obstacles are so much a part of black lives that they generally become a part of the societal woodwork. This "everydayness" of racist barriers means that for many black Americans a survey researcher's brief question about discrimination will bring quickly to mind primarily the more serious incidents that stay at the front of the mind—and sometimes not the many intrusions of more subtle racism that occur in one's life. A failure to recall some incidents with whites when questioned briefly does not mean these encounters are of little consequence. In order to survive in a racist society, black Americans cannot attend consciously to all the racist incidents that intrude on their lives. The personal and family cost of too-close attention to much discrimination is too great.

To my knowledge, there is no research on the frequency of the incidents and events of discrimination faced by individual black Americans over their lifetimes. In a few exploratory interviews with black respondents, I have asked a question about frequency and gotten large estimates in response. For example, I asked a retired printer from New York City how often he has faced discrimination over the course of his life. After some careful reflection, this man estimated that he confronts at least 250 significant incidents of discrimination from whites each year, if he only includes the incidents that he consciously notices and records. Blatant and subtle mistreatment by white clerks in stores and restaurants are examples he had in mind. Judging from my own field studies using in-depth interviews with black Americans, this man's experience seems representative. Over the course of a lifetime, a typical black man or woman likely faces *thousands* of instances of blatant, covert, or subtle discrimination at the hands of whites. Today, this omnipresent and routinized discrimination

remains a key mechanism in the social reproduction of systemic racism.

Racial Discrimination in Public Places

Racial oppression has a distinctive spatial dimension, and its character can vary as a black person travels from the private home site to more public spaces. In one study that interviewed a large number of middle-class black Americans, a professor at a major university noted the stress that comes from dealing with whites in public places:

> If I'm in those areas that are fairly protected, within gatherings of my own group, other African Americans, or if I'm in the university where my status as a professor mediates against the way I might be perceived, mediates against the hostile perception, then it's fairly comfortable. . . . When I divide my life into encounters with the outside world, and of course that's ninety percent of my life, it's fairly consistently unpleasant at those sites where there's nothing that mediates between my race and what I have to do. For example, if I'm in a grocery store, if I'm in my car, which is a 1970 Chevrolet, a real old ugly car, all those things—being in a grocery store in casual clothes, or being in the car—sort of advertises something that doesn't have anything to do with my status as far as people I run into are concerned (Feagin & Sikes 1994).

The increase in unpleasant encounters that comes as this professor moves from her home into public arenas such as stores in attributed to the absence of mediating factors such as whites knowing that she is a professor. Much antiblack discrimination occurs outside social contexts where there are family or friends or symbols of status that may reduce the likelihood of discrimination. On the way to work or school there can be unpleasant contacts with white police-officers, white clerks who will not touch your hand, white teenagers at a traffic light, or white customers in stores who are rude. These racist practices are not limited to one setting but rather take place across many public arenas.

DISCRIMINATION IN PUBLIC PLACES

Psychological researchers have staged situations of possible discrimination in public places, and have discovered that white bystanders will often not respond to a black person's call for help in a staged emergency situation. In contrast, whites are much more likely to respond to calls for help from a white person (Dovido 1993). One study found that when a black woman drops a bag of groceries in a public setting, a white person is less likely to help her than to help a white woman who has the same mishap (Crosby et al. 1980). The racial identity of the person needing help strongly affects white responses. Overt dislike of black people is one likely reason. One analyst has suggested yet another possible reason for the white reactions: The more whites see of black people suffering, such as in the media, the more they come to see that condition as normal, and the less sympathy they have for blacks in difficulty (Delgado 1996).

In a recent Gallup survey asking black respondents about discrimination in various settings in the preceding month, retail shopping was the area in which the largest percentage (30 percent) of the sample reported racial mistreatment. Indeed, 45 percent of the young men in this sample reported such discrimination. Twenty-one percent of the sample (and 32 percent of young men) also reported discrimination when dining out. Discrimination in dining includes very poor service that seems racially motivated and often being seated in an undesirable place, such as at the back of the restaurant near the kitchen. Discrimination in retail stores encompasses the extra surveillance often faced by black shoppers and other discrimination

by white sales clerks. In this survey, moreover, those black respondents with higher incomes reported encountering more discrimination than those with lower incomes (Gallup 1997). Leanita McClain, a prize-winning black columnist for the *Chicago Tribune*, once suggested an important difference between contemporary racist practices and the old segregationist practices: "The old racism wouldn't let blacks into some stores; the new racism assumes that any black person, no matter how well dressed, in a store is probably there to steal, not to buy." Undoubtedly drawing on her own experience, she added that the old racism "didn't have to address black people; the new racism is left speechless when a black, approached condescendingly, has an eloquent comeback" (McClain 1986).

Black customers face discrimination in the buying process. One major Chicago study examined more than 180 buyer-salesperson negotiations at ninety car dealerships. Black and white testers, with similar economic characteristics and bargaining scripts, posed as car buyers. White male testers got much better prices from the salespeople than did white women or black men and women. Compared to the markup given to white men, black men paid twice the markup and black women paid more than three times the markup. The average dealer profit in the final offers to each category of tester was as follows: white men, $362; white women, $504; black men, $783; and black women, $1237. In another study the researchers used thirty-eight testers who bargained for some 400 cars at 242 dealers. Again, black testers were quoted much higher prices that white men, though this time black men were quoted the highest prices. In some cases racist language was used by salespeople, but the researchers concluded that the more serious problem was stereotyping about how much black customers will pay. The cost of this commonplace discrimination is high. Given that black customers pay two to three times the markup offered to white men—if this holds across the nation—then black customers "annually would pay $150 million more for new cars than do white males" (Ayres 1991).

Discrimination has also been found in professional services. Recently, one group of researchers used actors to portray black and white patients with certain coronary disease symptoms. A total of 720 physicians were asked to look at these recorded interviews and other patient data, to assess the probability of coronary artery disease, and to suggest treatment. The researchers found differences in proposed treatment: blacks, and especially black women, were less likely to be recommended for cardiac catheterization, compared to whites with the same dress, occupations, and medical histories (Schulman et al. 1999; Bach et al. 1999). Another recent study reported in the *New England Journal of Medicine* found that black patients with lung cancer were less likely to receive the best surgical treatment than white patients. The reasons for these patterns of differential medical treatment along racial lines are yet to be delineated, but they may include not only traditional racial stereotypes but also specific stereotypes shared by some white medical practitioners, such as the notion that black patients who get special or expensive treatments are not as likely as whites to take proper care of themselves after treatment. The explanation for differences in surgery may also include the reluctance on the part of some black patients to trust the recommendations of white physicians. More research remains to be done, but there is no reason to expect that the racism of the larger society does not extend into the medical professions.

References

Ayres, Ian. 1991. "Fair Driving: Gender and Race Discrimination in Retail Car Negotiations." *Harvard Law Review* 104, (February).

Bach, Peter B. et al. 1999. "Racial Differences in the Treatment of Early-Stage Lung Cancer." *New England Journal of Medicine* (October 14).

Blendon, Robert J. et al. 1998. "The public and the President's Commission on Race." *The Public Perspective,* February.

Bobo, Lawrence. 1988. "Group Conflict, Prejudice and the Paradox of Contemporary Racial Attitudes." In *Eliminating Racism,* Phyllis A. Katz and Dalmas A. Taylor, eds., New York: Plenum.

Bobo, Lawrence, James R. Kluegel, and Ryan A. Smith. 1997. "Laissez-faire Racism: The Crystallization of a Kinder, Gentler, Antiblack Ideology." In *Racial Attitudes in the 1990s: Continuity and Change,* Steven A. Tuch and Jack K. Martin, eds. Westport, CT: Praeger.

Calmore, John O. 1989. "To Make Wrong Right: The Necessary and Proper Aspirations of Fair Housing." In *The State of Black America 1989.* New York: The National Urban League.

Crosby, Faye et al. 1980. "Recent Unobtrusive Studies of Black and White Discrimination and Prejudice: A Literature Review." *Psychological Bulletin* 87.

Culp, Jerome M., Jr. 1993. "Water Buffalo and Diversity: Naming Names and Reclaiming the Racial Discourse." *Connecticut Law Review* 26 (Fall).

Delgado, Richard. 1996. *The Coming Race War?* New York: New York University Press.

Devine, Patricia G. 1989. "Stereotypes and Prejudice: Their Automatic and Controlled Components." *Journal of Personality and Social Psychology* 56: 15–16.

Dovidio, John F. 1993. "The Subtlety of Racism." *Training and Development,* April.

Entman, Robert M. 1997. "Manufacturing Discord: Media in the Affirmative Action Debate." *Press/Politics* 2.

Essed, Philomena. 1991. *Understanding Everyday Racism.* Newbury Park, CA: Sage.

Feagin, Joe R., and Clairece B. Feagin. 1999. *Racial and Ethnic Relations, 6th Edition.* Upper Saddle River, NJ: Prentice-Hall.

Feagin, Joe R., and Hernan Vera. 1995. *White Racism: The Basics.* New York: Routledge.

Feagin, Joe R., and Melvin P. Sikes. 1994. *Living with Racism: The Black Middle-Class Experience.* Boston: Beacon Press.

Forman, Tyrone, David R. Williams, and James S. Jackson. 1997. "Race, Place, and Discrimination." In *Perspectives on Social Problems.* Carol Brooks Gardner, ed. Stamford, CT: Jai Press.

Frankenberg, Ruth. 1993. *White Women, Race Matters.* Minneapolis: University of Minnesota Press.

Gallup Organization. 1997. *Black/White Relations in the United States.* Princeton, NJ: Gallup Organization.

Hughes, Michael. 1997. "Symbolic Racism, Old-fashioned Racism, and Whites' Opposition to Affirmative Action." In *Racial Attitudes in the 1990s: Continuity and Change,* Steven A. Tuch and Jack K. Martin, eds. Westport, CT: Praeger.

Jhally, Sut, and Justin Lewis. 1992. *Enlightened Racism.* Boulder, CO: Westview Press.

King, Joyce E. 1991. "Dysconscious Racism: Ideology, Identity, and the Miseducation of Teachers." *Journal of Negro Education* 60.

Kluegel, James R., and Eliot R. Smith. 1986. *Beliefs about Inequality.* New York: Aldine de Gruyter.

Krieger, Nancy, and Stephen Sidney. 1996. "Racial Discrimination and Blood Pressure." *American Journal of Public Health,* 86.

Ladd, Everett C. 1995. "Rethinking the Sixties." *The American Enterprise,* May/June.

Lehigh, Scott. 1998. "Conflicting Views of Massachusetts; Poll Shows a Sharp Racial Divide over the State of Equality." *Boston Globe,* June 14.

McClain, Leanita. 1986. "The Insidious New Racism." In *A Foot in Each World,* Clarence Page, ed. Evanston, IL: Northwestern University Press.

NORC, 1990. *General Social Survey.* Chicago, IL: National Opinion Research Center.

Schulman, Kevin A. et al. 1999. "The Effect of Race and Sex on Physicians' Recommendations for Cardiac Catherization." *New England Journal of Medicine,* February.

Sears, David O. 1988. "Symbolic racism." In *Eliminating Racism,* Phyllis A. Katz and Dalmas A. Taylor, eds. New York: Plenum.

Sigelman, Lee, and Susan Welch. 1991. *Black Americans' Views of Racial Inequality: The Dream Deferred.* Cambridge: Cambridge University Press.

Smith, Matthew P. 1996. "Bridging the Gulf Between Blacks and Whites." *Pittsburgh Post Gazette,* April 7.

St. Jean, Yanick, and Joe R. Feagin. 1998. *Double Burden: Black Women and Everyday Racism.* New York: M.E. Sharpe.

Verba, Sidney, and Gary R. Orren. 1985. *Equality in America: The View from the Top.* Cambridge, MA: Harvard University Press.

Wellman, David. 1977. *Portraits of White Racism.* Cambridge: Cambridge University Press.

Questions

1. Make a list of the varieties of antiblack racist acts that were described by black people in Feagin's article. Assume that these kinds of discriminatory acts are familiar to just about every black person in the United States. Which discriminatory acts on your list are of the sort that the average white person is likely to have many opportunities to personally observe and understand as racist?

2. In reading #13 ("Separating the Men from the Girls") Michael Messner and his colleagues suggested that "subtle bias is no less dangerous than overt sexism" (in other words, that subtle bias is as dangerous as overt sexism). Can the same be said of racism; can it be said that subtle bias is as dangerous as overt racism? Why or why not? Then, consider this: are there any circumstances under which it could be said that *subtle bias is even more dangerous than overt racism?*

Confessions of a Nice Negro, or Why I Shaved My Head

Robin D. G. Kelley

No matter how much they distort reality, stereotypes exist and have an impact on people's lives. In this 1995 article, Robin Kelley recounts his experiences with what, to him, was a new stereotype.

It happened just the other day—two days into the new year, to be exact. I had dashed into the deserted lobby of an Ann Arbor movie theater, pulling the door behind me to escape the freezing winter winds Michigan residents have come to know so well. Behind the counter knelt a young white teenager filling the popcorn bin with bags of that awful pre-popped stuff. Hardly the enthusiastic employee; from a distance it looked like she was lost in deep thought. The generous display of body piercing suggested an X-generation flower child—perhaps an anthropology major into acid jazz and environmentalism, I thought. Sporting a black New York Yankees baseball cap and a black-and-beige scarf over my nose and mouth, I must have looked like I had stepped out of a John Singleton film. And because I was already late, I rushed madly toward the ticket counter.

The flower child was startled: "I don't have anything in the cash register," she blurted as she pulled the bag of popcorn in front of her for protection.

"Huh? I just want one ticket for *Little Women*, please—the two-fifteen show. My wife and daughter should already be in there." I slowly gestured to the theater door and gave her one of those innocent childlike glances I used to give my mom when I wanted to sit on her lap.

"Oh, god . . . I'm so sorry. A reflex. Just one ticket? You only missed the first twenty minutes. Enjoy the show."

Enjoy the show? Barely 1995 and here we go again. Another bout with racism in a so-called liberal college town; another racial drama in which I play the prime suspect. And yet I have to confess the situation was pretty funny. Just two hours earlier I couldn't persuade Elleza, my four-year-old daughter, to put her toys away; time-out did nothing, yelling had no effect, and the evil stare made no impact whatsoever. Thoroughly frustrated, I had only one option left: "Okay, I'm gonna tell Mommy!" Of course it worked.

So those five seconds as a media-made black man felt kind of good. I know it's a product of racism. I know that the myth of black male violence has resulted in the deaths of many innocent boys and men of darker hue. I know that the power to scare is not real power. I know all that—after all, I study this stuff for a living! For the moment, though, it felt good. (Besides, the ability to scare with your body can come in handy, especially when you're trying to get a good seat in a theater or avoid long lines.)

I shouldn't admit this, but I take particular pleasure in putting fear into people on the look-out for black male criminality mainly because those moments are so rare for me. Indeed, my *inability* to employ blackmaleness as a weapon is the story of my life. Why I don't possess it, or rather possess so little of it, escapes me. I grew up poor in Harlem and Afrodena (the Negro West Side of Pasadena/Altadena, California). My mom was single during my formative preadolescent years, and for a brief moment she even received a welfare check. A hard life makes a hard nigga, so I've been told.

Never an egghead or a dork, as a teenager I was pretty cool. I did the house-party circuit on Friday and Saturday nights and used to stroll down the block toting the serious Radio Raheem boombox. Why, I even invaded movie theaters in the company of ten or fifteen hooded and high-topped black bodies, colonizing the balconies and occupying two seats per person. Armed with popcorn and Raisinettes as our missiles of choice, we dared any usher to ask us to leave. Those of us who had cars (we called them hoopties or rides back in that day) spent our lunch hours and precious class time hanging out in the school parking lot, running down our Die Hards to pump up Cameo, Funkadelic, Grandmaster Flash from our car stereos. I sported dickies and Levis, picked up that gangsta stroll, and when the shag came in style I was with it—always armed with a silk scarf to ensure that my hair was laid. Granted, I vomited after drinking malt liquor for the first time and my only hit of a joint ended abruptly in an asthma attack. But I was cool.

Sure, I was cool, but nobody feared me. That I'm relatively short with dimples and curly hair, speak softly in a rather medium to high-pitched voice, and have a "girl's name" doesn't help matters. And everyone knows that light skin is less threatening to white people than blue-black

or midnight brown. Besides, growing up with a soft-spoken, uncharacteristically passive West Indian mother deep into East Indian religions, a mother who sometimes walked barefoot in the streets of Harlem, a mother who insisted on proper diction and never, ever, ever used a swear word, screwed me up royally. I could never curse right. My mouth had trouble forming the words—"fuck" always came out as "fock" and "goddamn" always sounded like it's spelled, not "gotdayum," the way my Pasadena homies pronounced it in their Calabama twang. I don't even recall saying the word "bitch" unless I was quoting somebody or some authorless vernacular rhyme. For some unknown reason, that word scared me.

Moms dressed me up in the coolest mod outfits—short pant suits with matching hats, Nehru jackets, those sixties British-looking turtlenecks. Sure, she got some of that stuff from John's Bargain Store or Goodwill, but I always looked "cute." More stylish than roguish. Kinda like W. E. B. Du Bois[1] as a toddler, or those turn-of-the-century photos of middle-class West Indian boys who grow up to become prime ministers or poets. Ghetto ethnographers back in the late sixties and early seventies would not have found me or my family very "authentic," especially if they had discovered that one of my middle names is Gibran, after the Lebanese poet Kahlil Gibran.

Everybody seemed to like me. Teachers liked me, kids liked me; I even fell in with some notorious teenage criminals at Pasadena High School because *they* liked me. I remember one memorable night in the ninth grade when I went down to the Pasadena Boys' Club to take

---

[1]W. E. B. Du Bois (1868–1963) was the first African American to earn a Ph.D. from Harvard University (1895). He taught sociology at several universities, was a strong advocate for racial integration, and in 1909 founded the National Association for the Advancement of Colored People. Ultimately, Du Bois lost faith in the possibility of integration and began to promote segregation. He was dismissed from the NAACP and moved to Ghana, where he lived until his death.—Ed.

photos of some of my partners on the basket-ball team. On my way home some big kids, eleventh-graders to be exact, tried to take my camera. The ringleader pulled out a knife and gently poked it against my chest. I told them it was my stepfather's camera and if I came home without it he'd kick my ass for a week. Miraculously, this launched a whole conversation about stepfathers and how messed up they are, which must have made them feel sorry for me. Within minutes we were cool; they let me go unmolested and I had made another friend.

In affairs of the heart, however, "being liked" had the opposite effect. I can only recall having had four fights in my entire life, all of which were with girls who supposedly liked me but thoroughly beat my behind. Sadly, my record in the boxing ring of puppy love is still 0–4. By the time I graduated to serious dating, being a nice guy seemed like the root of all my romantic problems. I resisted jealousy, tried to be understanding, brought flowers and balloons, opened doors, wrote poems and songs, and seemed to always be on my knees for one reason or another. If you've ever watched "Love Connection" or read *Cosmopolitan*, you know the rest of the story: I practically never had sex and most of the women I dated left me in the cold for roughnecks. My last girlfriend in high school, the woman I took to my prom, the woman I once thought I'd die for, tried to show me the light: "Why do you always ask me what I want? Why don't you just *tell* me what you want me to do? Why don't you take charge and *be a man?* If you want to be a real man you can't be nice all the time!"

I always thought she was wrong; being nice has nothing to do with being a man. While I still think she's wrong, it's an established fact that our culture links manhood to terror and power, and that black men are frequently imaged as the ultimate in hypermasculinity. But the black man as the prototype of violent hypermasculinity is as much a fiction as the happy Sambo. No matter what critics and stand-up comics might say, I know from experience that not all black

men—and here I'm only speaking of well-lighted or daytime situations—generate fear. Who scares and who doesn't has a lot to do with the body in question; it is dependent on factors such as age, skin color, size, clothes, hairstyle, and even the sound of one's voice. The cops who beat Rodney King and the jury who acquitted King's assailants openly admitted that the size, shape, and color of his body automatically made him a threat to the officers' safety.

On the other hand, the threatening black male body can take the most incongruous forms. Some of the hardest brothas on my block in West Pasadena kept their perms in pink rollers and hairnets. It was not unusual to see young black men in public with curlers, tank-top undershirts, sweatpants, black mid-calf dress socks, and Stacey Adams shoes, hanging out on the corner or on the basketball court. And we all knew that these brothas were not to be messed with. (The rest of the world probably knows it by now, too, since black males in curlers are occasionally featured on "Cops" and "America's Most Wanted" as notorious drug dealers or heartless pimps.)

Whatever the source of this ineffable terror, my body simply lacked it. Indeed, the older I got and the more ensconced I became in the world of academia, the less threatening I seemed. Marrying and having a child also reduced the threat factor. By the time I hit my late twenties, my wife, Diedra, and I found ourselves in the awkward position of being everyone's favorite Negroes. I don't know how many times we've attended dinner parties where we were the only African Americans in the room. Occasionally there were others, but we seemed to have a monopoly on the dinner party invitations. This not only happened in Ann Arbor, where there is a small but substantial black population to choose from, but in the Negro mecca of Atlanta, Georgia. Our hosts always felt comfortable asking us "sensitive" questions about race that they would not dare ask other black colleagues and friends: What do African

Americans think about Farrakhan? Ben Chavis? Nelson Mandela? Most of my black students are very conservative and career-oriented—why is that? How can we mend the relations between blacks and Jews? Do you celebrate Kwanzaa? Do you put anything in your hair to make it that way? What are the starting salaries for young black faculty nowadays?

Of course, these sorts of exchanges appear regularly in most black autobiographies. As soon as they're comfortable, it is not uncommon for white people to take the opportunity to find out everything they've always wanted to know about "us" (which also applies to other people of color, I'm sure) but were afraid to ask. That they feel perfectly at ease asking dumb or unanswerable questions is not simply a case of (mis)perceived racelessness. Being a "nice Negro" has a lot to do with gender, and my peculiar form of "left-feminist-funny-guy" masculinity—a little Kevin Hooks, some Bobby McFerrin, a dash of Woody Allen—is regarded as less threatening than that of most other black men.

Not that I mind the soft-sensitive masculine persona—after all, it is the genuine me, a product of my mother's heroic and revolutionary child-rearing style. But there are moments when I wish I could invoke the intimidation factor of blackmaleness on demand. If I only had that look—that Malcolm X/Mike Tyson/Ice Cube/Larry Fishburne/Bigger Thomas/Fruit of Islam look—I could keep the stupid questions at bay, make college administrators tremble, and scare editors into submission. Subconsciously, I decided that I had to do something about my image. Then, as if by magic, my wish was fulfilled.

Actually, it began as an accident involving a pair of electric clippers and sleep deprivation—a bad auto-cut gone awry. With my lowtop fade on the verge of a Sly Stone afro, I was in desperate need of a trim. Diedra didn't have the time to do it, and as it was February (Black History Month), I was on the chitlin' lecture circuit and couldn't spare forty-five minutes at a

barber shop, so I elected to do it myself. Standing in a well-lighted bathroom, armed with two mirrors, I started trimming. Despite a steady hand and what I've always believed was a good eye, my hair turned out lopsided. I kept trimming and trimming to correct my error, but as my flattop sank lower, a yellow patch of scalp began to rise above the surrounding hair, like one of those big granite mounds dotting the grassy knolls of Central Park. A nice yarmulke could have covered it, but that would have been more difficult to explain than a bald spot. So, bearing in mind role models like Michael Jordan, Charles Barkley, Stanley Crouch, and Onyx (then the hip-hop group of the hour), I decided to take it all off.

I didn't think much of it at first, but the new style accomplished what years of evil stares and carefully crafted sartorial statements could not: I began to scare people. The effect was immediate and dramatic. Passing strangers avoided me and smiled less frequently. Those who did smile or make eye contact seemed to be deliberately trying to disarm me—a common strategy taught in campus rape-prevention centers. Scaring people was fun for a while, but I especially enjoyed standing in the line at the supermarket with my bald head, baggy pants, high-top Reeboks, and long black hooded down coat, humming old standards like "Darn That Dream," "A Foggy Day," and "I Could Write a Book." Now *that* brought some stares. I must have been convincing, since I adore those songs and have been humming them ever since I can remember. No simple case of cultural hybridity here, just your average menace to society with a deep appreciation for Gershwin, Rodgers and Hart, Van Heusen, Cole Porter, and Jerome Kern.

Among my colleagues, my bald head became the lead subject of every conversation. "You look older, more mature." "With that new cut you come across as much more serious than usual." "You really look quite rugged and masculine with a bald head." My close friends dispensed with the euphemisms and went straight to the point: "Damn. You look scary!" The most painful comment was that I looked like a "B-Boy wannabe" and was "too old for that shit." I had to remind my friend that I'm an OBB (Original B-Boy), that I was in the eleventh grade in 1979 when the Sugar Hill Gang dropped "Rapper's Delight," and that *his* tired behind was in graduate school at the time. Besides, B-Boy was not the intent.

In the end, however, I got more questions than comments. Was I in crisis? Did I want to talk? What was I trying to say by shaving my head? What was the political point of my actions? Once the novelty passed, I began getting those "speak for the race" questions that irritated the hell out of me when I had hair. Why have *black men* begun to shave their heads in greater numbers? Why have so many black athletes decided to shave their heads? Does this new trend have some kind of phallic meaning? Against my better judgment, I found myself coming up with answers to these questions—call it an academician's reflex. I don't remember exactly what I said, but it usually began with black prizefighter Jack Johnson, America's real life "baaad nigger" of the early twentieth century, whose head was always shaved and greased, and ended with the hip-hop community's embrace of an outlaw status. Whatever it was, it made sense at the time.

The publicity photo for my recent book, *Race Rebels,* clearly generated the most controversy among my colleagues. It diverged dramatically from the photo on my first book, where I look particularly innocent, almost angelic. In that first photo I smiled just enough to make my dimples visible; my eyes gazed away from the camera in sort of a dreamy, contemplative pose; my haircut was nondescript and the natural sunlight had a kind of halo effect. The Izod shirt was the icing on the cake. By contrast, the photograph for *Race Rebels* (which Diedra set up and shot, by the way) has me looking directly into the camera, arms folded, bald head glistening from baby oil and rear window light, with a grimace that could give Snoop Doggy Dogg a

run for his money. The lens made my arms appear much larger than they really are, creating a kind of Popeye effect. Soon after the book came out, I received several e-mail messages about the photo. A particularly memorable one came from a friend and fellow historian in Australia. In the course of explaining to me how he had corrected one of his students who had read an essay of mine and presumed I was a woman, he wrote: "Mind you, the photo in your book should make things clear—the angle and foreshortening of the arms, and the hairstyle make it one of the most masculine author photos I've seen recently????!!!!!!"

My publisher really milked this photo, which actually fit well with the book's title. For the American Studies Association meeting in Nashville, Tennessee, which took place the week the book came out, my publisher bought a full-page ad on the back cover of an ASA handout, with my mug staring dead at you. Everywhere I turned—in hotel elevators, hallways, lobbies, meeting rooms—I saw myself, and it was not exactly a pretty sight. The quality of the reproduction (essentially a high-contrast xerox) made me appear harder, meaner, and crazier than the original photograph.

The situation became even stranger since I had decided to abandon the skinhead look and grow my hair back. In fact, by the time of the ASA meeting I was on the road (since abandoned) toward a big Black Power Afro—a retro style that at the time seemed to be making a comeback. Worse still, I had come to participate in a round-table discussion on black hair! My paper, titled "Nap Time: Historicizing the Afro," explored the political implications of competing narratives of the Afro's origins and meaning. Overall, it was a terrific session; the room was packed and the discussion was stimulating. But inevitably the question came up: "Although this isn't directly related to his paper, I'd like to find out from Professor Kelley why he shaved his head. Professor Kelley, given the panel's topic and in light of the current ads floating about with your picture on them, can you shed some light on what is attractive to black men about baldness?" The question was posed by a very distinguished and widely read African American literary scholar. Hardly the naif, he knew the answers as well as I did, but wanted to generate a public discussion. And he succeeded. For ten minutes the audience ran the gamut of issues revolving around race, gender, sexuality, and the politics of style. Even the issue of bald heads as phallic symbols came up. "It's probably true," I said, "but when I was cutting my hair at three-o'clock in the morning I wasn't thinking 'penis.'" Eventually the discussion drifted from black masculinity to the tremendous workloads of minority scholars, which, in all honesty, was the source of my baldness in the first place. Unlike the golden old days, when doing hair was highly ritualized and completely integrated into daily life, we're so busy mentoring and publishing and speaking and fighting that we have very little time to attend to our heads.

Beyond the session itself, that ad continued to haunt me during the entire conference. Every ten minutes, or so it seemed, someone came up to me and offered unsolicited commentary on the photo. One person slyly suggested that in order to make the picture complete I should have posed with an Uzi. When I approached a very good friend of mine, a historian who is partly my Jewish mother and partly my confidante and *always* looking out for my best interests, the first words out of her mouth were, "Robin, I hate that picture! It's the worst picture of you I've ever seen. It doesn't do you justice. Why did you let them use it?"

"It's not that bad," I replied. "Diedra likes it—she took the picture. You just don't like my bald head."

"No, that's not it. I like the bald look on some men, and you have a very nice head. The problem is the photo and the fact that I know what kind of person you are. None of your gentleness and lovability comes out in that picture. Now, don't get a swelled head when I say this, but you have a delightful face and

expression that makes people feel good, even when you're talking about serious stuff. The way you smile, there's something unbelievably safe about you."

It was a painful compliment. And yet I knew deep down that she was telling the truth. I've always been unbelievably safe, not just because of my look but because of my actions. Not that I consciously try to put people at ease, to erase conflict and difference, to remain silent on sensitive issues. I can't quite put a finger on it. Perhaps it's my mother's politeness drills? Perhaps it's a manifestation of my continuing bout with shyness? Maybe it has something to do with the sense of joy I get from stimulating conversations? Or maybe it's linked to the fact that my mom refused to raise me in a manner boys are accustomed to? Most likely it is a product of cultural capital[2]—the fact that I *can* speak the language, (re)cite the texts, exhibit the manners and mannerisms that are inherent to bourgeois academic culture. My colleagues identify with me because I can talk intelligently about their scholarship on their terms, which invariably has the effect of creating an illusion of brilliance. As Frantz Fanon said in *Black Skin, White Masks*, the mere fact that he was an articulate *black* man who read a lot rendered him a stunning specimen of erudition in the eyes of his fellow intellectuals in Paris.

Whatever the source of my ineffable lovability, I've learned that it's not entirely a bad thing. In fact, if the rest of the world could look a little deeper, beyond the hardcore exterior—the wide bodies, the carefully constructed grimaces, the performance of terror—they would find many, many brothas much nicer and smarter than myself. The problem lies in a

---

[2]The concept of cultural capital has gained currency through the work of Marxist sociologist Pierre Bourdieu, who uses the term to refer to specific skills and competencies (for example, the ability to use language and other social skills) that middle- and upper-class parents are able to pass on to their children. Ownership of cultural as well as economic capital provides advantages to members of the middle and upper classes and increases the probability of their success.—Ed.

racist culture, a highly gendered racist culture, that is so deeply enmeshed in the fabric of daily life that it's practically invisible. The very existence of the "nice Negro," like the model-minority myth pinned on Asian Americans, renders the war on those "other," hardcore niggas justifiable and even palatable. In a little-known essay on the public image of world champion boxer Joe Louis, the radical Trinidadian writer C. L. R. James put it best: "This attempt to hold up Louis as a model Negro has strong overtones of condescension and race prejudice. It implies: 'See! When a Negro knows how to conduct himself, he gets on very well and we all love him.' From there the next step is: 'If only all Negros behaved like Joe, the race problem would be solved'" (1946).

Of course we all know this is a bunch of fiction. Behaving "like Joe" was merely a code for deference and patience, which is all the more remarkable given his vocation. Unlike his predecessor Jack Johnson—the bald-headed prizefighter who transgressed racial boundaries by sleeping with and even marrying white women, who refused to apologize for his "outrageous" behavior, who boasted of his prowess in every facet of life (he even wrapped gauze around his penis to make it appear bigger under his boxing shorts)—Joe Louis was America's hero. As James put it, he was a credit to his race, "I mean the human race." (Re)presented as a humble Alabama boy, Godfearing and devoid of hatred, Louis was constructed in the press as a raceless man whose masculinity was put to good, patriotic use. To many of his white fans, he was a man in the ring and a boy—a good boy—outside of it. To many black folks, he was a hero because he had the license to kick white men's butts and yet maintain the admiration and respect of a nation. Thus, despite similarities in race, class, and vocation, and their common iconization, Louis and Johnson exhibited public behavior that reflected radically different masculinities.

Here, then, is a lesson we cannot ignore. There is some truth in the implication that race (or gender) conflict is partly linked to behavior and how certain behavior is perceived. If our society, for example, could dispense with rigid, archaic notions of appropriate masculine and feminine behavior, perhaps we might create a world that nurtures, encourages, and even rewards nice guys. If violence were not so central to American culture—to the way manhood is defined, to the way in which the state keeps African American men in check, to the way men interact with women, to the way oppressed peoples interact with one another—perhaps we might see the withering away of white fears of black men. Perhaps young black men wouldn't feel the need to adopt hardened, threatening postures merely to survive in a Doggy-Dogg world. Not that black men ought to become colored equivalents of Alan Alda. Rather, black men ought to be whomever or whatever they want to be, without unwarranted criticism or societal pressures to conform to a particular definition of manhood. They could finally dress down without suspicion, talk loudly without surveillance, and love each other without sanction. Fortunately, such a transformation would also mean the long-awaited death of the "nice Negro."

Not in my lifetime. Any fool can look around and see that the situation for race and gender relations in general, and for black males in particular, has taken a turn for the worse—and relief is nowhere in sight. In the meantime, I will make the most of my "nice Negro" status. When it's all said and done, there is nothing romantic or interesting about playing Bigger Thomas. Maybe I can't persuade a well-dressed white couple to give up their box seats, but at least they'll listen to me. For now. . . .

Reference

James, C. L. R. 1946. "Joe Louis and Jack Johnson." *Labor Action,* July 1.

Questions

1. Have you ever been a victim of stereotyping—for example, based on your gender, race, ethnicity, sexual orientation, or social class? If you have, how did it make you feel?

2. Early in the article Kelley refers to the "media-made black man." What did he mean by this?

3. Does a shaved head have a different meaning for a black man than for a white man? In other words, would people find a white man with a shaved head to be scary? Why or why not?

4. Kelley says that "any fool can look around and see that the situation for race and gender relations in general, and for black males in particular, has taken a turn for the worse—and relief is nowhere in sight." To what extent do you agree with this assessment?

·39·

The Model Minority Myth
Asian Americans Confront Growing Backlash

Yin Ling Leung

In this 1987 article, Yin Ling Leung reveals something of a social paradox: Members of some groups in our society are singled out for discriminatory treatment because they are judged by the dominant group to be "inferior," whereas others are singled out for discrimination because they are judged "superior." Note that here, the terms *Asians* and *Asian Americans* refer to a wide range of peoples, including Cambodians, Chinese, Filipinos, Hmong, Japanese, Koreans, Laotians, Thais, and Vietnamese.

The once predominant media caricatures of Asians such as the effeminate Charlie Chan, the evil Fu Manchu, the exotic dragon-lady Suzy Wong or the docile, submissive Mrs. Livingston are giving way to a more subtle but equally damaging image. The emerging picture of Asians as hardworking, highly educated, family-oriented, and financially successful—in short, a "model minority"—appears benign at first, even beneficial. However, Asians are experiencing a growing backlash against their "model minority" status. The pervasive perception that Asian Americans are "making it," even surpassing whites despite their minority status, is resulting in discriminatory college admittance practices and a rise in anti-Asian sentiment.

What is now being coined the "model minority myth" began to take root in the late 1960s, after increasing numbers of Asian immigrants came to the U.S. under the Immigration Act of 1965.[1] A 1966 *U.S. News and World Report* article, entitled "Success Story of One Minority Group in the U.S.," portrayed Asian Americans as hardworking and uncomplaining, and implied that discrimination is not an obstacle for Asian Americans. A rash of similar articles followed, each attempting to reveal the "formula" responsible for Asian American success and prosperity.

The increased numbers of Southeast Asian refugees (the Hmong, Vietnamese, Laotian, and Kampuchean/Cambodians) and the increased immigration from Taiwan, Korea and Hong Kong have made Asians the second-fastest-growing minority population in the U.S. With this increase in numbers, the media has increased its focus on the "success stories" of Asian Americans as a whole. Articles in popular

[1]Center for Third World Reporting. 1987. *Minority Trendsletter*, Winter, pp. 5–7.

magazines such as *Newsweek, U.S. News and World Report* and others, with titles like "Asian-Americans: A 'Model Minority,'" "The Drive to Excel," "A Formula for Success," "The Promise of America," and "The Triumph of Asian Americans," perpetuate a distorted image of universal Asian-American success. One article in *Fortune* magazine portrayed Asians as a super competitive force, or "super minority," outperforming even the majority white population.

Myth Versus Reality

A closer examination of the facts, however, reveals holes in both the "model minority" and "super minority" myths. For example, 1980 census figures place the mean family income for Asian American families in the U.S. at $26,456 — nearly $3,000 higher than white families. These figures dramatically change, however, if adjusted for the number of workers per family. Because Asians tend to have more workers per family, the total income of a family reflects less per individual. In addition, over 64 percent of Asian Americans live in urban areas of San Francisco, Los Angeles, New York and Honolulu, where the incomes and cost of living are correspondingly higher.

The model minority myth also masks the complexity of Asians in America and the different realities they face. In fact, Asian Americans come from sharply distinct backgrounds which determine their life in the U.S. Many of the "successful" Asian immigrants touted by the media as exemplifying the model minority phenomenon come from families that have been in the states for many generations or from aristocratic, elite, educated, economically advantaged backgrounds in their home countries. For example, the early Vietnamese refugee boat people were from wealthier and more educated communities than the more recent refugees from Vietnam. In addition, immigrants from China, Japan, and Korea tend to come from relatively more privileged backgrounds.

The more recent immigrants from Southeast Asia, like the Hmong, Laotian, Kampuchean/Cambodian, and the Vietnamese refugees arriving after 1976, do not mirror the image of instant success that the media perpetuates. These hundreds of thousands of Southeast Asian refugees suffer not only from language difficulties, but also from deep-seated emotional and psychological disorders, resulting from the trauma they experienced in the war-torn countries of Southeast Asia. Asian refugees also face limited work opportunities, substandard wages and lack of health benefits and unhealthy working conditions.

Another facet to [the] model minority myth is the belief that all Asians excel academically. There is no disputing that Asian Americans are "overrepresented" in the nation's colleges and universities. Asians make up approximately 3.7 million or 1.6 percent of the total U.S. population, but comprise 8 to 18 percent of enrollment in the nation's top colleges and universities. At the University of California at Berkeley, Asian students make up a quarter of the student population.

The media links Asian "success" in education with their strong familial bonds. This is, to some extent, an accurate portrayal. Many Asian cultures believe that social mobility is directly tied to education and therefore spend a disproportionate amount of family income on education, as compared to white families. Because it is a considerable sacrifice for most immigrant families to send their children to college, Asian students are often urged by their parents to pursue "safer" professions, such as medicine, engineering and other fields where the economic payback is proportionate to the number of years (and dollars) invested in education.

Even in these "safe" professions, however, Asians are discovering that quiet achievement and good job performance may not amount to promotions. A *Newsweek* article recently pointed to a phenomenon of Asian middle-management professionals, especially in corporate business fields, who "top-out," reaching a plateau beyond which their employers will not promote them.

Backlash: Asians Face Discrimination

Repercussions of the model minority myth on Asian Americans could be described as "the many being punished by the success of a few." Asians of all classes and generations are experiencing a rise in anti-Asian sentiment. This anti-Asian sentiment is expressed both through subtle, systematic discrimination, particularly in higher education, and through racially motivated violence.

Because of the disproportionate numbers of Asian Americans in the nation's universities, some colleges are denying Asians affirmative action consideration. At Princeton University, for example, where Asians make up approximately 8.5 percent of the entering class, admissions officials no longer consider Asian Americans as a minority group, despite federal regulations which define them as a protected subgroup.

Other prestigious colleges and universities are systematically excluding qualified Asians through the application of heavily subjective criteria. At the University of California at Berkeley, for example, despite a 14 percent rise in applications between 1983 to 1985, the number of Asian Americans admitted to UCB dropped 20 percent in 1984.

The Asian American Task Force on UC Admissions, which conducted a seven-month study, found that the university had temporarily used a minimum SAT verbal score to disqualify applicants. While Asian Americans excel on the math sections of the SAT, their national average on the verbal portion of the test was under 400. The Task Force also found that UCB now relies more heavily on subjective criteria for freshman admissions. For the fall of 1987, grades and test scores will determine

only 40 percent of admittees, while 30 percent will be chosen by subjective factors which tend to operate against Asians.

According to Henry Der, executive director of Chinese for Affirmative Action: "Qualified Asian students are being excluded from the Berkeley campus in substantial numbers. It is apparent that UC policy changes are conscious attempts to limit the growth of Asian students, to the benefit of qualified white students."

Discriminatory practices at UC Berkeley point to a nationwide trend. At Harvard University, where Asians make up 10.9 percent of the first-year class, admitted Asian students had scores substantially higher than white students who were admitted. At Brown University, a study conducted by Asian American students found that Asian American admittance rates in the early 1980s had been consistently lower than the all-college admittance rate.

There is increasing evidence that these and other select schools are designing "hidden quotas" to exclude otherwise qualified Asian applicants. For example, a recent survey of Asian American applicants at Stanford demonstrated that popular images of Asians as narrowly-focused math and science students influenced how admissions officers judged Asians for entrance to college campuses. Just as "regional diversity" was used as a mechanism to keep Jews, who tended to be concentrated in metropolitan areas like New York and Los Angeles, out of elite institutions prior to World War II, "extra-curricular and leadership" criteria are functioning in a similar manner for certain Asians. The Stanford study found that although Asian Americans participated in nearly the same proportion as whites in high school sports, in equal numbers in music and in greater numbers in social, ethnic and community organizations, "intentional or unintentional" biases have made many applicants the victims of racial stereotypes.

Black conservative Thomas Sowell and other neoconservatives applaud the divorce of

Asians from their minority status. Sowell believes that this will cause schools to be just as rigorous in selecting Asian students as they are at selecting majority white students. In this way, he continues, students will not be mismatched with their schools, a problem he attributes to quota requirements.

Anti-Asian Sentiment Rising

The model minority myth, coupled with the rising economic prowess of Pacific Rim Asian countries and the corresponding economic downturn in the U.S., has given rise to an increase in anti-Asian violence. In 1981, the Japanese American Citizens League recorded seven cases in which anti-Asian sentiment was expressed verbally, legislatively or physically; in 1982 they recorded four; in 1983, 20; in 1984, 30; in 1985, 48.

One explanation for this rise in anti-Asian violence is that Asians are being used as scapegoats[2] for the nation's economic problems. Both business and labor have waged explicitly anti-Asian media campaigns portraying Japanese competition as an explanation for the ills of American industry.

The case of Vincent Chin dramatically demonstrates the potential impact of such campaigns. Chin, a 27-year-old Chinese American resident of Detroit, was bludgeoned to death by two white unemployed auto workers. The two men, who were merely fined and put on probation, mistook him for Japanese. They saw Chin as a representative of the Japanese automobile imports business, which they blamed for the loss of their jobs. Violence against Asian refugees and immigrants who compete for scarce resources in low-income communities has also dramatically increased.

The Asian Community Responds

Asian Americans are contradicting the very stereotype of the hardworking, uncomplaining minority by protesting the discriminatory practices in the nation's colleges and in the job market. For example, the Chinese American Legal Defense Fund, a Michigan-based organization, has filed suit against UC Berkeley and several other elite institutions, including Stanford, Princeton, Yale, and MIT. They charge that campuses have imposed "secret quotas" on Asians because of their growing enrollments. In another case, Yat-Pang Au, valedictorian of San Jose's Gunderson High School, with "top test scores and an impressive array of extracurricular activities," is threatening a civil rights suit against UC Berkeley for denying his entrance to the competitive College of Engineering.

At least one school has responded to this pressure by re-examining its admittance policies. A recent study of Asian student admission at Stanford, Brown, Harvard, and Princeton by John H. Bunzel and Jeffrey K. D. Au, both from Stanford, found that Stanford was the only university to buck the trend of declining Asian admissions. The 1986 entering class of Asian Americans increased from 119 last year to 245 this year. Asians at Stanford make up 15.6 percent of the class, still lower than UC Berkeley, where 26.5 percent of this year's entering class are Asian Americans.

Mobilizations against anti-Asian violence have also begun on the national and the community level. The Japanese American Citizens League, the Violence Against Asians Taskforce, Chinese for Affirmative Action, and other Asian groups have monitored incidents of anti-Asian violence and pressured the U.S. Commission on Civil Rights and other government bodies to

---

[2]The concept of scapegoat comes to us from the Old Testament. As told in Leviticus (16:10), on the day of Atonement, the sins of the Jewish people were heaped upon the head of a goat who was then "let go . . . into the wilderness." The term *scapegoat* thus literally means "escaping goat." Today, the concept is used to refer to people who, though they may be completely innocent of any offense, are singled out, blamed, and punished for the misfortunes of others. — Ed.

confront and investigate the problem. Projects such as the Coalition to Break the Silence and the Community Violence Prevention Project, both in Oakland, CA, are fighting to raise community consciousness on the issue through community forums and legislative testimony. The Coalition to Break the Silence has also developed ties with other organizations doing similar work in Los Angeles, New York, and Boston.

Questions

1. What does Leung mean by "backlash"? Can you think of any other examples of this phenomenon?

2. Some people who oppose affirmative action and quotas for blacks and Hispanics are nonetheless in favor of setting limits on how many Asian Americans should be admitted to colleges and universities. What could explain this apparent contradiction?

3. For individual Asian Americans, what difficulties might be caused by being stereotyped as a "model minority"?

·40·

Tales Out of Medical School

Adriane Fugh-Berman, M.D.

Recall that the Sadkers (reading 20) observed that girls and boys may sit in the same classrooms, read the same books, and have the same teachers, but they often do not get the same education. In this 1992 walk down memory lane, Adriane Fugh-Berman suggests that medical school is similarly bifurcated by gender.

With the growth of the women's health movement and the influx of women into medical schools, there has been abundant talk of a new enlightenment among physicians. Last summer, many Americans were shocked when Frances Conley, a neurosurgeon on the faculty of Stanford University's medical school, resigned her position, citing "pervasive sexism." Conley's is a particularly elite and male-dominated subspecialty, but her story is not an isolated one. I graduated from the Georgetown University School of Medicine in 1988, and while medical training is a sexist process anywhere, Georgetown built disrespect for women into its curriculum.

A Jesuit school, most recently in the news as the alma mater of William Kennedy Smith, Georgetown has an overwhelmingly white, male and conservative faculty. At a time when women made up one-third of all medical students in the United States, and as many as one-half at some schools, my class was 73 percent male and more than 90 percent white.

The prevailing attitude toward women was demonstrated on the first day of classes by my anatomy instructor, who remarked that our

elderly cadaver "must have been a Playboy bunny" before instructing us to cut off her large breasts and toss them into the thirty-gallon trash can marked "cadaver waste." Barely hours into our training, we were already being taught that there was nothing to be learned from examining breasts. Given the fact that one out of nine American women will develop breast cancer in her lifetime, to treat breasts as extraneous tissue seemed an appalling waste of an educational opportunity, as well as a not-so-subtle message about the relative importance of body parts. How many of my classmates now in practice, I wonder, regularly examine the breasts of their female patients?

My classmates learned their lesson of disrespect well. Later in the year one carved a tick-tack-toe on a female cadaver and challenged others to play. Another gave a languorous sigh after dissecting female genitalia, as if he had just had sex. "Guess I should have a cigarette now," he said.

Ghoulish humor is often regarded as a means by which med students overcome fear and anxiety. But it serves a darker purpose as well: Depersonalizing our cadaver was good preparation for depersonalizing our patients later. Further on in my training an ophthalmologist would yell at me when I hesitated to place a small instrument meant to measure eye pressure on a fellow student's cornea because I was

"Tales Out of Medical School" by Adriane Fugh-Berman, M.D. Reprinted with permission from the January 20, 1992 issue of *The Nation*. For subscription information, call 1-800-333-8536. Portions of each week's Nation magazine can be accessed at http://www.thenation.com.

afraid it would hurt. "You have to learn to treat patients as lab animals," he snarled at me.

On the first day of an emergency medicine rotation in our senior year, students were asked who had had experience in placing a central line (an intravenous line placed into a major vein under the clavicle or in the neck). Most of the male students raised their hands. None of the women did. For me, it was graphic proof of inequity in teaching; the men had had the procedure taught to them, but the women had not. Teaching rounds were often, for women, a spectator sport. One friend told me how she craned her neck to watch a physician teach a minor surgical procedure to a male student; when they were done the physician handed her his dirty gloves to discard. I have seen a male attending physician demonstrate an exam on a patient and then wade through several female medical students to drag forth a male in order to teach it to him. This sort of discrimination was common and quite unconscious: The women just didn't register as medical students to some of the doctors. Female students, for their part, tended (like male ones) to gloss over issues that might divert attention, energy or focus from the all-important goal of getting through their training. "Oh, they're just of the old school," a female classmate remarked to me, as if being ignored by our teachers was really rather charming, like having one's hand kissed.

A woman resident was giving a radiology presentation and I felt mesmerized. Why did I feel so connected and involved? It suddenly occurred to me that the female physician was regularly meeting my eyes; most of the male residents and attendings made eye contact with only the men.

"Why are women's brains smaller than men's?" asked a surgeon of a group of male medical students in the doctors' lounge (I was in the room as well, but was apparently invisible). "Because they're missing logic!" Guffaws all around.

Such instances of casual sexism are hardly unique to Georgetown, or indeed to medical schools. But at Georgetown female students also had to contend with outright discrimination of a sort most Americans probably think no longer exists in education. There was one course women were not allowed to take. The elective in sexually transmitted diseases required an interview with the head of the urology department, who was teaching the course. Those applicants with the appropriate genitalia competed for invitations to join the course (a computer was supposed to assign us electives, which we had ranked in order of preference, but that process had been circumvented for this course). Three women who requested an interview were told that the predominantly gay male clinic where the elective was held did not allow women to work there. This was news to the clinic's executive director, who stated that women were employed in all capacities.

The women who wanted to take the course repeatedly tried to meet with the urologist, but he did not return our phone calls. (I had not applied for the course, but became involved as an advocate for the women who wanted to take it.) We figured out his schedule, waylaid him in the hall and insisted that a meeting be set up.

At this meeting, clinic representatives disclosed that a survey had been circulated years before to the clientele in order to ascertain whether women workers would be accepted; 95 percent of the clients voted to welcome women. They were also asked whether it was acceptable to have medical students working at the clinic; more than 90 percent approved. We were then told that these results could not be construed to indicate that clients did not mind women medical students; the clients would naturally have assumed that "medical student" meant "male medical student." Even if that were true, we asked, if 90 percent of clients did not mind medical students and 95 percent did not mind women, couldn't a reasonable person assume that female medical students would be acceptable? No, we were informed. Another study would have to be done.

We raised formal objections to the school. Meanwhile, however, the entire elective process had been postponed by the dispute, and the blame for the delay and confusion was placed on us. The hardest part of the struggle, indeed, was dealing with the indifference of most of our classmates—out of 206, maybe a dozen actively supported us—and with the intense anger of the ten men who had been promised places in the course.

"Just because you can't take this course," one of the men said to me, "why do you want to ruin it for the rest of us?" It seemed incredible to me that I had to argue that women should be allowed to take the same courses as men. The second or third time someone asked me the same question, I suggested that if women were not allowed to participate in the same curriculum as men, then in the interest of fairness we should get a 50 percent break on our $22,500 annual tuition. My colleague thought that highly unreasonable.

Eventually someone in administration realized that not only were we going to sue the school for discrimination but that we had an open-and-shut case. The elective in sexually transmitted diseases was canceled, and from its ashes arose a new course, taught by the same man, titled "Introduction to Urology." Two women were admitted. When the urologist invited students to take turns working with him in his office, he scheduled the two female students for the same day—one on which only women patients were to be seen (a nifty feat in a urology practice).

The same professor who so valiantly tried to prevent women from learning anything unseemly about sexually transmitted diseases was also in charge of the required course in human sexuality (or, as I liked to call it, he-man sexuality). Only two of the eleven lectures focused on women; of the two lectures on homosexuality, neither mentioned lesbians. The psychiatrist who co-taught the class treated us to one lecture that amounted to an apology for rape: Aggression, even hostility, is normal in sexual relations between a man and a woman he said, and inhibition of aggression in men can lead to impotence.

We were taught that women do not need orgasms for a satisfactory sex life, although men, of course, do; and that inability to reach orgasm is only a problem for women with "unrealistic expectations." I had heard that particular lecture before in the backseat of a car during high school. The urologist told us of couples who came to him for sex counseling because the woman was not having orgasms; he would reassure them that this is normal and the couple would be relieved. (I would gamble that the female half of the couple was anything but relieved.) We learned that oral sex is primarily a homosexual practice, and that sexual dysfunction in women is often caused by "working." In the women-as-idiots department, we learned that when impotent men are implanted with permanently rigid penile prostheses, four out of five wives can't tell that their husbands have had the surgery.

When dealing with sexually transmitted diseases in which both partners must be treated, we were advised to vary our notification strategy according to marital status. If the patient is a single man, the doctor should write the diagnosis down on a prescription for his partner to bring to her doctor. If the patient is a married man, however, the doctor should contact the wife's gynecologist and arrange to have her treated without knowledge of what she is being treated for. How to notify the male partner of a female patient, married or single, was never revealed.

To be fair, women were not the only subjects of outmoded concepts of sexuality. We also received anachronistic information about men. Premature ejaculation, defined as fewer than ten thrusts(!), was to be treated by having the man think about something unpleasant, or by having the woman painfully squeeze, prick or pinch the penis. Aversive therapies such as these have long been discredited.

Misinformation about sexuality and women's health peppered almost every course (I can't recall any egregious wrongs in biochemistry). Although vasectomy and abortion are among the safest of all surgical procedures, in our lectures vasectomy was presented as fraught with long-term complications and abortion was never mentioned without the words "peritonitis" and "death" in the same sentence. These distortions represented Georgetown's Catholic bent at its worst. (We were not allowed to perform, or even watch, abortion procedures in our affiliated hospitals.) On a lighter note, one obstetrician assisting us in the anatomy lab told us that women shouldn't lift heavy weights because their pelvic organs will fall out between their legs.

In our second year, several women in our class started a women's group, which held potlucks and offered presentations and performances: A former midwife talked about her profession, a student demonstrated belly dancing, another discussed dance therapy and one sang selections from *A Chorus Line*. This heavy radical feminist activity created great hostility among our male classmates. Announcements of our meetings were defaced and women in the group began receiving threatening calls at home from someone who claimed to be watching the listener and who would then accurately describe what she was wearing. One woman received obscene notes in her school mailbox, including one that contained a rape threat. I received insulting cards in typed envelopes at my home address; my mother received similar cards at hers.

We took the matter to the dean of student affairs, who told us it was "probably a dental student" and suggested we buy loud whistles to blow into the phone when we received unwanted calls. We demanded that the school attempt to find the perpetrator and expel him. We were told that the school would not expel the student but that counseling would be advised.

The women's group spread the word that we were collecting our own information on possible suspects and that any information on bizarre, aggressive, antisocial or misogynous behavior among the male medical students should be reported to our designated representative. She was inundated with a list of classmates who fit the bill. Finally, angered at the school's indifference, we solicited the help of a prominent woman faculty member. Although she shamed the dean into installing a hidden camera across from the school mailboxes to monitor unusual behavior, no one was ever apprehended.

Georgetown University School of Medicine churns out about 200 physicians a year. Some become good doctors despite their training, but many will pass on the misinformation and demeaning attitudes handed down to them. It is a shame that Georgetown chooses to perpetuate stereotypes and reinforce prejudices rather than help students acquire the up-to-date information and sensitivity that are vital in dealing with AIDS, breast cancer, teen pregnancy and other contemporary epidemics. Female medical students go through an ordeal, but at least it ends with graduation. It is the patients who ultimately suffer the effects of sexist medical education.

Questions

1. According to Fugh-Berman's account, the gender ratio was usually skewed at Georgetown's medical school. In your judgment, would there be less sexism if the ratio of men and women was more equal? Why or why not?

2. To what extent might it be said that the women medical students were victims of hate crimes? What would be the motive behind these attacks?